TEACHING BIBLIOGRAPHIC SKILLS IN HISTORY

Teaching Bibliographic Skills in History

A SOURCEBOOK FOR HISTORIANS AND LIBRARIANS

EDITED BY

Charles A. D'Aniello

Greenwood Press
Westport, Connecticut • London

Library of Congress Cataloging-in-Publication Data

Teaching bibliographic skills in history : a sourcebook for historians
  and librarians / edited by Charles A. D'Aniello.
      p. cm.
   Includes bibliographical references and index.
   ISBN 0–313–25266–1 (alk. paper)
   1. Historical libraries—Handbooks, manuals, etc. 2. History
students—Library orientation—Handbooks, manuals, etc. 3. History—
Bibliography—Methodology—Study and teaching—Handbooks, manuals,
etc. 4. Libraries—Special collections—History—Handbooks,
manuals, etc. I. D'Aniello, Charles A.
Z675.H5T4   1993
025.5'669—dc20   92–8833

British Library Cataloguing in Publication Data is available.

Library of Congress Catalog Card Number: 92–8833
ISBN: 0–313–25266–1

First published in 1993

Greenwood Press, 88 Post Road West, Westport, CT 06881
An imprint of Greenwood Publishing Group, Inc.

Printed in the United States of America

The paper used in this book complies with the
Permanent Paper Standard issued by the National
Information Standards Organization (Z39.48–1984).

10 9 8 7 6 5 4 3 2 1

Copyright Acknowledgments

This work is dedicated to Dr. Warren F. Kuehl (1924–1987),
who contributed much
in spirit and labor to the
bibliography of history.

Contents

FIGURES   XV

PREFACE   xvii

Part I. The Study of History

1.   Historical Methodologies and Research

    Georg G. Iggers   3

       Selected Bibliography   19

2.   History and Interdisciplinary History

    Harry Ritter   25

       Origins and Growth of the Idea of Interdisciplinary
History   26

       Selected Examples of Recent Interdisciplinary Work   28

Part II. Bibliographic Instruction in History

3.   Finding and Using Historical Materials

    Jane A. Rosenberg and Robert P. Swierenga   51

       Research on Library Use   51

       Historians and Library Services   55

       Historians and the Research Process   57

       Students and the Research Process   59

Designing the Course: The Historian's View
Robert P. Swierenga 62

4. Bibliographic Instruction in History

Charles A. D'Aniello 69

A Historical Education 69

The Nature of Research 70

Bibliographic Instruction for History Students:
Opportunities and Realizations 70

The Best Approach 71

Librarian–Historian Collaboration 72

What to Teach and When to Teach It 73

Contexts in Which Instruction May Be Offered 75

How to Teach Conceptual Frameworks: Basic
Instructional Designs 76

Instructional Designs Based on Conceptual Frameworks 77

Type of Reference Tools 78

Systematic Literature Searching 80

Form of Publication 84

Index Structure 84

Primary and Secondary Sources 86

Publication Sequence 86

Citation Patterns 87

Sociohistorical Analysis 89

A Word on the Design of Guides to Library Resources 90

Plagiarism: So Many Things to Copy From 90

How Effective Is Bibliographic Instruction? 91

Part III. Special Topics

5. Using Catalogs and Indexes

David Y. Allen and John Attig 97

Library Research 97

The Catalog 99

Scope of the Catalog 100

Principles of Catalog Construction: Description   100

Principles of Catalog Construction: Indexing   102

Traditional Forms of Library Catalogs   107

The Online Catalog   109

Reference Tools   111

Published Catalogs of Books   111

Periodical Literature   114

Other Types of Library Materials   121

6. Using Reference Sources

Charles A. D'Aniello   129

How to Read a Reference Book   129

Beginnings, Overviews, and Clarifications   131

Miscellaneous Ready-Reference Aids   136

Indexes and Abstracts, Bibliographies, and Union Lists
and Catalogs   139

Evaluative Sources   141

Primary Sources   143

An Illustration of Use   143

7. Sources for Interdisciplinary Research

Raymond G. McInnis   167

Quantitative Methods   169

General and Area Studies   172

Social Sciences   183

Anthropology   183

Business and Labor   186

Communication, Mass Media, and Journalism   188

Demography   190

Economics and Economic Thought   192

Education   195

Political Science   198

Psychology   202

Sociology   205

Women's Studies 210

Humanities 214

    Fine and Applied Arts 214

    Language and Literature 217

    Philosophy and Religion 221

History of Science and Technology 224

8. Using Electronic Information Sources

Joyce Duncan Falk 229

    Definitions 230

    Databases 231

        Types of Databases 231

        Critical Evaluation of Databases for History Topics 232

        Examples of Databases for History Topics 234

    The Search Process 238

        Advantages of Online Searching and How It Functions 238

        When to Use Electronic Database Searching 244

        When Not to Use Electronic Database Searching 244

        Additional Points to Consider 246

    How to Obtain an Electronic Database Search 250

        Costs 252

    Electronic Searching, Bibliographic Instruction, and the Research Process 253

    APPENDIX 258

        Databases 258

        Directories of Databases (Selected) 263

        Major Information Retrieval Systems with Databases of Interest to Historians 263

        Instructional Materials 264

9. Using the Finding Aids to Archive and Manuscript Collections 265

Trudy Huskamp Peterson

Published Primary and Secondary Sources 266

Unpublished Sources 267

   Defining Terms 267

   Understanding the Institutions 268

   Finding the Finding Aids 272

   Automating the Documents 285

   Working with an Archivist 287

   Searching for Other Sources 290

Part IV. Bibliography

10. Teaching the Bibliography of History: A Selected Annotated
Bibliography

   Charles A. D'Aniello 295

   General Ideas, Issues, and Assumptions 295

   A Selection of Overviews of Historical Research 302

   Historical Research, Library Collections, and the
Characteristics of Publication 303

   Research Methodology: The Humanities 312

   Research Methodology: The Social Sciences 314

   Relevant Instructional Designs from Other Disciplines 316

   Workbooks, Courses, Exercises, and Instructional
Designs 319

   Early Bibliographic Instruction Programs in History and
Related Disciplines 334

   Electronic Information Sources 337

   Abstracting and Indexing History 343

   Historians' Use of U.S. Government Documents 346

   Relations Between Historians and Librarians 346

   Research Guides and Manuals 347

   Ethical and Intellectual Issues in Documenting
Historical Research 354

INDEX 357

ABOUT THE EDITOR AND CONTRIBUTORS 383

Figures

5.1   Typical Catalog Card   101

5.2   Online Catalog Record: Captioned Format   101

5.3   Typical Catalog Card: A Translation   102

5.4   Extract from *Library of Congress Subject Headings*   106

5.5   Sequence of Subject Headings   108

5.6   Extract from *Humanities Index*   115

5.7   Extract from *America: History and Life*   117

5.8   Extract from Citation Index of *Arts & Humanities Citation
      Index*   120

9.1   Levels of Arrangement and Description   272

9.2   Extract from the *Directory of Archives and Manuscript
      Repositories in the United States*   274

9.3   Extract from *National Union Catalog of Manuscript
      Collections*   275

9.4   Example of a Guide Entry   276

9.5   Example of an Inventory   277

9.6   Example of a Register   278

9.7   A Series Entry   279

9.8   Example of a Folder–Title List   280

9.9   Example of a Calendar Item List   281

9.10 A MARC/Archives and Manuscripts Control (AMC)
      Record from the RLIN Database   284

Preface

This work is intended as a source of ideas for historians and librarians who teach history students how to use the library and do bibliographic research. It is neither a guide to history reference sources nor a fully developed instructional program. Although some exercises are included, I hope readers will use them only as models for creating their own learning experiences because, as instructors, we do our best when we know what we teach and are energized by the pride and passion of creation.

Historians ponder the nature of history as a discipline; librarians are less likely to do so. Included for both groups, therefore, is an essay by Georg G. Iggers on the evolution of historical study and an essay by Harry Ritter on the nature of interdisciplinary history. Such broad knowledge of the discipline and its needs may be unnecessary for work with beginning undergraduates, but a historical sense is vital for work with more advanced students. In addition, these essays will serve as useful introductory reading for advanced undergraduates and graduate students.

Relying upon personal experience as a librarian and a historian, and upon empirical studies conducted over the past twenty years, Jane A. Rosenberg considers how historians conduct research and how the bibliographic needs of students differ from those of professionals. Following Rosenberg's discussion, Robert P. Swierenga offers his personal response to the needs of beginning graduate students. In the following chapter I outline approaches and contexts for instruction and provide exercises. Then I briefly discuss the design of library guides, issues in plagiarism and documentation, and comment on the effectiveness or benefits of instruction.

Next, David Y. Allen and John Attig introduce the concepts of cataloging and indexing, the basic systems for finding books and periodical articles as well as other materials. I then discuss the full range of reference sources and demonstrate their use in an editing exercise that can be adapted for use with students.

Interdisciplinary history is a burgeoning enterprise, and it is important that advanced students know how to tap into the bibliographic and reference literature of a range of disciplines. Raymond G. McInnis offers a guide and conceptual structure that introduces major sources in quantitative methods; general and area studies; anthropology; business and labor; communication, mass media, and journalism; demography; economics and economic thought; education; political science; psychology; sociology; women's studies; fine and applied arts; language and literature; philosophy and religion; and the history of science and technology. His emphasis on research guides is especially useful.

Electronic databases are changing the way information is found in all fields. Joyce Duncan Falk describes the nature and use of these resources in historical study, concentrating on issues to be noted when offering instruction and points to remember when using these services either on one's own or with the assistance of a librarian.

Primary source material is at the heart of all historical work, and although archival and manuscript materials are not the only primary sources they occupy center stage. Trudy Huskamp Peterson discusses the full range of finding aids to this material.

In the concluding annotated bibliography, I have tried to capture a wide range of relevant material. Here the reader will find fuller discussions of some of the points made in various chapters, issues to ponder, background information for lectures, and exercises.

Before directing the reader to the text, I must thank all of the contributors for lending their expertise and insights to this project. I especially thank David Y. Allen and Jane A. Rosenberg for their labors. In addition to their written contributions, they read several of the essays and contributed significantly to their editing at various stages. Their advice, friendship, and patience throughout has been invaluable. I have learned much over the years from colleagues and students, and they deserve special thanks; I especially thank those in the various sections of "History 500: Historical Methods and Research," offered by the history department of the State University of New York at Buffalo. I taught this course for several years with Melvin J. Tucker, to whom I am particularly indebted as a friend and colleague. Colleagues within the Association for the Bibliography of History have also been helpful. Ruth Clinefelter, a former president of the Association for the Bibliography of History, deserves special thanks for her enthusiasm, steadfast commitment, and kind and generous encouragement, as well as for her advice and research in the early stages of the bibliography's compilation. I also thank my editor and copyeditor at Greenwood Press, Sally Scott and Brenda Hanning. Needless to say, as editor, I accept responsibility for any errors of overall emphasis, inclusion or exclusion, or focus. And I thank my family—Rona, Jacob, and Sarah—without whose support this project would have remained unfinished.

Charles A. D'Aniello

Part I
The Study of History

1

Historical Methodologies and Research

Georg G. Iggers

History since its beginning has had the dual characters of literature and science. Indeed, the term *history* requires definition.[1] It refers not only to the course of events, to what has actually happened, but also to the reconstruction of this past by the historian. History in the latter sense has often been called historiography, *Geschichtschreibung* in German, to distinguish it from the actual past. Until relatively recently it was assumed that history as a field of study presupposed the occurrence of writing and the existence of written records. Whatever occurred prior to the existence of the art of writing constituted prehistory. This view left little space for oral history and nonwritten sources. This notion, which was never held unanimously by those who occupied themselves with history, however, has long been questioned. Already in the eighteenth century, thinkers such as Giambattista Vico and Johann Herder recognized the extreme antiquity of human existence and culture and emphasized the value of what they called "mythhistory," which took seriously the orally transmitted traditions of early cultures or of modern peoples living outside the fold of western civilization.

The problems of historical method appear much more complex than they did only a few decades ago. One great turning point came in the course of the nineteenth century with the professionalization of historical studies.[2] History was increasingly conceived of, not as a literary art, but as a scholarly discipline. In the languages of continental Europe, though less frequently in English, the term *science* was applied to this new discipline. Science here had two meanings, an institutional one and a methodological one. On the institutional level, it meant that the study of history was now located at universities or at research institutes. It was pursued by professionals who had been trained in the craft of history and who constituted a scholarly or scientific community that would apply criteria of criticism accepted by the profession to judge the soundness of a historical work. History could no longer be left to amateurs, the men of letters or the statesmen who had written history in the West since the days of Thucydides although not trained as historians, or to the antiquarians who had dabbled with the past.

This conception of history as a science, which was shared by almost all professional historians from Leopold von Ranke in the mid-nineteenth century to G. R. Elton[3] in the late-twentieth century, assumed that historians, if they analyzed the historical record with proper care, could reconstruct the past ''as it had actually occurred.''[4] This assumed that history was a rigorous discipline, as rigorous as the natural sciences, concerned with research using ''objective'' methods to study an ''objective'' reality. The model for scientific research was presented by the natural sciences, which had since the seventeenth century revolutionized the study of the world. From these sciences, the historians took over the notion of systematic, methodological inquiry. At the same time they recognized and emphasized fundamental differences between the natural sciences and the sciences dealing with intentional human behavior.[5] The latter could never be defined in mechanistic terms. They involved meanings that could not be analyzed in abstract terms but that had to be ''comprehended'' in their concrete reality. But the gap between historical and natural science was lessened, at least for the German historical scholars of the nineteenth century, by the fact that for them biology,[6] not physics, was the key natural science. Like history, biology involved living organisms, governed by internal principles of growth, not dead matter acted upon by external agents.

Yet no matter how different Leopold von Ranke's notion of science was from that of Isaac Newton, both agreed that scientific study required strict, clearly defined procedures. The aim of Newtonian physics was different from that of Rankean history. Each involved a different conception of what constituted science. The former sought to formulate laws, capable of being expressed in mathematical terms and universally valid. The latter sought to do justice to the variety of persons, institutions, and cultures that composed mankind and that each needed to be understood as a unique expression of meaning. What both conceptions shared was the belief that the scientist or scholar must confront evidence ''objectively,'' free of personal bias and guided by a clearly defined methodology and logic of inquiry. Written records were the prime, even if not the sole, source of historical study. These records were to be tested for their truth content. Historians in the past had written histories on the basis of accounts that had been considered reliable, but this was no longer deemed sufficient.

Since the Renaissance, two criteria of historical criticism had increasingly been applied to the sources: the genuineness of the documents and their credibility. Now historians insisted that history not be written on the basis of past accounts, no matter how reputable, but be based entirely on primary sources, the best being records, diaries, letters, or accounts by reliable eye witnesses.[7] Behind this was the confidence that if all the sources relating to a historical topic of study were examined, a definite version of a set of events would be possible.[8] Two problems hindered this noble aim, of which the new critically oriented historians were only vaguely aware. For one, they relied increasingly on documents of state without sufficiently taking into account the bias that they contained. Ranke thus based his history of the emergence of the modern state system at the turn of the sixteenth century in part on the reports that the Venetian ambassadors had sent to their home government, without taking into account the extent to which these ambassadors reported what they thought would gain favor.[9] Moreover, although he and many practitioners in this tradition realized that philological methods of textual criticism did not suffice for historical synthesis and that the work of the historian involved interpretation, they remained confident that the interpretation that did justice to the objective character of past reality revealed itself through immersion in the sources.[10] Yet there was a fundamental contradiction between the strict rules that governed the establishment of a reliable text and the lack of rules that guided historical interpretation and synthesis.

These two problems, the perspective if not bias of an approach that relied so heavily and so uncritically on documents of state, and the subjectivity of the syntheses that came out of the critical examination of texts, were to trouble future historians. Nevertheless, from Leopold von Ranke's famous critical appendix of 1824 on past historians to the standard manuals of historical method that appeared well into the second half of the twentieth century,[11] historians perpetuated these notions of method and interpretation as the model of a scholarly, that is, scientific, history.

In the course of the twentieth century the adequacy of the documentary approach was increasingly questioned, as was the notion of what constituted "historical science." I shall discuss later the change in the subject matter of history that took place in recent decades and the implications that this change had for the documentary method. Equally significant are the changes in the conception of what constituted the scientific character of historical studies, changes that went in two very different directions. By the 1890s, when history in many countries had become a professionalized discipline after the German model, historical studies were criticized not because they were overly scientific and hence removed from life, as Friedrich Nietzsche had claimed, but because they were insufficiently scientific and therefore inadequate to meet the intellectual demands of a modern industrial and democratic world.

The mainline professional historians had argued that history as a science of man required a logic of inquiry fundamentally different from the sciences of nature, namely one that took into account the elements of meaning and value inherent in culture. Their critics now argued for the unity of scientific method. Historical reasoning, such critics as Wilhelm Dilthey, Benedetto Croce, and R. G. Collingwood argued,[12] involved reexperiencing the internal mental and emotional operations of living human beings, natural science involved the application of artificial conceptual constructs from without. The extreme argument, as advocated by certain of the neo-Kantian philosophers of historical knowledge such as Wilhelm Windelband or an intellectual historian such as Friedrich Meinecke,[13] was that the two were incompatible. At the other extreme was the

argument advanced by sociologists such as Emile Durkheim and François Simiand and historians such as Karl Lamprecht and Kurt Breysig that all science
presupposed theory and that history, if it were to be a science, would have to
do the same and approach its subject matter with theory-guided hypotheses.
Durkheim assumed that history could not fulfill this task and thus could only be
a handmaiden to sociology as a science of society that would seek to do just
that.[14] Involved here was not only the question of what constituted historical
science but also the question of what constituted social science.

Two very different conceptions of history as a social science emerged: One
corresponded to the two differing conceptions of science discussed earlier, sometimes described as positivistic, which took the empirical social sciences as a
model and placed a premium on quantification; the other was closer to the German
historical tradition in stressing the central role of meaning in all human activity
while also arguing that mere immersion in the evidence did not suffice, but had
to be supplemented by clearly formulated questions with which the scholar
approached his evidence.

The most important exponent of this second orientation was Max Weber. He
rejected the reliance of German historical scholarship, of political historians in
the tradition of Ranke, as well as of historical economists like Karl Roscher on
intuition and the preference for narration; he emphasized that no science was
possible without clear analytical concepts. He also recognized that these concepts
must be instruments for clearly formulating the values and intentions that directed
human social behavior. He sought to introduce a rational method into historical
studies, which in his opinion had been absent from the German historical school.
Weber shared with neo-idealist theorists of history and the cultural sciences like
J. G. Droysen, Wilhelm Dilthey, Wilhelm Windelband, and Heinrich Rickert
the belief that all studies of society and culture involved the comprehension of
meaning. But he rejected the notion that this meaning could be grasped by
subjectively reexperiencing the thought processes of individuals or social groups.
The scientific study of society for Weber required a strict methodology, the use
of analytic constructs or "ideal types," which sought to formulate how historical
agents, individuals, institutions, or social systems would act ideally in terms of
their convictions and then would test these formulations against the historical
record. Yet "objectivity" in social and historical inquiry was still possible for
Weber even if objectivity now resided in the method of study and not in the
object under study.[15]

Historians seldom tend to be consistent theorists, however. They leave the
questions of theory to the philosophers or the sociologists and pursue their work
in a pragmatic manner, although their work is always guided by certain theoretical
assumptions that are often unexamined and merely implicit. Thus Durkheim and
Weber are much more significant for the different directions that sociological
rather than historical studies took. A large number of historians, the New Historians and the Progressive Historians in the United States,[16] and social and
economic historians in the French-speaking world such as the Belgian Henri

Pirenne,[17] borrowed relatively eclectically from the various social sciences without formulating a systematic logic of inquiry. In fact the very nature of history with its rich diversity was incompatible with any attempt to introduce a systematic view.

Parallel to these attempts to reformulate the scientific character of history arose an increasing skepticism in regard to the notion that history was a science at all. The professionalization of history had been based on the assumption that history was a science even if the character of this science was disputed. From Friedrich Nietzsche[18] in the late-nineteenth century to Roland Barthes[19] and Michel Foucault in the late-twentieth century, theorists of history, more often than its practitioners, rejected the notion that had been so dear to the professional historians that history in its claim to secure knowledge was fundamentally different from literature. Foucault suggested that the intense concern with history and historical studies since the late-eighteenth century represented the arrogance of modern western man, proud of a civilization that, according to Foucault, claimed to be humane but was basically and fundamentally inhumane.[20] In Foucault's opinion this worldview, which dominated the thinking of the nineteenth century, in its arrogant anthropocentric belief that man should dominate nature had destroyed the harmony between man and nature. Basic to this criticism was the notion that modern science itself was an illusion. Claude Lévi-Strauss has denied a fundamental distinction between "civilized" and "primitive" societies and argued that the "savage mind" represented as dignified and proper a way of dealing with reality as modern "science."[21]

History in a very essential sense was not science but myth, for which the term *mythistory*, first used in the eighteenth century, was revived.[22] This new critique involved more than the traditional question of the relationship between history and literature. Only the most radical exponents of professional history, among them few historians of real stature, had argued that literary quality was immaterial for historical writing. Ranke had emphasized that history was both a science and an art and that it was a prime task of the historian to combine scientific history with literary elegance.[23] In fact the great professional historians of the nineteenth century had written not merely for specialists but also for a broadly educated public that appreciated them as great writers. It was no coincidence that historian Theodor Mommsen received the Nobel Prize for literature in 1902. Only in the period after about 1890, when specialization won out, did historians write increasingly for other historians rather than for the educated reader, but even then the writer who combined scholarship with literary eloquence, such as Lord Acton, Friedrich Meinecke, and Marc Bloch, occupied a place of eminence in the profession.

The new challenge to historical science, however, was the insistence that history was a form of literature, nothing more or less, and that the search for a science of history based on strict methodological procedures was a chimera. This challenge took more or less extreme forms. The most extreme one rejected the notion of the scientific character of science itself. Oswald Spengler had denied the universal character of science and insisted that every science, including mathematics, reflected the basic worldview of the culture in which it arose.[24] Gaston Bachelard had argued that science was merely a form of poetry and myth.[25] Hayden White, in a study of four major historians and four major philosophers of history in the nineteenth century, had come to the conclusion that there was no fundamental distinction between empirical history and speculative philosophy of history. He did not go as far as Roland Barthes in denying the distinction between fact and fiction.[26] History in fact was different from fiction in seeking to regrasp a past as it had occurred. Hence in a very restrictive way, the critical method of historical inquiry was justified in creating the factual basis of historical writing. But historical writing always involved interpretation, and interpretation followed no clear methodological procedures.

In presenting a synthesis, the historian proceeds very much like the novelist. He or she "performs an essentially *poetic* act" in constructing a story determined by a choice among the limited forms of "emplotment" that are available to the writer of literature. Literary criticism is thus the key to evaluating and understanding a historical work. History is obviously not a "genuine science," if in fact such exists, and thus "in any field of study not yet reduced (or elevated) to the status of a genuine science, thought remains the captive of the linguistic mode in which it seeks to grasp the outline of objects inhabiting its field of perception."[27]

This emphasis that historical writing must be understood in linguistic rather than scientific terms has been shared by a broad segment of thinkers in the past several decades who have sometimes been labeled "structuralists," "poststructuralists," and "deconstructionists."[28] Fundamental to the structuralist position is the assumption that the basis of all human reality is language. It is not men who use language to communicate ideas but language that determines their thoughts. From this position history has no reality apart from language. Society and culture, which constitute the subject matter of history, represent texts, which like any literary texts must be understood. But the meaning of these texts is not obvious from the words; it is hidden in "deep structures" that underlie consciousness and that must be "deciphered."[29] In the extreme form of Jacques Derrida's deconstructionism, the text must be cleansed of every intentional expression, of all "ideology," and reconstructed on a formal, depersonalized level. The linguistic critique or reconstitution of historical science contains an obvious element of validity but also carries with it deep-seated contradictions. Clearly the ideal of a history that speaks through the historian free of subjectivity, of which Ranke dreamed, is an illusion. Without the explicit questions that the historian puts to the past and that, as Enlightenment historians already recognized, reflect his or her standpoint, no historical writing is possible.

The linguistic structuralists fall into a new kind of objectivism. They assume that a culture is a thoroughly integrated system, an organism in a sense. For them every manifestation of the culture has a symbolic significance. By viewing these manifestations as they occur on the level of a microhistory, the historian can grasp the broader context and penetrate the "code" that determines the culture. The question remains, however, what rational guidelines direct such a study. Intuition, the confrontation with a "thick description" of symbolic acts, remains the primary tool for breaking the code, but this immersion contains no explicit methodology nor does it desire one.[30] The result is a new epistemological irrationalism that is even welcomed as such. But this is an abdication of reason. This abdication rests on a conscious rejection of the humanistic tradition of the Enlightenment, which in seeking to enthrone man as the master of the world and thus introducing modern technological civilization, is seen as destructive of human and humane values and accused of upsetting the balance between man and nature.

In its extreme form, the new symbolic approach to history seeks to deny the very concept of personality that has been crucial to historical writing since antiquity—and thereby to reject the notion that man has a history. Michel Foucault viewed historical consciousness as a prejudice of modern western man, although ironically his own work proceeded largely historically. In this context, the recognition by a broad segment of very diverse historical thinkers in the twentieth century from Max Weber and Karl Mannheim to Raymond Aron and Jürgen Habermas of the limits of rational method, coupled with an insistence on the necessity of rational communication within these limits, constitutes an important attempt to rescue historical theory from obscurantism.

This whole discussion nevertheless emphasizes that the problems of historical method are much more complex than the courses and seminars for graduate students suggested until recently. The crucial questions of what constitutes a source and what is historical evidence are not new but go back to the very beginnings of a secularized historiography. The basic issues in the later debates were already foreshadowed in the differences between Herodotus and Thucydides,[31] between a broad cultural approach relying heavily on oral traditions and a more narrow political one seeking to reestablish critically what happened. The Thucydidean conception of political history was revived among the humanists of Renaissance Italy by Machiavelli and Guicciardini.[32] At the same time, a new tradition of erudition and textual criticism emerged among the humanists and later among scholars in both the Catholic and the Protestant world, which prepared the way for the philological studies of the Bible and the ancient classics at the eighteenth-century German universities that in turn laid the foundations for the source criticism of the professional scholarship of the nineteenth century.[33]

Voltaire represented a different approach. In the final chapters of his essentially conventional political history of the *Age of Louis XIV* and even more so in his *History of Manners*, he broadened the scope of history to embrace many aspects of society, culture, and technology. This attempt at a history of culture for which poetry, art, and religion were crucial was widespread in the Enlightenment, particularly among those writers who are generally seen as standing on the threshold of romanticism. For philologists like Christian Heyne and Friedrich

Wolf, the classical texts must be understood as an expression of a folk culture. This required on the one hand a rigorous critique of the texts to reconstruct their original form, and on the other hand a belief that it is not sufficient to read the texts in terms of their lexicographical significance but in a deeper sense, as symbolic reflections of a culture.[34]

Yet the Rankean conception of scientific history by no means possessed a monopoly even in the age of professionalization. A broad and very diverse tradition of cultural history maintained itself in the first half of the nineteenth century, finding its most developed expression in France where historians closely linked culture with social, economic, and political factors. Marx later emphasized the great debt that he owed to this historiography.[35] But this history also utilized very different sources from those of the dominant school of professional historiography. The stress on careful work with documents, preferably in archives, was widespread. Yet even political history could be approached very differently from Ranke's person- and event-oriented manner.

A historian such as Alexis de Tocqueville could demonstrate that one could work very differently with archival sources than Ranke had done and write a very different kind of history. He was keenly interested in political history, but from a different perspective than Ranke, not primarily in diplomatic and military activity but in the administrative institutional framework within which political life took place. The overall direction of the development of modern political institutions interested Tocqueville, not the concrete actions of politicians.[36] From a very different political stance and with little attention to the archives, these were also the concerns of Karl Marx and Friedrich Engels, for whom the affairs of state could not be taken at their face value but needed to be understood in the broader context of conflicting social forces.[37]

The early work of Fustel de Coulanges on family and religion in the ancient Greek and Roman world and of Jacob Burckhardt on the Italian Renaissance proceeded with a still more radically different conception of sources and evidence.[38] Burckhardt had studied in Ranke's seminar, yet art, literature, and manners, not documents, were important for him as were religious rites to Fustel de Coulanges. The quality of these sources, however, was much more symbolic than verbal and required approaches that sought to grasp the underlying quality of a culture.

After 1890 the dominant role of the Rankean type of historical scholarship, which had served as a model for historians throughout the world wherever historical studies became a professional discipline, declined. In a sense this self-proclaimed scientific school of history had violated its own principles. It wanted to be politically impartial, to stand above the parties, to preserve strict value neutrality, but never fulfilled this claim. Ranke himself identified impartiality with the attachment to a state that stood above the conflicts of the society and followed dispassionately the logic of national self-interest on the international scale.[39] In truth this state did not stand above parties, and Ranke in endorsing it carried a bias in favor of the established order into his historiography. A later generation of historians went into the archives to find weapons for its political goals, whether it was the unification of the nation under a semiautocratic Prussian monarchy in Germany,[40] the stabilization of the Third Republic in France,[41] the maintenance of a national consensus in the United States that skirted class or racial tensions,[42] or the assertion of nationality and ethnicity in Eastern Europe. Far from bringing about a depoliticization of historical studies, professionalization contributed to an increased politicization that reached its high point in the response of historians to World War I and its aftermath.

Historical writing and historical theory almost always go different ways because historians generally do not reflect profoundly on the assumptions that underlie their practice. Therefore, the sharp theoretical distinctions on the nature of history as a scientific enterprise that I discussed earlier were only partly reflected in the writing of the historians. The great theoretical debate began at the end of the nineteenth century.[43] The reorientation of professional historiography proceeded more slowly. And this reorientation affected the subject matter of historical studies, the methods and the sources that this subject matter required, and the mode of discourse that was considered proper for writing history. Social history became increasingly important and for many, although by no means all social historians, was conceived of as social science.[44]

Particularly after World War II new areas of study emerged. Broad segments of the population that had previously been neglected, such as workers, women, and ethnic minorities, became subjects of historical study. New aspects of life such as the family, sexuality, working conditions, recreation, disease, and crime interested historians.[45] The nonwestern world received greater attention. A good deal of social history continued to be discursive. In Great Britain, George Trevelyan saw social history essentially as an anecdotal history with the politics left out.[46] In Germany an older tradition of social and economic history followed the patterns of narrative of the political historians in examining how economics and society were integrated into the state.[47] Increasingly, narration ceded to analysis. Politics, including international relations, continued to be a central concern of historians, but these were now seen in the context of social and economic forces, whether from a Marxist class perspective or not.

The notion that history should be a social science increasingly won favor, although very different models of such a science competed with each other. As already mentioned, concepts from the social sciences—from economics, sociology, anthropology, social psychology, psychoanalysis, and, particularly in France, geography—were borrowed to illustrate a narrative account or strengthen explanations. Marxism constituted one available model of a historical social science that in fact deeply influenced writing in social and economic history by emphasizing the role of economic and social conflict.

Few social historians were not in some way affected by Marxist concepts of class analysis but few, outside the socialist countries, accepted Marxism as a system.[48] Except in the more dogmatic presentations of dialectical materialism, Marxism turned out to be much too flexible and many sided to be reduced to a system. As Georg Lukács argued emphatically in the early 1920s, the method not the system was central to Marx's thought.[49] For Lukács the important element of a Marxist approach, which distinguished it sharply from a narrow empiricism, was that all human events needed to be seen in the broad historical context of society. At this point much of Marxist thought agreed with broad segments of non-Marxist thought, abandoning a narrow economic determinism and recognizing the significance of cultural factors.

Two aspects of Marxism that affected the historical thinking of non-Marxists need to be mentioned as well. Marxism provided a theory of modernization, an attempt to explain the emergence of the modern industrial world, which as formulated by Marxists remained controversial but was the starting point for the analysis of modern society for many historians who rejected its particular conception of the sequence of stages and its utopian vision of the future.[50] Marxism also contained a populist aspect, a concern for the masses and their conditions of life and consciousness, which was assimilated by many historians who did not share the political aims of the Marxist parties.[51]

The significance of Marxism for modern social history should neither be overemphasized nor played down. Outside the socialist block it was more important in the Latin countries of Western Europe, in Latin America, and Japan than in the English-speaking countries or West Germany.[52] In West Germany in the years after 1960 historians sought to create a "historical social science" as deeply indebted to Max Weber as to Karl Marx, in order to understand by means of a social analysis of politics the forces that led to fascism in Germany.[53] In Great Britain and to a lesser extent the United States, cultural explanations of social and economic domination, often utilizing notions of cultural "hegemony" as formulated by the Italian Marxist Antonio Gramsci, found their counterpart in the critique of the modern social order by many non-Marxist populist historians who similarly emphasized cultural factors.

In sharp contrast to these forms of social history stood the attempts to model history on the empirical social sciences.[54] In a sense the old dispute of the nineteenth century was revived, between the advocates of a positivistic history such as Thomas Buckle[55] who believed that history as a science must discover general laws capable of quantification, and the historicists who argued that the very nature of human history as a meaning-filled enterprise made such an approach impossible.[56] Only now, the positivists had the means of mathematizing history.

The new social science history was less concerned with the formulation of broad laws of historical development, which had fascinated nineteenth-century writers from Auguste Comte and Herbert Spencer to Karl Lamprecht, than in formulating more limited theories of historical development that were capable of empirical testing.[57] As late as the 1970s Geoffrey Barraclough, in his survey of developments in contemporary historical writing, observed that "the search for quantity is beyond all doubts the most powerful of the new trends in history, the fact above all others which distinguishes historical attitudes in the 1970's from historical attitudes in the 1930's."[58] This was perhaps most true of economic history, which turned increasingly to quantitative models.

Quantification played an important role in other areas of historical studies too, in demography, social mobility, and electoral behavior, among others. The sources that were studied were fundamentally different from those of traditional historiography. Unlike literary or "soft" sources, they were "hard" data such as quantitative measures like price and wage indices, vital statistics, voting results, and so forth, which could be fed into the computer without deep analysis of what their authors meant. Hence the subjective element that was so crucial in traditional historical writing was supposed to be excluded. The question remained, however, whether important problems of historical interpretation could be settled by these methods. Robert Fogel and Stanley Engerman in their book on American slavery, *Time on the Cross* (1974), thought that not only the question of the profitability of slavery but also of certain of its qualitative aspects could receive a definite, irrefutable answer on the basis of computerized analysis. The controversy that followed led to the general acknowledgment that quantitative historians could no more do without a critical examination of the reliability of their sources than other historians, and that quantity could only answer questions regarding the qualitative aspects of human life in a very limited sense.[59]

Cliometrics in this form was predominantly, although not exclusively, an American phenomenon. Elsewhere too, although primarily in economic and to a lesser extent in demographic history, quantitative methods were applied to historical analysis, even in the Soviet Union. In France, the group of historians associated with the famous journal *Annales* at times adopted similar positions, but with significant differences. One of their most important representatives, Emmanuel Le Roy Ladurie, still wrote in 1973 that "history that is not quantifiable cannot claim to be scientific."[60] But quantification was essentially a means, and was not at the core of the historical concerns of the *Annales* group.

One often speaks of an *Annales* school, but this term disregards the tremendous diversity within the group and the transformations it has undergone. The journal was founded in 1929 by Lucien Febvre and Marc Bloch, who wished to create a counterpart to the traditional event-oriented political history, namely a social history that sought to lay bare the long-lasting "structures" within which human life occurred. Marc Bloch examined the institution of feudalism in its political, social, and intellectual aspects with virtually no reference to individual persons.[61] Lucien Febvre, in a book on the age of Rabelais, attempted through an analysis of language to establish the mental patterns of the age.[62] In his study of medieval rural France Bloch sought on the basis of hard archeological evidence, particularly tools and aerial photographs of field usages, to write a history of medieval agriculture.[63] This work foreshadowed the great interest in "material" factors— climate, food, disease, and so forth—that marked much of the *Annales* work of the 1960s. The fascination with statistics set in at this time, also. Historians like Le Roy Ladurie became interested in the interrelation of demographic cycles and food supply, which could be quantified.[64] In fact "serial history," the establishment of long chains of quantifiable data, now played as significant a role in France as it did in the United States. At all times, however, the "history of mentalities" played an important role in *Annales* writings, with a conscious attempt to study attitudes through the use of hard data. One example is secularization as it became apparent in the measurable declining provisions in eighteenth-century wills for masses for the dead.[65]

The late 1970s and the 1980s saw a worldwide reaction against these forms of objectivism. The history of consciousness increasingly gained in importance, while at the same time new stress was placed on qualitative aspects that could not be adequately measured. Lawrence Stone, in an important article in 1979, spoke of a "Revival of Narrative" that had taken place.[66] This revival took two forms: The first was one that Stone touched on only briefly, a return to older forms of political history, particularly biography, often linked with forms of social and political conservatism, which was the key concern of the article; the other, an attempt by populist historians to recreate the life of simple people.

This second kind of narrative was fundamentally different in its aim and method from the older, traditional forms of narrative. It too argued that the historian must not approach his subject matter with previously formulated theoretical constructs and questions but must derive theory and explanation from the sources themselves. The content of these sources, however, took on a different form. First of all sources were sought that revealed the lives and thoughts of the humble, including the poor, the deviant, and women, rather than of the eminent who had dominated society. A shift took place from high politics and high culture to everyday life and popular culture. But this new history approached these sources very differently from traditional narrative historiography. It was less concerned with the specific actions and intentions of leading individuals than with the existential aspects of the lives of average people. To understand these required a different methodology. Symbolic action, not the written word, was important.[67]

In a very fundamental way the new social history, which stressed so much its concern for the concrete lives of the people it studied, was less interested in the individuals for their own sake than in the culture, viewed as popular culture, of which these individuals were only a part. Deeply influenced by French and American anthropological theory, by Pierre Bourdieu and Clifford Geertz, the historians in this new orientation viewed culture as "an historically transmitted pattern of meanings embodied in symbols, a system of inherited conceptions expressed in symbolic form by which men communicate, perpetuate, and develop their knowledge about attitudes toward life."[68] What people said and meant was not important; their beliefs, attitudes, and actions, signified on a "deeper" level of which they often were unaware, was. The task of the historian was to break the "code" that governed the culture.

Geertz's "thick description" of a Balinese cock fight[69] offered the model for Robert Darnton's recent historical attempt to relate the ritualized massacre of cats by French printers' apprentices in the eighteenth century as a key to understanding social relations and conflicts in Old Regime France.[70] All this makes good reading—which fits in well with the writers who insist that history is indeed a literary genre—but it does not solve the question of the relationship between behavior that the authors regard as symbolic and the fundamental context to which these symbols refer. The notion of a popular culture as it is conceived by these writers remains basically speculative, certainly as long as it contains no conceptual means for testing this relationship. But the very idea of "thick description" assumes an immediate perception of the "deep structure," which permits of no rational controls. Without concepts of social structure the stories that Darnton and others tell remain a set of interesting anecdotes.

We thus find ourselves at a crossroads in the discussion of historical methodology and research techniques. The question as to what constitutes method in history is much more complex today than it was a century or so ago when a broad consensus existed among professional historians. That consensus no longer exists and will not be reestablished soon, if at all. Historical thinking and writing always reflect in some ways the social, political, and intellectual contexts in which they occur, and this context continues to change—resulting in changes not only in historical interpretation but also in historical method. This diversity in historical method can be used to argue against the idea that any sort of secure historical knowledge is possible. In recent years this has led to the insistence that history and poetry are basically akin.[71] Poetry, too, of course, can be a means to achieve human understanding, but for most historians the two continue to be qualitatively different. Historians will continue to recognize that the past has a degree of autonomy, that this autonomy must be respected even if the views of the historian are always colored to some degree by the conceptions of the present. They know that the search for the historical past will always be guided by methodological standards and critical control shared by a community of people who seek to recover aspects of this past, no matter how partial and pluralistic in focus they may be.

NOTES

1. The term *history* has been in use since Greek antiquity. The Greek term ἱστορία (historía) originally meant inquiry and was used by Herodotus to refer to a narrative account. Almost from the beginning the term referred both to the actual course of events and to the historian's reconstruction of these events. Quite frequently until the early nineteenth century, historians, including Leopold von Ranke in his earliest work of 1824 (see n. 4), narrated "histories" rather than a continuous "history." The notion that there was one history that linked earliest times with the future, although present in Judeo-Christian eschatologies, was first widely accepted in its secularized form in the Enlightenment. With the decline of the idea of progress, historians in the twentieth century again questioned the notion that there was one history. Cyclical theorists such as Oswald Spengler and Arnold Toynbee believed that every civilization had its own history portraying its rise and decline. Fernand Braudel spoke of a variety of historical times, of enduring social structures and rapidly changing political events, each of which required a different kind of history. For a discussion of the concept of historical time, see Reinhard

16 The Study of History

Koselleck, *Futures Past: On the Semantics of Historical Time* (Cambridge, Mass.: MIT Press, 1985).

2. On the professionalization of historical scholarship, see Herbert Butterfield, *Man on His Past: The Study of the History of Historical Scholarship* (Cambridge, U.K.: Cambridge University Press, 1955); and John Higham, Leonard Krieger, and Felix Gilbert, *History: The Development of Historical Studies in the United States* (Englewood Cliffs, N.J.: Prentice-Hall, 1965).

3. G. R. Elton, "Two Kinds of History," in *Which Road to the Past? Two Views of History*, G. R. Elton and Robert Fogel (New Haven, Conn.: Yale University Press, 1983), 71–121.

4. "Wie es eigentlich gewesen." See Leopold von Ranke, in "Introduction to the *Histories of the Latin and Germanic Nations*," in *The Theory and Practice of History*, ed. Georg G. Iggers and Konrad von Moltke (Indianapolis, Ind.: Bobbs-Merrill, 1973), 135–38.

5. On the distinction between history and philosophy, see Ranke, "On the Relations of History and Philosophy," ibid., 29–32, and "On the Character of Historical Science," ibid., 33–46; Dilthey, "An Introduction to the Human Studies," in his *Selected Writings*, ed. H. P. Richman (New York: Cambridge University Press, 1976), 157–67, and "The Construction of the Historical World in the Human Studies," ibid., 168–245; Wilhelm Windelband, "Geschichte und Naturwissenschaft," in *Präludien. Aufsätze und Reden zur Philosophie und ihrer Geschichte*, 7th and 8th ed. (Tübingen: Mohr, 1921), vol. 2.

6. Peter Hanns Reill, "History and the Life Sciences in the Early Nineteenth Century: Wilhelm von Humboldt and Leopold von Ranke," in *Leopold von Ranke and the Shaping of the Historical Discipline*, ed. James T. Powell and Georg G. Iggers (Syracuse, N.Y.: Syracuse University Press, 1990), 21–35.

7. Ranke, "Introduction to the *Histories of the Latin and Germanic Nations*," 137.

8. See Charles V. Langlois and Charles Seignobos, *Introduction to the Study of History* (New York: H. Holt, 1926), 316.

9. See Gino Benzoni, "Ranke's Favorite Source: The Venetian Relazioni," in *Leopold von Ranke and the Shaping of the Historical Discipline*, ed. Powell and Iggers, 45–57.

10. See Johann G. Droysen, *Outline of the Principles of History* (Boston: Ginn, 1893).

11. Ernst Bernheim, *Lehrbuch der historischen Methode und der Geschichtsphilosophie*, 6th ed. (Leipzig: Duncker & Humbolt, 1908); Langlois and Seignobos, *Introduction to the Study of History*; Louis Gottschalk, *Understanding History* (New York: Knopf, 1958).

12. Dilthey, *Selected Writings*; Croce, *History: Its Theory and Practice* (New York: Harcourt, Brace and Company, 1921); R. G. Collingwood, *The Idea of History* (Oxford: Clarendon Press, 1946).

13. Windelband, "Geschichte und Naturwissenschaft"; Meinecke, *Historism: The Rise of a New Historical Outlook* (New York: Herder and Herder, 1972).

14. See Durkheim's inaugural address in his course on "social science" at the University of Bordeaux published in 1888, and also William R. Keylor, *Academy and Community: The Foundation of the French Historical Profession* (Cambridge, Mass.: Harvard University Press, 1975), 112–13.

15. " 'Objectivity' in Social Science and Social Policy," in *Max Weber on the Methodology of the Social Sciences*, trans. and ed. Edward A. Shils and Henry A. Finch (Glencoe, Ill.: Free Press, 1949).

16. See John Higham in Higham, Krieger, and Gilbert, *History*, chapters 2 and 3, 87–232.

17. See Bryce Lyon, *Henri Pirenne: A Biographical and Intellectual Study* (Ghent: Story-Scientia, 1974).

18. "The Use and Abuse of History" in *Thoughts Out of Season*, part 2 (New York: Russell & Russell, 1964), 1–100.

19. See Hayden White's discussion of Barthes and French theories of the narrative in "The Question of Narrative in Contemporary Historical Theory," *History and Theory*, vol. 23 (1984), 1–33, esp. 10–15.

20. This note runs through all of Michel Foucault's writings from *Madness and Civilization* (New York: Pantheon Books, 1965) to *A History of Sexuality* (New York: Pantheon Books, 1978–).

21. Lévi-Strauss, *The Savage Mind* (Chicago: University of Chicago Press, 1966).

22. Cf. Donald Kelley, "Mythistory in the Age of Ranke," in *Leopold von Ranke and the Shaping of the Historical Discipline*, ed. Powell and Iggers, 3–20.

23. See Rudolf Vierhaus, "History Between Science and Art," in *Leopold von Ranke and the Shaping of the Historical Discipline*, ed. Powell and Iggers, 61–69.

24. Spengler, *The Decline of the West* (New York: Knopf, 1926), esp. chapter 2, "Meaning of Numbers."

25. See Bachelard, *The Philosophy of No: A Philosophy of the New Scientific Mind* (New York: Orion Press, 1960).

26. See n. 19.

27. Hayden White, *Metahistory: The Historical Imagination in Nineteenth-Century Europe* (Baltimore: Johns Hopkins University Press, 1973), x, xi.

28. See Hans Kellner, "Narrativity in History: Post-Structuralism and Since," *History and Theory*, Beiheft 26 (1987), 1–33.

29. Cf. White, *Metahistory*, x, xi; see also Dominick LaCapra, "Chartier, Darnton, and the Great Symbol Massacre," *Journal of Modern History* 60 (1988): 95–112.

30. See Clifford Geertz, "Thick Description: Toward an Interpretive Theory of Culture," in his *Interpretation of Culture* (New York: Basic Books, 1973), 3–30, and his "Deep Play: Notes on the Balinese Cockfight," ibid., 412–53; Marshall Sahlins, *Islands of History* (Chicago: University of Chicago Press, 1985); also Hans Medick, "Missionaries in the Rowboat: Ethnological Ways of Knowing as a Challenge to Social History," *Comparative Studies in History and Society* 27 (1987): 76–98.

31. Arnaldo Momigliano, "The Place of Herodotus in the History of Historiography," in *Studies in History* (New York: Oxford University Press, 1966), 127–42; on Thucydides, "Tradition and the Classical Historian," in *Essays in Ancient and Modern History* (Middletown, Conn.: Wesleyan University Press, 1977), 161–77.

32. Felix Gilbert, *Machiavelli and Guicciardini: Politics and History in Sixteenth-Century Florence* (Princeton, N.J.: Princeton University Press, 1965).

33. See Hans-Erich Bödeker et al., *Aufklärung und Geschichte: Studien zur deutschen Geschichtswissenschaft* (Göttingen: Vandenhoeck & Ruprecht, 1986); and Peter H. Reill, *The German Enlightenment and the Rise of Historicism* (Berkeley: University of California Press, 1975).

34. See F. A. Wolf, *Prolegomena to Homer*, ed. Anthony Grafton (Princeton, N.J.: Princeton University Press, 1985).

35. See Marx's letter to Wedemeyer, 5 March 1852, in Karl Marx and Friedrich

Engels, *Correspondence, 1846–1895* (New York: International Publishers, 1936), 56–57.

36. Tocqueville, *The Old Regime and the Revolution* (1856).

37. Karl Marx, *The Eighteenth Brumaire of Louis Bonaparte* (1852).

38. Jacob Burckhardt, *Civilisation of the Period of the Renaissance in Italy*, 2 vols. (London: C.K. Paul & Co., 1878).

39. "A Dialogue on Politics," in *The Theory and Practice of History*, Iggers and Moltke, 102–30.

40. Georg G. Iggers, *The German Conception of History: The National Tradition of Historical Thought from Herder to the Present*, 2d ed. (Middletown, Conn.: Wesleyan University Press, 1983).

41. Keylor, *Academy and Community*.

42. Cf. John Higham, "Beyond Consensus: The Historian as Moral Critic," *American Historical Review* 67 (1961–62): 609–25; Richard Hofstetter, *The Progressive Historians: Turner, Beard, Parrington* (New York: Knopf, 1968).

43. See Georg G. Iggers, "Social History, the Social Sciences and Political Culture, 1890–1914: An International Perspective," *Tel Aviver Jahrbuch für deutsche Geschichte* 17 (1987): 117–34.

44. See Georg G. Iggers, *New Directions in European Historiography*, 2d ed. (Middletown, Conn.: Wesleyan University Press, 1984); also Geoffrey Barraclough, *Main Trends in History* (New York: Holmes & Meier, 1978).

45. See Michael Kammen, *The Past Before Us: Contemporary Historical Writing in the United States* (Ithaca, N.Y.: Cornell University Press, 1980).

46. George Trevelyan, *English Social History* (London: Longmans, Green, 1942).

47. Georg G. Iggers, ed., *The Social History of Politics: Critical Perspectives in West German Historical Writing since 1945* (Leamington Spa: Berg, 1985), esp. the Introduction.

48. See Barraclough, *Main Trends*, 17–27; and Iggers, *New Directions*, chapter 4 and Epilogue.

49. Lukács, "What Is Orthodox Marxism?" in his *History and Class Consciousness: Studies in Marxist Dialectics* (Cambridge, Mass.: Harvard University Press, 1971), 46–82.

50. See Barraclough, *Main Trends*, 17–28.

51. Two very important works in this connection are E. P. Thompson, *The Making of the English Working Class* (London, 1963); and Carlo Ginzburg, *The Cheese and the Worms: The Cosmos of a Sixteenth-Century Miller* (Baltimore: Johns Hopkins University Press, 1982).

52. See Georg G. Iggers and Harold T. Parker, *International Handbook of Historical Studies* (Westport, Conn.: Greenwood Press, 1979).

53. See Iggers, *Social History of Politics*.

54. Cf. Robert Fogel, "Two Kinds of History," in *Which Road to the Past?* Elton and Fogel, 5–70.

55. Buckle, "From General Introduction: *History of Civilization in England*," in *The Varieties of History* ed. Fritz Stern (New York: Vantage Books, 1973), 121–37.

56. "Art and Method," in ibid., 137–44.

57. Cf. François Furet, "Quantitative History," in *Historical Studies Today*, Felix Gilbert and Stephen R. Graubard (New York: W.W. Norton, 1971), 45–61.

58. Barraclough, *Main Trends*, 89.

59. See Herbert Gutman, *Slavery and the Numbers Game* (Urbana: University of Illinois Press, 1975); for a defense of Fogel and Engerman, see J. Morgan Kousser, "Quantitative Social-Scientific History," in *The Past Before Us*, Kammen, 446–47.

60. Emmanuel Le Roy Ladurie, *The Territory of the Historian* (Chicago: University of Chicago Press, 1979), 15.

61. Marc Bloch, *Feudal Society*, 2 vols. (Chicago: University of Chicago Press, 1964).

62. Lucien Febvre, *The Problem of Unbelief in the Sixteenth Century: The Religion of Rabelais* (Cambridge, Mass.: Harvard University Press, 1982).

63. Marc Bloch, *French Rural Society* (Berkeley: University of California Press, 1966).

64. Emmanuel Le Roy Ladurie, *The Peasants of Languedoc* (Urbana: University of Illinois Press, 1974).

65. On studies of death by François Lebrun, Michel Vovelle, Philippe Ariès, and Pierre Chaunu, see Iggers, *New Directions*, 245, n. 60.

66. Stone, "The Revival of Narrative: Reflections on a New Old History," *Past and Present* 85 (November 1979): 3–24.

67. On the question of symbolism and semiotics, see Roger Chartier's critique of Robert Darnton, *The Great Cat Massacre and Other Episodes in French Cultural History* (New York: Basic Books, 1984), in "Text, Symbols and Frenchmen," *Journal of Modern History* 57 (1985): 682–95; and Darnton's reply, "The Symbolic Element in History," ibid. 58 (1986): 219–34; also LaCapra, "Chartier, Darnton, and the Great Symbol Massacre."

68. Geertz, *Interpretation of Culture*, 89.

69. Geertz, "Deep Play: Notes on the Balinese Cockfight," 412–53.

70. Darnton, *The Great Cat Massacre*.

71. Hayden W. White, *Metahistory: The Historical Imagination in Nineteenth-Century Europe* (Baltimore: Johns Hopkins University Press, 1973), x.

SELECTED BIBLIOGRAPHY

Bibliographical Guides

A useful introduction to the literature on historical method and the history of historiography is provided by the American Historical Association's annotated *Guide to Historical Literature*. A first edition appeared in 1931, a second in 1961 (see esp. 1–21), and a third edition is in preparation and publication is planned for the mid–1990s. Also important are the bibliographies that are published every few years in the *Beihefte* of *History and Theory*. ABC-Clio, the publishers of *Historical Abstracts* and *America: History and Life* in 1987, published the two-volume work *Historiography: An Annotated Bibliography of Journal Articles, Books and Dissertations*, ed. Susan K. Kinnell. A bibliography even more extensive in its international and chronological scope has been prepared by Attila Pók entitled *A Selected Bibliography of Modern Historiography* (Westport, Conn.: Greenwood Press, 1992). For theory of history, see also Helmut Berding, *Bibliographie zur Geschichtstheorie* (Göttingen, Ger.: Vandenhoeck und Ruprecht, 1977); for historiography, particularly the excellent and comprehensive bibliography in Ernst Breisach, *Historiography: Ancient, Medieval, Modern* (Chicago: University of Chicago Press, 1983), 429–64.

Philosophy and Theory of History

A distinction has been commonly made between "speculative" and "critical" philosophies of history. The former, which interests us less in the context of this essay, attempts to fathom the direction and meaning of human history; the latter, perhaps better called "analytical" philosophies of history because of their close relationship to Anglo-American analytical philosophy, are more concerned with the problem of historical knowledge. Aside from very brief remarks by ancient writers (Aristotle, Lucian), the first serious attempts to deal with the question of the nature of historical knowledge and method appear in the Renaissance and post-Renaissance period (e.g., Lorenzo Valla, Jean Bodin). See George Huppert, *The Idea of Perfect History: Historical Erudition and Historical Philosophy in Renaissance France* (Urbana: University of Illinois Press, 1970); Donald R. Kelley, *Foundations of Modern Historical Scholarship: Language, Law, and History in the French Renaissance* (New York: Columbia University Press, 1970); and J. G. A. Pocock, *The Ancient Constitution and the Feudal Law: A Study of English Historical Thought in the 17th Century* (Cambridge: Cambridge University Press, 1987). In Giambattista Vico's *New Science* (3d ed. of 1744, trans. T. G. Bergin and Max H. Fisch; Ithaca, N.Y.: Cornell University Press, 1968), a grandiose conception of historical cycles and progress is combined with an attempt to distinguish history as something made by human beings from nature that is not the direct product of men—and hence to call for a unique science of history. This concern with the unique character of historical knowledge is also typical of Johann Martin Chladenius's *Allgemeine Geschichtswissenschaft* of 1752, recently reissued (Wien: Böhlau, 1985) and other eighteenth-century thinkers; see Horst Walter Blanke and Dirk Fleischer, eds., *Theoretiker der Aufklärung*, 2 vols. (Stuttgart-Bad Cannstatt: Frommann-Holzboog, 1990). On the origins of a historical outlook in eighteenth-century German scholarship, see Peter Reill, *The German Enlightenment and the Rise of Historicism* (Berkeley: University of California Press, 1975). From a broadly European but very partisan perspective, see Friedrich Meinecke, *Historism: The Rise of a New Historical Outlook* (1936; London: Routledge and Kegan Paul, 1972). For French Enlightenment thought, Voltaire's article "Histoire" in the *Encyclopédie ou dictionnaire raisonné des sciences, des arts et des métiers*, vol. 17 (Lausanne: Sociétés Typographiques, 1782), 555–64, is instructive. On early nineteenth-century approaches to historical knowledge, particularly in Germany, see Joachim Wach, *Das Verstehen*, 3 vols. (Tübingen: Mohr, 1926–1933); for the German idealistic tradition generally, see Hans-Georg Gadamer, *Truth and Method* (New York: Seabury Press, 1975). The most comprehensive examination of thought on historical method in the late-nineteenth and early-twentieth centuries in Europe and North America is contained in the work by the Soviet philosopher and sociologist Igor Kon, *Filosovskiĭ idealizm i krizis burzhuaznoĭ istoricheskoĭ mysli* (Moscow: Izdvo sotsial noekohomichesko i literatury, 1959); German translation: *Geschichtsphilosophie des 20. Jahrhunderts*, 2 vols. (Berlin, East Germany: Akademie-Verlag, 1964). On late-nineteenth and early-twentieth century idealistic notions of historical method and knowledge, see Maurice Mandelbaum, *The Problem of Historical Knowledge: An Answer to Relativism* (New York: Liveright, 1938); and his more recent *History, Man, and Reason: A Study in 19th Century Historical Knowledge* (Baltimore: Johns Hopkins Press, 1971). A brief survey of speculative and critical discussions is contained in William Dray, *Philosophy of History* (Englewood Cliffs, N.J.: Prentice-Hall, 1964). On very recent discussions, see Hayden White, "The

Question of Narrative in Contemporary Historical Theory,'' *History and Theory* 23 (1984): 1–33; and Hans Kellner, ''Narrativity in History: Post-Structuralism and After,'' *History and Theory*, Beiheft 26 (1987).

There are three very useful anthologies of writings on problems of historical knowledge, none unfortunately recent enough to include the discussions of the past two decades, namely: Patrick Gardiner, ed., *Theories of History* (Glencoe, Ill.: Free Press, 1959); Hans Meyerhof, ed., *Philosophy of History in Our Time* (Garden City, N.J.: Doubleday, 1959); and Ronald Nash, ed., *Ideas of History*, 2 vols. (New York: Dutton, 1969), esp. vol. 2 on critical philosophies of history.

Historical thought in recent years has gone in different directions. The so-called critical philosophy of history, particularly in the Anglo-American world, was strongly influenced by analytical philosophy of history. The discussions on the narrative, mentioned earlier, marked a transition to a very different approach, influenced by continental philosophy and especially by recent French and American literary theory. As in analytical or critical philosophy, the emphasis was on language, but language was conceived very differently, as neither referential nor consisting of clearly definable concepts. The new language-oriented approach to historical writing is no longer interested in historical explanation but in examining historical texts as literary products. An important work that helped initiate the new orientation was Hayden White, *Metahistory: The Historical Imagination in Nineteenth-Century Europe* (Baltimore: Johns Hopkins University Press, 1973). Since then there has been a wealth of literature produced. A selection of titles includes: Dominick LaCapra, *History and Criticism* (Ithaca, N.Y.: Cornell University Press, 1985); John Toews, ''Intellectual History after the Linguistic Turn,'' *American Historical Review* 92 (1987): 879–907; Hans Kellner, *Language and Historical Representation: Getting the Story Crooked* (Madison: University of Wisconsin Press, 1989); Allan Megill, ''Re-counting the Past: 'Description,' Explanation, and Narrative in Historiography,'' *American Historical Review* 94 (1989): 627–53; F. R. Ankersmit, ''Historiography and Postmodernism,'' *History and Theory* 28 (1989): 139–53; Perez Zagorin, ''Historiography and Postmodernism: Reconsiderations,'' *History and Theory* 29 (1990): 263–74; F. R. Ankersmit, ''Reply to Professor Zagorin,'' ibid., 275–96.

Historical Method

A classical attempt to apply criteria of historical criticism to historical works is Leopold von Ranke's ''Zur Kritik neuerer Geschichtschreiber'' (Toward a critique of modern historians) of 1824. The two major German textbooks in historical method in the nineteenth century were J. G. Droysen's *Grundriss der Historik,* a small section of which was published in English as *Outline of the Principles of History* (Boston, Mass.: Ginn, 1893); and Ernst Bernheim's *Lehrbuch der historischen Methode und der Geschichtsphilosophie* (Leipzig, 1889; 5th and 6th rev. ed., Duncker & Humbolt, 1908). Bernheim became a standard work and a guide for manuals in other countries but interestingly enough was never translated into English. Droysen, whose manual received much less attention at the time, has experienced a revival, but less for his methodological guidelines than for his broader philosophical and theoretical scope. The link between theory and methodological practice is also important in Bernheim's manual, as the title suggests. Bernheim provided a basis for Charles V. Langlois and Charles Seignobos's *Introduction to the Study of History*, published in Paris in French in 1898 and translated in the same year into English. Langlois and Seignobos consciously avoided the theoretical concerns of

Bernheim, however, and emphasized methodological procedures. They basically continued Ranke's conception of critical method but separated it from its philosophical foundations. A number of textbooks appeared in English along practical lines similar to those of Langlois and Seignobos, including Homer C. Hockett, *The Critical Method in Historical Research and Writing* (New York: Macmillan, 1955); Louis Gottschalk, *Understanding History: A Primer of Historical Method* (New York: Knopf, 1969); and Jacques Barzun and Henry F. Graff, *The Modern Researcher*, which has appeared in several editions since its first publication in 1957. None of these books, with the exception of very brief sections in the revised 1977 and 1985 editions of *The Modern Researcher* (Fort Worth, Tex.: Harcourt Brace Jovanovich), deal with the methods that have transformed historical research.

A number of texts have dealt with aspects of contemporary historical method, such as Robert F. Berkhoffer, *A Behavioral Approach to Historical Analysis* (New York: Free Press, 1969); William O. Aydelotte et al., eds., *The Dimensions of Quantitative History: Selected Readings* (Princeton, N.J.: Princeton University Press, 1972); and Robert Fogel, "Scientific History and Traditional History," in *Which Road to the Past? Two Views of History*, G. R. Elton and Robert Fogel (New Haven, Conn.: Yale University Press, 1983); but these books too are already partly outdated, and none offers a systematic and comprehensive approach to contemporary practices. On oral history, see Michael Frisch, *A Shared Authority: Essays on the Craft and Meaning of Oral and Public History* (Albany: State University of New York Press, 1990).

There is as yet no good manual in the English language, or for that matter in French or German, that does justice to the variety of present-day methods and conceptualization of historical research. Perhaps the most comprehensive and up-to-date guide, which goes beyond traditional historical criticism in the Rankean manner to a variety of modern approaches, is *L'Histoire et ses méthodes*, ed. Charles Samaran (Paris: Gallimard, 1961), which is now three decades old. Four French works, Jacques LeGoff and Pierre Nora, eds., *Faire l'histoire*, 3 vols. (Paris: Gallimard, 1974); the small encyclopedia, *La Nouvelle Histoire* (Paris: Retz, 1978); and Emmanuel Le Roy Ladurie's two collections of essays, *The Territory of the Historian* (Chicago: University of Chicago Press, 1979) and *The Mind and Method of the Historian* (Chicago: University of Chicago Press, 1981), deal with aspects of modern methodology in a less systematic fashion. On more recent discussions and trends, see Lynn Hunt, ed., *The New Cultural History* (Berkley: University of California Press, 1989). Several journals should be mentioned that deal with problems in the philosophy and theory of history and also with the history of historiography, namely the international journal *History and Theory: Studies in the Philosophy of History*; *Clio: A Journal of Literature, History, Philosophy of History*; *History and Memory*; and a journal also called *History and Theory*, published in the People's Republic of China in Chinese from the mid–1980s until its suspension in the summer of 1989.

The History of Historical Writing

The most up-to-date history of western historical writing is Ernst Breisach, *Historiography: Ancient, Medieval, Modern* (Chicago: University of Chicago Press, 1983), which seeks to place historical writing in the context of the history of ideas and thus overcome what otherwise might be an encyclopedic undertaking. This is the only history of western historiography that follows the development of historical practice into the second half of the twentieth century. Two previous attempts to span the full scope of historical writing from the ancient to the modern period are Harry Elmer Barnes, *A History of Historical Writing*, 2d rev. ed. (New York: Dover, 1963), which seeks to trace the evolution of history from lore to science; and James Westfall Thompson's two volumes by the same title (New York: Macmillan, 1942). Herbert Butterfield's article "Historiography" in the *Dictionary of the History of Ideas*, vol. 2 (New York: Scribner, 1972), 464–98, is a skillful and well-written examination of major traditions of historical writing, including a brief excursion into nonwestern historiography. See also Arnaldo Momigliano's entry, "Historiography: Western Studies," in *The Encyclopedia of Religion*, vol. 6 (New York: Macmillan, 1987), 383–90. The collections of essays edited by Mathew A. Fitzsimons, *The Development of Historiography* (Harrisburg, Pa.: Stackpole, 1954), contain separate informative chapters on historical writing in various epochs, regions, and countries without any attempt at synthesis. Still missing is a comprehensive history of historiography that also gives extensive consideration to the nonwestern world. Ernst Breisach attempts this within the confines of an encyclopedia article in his entry, "Historiography: An Overview," in *The Encyclopedia of Religion*, vol. 6, 370–83; as does the slender volume in French by Charles-Olivier Carbonell, *L'Historiographie* in the *Que Sais-Je?* series (Paris: Presses Universitaires de France, 1981). A special journal for the history of historiography, *Storia della Storiografia* (History of historiography) was founded in 1982 and carries articles in English, Italian, French, and German. Momigliano's essays in *Studies in Historiography* (New York: Harper & Row, 1966) and *Essays in Ancient and Modern Historiography* (Middletown, Conn.: Wesleyan University Press, 1977) deserve particular attention.

There are few studies on nonwestern historiographical traditions. Volumes that can be cited include *Historians of China and Japan*, ed. W. G. Beaseley and E. G. Pulleyblank (London: Oxford University Press, 1961); *Chinese Traditional Historiography*, a collection of readings edited by Charles Sidney Gardner (Cambridge, Mass.: Harvard University Press, 1961); *Historians of India, Pakistan, and Ceylon*, ed. Cyril Henry Philips (London, 1961); Franz Rosenthal's *A History of Muslim Historiography*, 2d ed. (Leiden: E. J. Brill, 1968). On black Africa no parallel work exists yet, but the essay by J. F. Ade. Ajayi and E. J. Alagoa, "Sub-Saharan Africa," in *International Handbook of Historical Studies*, ed. Georg G. Iggers and Harold T. Parker (Westport, Conn.: Greenwood Press, 1979), contains a valuable bibliography, 416–18.

On pre-ancient historiography, see H. C. Dent, ed., *The Idea of History in the Ancient Near East* (New Haven, Conn.: Yale University Press, 1955). Among works on Greek and Roman historians, the following should be included: Michael Grant, *The Ancient Historians* (New York: Scribner, 1970); Moses I. Finley, ed., *The Greek Historians* (London: Chatto & Windus, 1959); and Momigliano's essays, already mentioned. A good survey of medieval historiography is contained in the previously cited work by Ernst Breisach, *Historiography*. On the Renaissance, see Eric Cochrane, *Historians and Historiography in the Italian Renaissance* (Chicago: University of Chicago Press, 1981); Peter Burke, *The Renaissance Sense of the Past* (London: Edward Arnold, 1970); and Felix Gilbert, *Machiavelli and Guicciardini: Politics and History in 16th Century Florence* (Princeton, N.J.: Princeton University Press, 1965). On the early modern period, the works by Huppert, Kelley, and Pocock listed above should be mentioned. The classical work on modern historical writing from the Renaissance until the late nineteenth century remains Eduard Fueter's *Geschichte der neueren Historiographie*, 3d ed. (Munich: R. Oldenbourg, 1936), unfortunately never translated into English. A good view of the emergence of modern scholarly methods in the eighteenth century and its impact on the nineteenth century is contained in Herbert Butterfield, *Man on His Past: The Study of the History of Historical Scholarship* (London: Cambridge University Press, 1955). A very good collection of programmatic statements by historians from Voltaire in the eighteenth century to Fernand Braudel in the twentieth century is contained in Fritz Stern, ed., *The Varieties of History: From Voltaire to the Present*, expanded ed. (New York: Random House, 1973). For history of nineteenth-century historiography with extensive intellectual biographies of major historians, see George P. Gooch, *History and Historians in the Nineteenth Century* (London, 1914; rep. Boston: Beacon Press, 1959); also Felix Gilbert, *History: Politics or Culture? Reflections on Ranke and Burckhardt* (Princeton, N.J.: Princeton University Press, 1990). On nineteenth- and twentieth-century historians of Europe, see Bernadotte E. Schmitt, ed., *Some Historians of Modern Europe* (Chicago: University of Chicago Press, 1942); S. W. Halperin, ed., *Some 20th Century Historians* (Chicago: University of Chicago Press, 1961); S. W. Halperin, comp., *Essays in Modern European Historiography* (Chicago: University of Chicago Press, 1970); and Hans A. Schmitt, ed., *Historians of Modern Europe* (Baton Rouge: Louisiana State University Press, 1971).

For histories that deal with national developments, for the United States see Michael Kraus, *The Writing of American History* (Norman: University of Oklahoma Press, 1985); Richard Hofstadter, *The Progressive Historians* (New York: Knopf, 1968); John Higham, Felix Gilbert, and Leonard Krieger, *History: The Development of Historical Studies in the United States* (Englewood Cliffs, N.J.: Prentice Hall, 1965); and Michael Kammen, ed., *The Past Before Us: Contemporary Historical Writing in the United States* (Ithaca, N.Y.: Cornell University Press, 1980). For France, see François Furet, *In the Workshop of the Historian* (Chicago: University of Chicago Press, 1984); William Keylor, *Academy and Community: The Foundations of the French Historical Profession* (Cambridge, Mass.: Harvard University Press, 1975); and Troian Stoianovich, *French Historical Method: The Annales Paradigm* (Ithaca, N.Y.: Cornell University Press, 1976). On Germany, see Georg G. Iggers, *The German Conception of History: The National Tradition of Historical Thought from Herder to the Present*, 2d rev. ed. (Middletown, Conn.: Wesleyan University Press, 1983).

For treatments of historiographic trends in the second half of the twentieth century, see Geoffrey Barraclough, *History in a Changing World* (Norman, Okla: Oklahoma University Press, 1956); *Main Trends in History* (New York: Holmes & Meier, 1979); Georg G. Iggers, *New Directions in European Historiography*, 2d rev. ed. (Middletown, Conn.: Wesleyan University Press, 1984); Felix Gilbert and Stephen R. Graubard, eds., *Historical Studies Today* (New York: W.W. Norton, 1971); Charles F. Delzell, ed., *The Future of History* (Nashville, Tenn.: Vanderbilt University Press, 1977); Georg G. Iggers and Harold T. Parker, eds., *International Handbook of Historical Studies* (Westport, Conn.: Greenwood Press, 1979); and Theodore K. Rabb and Robert I. Rotberg, eds., *The New History: The 1980's and Beyond: Studies in Interdisciplinary History* (Princeton, N.J.: Princeton University Press, 1982); also see the two special issues of *Storia della Storiografia*, no. 17 (1990) and no. 18 (1991), on the writing of social history in the 1980s.

2

History and Interdisciplinary History

Harry Ritter

History, it has been aptly observed, is an "omnivorous" discipline. Few present-day scholars would contest the notion that historians are free to study anything at all, provided that it happened in the past and that it affected human beings. It is also widely agreed that historians may employ a broad range of methods, theoretical categories, and literary devices—from statistical theory to the rhetorical strategies of romance or tragedy—providing that their choice of technique and style illuminates the data they wish to explain.

Such ecumenical views have not always prevailed. At the turn of the present century, for instance, history was often a staid affair, narrowly identified with the evolution of political institutions. Students of the time, even at the higher levels, were commonly expected to vie with one another in memorizing chronologies of political facts dictated by their instructors. This approach was an exaggerated extension of the ancient tradition associating history with the record of great deeds, and it persists in popular notions of history even today. The idea that a historical work may properly deal with demographic trends, collective emotions, or human fertility rates (as opposed to political campaigns or presidential administrations) might well come as a surprise to many members of the American public. Even in the eighteenth century, however, authors such as Voltaire and Herder published philosophical histories that centered on themes such as popular mores, folk customs, art, technology, and so on, at the expense of politics. Indeed, the late nineteenth century produced the classic example of "cultural" (as opposed to narrowly political) historiography: Jacob Burckhardt's *The Civilization of the Renaissance in Italy* (1860). Thus, the view that history is reducible to "past politics" was really little more than the favored approach of some prominent historians of the late Victorian era.

The author wishes to thank professors Amanda Eurich and Louis Truschel for their comments on this chapter.

All the same, the growth of a self-consciously interdisciplinary approach in history had to await the turn of the twentieth century.[1] This is because the idea of systematic borrowing from other disciplines depended on the establishment of those disciplines. In the mid- and late-nineteenth century the modern social sciences—geography, sociology, economics, psychology, anthropology—became academic subjects. The founders of these new fields devised novel methods to study human phenomena—innovations distrusted by conservative members of the historical guild but gradually embraced and adapted by a small group of experimenters.[2] The stage was thus set for a period of increasingly frequent cross-fertilization between history and the other human sciences. This process has since become so significant that one may hazard the view that twentieth-century historiography's most important feature has been its tendency to become more comprehensive in scope and more experimental and eclectic in method.

In this chapter, I wish to do two things: (1) present a brief survey of the origins and growth of this interdisciplinary movement; and (2) discuss some recent examples of cross-disciplinary historical research, as well as their critical reception by historians and authorities in other fields.

ORIGINS AND GROWTH OF THE IDEA OF INTERDISCIPLINARY HISTORY

Perhaps the most dramatic instance of a self-consciously interdisciplinary historiographical movement arose in early twentieth-century France. There, in 1900, Henri Berr (1863–1954) founded the *Revue de synthèse historique*, describing his program for "historical synthesis" as "basically an appeal for greater cooperation between social scientists and historians."[3] Berr's *Revue de synthèse* soon became a major platform for international discussion of interdisciplinary research and theory. Most important, perhaps, it helped create the climate in which the now famous *Annales* school of French historiography originated. The *Annales* school, led by Lucien Febvre and Marc Bloch (founders and editors of the journal *Annales d'histoire économique et sociale* from 1929 onward), championed the view that history "must be wide open to the findings and methods of other disciplines—geography, economics, sociology, psychology."[4] The *Annales* historians led a crusade in favor of "total history"—the history of all aspects of human life in the past—and against *histoire événementielle*, an expression they used to denote history narrowly conceived as the record of political events.

From the 1930s onward the *Annales* school functioned as a historiographical avant-garde, not only in France but also internationally. In 1947 Febvre became president of a new "Sixth Section" of the French Ecole des Hautes Etudes, an agency that sought to promote advanced research in the social sciences.[5] Under Febvre's guidance, the Sixth Section became the world's most important center for the development of interdisciplinary theory, methodological innovation, research, and publication. By the 1960s the *Annales* provided a major source of inspiration for interdisciplinary history in Europe and the Americas.

Conditions in late-nineteenth-century Germany were not as favorable for the growth of interdisciplinary history as they were in France. In German-speaking Europe, historical studies were professionalized in the late-eighteenth and early-nineteenth centuries—ahead of France, England, and America. Thus, before the complete emergence and legitimization of the social science disciplines, a strong tradition of historiographical orthodoxy had been established, revolving around the idea of painstaking archival research, philological criticism, and the notion of the political state as a spiritual organism. In this context of solid scholarly and theoretical accomplishment, identified with revered names such as Niebuhr, Ranke, Waitz, Sybel, and Droysen, the idea of methodological experimentation found few supporters.

There was, nonetheless, one noteworthy German champion of interdisciplinary studies: Karl Lamprecht (1865–1915). Lamprecht, who taught at Leipzig from 1891 until his death in 1915, employed the label *Kulturgeschichte* (cultural history) to designate a comprehensive approach in which he sought to blend the methods of traditional historiography with those of economics, art history, and psychology (particularly the theories of Wilhelm Wundt and Theodor Lipps). Lamprecht considered psychology especially crucial and defined his version of cultural history as "the comparative history of the factors of socio-psychic development."[6] To make psychology genuinely useful to history, however, he maintained that it would have to be transformed from an introspective science into a collective social psychology based on the study of groups and situations rather than single individuals.

In his ambitious, twenty-one-volume *Deutsche Geschichte* (1891–1915), Lamprecht tried to demonstrate his method by describing the evolution of the collective German psyche (*Volksseele*) through a series of stages from ancient times to his own day. The result was disappointing; it is now agreed that Lamprecht's aspirations were simply too vast for the methods available to him (social psychology and statistics were still in their infancy), and that his books were written too rapidly, without sufficient attention to accuracy.

Lamprecht's work sparked a furious controversy within the German historical profession, and before the outbreak of World War I his ideas had been discredited in the minds of the majority of his peers as "eclectic trifling."[7] Thus he established no lasting tradition in German scholarship, and it is only since the 1960s that some West German historians, in conscious revolt against the state-worshiping historiography that prevailed in central Europe from Ranke's day to that of Friedrich Meinecke, have begun to cultivate an interdisciplinary approach oriented especially toward the use of Weberian sociology and Marxist social and economic theory.

But if Lamprecht's work was ridiculed in turn-of-the-century Germany, his ideas were welcomed in the United States, where they helped to inspire an interdisciplinary "New History" on the eve of World War I. A basic feature of the New History doctrine, which flourished from about 1912 (the publication date of James Harvey Robinson's collection of essays entitled *The New History*) to the mid–1930s, was an appeal for an "enthusiastic alliance with the social sciences."[8] Among those prominently associated with the New History were Harry Elmer Barnes, Charles Beard, James T. Shotwell, Conyers Read, Frederick J. Teggart, and Crane Brinton. For these men the expression "New History" was a battle cry designating a "synthetic," present-oriented approach to the past that was pitted against the "political fetish" of late-nineteenth-century historiography.[9]

The influence of these ideas on historical scholarship in America was much greater than that of Lamprecht on German historiography. As a label for innovators, it is true, the term *New History* temporarily lost favor after the mid–1930s, when the first generation of the movement began to decline due to its perceived association with presentism, relativism, and "indiscriminate eclecticism."[10] Still, the New History unquestionably helped to reorient thinking and paved the way for a broader and more methodologically ecumenical view of history after World War II. Today the expression "new history" is once again in vogue, primarily in conjunction with the growing list of specialized subfields of historical scholarship—as in "new social history," "new political history," or "new economic history."

In fact it has really been since 1945 that a large-scale shift in the direction of consciously interdisciplinary *practice* (as opposed to theory) has begun to take place. This development has to some degree been intertwined with two other postwar trends: (1) widening the scope of historical inquiry to include the social traditions of the nonwestern world as well as those of Western Europe and North America; and (2) a more "democratic" emphasis on efforts to tell the stories of "the people" as a whole, that is, to write histories of the inarticulate masses as well as political and cultural elites.[11] Indeed, the urge to broaden history's focus in these two ways has led historians to look increasingly to other disciplines for new strategies. The countries that have led in this work of rejuvenation and liberalization are France and the United States, where interdisciplinary research has been fostered by such internationally prestigious journals as Bloch and Febvre's *Annales* (now rechristened *Annales: Economies, Sociétés, Civilisations*) and the *Journal of Interdisciplinary History* (founded in 1970).

SELECTED EXAMPLES OF RECENT INTERDISCIPLINARY WORK

It is now time to shift attention to some instances of this research, in order to assess its reception by historians as well as specialists in other disciplines.

One of the more interesting examples of interdisciplinary historical scholarship to appear in recent years—in terms of both commercial success and academic recognition—is Carl E. Schorske's *Fin-de-Siècle Vienna: Politics and Culture*. Schorske's study is a hybrid of traditional cultural history,[12] sociology of knowledge, and psychoanalytic interpretation that seeks to illuminate relationships between sociopolitical change and high culture in Vienna in the decades around 1900. In 1981 it received the Pulitzer Prize for general nonfiction—an indication of its appeal to a broad audience. While most academic reviewers were adversely critical, they also agreed that the book was one of special significance, and a leading student of Austrian history called it a "stunning achievement," predicting that it would attain the "status of a modern classic."[13]

Schorske's book is a convenient place to start our survey of individual works since its introduction contains a clear statement of the centrality of the interdisciplinary orientation to its content. These remarks are not presented as a manifesto, but rather as personal testimony of the author's gradual discovery of the need to use a cross-disciplinary strategy to make sense of his subject matter. As a beginning teacher in the late 1940s, Schorske relates, he sought to design a course that would introduce college students to the linkages between high culture and social change. To package such a course he needed suitable interpretive generalizations under which to classify, contextualize, and so historically explain the various data. Earlier historians had already devised many such "conceptual premises" in the course of their efforts to explain modern change: rationalism, progress, liberalism, romanticism, individualism, realism, and so forth. Schorske soon concluded, however, that the optimistic controlling assumptions of previous histories were inadequate to the task of the scholar who, living in the aftermath of two world wars, wished to elucidate the sources of contemporary disillusionment, and was himself an intellectual product of this modern temper. The consensus that once existed on the adequacy of these concepts for social analysis had broken down, and a series of separate social disciplines had emerged, each with its own highly specialized vocabulary for explaining recent change.

Schorske turned to colleagues in other fields in search of new interpretive structures, models, and paradigms. This was initially disheartening since he found that other disciplines were evidently turning away from history as a means of understanding the modern world. Despite the apparent disinterest of nonhistorians in history as a mode of understanding, however, Schorske became convinced that "the autonomous analytic methods of the several disciplines, however a-historical in general import, posed to the intellectual historian a challenge he could no longer ignore with impunity."[14] Eventually he devised a strategy that he calls "post-holing." He conducted a number of methodologically distinct inquiries, each a "separate foray into the terrain," all linked by his desire to understand the relationship between high culture and politics. Schorske based his method on the belief that it was necessary to examine each facet of high culture in the terms devised by those who specialized in its study—simply because the representatives of the "specialized disciplines" would "know better than the historian what in their métier constitutes stout yarn of true color."[15]

Thus, to depict the advent of modernity in architecture and city planning one would have to read city plans and urban structures as "texts" (after the fashion of literary critics), and to do so one would have to employ the "specialized internal analysis'' of fields such as architecture, art history, urban geography, and city planning. In his widely praised chapter on ''The Ringstrasse, Its Critics, and the Birth of Urban Modernism,'' Schorske cites works in these fields. In other areas, also, Schorske's choice of ''texts''—the murals and paintings of Gustav Klimt, a musical score of Arnold Schönberg, one of Freud's dreams, a Hofmannsthal libretto, and so on[16]—demanded the use of ''specialized internal analysis.''

Connecting these interdisciplinary ''post-holes'' was the traditional historian's desire to relate various expressions of the human spirit to one another and to the idea of social process, that is, development in time. Here Schorske employs the terminology of *diachrony* and *synchrony* popularized by anthropologists, reporting that the cultural historian

> seeks . . . to locate and interpret the artifact temporally in a field where two lines intersect. One line is vertical, or diachronic, by which he establishes the relation of a text or a system of thought to previous expressions in the same branch of cultural activity. . . . The other is horizontal, or synchronic; by it he assesses the relation of the content of the intellectual object to what is appearing in other branches or aspects of a culture at the same time.[17]

The synthetic power to pull these synchronic and diachronic strands together is supplied by a variety of techniques, all less novel than the post-holing strategy. One device is the familiar method of selecting recurring motifs as focal points for the separate essays, such as the theme of the garden in Austrian literature and representational art. Even more basic is Schorske's belief—influenced by men such as the literary critic Lionel Trilling, the philosopher Herbert Marcuse, and the historian William L. Langer—that the relations between culture and politics are best explained by combining ideas of Karl Marx and Sigmund Freud. Like many other current historians, Schorske leans heavily on the idea of ''ideology,'' a concept closely identified with Marxist theory and Karl Mannheim's ''sociology of knowledge.''[18] Equally fundamental to Schorske's synthetic imagination are the categories of Freudian psychology, which he absorbed most directly from Marcuse (whose *Eros and Civilization* seeks to blend Marxist and Freudian theory into a tool of social criticism), and the classicist Norman O. Brown (author of *Life Against Death* and *Love's Body*, popularizations of psychoanalytic theory intended as therapy for western culture). Schorske employs Freudian concepts most explicitly in his fourth essay, where he interprets Freud's own political sensibility, but psychoanalytic theory—especially the notion of the Oedipus complex—underpins his entire understanding of political rebellion and cultural innovation; the ''new culture makers in the city of Freud,'' Schorske believes, ''repeatedly defined themselves in terms of a kind of collective oedipal revolt.''[19]

We now turn to the book's critical reception, especially the response to its interdisciplinary approach. As noted, criticism was not universally positive. A scholar who borrows from specializations outside his or her own field naturally risks some technical gaffes, and Schorske is no exception. An art historian, for instance, complained that he mistakenly identified the pre–1914 Viennese Secession style with the "art deco" movement of the 1920s and 1930s.[20] On the whole, however, Schorske appears to have been quite successful in avoiding such errors.[21]

Much criticism centered on Schorske's post-holing technique, which required him to look intensely at a few select cases instead of viewing Vienna's cultural life comprehensively. The historian William Johnston, for instance, complained that Schorske wrote only about people who happened to interest him. "Schorske has chosen narrowly and unsystematically," Johnston asserted, "eschewing all obligations to justify his omissions, and thus these essays reflect a personal taste rather than a rigorous scholarly ethos."[22] Echoing Johnston, the philosopher Stephen Toulmin complained that Schorske's picture of Viennese life "remains surprisingly thin and sketchy," a collection of "vignettes" rather than a "comprehensive politico-psychological analysis of Habsburg culture and society."[23] In the same spirit, Alessandra Comini asked why Schorske did not discuss such key figures as the philosophers Ernst Mach or Ludwig Wittgenstein, the architect Adolf Loos, the writer Karl Kraus, or any natural scientists.[24]

One senses that Schorske's topics were indeed not chosen in rigorously systematic fashion; he seems to have proceeded less like the detached social scientist than the connoisseur whose impulses draw him to the contemplation of a given objet d'art. Yet complaints based on the narrowness of this aspect of Schorske's approach seem unfair if we recall the traditional critic's rule that an author should be judged on the basis of the book he has written, not the one reviewers may wish him to write.[25] On the other hand, such objections indicate an important aspect of Schorske's personalized brand of post-holing: the strategy causes him to present an extremely selective picture of Vienna's intellectual life.

A final aspect of Schorske's method that aroused opposition was his use of psychoanalytic theory. Such hostility typifies most historians' suspicions of the interdisciplinary orientation known as "psychohistory"[26]—a distrust shared by many scholars in other fields. Though commentary on this point was not always negative,[27] reviewers were usually decidedly unhappy. For example, Peter Davey, an architecture critic, disliked Schorske's "post-Freudian vapouring."[28] The art historian Comini agreed; she was especially skeptical of the "incessantly stressed Oedipal theme that unites the seven chapters of Schorske's book."[29] Johnston found that the pivotal psychohistorical essay on Freud suffered from "overinterpretation,"[30] while Toulmin regretted Schorske's evident belief that intellectual accomplishments are "significant only to the extent that they are sublimations of a deeper creative/sexual libido."[31] The historians Robert A. Kann, Peter Pulzer, and Hugh Trevor-Roper, all general admirers of the book, found that Schorske's ideas in this specific regard lacked adequate factual basis.[32]

As controversial as Schorske's study of Vienna was, its reception did not match the "tidal wave"[33] of response to my second example of interdisciplinary scholarship: *Time on the Cross: The Economics of American Negro Slavery* by Robert William Fogel and Stanley L. Engerman published six years earlier in 1974. Scant months after its publication, *Time on the Cross* was already recognized as a "tradition-shattering cliometric study . . . almost as controversial as its subject."[34] Aggressively marketed by its publisher and authors, the book's appearance became a media event in which the study was itself practically buried under a landslide of publicity and criticism.

The controversy was a consequence of several causes. First, *Time on the Cross* was a self-consciously iconoclastic study based on a number of striking propositions. Slavery, the authors argued, was an economically profitable institution under which bondsmen were generally treated humanely and enjoyed a much higher material living standard than was commonly presumed. Moreover, the book was "relevant" scholarship explicitly designed to supply modern black Americans with a heroic, socially usable past: under slavery, Fogel and Engerman maintained, Negroes achieved dignity by contributing to their own self-improvement as well as overall southern prosperity. (A principal target of their attack was Stanley Elkins, whose *Slavery* [1959] likened the plantation economy to a prison system in which blacks became lazy, deferential "Samboes.") Today's blacks could build on this record of accomplishment if racist barriers to opportunity—ingrained primarily during the postbellum Reconstruction era—were finally demolished.[35] To make this polemical message more congenial to the general public, Fogel and Engerman divided their study into two separate volumes. The first was a narrative of their findings, written in nontechnical language and without footnotes; the second volume explained their methods in technical terms and offered documentation to support their conclusions.

Finally, the study was controversial because Fogel and Engerman championed a novel and allegedly more rigorously "scientific" approach to history based on computer-assisted quantitative methods borrowed from mathematics and econometrics. Thus, the book provides a convenient focus for assessing the reception of quantification in history.

Before discussing response to the book, it is useful to summarize briefly some aspects of the history of quantitative history. As early as 1896 the American historian Orin G. Libby called for quantitative analyses of congressional roll calls, and in the early 1930s the British scholar J. H. Clapham declared that all economic historians need a "statistical sense."[36] The notion that the systematic use of mathematics and statistical theory might be *indispensable* to the advancement of historical science, however, has usually encountered stiff opposition from defenders of conventional methods and humanistic values in historiography. Arthur Schlesinger, Jr., reflected traditional opinion when he claimed that "almost all important questions [in human affairs] are important precisely because they are *not* susceptible to quantitative answers."[37] In the same spirit Carl Bridenbaugh warned historians against "that Bitch-goddess QUANTIFICATION" in his 1962 presidential address to the American Historical Association,[38] and Jacques Barzun, in a furious attack on "quanto-history," proclaimed that one "knows as his eye ranges across a chart in all directions that he is not *reading history*."[39]

The possibility of an intensively quantitative approach to history had in the meantime, however, been significantly advanced by refinements in statistical theory and the advent of computers. The work of Conrad and Meyer on economic conditions in the antebellum South,[40] and of Fogel on the place of railroads in American economic growth[41]—initially the focus of acrimonious debate—nevertheless established quantification as an approach that could not be ignored, at least by economic historians. Moreover, during the debate quantifiers scored one undeniable point: The question of whether "counting" should or can be used in history is spurious. Whenever historians employ terms such as *many*, *widespread*, *representative*, *typical*, and so forth, they tacitly engage in quantitative reasoning, whether their prose is supplemented by equations or not. Thus, the question is not "*can* there be a quantitative history?" but "*when* should formal quantitative methods be utilized in historical research and explanation?"[42]

Today many historians remain skeptical about quantification; nevertheless, computers are no longer the frightening novelties they were in the 1950s and 1960s and they are now readily available to any scholar who wishes to use them. An atmosphere of qualified acceptance is growing, based on the realization that quantitative methods can bring fresh perspectives to historical controversies.[43] The possibility of the easy acceptance of "cliometrics" into the disciplinary mainstream is lessened, however, by the fact that mathematics and statistics are not now (and are unlikely soon to become) part of the required training of most historians. This means that the majority of historians are likely to remain unqualified to evaluate the more technical aspects of quantitative scholarship.

The stormy critical reception of *Time on the Cross* must be understood in this context. It should be noted at the outset that reviewers usually appreciated the book's considerable significance for future research. C. Vann Woodward, the country's leading student of southern history, believed that it would inaugurate a "new period of slavery scholarship,"[44] while Stanley Lebergott reflected informed opinion in asserting that "historians of slavery will have to reckon with [Fogel's and Engerman's] insights—just as surely as with those of Cairnes, Olmstead, Phillips, Frazier, or Stampp."[45] Despite reservations, William G. Whitney called the book a "monumental work of historical scholarship when viewed on its own terms and an unavoidable challenge to historians who wish to argue from a different perspective."[46] Even hostile reviewers often indicated sympathy, at least in principle, with quantitative methods,[47] and endorsed the assertion that slavery was profitable (though economists noted that this claim had already been established by earlier quantitative research).[48] A few critics were enthusiastic about the book as a whole. A geographer, for instance, praised its quantitative, "problem-solving" strategy, hoping that it would inspire similar efforts in his own field.[49] Jerome M. Clubb, himself a quantitative historian, predicted that the work would become a "model" for quantitative research.[50]

Yet, in the end, most critics expressed profound dissatisfaction. Even strong admirers of the work could not deny that it had serious flaws,[51] and virtually none of the authors' propositions escaped attack from one quarter or another, either on scholarly or ethical grounds, or a combination of both.

In the area of ethics, it is true, some objections were either wrongheaded or irrelevant. Included in this category were allegations that the book was an apology for slavery that would encourage further injustice toward blacks.[52] Yet there was a compelling ring to charges that the book's logic suffered from a certain moral insensitivity.[53] Quite simply, Fogel and Engerman displayed a conception of black "achievement" that affronted certain fundamental western values, especially insofar as they tended (deliberately or not) to depict nineteenth-century slaves as free producers and consumers in the late-twentieth-century sense: "Can one say [asked two economists] what is fit and proper behavior for individuals caught up within a coercive institutional situation?"[54] It was no use objecting that Fogel's and Engerman's findings were "simply descriptions based upon analysis of empirical data";[55] mere "description" and value judgment are seldom, if ever, discrete categories in history,[56] and certainly not where bondage is involved. A major problem was that it hardly seemed to occur to Fogel and Engerman that it was even "appropriate for the slaves to have resisted their bondage," and in this they differed strikingly from other major recent interpreters.[57] The issue was addressed from another angle in an economist's observation that slavery was a "relationship involving men who happen[ed] to be white and *property* which [was] black"—a fact largely lost in the book's saga of industrious slaves and capitalist planters.[58] Two commentators concluded that the authors wrote from a narrow, "technocratic point of view that admires economic efficiency as an end in itself; their computers badly need a quiet period of reflection by Walden Pond."[59]

Reference to the book's "technocratic" perspective calls to mind another problem on the methodological frontier where ethics, ideology, and scholarship overlap—namely, the strongly presentist cast of the authors' overall interpretive framework. There is much truth to the charge that Fogel and Engerman rather crudely projected their own ideological preferences on another time and place.[60] Their vision of the proper role for blacks idealized the achiever who, driven by a work ethic, acts within the framework of existing society to improve his material lot; it is the idea of the black bourgeoisie, buttressed in their case by certain premises of neoclassical economic theory.[61] The result was a "shaky theoretical foundation" that was allowed, often quite naively, to guide and inform the authors' quantitative operations.[62]

I turn now to methodological flaws in the narrower sense—that is, apart from questions of general interpretive perspective. Careful inspection of the authors' argument revealed—in ironic contrast to their rather pretentious claims to scientific rigor—that an embarrassing number of the book's conclusions rested on guesswork, rhetorical ploys, question begging, a priori assumptions, or disingenuous fudging—and possibly willful distortion.[63] Fogel and Engerman's statistical operations may have been largely unintelligible to nonquantifiers,[64] but hostile critics nevertheless found *Time on the Cross* an easy mark. Not infrequently, the authors ignored crucial primary evidence or secondary scholarship, misrepresented mainstream interpretations, or smuggled in unrepresentative, impressionistic, discredited, or otherwise inappropriate evidence.[65] In arguing that slave housing compared favorably with that of northern workers, for instance, the authors drew their data for the north from a New York housing survey of 1893.[66] Even in their technical applications of statistical methods, Fogel and Engerman sometimes made errors of inference or employed questionable assumptions.[67]

Critics were dismayed by the authors' evident belief that even highly biased statistical samples were more reliable than nonquantitative evidence, and frequently stressed that any data—whether quantitative or literary—must be subjected to interpretation.[68] Indeed, a survey of the reviews of *Time on the Cross* provides an object lesson in the issues involved in the use of evidence in history.[69] Difficulties surrounding this most fundamental of points led one historian to conclude that the "scholars who will be most disappointed with *Time on the Cross* are statisticians, mathematical economists, historians who are quantifiers, and those . . . sympathetic to their objectives and methodology."[70]

Considerations of space permit discussion of only the more serious points of contention.[71] Most problems boiled down to slipshod scholarship that led to yawning gaps between the assertions in volume 1 and the documentation in volume 2. Especially devastating were revelations concerning the unrepresentative nature of much of the evidence cited by Fogel and Engerman—particularly in light of the authors' claim to have established warranted inferences regarding the *typical* anatomy of the plantation system. Some key arguments rested on samples drawn from only about thirty large cotton plantations (the authors failed to specify the exact number!), records of the New Orleans slave market, and a relatively small selection of census records. Evidence regarding plantations with less than fifty slaves was overlooked, no data from rice or sugar plantations was considered, and even for cotton the sample was so scant that "any pretense of representativeness is easily dismissed."[72] A political scientist noted that calculations supporting the contention that slave plantations were 35 percent more efficient than northern farms entirely excluded relevant statistics—for example, data on corn, the South's second most valuable crop—and were based on the arbitrary assumption that "capital earned 10 percent on both northern and southern farms."[73]

Critics were quick to challenge the authors' contention that the integrity of slave families was typically unaffected by the sale of slaves.[74] This claim rested not only on unsupported initial assumptions (for example, that "when planters moved west with all their slaves 50 per cent of these slaves were male"[75]), but also was narrowly based on records of interregional sales at the New Orleans slave market. The authors overlooked data regarding local slave markets and largely ignored other interregional markets, leading one commentator to assert that their conclusions were the result of massive bias and guesswork.[76]

Claims regarding the slave diet were equally controversial. One scholar re-
marked that "(t)he reader is told that the sources are a sample of plantations
with more than fifty slaves in counties at least fifty wagon miles from the nearest
city. Unmentioned are locations or even the total number of plantations, what
constitutes a city, and variations from one plantation to another."[77] As for Fogel
and Engerman's argument on the frequency of slave punishment, the same author
observed: "To offer a figure and a text average (0.7 whippings per hand per
year) on the basis of one plantation record for two years is to make a caricature
of quantitative methods."[78]

Historians are traditionally concerned with the categories of particularity and
temporal process; they were quick to complain that Fogel and Engerman overlooked variations according to region or period. The authors lost sight, in other
words, of the *historical* dimension—the dynamics of slavery as a process of
change and development. "We learn little," wrote one commentator, "about
variations arising from different locations, crops and plantation size. Their 'typical' or 'average' slave usually turns out to be one residing on a plantation with
fifty or more fellows."[79] Another historian complained that

the element of time, stressed in the title, is itself crucified in paragraph one—where the
"years of black enslavement" stretching over eight generations are reduced to "the
antebellum era"—and is never adequately resurrected. By drawing data primarily from
the mid-nineteenth century, the authors continue to minimize evolutionary factors in the
overall equation of slavery."[80]

Furthermore, the statistical paraphernalia in volume 1—tables, graphs,
charts—seemed to some reviewers misleadingly tailored to "throw the best light
on the authors' conclusions."[81] In the second volume the authors themselves
occasionally admitted that they had either just begun or not yet completed their
analysis of some sources. Yet critics maintained that conclusions based on such
preliminary research were presented as fact in volume 1.[82] The entire notion of
splitting the study into two separate volumes, one for narrative and the other for
evidence, was widely attacked on the grounds that it discouraged easy inspection
of the book's supporting documentation—which was itself often confusing or
opaque, even to specialists. "For most purposes the second volume is a waste
of paper," declared one commentator. "It is not detailed or complete enough
for the professional student and is worthless to the lay reader."[83]

In summary, Fogel and Engerman posed many new and provocative questions
regarding slavery, and it is possible that the spirit of some of their inadequately
documented claims may be substantiated by future research (e.g., their arguments
regarding the relatively high material living standard of slaves).[84] On the other
hand, John Hope Franklin, in the fifth edition of the major textbook on black
history (*From Freedom to Slavery: A History of Negro Americans* [1980]),
dismissed Fogel and Engerman's work with a few asides.[85] *Time on the Cross*
is doubtless an important book; but it is also seriously flawed. It is thus unlikely

that it will ever be considered the exemplary "model" of quantitative historiography that Jerome Clubb hoped it would be. Far more possible is the danger that this "paradoxical . . . historical naïveté" will reinforce the prejudices of many historians against quantitative and interdisciplinary scholarship.[86] At the present time the safest thing to say about the book and the controversy it generated is that future historians should be less likely than before to overlook John Blassingame's point: "Statistics and mathematical models may become mandatory ancillary tools for the historian, but they cannot totally replace logic and systematic research."[87] "Perhaps the main value of the Fogel and Engerman opus," another critic sensibly concluded, "will be to stimulate other historians to do more research not only on slavery but also on the techniques of the cliometricians."[88]

I now turn to a third instance of modern interdisciplinary scholarship, Hayden White's *Metahistory: The Historical Imagination in Nineteenth-Century Europe.* Unlike Schorske's collection of essays on Vienna, or Fogel and Engerman's controversial inspection of slavery, White's complicated and sometimes abstruse analysis of the nature of historical conceptualization was too arcane and mentally taxing to appeal to the general public. It had a dramatic impact on academic audiences, however, creating waves of controversy in history and related fields that have yet to subside. White's ideas are already being adapted for use in other disciplines such as anthropology and literary criticism.[89]

Metahistory is an ingenious anatomy of the "deep structure of the historical imagination" as manifested in the work of several historians and philosophers of history of the nineteenth century: Hegel, Michelet, Ranke, Tocqueville, Burckhardt, Marx, Nietzsche, and Croce. Methodologically, the book combines theories and concepts drawn from workers in an array of other fields: for instance, the literary critics Northrop Frye and Kenneth Burke; structural linguists and critics such as Roman Jakobson, Jacques Lacan, and Lucien Goldmann; and philosophers and social theorists such as Giambattista Vico, Stephen Pepper, and Karl Mannheim. White approaches the writing of his subjects as "what it most manifestly is: a verbal structure in the form of a narrative prose discourse." His thesis is that their works "contain [an unconscious] deep structural content which is generally poetic, and specifically linguistic" and that this content "serves as the precritically accepted paradigm of what a distinctively 'historical' explanation should be. This paradigm functions as the 'metahistorical' element in all historical works that are more comprehensive in scope than the monograph or archival report."[90]

White defines three basic explanatory "strategies" that his historians used: explanation by formal argument, explanation by emplotment, and explanation by ideological implication. Under each of these headings he distinguishes four possible types of articulation: formism, organicism, mechanism, and contextualism (for arguments); romance, comedy, tragedy, and satire (for emplotments); anarchism, conservatism, radicalism, and liberalism (for ideological implication). The *style* of a given historical thinker, he concludes, is the product of a unique synthesis of these strategies and modes of articulation. The entire theory is built on the assumption that there is a deep level of consciousness from which historians select the conceptual frameworks they will use to explain their evidence. To identify these "types of [unconscious] prefiguration" or "frames of mind," White uses the four tropes of poetic language: metaphor, metonymy, synecdoche, and irony. He argues that the "dominant tropological mode and its attendant linguistic protocol comprise the irreducibly 'metahistorical' basis of every historical work." Thus, the thought of the great historians actually "represents the working out of the possibilities of tropological prefiguration of the historical field contained in poetic language in general."[91]

White's complicated analysis radically contradicted the commonsense notion of history that many (and perhaps most) modern historians share, that is, that the historian's task is simply and realistically to retell the story of the past "as it actually happened." It contradicted, as well, the notion that historians are rhetorically prosaic "subalterns" in the realm of letters,[92] a widespread attitude reflected, for instance, in Samuel Johnson's belief that "great abilities are not requisite for an Historian, for in historical composition all the greatest powers of the human mind are quiescent. He has facts ready to his hand, so there is no exercise of invention. Imagination is not required in any high degree; only about as much as is used in the lower kinds of poetry."[93]

Partially because White's book challenged such well-established beliefs, and partly because its highly abstract and demanding argument was not always presented in a clear or graceful style, it was simply ignored or dismissed out of hand in many circles. Those historians who took the book seriously tended to reject its relativist implications,[94] while complaining that White's highly formalistic argument lacked the necessary historical concreteness; that is, it failed to relate systematically the work of nineteenth-century historians to the specific historical settings in which they operated.[95] Michael Ermarth was correct, however, in heralding the work as a "daring, ingenious, and sometimes bewildering tour de force," an "impressive synthesis [that] casts a very new light" on the nature of historical consciousness.[96] John Clive agreed that the book was an "important and pioneering work," an "immensely ambitious undertaking, requiring mastery of philosophy and historiography as well as of linguistic theory."[97] Clive underscored the unique nature of the book's general significance when he said: "That historians are to some extent poets as well has been a commonplace since classical times. But White is the first to have tried to grapple systematically with the manner in which literary artistry is not merely decorative or ancillary but integral to the historical work in hand."[98]

No further comment is needed on the wide-ranging interdisciplinary nature of *Metahistory*; the reader may easily obtain graphic verification of this aspect of White's study by consulting the footnotes in the book's methodological introduction on "The Poetics of History," which bristle with references to work in literary history, poetics, rhetoric, philosophy of history (both analytical and speculative), social theory, sociology of knowledge, aesthetics, anthropology, linguistics, stylistics, and so forth. (The one major relevant field that White ignores is psychology.[99]) The book is indeed an interdisciplinary "tour de force."

What needs to be highlighted are any of the book's limitations that bear specifically on White's interdisciplinary style. This question has been incisively addressed by the literary scholar Carl A. Rubino. Rubino admires White's interdisciplinary élan and stresses that *Metahistory* is an "exciting and important book that deserves careful reading and much discussion."[100] Yet he expresses serious reservations concerning the way White develops his argument, especially White's failure to blend fully theories borrowed from other fields into a tight system of his own.

The detailed mediation that is essential to true integration is missing [Rubino writes]; instead, the borrowed categories seem to be rather crudely abstracted from their native contexts, cut off from the detailed arguments that gave them conceptual flesh and blood. Such excessively violent uprooting and hasty replanting in a soil not made ready for them deprives those 'tender plants' of much of their force and beauty, creating a disordered intellectual landscape where it is often difficult to follow the path of White's argument.

The result is "a kind of conceptual cacophony" that is compounded by White's awkward style, making the book "needlessly difficult and even painful to read." Thus, Rubino concludes, "damage is done to the force of White's argument; and [he rightly predicts] we might well suspect that his failings will prove convenient for those who seek a way to avoid confronting the issues he raises."[101]

Thus Rubino highlights a problem that many reviewers identify as the "overly schematic" nature of White's argument.[102] His comments suggest a general lesson for those who would practice interdisciplinary scholarship: namely, that to be fully effective, methods and ideas borrowed from other fields must be thoroughly combined and polished into a system and style of one's own.

My fourth example of interdisciplinary history manages to do just this—at least in the opinion of most reviewers. Emmanuel Le Roy Ladurie's *Montaillou: The Promised Land of Error*,[103] while reflecting a "strikingly sophisticated knowledge of the modern social sciences," nonetheless "never allows theoretical constructs to come between the reader and the people being studied."[104] Le Roy Ladurie, a leading champion of *Annales* historiography, exemplifies the author who seeks to fuse the theory and methods of discrete fields into a highly integrated and refined interdisciplinary style. In *Montaillou*, even historical methodology virtually disappears behind the narrative,[105] arousing in readers a feeling of intimacy with the story's setting and characters to an extent rare in the literature of fact. Not surprisingly, the book became a best-seller in France and was widely praised for its literary excellence in the United States. It is now routinely cited as an authoritative source by specialists in various branches of the social sciences.[106]

Seldom have academic reviewers been so uniformly enthusiastic about a work of historical scholarship. "When a scholar inquires of a medievalist which one

work would they recommend that encapsulates the new scholarship on the medieval period," writes Susan Stuard, "they are likely to be told: *Montaillou*."[107]
Soon after its appearance in 1975, reviewers from a variety of fields praised the
book as "stunning," "superbly invigorating and original," a "monumental
work" that "radically alters one's view of the entire medieval period."[108] The
anthropologist Laurence Wylie called it "the most comprehensive historical study
ever made of a community. . . . a new classic in both history and anthropology."[109] Perhaps the highest praise from a historian came from Charles T. Wood,
who claimed that *Montaillou* "does more to enrich our understanding of life in
the Middle Ages than any book since Marc Bloch's *Société féodale*."[110]

   Montaillou is an *Annales*-style "total" history of a small village in the French
Pyrenees at the beginning of the fourteenth century. It describes virtually the
entire way of life of this tiny world of peasants and shepherds, from demographic
patterns and everyday behavior to religious beliefs and social mentality. Historian
Keith Thomas sees it as the "first wholly successful attempt to write the total
history of a small community with as much regard for the mental attitudes of
the inhabitants as for their social and economic situation."[111] "The whole is an
integrated analysis," writes Thomas, "reminiscent of the best kind of village
study by a modern social anthropologist."

   Le Roy Ladurie was able to write the history of this community, so remote
in time, due to the existence of Inquisition registers compiled between 1318 and
1325 by Jacques Fournier, the bishop of Pamiers. Fournier (later Pope Benedict
XII) was a fanatical inquisitor, and the records of his court contain information
not only on the Albigensian (or Cathar) heresy that triumphed in Montaillou but
also on many aspects of village life. Scholars have of course often used Inquisition
records to study the history of the church's war against heresy; Le Roy Ladurie's
orginality lies in the idea of exploiting them to write about the *everyday life* of
an obscure medieval community. In interpreting the registers, the French scholar
displays his command of the skills of both the historian and the ethnographer:
"His basic approach . . . is to treat the material as a reasonably adequate field
report. He erects a society step by step and returns repeatedly to the principals
of his cast and the critical events of their lives as meaning is layered on meaning.
This is a trustworthy technique of ethnography which creates comprehensible
order but not at the price of complexity."[112] From the resulting "ethnographic
report"[113] readers know the village's inhabitants on a surprisingly intimate
level—their vocabulary, daily routines, diet, folklore, sexual mores, social structure and patterns of authority, and so forth. The political scientist Roger Masters
asserts that *Montaillou* is useful for the study of comparative social processes
and "the dynamics of traditional societies."[114] But the book works on the personal as well as the collective level: We recognize the characters as individuals,
with specific desires, personality quirks, fears, and so on. *Montaillou* has been
widely praised as simply a "good yarn."[115]

   Of course, there were some criticisms. Susan Stuard, a feminist, complains
that Le Roy Ladurie's use of certain ideas of the French anthropologist Claude

Lévi-Strauss leads him erroneously to "perpetuate the medieval stereotype of women rather than reinterpret it in the light of new historical thinking."[116] Le Roy Ladurie, she maintains,

adopts Lévi-Strauss's basic understanding of society, namely that a society possess [sic] three languages or means of exchange: messages, goods or services, and women. . . . Women are treated not as an integral part of the social order but rather as a means of facilitating exchange between social units. LeRoy Ladurie can only do this by manipulating the evidence of the registers, in rather tortuous ways.

The problem, according to Stuard, is the "danger in perceiving women as a means of exchange rather than a component part of the social order."[117] Even when his own research contradicts Lévi-Strauss's construct, she argues, he continues to use it. Thus she claims that his findings show that although "males tended to dominate over females, in the last analysis age was a greater determinant of authority than sex."[118] In short, Stuard believes that in this instance Le Roy Ladurie becomes the prisoner of borrowed theory.

The historian Rodney Hilton has broader, though related, reservations about Le Roy Ladurie's use of social science theory.[119] Indeed, Hilton is one of the few reviewers who believes that Le Roy Ladurie generally allows interdisciplinary theory and social science pretensions to stand in the way of his work as a historian. While conceding that *Montaillou* is characterized by "brilliance," he cautions that there is

evidently a considerable uncertainty about the conceptual framework. Having rejected Ferdinand Tönnies (*Gesellschaft-Gemeinschaft*) and Marx (the class analysis), the author opts for what he terms a "historiographic-regional model" which is, of course, not a theoretical model at all, but a practical convenience. Although the book makes absolutely clear that the situation in the Sabarthès at the time of the Inquisition was historically specific, he refers to a wide range of anthropological writers—Lévi-Strauss, Redfield, Wylie, Mauss, Riesman, Chayanov, Polyani, Sahlins.

Le Roy Ladurie's intent, Hilton contends, is to "assimilate Montaillou and the Sabarthès to a model of a worldwide, or at least a Mediterranean, peasant culture of all time." But, he insists, whatever the case of Montaillou has to tell us about peasant life is time- and place-specific; to use data from the Fournier registers to build general theory concerning traditional societies is, in his view, inappropriate. In the final analysis, he believes, "it is M. Le Roy Ladurie the historian rather than the anthropologist who impresses. The disciplines of history and anthropology have much to offer each other but not at the price of surrender. In fact, perhaps in spite of himself, Le Roy Ladurie remains absolutely a historian."

In principle, of course, all responsible historians would agree that the best interests of the human studies require that history never "surrender" to another discipline, whether anthropology or any other field. It is widely believed (and not only within the field of history) that the human sciences require a branch that emphasizes the particular or nonrecurrent aspects of social experience at the expense of generalization. History has traditionally filled this need. Whether Le Roy Ladurie in fact surrenders is a matter for debate. That so few other historians found theory to be an intrusion in his work, however, suggests the degree to which it has now become common to believe that the traditional particularistic concerns of historiography can be wedded to the utilization of the paradigms and techniques of other fields, even though these fields may aspire to establish general truths.

NOTES

1. For fuller accounts of the following, see "Interdisciplinary History" in Harry Ritter, *Dictionary of Concepts in History* (Westport, Conn.: Greenwood Press, 1986), and esp. T. C. R. Horn and Harry Ritter, "Interdisciplinary History: A Historiographical Review," *The History Teacher* 19 (1986): 427–48.

2. On these developments see H. Stuart Hughes, *Consciousness and Society: The Reorientation of European Social Thought, 1890–1930* (New York: Knopf, 1958); also Alexandra Oleson and John Voss, *The Organization of Knowledge in Modern America, 1860–1920* (Baltimore, Md.: Johns Hopkins University Press, 1979).

3. Martin Siegel, "Henri Berr's *Revue de Synthèse Historique*," *History and Theory* 9 (1970): 332.

4. Geoffrey Barraclough, "History," in *Main Trends of Research in the Social and Human Sciences*, Part 2, *Anthropological and Historical Sciences, Aesthetics and the Sciences of Art*, ed. Jacques Havet (Paris: Mouton, 1978), 264.

5. Emmanuel Le Roy Ladurie, *The Territory of the Historian* (Chicago: University of Illinois Press, 1979), 17.

6. Cited in Annie M. Popper, "Karl Gotthard Lamprecht (1856–1915)," in *Some Historians of Modern Europe: Essays in Historiography,* ed. Bernadotte E. Schmitt (1942; repr. Port Washington, N.Y.: Kennikat Press, 1966), 223.

7. Cited in Hans-Josef Steinberg, "Karl Lamprecht," in *Deutsche Historiker*, ed. Hans-Ulrich Wehler (Göttingen: Vandenhoeck & Ruprecht, 1971), 58.

8. John Higham, *History* (Englewood Cliffs, N.J.: Prentice-Hall, 1965), 113.

9. Harry Elmer Barnes, *The New History and the Social Studies* (New York: The Century Co., 1925), 11.

10. Higham, *History*, 119.

11. Leonard Krieger, "Reassessing Slavery," *Partisan Review* 46 (1979): 152–53.

12. It should be stressed that, though methodologically innovative, *Fin-de-Siècle Vienna* (New York: Alfred A. Knopf, 1980) has solid roots in historiographic tradition; it is cultural history in the fashion of Burckhardt's *Civilization of the Renaissance in Italy* and Johan Huizinga's *Waning of the Middle Ages*. Like these books, it creates a cross-sectional view of high culture at a specific point in time and space.

13. John Boyer, *The Journal of Modern History* 52 (1980): 725, 726.

14. Schorske, *Fin-de-Siècle Vienna*, xxi.

15. Ibid., xxii, xxv, xxvi, xxviii.

16. Cf. Barry M. Katz, *New German Critique*, 20 (Spring/Summer 1980): 199.

17. Schorske, *Fin-de-Siècle Vienna*, xxii.

18. Boyer, *The Journal of Modern History* 52 (1980): 725, correctly notes that a key

assumption of Schorske's book is the belief that "political values, both explicit and implicit, reflect material circumstances and, in turn, condition cultural-aesthetic styles." Cf. "Ideology" in Ritter, *Dictionary*.

19. Schorske, *Fin-de-Siècle Vienna*, xxvi. Schorske pays tribute to Marcuse and Brown on pages xv and xxiv.

20. Alessandra Comini, *The Art Bulletin* 63 (September 1981): 523.

21. Although Comini concludes that Schorske is uncomfortable in art history (ibid., 522), others praise his work in this field: for example, Stephen Toulmin, *Commonweal*, 29 August 1980, 476; Bernard Michel, *Annales* 39 (January/February 1984): 208.

22. Johnston, *The American Scholar* 50 (1980–81): 262.

23. Toulmin, *Commonweal*, 29 August 1980, 476.

24. Comini, *The Art Bulletin* 63 (September 1981): 523.

25. Cf. Katz, *New German Critique*, 20 (Spring/Summer 1980): 201. Boyer, *The Journal of Modern History* 52 (1980): 726, agrees that "to criticize the book for its scope and biographical omissions is ultimately unfair."

26. For a summary of objections to the use of psychoanalytic theory in history, see David E. Stannard, *Shrinking History: On Freud and the Failure of Psychohistory* (New York: Oxford University Press, 1980). For defenses of psychohistory by historians see Robert J. Brugger, ed., *Our Selves, Our Past: Psychological Approaches to American History* (Baltimore, Md.: Johns Hopkins University Press, 1981); Dorothy Ross, "Woodrow Wilson and the Case for Psychohistory," *The Journal of American History* 69 (December 1982): 659–68; and Peter Gay, *Freud for Historians* (New York: Oxford University Press, 1985).

27. Robert Alter, a literary critic (*Commentary*, March 1980, p. 81), believes that Schorske uses psychoanalytic theory "with discretion." The reviewer for the *American Journal of Psychiatry* 137 (September 1980): 1134, praises the book for its "richness and density." Boyer, *The Journal of Modern History* 52 (1980): 726, sidesteps the issue, arguing that "it is irrelevant to complain of [the book's] use of psychoanalytic interpretive schemes" since "such views fail to do justice to [its] powerful vision" (p. 726).

28. Davey, *Architectural Review* 168 (July-December 1980): 320.

29. Comini, *The Art Bulletin* 63 (September 1981): 522–23.

30. Johnston, *The American Scholar* 50 (1980–81): 264.

31. Toulmin, *Commonweal*, 24 August 1980, 477.

32. Kann, *Central European History* 14 (1981): 170; Pulzer, *Historische Zeitschrift* 233 (December 1981), 713; Trevor-Roper, *The New York Times Book Review*, 27 January 1980, 31.

33. Thomas B. Alexander, *The Journal of Modern History* 62 (1975): 686.

34. John H. Pruett and Robert M. McColley, *The Journal of Southern History* 40 (1974): 637.

35. See especially Fogel and Engerman's Epilogue, entitled "Implications for Our Time," *Time on the Cross*, vol. 1 (Boston: Little, Brown, 1974), 258–64.

36. "Economic History as a Discipline," *Encyclopedia of the Social Sciences* 5: 328.

37. Schlesinger, "The Humanist Looks at Empirical Social Research," *American Sociological Review* 27 (1962): 770.

38. Bridenbaugh, "The Great Mutation," *The American Historical Review* 68 (1963): 326.

39. Barzun, *Clio and the Doctors: Psycho-History, Quanto-History, and History* (Chicago: University of Chicago Press, 1974), 24.

40. Conrad and Meyer, "The Economics of Slavery in the Ante-Bellum South," *Journal of Political Economy* 66 (April 1958): 95–130.

41. Fogel, *Railroads and American Economic Growth: Essays in Econometric History* (Baltimore, Md.: Johns Hopkins Press, 1964).

42. William O. Aydelotte, *Quantification in History* (Reading, Mass.: Addison-Wesley, 1971), 40.

43. Peter D. McClelland, *Causal Explanation and Model Building in History, Economics, and the New Economic History* (Ithaca, N.Y.: Cornell University Press, 1975), 218. See also David Hackett Fischer, *Historians' Fallacies: Toward a Logic of Historical Thought* (New York: Harper & Row, 1970), 90.

44. Woodward, *The New York Review of Books* 21 (2 May 1974), 6.

45. Lebergott, *The American Political Science Review* 69 (1975): 697.

46. Whitney, *The Annals of the American Academy of Political and Social Science* 419 (May 1975): 197.

47. E.g., John W. Blassingame, *Urban League Review* 1 (1975): 54.

48. Paul A. David and Peter Temin, *Journal of Interdisciplinary History* 5 (1975): 450; cf. Marcus Alexis, *Urban League Review* 1 (1975): 56–57; Thomas Weiss, *Monthly Labor Review* (June 1975): 68; Pruett and McColley, *The Journal of Southern History* 40 (1974): 637.

49. Stanley D. Brunn, *Journal of Historical Geography* 2 (1976): 277–78.

50. Clubb, *Computers and the Humanities* 9 (1975): 248; see also the admiring review by George C. Rogers, Jr., *Societas* 6 (1976): 216–18.

51. E.g., Brunn, *Journal of Historical Geography* 2 (1976): 278; Clubb, *Computers and the Humanities* 9 (1975): 247–51.

52. E.g., Marcus Alexis, an economist, finds Fogel and Engerman "guilty" of writing "another proslavery apology" (*Urban League Review* 1 [1975]: 58); see, as well, Gregory Branch, *The Black Scholar* 7 (1975): 48–49, and Mildred C. Fierce, *Phylon* 36 (1975): 89–93, whose remarks on pages 92–93 reflect an especially serious misreading. For a corrective, see Seymour Mandelbaum, *The American Political Science Review* 69 (1975): 700–701; also, Whitney, *The Annals of the American Academy of Political and Social Science* 419 (May 1975): 196, who nevertheless acknowledges that the authors' approach "reifies the hell out of the physical pain and psychological suffering experienced by human beings caught up in involuntary servitude" (p. 197).

53. Cf. Peter H. Wood, *The American Historical Review* 80 (1975): 1394, who notes the "unintentionally partisan tone" in which "the slave system seems to be defended."

54. David and Temin, *Journal of Interdisciplinary History* 5 (1975): 448; cf. John McManus, *Canadian Journal of Economics* 9 (1976): 196.

55. E.g., Clubb, *Computers and the Humanities* 9 (1975): 248.

56. See Ritter, *Dictionary*, 447–54; also David Harris Sacks, "The Hedgehog and the Fox Revisited," *Journal of Interdisciplinary History* 16 (1985): 276–77.

57. David and Temin, *Journal of Interdisciplinary History* 5 (1975): 455.

58. Alexis, *Urban League Review* 1 (1975): 57.

59. Pruett and McColley, *The Journal of Southern History* 40 (1974): 639.

60. E.g., Alexis, *Urban League Review* 1 (1975): 57.

61. Keith Aufhauser, *Social Policy* 7 (May/June 1976): 60–63; Jay R. Mandle, *Studies in Comparative International Development* 11 (1976): 114.

62. McManus, *Canadian Journal of Economics* 9 (1976): 197; cf. Herbert G. Gutman, "The World Two Cliometricians Made," *Journal of Negro History* 60 (January 1975): 53–227. Many critics concluded that Fogel and Engerman were bondsmen of their own ideological premises and that all too often these assumptions distorted their use of statistics and econometric theory (e.g., David and Temin, *Journal of Interdisciplinary History* 5 [1975]: 447—see also the following article by the same authors, "Slavery: The Progressive Institution?" *Journal of Economic History* 34 [1974]: 739–83), reducing their work in places to an "Alice in Wonderland" level. For instance, their idea that slaves enjoyed a relatively high "pecuniary income" is, in John Blassingame's words, "such a theoretical construct that anyone using it should probably spend some time chopping and picking cotton before applying it. Then, the 'return on labor' will not appear as high as Fogel and Engerman imply" (*Urban League Review* 1 [1975]: 55).

63. Marc Egnal, *The Canadian Review of American Studies* 6 (1975): 114.

64. E.g., Woodward, *The New York Review of Books* 21 (2 May 1974), 6.

65. Maris Vinovskis, *Journal of Interdisciplinary History* 5 (1975): 464–65; Peter Kolchin, *Journal of Social History* 9 (1975): 101–2, 107; Jim E. Reese, *Social Science Quarterly* 56 (1975): 145; Woodward, *The New York Review of Books* 21 (2 May 1974), 3; Alphonso Pinkney, *Urban League Review* 1 (1975): 51; Brunn, *Journal of Historical Geography* 2 (1976): 278; Clubb, *Computers and the Humanities* 9 (1975): 247, 249.

66. Egnal, *The Canadian Review of American Studies* 6 (1975): 111.

67. David and Temin, *Journal of Interdisciplinary History* 5 (1975): 450, 452; McManus, *Canadian Journal of Economics* 9 (1976): 195.

68. Duncan J. Macleod, *The Historical Journal* 18 (1975): 203, 204; Kolchin, *Journal of Social History* 9 (1975): 106; Blassingame, *Urban League Review* 1 (1975): 56.

69. On problems surrounding the idea of evidence in history, see Ritter, *Dictionary*, 143–46; also Sacks, "The Hedgehog and the Fox Revisited," *Journal of Interdisciplinary History* 16 (1985): 267–80, esp. 274ff.

70. Blassingame, *Urban League Review* 1 (1975): 54. A longer version of this review appeared in the *Atlantic Monthly* (August 1974). Blassingame's generally intelligent gloss unfortunately misrepresents counterfactual reasoning—a favorite device of many quantifiers—as "an anachronistic and thoroughly discredited form of historical inquiry" (p. 54). Cf. "Counterfactual Analysis" in Ritter, *Dictionary*; also Whitney, *The Annals of the American Academy of Political and Social Science* 419 (May 1975): 196, who refers to the authors' "judicious use of counterfactual arguments."

71. For an exhaustive catalog of the book's flaws see Herbert G. Gutman, *Slavery and the Numbers Game* (Urbana: University of Illinois Press, 1975), as well as the review by Peter Kolchin in the *Journal of Social History* 10 (1976): 107–9; see also Richard Sutch, "The Treatment Received by American Slaves: A Critical Review of the Evidence Presented in *Time on the Cross*," *Explorations in Economic History* 12 (1975): 335–438.

72. Alexis, *Urban League Review* 1 (1975): 58; Alexander, *The Journal of Modern History* 62 (1975): 689; Blassingame, *Urban League Review* 1 (1975): 54.

73. Lebergott, *The American Political Science Review* 69 (1975): 698–99.

74. Egnal, *The Canadian Review of American Studies* 6 (1975): 112; John Leggett, *Society* 12 (Sept./Oct. 1975): 94–95; Blassingame, *Urban League Review* 1 (1975): 55.

75. Lebergott, *The American Political Science Review* 69 (1975): 699.

76. Blassingame, *Urban League Review* 1 (1975): 55; also Pruett and McColley, *The*

Journal of Southern History 40 (1974): 638; Lebergott, *The American Political Science Review* 69 (1975): 699.

77. Alexander, *The Journal of Modern History* 62 (1975): 689; cf. Pruett and McColley, *The Journal of Southern History* 40 (1974): 638; Egnal, *The Canadian Review of American Studies* 6 (1975): 111.

78. Alexander, *The Journal of Modern History* 62 (1975): 690.

79. Macleod, *The Historical Journal* 18 (1975): 202.

80. Wood, *The American Historical Review* 80 (1975): 1394; cf. Macleod, *The Historical Journal* 18 (1975): 205.

81. Macleod, *The Historical Journal* 18 (1975): 203.

82. Kolchin, *Journal of Social History* 9 (1975): 102–3; Blassingame, *Urban League Review* 1 (1975): 54.

83. Reese, *Social Science Quarterly* 56 (1975): 145; cf. McManus, *Canadian Journal of Economics* 9 (1976): 197; Alexander, *The Journal of Modern History* 62 (1975): 689–90; Clubb, *Computers and the Humanities* 9 (1975): 250.

84. Macleod, *The Historical Journal* 18 (1975): 203, 205; Kolchin, *Journal of Social History* 9 (1975): 103; cf., however, Egnal, *The Canadian Review of American Studies* 6 (1975): 113; also H. Shelton Smith, *Church History* 45 (1976): 264.

85. John Hope Franklin, *From Freedom to Slavery: A History of Negro Americans*, 5th ed. (New York: Knopf, 1980), 138, 521.

86. Kolchin, *Journal of Social History* 9 (1975): 111; Alexander, *The Journal of Modern History* 62 (1975): 690.

87. Blassingame, *Urban League Review* 1 (1975): 56.

88. Reese, *Social Science Quarterly* 56 (1975): 145.

89. E.g., George E. Marcus, "Rhetoric and the Ethnographic Genre in Anthropological Research," *Current Anthropology* 21 (August 1980): 507–10; George E. Marcus and Dick Cushman, "Ethnographies as Texts," *Annual Review of Anthropology* 11 (1982): 25–69, esp. 54–55; Peter McInerney, " 'Straight' and 'Secret' History in Vietnam War Literature," *Contemporary Literature* 22 (1981): 187–204.

90. White, *Metahistory: The Historical Imagination in Nineteenth-Century Europe* (Baltimore, Md.: Johns Hopkins University Press, 1973), ix–x.

91. Ibid., x–xii.

92. Robert E. Bonner, *History and Theory* 14 (1975): 350.

93. James Boswell, *The Life of Samuel Johnson* (New York: The Modern Library, n.d.), 258.

94. White argues that "the best grounds for choosing one perspective on history rather than another are ultimately aesthetic or moral rather than epistemological" (*Metahistory*, xii).

95. E.g., Georg G. Iggers, *Reviews in European History* (June 1976): 174, 180. Nevertheless, Iggers recognizes the book as "one of the important works of historical theory of the twentieth century" (p. 172). The remarks of the literary critic Frederic Jameson (*Diacritics* 6 [1976]: 2–9) are to some extent related in spirit to those of Iggers.

96. Ermarth, *The American Historical Review* 80 (1975): 962, 963.

97. Clive, *The Journal of Modern History* 47 (1975): 543.

98. Ibid.

99. He does so on the debatable grounds that current psychology is in a "state of conceptual anarchy" (*Metahistory*, 430) and that in any case little would be "added to the understanding of a given writer's thought by the revelation of the personality type

which supposedly underlay and gave form to [a historian's] work" (p. 431). Cf. the comments of Ross, "Woodrow Wilson and the Case for Psychohistory," 660, n. 1.

100. Rubino, *Modern Language Notes* (MLN) 91 (October-December 1976).

101. Ibid., 1131–32, 1134.

102. Clive, *The Journal of Modern History* 47 (1975): 542. For additional remarks on other facets of this aspect of the work, see Ermarth, *The American Historical Review* 80 (1975): 962; Jameson, *Diacritics* 6 (1976): 4; Gordon Leff, *The Pacific Historical Review* 43 (1974): 600; Adrian Kuzminski, *Comparative Studies in Society and History* 18 (1976): 139–40; John S. Nelson, *History and Theory* 14 (1975): 79.

103. Le Roy Ladurie, *Montaillou: The Promised Land of Error* (Paris: Editions Gallimard, 1975; New York: George Braziller, 1978).

104. Charles T. Wood, *The American Historical Review* 81 (December 1976): 1090.

105. Roger D. Masters, *The American Political Science Review* 71 (December 1977): 1708.

106. E.g., Anthony Synnott, "Little Angels, Little Devils: A Sociology of Children," *Canadian Review of Sociology and Anthropology* 20 (1983): 82; Rosamond Faith, Review of *The Origins of English Individualism* by Alan Macfarlane, *The Journal of Peasant Studies* 7 (April 1980): 387–88; Richard A. Peterson, "Revitalizing the Culture Concept," *Annual Review of Sociology* 5 (1979): 141; W. R. Mead, "The Discovery of Europe," *Geography* 67 (July 1982): 199.

107. Stuard, "An Unfortunate Construct: A Comment on Emmanuel Le Roy Ladurie's *Montaillou*," *Journal of Social History* 15 (Fall/Summer 1981–82): 153.

108. Wood, *The American Historical Review* 81 (December 1976): 1090; Keith Thomas, *The New York Review of Books*, 25 (12 October 1978): 53; Masters, *The American Political Science Review* 71 (December 1977): 1707, 1708.

109. Wylie, *Book World*, 20 August 1978, 1, 4.

110. Wood, *The American Historical Review* 81 (December 1976): 1090.

111. Thomas, *The New York Review of Books*, 25 (October 1978): 52.

112. Stuard, "An Unfortunate Construct," 155.

113. Masters, *The American Political Science Review* 71 (Dec. 1977): 1708.

114. Ibid.

115. Stuard, "An Unfortunate Construct," 153.

116. Ibid.

117. Ibid., 154.

118. On this subject see also Susan Mosher Stuard, "The Annales School and Feminist History: Opening Dialogue with the American Stepchild," *The Journal of Women in Culture and Society* 7 (1981): 142.

119. Hilton, *Times Literary Supplement*, 26 Mar. 1976, 353.

Part II

Bibliographic Instruction in History

3

Finding and Using Historical Materials

Jane A. Rosenberg and Robert P. Swierenga

Both librarians and teachers try to anticipate research needs—librarians, to prepare to meet the needs, and teachers, to expedite their own and their students' work. But the perspectives of those who use research materials frequently differ from those who organize and make them available. Their assessments of needs and priorities are not only dissimilar; in some cases they conflict. In this chapter Jane A. Rosenberg reviews historians' needs for various types of research materials and suggests some strategies for helping both expert and novice scholars learn about the complexities of working in libraries and archives. In the final section Robert P. Swierenga describes his efforts to make students aware of the value of standard reference sources for research, within the context of basic education for the history profession.

RESEARCH ON LIBRARY USE

Attempts to distinguish among types of needs for research materials for the social sciences and humanities began some twenty years ago. Borrowing from earlier studies of the information needs of scientists and general library use studies, librarians and information scientists attempted to identify the library and literature use habits of groups of scholars and students. Their efforts were intended to help librarians understand not only what kinds of materials researchers in various disciplines were likely to require in the future, but also the types of services they would find most helpful. These studies fall into three broad categories:[1]

Jane A. Rosenberg is grateful to David Allen for his comments on an earlier version of this chapter. The opinions expressed here are her own and should not be attributed in any way to the National Endowment for the Humanities.

Citation analysis considers the materials scholars actually use in producing their works, as revealed by the characteristics of items cited in footnotes in journals, books, theses, or other research material.

Library use studies report on demand for library materials, employing circulation records, surveys, interviews, and other means to ascertain which items are used internally or borrowed.

Studies of historians' research habits examine the choice of research topics and subsequent use of sources among small groups of scholars.

The major conclusions of these studies are elementary: First, books, journals, and manuscripts are, and have always been, of primary importance to historical research. Furthermore, because most historical writing is time- and place-bound and professional historians employ contemporary source materials, retrospective materials are more important for history than for some other disciplines. But the studies also revealed a significant demand for very current secondary sources; this demand falls off fairly quickly as journals age and somewhat more slowly in the case of monographs.[2]

This brief characterization may help to differentiate history research needs from those of fields such as journalism or philosophy, but it does not probe deeply enough. Most historians acknowledge that the choice of primary source materials can be influenced by historical fashion: The issues and subjects they study are partly determined by activity in the field and the opinions of their peers. Use studies, for example, seem to indicate that the demand for newspapers and government documents varies depending on the subject of the research, but there is some evidence that these traditional sources are less popular with historians than they used to be. No one has systematically assessed the extent to which other types of primary sources have replaced them, however.

To take another example, the results of several studies indicate that thesis and dissertation literature is not very important to historians. But many scholars would dispute this claim. Whether or not theses and dissertations are actually used, they say, most historians are quite conscious that these sources are sometimes worth investigating. Moreover, no one has tried to ascertain whether dissertations and theses are read but not cited.

The use of foreign-language materials is similarly controversial. Although historians frequently emphasize the importance of foreign scholarship and imply that they attempt to keep up with it, the results of use studies suggest that relatively few actually read much foreign-language material. Many historians confess that their work is constrained by language restrictions. Most academics do rely heavily on libraries for foreign materials, however, so that when there is a demand it is likely to be most apparent in library-related studies.

Use studies also reveal that current awareness is important to research in history. Like other humanities scholars, historians are inclined to work alone and to rely heavily on printed materials. They cite bibliographies and book reviews as the most useful sources of up-to-date information. Both are readily available in the journal literature, which historians, like other scholars, consult first when they want updated information. Specialists prefer journals of broad geographic coverage (e.g., the *Journal of American History*, *Hispanic American Historical Review*, *Slavic Review*) as aids to current awareness; frequently, these journals are the ones published by scholarly professional societies. Professional historians often want to range more widely than a specific research subject requires and to review new materials systematically in a fairly broad field. When pursuing more specialized investigations, however, they tend to confine their attention to journals that concentrate on a specific period or subfield.

Historians' second choice for a current awareness mechanism is consultation with colleagues who work on similar subjects or in related areas. Few historians report that they consult with specialists outside the discipline. Nor do they tend to consult general reference librarians, although the assistance of special collections librarians and archivists is considered essential.[3] Similarly, scholars report that they do not use library-based tools such as indexing or abstracting services very frequently. They are inclined to consult such sources, however, when they are investigating a topic that is unfamiliar. The apparent lack of interest in general reference sources and reference librarians does appear to be due less to a lack of confidence in librarians than to other factors. Professional historians believe that they should be able to locate and use materials themselves; moreover, the categories chosen by professional indexers and the means of access the indexes offer frequently do not suit their needs. Sophisticated indexing and abstracting services are employed less than simpler sources such as the ever-popular *Readers' Guide to Periodical Literature*. When historians cite library sources, they most often emphasize the card catalog, and many advocate browsing the shelves to find serendipitously items that they otherwise might miss.[4]

Thus studies of the use of historical materials describe the world of historians as a print-centered culture, dependent on primary sources, books, and journals. History scholars often consult the journal literature, their colleagues, and, when necessary, special collections librarians or archivists—but they rarely employ the library-oriented reference apparatus.

Again, however, these generalizations do not adequately describe research needs in the discipline. Most of the use studies performed thus far concentrate on recorded use of materials, and these studies reveal only partially the real needs of any researcher. A study of actual needs would include the range of materials used but never actually cited, the researcher's assessment of the relative importance of the works he or she has used, lists of items or types of sources that are sought but never obtained, and attempts to obtain material from sources other than libraries, archives, and publishers.[5]

Second, the studies ignore differences among historians and fail to allow for changes in the discipline over time. Most historians specialize in one or two subfields; thus, generalizations about the types of sources used mask wide variations in research needs. It has occasionally been asserted, for example, that historians are biased against nonprint media, but there are good reasons for why some historians have not used such resources. Those who specialize in ancient or medieval history will find little of interest in photographs, sound recordings, or films, but they may be heavy users of museum collections. Specialists in African-American history, women's history, and political or diplomatic history, however, may consider all of these media useful. Some of them also make heavy use of oral histories and material culture collections.

Of course, many of the nonprint collections are themselves fairly new because more material of this kind is becoming available to researchers than in the past. Whereas a historian has always been expected to interview anyone who could shed light on events he or she is studying, the systematic collection of interviews in the expectation of future need is largely a phenomenon of the past two decades. So, too, is the availability of collections of artifacts of everyday life. New cataloging standards for these nontraditional kinds of collections, where they are employed, require systematic recording of authoritative information about individual items. In the past, this kind of information has not been readily available to researchers.

Also fairly new to the field are collections of machine-readable information. Two investigators reported finding computer printouts among the materials researchers employed; another study revealed enhanced computer use among a small group of humanities scholars. Another study revealed widespread appreciation for word processing and several other types of computer software. Many tend to consider computers as tools, however, rather than as transformers of research patterns. Whether many historians find online information useful is uncertain since there has been no systematic study of the extent to which they employ numeric databases, bibliographic databases, or text bases. The real agent of change for historians' data gathering remains a device now taken for granted—the photocopier.[6]

The number of databases continues to increase, however, and so does the adoption of technology for classroom teaching. Huge, up-to-date union listings of library and archival materials are now available only via a computer search. Electronic projects such as the *Thesaurus Linguae Graecae*, Harvard's Perseus project, the ARTFL database of French texts, and the Medieval and Early Modern Data Bank are assisting classicists, medievalists, and literature scholars. Some historians have used the machine-readable data available from centers such as the University of Michigan's Inter-University Consortium for Political and Social Research. A very few deposit their own data there. But with the increasing availability of electronic information, and with the coming-of-age of generations that were introduced to computers in grade school, are databases becoming more important for historical research? We do not know.[7]

Use studies have ignored other issues that are of considerable importance to researchers. The rapid increase in publication of journals and monographs threatens to inundate scholars in every branch of the discipline. Historians are acutely aware that they have limited time to cover a huge and growing mass of potentially relevant literature. Are surrogates becoming more important? Guides to the literature and state-of-the-art reports, which most historians of the 1960s found less than essential, are appearing more regularly. So are guides to library and archival collections and current awareness tools such as *Current Contents*. Sensing a need within the field for wider knowledge and understanding of microform products, oral history methodology and reference tools, the *Journal of American History* has inaugurated review sections for these materials, and the American Historical Association features articles on library and archival matters in its newsletter, *Perspectives*. Concerns relating to the use of both secondary and primary sources are similarly beginning to receive more attention as controversies over the "fair use" of published and unpublished material and delays in declassifying government records pose major stumbling blocks to research.[8]

These are only a few of the current issues and trends that affect scholars' work. Important developments are also occurring in the methods of organizing materials and making them available for research use in libraries and archives—developments that influence both research and teaching. The following section addresses the effects of some of the changes in libraries on historical research.

HISTORIANS AND LIBRARY SERVICES

Barzun and Graff caution that it is essential to understand the methods of librarians to locate materials in the largely library-resident reference and bibliographic system. Many historians have ignored this elementary caution—albeit, undoubtedly, with good reason. Historians are disadvantaged when it comes to using the library apparatus. They cannot afford to discriminate between the utility of a book that is one hundred years old and one that appeared yesterday, for both are necessary—the first as a primary source and the second as a new interpretation. Bibliographers and librarians, on the other hand, do discriminate among materials by age and format. A prime example is the order in which bibliographic records for library materials are entered into machine-readable catalogs. Older books, manuscripts, and other media generally become available through an electronic catalog only after the current materials and new acquisitions are handled. The enormous human and financial resources required to convert records for an entire library are frequently not available. Too often, the materials historians need are left until last or they are left out completely.[9]

Thus for historians, new technologies and changes in libraries often appear counterproductive. There is no choice but to add the computer catalog (and the time required to learn to use it) to a list of library stops that may include the old card catalog, the serials list, printed indexes, and specialized library files and inventories as yet unintegrated into the main database. And since it has been discovered that old books—or at least books of a certain age—are likely to crumble into yellow dust unless microfilmed or otherwise preserved, historians may find that some sources are becoming less accessible. Unless they are reprinted, such books may be available only in microform. Most scholars have a love–hate relationship with microform viewing and copying devices. While they make it possible to do away (at least in part) with the expense of travel to use original sources, the imposition of balky, poor-quality equipment between the scholar and the sources means that work must be done in inconvenient places and at less desirable times. Using an index to microformed materials may also be a problem, for the index may be of poor quality or inconvenient to use; in some libraries printed indexes are stored far away from the microform equipment. Copies made from microform are usually more expensive than regular photocopies, of poorer quality, and take more time and trouble to produce.[10]

Nor has the publishing revolution served historians well. At the same time that current secondary sources multiply, the discovery and exploitation of more and more primary sources requires broadening or deepening the scope of historical inquiries. New fields and subfields have spawned large literatures. Specializations have become narrower and generalizations less confident. When reviewing the literature, therefore, most scholars subject it to a rigorous winnowing but recognize that they must still look at all items that appear to be pertinent.

Another issue is whether this secondary literature is likely to be available when needed. While libraries have responded favorably to all of historians' requests, they are now much less likely to do so than in the balmy days of the 1960s when budgets rose annually and acquisitions kept pace with book and serial publication. Even the largest libraries now acquire only a carefully selected proportion of the total published output. Many of them do not purchase large collections of primary source materials. Journal subscription lists have been subject to numerous cuts since the mid–1970s. Thus specialists in narrow or exotic fields, or in areas that are not considered important for their institution's library collection, cannot readily obtain even relevant secondary sources. Moreover, many libraries have such limited space that it has been necessary to place some classes of material in storage—which frustrates the researcher's wish to browse.

To help satisfy mushrooming demands from users, librarians have formed cooperative agreements among institutions to make individual items available. Sometimes they can provide access to whole classes of materials and collections, but the advantages of cooperation for scholarly needs have yet to be realized because the result is an intricate maze of special interlibrary arrangements that may or may not address the needs of an individual researcher. Perhaps the best news for scholars was a development that is now considered by the library profession to be rather old hat—the establishment of deposit libraries where little-used materials could be placed. The formation of the Center for Research Libraries more than a quarter of a century ago was a significant step toward making the research library community more responsive to scholars' needs. Another was the establishment of bibliographic networks such as the Online Computer Library Center (OCLC) and the Research Libraries Information Network (RLIN). Many libraries contribute information on their holdings to these networks. But the library world is still struggling with the problem of effectively addressing scholarly needs that go beyond the institutional level.

The historian cannot afford to limit his or her work artificially by using only sources that are readily available. As noted above, looking at everything likely to be pertinent to the current research project is still the norm. But nearly half of a survey group of American scholars in the humanities and social sciences thought their home institution facilities did *at best* a "fair" job of making available the books they needed. Historians usually use more than one research library, and many travel to obtain materials; most also rely on the vital service of interlibrary loan (ILL). Every researcher is aware that the process is painfully slow and inefficient, that it is sometimes difficult to locate materials, and that the expenses attached to providing this customized service have forced many librarians to institute fees. Where it used to be the case that only photocopied materials were not provided free of charge, ILL users now sometimes pay fairly heavy charges for borrowing books. Nevertheless the expenses and inconveniences of ILL are still patiently suffered—especially by those who are most in need, such as individuals at institutions with small libraries or poor collections.[11]

This long litany of difficulties that attend historical research is intended more to document the situation than to criticize librarians or urge reforms. Each library user has his or her own perspective on library problems and the ideal remedies. One theme does, however, predominate: Libraries and archives do not accommodate all user groups' needs equally well. Sometimes, where there is a better awareness of the needs, improvements in services or collections are possible. In other situations, they are not. Generally, scholars have been more than patient with institutional failings—either because they become used to surmounting difficulties or because they do not know what kinds of remedies are possible or appropriate.

HISTORIANS AND THE RESEARCH PROCESS

With most, if not all, historians dependent on libraries and archival repositories, one might assume that they are knowledgeable and expert in using them. Some—perhaps many—are. But librarians and curators often find the assumption unwarranted, and they have evolved elaborate programs to socialize students and faculty in methods of searching for information. If these programs have not always been successful, it is at least partly because there are differences in the ways in which researchers and librarians approach their work.

Researchers often generate an agenda of sources to be read or consulted by following footnotes or references in pertinent articles or books. They supplement their lists by browsing library shelves, scanning book reviews, reading current journals, or consulting their colleagues—that is, with a kind of informed serendipity that has its own logic. It often makes no particular difference in which order research tasks are accomplished—except that it usually makes eminently good sense to let one's excursions through the primary sources dictate one's agenda. The librarian's access tools—indexes, abstracts, bibliographies—often are not consulted at all. Librarians have long wondered about this apparently cavalier neglect of aids to research, and they have (until relatively recently) either scorned or cautioned against the scholar's habit of serendipitous browsing.[12]

One reason that historians neglect indexes and abstracts is that they are inconvenient—they are usually available only in libraries. But there are other reasons that relate more directly to research habits. Major bibliographies and other published finding aids, historians complain, are too often out of date. Reference sources omit the context within which a researcher is trying to work: Not only does indexing terminology often not capture either the nuances or connections of topics in a researcher's mind, but also it is often archaic and may vary, due to the individual differences among those who assign the terms. Indexing and abstracting services describe rather than evaluate material and may misstate the emphasis of articles or fail to indicate connections to related topics. Full-text searching is more helpful because it not only allows use of all relevant terms, but also can ignore nationality or chronology to produce references to similar phenomena in other cultures or time periods. Use of computerized indexing and abstracting services, however, often involves arranging a search with a librarian and, all too frequently, a hefty bill.[13]

Librarians, on the other hand, are close to their sources. They have the luxury of conducting each search de novo, beginning with the most relevant bibliography, index, handbook, or other tool, and following all relevant paths to produce a comprehensive bibliography or compilation of information. They have been trained to visualize an ordered set of reference materials, each with a specific purpose and structure, and each with different features that can be used to answer specific inquiries. They know the ways in which indexing systems are constructed and they are used to the terminology employed. It is, for librarians, largely a matter of matching the inquiry with the right source. And it is this habit of mind that Barzun and Graff—and others—ask the researcher to understand. For reference librarians, the discrete inquiry is the usual unit of work. And while an individual librarian may not know a great deal about the substance of the inquiry, he or she has all the options for finding information well in mind.[14]

It is a very unusual scholar who is able to engage such a range of options without assistance. Yet, if historians have ignored the range of solutions to information problems that librarians have at their fingertips, librarians also have taken a rather narrow outlook. While the methods and types of tools utilized can vary depending on the questions being asked, librarians have generally assumed that their systematic approach is applicable to all disciplines and inquiries. Only fairly recently have the results of use studies and the testimony of users made it clear that such an approach is not accepted by the very population librarians are trying to serve.[15]

The library-oriented approach to research ignores one simple truth: It is difficult to codify an inquiry. The process of discovery varies according to topic, period, country, subject, method, and, most important, the researcher's personal pre-dilections and agenda. Like the best history, good research depends on under-standing where one needs to go next in a continuing search to capture some concept, sequence of events, or analytical angle. Fitting bits and pieces together, paying attention to suspicions, and intuiting relationships all inform the re-searcher's agenda; the hard choices concern whether or not a particular hunch is worth following up or whether more searching will in fact turn up information that seems to be unavailable. In fact, the separate tasks involved in acquiring information are amenable to nearly any order that an individual wants to impose. The same task may yield different results as one works into a project; information may be needed at different stages and in varying levels of detail. New questions emerge as problems are solved and more information is collected. No one but the researcher determines how much digging is enough. Seen in this light, the historian's predilection for working alone and doing intermittent bibliographical or reference work has much to recommend it.[16]

Yet each profession has something to offer the other. Librarians need to recognize that research is both a complex and an extremely individualized pro-cess, that the literature of a discipline to a considerable extent sorts and indexes itself through citations, and that a researcher may simultaneously be in more than one stage of a project and infrequently conduct a single comprehensive search for anything. Historians should recognize that their research habits could also mesh efficiently with library reference tools, that scholars often depend on librarians and archivists to provide at least information on the location of the materials they need, and that at times the help of a skilled intermediary is essential for finding the most promising channels to pursue. Neither research decisions nor searching skills are mechanical. One must know how to select, when and where to look, and how to combine sources creatively to extract the maximum assistance.

STUDENTS AND THE RESEARCH PROCESS

As described above, historians' lack of interest in the library reference ap-paratus can indicate a genuine absence of need or an ignorance that such tools can be helpful. More likely, however, it is due to research habits that have persisted throughout a scholarly career. In most cases, scholars are building on a career spent researching and writing within a fairly narrow area of speciali-zation. Immersed in a culture of refereeing articles, reviewing books, and pre-senting papers, historians need not, in many cases, do more than turn out their own capacious files when information is needed. In the small world of the specialist, nearly all quantities are known. Conversations with the handful of scholars working in the same area provide much of the essential current awareness.

Knowledge of the specialist's research habits has come to the library world relatively recently and has brought with it a certain amount of frustration. Librarians find it hard to reconcile the apparent indifference of scholars to reference materials with their knowledge that these tools are widely used and useful and that publishers continue to turn them out. They know that a library subject specialist who is knowledgeable about a field can develop an ongoing current awareness and a broad perspective on sources and collections that surpasses that of the scholar. And these specialists find that many researchers are glad to learn of the availability of sources that lie outside the normal channels.

Librarians assume that the upcoming generation of researchers will benefit by being tutored in library research methods. Students should not learn by implication that haphazard information gathering is fruitful, they say, any more than librarians should consider it essential to begin with an established sequence of library tools. Students should not, above all, learn to consider it acceptable to approach research with only vague impressions of the types of materials that may be helpful. Because novice researchers all too rapidly realize the frustrations inherent in locating and using historical materials in libraries and archives, some orientation is needed. Librarians recognize that some of the problems relating to the use of reference materials are unique to the discipline, others are generic to libraries and archives, and still others are simply idiosyncrasies. They would like researchers to become sophisticated enough to recognize that these differences exist.

In trying to convince practicing historians that knowledge of reference and research tools can greatly ease their students' (and sometimes their own) work, librarians couch their arguments in the following terms: Students do not have all the avenues of peer assistance at their command that their instructors are apt to take for granted. They generally cannot attend conferences and they cannot call a colleague at another institution when they need assistance. If it becomes embarrassing to reveal a lack of knowledge to mentors or contemporaries, they have a recourse: the time-honored method called "looking it up." Thus, when students begin to do research, they should already be aware of some of the methods of finding basic information. Later, when they want to conduct systematic searches, they will then have some basis on which to proceed. At the very least, this may save the history faculty some time and trouble. Furthermore, if new technology is involved (and in most medium-sized and large libraries these days it is impossible to escape it), some advice on its uses, advantages, and disadvantages is helpful. If not all historians have been convinced by these arguments, a substantial number now acknowledge the need to provide for students at least minimal acquaintance with the increasing number of reference sources and a moderate awareness of library services. Many more readily concede the necessity of consulting specialists when special collections or archives are involved.

An initial history department methods course is usually intended to tutor new graduate students, most often at the master's degree level, in the basics of advanced historical research. Some undergraduate preparation is assumed, and perhaps even some knowledge of library tools and their uses, but for the most part these courses emphasize basic sources and techniques. If beginning students complete such a course first, the matter of providing assistance with term papers, seminar presentations, theses, and dissertations assumes a progression in which the student may become more proficient in research techniques as he or she is exposed to the tutelage of a succession of faculty members.[17]

Unfortunately, not much is known about possible changes in research habits accompanying progression in graduate or undergraduate programs. While it is comforting to assume improvement and increasing sophistication, such hopes are undocumented. The suspicion is that students will adopt the good (and bad) habits of the faculty and also their biases. It is an unusual teacher who decides well in advance which research habits to encourage and which ones to watch out for. After all, fitting one's teaching style and level of instruction to the carefully assessed level of sophistication of one's students is a luxury many never experience. Too often the level of sophistication is nil or the experience is diverse. Those who take the basic research course will probably profit from it if they have a base to build upon; their progress in understanding research techniques will depend greatly on whether subsequent course work and advisers require thorough and sophisticated mining of the sources.

Librarians have long understood that instruction is most effective when it accompanies a real need: Experience with sources when a particular problem makes their use essential prompts better recall. They also have found that an introduction to libraries and archives fits best and reaches the greatest number within the framework of the methods course. One option is to have an entire course devoted to learning the reference and bibliographical apparatus. Some schools have provided such a course. But the usual allocation of time for library learning in a course is still the single class period, and the problem is to transmit basic information in a stimulating way. While patently insufficient for the more complicated tools and inadequate for addressing individual needs, the introductory session provides an opportunity for students to gain a cursory acquaintance with materials and, more important, with the library staff. Not covering everything is the least of the worries. The most pressing concern is to emphasize the variety of materials available and the many approaches to information. At a later time, and under the stimulus of specific individual research needs, working sessions or consultations can be highly effective.

A second major task of library instruction is socialization—the introduction of the folkways, highways, and byways of doing research in libraries and archives. It is essential to address the frustration factors, from unreadable microfilm to arbitrary regulations and difficulties with fee-based services. Reasonable expectations need to be established, and the limitations of reference sources and finding aids should be emphasized. It had better be sooner rather than later that a budding researcher finds out that indexes have to be understood on their own terms; that it may be necessary to piece data together or to calculate it from a variety of widely dispersed sources of varying accuracy; and that neither a computerized catalog nor a computer search is usually comprehensive.

There are some additional benefits to this kind of exercise that are not usually recognized by historians. Dealing with reference sources requires both conceptual and technical precision. Having to translate one's own views and preconceptions into others' language to further one's work can also inculcate the habits of defining terms, assessing assumptions, and checking details. But because students may balk at such complexities and because they quickly feel inundated by the wide range of available material, history faculty support is essential. Coping with the advantages and disadvantages of the reference and research apparatus requires much time, and it is important that both librarian and historian convey the message that it is time well spent. In one field, at least, it appears that the task is an easy one: Most students are easily convinced that the use of new technology is both important and pertinent.

Third, and of utmost importance, it is essential to emphasize that for most historians it is not possible to deal with only one library or only one archival repository. Sophistication about these institutions is not widespread among graduates of history programs, yet socializing students to locate and use primary sources in various places and under various conditions partakes of a nuts-and-bolts mentality that is often disparaged. The few practical articles on these topics, however, are in journals and books that history students are unlikely to encounter. Particularly in cases where work abroad is contemplated, the assistance of a student's adviser is important, although an abundance of printed aids and catalogs continue to be published and more and more microfilming projects are making the contents of foreign repositories available in this country. Librarians follow the bibliography of guides and catalogs and the progress of archival projects, whereas historians may miss such information.[18]

Cooperative programs such as the one described below bring library and academic department together to give students the benefit of the best that both can offer. Mutual support and consultation between members of the two cultures is indispensable. In an atmosphere of proliferating secondary literature, an increasing reference apparatus, and a growing body of machine-readable files, that consultation and cooperation offers the best assurance that the research function will be well served.

DESIGNING THE COURSE: THE HISTORIAN'S VIEW

Robert P. Swierenga

While historians are acutely library dependent, they are often intimidated by the library environment and uninformed about its reference collections. For novices the problem of gaining bibliographic skills means addressing lack of knowledge of what tools exist and the inability to use the tools effectively. There has been an exponential growth in reference works. The "professional informers" are inundating the scholarly community with thousands of finding aids, guides, handbooks, and catalogs. There are several hundred in the field of history alone. Coupled with the plethora of new reference titles is their increasing specialization and complexity. It takes considerable skill and effort, for example, to master the *Social Science Citation Index*, with its several sophisticated indexes.

Even locating the needed reference tools can be a challenge. Customarily, historical reference works are interspersed among thousands of other reference books according to the classification system, and the only entrée is through the catalog. But this avenue is a difficult one if a researcher does not have specific authors and titles in mind. A good solution is a current, compact, annotated historian's handbook for reference works; Helen J. Poulton's *The Historian's Handbook* (1972) was useful in its time but is now seriously outdated. *Reference Sources in History: An Introductory Guide*, by Ronald H. Fritze, Brian E. Coutts, and Louis A. Vyhnanek is the new update to Poulton's work. For Americanists, Francis Paul Prucha's *Handbook for Research in American History* (1987) is a useful tool.

Because of my convictions about the primacy of reference tools, I have always incorporated training in their use early in the curriculum of my graduate methods course in history, which is one of the first courses students take in our graduate program.[19] To insure that students are introduced to the widest spectrum of reference works, and also to the best and most current ones, I rely wherever possible on the expertise of professional librarians with subject specialties in history or related disciplines. Fortunately for me and my students, during the past two decades our library staff has included such persons. If this were no longer the case, I would attempt the job myself, drawing on the foundation already laid. A specialist in one discipline, however, cannot hope to master many other disciplines. It is the better part of wisdom to acknowledge this reality. As an editor of an interdisciplinary journal, *Social Science History*, I continually rely on experts to evaluate manuscripts in the various social sciences that lie beyond my competence. Similarly, my research projects take me into the fields of social statistics and computer programming, where I again gladly accept the help of statisticians and skilled programmers. In the same manner, I maintain an ongoing alliance with reference librarians and archivists.

DeLloyd Guth, in a 1980 essay in the *AHA Newsletter* feature "Teaching History Today," approvingly reiterated the advice of his own graduate mentor some years earlier: "You now need to rely on two, and only two, people: Your nearest [reference] librarian and your nearest archivist."[20] Guth has the right idea, but why be limited to only two experts? Your nearest computer programmer, statistician, or CAI (computer-assisted instruction) instructor may be equally vital. That is why I introduce my students to computer specialists as well as to library specialists. Fortunately, given the recent developments in librarianship, the two may even be one and the same person. On our campus, the computer center itself has been relocated to the library and the CAI laboratory occupies another section of the building.

The mechanics of bibliographic instruction in my graduate methods courses are simple. Early in the semester, I schedule a two-hour session with the reference librarian. The seminar (usually consisting of ten to twelve students) meets in a classroom in the library, and the specialist assembles several dozen of the most important reference works—first consulting me about the composition of the class in terms of disciplines or subfields within history. The librarian also updates a ten-page syllabus listing approximately 150 major bibliographic and reference sources that was initially prepared by Jane Rosenberg, author of the first part of this chapter. The syllabus is divided into seven sections: library guides; national bibliography and library catalogs; general and specialized guides and bibliographies; periodicals and newspapers (including directories); encyclopedias and dictionaries, biographies, statistical sources, and book reviews; government document guides and bibliographies; and manuscript and archival sources.

In the class session, the library specialist begins with a brief description of the physical layout of the library and the workings of its major specialized departments for graduate research: interlibrary loan, microform, archives, and computer search services. The bulk of the period is devoted to a *seriatim* description of each of the items in the syllabus, taking care to spend more time with the most useful and complex items. It is a hands-on class. After the librarian has described each item, books are passed around so that students can scan them and gain an impression of content and usefulness.

Of course, the items blur in the mind long before handling the last of them. Thus, a follow-up assignment is required to ensure that students again consult and interact with the books. I require students to prepare a five-page paper in which they select a specific topic of their own choice and describe the usefulness of at least ten of the reference or bibliographical works in helping to locate sources and research materials on their topic. For heuristic purposes, I encourage them to select a midrange topic, one broad enough to be treated in a wide variety of reference works and yet limited enough to be isolated for detailed study. The topic of Dutch immigration, for example, is preferable to the topic immigration in general. Such delimitation is important because students are required to consult at least one item, preferably the most pertinent, from each of the seven major sections of the syllabus. Since the purpose of the assignment is to encourage students to work with the reference sources, rather than to construct an actual bibliography on the topic, I direct them to describe the process more than the results. It is sufficient, for example, to note that *Dissertation Abstracts International* since 1960 contains twenty titles on various aspects of Dutch immigration to the United States. The entries themselves need not be copied and listed. Similarly, if the *Monthly Catalog of United States Government Publications* contains no entry on Dutch immigration in the nineteenth century, the student need only note this fact and perhaps hazard an opinion as to why this particular source is silent on this subject. Again, I repeat, the purpose is to enable students to use library resources to compile a working bibliography of a given topic in a thorough and efficient manner.

I should also mention that at the conclusion of the introductory session all students unfamiliar with the library's computer cataloging system are taken to a terminal, given a brief introduction, and referred to the self-instructional guides located at the terminals. The benefits and costs of the university's computer bibliographic search capability are also explained for future reference.

Student reaction has been very positive. Students clearly realize the immediate and potential benefits derived from having a working knowledge of the burgeoning shelves of reference and bibliographical guides in college and university libraries today. Graduate students who have already staked out a thesis or dissertation topic often express pleasure at finding materials quickly and comprehensively, including items that might otherwise have eluded them. As one student wrote, ''Finding the right source is often the key to a good research paper. Hence the greater the volume and wider the variety of materials consulted, the greater the chance that the topic can be covered comprehensively.''

Other library holdings that I view as a ''must'' for graduate students to master are the periodicals and serials collection, the historical archives, and the microform materials. The journals are the knowledge frontier of the disciplines. All students will, of necessity, consult the journal literature in their studies, and a few will even publish the first fruits of their work in periodicals. The key to success in these endeavors is familiarity with the entire stable of journals so that one can submit one's work to the most conducive outlet. Every journal has its special scholarly niche and readership. The ability to identify that unique role and pitch one's research questions and findings to that audience is the key to success in publishing. On this assumption, I have prepared a listing of approximately fifty leading English-language scholarly journals in history and the social sciences with which graduate students must familiarize themselves. I require them to browse the shelves; to speed-read an issue or two of each serial, noting the beginning date of publication, the purpose and objectives of the journal, and its sponsoring organization (if any); and most important, to prepare a brief, one-paragraph evaluation. This assignment is quite time-consuming, but like the reference session and the paper, it ensures that students begin to build the foundational skills needed for a successful professional career.

In addition to the reference and journal assignments, I require my students to peruse the card catalog and inventory file of the archives division in order to gain a sense of the varieties of primary historical documents and manuscript collections available on each campus. Microform materials likewise offer a vast treasury of historical records, especially newspapers and census records. To ensure that graduate students know about the census materials, I require them to transcribe several pages of the nineteenth-century population censuses, according to a set of guidelines prepared by the Ohio Historical Society for converting census records into computer-driven files. This exercise, along with several class lectures, introduces students to the problems and possibilities of collective biography and quantitative social history.

Advanced students must master the specialized reference works in their own and related disciplines. The success of their academic careers depends upon it. When professors and library specialists pool their expertise in the teaching of graduate and undergraduate seminars, students assuredly benefit from such team teaching, and their professors even learn a thing or two.

Developing bibliographic searching skills is an art as well as a science. Advanced history students must appreciate the complexity of today's reference works and be introduced to them both by library specialists and by their history professors. The librarians can provide rigorous scientific knowledge about reference works, their organizing principles, and inner logic. Librarians can also best explain the uses of online bibliographic databases and computer bibliographic searching techniques. Professors, on the other hand, have mastered the subject matter and bibliographic sources of their particular areas of research; hence, they can teach students the art of pursuing hunches, following leads, and even utilizing the same informal scholars' networks upon which professionals often rely. The goal is to replace idiosyncratic and haphazard methods with systematic, efficient methods of library use. Only in this way will the frustration factors in research give way to satisfaction factors, as the tools and their keepers become friends instead of enemies.

NOTES

1. Cf. Donald Owen Case, "The Collection and Use of Information by Some American Historians: A Study of Motives and Methods," *Library Quarterly* 61 (January 1991): 61–82.

2. Margaret F. Stieg, "The Information Needs of Historians," *College & Research Libraries* 42 (November 1981): 549–60; Cynthia Corkill and Margaret Mann, *Information Needs in the Humanities: Two Postal Surveys* (Sheffield: University of Sheffield, Center for Research on User Studies, 1978); Clyve Jones, Michael Chapman, and Pamela Carr Woods, "The Characteristics of the Literature Used by Historians," *Journal of Librarianship* 4 (July 1972): 137–56; Dagmar Horna Perman, "Bibliography and the Historian," in *Bibliography and the Historian, The Conference at Belmont of the Joint Committee on Bibliographic Services to History*, ed. Dagmar Horna Perman (Santa Barbara, Calif.: Clio, 1967), 7–19. We have not included the findings of several social science use studies that are sometimes cited in connection with historians' use habits.

3. Herbert C. Morton and Ann Jamieson Price, "The ACLS Survey of Scholars: Views on Publications, Computers, Libraries," *Scholarly Communication* no. 5 (Summer 1986); Corkill and Mann, *Information Needs*; Jan Horner and David Thirlwall, *Personal Online Information and the Social Sciences and Humanities Researcher,* Final report to the Social Sciences and Humanities Research Council of Canada (Winnipeg, Manitoba: University of Manitoba Libraries, August 1986), 6.c.

4. Stephen E. Wiberley, Jr., and William G. Jones, "Patterns of Information Seeking in the Humanities," *College & Research Libraries* 50 (November 1989): 641; Perman, "Bibliography and the Historian," 18.

5. Maurice B. Line, "Information Needs of the Social Sciences," *INSPEL: International Journal of Special Libraries* 8 (April 1973): 29–39.

6. Jerome M. Clubb, "Computer Technology and the Source Materials of Social Science History," *Social Science History* 10 (Summer 1986): 97–114; Jitka Hurych, "After Bath: Scientists, Social Scientists, and Humanists in the Context of Online Search-

ing," *Journal of Academic Librarianship* 12 (1986): 158–65; Wiberley and Jones, "Patterns of Information Seeking," 639–40; Case, "Collection and Use," 75–76.

7. *Humanities Communication Newsletter* no. 4 (April 1985): 15–16; Stieg, "Information Needs," 551; May Katzen, *Technology and Communication in the Humanities* (Boston Spa: British Library, 1985); Horner and Thirlwall, *Personal Online Information*, 6.b, 6.c; Sue Stone, "Humanities Scholars: Information Needs and Uses," *Journal of Documentation* 38 (December 1982): 299–300.

8. Walter Rundell, Jr., *In Pursuit of American History* (Norman, Okla.: University of Oklahoma Press, 1970), 234–59; Perman, "Bibliography and the Historian," 18–19; Stanley I. Kutler and Stanley N. Katz, "The Promise of American History: Progress and Prospects," *Reviews in American History* 10 (December 1982); James B. Gardner and George Rollie Adams, eds., *Ordinary People and Everyday Life* (Nashville, Tenn.: American Association for State and Local History, 1983); Thomas Bender, "Wholes and Parts: The Need for Synthesis in American History," *Journal of American History* 73 (June 1986): 120–36; Alan Solomon, "Microform Reviews: Introduction," *Journal of American History* 73 (March 1987): 1086–87; John D. Buenker, "Research and Reference Tools Reviews," *Journal of American History* 73 (March 1987): 1096–97; Michael Les Benedict, "Historians and the Continuing Controversy Over Fair Use of Unpublished Manuscript Materials," *American Historical Review* 91 (October 1986): 859–81.

9. Jacques Barzun and Henry E. Graff, *The Modern Researcher*, 4th ed. (San Diego, Calif.: Harcourt Brace Jovanovich, 1985), 69.

10. J. S. Morrill, "Microform and the Historian," *Microform Review* 16 (Summer 1987): 204–12.

11. Joel Rudd and Mary Jo Rudd, "Coping with Information Load: User Strategies and Implications for Librarians," *College & Research Libraries* 47 (July 1986): 315–22; Morton and Price, "The ACLS Survey."

12. See Thomas Mann, *A Guide to Library Research Methods* (New York: Oxford University Press, 1987), 27–35, for a helpful discussion by a librarian of systematic browsing using the classification scheme and comparing the advantages of browsing to those of using the reference apparatus of the catalog. Also, see Robert Grover and Martha L. Hale, "The Role of the Librarian in Faculty Research," *College & Research Libraries* 49 (January 1988): 9–15; and Case, "Collection and Use," 76–79.

13. Stephen K. Stoan, "Research and Library Skills: An Analysis and Interpretation," *College and Research Libraries* 45 (March 1984): 99–109; Stoan, "Historians and Librarians: A Response," *College and Research Libraries News* 47 (September 1986): 503; Perman, "Bibliography and the Historian," 12; Case, "Collection and Use," 79. A rebuttal to Stoan is in Joyce Duncan Falk, "Librarians and Historians at the American Historical Association," *College and Research Libraries News* 47 (September 1986): 501–2. For an interesting exposition of the complexities attached to using online bibliographic search services, see Falk's article in this volume, and for a detailed exposition of the advantages and shortcomings of abstracts, see Joyce Duncan Falk, "Why Abstracts," *Editing History* 5 (Spring 1988): 6–8.

14. See also Mann, *Guide to Library Research Methods*, 158.

15. For example, when the designers of indexing and abstracting systems met with historians, bibliographers, and librarians in the late 1960s to try to improve the reference apparatus, the implicit assumption remained that researchers would deal in a systematic way with bibliographies and other reference tools. The solution to assisting history scholars appeared to be to execute a straightforward study of how historians do their work and

subsequently design information services and access tools that would more nearly fit their needs. See Paul L. Ward, "Clarification of Needs and Formulation of Recommendations," in *Bibliography and the Historian*, ed. Perman, 164.

16. Line, "Information Needs," 33.

17. Walter Rundell's survey of the training given graduate students makes it evident that many history departments have proceeded under these assumptions in designing courses. The librarians and curators he questioned, however, made it evident that many faculty members were not acquainted specifically with the sources their students needed to use. See Rundell, *In Pursuit of American History*, 3–36. The National Archives is currently supporting a new survey of scholars' use of original documentary sources.

18. An example is Michele L. Fagan, "Practical Aspects of Conducting Research in British Libraries and Archives," *RQ* 26 (Spring 1987): 370–76.

19. This description of the course offered at Kent State University was published in a slightly different form in *The History Teacher* 17 (May 1984): 391–96. It is used here with permission.

20. DeLloyd J. Guth, "History as Epistemology," *AHA Newsletter* 18, no. 4 (April 1980): 6–7, 10.

4

Bibliographic Instruction in History

Charles A. D'Aniello

A HISTORICAL EDUCATION

When considering bibliographic instruction in history it is appropriate to reflect on the purpose of a historical education. When one does, one realizes that the goals of historical and bibliographic education are complementary. Question analysis and the finding of information are common to both endeavors. An education is more than an accumulation of facts, and historians have long argued that a historical education prepares one to search for understanding. Yet the past cannot be reconstructed or imagined unless the searcher commands the skills necessary to identify, find, and interpret the records or objects in which it is remembered. And information cannot be found and turned into knowledge unless the searcher possesses sufficient background knowledge, organized into a web of associative relationships or schemata, that enable him or her to make sense of new information and to anticipate probable evidence, connections, and conclusions. Practically, like the reference librarian, the historian works with an incomplete picture, and what he or she finds plays an important role in determining the history that is written.

Expanding references is central to the process of scholarship. In this sense, many reference tools may be broadly defined as dictionaries, because they either give meaning to a term directly or identify other sources that do. Cultural historian Eric Weil echoes the earlier words of Samuel Johnson when he writes: "Education is not a question of cramming but of discovering and showing lines and problems and an orientation, the cultivated man is not he who can quote the contents of an encyclopedia, but he who knows what you look for and where to look for it."[1]

The ability to verify facts and establish context are critical to the analysis of information. Practically, the less easily one is able to verify the less likely one is to question. Documents become indecipherable when one knows neither the meaning of a term or event nor where to find a definition of it. But often even to know that the answer has been found requires a knowledge of the discipline as well as of bibliography. Thus historical and bibliographic skills are complementary.

The range of contemporary information sources is enormous. For all researchers, resources have become more varied and available, but the knowledge necessary to take full advantage of them has increased as well. Online catalogs and bibliographic databases enable searchers to employ Boolean logic in their searching with powerful results. (Boolean techniques are commonly used with manual searches; for instance, one can look up Marxism in a Soviet encyclopedia and identify a sympathetic essay from a Soviet perspective. The computer, however, facilitates linkages.) And the extent of indexing and the array of dictionaries, encyclopedias, and handbooks far exceeds that available even a decade ago. Two recent surveys conducted by the Research Libraries Group, profiling the research techniques and needs of various disciplines, census the already burgeoning array of machine-readable files and point the way to an even richer electronic future.[2]

THE NATURE OF RESEARCH

What constitutes good research, whether conducted by a student or by a scholar? The age-old prerequisite of sensing and being open to the existence of what one is looking for remains at the heart of successful research, bibliographic or otherwise. But good research is only likely to occur when questions have been carefully formulated and, as noted above, when substantive knowledge is great enough to suggest context and research skill is developed sufficiently to enable one to search and reason for information and explanation. Research does not consist of a series of mechanical steps. Though there are tests of reliability and intent that can be applied to evidence, a confluence of understandings and perceptions held by the researcher come together in the form of imagination and insight to propel good research forward. It is ultimately an art form. For as librarian and historian C. Paul Vincent writes, "Good research is the product of clear and imaginative thought, accompanied by a logical and not overly dependent use of indexing tools and other reference sources," and "research has not ensued until the results of an index search have been confronted; until a meeting-of-the-minds takes place between the author and student."[3]

BIBLIOGRAPHIC INSTRUCTION FOR HISTORY
STUDENTS: OPPORTUNITIES AND REALIZATIONS

In 1967 Charles Tilly and David Landes, writing for the Social Science Research Council, advocated that students receive instruction in research design and the use of social science concepts, and that they be led to develop a sensitivity to existing but ignored information sources.[4] In 1991, writing for the Association of American Colleges Project on Study In-Depth, the Task Force on the History Major advised, concerning undergraduate history students: "Traditional library resources and new technologies for use in research provide students with experiences that go far beyond their immediate application in history courses."[5] And the American Library Association's Presidential Committee on Information Literacy recently declared: "To be information literate, a person must be able to recognize when information is needed and have the ability to locate, evaluate, and use effectively the needed information."[6]

To achieve their ends Landes and Tilly recommended that "departments of history offer formal courses in historical method that include the appropriate literature of the other social sciences."[7] Historian and founder of ABC-Clio Eric Boehm recommended a special course of bibliographic study in doctoral programs and for postgraduates.[8] Most recently, the Task Force on the History Major recommended a course in historical methods and a research seminar with a writing requirement as well as a strong foundation course and a course to acquaint students with global diversity.[9]

THE BEST APPROACH

Jane Rosenberg identifies socialization as one of the goals of bibliographic instruction, and I suggest that the very first thing students of any discipline should be taught is not explicitly how to use the library and reference sources but, rather, to look to the library, electronic systems, traditional reference sources, and librarians as friends. Students should not approach the library with more anxiety than hopefulness. To those who give library assignments—historians and librarians—this means that an undergraduate's first experience using the library should be well conceived and well programmed for obvious success. Certainly, we all harbor within us, at one time or another, a self-defeating voice that whispers, "I am scared to ask questions. I don't want to bother anyone. I just don't want them to think I'm stupid." Giving students a frustrating library research assignment that cannot be successfully completed is a sure way to make future independent library use problematic. Whatever you ask students to do, be sure you yourself have done it and are confident it can be done by them. Further, students cannot be asked to do too many things at once, nor should one assume that even the names assigned to library items and procedures are known to them.[10]

Basic instructional objectives should always be the same: to equip students with the skills and knowledge to complete the assignment they are working on successfully, with some independence and ease, and to add to or reinforce a body of bibliographic awareness and skills that will enable them to pursue information independently throughout their formal education and beyond. Such instruction is especially important for graduate students.

The conditions under which learning most easily occurs should inform the manner in which instruction is offered. Briefly, there are two types of learning:

insightful and meaningful. Insightful learning is achieved through intense inquiry and interest but it is difficult to evaluate and produce. Meaningful learning, on the other hand, is much easier to achieve and understand. It occurs when what one learns is meaningful because it finds a ready home in already existing mental structures. It is defined as an understanding of conceptual relationships, and the teaching of concepts rather than sources should be the underlying aim of all bibliographic instruction.[11] When a librarian uses an appropriate reference tool that he or she has never used before, after first determining the type of tool needed, that librarian is demonstrating the consequence of meaningful learning.

In addition to being taught the concepts on which bibliography is organized, students should be taught to be flexible and inventive and not to approach library research as a mere progression of mechanical steps. In the process of research and writing, questions and information needs emerge and evolve. As Donald Owen Case has argued, historians are "guided less by sources and more by questions or problems that lead them to particular sources." In fact, unlike many investigators whom he cites, Case "found historians to be well-organized and methodical in their research"; but historical research is a back-and-forth activity, not a linear process.[12]

Of course, none of this precludes considerable and distressing ignorance of bibliographic tools on the part of some faculty who would benefit richly from such knowledge. But, as Jane Rosenberg succinctly shows, faculty pursue information needs differently than students and sometimes may simply not need to rely heavily on bibliographic tools. Yet if mature library use is seldom a systematic series of steps, it is, as many commentators have pointed out, an exercise in logic and art. But to teach students this requires structure, as developmental and educational theorists have long argued: it is best for our mental development if we are able to crawl before we walk, and walk before we run. Therefore, the way in which basic library skills are taught may well not initially reflect the way in which instructors may hope they will ultimately be utilized. Thus highly structured learning experiences are appropriate, because intuitive links, leaps of insight, do not occur in a vacuum, and the more one knows, the more one can then imagine.

LIBRARIAN–HISTORIAN COLLABORATION

Professionals across the disciplinary map consult professionals in other fields as they proceed with their work. One steeped in the concepts and tools of a particular field cannot help but utilize its resources more effectively than an outsider. The extent to which a librarian understands a discipline will vary, just as the knowledge a practitioner of a discipline has of bibliography and library skills will vary. But while specialized disciplinary knowledge is not uniform, inevitably a librarian will know far more about manipulating the library as an organization than the vast majority of professors. The historian may be an expert bibliographer but the librarian will have broader bibliographic knowledge and, generally, far more insight into ways in which to expand that knowledge easily.[13] In short, librarians and library resources enable the neophyte to mine for ideas and information in material that would otherwise be largely inaccessible.

WHAT TO TEACH AND WHEN TO TEACH IT

Beyond the underlying goals discussed above, students should be taught to analyze a problem bibliographically: to determine the questions that must be asked to explore it; to anticipate the types of sources of information that may solve it; and, finally, to identify the specific reference sources that identify, contain, and/or provide access to the needed information. They should be taught what the various types of reference sources and publication formats do, given the variations within each, as well as an awareness of the way a discipline's literature is indexed through footnotes and references. And they should be given an appreciation of the increasing interdisciplinarity of contemporary historical scholarship and a basic familiarity with the reference sources that serve other disciplines.

When to teach? Some undergraduates use the library extensively, but analytical learning can occur without such effort. Some instructors may encourage intensive rather than extensive reading—although one need not preclude the other. Yet the searching of the stacks is important not because it teaches analytical skills— there are many ways to do that—but because it teaches something about information. It instills an attitude about the accessibility of information, which if done properly will suggest to students that they really can with ease and flexibility significantly and independently increase their stock of knowledge.

Listed below are the minimum skills that I believe should be taught at each educational level. The needs of a particular course may justify some movement between levels. It is assumed that once introduced, skills in each area will be pursued in greater depth and intensity at succeeding levels.

Beginning Undergraduates
(Freshmen and Sophomores)
Should Be Taught

- Use of the catalog in its traditional and/or electronic forms.
- Use of general periodical abstracts and indexes in their traditional and electronic forms.
- Use of Boolean search techniques in accessing electronic catalogs and general abstracts and indexes.
- Use of each of the genres of reference sources.
- Use of a systematic generic library research model with an appreciation that library research is not a linear process.

Sometimes, these goals are addressed by the completion of a freshman work-book and/or work in an undergraduate composition course. It is best to introduce students first to a generic rather than a discipline-specific library research model. In so doing they are introduced to tools that have the broadest focus and thus the greatest likelihood of satisfying the most diverse needs. Whenever the opportunity arises, beginning undergraduate history courses should largely, though not exclusively, follow this generalist approach.

Advanced Undergraduates
(Juniors and Seniors)
Should Be Taught

- How to analyze complicated questions to determine the type of information needed and the type of reference source likely to be useful.

- Use of specialized indexes and abstracts in their traditional and electronic forms.

- Use of a systematic discipline-specific library research model with an appreciation that library research is not a linear process.

- Evaluation of information for bias through contextual understanding.

- Awareness that the literature of a discipline indexes itself, through footnotes and bibliographies in books, articles, and so forth, and a sensitivity to the strengths and weaknesses of relying upon this referencing.

- An appreciation of the importance of correct referencing and the role of citation in argumentation.

The achievement of these goals has traditionally been guaranteed with a research project in a methods seminar offered in the major's junior year, but may be taught in the writing and research component of any course.

Graduate students enter their programs with wholly unpredictable levels of bibliographic and library knowledge and skills; therefore, the goals listed below may often be approached only after remedial instruction. Such instruction, however, need not be time-consuming. Instruction for graduate students is sometimes offered in a methodology course that initiates students to graduate work; otherwise it is presumed to occur within graduate research seminars.

Graduate Students
Should Be Taught

- Knowledge of the nature and structure of communication (the role of professional organizations, conferences, newsletters, dictionaries and encyclopedias, etc.) among the discipline's practitioners.

- Extensive practice in bibliographically analyzing questions and identifying bibliographic, reference, and secondary and primary source materials that either provide needed information or identify materials likely to contain needed information.

- Techniques for tapping into the literature of other disciplines by using reference sources.

- Use of printed and electronic resources that identify books, serials, and primary source materials across libraries and research institutions.

CONTEXTS IN WHICH INSTRUCTION MAY BE OFFERED

The ideal setting in which to offer advice is the private consultation. However, the less informed students are the more time-consuming such sessions can be and economy demands that basic library skills be taught in some sort of group setting. For undergraduates private or semiprivate sessions often take the form of term-paper clinics; for graduate students, required consultations with a librarian during the term-paper or thesis-writing process would be ideal. A form of the latter would require consultation with a librarian before a student was given permission to proceed with the writing of a dissertation or a thesis.[14] For some, the meeting might result in a long-term working relationship, for others not, but an opportunity for interaction would be assured.

The manner in which bibliographic instruction is offered and its extent and content are a consequence of a discipline's research methods and logistical considerations. Concerns related to class size and personnel are often the determining factors, for the methods and means of offering instruction are diverse: lectures, workshops, workbooks, and video productions may all be utilized to good advantage. Yet single-session or one-night stand instructional opportunities predominate.

Distinctions must be made between course-related, course-integrated, and curriculum-integrated instruction. Librarian Frances Hopkins has done an excellent job of describing differences between the approaches. Course-related instruction is designed to support a specific assignment. For instance, a librarian might be asked to present the strategy for researching a given topic to a group of students or might perceive this need independently and offer a workshop. As an example, all students might be instructed in strategies for identifying research material using the *National Union Catalog of Manuscript Collections* or *America: History and Life* and *Historical Abstracts*, or a workshop might be offered in tracing legislative histories using Congressional Information Service's various indexes as well as official sources.

Course-integrated instruction differs from these instructional designs because it requires collaboration between librarian and instructor and sustains an ongoing bibliographic instruction component. Examples of such integration might be a course built around the gathering of evidence for argumentation or the careful consideration and editing of a historical text, or the completion of a series of bibliographic exercises throughout the course.

Curriculum-integrated instruction, Frances Hopkins points out, "requires that an academic department, in cooperation with a teaching librarian, establish library competency goals for majors and plan its curriculum so that every major's program includes the required levels of library research experience." A bibliography course required of all majors or graduate students, offering guidance and practice in the answering of specific questions as well as in the compilation of a bibliography, is perhaps the easiest way to achieve this end. For instance, curriculum-integrated instruction alone seeks to guarantee that all students will,

through their formal course work, have the opportunity to attain the same previously agreed-upon competencies.[15] However instruction is offered it should
reflect, especially at the graduate level, the interdisciplinary nature of much
contemporary historical work (see chapter 2) and, at all levels, the ever-increasing
importance of electronic resources (see chapter 8).

HOW TO TEACH CONCEPTUAL FRAMEWORKS: BASIC INSTRUCTIONAL DESIGNS

Librarians Pamela Kobelski and Mary Reichel have summarized the essential
hooks on which bibliographic instruction in any discipline may be hung. While
the above concerns are strategic, the approaches for lessons and assignments
that follow are more a matter of tactics and techniques. *Type of Reference Tools*
(This is an abstract and this is what abstracts do . . .): even when examples of
each type of reference tool are grouped together, this approach is best suited to
teaching reference rather than research skills because it does not encourage
explanation of the structure of the discipline or how tools work together, or
materials that are not reference tools. *Systematic Literature Searching* (First look
in this type of source, then this type of source . . .): presents sources in a logical
sequence and appreciates the function and interrelationship of various tools but
it encourages a linear perception of library research. It is the best approach for
beginning researchers. *Form of Publication* is a useful tactic for the beginning
of an instructional session. Groupings may range from books and periodicals to
newspapers, government documents, and maps. This approach makes immediately clear to students that bibliographic tools and library organization are a
response to organizational problems produced by the common as well as unique
characteristics of publication formats. *Primary/Secondary Sources* provides a
natural context for librarian-historian collaboration in the consideration of what
constitutes a primary source, the tools that provide access to such material, and
the reliability of various sources. *Publication Sequence* (The study of *x* was first
announced in an article and ten years later an encyclopedia specifically devoted
to the topic was published . . .): is an exercise in intellectual history best used
as an aside in a presentation to a research seminar. *Citation Patterns* (Who cites
who, and why . . .): familiar to librarians in citation indexes and to historians
in footnotes, this is another approach that is useful in any study of the evolution
of ideas, and it clearly illustrates the dynamic nature of research as reflected in
bibliography. *Index Structure* (These are the types of headings that appear in
the tool of this discipline and its indexes provide access to this type of literature
in these ways . . .): asks students to reflect on what and why certain things are
important in a particular discipline. It invites consideration of the strengths and
weaknesses of using various types of indexes and of their fallibility.[16] *Sociohistorical Analysis*, although applicable to all of the above, is not explicitly part
of Kobelski and Reichel's original taxonomy (This is the meaning of this work
in its historical context and it reflects the environment in which it has been

created in these ways . . .): should appeal to history students and, often using *Citation Patterns* or *Publication Sequence*, is an exercise in intellectual history. In fact, this conceptualization can be an aspect in any of the other approaches.

Successful presentations often incorporate more than one of these approaches, and multiple sessions or a bibliography course might use all or nearly all of them. In the compressed time and format in which bibliographic instruction is generally offered, the most economical approach to be used with beginning students is the *Systematic Literature Search* model. As outlined by librarian Gemma DeVinney, the process is straightforward. The model encourages students to approach research as a process rather than an accident. In outline form, it moves from overviews to books to articles to supporting material. Starting from a chosen topic the librarian first presents the encyclopedic overviews that will quickly inform the students of the dimensions of the chosen topic. The fact that these sources often contain valuable bibliographies is also pointed out. The next stage revolves around finding books on the topic. Here issues concerning controlled vocabulary as used in the *Library of Congress Subject Headings* list may be considered. Next, the nature of periodical literature and the tools that provide access to it are studied. It is an easy leap from the *Readers' Guide to Periodical Literature* to the Wilson academic indexes such as *Social Sciences Index* and *Humanities Index*. Finally, as appropriate, special resources such as newspapers or statistics are considered.[17]

INSTRUCTIONAL DESIGNS BASED ON CONCEPTUAL FRAMEWORKS

Exercises that librarians or historians and librarians working together might wish to use with history students follow. These exercises also offer ideas for classroom presentations. Some are alternatives to the more common show-and-tell presentations simply structured around a particular topical concern, and they teach lessons about reference and bibliographic sources and bibliography itself. They are not intended to be more than models, nor do they constitute an instructional program. Citations and abstracts for pertinent articles and books describing courses and classes as well as appropriate workbooks and guides are found in the concluding chapter of this book. Completing bibliography exercises is a way of learning and practicing library skills. Instructors are encouraged to design their own exercises and, in so doing, increase their own bibliographic skills and understanding.

The exercises that follow may be modified to nurture independence, and the degree of instructor guidance may be easily manipulated. For instance, in many of the exercises that follow students might be told exactly what source to use to complete an exercise, be required to select from a list of sources, or be required to find the appropriate source on their own using either the catalog or a general or specialized guide to reference materials (see chapters 6 and 7). The intellectual level students have attained either on their own or as a consequence of instruction must determine what they are asked to do.

Before giving an assignment, be sure that students have acquired sufficient knowledge and skill to complete the exercise and that they know their way around the facility they will be using. I assume one or more meetings with a librarian will precede the assignment of an exercise and, ideally, that a follow-up meeting will occur after the exercise's completion. At the first meeting(s) the tools or strategies to be used should be clearly explained and illustrated with either handouts or overheads and, at the concluding session, students should be encouraged to discuss problems, make observations, and share information and perspectives. Be sure that an appropriate individual at the library has been notified about the assignment and given a copy of it. The best library assignments are the fruits of librarian–historian collaboration, the sharing and merging of different approaches and knowledge resulting in a product to which both parties are committed. If you are a librarian and are asked to offer instruction, ask the historian how he or she is pedagogically and historiographically pursuing the subject of the course and determine the types of resources he or she would like students to use and the ultimate objective of the exercise. Be sure to obtain a copy of the course's syllabus. If you are a historian, reverse the procedure. Perhaps one or more of the exercises given below may be appropriately adapted by both of you for use in a course where the initial request was for basic instruction.

Notes to the instructor are included for particular exercises only when judged necessary. Many of the exercises that follow are indebted to exercises described or suggested in works cited in sections 1, 6, and 7 of the concluding bibliography. Some are adaptations of one or more of these exercises. Please refer to these sections for the discussions and for additional instructional ideas. (The influence of Raymond G. McInnis's many contributions, cited in the concluding bibliography, requires special acknowledgment. The sample exercise on cycling references is based on material McInnis shared with the author.)

Type of Reference Tools

Students can be taught the characteristics of the various categories of reference tools by requiring them to examine individually representative examples. Unless the number of titles is modest and the utility of the effort is obvious, this exercise may be rather tedious. Categories, which have been previously defined, should be arranged in a logical sequence. The assumption is that students will familiarize themselves enough with these resources to relate them to one another and that they will develop both a cognitive and a locational map of the reference collection.

Sample Exercise
Annotating a List of Reference Sources

Student: Teach yourself what is in the reference collection by walking through it and becoming familiar with some of its most useful works. The following reference

sources are listed under the categories: guides, dictionaries and encyclopedias, reference sets, biographical dictionaries, atlases and gazetteers, abstracts and summaries, commentaries, chronologies, yearbooks and almanacs, quotation dictionaries
and concordances, statistical sources, indexes and abstracts, bibliographies of bibliographies, bibliographies, current awareness sources, research reviews and book
reviews, book review indexes, source collections and collected works, pictorial
works, indexes to archival and manuscript material, United States government documents. For each tool listed describe on a four-by-six-inch card, in 150 to 200 words,
its function, scope, basic organization, and special features and provide its call
number.

For example: *America: History and Life* (AHL), 1964–. Santa Barbara, Calif.: ABC-
Clio. Available online (1980–   ) and on CD-ROM (1982–   ).

AHL indexes and abstracts approximately 2,100 serial publications in over forty languages
on all historical aspects of Canadian and American history. Articles published in
languages other than English are abstracted in English. Abstracts capture the essential
points of the article and indicate the sources upon which the article is based. Indexing
provides access geographically and topically, and chronology is clearly indicated.
Articles abstracted may also be searched by author. Retrospective volumes extend
coverage back to 1954. Since its inception, AHL has been organized in various ways
and is currently published in five issues. Each contains article abstracts and citations
for reviews of books and films and citations for dissertations. Except for the fourth
issue, each contains an author index, a subject index, a book and film title index,
and a reviewer index. The fifth issue is an annual cumulative index. Entries are
organized under six major groupings: North America; Canada; United States of
America: National History (to 1945); United States of America: 1945 to Present;
United States of America: Regional, State, and Local History; History, the Humanities, and Social Sciences.

Having students answer a series of questions using tools that you would like
them to use is a more interesting way to proceed, although the two exercises
can be combined.

Sample Exercise
Using Specific Sources[18]

Student: Consult the *Encyclopedia of the Social Sciences* (ESS) and the *Kodansha Encyclopedia of Japan* (KEJ) and (a) cite discussions of the similarities and dissimi-
larities between European and Japanese feudalism, and (b) cite a discussion of the
perception of women in Bushidō.

Instructor: (a) ESS, "Feudalism—Japanese," vol. 6, 217–18, and KEJ, "feudalism,"
vol. 2, 263. The latter is a historiographical summary. The former appears in a
grouping of essays about feudalism around the world, and similarities are both
assumed and emphasized. (b) ESS, "Feudalism—Japanese," vol. 6, 217–18. None
of KEJ's essays addresses this topic.

Questions can be designed to teach both the use of reference sources and critical
thinking by helping students identify bias and opposing perspectives in different
reference sources.

Student: To which race did the ancient Egyptians belong? Consult the *Cambridge Encyclopedia of Africa* (CEA) and UNESCO's *General History of Africa* (GHA), vol. 2, *Ancient Civilizations of Africa*. First (a) compare and contrast the conclusions of each; then consult only the latter work and summarize, in light of this controversy, its discussion of (b) melanin dosage tests, (c) osteological measurements, (d) blood types, and (e) linguistic analysis.

Instructor: Students may be told at some point that ancient Egypt is included in the *Cambridge Ancient History*, and in the *Cambridge History of Africa*. (a) CEA notes that "Despite claims and counterclaims the population of ancient Egypt cannot be characterized either as 'Asiatic' or as 'Negroid,' " p. 93. The only index entry that works here is " 'Negroid' population of Egypt." GHA strongly insists that the ancient Egyptians were unquestionably among the black races, pp. 49–51. In GHA see the index entry "race question, see color question," that is, "Color question on Egypt"; (b) chemical responsible for skin pigmentation, unquestionably black, p. 35; (c) body proportions, unquestionably black, p. 35; (d) even today Group B as in Western Africa predominates, p. 36; (e) a connection with African languages, pp. 44–48.

Systematic Literature Searching

Answering a reference question takes different skills than compiling a bibliography. Bibliographic exercises can lend themselves to the exploration of a topic across a breadth of concerns and approaches. But for teaching bibliographic knowledge the construction of a pathfinder, or bibliographic guide to reference sources, is a more certain exercise than simply asking for a bibliography. Beginning students may be given a completed pathfinder to guide them in their work. Pathfinders are synthetic and are ideal concluding exercises for a library skills course or as a component of a seminar or course requiring a research paper. The pathfinder assignment below is elaborate, but an instructor can easily adapt it to any level of difficulty by shortening it and/or by telling students precisely what sources to use or by meeting with individual students and, based on the topic that has been selected, indicating the sources that should be consulted. The basic form of this exercise is briefly discussed earlier in this chapter, p. 77.

Sample Exercise
Pathfinders

Student: Begin by defining a topic for investigation. As you identify reference sources using the various guides to reference books and the catalog, provide a bibliographic citation, call number, and a description of the source's structure: note its special features, strengths, weaknesses, and coverage, if it gives bibliographic references, and if it is available in electronic form(s) (online and/or CD-ROM). Annotations should be between 150 and 200 words in length. Then, proceed as directed.

Pathfinder I—Secondary Literature

1. Topic Statement. In not more than one hundred words describe the specific topic

you will investigate, indicating its historical importance and its intellectual, chronological, and geographical contexts. Indicate if work in disciplines other than history is relevant.

2. Subject Headings. Consult *Library of Congress Subject Headings* and attach a photocopy of relevant headings and list especially significant proper nouns that should be searched.

3. Books. Cite two appropriate books, and in several sentences per book indicate the significance of each for the topic. Comment not only on each book's thesis and quality but also on the sources it is based on, the methodology employed, and the nature and extent of its bibliographic apparatus: footnotes, bibliography, bibliographic essay, and so forth.

4. Book Reviews. Cite two reviews for each of the above books and cite and annotate the book review index(es) used to find them. Use *Book Review Digest* and *Combined Retrospective Index to Book Reviews in Scholarly Journals, 1886–1974* and *Combined Retrospective Index to Book Reviews in Humanities Journals, 1802–1974* (if publication dates are appropriate) as well as other indexes that may be useful, including *America: History and Life*, *Arts and Humanities Citation Index*, and *Social Sciences Citation Index*.

5. Essays. Cite and annotate *Essay and General Literature Index* and cite two relevant essays found using it.

6. General Guides to Research and Reference Materials. Cite and annotate the American *Guide to Reference Books* and the British *Walford's Guide to Reference Materials* and note the sections of each likely to be especially useful.

7. Specialized Guides to Research and Reference Materials. As appropriate, cite and annotate tools such as Fritze, Coutts, and Vyhnanek's *Reference Sources in History: An Introductory Guide* and Francis Paul Prucha's *Handbook for Research in American History: A Guide to Bibliographies and Other Reference Works* and note the sections of each likely to be especially useful. You can identify specialized guides—there are ones for special subjects as well as for various disciplines—by using the general guides noted above in #6.

8. Specialized Dictionaries, Encyclopedias, and Reference Sets. Include such reference sets as the Cambridge histories on various topics, and, for dictionaries and encyclopedias, such sources as the *Dictionary of the History of Ideas*, the *International Encyclopedia of the Social Sciences*, and highly specialized sources such as James S. Olson's *Historical Dictionary of the 1920s: From World War I to the New Deal, 1919–1933* (Westport, Conn.: Greenwood, 1988). Cite at least five sources likely to be useful, annotate each, and, from each, note three useful entries.

9. Biographical Sources. Cite and annotate such sets as the *Dictionary of American Biography* (United States) and the *Dictionary of National Biography* (Great Britain) as well as works on specific groups such as John N. Ingham's *Biographical Dictionary of American Business Leaders* (Westport, Conn.: Greenwood, 1983).

10. Reference Sources. Excluding the above, cite and annotate relevant chronologies, directories, digests and summaries, statistical compilations, geographical sources, and so forth. Following the citation and annotation of each source, give three useful entries from it.

11. Bibliographies of Bibliographies. Cite and describe the standard works: Theodore

Besterman's *A World Bibliography of Bibliographies*; Alice F. Toomey's *World Bibliography of Bibliographies, 1964–1974*; and *Bibliographic Index*. Then cite and annotate specialized bibliographies of bibliographies found using them, guides to reference sources, or our library's catalog. Patricia K. Ballou's *Women, A Bibliography of Bibliographies* (Boston: G.K. Hall, 1980) is an example of a specialized bibliography of bibliographies.

12. Topical Bibliographies. Cite and annotate up to three topical bibliographies and, from each, cite a relevant publication. Use the above sources (see #11), but also the library's catalog to find topical bibliographies such as Gerold Cole's *Civil War Eyewitnesses: An Annotated Bibliography of Books and Articles, 1955–1986* (Columbia: University of South Carolina Press, 1988).

13. Catalogs of Special Libraries. Cite and annotate Bonnie R. Nelson's *A Guide to Published Library Catalogs* and note three catalogs likely to be useful. Explain in your annotation why each of these catalogs may be helpful.

14. Online Union Catalogs. The online union catalogs of the Online Computer Library Center (OCLC) and of the Research Libraries Group (RLG) are powerful bibliography-building tools. They are important complements to the traditional bibliographic tools indicated above. If available, conduct a search in either or both of these systems and attach a printout of relevant citations.

15. Journal Articles. Cite and annotate abstracts, bibliographies, and indexes likely to be useful and, for each, indicate whether or not it is available in electronic form. Useful in this latter regard are such sources as the American Society for Information Science's annual publication *Computer-readable Data Bases*. After the annotation of each source cite one relevant article found using it. Most of the bibliographies and indexes you might wish to use are included in *Reference Sources in History*, among them: *America: History and Life; Historical Abstracts; C.R.I.S. The Combined Retrospective Index Set to Journals in History, 1838–1974; Social Sciences Index; Humanities Index; Writings on American History*; and *P.A.I.S.* More specialized sources may be identified by using *Walford's Guide to Reference Material* and *Guide to Reference Books*.

16. Journals. Cite and briefly describe the scope and special features of three academic journals likely to carry articles on the topic. As appropriate, give preference to specialized journals such as *Agricultural History, Journal of Library History*, and *Journal of Psychohistory*. Consult Janet Fyfe's *History Journals and Serials: An Analytical Guide* and Eric Boehm and Barbara H. Pope's *Historical Periodicals Directory*.

17. Electronic Sources. Describe the basic contents of each electronic source available at our library that may be useful to you, for instance: ERIC, PsycLit, MLA, and Sociofile as well as the CD-ROM versions of *America: History and Life* and *Historical Abstracts*. From each source cited provide a printout of five relevant citations.

18. Master's Theses and Dissertations. Cite and annotate sources you will use to identify relevant work in these formats. From each source cited, note one relevant thesis or dissertation. Provide copies of the abstracts for the dissertations or theses you cite. You can obtain copies of abstracts for dissertations from the CD-ROM or online dissertation database or from the hardcopy *Dissertation Abstracts International*. Re-

member, DAI has its own separately published and comprehensive index, *Comprehensive Dissertation Index, 1861–1972*, and CDI is ongoing from 1973.

19. Traveling to Other Institutions. Consult and annotate Lee Ash and William G. Miller's *Subject Collections: A Guide to Special Book Collections and Subject Emphases as Reported by University, College, Public, and Special Libraries in the United States and Canada* and *Special Collections in College and University Libraries*, compiled by Modoc Press. From each source identify up to three institutions that have reported strength in your area of interest.

Pathfinder II—Primary Literature

1. Books. If you will be using books published in earlier periods, cite and annotate the catalogs or bibliographies you will use to identify them. Include such sources as the *Eighteenth-Century Short Title Catalogue* (a machine-readable database), the catalog of the British Museum, or Charles Evans's *American Bibliography* and Ralph Robert Shaw and Richard H. Shoemaker's *American Bibliography: A Preliminary Checklist for 1801–1819*. For each bibliography or catalog you consult, cite a book you found using it.

2. Magazine and Journal Articles. Same as above. Remember to include periodical indexes that provide retrospective coverage or indexes published during the period under study. For instance, if you are researching nineteenth-century American history you will cite the *Nineteenth Century Readers' Guide to Periodical Literature* and *Poole's Index to Periodical Literature*. If you are interested in the reaction of American historians in the 1930s to a particular historical event you will want to search appropriate volumes of *Writings on American History*.

3. Manuscript and Archival Collections. Cite and annotate such sources as the *National Union Catalog of Manuscript Collections* and the *Guide to the National Archives of the United States* and other useful general and specialized indexes and guides as well as directories, such as the *Directory of Archives and Manuscript Repositories in the United States*. Cite a relevant collection or repository identified through each.

4. Printed and Microfilmed Collections. Include such things as the collected works and papers of individuals and collections of documents focused on a particular event or topic. Among sources through which printed collections may be found are our library's catalog, RLIN, OCLC, the *Harvard Guide to American History*, and the American Historical Association's *Guide to Historical Literature*; for microform collections use Suzanne Cates Dodson's *Microform Research Collections: A Guide*. Cite two printed collections and two microform collections.

5. Newspapers. Cite and annotate, as appropriate, union lists of newspapers such as *American Newspapers, 1821–1936: A Union List of Files Available in the United States and Canada* and Winfred Gregory's *American Newspapers, 1821–1936: A Union List of Files Available in the United States and Canada*, and for bibliographies/union lists such works as Clarence S. Brigham's *History and Bibliography of American Newspapers, 1690–1820*. Cite five newspapers you might consult.

6. Government Documents. Cite a guide that describes the government publications of the nation (or state) or organization appropriate to your research. For instance, if your topic concerns Great Britain you should cite Frank Rodger's *A Guide to British Government Publications*. Then refer to this source to determine the types of docu-

mentation likely to be of use to you and describe the types of material you might consult. Therefore, if you are researching the history of a piece of legislation, briefly describe the documentation generated by the legislative process.

7. Other Categories of Primary Source Material. Describe the types of materials you might use—diaries, physical objects, radio or television tapes, works of art, statistical records (list governmental statistics above), maps, and so forth—and cite and annotate indexes, bibliographies, books, and other sources helpful in accessing them. For instance, if you wish to use American diaries you will list William Mathew's *American Diaries: An Annotated Bibliography of American Diaries Written Prior to the Year 1861* as well as Mathew's *American Diaries in Manuscript, 1580–1954*. As you have done in similar instances, look for such aids in the *Guide to Reference Books* and in *Walford's Guide to Reference Material*.

While a pathfinder is designed to lead students to bibliographic and reference sources, the compilation of a resource bibliography asks for the compilation of a list of sources from which one might study, teach, or write. It can be incorporated as part of a pathfinder exercise as I have done to some extent here or as an exercise that follows the construction of the pathfinder(s).

Form of Publication

When students are working on a specific project they often need to acquire competence in the identification and use of a specific format. Different formats convey information differently, and in addition, libraries often organize and provide access to diverse formats differently. For instance, a class that will be using government documents should receive background information on the nature of the materials they will be accessing as well as instruction in their organization, and they should complete exercises that teach and practice the use of the specialized tools that provide access to them.

Sample Exercise
The Purpose and Nature of a Journal

Student: Academic and professional journals are important information sources for their readers. Analyze the structure, design, format, and special features of the *American Historical Review*. Based on your analysis explain the role the journal plays for its readers and indicate the bibliographic tools, both particular title and type, that provide access to it. Then perform the same analysis for the American Historical Association's *Perspectives* and explain the different roles the two publications play. Last, use the *Historical Periodicals Directory* or Janet Fyfe's *History Journals and Serials: An Analytical Guide* to identify the journal and newsletter of the Organization of American Historians and perform the same analyses as above.

Index Structure

Simple as using an index may initially appear, indexes are not simple. In fact, there are many different types of indexes, which reflect a host of technical and intellectual decisions by the compiler. Apart from the challenges of name authority, the subject headings and index entries chosen reflect the perspectives of the cataloger or indexer. If an author's terms are used, inconsistencies across a large number of articles by different authors can be mind-boggling. To the student of history, index structure can be an intellectual map, a journey through levels of terminology and conceptualization.

Sample Exercise
Library of Congress Subject Headings

Student: Books are cataloged using a controlled vocabulary, and you must use the subject terms applied when using the subject catalog. The less focused your search, the less likely you are to miss pertinent material; however, the broader your search, the more difficult it becomes to focus on precisely what you need. Regardless of the terminology employed by a work's author, books on the same or similar topics are linked to one another by this controlled vocabulary. Use the *Library of Congress Subject Headings* list to compile a list of subject headings on a well-defined topic, include headings that may be used to broaden or narrow your search. Also include proper nouns: names of institutions, people, and places.

Much contemporary indexing is based on abstracts. In many fields authors compose abstracts of their work to accompany it at its time of submission. This is generally not the case with history journals, and the abstract services, *America: History and Life* and *Historical Abstracts*, rely on abstracts written largely by volunteers. These abstracts are available for full free-text searching in these databases. To illustrate to students the importance as well as imperfections of abstracts, ask all students in a class to abstract the same article.

Sample Exercise
Abstracting an Article

Student: Abstracts can save you time by giving you enough information to decide whether or not you should read a work, and full-text electronic searching depends on the quality of abstracting; if important terms are missing from an abstract the computer will not be able to find them. The efficiency of online searching begins with a high-quality abstract. All students will abstract the same journal article referring to the model abstracts provided as examples. Abstracts should be 150–200 words in length and should summarize the theme(s) of the article, noting its thesis, methodology, and sources. Be sure to address the basic facts: who (include life dates if available), what, when, and where. When citing non-English language material, give an English translation in brackets. Stylistic points made in the guidelines sent to prospective abstracters by ABC-Clio's editors include: "The first sentence may be a phrase, assuming the article as a subject, e.g., 'Discusses the impact of the Franco-Prussian War on British public opinion.' " "Omit such circumlocutions as 'Argues that' or 'Concludes that.' " "Avoid the passive voice. . . . Avoid long quotations from the article; if you do use quotations, put them in quotation marks."

Before abstracts are discussed in class, each student will be provided with a set of abstracts completed by other class members. Abstracts will be evaluated on the basis of their usefulness and on the extent to which they capture all aspects of the article in conformity with distributed guidelines.

Primary and Secondary Sources

What is a primary source? What is a secondary source? When is someone else's secondary source your primary source? How does one evaluate the trustworthiness of a primary source? What are the types of primary sources appropriate for addressing a specific research problem? The questions are pivotal to the historical enterprise. This is a good framework in which to have students match bibliographic tools to the types of sources they believe will address a specific research problem, and it provides a relevant context in which to discuss the design and use of appropriate access tools.

Sample Exercise
Matching Source to Topic

Student: For each of the problems listed below indicate the type of primary sources that may provide appropriate information; then cite and annotate the tools that identify and/or provide access to them.

1. How might one go about probing the personal lives and innermost thoughts of early nineteenth-century American men and women?

Source(s): Autobiographies, diaries, and personal papers.

Access Tool(s): Use such tools as: William Mathews, *American Diaries: An Annotated Bibliography of American Diaries Written Prior to the Year 1861* (Los Angeles: University of California Press, 1945); William Mathews, *American Diaries in Manuscript, 1580–1954* (Athens: University of Georgia Press, 1974); Laura Arksey, Nancy Pries, Marcia Reed, *American Diaries: An Annotated Bibliography of Published American Diaries and Journals*, 2 vols. (Detroit: Gale, 1983–87).

Publication Sequence

Although it is not always the case, research ideas generally progress through a series of stages before they become fully integrated into a discipline as a subfield, become a discipline in their own right, or emerge as a topic that has attained a level of mature and intense investigation. Ideas or findings are first discussed among a group of concerned experts; thoughts and findings are next shared at conferences and become available to an even wider public as proceedings; journal articles and their indexing in appropriate tools follow; these articles exert influence, which is evidenced by their citation by other researchers; then books appear; and finally the idea or concern is included in standard synthetic reference works such as encyclopedias, or is treated in its own reference sources.

This basic mode of analysis can be adapted to deal with topics as well as ideas. Chronologically mapping the beginning and, if desired, intensity of coverage of a topic across formats reveals the evolution of an idea or concern and, if works within formats are distinguished by the audience they serve, the temporal prominence of the idea or topic across various communities: professions, the lay public, and special-interest groups. One can then discuss the role various formats play in disseminating information, the significance of the formats, what treatment in a particular format says about the maturity of the concern, and, as applicable, the sources that provide access to formats. See also the reference to the work of Michael Keresztesi on pages 296–97 and the exercise "The Development of a Discipline's Bibliographic Apparatus" under *Sociohistorical Apparatus* on page 89.

Sample Exercise
Tracing the Evolution of an Idea or Concern

Student: The bibliography of a topic, examined across time and format, reveals the evolution of a concern, both its intensity and its characteristics. Recognition of Acquired Immune Deficiency Syndrome (AIDS) was represented by eight articles in periodicals covered by *Magazine Index* in 1982. Searching under the acronym AIDS, when was its coverage picked up by such general newsmagazines as *Time*, *Newsweek*, and *U.S. News & World Report*? Since 1982 what has been the annual volume of article publication represented in *Magazine Index*? Identify periodicals between 1982 and 1985 that provided the most coverage for the lay public. How have the types of magazines providing coverage changed? Since its first coverage, has the alternative press had different concerns than the popular press? Using titles of articles and magazines, explain how the nature or concerns of coverage has changed. When was the first book solely devoted to the topic published? Give an indication of the annual volume of book publication over the past ten years. Are there periodicals devoted solely to the topic? Give their dates of initial publication. Are there reference sources devoted solely to the topic? Give their dates of initial publication.

Instructor: *Ulrich's International Periodicals Directory* may be used to determine the existence of relevant periodical titles and their dates of initial publication. *Alternative Press Index* covers several gay periodicals as well as some feminist journals and the journals of various social movements. *Magazine Index* covers a larger number and greater diversity of titles than *Readers' Guide to Periodical Literature*, which is by far the most conservative of the indexes mentioned. In addition, either RLIN or OCLC may be searched in a multitude of ways to identify appropriate titles, and searches may be limited by date of publication. However, one must be careful to distinguish multiple cataloging entries for the same title. *Books In Print* may be searched by year if editions are retained. *Ulrich's*, *Books in Print*, *Magazine Index*, and *Readers' Guide* are searchable online and in CD-ROM.

Citation Patterns

Ideas are preserved in the bibliographic record even after they are no longer operative, and who current researchers cite reflects the contemporary importance of particular ideas. Ultimately, the study of citation patterns shows that research is an organic process and that researchers in all fields are likely to draw upon the insights and discoveries of others. Examination of the bibliographic citations or footnotes in various publications over a period of time—for the falloff, persistence, or pairing of particular citations—is an exercise in intellectual history and reveals changing views and perspectives. But students are most likely to benefit from using citation indexing or footnote cycling as a means for obtaining information and understanding the research process.

Sample Exercise
Verifying References

Student: As you follow an author's thinking through an examination of his or her footnotes you will see the way in which the work of others is used and the way in which the footnotes and bibliography index the literature of a topic. But this indexing cannot be without nuance and interpretation. Use the text provided and collected copies of publications represented by footnotes. Are the author's conclusions supported by references to appropriate primary or secondary material? If footnotes seem to be missing indicate where they should be placed. Consult the source to which each reference is made and verify the correctness of each citation. With the cited text before you, consider whether or not the author has fully indicated his or her debt to the cited work. Is any quoted or cited material used in a way inconsistent with the intent of its author? If quoted material is truncated, indicate if truncation has changed its original meaning.

Instructor: Select a brief scholarly article or book chapter, make available to students the full text of all referenced pieces, and be sure to complete the exercise before assigning it. You may wish to divide this assignment between groups. See descriptions of pertinent instructional experiences in annotations for articles by Ernest Cassara, page 322, and by Raymond G. McInnis and Dal S. Symes, page 328.

Sample Exercise
Cycling References

Student: Footnotes index the ideas or concepts an author borrows from other sources. They may refer to the raw data of a primary source or to the refined conceptualizations of a scholarly article or monograph. Of course, the same ideas or concepts may also be used in different ways by different authors. Examine the scholarly article provided and the representation of its footnotes from the Source Index of *Arts and Humanities Citation Index* (1975–1979 five-year cumulation). Are the footnote references in the Source Index complete enough to be useful? Then select five journal references from this article and, using the Citation Index, identify two citing journal articles for each of these five references (for a total of ten citations). Complete these references by returning to the Source Index. Next examine the articles by the five cited authors and the articles citing them that you have identified by using the Citation Index. What is the intellectual connection between these two groups? Compare and contrast the role of the citations in the citing articles, including the article with which the exercise began. Are references used to make the same point? Are the articles on the same topic? Are they written within the same discipline? Do the parts, that is, pages, of each of the articles referenced differ or are they the same?

Instructor: A discussion of why one author has cited another is a natural follow-up to this exercise. It is also interesting to consider the disciplines in which citing authors are working; for instance, historians citing the work of psychologists or librarians citing the work of sociologists. Make copies available to students of all the materials with which they will be working. Also, be certain that the volume of citation required for the exercise is present. Beginning with an article in the five-year cumulation greatly facilitates work on this exercise, and students should restrict their searching to the cumulation.

Sociohistorical Analysis

Reference tools are themselves important subjects for historical and sociological analysis. The bibliographic tools of history are no less a part of the literature of history than a recent monograph. Bibliographic and reference sources exist not only to serve a discipline, but also as an expression of it. In many instances they are what is generally consulted for information, and they serve a synthetic function. The reference tools of a discipline identify but also canonize the prevailing perception of knowledge. These sources are generally the creations of individuals and organizations central to the concerns of the discipline. Studied across time, place, or perspective, they reveal differing as well as changing biases and perceptions.

Sample Exercise
Encyclopedia Articles from Different Perspectives

Student: Different groups have different perspectives, perceptions, emphases, and interpretations of both current and past events. Compare, contrast, and explain differences in the essays on anti-Semitism in the *New Catholic Encyclopaedia* and *Encyclopaedia Judaica*. What does this exercise reveal about the nature of reference sources in general and in the humanities in particular?

Sample Exercise
The Development of a Discipline's Bibliographic Apparatus

Student: Begin by reading either Michael Keresztesi, "The Science of Bibliography: Theoretical Implications for Bibliographic Instruction" in *Theories of Bibliographic Education: Designs for Teaching* (1982) or Deborah Fink, *Process and Politics in Library Research: A Model for Course Design* (1989), 44–50. Trace the evolution of psychohistory as a discipline through the initial dates of publication of its bibliographic apparatus and the appearance of specialized periodicals. What are the types of resources that are specifically available to researchers, and what has been the chronological and conceptual evolution of coverage of this field in the full range of standard scholarly reference tools? Does the appearance of various reference tools, coverage in standard reference sources, and the organization of associations, meetings, and periodicals and newsletters correspond with Keresztesi's stages of development—pioneering, elaboration and proliferation, and establishment—and with the corresponding bibliographic manifestations that he identifies?

A WORD ON THE DESIGN OF GUIDES TO LIBRARY RESOURCES

The best way to ensure library use is to tell students which library resources to use. Librarians, in consultation with faculty, can contribute significantly to library usage by preparing resource sheets or pathfinders for distribution to students. These aids should identify and describe the resources—reference materials, books, microform collections, and so forth—that students should use. Traditionally professors have given students a bibliography of suggested readings; this suggestion carries the practice further.

Instructional materials should be clearly formatted and attractively printed. Tables and charts may be used to illustrate research strategies. Annotations should compare works whenever appropriate, resources should be presented under genre headings, and groupings should proceed logically. A general to specific organization structure should be used, and library jargon should be avoided: for instance, as a heading try using "Finding Periodicals" rather than "Abstracts and Indexes."[19] For citations to examples of published guides see the bibliography that concludes this book.

PLAGIARISM: SO MANY THINGS TO COPY FROM

Plagiarism and proper forms of attribution come up repeatedly in library use articles. After all, once students know how to access a wealth of synthesized information—specialized encyclopedia articles, plot summaries, and so forth, not to mention articles and books—how will one ever know if they are presenting their own work? And now the manipulation of machine-readable full-text files and abstracts offers imponderable opportunities for intellectual thievery. Historians have thought often about plagiarism but the profession has not welcomed the unpleasant task of policing itself. When a pattern of plagiaristic activity is discovered the consequences are painful for all concerned. A reading of Thomas Mallon's account of Jayme Sokolow's *Eros and Modernization: Sylvester Graham, Health Reform, and the Origins of Victorian Sexuality in America* (Rutherford, N.J.: Fairleigh Dickinson University Press, 1983) and of Sokolow's other plagiarisms in Mallon's *Stolen Words: Forays into the Origins and Ravages of Plagiarism* is a sobering experience.[20] Although not a tale of plagiarism, David Abraham's ordeal concerning accusations that he was guilty of slovenly documentation and, far more serious, of falsifying and purposely distorting and misconstruing archival evidence in his *Collapse of the Weimar Republic: Political Economy and Crisis* (Princeton, N.J.: Princeton University Press, 1981) is also worth considering.[21]

Honest and careful documentation is both the obligation and the last refuge of the historian. The art and purpose of documentation as well as its importance to researchers should be fully explained to students. Aside from concerns of intellectual property rights, skillful footnoting indexes primary and secondary literature with a specificity not to be matched by library tools.[22]

The "Statement on Plagiarism" of the American Historical Association is well worth discussing with a class. Describing the nature of plagiarism, its authors write:

> The plagiarist's standard defense—that he or she was misled by hastily taken and imperfect notes—is plausible only in the context of a wider tolerance of shoddy work. A basic rule of good notetaking requires every researcher to distinguish scrupulously between exact quotation and paraphrase. A basic rule of good writing warns us against following our own paraphrased notes slavishly. When a historian simply links one paraphrase to the next, even if the sources are cited, a kind of structural plagiarism takes place; the writer is implicitly claiming a shaping intelligence that actually belonged to the sources.[23]

HOW EFFECTIVE IS BIBLIOGRAPHIC INSTRUCTION?

How will bibliographic instruction affect the performance of students? The obvious answer: all students will be affected differently, and the quality and pertinence of the instruction that is offered will be the key factors in ensuring the acquisition and retention of library skills.[24]

Information-gathering skills are invaluable, but they are generally learned as they are needed and they are used only when they are necessary. If students are not asked to interpret historical documents closely or to argue hypotheses or interpretations, or to do research, then any instruction other than the most basic introduction to the library is thoroughly unnecessary and, ultimately, a complete waste of time. If we want students to learn to do history by studying the same textual evidence that professional historians study, then we must instruct them in ways to expand their knowledge base quickly to provide the specific and contextual information without which historical analysis cannot occur. Information is organized, it can be found and questioned, and in its finding and questioning it becomes appreciated for what it is—definition and evidence. It is my contention that only by practicing on specific problems will general organizational schemata be learned. After acquiring a general conceptual understanding through the completion of carefully designed exercises, students must practice their skills in research and writing.

NOTES

1. Eric Weil, "Supporting the Humanities," *Daedalus* 102, no. 2 (Spring 1973): 30–31.

2. Constance C. Gould, *Information in the Humanities: An Assessment* (Stanford, Calif.: The Research Libraries Group, 1988); Constance C. Gould and Mark Handler, *Information Needs in the Social Sciences: An Assessment* (Mountain View, Calif.: The Research Libraries Group, 1989).

3. C. Paul Vincent, "Bibliographic Instruction in the Humanities: The Need to Stress Imagination," *Research Strategies* 2, no. 4 (Fall 1984): 179–84; see also Stephen K. Stoan, "Research and Library Skills: An Analysis and Interpretation," *College & Research Libraries* 45, no. 2 (March 1984): 99–109.

4. David S. Landes and Charles Tilly, eds., *History as Social Science: The Behavioral and Social Sciences Survey* (Englewood Cliffs, N.J.: Prentice-Hall, 1971), 91.

5. American Historical Association Task Force on the History Major, "Liberal Learning and the History Major," *Perspectives* (American Historical Association) 28, no. 5 (May/June 1990): 14–15.

6. On information literacy see ALA Presidential Committee on Information Literacy, *Final Report* (Chicago: American Library Association, 1990); Patricia Senn Breivik, *Information Literacy: Revolution in the Library* (New York: American Council on Education, 1989); Breivik, "Library Based Learning in an Information Society," *New Directions in Higher Education* 56 (Winter 1986): 47–55; Breivik, "Making the Most of Libraries in the Search for Academic Excellence," *Change* 19, no. 4 (July/August 1987): 44–52; a critical rejoinder is Lawrence J. McCrank, "Information Literacy: A Bogus Bandwagon?" *Library Journal* 116, no. 8 (1 May 1991): 38–42.

7. Landes and Tilly, eds., *History as Social Science*, 94–95.

8. Eric H. Boehm, "On the Second Knowledge: A Manifesto for the Humanities," *Libri* 22, no. 4 (1972): 312–23.

9. American Historical Association Task Force on the History Major, "Liberal Learning and the History Major," 18.

10. Constance A. Mellon, "Library Anxiety: A Grounded Theory and Its Development," *College & Research Libraries* 47, no. 1 (January 1986): 160–65; Deborah Fink, "What You Ask for Is What You Get: Some Dos and Don'ts for Assigning Research Projects," *Research Strategies* 4, no. 2 (Spring 1986): 91–93; Mary George and Sharon Hogan, "What Anxiety?" *Research Strategies* 7, no. 2 (Spring 1989): 50–51. On the dangers of jargon see Rachel Naismith and Joan Stein, "Library Jargon: Student Comprehension of Technical Language Used by Librarians," *College & Research Libraries* 50, no. 5 (September 1989): 543–52.

11. Rao Aluri, "Application of Learning Theories to Library-Use Instruction," *Libri* 31, no. 2 (August 1981): 140–52; See also Elizabeth J. McNeer, "Learning Theories and Library Instruction," *Journal of Academic Librarianship* 17, no. 5 (November 1991): 294–97.

12. Donald Owen Case, "The Collection and Use of Information by Some American Historians: A Study of Motives and Methods," *Library Quarterly* 61, no. 1 (January 1991): 61–82.

13. On librarians as tool experts see Sharon J. Rogers, "Science of Knowledge," in *Bibliographic Instruction: The Second Generation*, ed. Constance A. Mellon (Littleton, Colo.: Libraries Unlimited, 1987), 125–33; on the needs of students as opposed to the needs of faculty see Constance McCarthy, "The Faculty Problem," *Journal of Academic Librarianship* 11, no. 2 (July 1985): 142–45.

14. Bill Bailey, "Thesis Practicum and the Librarian's Role," *Journal of Academic Librarianship* 11, no. 2 (May 1985): 79–81; Mary R. Ishaq and Donna P. Cornick, "Library Research Consultation (LaRC): A Service for Graduate Students," *RQ* 18, no. 2 (Winter 1978): 168–76; Richard A. Dreifuss, "Library Instruction and Graduate Students: More Work for George," *RQ* 21, no. 2 (Winter 1981): 121–23; Denise Madland, "Library Instruction for Graduate Students," *College Teaching* 33, no. 4 (Fall 1985):

163–64; Thomas J. Michalak, "Library Services to the Graduate Community: The Role of the Subject Specialist Librarian," *College & Research Librarianship* 37, no. 3 (May 1976): 257–65; Marilyn Parrish, "Academic Community Analysis: Discovering the Needs of Graduate Students at Bowling Green University," *College & Research Libraries News* 50, no. 8 (September 1989): 644–46. For undergraduates see Gillian Debreczeny, "Coping with Numbers: Undergraduates and Individual Term Paper Consultation," *Research Strategies* 3, no. 4 (Fall 1985): 156–63.

15. Frances L. Hopkins, "User Instruction in the College Library: Origins, Prospects, and a Practical Program," in *College Librarianship*, ed. William Miller and D. Stephen Lockwood (Metuchen, N.J.: Scarecrow Press, 1981), 173–204.

16. Pamela Kobelski and Mary Reichel, "Conceptual Frameworks for Bibliographic Instruction," *Journal of Academic Librarianship* 7, no. 2 (May 1981): 73–77; repr. in Mary Reichel and Mary Ann Ramey, eds., *Conceptual Frameworks for Bibliographic Education* (Littleton, Colo.: Libraries Unlimited, 1987).

17. Gemma DeVinney, "Systematic Literature Searching as a Conceptual Framework for Course Related Bibliographic Instruction for College Freshmen," in *Conceptual Frameworks for Bibliographic Education: Theory into Practice*, ed. Mary Reichel and Mary Ann Ramey (Littleton, Colo.: Libraries Unlimited, 1987), 13–23.

18. Reprinted with permission from Gerald H. Davis and Charles A. D'Aniello, *Instructor's Manual with Instructional Objectives and Library Research Problems to Accompany* A History of the World by Stanley Chodorow, Hans W. Gatzke, Conrad Schirokauer (San Diego: Harcourt Brace Jovanovich, 1986), 132, 171.

19. William J. Jackson, "The User-Friendly Library Guide," *College & Research Libraries News* 45, no. 9 (October 1984): 468–71.

20. Thomas Mallon, "Quiet Goes the Don: An Academic Affair," in *Stolen Words: Forays into the Origins and Ravages of Plagiarism* (New York: Ticknor and Fields, 1989), 144–93. For a review, see Ralph D. Gray, "A Pinocchio in Academe: A Review, with Elaborations of Thomas Mallon's *Stolen Words*," *Editing History* 6, no. 2 (Fall 1990): 7–8.

21. For a sense of this affair see T. W. Mason, [review] *American Historical Review* 87, no. 4 (October 1982): 1122–23; Henry A. Turner, T. W. Mason, and David Abraham, [exchange] *American Historical Review* 88, no. 4 (October 1983); 1143–49; Gerald D. Feldman, David Abraham, Douglas A. Unfug, "Debate: Abraham's *The Collapse of the Weimar Republic*," *Central European History* 17, nos. 2/3 (June/September 1984): 159–293.

22. Mary Reichel, "Ethics and Library Instruction: Is There a Connection?" *RQ* 28, no. 4 (Summer 1989): 477–80; Janell Rudolph and Deborah Brackstone, "Too Many Scholars Ignore the Basic Rules of Documentation," *Chronicle of Higher Education* 36, no. 30 (April 11, 1990), A56.

23. American Historical Association (prepared by John Higham and Robert Zangrando), *Statement on Plagiarism* (adopted May 1986; amended May 1990), [4].

24. The literature is vast; see esp. Richard Feinberg and Christine King, "Short-Term Library Skill Competencies: Arguing for the Achievable," *College & Research Libraries* 49, no. 1 (January 1988): 24–28; Larry Hardesty, Nicholas P. Lovrich, Jr., and James Mannon, "Library-Use Instruction: Assessment of the Long-Term Effects," *College & Research Libraries* 43, no. 1 (January 1982): 38–46; David F. Kohl and Lizabeth A. Wilson, "Effectiveness of Course-Integrated Bibliographic Instruction in Improving Course Work," *RQ* 26, no. 2 (Winter 1986): 206–11; Richard H. Werking, "Evaluating

Bibliographic Education: A Review and Critique," *Library Trends* 29, no. 1 (Summer 1980): 153–72; Richard J. Wood, "The Impact of a Library Research Course on Students at Slippery Rock University," *Journal of Academic Librarianship* 10, no. 5 (November 1984): 278–84.

Part III

Special Topics

5

Using Catalogs and Indexes

David Y. Allen and John Attig

This is the first of several chapters on teaching the essentials of library research in history. This chapter will focus on the use of such basic information sources as library catalogs and periodical indexes. Something will also be said about the various services, such as interlibrary loan, that may be encountered in a research library.

Most of the sources and services discussed in this chapter will be familiar to librarians and history faculty. They are not familiar to most students, however, including beginning graduate students. College instructors quickly become aware of the depth of their students' ignorance concerning the subject matter of the courses they teach, but they often forget that this same ignorance extends to the use of the library.

The information presented in this chapter can be adapted for use at all levels, from upper-division undergraduate on up. We have included some specialized material—such as information on maps and government publications—that is suitable primarily for classes working on special topics, rather than material for the usual introductory "how to do research in history" courses. It is up to the reader to select what is most important for his or her needs.

LIBRARY RESEARCH

The instructor in a research methods course needs to reassure students that they do not have to master all of the techniques of bibliographic research at once and that help is available for library users. The best advice an instructor can give is: First, reduce the problem at hand to a series of questions that are as specific as possible; and second, ask for help from library staff if you do not seem to be finding the answers after making a reasonable effort.

One strategy that might help illustrate these points to students is to use a simple example showing some of the different kinds of questions that might need to be answered and the different kinds of sources that might contain the answers. In the following paragraphs, we take the topic of criminals in fifteenth-century Italy and look at a number of possible questions.

To some extent, the nature of these questions depends on the level of the student. An advanced student, for example, might require the use of primary sources. Locating archival source material is covered in chapter 9. However, a great deal of source material has been published, either in printed editions or in microform reproductions. Some of these sources can be found by consulting the catalog of the local library or by searching published catalogs of other collections. Others, particularly microform collections, may not be included in these catalogs; there are some hints about locating microform source material later in this chapter.

The first problem that might confront a student in any kind of project is to compile a reading list of books and articles relevant to the topic. It is important to define the topic as precisely as possible. In our example, there are three clear elements: PLACE—Italy; TIME—the fifteenth century; and TOPIC—criminals and criminal activities. These elements give the student tools to query the reference sources, words to look up in a catalog or index. The next step is to find catalogs and indexes to query. The catalog of the local library is a good place to start. For articles, periodical indexes will need to be consulted. The student looks for items that are related to all (or most) of the elements of the topic and adds them to a reading list. As our student reads items on the list, he or she may find bibliographies or notes that suggest additional items; in this way, the list grows from a working list to a more comprehensive bibliography of works on the topic.

The result may be a list that is too long for the scope of the project. A list of dozens of books and articles is no help to a student who has a week to prepare a paper. That student needs to find a few of the most important works on a topic. Even in a larger project, a researcher will find particular subtopics that need to be looked into but are not worth extended research. For example, in our study of Italian criminals, a scholar might need some background on the fifteenth-century Italian legal system. He or she will not need to read everything about it, but would like to feel that the information comes from a standard work on the subject. This involves more than a simple identification of a relevant item; it requires an evaluation of the item. There are certain sources—abstracts, reviews, comments by other historians—that provide evaluations of books and articles. The future historian needs to know when such sources are needed and how to find them.

Sometimes a scholar wants the most recent research on a topic, for example, in order to verify that the standard work has not been superseded by a recently published article. The most up-to-date research can usually be found by browsing recent issues of relevant journals or by using periodical indexes, which are covered later in this chapter.

In other cases, all that the researcher needs is one particular fact. For instance, it may be necessary to determine the value of the Venetian ducat circa 1450 in order to indicate the significance of a fine levied on a convicted criminal. It does not matter where the fact is found, so long as the source is reliable. It is also unlikely that there will be a complete book or article devoted to this fact. The need here is to find a source that contains the particular fact needed. This usually means a paper chase through the library's reference collection. The approach will often need to be indirect. It is unlikely that one will find a work on medieval Italian money; instead, a bibliography or reference guide to European economic history may have to serve. If there is nothing that looks right in the library catalog, one should consult a general guide to reference works, such as the *Guide to Reference Books*,[1] or seek out a reference librarian. This topic is covered in chapter 6.

The discussion of types of research questions shows clearly that there are all kinds of information needs involved in historical research and that many of them require the use of reference books collected by the library. Not all of them do, however, and often the most valuable sources of information are the comments and citations of other historians. Students need to be encouraged to examine not only the substance of the books and articles they read, but also the author's notes on the sources of his or her information. These notes are often the best source for identifying relevant works to consult. They are also one of the best sources for evaluating those works; students who have decided that the book or article they are reading is a standard (or at least reliable) work should then be able to trust the judgments the author makes on the work of other historians or on the primary sources the students consulted.

Many of the questions discussed above lead to searches for books on a known subject; others will give the researcher the author and title of a specific work. Whenever a question has developed to the point where something like this is known but the specific item has not been found, the researcher will need to consult the catalog of the local library. This may have to be done at least twice in a search: first to locate a relevant reference book (bibliography or index), and then to locate the specific items listed in the bibliography or index. There may even be further steps, as one is led to further citations of relevant material. A search for journal articles almost always involves at least two steps: first one needs to locate and use a periodical index to find a list of articles, then one has to use the catalog to find the location of the journals in which the articles were published.

THE CATALOG

The library catalog is one of the most commonly used tools for locating materials within a particular collection. Moreover, the catalog has much in common with other reference sources that list the authors, titles, and subjects of books and other library materials. The researcher who understands the general principles upon which such catalogs are constructed will have more success using all kinds of reference materials. So the library catalog is a good place to begin an introduction to library research.

Library catalogs are deceptively easy to use, and most students think they have mastered the local one. However, both students and scholars tend to underestimate the complexity of library catalogs and the amount of thought and ingenuity that has gone into their construction.[2] As a result, they also fail to take advantage of the full power of the catalog. Instructors should try to remedy this underestimation by informing their students about the principles of catalog construction and the ways catalogs can be used most effectively.

Scope of the Catalog

The first surprise in store for students is that the catalog does not list everything in the library. In fact, most of the works available in the library can *not* be found by looking directly in the catalog.

Library catalogs are primarily lists of books and serials (also known as periodicals or journals). Each individual book or serial title is listed, but the contents (the articles in a journal, the chapters in a book) are not. In addition, materials other than books and serials are often excluded completely from the catalog. Although the policies of individual libraries differ, material not listed in the catalog may include government documents, manuscripts, microforms, and maps. This material is invisible to users of the catalog, yet it constitutes a significant portion of the resources of any library collection.

How can such material be located? For some types of material, the answer may simply be a separate catalog located near where the materials are stored. In other cases, such as government documents or titles within a microform set, access may be provided through published catalogs. In the case of journal articles, a two-stage search will be necessary. The articles themselves will not be found in the catalog, but the journals will. It is necessary to use appropriate reference tools to identify relevant articles and then to consult the card catalog to locate the journal volumes. The use of catalogs and indexes is dealt with in the second part of this chapter.

Principles of Catalog Construction: Description

Library catalogs take many forms, including card catalogs, book catalogs, and computerized catalogs. Regardless of form, however, the principles underlying their construction remain much the same. In the typical library catalog, each book or serial is represented by a description made up of bibliographic information such as title, publisher, and date of publication. This information is copied exactly as it appears in the item itself. Note that these basic descriptive elements are similar to those prescribed for bibliographic citations in style manuals such as the *Chicago Manual of Style*. The conventions of bibliographic

Figure 5.1
Typical Catalog Card

```
Ruggiero, Guido, 1944-
   Violence in early Renaissance Venice / Guido Ruggiero. -- New
Brunswick, N.J. : Rutgers University Press, c1980.
   xv, 235 p. ; 24 cm. -- (Crime, law, and deviance)
   Bibliography: p.211-221.
   Includes index.

   1.  Crime and criminals--Italy--Venice--History.  2. Violence
--Italy--Venice--History.  3. Venice (Italy)--Social conditions.
4. Venice (Italy)--History--697-1508.
```

Figure 5.2
Online Catalog Record: Captioned Format

```
   AUTHOR:  Ruggiero, Guido, 1944-
    TITLE:  Violence in early Renaissance Venice / Guido
            Ruggiero.
    PLACE:  New Brunswick, N.J.
PUBLISHER:  Rutgers University Press.
     DATE:  c1980.
   EXTENT:  xv, 235 p. ; 24 cm.
   SERIES:  Crime, law, and deviance.
    NOTES:  Bibliography: p.211-221.
            Includes index.
 SUBJECTS:  Crime and criminals--Italy--Venice--History.
            Violence  --Italy--Venice--History.
            Venice (Italy)--Social conditions.
            Venice (Italy)--History--697-1508.
```

description found in the library catalog can be thought of as a special type of
style manual.

The description may be presented in various ways. The typical catalog card
groups the main elements into a single paragraph beginning with the title and
ending with the date of publication; this is followed by additional paragraphs of
notes. Figure 5.1 illustrates this kind of display. On the other hand, many online
catalogs give each element on a separate line, each with a caption that identifies
its function. Figure 5.2 shows the same description in a captioned format. This
type of display is useful for an inexperienced user because it clearly identifies
all the separate elements that make up the description.

The purpose of the description is to identify the item, to distinguish it clearly
from all other items, and to indicate any special relationships it might have with
other items. In most cases, the title is sufficient to identify the item. In other
cases, however, the specific edition may be identified by a formal edition statement (''3rd ed.''), by the date of publication, or by the name of the publisher.
Researchers may not care which edition they use, in which case these details
may be ignored. On the other hand, one edition may be more up-to-date or more
accurate than another, and then this information is very important.

Figure 5.3
Typical Catalog Card: A Translation

```
Le Roy Ladurie, Emmanuel.
  The mind and method of the historian / Emmanuel Le Roy Ladurie
; translated by Sian Reynolds and Ben Reynolds. -- Chicago :
University of Chicago Press, c1981.
  v, 310 p. ; 22 cm.
  Translation of Le territoire de l'historien, v. 2. Translated
from a selection of 9 of the 15 essays.
  Includes bibliographical references

  1. France--Historiography.
```

The description may include other kinds of useful information. For example, the number of pages in a book is usually given. The presence of illustrations or of bibliographic references may be indicated. The relation of the work to other works is particularly important. In figure 5.3 a note indicates that the work is a translation of a part of one volume of a French original. The fact that this is a translation has a further significance. Although the translation was published in 1981, the French original and the ideas it contains were written earlier (in 1978, in this case, although this is not stated in the description of the translation). Another kind of relationship is particularly important for serials or journals. When a journal changes its title—when, for example, the *Mississippi Valley Historical Review* changed its title to *Journal of American History* in 1964— each title will be described separately, but each record will have a note giving the earlier or later title.

The description may also contain valuable information about the content of the item: a summary or abstract, a listing of the contents of a collection of essays or of the individual volumes of a multivolume set. Perhaps the most common clue to the nature of the item is the list of subject terms under which the item has been indexed. In figure 5.1, the subjects are listed at the end of the description, each preceded by an arabic number. For hints about using these tracings, as they are called, for enhanced subject searching, see p. 105 below.

Principles of Catalog Construction: Indexing

In the bibliography of a book, the descriptive citations are arranged in order, usually by author. This simple arrangement is sufficient for a limited list. However, for the large number of descriptions in a typical library catalog, a single arrangement is not sufficient. Instead, each item is indexed by a number of different elements: names of persons (authors, editors, etc.) and corporate bodies, titles, and subjects. The description of the item is either repeated with each index term (as in a card catalog, where each card is a copy of the bibliographic description with an index term at the top) or the descriptions are listed in one part of the catalog and the indexes point to the descriptions through some sort of serial number, much as the index to a book points to the text through page numbers.

One of the principles of traditional library cataloging is that each indexed entity (each name, title, or subject) is represented in the catalog by one and only one index term. Thus, if an author uses different forms of a name (H. S. Commager versus Henry Steele Commager), one form will be chosen for use in the catalog. The same applies to subjects. If a word has alternate spellings (*color* and *colour*, for example), one spelling is chosen. And if a topic has several synonymous names (monasteries and abbeys), only one term is used in the catalog. This ensures that all items relating to a name or subject will be brought together under a single term in the catalog.

Choosing a single conventional form for each name or subject does not necessarily mean that only the correct form can be found in the catalog. Alternative forms may be provided as references ("Colour, see Color") that guide the user to the correct form. However, this practice cannot always be relied upon, especially in computerized catalogs. Thus the user who searches under the incorrect form of an author's name in an online catalog may receive the misleading impression that there are no works by that author in the library. In such catalogs, the user must know—or guess—the form that has been chosen by the catalogers.

The whole body of chosen forms, together with cross-references from unused forms, constitutes an authority file or thesaurus. It is used by the creators of the catalog as a record of their decisions and as a guide to promote consistency of practice in the future. In many cases, the authority file or thesaurus may be available to users of the catalog. It is common, for example, for libraries to place copies of the *Library of Congress Subject Headings*, the subject authority file used by most research libraries, near the catalog.

There are three basic types of index terms used in catalogs: names, titles, and subjects. Of these, titles are the most straightforward. The title is the most distinctive piece of bibliographic information about a work, because an author may have written several books. There are probably several works on any given topic, but it is rare for two works to have exactly the same title. Therefore, a title search is the most effective way of locating a particular item if you are certain of the correct title. Remember that the title is indexed exactly as it appears on the item itself. Be wary of title citations in other works, in advertisements or reviews, and in reference sources; such citations may be incorrect or incomplete. If you search an inaccurate title, you may not be able to find the item. (It is a good idea to remind students to be totally accurate in their own citations, lest they cause similar grief to future researchers.)

Perhaps the most familiar index term is the name of the author. While this is not the most specific way to search for a particular work, there are advantages to searching by author. The author's name is easiest to determine accurately and to remember correctly. In addition, an author search will retrieve all works by the author, and there may be other relevant works by the same author. Author indexes are quite familiar to most students and should present few problems to anyone who has already learned to invert the name (last name first). It is unwise to assume that all students have already learned this. And there are names that do cause problems: compound names (such as Emmanuel Le Roy Ladurie in fig. 5.3) and names containing prefixes (Leopold von Ranke); medieval and Renaissance names (John of Salisbury or Leonardo da Vinci); or names of rulers that do not include a surname or family name (Henry VIII, king of England). The catalog should provide adequate cross-references, but a librarian should be consulted if a name cannot readily be located.

Besides authors, other persons may be indexed: editors, translators, or compilers of collections. In addition, library catalogs also include corporate names, such as names of government departments and agencies, business corporations, institutions, and so forth. Such names are usually indexed as they appear in publications of the body, although government agencies will be indexed under a geographic name ("Pennsylvania," not "Commonwealth of Pennsylvania"). Corporate bodies often form complex hierarchies of subordinate units. In the catalog heading, the middle levels of the hierarchy are usually omitted: for example, "United States. Bureau of Indian Affairs" rather than "United States. Dept. of the Interior. Bureau of Indian Affairs."

The choice of a single conventional name for each person or corporate body has now become standardized within American libraries thanks to their use of the authority files developed and maintained by the Library of Congress. Future scholars should be encouraged to use these standardized forms of names in their bibliographic citations. This will make it easier for their readers to locate the works they cite in library catalogs.

Name and title searches are usually for specific items, such as for the title of a particular work or the name of a particular author. Subject searches, on the other hand, are fishing expeditions for something about a general topic. There are many ways of finding material on a topic, and the library catalog is only one of them. Given the limitations on the scope of the catalog (only books and serials are routinely included) and given the nature of subject indexing in the catalog, a serious researcher will usually rely on subject bibliographies and on the citations in the works of other historians. However, there are cases in which subject searching in the library catalog may be useful or necessary; after all, one has to find that subject bibliography we just mentioned.

The first thing to remember about subject indexing is that the catalog does not deal with the parts of an item. Books are assigned subject terms that attempt to match as closely as possible the subject of the entire item. For example, a study of American labor unions may contain a chapter on the United Mine Workers, but there will be no subject heading for this book under mine workers, only the general term "Trade-unions—United States." Because of this, it is often necessary to search under terms that are either broader or narrower than the topic in which you are interested. At this point, it is important to take advantage of one of the features of a subject thesaurus: the identification of the broader topic or topics that include the topic sought and of the narrower topics into which the topic is divided. In figure 5.4, the chosen terms appear in bold type; *BT* indicates broader terms and *NT* indicates narrower terms; *UF* indicates references from synonyms or other forms not used in the catalog. Employing this structure of broader and narrower terms, a careful searcher can compile a list of appropriate terms for a particular search.

The most common list of subject terms used by research libraries in North America is the *Library of Congress Subject Headings* (from which fig. 5.4 is taken).[3] This list has been in use since the early years of this century and has been evolving ever since to keep pace with changes in vocabulary over time. Because of the cost of changing headings in a card catalog, the list has changed slowly, and many obsolete terms are retained. Over the past ten years, significant changes have been made to update terminology and structure of headings. However, libraries usually have not applied these changes to their older records, so their catalogs contain the outdated terms. Thus the researcher looking for works on 1960s-style communes will probably find most of them listed under the heading ''Collective settlements,'' and many of the older works on the Vikings are cataloged under the subject ''Northmen.'' At various times, ''Negroes,'' ''Blacks,'' and ''Afro-Americans'' have all been used as subject headings for dark-skinned people of African descent.

Names (personal, corporate, and geographic) may be used as subject headings for works about persons, places, and so forth. In libraries with separate subject catalogs, students should be reminded that they will have to look in two separate places to find books by and about a particular person or institution. Names of geographical areas and political jurisdictions are particularly important for historians. Usually, a common English name is used (e.g., ''Vienna'' rather than ''Wien''). Only the latest name of the place is used in subject headings (e.g., always ''Sri Lanka,'' never ''Ceylon,'' no matter what time period is involved). Under each place name, the catalog will include a variety of subdivisions covering such aspects as the geography, history, politics and government, economic conditions, and social conditions of the place. In addition, topical subjects (''Castles'' or ''Trade unions'') may be divided by geographical place. Geographic subdivision is usually hierarchical (e.g., ''Archives—France—Paris'').

Clearly, subject headings are complex and difficult to use. Fortunately, there is a feature of subject cataloging practice that can be of considerable assistance to a researcher. The subject terms assigned to each item are usually listed below the description (see figs. 5.1, 5.2 and 5.3). The terms assigned to a particular item may provide clues for further searches. For example, suppose our researcher has a citation to Ruggiero's *Violence in Early Renaissance Venice* (fig. 5.1). The first subject listed for this title is ''Crime and criminals—Italy—Venice—History.'' A search under ''Crime and criminals—Italy'' should therefore retrieve other books on Italian criminals, and a search under ''Violence'' (the second heading listed for the Ruggiero book) might also yield relevant material.

Figure 5.4
Extract from *Library of Congress Subject Headings*

Violence *(May Subd Geog)*
  UF Political violence
  BT Aggressiveness (Psychology)
       Psychology
       Social psychology
  RT Collective behavior
  NT Conjugal violence
       Family violence
       Fighting (Psychology)
       Prison violence
       School violence
       Violent crimes
       Violent deaths
  — Forecasting
  — Prediction
     USE Violence—Forecasting
  — Religious aspects
  — — Baptists, ₍Catholic Church, etc.₎
  — — Buddhism, ₍Christianity, etc.₎
  — Research *(May Subd Geog)*
    UF Violence research
Violence (Law) *(May Subd Geog)*
  UF Force (Law)
  NT Assault and battery
       Rape
       Robbery
       Violent deaths
Violence in art
Violence in children
  ₍RJ506.V56₎
  BT Aggressiveness in children
       Child psychopathology
Violence in hospitals *(May Subd Geog)*
  UF Hospital violence
  BT Hospitals
  NT Violence in psychiatric hospitals
Violence in literature
  Here are entered works on violence as a theme in
  literature, including violence in drama from a literary
  point of view. Works on violence as presented upon
  the stage are entered under Violence in the theater.
  BT Literature
Violence in mass media *(May Subd Geog)*
  ₍P96.V5₎
  BT Mass media
  NT Violence in motion pictures
       Violence in television
  — Law and legislation *(May Subd Geog)*
    BT Mass media—Law and legislation
Violence in motion pictures
  BT Moving-pictures
       Violence in mass media

Violence in nursing homes *(May Subd Geog)*
  BT Nursing homes
Violence in prisons
  USE Prison violence
Violence in psychiatric hospitals
  (May Subd Geog)
  ₍RC439.4₎
  Here are entered works on violence by patients or
  mental health personnel in psychiatric hospitals.
  BT Psychiatric hospital care
       Psychiatric hospitals
       Violence in hospitals
Violence in rabbinical literature
  BT Rabbinical literature
Violence in sports *(May Subd Geog)*
  ₍GV706.7₎
  BT Sports
  — Law and legislation *(May Subd Geog)*
Violence in television *(May Subd Geog)*
  UF Violence on television
  BT Television
       Television programs
       Violence in mass media
  RT Crime in television
  — Law and legislation *(May Subd Geog)*
Violence in the Bible
  ₍BS1199.V56₎
  UF Bible—Violence
Violence in the theater
  Here are entered works on violence as presented
  upon the stage. Works on violence as a theme in
  literature, including violence in drama from a literary
  point of view, are entered under Violence in litera-
  ture.
  BT Theater
  NT Stage fighting
Violence on television
  USE Violence in television
Violence-research
  USE Violence—Research
Violent crimes *(May Subd Geog)*
  UF Crimes, Violent
       Crimes of violence

This practice of expanding a search based on the information found is another example of one of the most basic rules of using the library catalog: look for and take advantage of clues that are provided in the catalog itself.

Traditional Forms of Library Catalogs

So far we have been talking primarily about the description and indexing of individual books and serials and about the use of specific index terms. In a catalog, however, all these individual descriptions and index terms come together into a grand totality. The precise manner in which a particular catalog is constructed depends primarily on the physical form in which it is stored. For most of this century, the most common form of library catalog was the familiar card catalog. Each card consists of the description of an item with one index term at the top of the card. The cards are filed in alphabetical order under the index terms.

The result is a fixed sequence of information. The order and presentation of this information are controlled by the creators of the catalog. It has a very complex structure, because it deals with a vast quantity of very different kinds of information and attempts to present it to users in an organized fashion. While this structure is sometimes confusing and intimidating, it can also assist the user in finding relevant information. A couple of examples may serve to illustrate both the complexity and the structure underlying it.

Most authors write only one or a few books. However, some authors are so prolific that it is hard to keep their works straight. They may write many books; their books may be translated or appear in abridgments and collections. The same works may appear under different titles (this is almost inevitable in the case of translations). As we saw, in the catalog all the works of an author are brought together under a single heading for that author. In addition, when a work has appeared under more than one title, all versions of that work are brought together under what is called a "uniform title." Thus all versions of Aristotle's *Politics* will be found under "Aristotle. Politics," usually subdivided so that texts in the original Greek are listed first, followed by translations (arranged alphabetically by language). Likewise, all works *about* the *Politics* will be found under the same uniform heading: "Aristotle. Politics."

Subject headings provide even greater complexity. Figure 5.5 represents a sequence of subject headings in a library catalog. If you compare it with figure 5.4, which represents the same sequence in the printed *Library of Congress Subject Headings*, note first that the order of the headings is somewhat different. In figure 5.5, the headings are filed word-by-word without regard to punctuation. In figure 5.4, there is a definite hierarchy of punctuation: single words first, then dashes, then parentheses, then phrases. Thus, in figure 5.4, headings appear in the following order: Violence; Violence—Forecasting; Violence—Religious aspects—Baptists; Violence—Research; Violence (Law); Violence in art; and so forth. Each catalog has its own filing rules. The only way to cope with this diversity is to be on guard. Always browse forward and backward to make sure nothing has been missed.

In figure 5.5, notice the extensive use of subdivisions. There are considerably more of them even than in figure 5.4. This is because certain types of subdivisions

Figure 5.5
Sequence of Subject Headings

Violence
Violence--Africa
Violence--Africa--Case studies
Violence--Argentina--History--20th century
Violence--Australia
Violence--Bibliography
Violence--California
Violence--California--Case studies
Violence--Canada
Violence--Canada--History
Violence--Case studies
Violence--China--History
Violence--Congresses
Violence--Cross-cultural studies--Congresses
Violence--Data bases
Violence--Developing countries
Violence--Europe--History--Congresses
Violence--Forecasting
Violence--Germany
Violence--Germany--History
Violence--Great Britain
Violence--Great Britain--Case studies
Violence--Great Britain--History
Violence--Great Britain--History--19th century
Violence--History
Violence--History--Congresses
Violence in art
Violence in motion pictures
Violence in motion pictures--Great Britain
Violence in motion pictures--United States
Violence in television
Violence in television--Congresses
Violence in television--Cross-cultural studies
Violence in television--Great Britain--Congresses
Violence in television--Great Britain--Public opinion
Violence in television--Law and legislation--United States
Violence in television--Social aspects
Violence in television--Social aspects--United States
Violence in television--United States
Violence--Italy
Violence--Italy--History--Congresses
Violence--Italy--Venice--History
Violence--Latin America
Violence (Law)
Violence (Law)--United States
Violence (Law)--United States--Abstracts
Violence--Michigan--Detroit--History--20th century
Violence--Pennsylvania--Philadelphia
Violence--Pennsylvania--Philadelphia--History--19th century
Violence--Periodicals
Violence--Peru
Violence--Peru--Congresses
Violence--Prediction
Violence--Prevention
Violence--Psychological aspects
Violence--Psychological aspects--Congresses
Violence--Religious aspects
Violence--Religious aspects--Christianity
Violence--Religious aspects--Islam
Violence--Religious aspects--Judaism
Violence--Social aspects
Violence--Soviet Union
Violence--Spain--Case studies
Violence--Spain--Castile--History
Violence--Spain--Folklore
Violence--United States
Violence--United States--Bibliography
Violence--United States--Case studies

such as geographic names and types of material ("Bibliography" and "Congresses") and common topics ("History" and "Psychological aspects") do not appear under all relevant subjects in the printed list, but may be used whenever they are applicable. It should also be noted that the order of the subdivisions is not completely predictable. Usually the geographic subdivisions come first, but some form subdivisions (e.g., "Law and legislation") are followed by geographic subdivisions. Again, the only way to cope is to browse through the entire file under a general topic to make sure nothing has been overlooked.

Library of Congress subject headings as applied by most libraries to their collections allow subjects to be identified with a degree of precision and are organized into a structure that attempts to bring together the most significant aspects of a subject. This structure is there to be exploited by researchers who know how to use it—or to bewilder those who do not.

The Online Catalog

The newest form of library catalog is the online catalog. All information is stored in computer-readable form and is searched via a terminal. Instead of flipping through cards in a drawer or pages in a book, the searcher types a search term. Results—such as bibliographic records, lists of titles, portions of an index, or help messages—are displayed on the terminal screen. These results can generally be printed or even downloaded for manipulation on a computer. (For a discussion of downloading see p. 117 and notes 11 and 12 of this chapter.)

The capabilities of online catalogs vary from system to system. Almost all online catalogs allow the user to search by author, title, and subject, much as in a traditional card catalog. Most online catalogs also provide for some form of keyword searching. While the user of the traditional catalog must depend on the order of words in the index term, the user of the online catalog with keyword searching can find words anywhere in a heading. For example, a search for "criminal" would retrieve a list of names, titles, or subjects containing the word *criminal*. In some online catalogs, keyword searches must be limited to specific fields (such as title or subject). In others, searchers can look for words in most or all of the fields in a record.

Keyword searching allows a user to break out of the structure of the traditional catalog. No longer governed by the organization imposed by the creator of the catalog, the user can define the structure of the search. Keyword searching allows the user access to the author's vocabulary (at least that part of it found on the title page) as well as the vocabulary of the cataloger's authority files. The user may not be confined to designated index terms, but can often search the entire description, including notes, abstracts, and contents listings. The user may also be able to combine concepts in ways not anticipated by the cataloger, using what is called Boolean searching. This involves the combination of search terms with the logical operators AND, OR, and NOT. For example, one might search for "terrorism" AND "airplanes" OR "aircraft" OR "airports" but NOT in the

"Middle East." It is also possible to make a search more precise by limiting the search term to a particular data element (field). For example, a researcher with an imprecise citation might look for "Smith" as an author and "Renaissance" in a title.

Keyword searching is thus quite powerful and flexible. However, it does have its limitations. While the searcher has access to the author's vocabulary, he or she is also often at the mercy of that vocabulary. Titles do not always accurately or precisely reflect the nature of the works, and the words retrieved by a keyword search may not have the meaning or significance the searcher anticipates. Boolean searching also has its dangers; combinations of words may be coincidental rather than intentional. For example, a search using "art" and "Japan" may retrieve the following title: *The Art of Business in Japan.* An inevitable limitation of keyword searching is that it depends on the language of the user coinciding with the language of the information being searched. This means, among other things, that an English-speaking searcher who does not use foreign words in a search is likely to retrieve only English-language items. The fundamental problem with keyword searching in an online catalog, however, is the loss of the consistency provided by the traditional structured catalog, which indexes all material under a single form of each name, title, or subject. Keyword searching can find things that the traditional approach cannot, but it will not provide a listing of all relevant material without tapping into the structured indexing vocabulary.

Fortunately there are ways to overcome the limitations of keyword searching in online catalogs and to take advantage of the authority work done by catalogers. A small number of relevant titles may be located through keyword searching. The astute searcher will then display the records retrieved, ignore the works not of interest, and use the information from the relevant records as the basis for more intensive searching. Thus, students should be encouraged to search under the names of authors of relevant works, employing the form used in the catalog, in the hope that these authors may have written other works on the topic. Similarly, as was noted above on page 105, students should look at the subject headings assigned to relevant works and use them to locate other works on the same subject.

A concrete illustration can provide dramatic evidence of the importance of this practice. This example uses our favorite topic: criminals in Renaissance Italy. A title keyword search under "crime" and "Renaissance" in one large catalog retrieved eight titles, most of them relevant to the topic at hand. Among these works was Ruggiero's *Violence in Early Renaissance Venice* (fig. 5.1). Note that the word *crime* does not appear in the title of this work; the search retrieved it from the series title: "Crime, law, and deviance." Note also that the first subject heading for this work is "Crime and criminals—Italy—Venice—History," which closely matches the topic of our search (although it is a bit too specific). By omitting "Venice" (which is too specific) and "History" (which is too common a word), we can search under "Crime and criminals—Italy." In our large catalog, this search retrieved a total of 136 titles, most of them in

Italian and other continental languages. Note that this search is likely to be fairly complete, since it uses the cataloger's standardized subject terminology. It also allows the searcher to overcome the language specificity of keyword searching on titles. Our sample search need not end with these 136 titles; each of these titles can be examined for additional authors, subject headings, or title keywords to be searched to locate even more works on the topic. This concept of cycling or using information in the bibliographic records to locate additional materials is a key to effective searching in any environment, but nowhere more so than in an online catalog.

REFERENCE TOOLS

The library catalog is, of course, only one of the many tools used in bibliographic research. Even the undergraduate writing his or her first research paper is going to need to consult a few other sources—such as periodical indexes, encyclopedias, sources of biographical information, and possibly some bibliographies. Advanced researchers have at their disposal a bewildering array of indexes, specialized bibliographies, retrospective imprint catalogs, computerized databases, union catalogs, and other reference sources.

Students should not be deluged with long lists of these specialized sources. Except for a small number of titles, it is not important for students to learn lists of reference sources. What students mainly need to know is what *kinds* of information can be found in the library. They need to have some idea of how different *types* of library materials are organized. And they need to know about the different types (or genres) of reference sources they can consult to get at the information they need.

Published Catalogs of Books

A logical first step beyond the catalog of the local library into the world of reference tools is the published catalog of books. This type of reference tool is similar to the local catalog. Some are even made by photographing in order all the cards in a card catalog. In addition, this category of material is a good place to introduce students to some of the concepts that organize types of reference works.

For example, some reference books cover all subjects while others are confined to a very specific subject or even to a particular collection. Many published catalogs of specialized libraries exist, such as the *Catalog of the Latin American Collection* at the University of Texas, or the *Catalogs of the Sophia Smith Collection, Women's History Archive* at Smith College.[4] Many types of reference works cover only one nation or language group. This is true, for example, of biographical dictionaries such as the *Dictionary of American Biography*. It is particularly true of catalogs of books, which tend to be compiled by national publishing organizations or by national libraries.

Trade catalogs (*Books in Print* is the American example) are usually issued by book publishers' organizations. They are generally limited to commercial publishers and may not cover the publications of small presses or of government agencies. They are confined to currently available titles and contain the sort of information needed by booksellers, such as price and restrictions on sale outside the country. National bibliographies, on the other hand, are usually compiled by the national library as part of the government's mission to record the national imprint (the total output of the nation's publishers); the compilation of the national bibliography is often connected both with the building of the national library's collections and with copyright registration. A good example of a national bibliography is the *British National Bibliography*. Unfortunately, the United States has no national library and therefore no national bibliography. The Library of Congress is precisely that: its primary mission is to support the work of the Congress. There are also two other "national libraries" in the country: the National Library of Medicine and the National Agricultural Library. All three produce catalogs, but neither separately nor together do they constitute a truly national bibliography.

Another distinction among catalogs of books is between current and retrospective bibliographies. Most national bibliographies and trade catalogs began coverage sometime in the present century, many of them since 1950. For searches prior to that time, the researcher must rely on rather primitive catalogs issued by commercial publishers and on the efforts of individual scholars, the latter usually working on a distinct time period. British imprints, for example, are covered by the *Short-Title Catalogue* (to 1640), Donald Wing's *Short-Title Catalogue (1641–1700)*, the *Eighteenth-Century Short-Title Catalogue*, and the *Nineteenth-Century Short-Title Catalogue*.[5] For the United States, there is Evans's *American Bibliography* and its continuations.[6]

While all these reference works hold endless fascination for the librarian, they are unlikely to be of significant help to most students, who can safely rely instead on the books in the local library. Catalogs of books are most useful when a researcher needs to locate material not available nearby. As this may not be necessary for students in many history courses, the instructor might be wise to use this type of material as a fairly clear and well-organized example of how types of reference tools are structured. The concepts we discussed above—comprehensive versus focused on a specific subject, national/language scope, current versus retrospective coverage, compilation by commercial organizations or government agencies or individual scholars—are applicable to many other types of reference works.

One particular type of catalog deserves special treatment. The logical extension of the catalog of an individual library is a catalog covering many libraries (called a "union catalog"). The ultimate union catalog would be one that includes all materials in all libraries. The closest approximation to such a catalog in print is the *National Union Catalog Pre–1956 Imprints*, which covers a large number of books published prior to 1956 held by many libraries in the United States.[7] In addition, there are a number of printed union catalogs that are regional in scope.

Thanks to the power of the computer, there are now also computerized union catalogs that are national in scope. Such systems were designed for shared cataloging, for allowing libraries to use catalog records created by other libraries. A by-product of these systems is a file of bibliographic descriptions, extensively indexed, and including a listing of the libraries holding each title. These online files now contain tens of millions of records, and they are the most up-to-date listings of bibliographic information. At the heart of these systems (and of most local online catalogs) are the authoritative machine-readable cataloging records (MARC) provided by the Library of Congress.[8]

At present, there are two computerized union catalogs commonly available in American libraries: OCLC and RLIN. It should be noted that merger negotiations have been held between administrators of these two systems, and some sort of merger or link between them may be a possibility for the future.[9]

OCLC—the Online Computer Library Center—is a nonprofit computer library service and research organization. The OCLC online union catalog contains over twenty million records, contributed by over eleven thousand libraries of all types in thirty-seven countries and territories. The database includes all the cataloging produced by the national libraries in the United States and Canada, by the Government Printing Office in Washington, D.C., and by the British Library. In the past, OCLC provided very limited indexing of the data in its records and no subject indexing at all. However, in 1990 OCLC introduced a new service called EPIC, which provides the sort of access usually available in online catalogs and bibliographic databases—keyword access to virtually the entire bibliographic record, Boolean searching capabilities, and ability to download records into files on a personal computer. OCLC is also providing the same search capabilities to a number of online periodical indexes.

RLIN—the Research Libraries Information Network—is the database maintained by the Research Libraries Group (RLG), a not-for-profit enterprise of about thirty major universities and research institutions in the United States (as well as a larger number of associate and special members). Its members collaborate in operating a set of ongoing programs that focus on collecting, organizing, preserving, and providing information necessary to education and scholarship. RLG has several special programs that enhance the value of the RLIN database. RLIN has an active East Asian program, and the system offers sophisticated support for storage, display, and indexing of East Asian languages in their original characters; the database includes over 100,000 Chinese, Japanese, and Korean records. RLIN provides support for the description and processing of archival collections; sixty-one institutions participate in this program, and there are over one-third of a million records for unique collections of archival materials. In addition to the RLIN database itself, there are a number of resource files including the *Eighteenth-Century Short-Title Catalogue*. All RLIN records are accessible through word and phrase indexes; Boolean searching is supported, as well as limiting the results of a search.

As comprehensive as these databases are, they are still part of the same world as the card catalog. They still specialize in books and other separate bibliographic items, such as sound cassettes or videotapes. These catalogs and databases thus exclude many works of importance to historians. The most significant of these missing works are periodical articles—to which we now turn.

Periodical Literature

Reference librarians get more questions about how to find articles in journals than on any other topic. Locating citations in periodical indexes and then tracking down those citations in a particular library's periodical catalog seems to cause beginning students more trouble than any other form of bibliographic research. Therefore even a brief introduction to the library should devote considerable time to an explanation of how to locate periodical articles. The number of specialized periodical indexes is so great that even the most experienced scholar is unlikely to be aware of all the useful titles outside of his or her immediate specialty.

Many instructors are surprised to learn how little even beginning graduate students know about how to find periodical literature on a subject. Few of them have heard of the *Humanities Index*, much less of *Historical Abstracts*. And how many of them know that most historical literature is indexed in the *Humanities Index* rather than in its companion publication, the *Social Sciences Index*? Or that American and Canadian history is indexed in *America: History and Life* rather than in *Historical Abstracts*, which is published by the same company (ABC-Clio)? A good measure of the sophistication of a group of students in conducting library research can be obtained by asking them to interpret an entry in a periodical index, or by asking them what steps they must take to find a journal article in a particular institution's library. We would recommend this exercise to every instructor who has not tried it—the results are likely to be an impressive testimonial to the need for bibliographic instruction.

Several generalizations about periodical indexes should be conveyed to beginning students. The first is that these indexes tend to come in "families," the members of which share many basic characteristics. The indexes most likely to be used by all except the most advanced graduate students follow a common format—for the good reason that most of them are compiled by the same organization, the H.W. Wilson Company. The "Wilson indexes" include such standards as *Readers' Guide to Periodical Literature*, *Humanities Index*, and *Social Sciences Index*, as well as such lesser-known but useful tools as *Biography Index*, *Bibliography Index*, and *Essay and General Literature Index*. These indexes are relatively easy to use, in part because they have standardized subject headings and fairly extensive cross-references. The existence of this subject

Figure 5.6
Extract from *Humanities Index*

> Sovereignty, absolutism and the function of the law
> in seventeenth-century France. D. Parker. *Past Present*
> no122:36-74 F '89
> Tradition and agrarian protest in nineteenth-century
> England and Wales. G. Seal. *Folklore* 99 no2:146-69
> '88
>
> Justice, Administration of
>> *See also*
>>> Courts
>>> Criminal justice, Administration of
>>> Government investigations
>>> Judges
>>> Judicial error
>>> Judicial review
>>> Law enforcement
>>> Obstruction of justice
>>> Punishment
>>> Searches and seizures
>>> Trials
>
>>> **Great Britain**
>>> *History*
> Chapman's The widow's tears: the governor's scene and
> Coke's opinion on Prohibitions del roy. W. Dean.
> *ANQ* ns2:7-10 Ja '89
>>> **Quebec (Province)**
>>> *History*
> Some aspects of civil litigation in Lower Canada, 1785-
> 1825: towards the use of court records for Canadian
> social history. E. Kolish. *Can Hist Rev* 70:337-65
> S '89
>
> Justice, Miscarriage of *See* Judicial error
> Justice Dept. (U.S.) *See* United States. Dept. of Justice
> Justice in literature
> Sexual oppression and social justice in Marguerite de
> Navarre's Heptaméron. J. D. Bernard. *J Medieval
> Renaiss Stud* 19:251-81 Fall '89

heading and cross-reference structure should be pointed out to students, and it can be profitably compared to the *Library of Congress Subject Headings*. It would be useful to illustrate these points by showing students a sample page from one of these indexes, such as that shown in figure 5.6. Most users find the subject headings in the Wilson indexes easier to use than LC subject headings, although the subject terms used in the Wilson indexes are derived from LC headings. The index terms used for periodical articles tend to be more current and less complex than LC headings. There are three main reasons for this relative ease of use: the indexes cumulate annually, each addresses a reasonably well-defined group of readers, and each covers a relatively narrow range of subjects. Hence they do not have to cover the whole universe of published materials as do the LC headings. For these reasons, the terms used in periodical indexes are likely to be relatively recent ones, direct, and precise.

Students using the Wilson indexes (as well as most other periodical indexes) often have trouble interpreting the entries. Some effort should be made to teach students how to decipher the abbreviations used in these indexes. It is important that they know to look up abbreviations of the titles of periodicals in the front of the indexes. All too often students have to return to the indexes a second time after copying down a long list of abbreviations like "Br J Hist Sci." To those who cannot interpret them exactly, these abbreviations are virtually useless for finding the actual journals. Most periodical catalogs require their users to look up journal titles word for word, exactly as they appear in the name of the journal. Students need to be told to look out for such minor differences as prepositions ("Journal of" and "Journal for").

Students should also be informed about the differences between the Wilson indexes and other types of periodical indexes. Even most beginning graduate students are likely to be unclear about the distinction between an index and an abstract. They may be bored or insulted if such distinctions are explained too pedantically, but such information can be introduced casually in an exposition of specific abstracting sources, such as *Historical Abstracts* and its counterpart for the history of the United States and Canada, *America: History and Life*. Sample pages, such as that shown in figure 5.7, might be given to students. Students are often delighted when they learn for the first time that they can get summaries to help them decide whether they actually need to read the article itself. The organization of abstracting sources, with the indexes and the summaries often in separate volumes, should be explained. Instructors may want to assign exercises, such as compiling a bibliography for a term paper, that require students to use several different types of indexes.

At some point in a discussion of indexes and abstracts, the existence of computerized versions of many of these sources should be mentioned. Fairly long runs of *Historical Abstracts* and *America: History and Life* can now be searched by computer, as well as recent years of the Wilson indexes and many other indexes of interest to historians. The computerized versions of these indexes are usually searched for a fee from commercial vendors, such as Bibliographic Retrieval Services (BRS) and Lockheed's Dialog. For a comprehensive discussion of computer searching, when to use it, and how to teach it, see chapter 8.

The most recent offspring of the electronic revolution in libraries is the database stored on CD-ROM (Compact Disk—Read Only Memory). CD-ROM is a form of information storage, technically related to the familiar CDs that are played on home stereos. Vast amounts of information can be stored on these disks and searched using microcomputers. Because databases on CD-ROM usually can be searched without direct cost to the user or a charge to the library for "connect time," they appear to mark the beginning of a shift from librarian-assisted database searching to direct "end-user" searching by the researcher. The most recent five years of *Historical Abstracts* and *America: History and*

Figure 5.7
Extract from *America: History and Life*

C. Spanish-American War

Articles

26:4935.   1898-99
Contosta, David R. WHITELAW REID AND THE INADVER-
TENT EMPIRE. *Old Northwest 1986 12(1): 27-40.* The journalist and
politician Whitelaw Reid (1837-1912) readily accepted the imperial
consequences of the Spanish-American War. Through speeches, letters,
and his control of editorial opinion at the *New York Tribune,* Reid
presented strong historical and economic arguments for American
overseas expansion. As one of the peace commissioners, Reid helped
conclude a treaty that embodied his, and the nation's, imperial ideas.
Based on the Whitelaw Reid Papers, Library of Congress, Washington,
D.C., and other primary sources; 26 notes.   P. L. McLaughlin

26:4936.   1898-99
Reilly, Margaret Inglehart. ANDREW WADSWORTH, A NE-
BRASKA SOLDIER IN THE PHILIPPINES, 1898-1899. *Nebraska
History 1987 68(4): 183-199.* Discusses Andrew S. Wadsworth's two-
year military career during the Spanish-American War and the Filipino
Insurrection by quoting frequently from his letters. A transplanted
New Yorker, Wadsworth rose from the ranks to become an officer in
the 1st Nebraska Volunteer Infantry Regiment. The article recounts his
enlistment, the long trip to the Philippines, battles, his wounding at
Quingua, hospitalization, and homecoming. Based on the Andrew S.
Wadsworth Letters in the Hussey-Wadsworth Papers, Clements Library, University of Michigan; map, 12 photos, 73 notes.
                                                          R. S. La Forte

Source: *America: History and Life.* Copyright © by ABC-Clio. Reprinted by permission.

Life have recently appeared on CD-ROM. Many other indexes and abstracts of
interest to historians are also available in this format. These include the Wilson
indexes, *Dissertation Abstracts*, *Sociological Abstracts* and the ERIC indexes.[10]
The techniques for searching these indexes vary from system to system, but the
more sophisticated of them have most of the capabilities found in their online
counterparts.[11]

In a discussion of indexes on CD-ROM, the possibility of downloading bibliographic records from CD-ROM onto a floppy disk should be mentioned.
Downloading of records is also possible from computerized card catalogs, OCLC
and RLIN, and commercial database vendors, such as BRS and Dialog. Downloaded records can be used by special bibliographic software packages that
manipulate them to produce footnotes and bibliographies.[12]

The computer has also affected the production of printed indexes and has led
to the creation of new types of indexes. Many of the new indexes produced with

the aid of the computer are essentially keyword indexes derived from the words in titles and sometimes from other parts of the description of the items indexed. The special characteristics of keyword indexes should be noted. The advantages and disadvantages associated with keyword indexes resemble those mentioned above in the discussion of keyword searching in online catalogs. Many researchers and professional indexers have a low opinion of keyword indexes. The main objection to such indexes is their lack of a "controlled vocabulary" based on a thesaurus, such as the Library of Congress list of subject headings or the terms used in the Wilson indexes. The lack of a controlled vocabulary means that you have to guess, without the benefit of cross-references, what words might appear in the titles of articles on a subject of interest. As a consequence, the user of these indexes will probably have to look under a number of terms and will probably miss some relevant titles, especially if research is being done in a field that favors "literary" titles, which allude only indirectly to the subject of an article. Users of these indexes also have to plow through large numbers of titles that have nothing to do with their subject, but in which the keywords they are looking under happen to appear. In some keyword indexes, the names of authors may also appear under several different forms. In spite of these drawbacks, keyword indexes are becoming increasingly common—mainly because they are relatively inexpensive to produce.

Users of keyword indexes may take some consolation from the fact that although they have to eschew the benefits of a controlled vocabulary, they also do not have to suffer the drawbacks of an indexer's "control." A controlled vocabulary puts one at the mercy of the indexer—if the indexer is ignorant or careless, or if the thesaurus is inadequate, important items may not be found. If research is being done on a subject so new or so specialized that it is not adequately reflected in the terminology used by indexers, a keyword index may be preferable to a conventional index. As noted previously, users of computerized catalogs and online indexes often have the advantage of being able to search for subjects using both keywords and controlled index terms. But it is very unusual for a printed index to include both a keyword index and a controlled-vocabulary index (an exception is the *Monthly Catalog of United States Government Publications*, which will be discussed under government publications reference sources, below).

The power of the computer to index massive quantities of material at low cost has led to the production of some important and innovative indexes in recent years. One of the most notable of these is *The Combined Retrospective Index Set to Journals in History, 1838–1974*. The unique organization of this index enables researchers to find in a single place scholarly articles in English appearing over a long period of time, rather than having to go through a series of annual indexes. Its reliance on keyword indexing, however, makes it an unreliable tool for the researcher who tries to depend on it as the sole source for all of the important articles on a subject.

Citation indexes. Another type of computer-produced index is the citation index. The one and only publisher of citation indexes is the Institute for Scientific Information (ISI), which issues *Science Citation Index*, *Social Sciences Citation Index*, and *Arts and Humanities Citation Index* (which covers most of the historical literature). These indexes are complex, and they are notoriously difficult to use. At the very least, the first-time user will need to read the introduction to these indexes carefully. It might be worthwhile to have students view one of the slide-tape presentations that ISI has prepared on its indexes. These publications can be viewed as bundles of indexes. Each annual volume includes the following: an author index, a title index, a subject index, a source index, a citation index, and a corporate name index. Among the various subindexes contained within the citation indexes, two are of particular note: The first is the subject index, which is a typical keyword index. The second is the citation index itself, for which the citation indexes are named (see figure 5.8).

The citation indexes in ISI's publications perform the truly unique function of indexing footnotes. In other words, you can use these indexes to find out who has footnoted a particular book or article in a given year. This feature makes it possible to get at information that would otherwise be difficult to locate. One can, for example, find out how often and where a particular author's works have been cited. More important for the researcher, citation indexing provides a valuable supplementary approach for obtaining information on certain subjects. Let us say one is studying the influence of Hayden White's *Metahistory* on recent historiography. A great deal of information that could not be obtained easily in any other way could be found by tracking down through the citation indexes who has cited White's work in the last decade or so. Or, if one is writing on a specialized subject in which there are one or two classic articles, research may be facilitated by using these indexes to locate works that have cited them. This technique is particularly valuable if one is dealing with a subject so specialized or recent that it is not adequately reflected in conventional indexing. This technique also has the advantage of leading one forward in time to the most recent literature on a subject. Most conventional literature searches using footnotes and bibliographies lead backward to ever-earlier works. Citation indexes reverse this process and therefore work well in tandem with conventional literature searches for scholars who are attempting to locate all of the published information on a subject.

Locating periodical issues. Once a student has negotiated the periodical indexes, it is still necessary to locate the article. Classes should be given some instruction on how periodicals are listed and arranged in a particular institution's library. Practices here vary greatly from library to library. Periodicals may be listed in the same catalog(s) as books, or they may be listed in a separate periodicals catalog. Bound journals may be shelved with the books or shelved separately. A major problem for most students is interpreting the source that gives a library's holdings of a particular periodical. Different libraries have

Figure 5.8
Extract from Citation Index of *Arts & Humanities Citation Index*

WHITE H

		VOL	PG	YR
LIFE L TRUMBULL 1913				
COLLINS B	J AM STUD	20	391	86
LIFE L TRUMBULL p272 1913				
KACZOROW.RJ	NY U LAW RE	61	863	86
LIT FACT SELECTED PA 1976				
WRIGHT SK	STUD MONAST	28	311	86
METAHISTORY				
RICOEUR P	REV OCCIDEN		41	87
SZEGEDYM.M	NEOHELICON	13	133	86
METAHISTORY 1973				
ANKERSMI.FR	HIST THEORY	25	1	86
BELLVILL.GH	SCI SOC	50	415	86
BENELLI D	SUB-STANCE		20	86
BERNARD C	POETIQUE		333	87
BLEIKAST.A	REV FR ETUD		7	87
BRODY R	HISPAN REV	55	323	87
BURKE WM	STUD MYST	10	3	87
CEBIK LB	HIST THEORY	25	58	86
CEVALLOS FJ	REV EST HIS	20	55	86
DIPUCCIO DM	LAT AM THEA	20	29	86
DOHERTY G	PARAGRAPH	9	49	87
DUBROW H	ENGL LIT RE	16	425	86
EGAN K	WALT WHIT Q	4	1	87
ELLIS RJ	J AM CULT	9	9	86
HEYNE E	MOD FICT ST	33	479	87
IGGERS GG	HIST THEORY	B	26	114	87
KENT CA	CAN J HIS	21	371	86
KERR J	TEX ST LIT	29	237	87
KITCH SL	ROCKY MT R	41	7	87
KRAMER LS	HIST REFLEC	13	517	86
KRONICK JG	CLIO	15	391	86
LAURENCE D	PMLA	102	55	87
LOUVRE A	LIT HIST	13	58	87
MCCORD PF	GENRE	19	59	86
MCKINNEY RH	PHILOS TOD	30	234	86
MERWICK D	REV AM HIST	14	487	86
MURRAY K	S REV-ADEL	20	49	87
NICHOLS B	FILM Q	41	9	87
POOLE FJP	J AM A REL	54	411	86
RE L	ITAL QUART	26	47	85
RICOEUR P	AUT AUT		23	86
RIGNEY A	NEW LIT HIS	18	77	86
ROBINSON A	MOD LANG R	82	830	87
ROSKILL M	CRIT INQ	14	173	87
RUSEN J	HIST THEORY	26	275	87
SAMMARCE.F	REV FR ETUD		93	87
SCHUSSLE.E	NEW TEST ST	33	386	87
SCHWANIT.D	LILI	N	17	131	87
SEWELL WH	AM J SOCIOL	N	93	166	87
SHAPIRO G	T C PEIRCE	23	31	87
STEINBER.S	AM J SEMIOT	4	29	86
STEINER P	POETICS TOD	7	759	86
STRASSER S	PHILOS RUND	B	34	1	87
TINKLER JF	HIST THEORY	26	32	87
WEILAND S	COLL ENGL	B	49	816	87
WOLF W	POETICA	18	305	86
WRIGHT SK	STUD MONAST	28	311	86
YOUNG JE	PHILOL Q	66	127	87
ZANTOP S	MLN-MOD LAN	102	570	87

Source: Citation Index of *Arts & Humanities Citation Index*, 1987, column 10796. Copyright ©1988 by Institute for Scientific Information. Reprinted by permission.

different methods for indicating holdings, and some of them are quite confusing to the neophyte. (A common error is confusing the statement that gives the publication dates for a journal with the volumes actually held by a library.)

Users of periodical indexes will often find that their library does not have the journals they need. Therefore, this is a good context in which to mention interlibrary loan. Interlibrary loan practices vary from library to library, but most graduate students (and often undergraduates) may use interlibrary loan to obtain books and articles not in the local library. Most libraries have at least some restrictions on the use of interlibrary loan. Once again, it is important that specific policies be explained to students.

An alternative to interlibrary loan for many students and scholars is to use materials at other libraries. If students expect to visit other libraries, they may want to know in advance in which libraries a particular periodical is located. Here they have a number of tools at their disposal. The *Union List of Serials* and its continuation, *New Serial Titles*, are the most comprehensive listings in print of periodicals available in American libraries. These publications also have foreign counterparts, such as the *British Union Catalogue of Periodicals*. There are also many state and regional union catalogs of serials. These often pick up holdings not mentioned in the national listings and may be of more immediate use to researchers who are unable to travel outside of a particular area. Finally, serial titles can be located through OCLC and RLIN.

Other Types of Library Materials

The majority of works that fill the shelves of reference rooms in academic libraries consist of works such as encyclopedias, dictionaries, biographical sources, and bibliographies. These works are so important for historical research that a separate chapter is devoted to them (see chapter 6).

Every research library also has a number of specialized departments that contain stores of materials likely to be heavily used by some historians. Often these materials are uncataloged and are overlooked by the unprepared. In many libraries, the number of uncataloged items greatly exceeds the cataloged ones. Uncataloged materials are usually located through specialized printed indexes or informal in-house "finding aids." Maps, microforms, government publications, and special collections departments are among the places where such materials are found. Not all researchers will need to use these collections, but students should at least be sufficiently aware of them to think of going to them in time of need. Those who are teaching an introduction-to-library-research class should at least mention the existence of these partially hidden resources. Teachers of more specialized courses may want to describe one or more of these areas in detail, and possibly schedule a tour of a map collection or a government documents depository. Those who are teaching archival research should consult chapter 9 of this book. Those who have the need or opportunity to lead students to other more specialized areas of the library may want to keep the following pointers in mind.

Government publications. These are a treasure trove of original source material—particularly for students of American history. Thanks to the Federal Depository Libraries Program, most academic libraries have large collections of U.S. government publications—at least of recent date. Micropublishers have produced extensive sets of government publications reaching back to the founding of the republic. There are few matters of public interest that are not documented in the publications of the federal government.

Although some libraries have cataloged all or a portion of their government publications—and cataloging records are frequently available on OCLC and RLIN—the primary means of access to these publications is through indexes. The most comprehensive "official" index to federal documents, *The Monthly Catalog of United States Government Publications*, was greatly improved in 1976. The *Monthly Catalog* used to be notorious for its inadequate and unpredictable indexing. Now, thanks in part to the ubiquitous computer, it appears resplendent with no less than nine separate indexes, including a subject index based on Library of Congress subject headings, a computer-produced keyword index, and an author index. There are also several privately produced versions of the *Monthly Catalog* on CD-ROM, which can be searched much like a computerized library catalog. These CD-ROM indexes are now widely available and are usually considered the most convenient means to search for recent U.S. government publications. The federal government is also starting to distribute many of its statistical publications on CD-ROM, and those with an interest in using statistics in computerized form should inquire about what is available at the local depository library.

Also available for recent government publications are a number of excellent privately produced indexes and abstracts. These include the *CIS Index* (for congressional publications) and the *American Statistics Index* (ASI Index), which provides detailed coverage for all of the statistical publications of the U.S. government. For the electronically inclined, these indexes are also searchable by computer and on CD-ROM.

Users of older federal publications are also better served than in the past. The inadequate indexing of the earlier volumes of the *Monthly Catalog* is now made up for in part by the recent appearance of a *Cumulative Subject Index to the Monthly Catalog of U.S. Government Publications* and a *Cumulative Title Index to United States Public Documents*. Two particularly useful categories of congressional publications also have detailed retrospective indexes: *The U.S. Congressional Committee Hearings Index* and the *U.S. Serial Set Index*. There are several other indexes for government publications too specialized to mention in a brief overview, but which may be useful for researchers working on certain topics. Here, too, students should be encouraged to consult with a librarian to find out what reference sources may be useful.

If the user of U.S. government publications is now well served by indexes, the same cannot be said for the user of state, local, foreign, and international documents. Indexes of one sort or another exist for most of these publications, but they are almost all of inferior quality. Because of the diversity of these publications and their indexes, not even an overview of the available tools is possible in a short chapter. The researcher interested in these areas would do well to consult directly with the person in charge of the nearest government publications department.

A few hints might be kept in mind by those interested in the publications of foreign governments. Most countries have an official list of government publications similar to the U.S. *Monthly Catalog*—the *British Catalogue of Government Publications* is an example. A useful guide to reference sources for foreign governments is Vladimir Palic's *Government Publications: A Guide to Bibliographic Tools*.[13] Keep in mind also that most libraries catalog their foreign government publications. This means that many of the holdings of other libraries (especially for recent years) can be found on OCLC and RLIN. Many important older titles can be tracked down through the *Catalog of Government Publications in the Research Libraries of the New York Public Library*.

Microforms. Another area where large research libraries usually have vast quantities of uncataloged material is in their microforms collections. It surprises most students that there is more than one kind of microform. In addition to microfilm, there are also microfiche, microcards, and microprint, all known collectively as microforms. It is often a good idea to illustrate an introduction to research using microforms with a few samples of the various types of microforms.

The sheer quantity and variety of material stored in one microformat or another surprises just about everybody. Here, too, specific holdings vary greatly from library to library, and a researcher would do well to begin by inquiring of the microforms librarian what holdings are available in his or her particular area of interest. Keep in mind that individual titles in microforms collections are frequently not listed in library catalogs, but must be located through printed indexes. Although it is impossible here even to begin to summarize the materials available on microform, we will mention a few collections to give readers some idea of the scope and variety of materials available. Newspapers are among the most heavily used items on microform, and their indexes frequently reside in the microforms department. It is through using such sources as *The Times* of London or the *New York Times* that most students make their first acquaintance with microforms.

Large research libraries hold numerous specialized microform collections of potential interest to historians. No library, however, has the financial resources to purchase more than a fraction of the total number of collections available. As researchers generally want to minimize the time they spend working at other libraries and archives, they should keep in mind that a great deal of source material, both printed and manuscript, is available in microform, and that this material can sometimes be obtained through interlibrary loan. Most libraries have special catalogs or lists of their own microform collections. There are also a number of reference works that can be used to locate microform collections that may be available from other libraries. Two of the most useful of these are the comprehensive *Guide to Microforms in Print* and the more selective but more descriptive *Microform Research Collections: A Guide*.[14]

There are so many microform collections that is impossible for an instructor to give more than a hint of what is available. First, there are a number of large and comprehensive collections that can be found in many research libraries. These include *Early American Imprints*, which consists of the text of every extant book, pamphlet, and broadside published in colonial America and the United States from 1613 to 1819. There are ongoing projects to film all of the titles in the major British imprint catalogs (such as Pollard and Redgrave's *Short Title Catalogue*), and most books published in Great Britain prior to 1700 are now available on microfilm. There are also massive collections of English, French, German, and Spanish drama covering extensive time periods. Another major microform set, *Landmarks of Science*, includes the texts of major works in the history of science.

Other microform collections are much less comprehensive. These include individual books and journals, many newspapers, parliamentary debates, and private papers (such as those of the Adams family in the United States). Libraries of important figures such as British economist Adam Smith (1723–1790) have been microfilmed. Particularly useful for graduate students and faculty are collections covering the entire contents of archives or the papers of historically important people. Examples of such collections are the *Archivo de Hidalgo del Parral*, the main archive of the German National Socialist party, the *Records of the Socialist Labor Party of America*, the correspondence of Robert Peel, and the papers of Eugene Debs.

A final type of microform collection, which has been appearing more frequently in recent years, takes a selective or thematic approach. Such collections purport to present the ''key documents'' on a subject, often one of topical interest. Serious researchers are likely to find such collections inadequate, since they will want to decide for themselves what is important rather than view their subject through the eyes of an editor. But these thematic collections may be useful for undergraduate assignments.

Cartographic materials. Maps, atlases, aerial photographs, and the like are usually housed in separate map collections. These materials should be of use to practically all students of history. Lack of basic geographic information is a major problem for many undergraduates, apparently because of a total lack of education in geography at all grade levels. If you doubt this, try asking a class of undergraduates to locate the major European countries on a blank map. History instructors may well want to consider giving assignments using cartographic materials—perhaps accompanied by a brief orientation from the map librarian— to remedy this ignorance. Certainly by the time they reach the graduate level, future historians should be aware of the existence of historical atlases and have some knowledge of the uses of maps for historical research. They should know something about such basic cartographic concepts as projection, relief, and scale. They should also know that large-scale maps are usually found in sheet-map collections, not in atlases. Students should have some idea of the types of information that may be conveyed by maps (including vegetation, climate, soil types, human structures, population densities, political boundaries, and military movements). They should also be acquainted with the different uses of historical and contemporary maps, and with the problems of interpreting old maps. Early maps are often effective tools for introducing students to historical research using original source materials. The visual and aesthetic appeal of these artifacts often seems to convey to students a sense of the past more directly than other types of source materials.[15]

In map collections, as elsewhere, instructors should keep an eye out for recently introduced computerized information sources. A number of sophisticated mapping programs have been developed that may be available in your library. One of the most interesting of these is Chadwyck-Healey's *Supermap*, which allows students to make their own detailed thematic maps using census data. Several libraries are also testing *The Great American History Machine*, developed by David W. Miller and Stephen Greene at Carnegie-Mellon University, which allows students to create detailed maps using a variety of historical statistics.[16]

Computer files. Computerized data archives are becoming increasingly important to historians. Files of machine-readable data are occasionally found in libraries, although they are at least as likely to be housed at campus computing centers or at special facilities bearing such names as "social sciences data laboratory." There are national organizations that make available computerized data files, most notably the Roper Public Opinion Research Center, the National Technical Information Service, and the Inter-university Consortium for Political and Social Research. In part because of the existence of these organizations and the activities of government agencies such as the Bureau of the Census, many large data files are widely distributed on the academic scene. These files include extensive records from many U.S. censuses, the results of public opinion polls, and the files accumulated by scholars in the course of their research.

Visiting other libraries. In addition to interlibrary loan, mentioned earlier, students and faculty are likely to have some access to research collections in other libraries (in addition to public libraries, which are open to everyone). Such access should not be assumed, however, for every major research library. Many institutions belong to regional consortia, which allow their members to use each other's libraries. The membership and user policies of these consortia are unpredictable, and this is another matter that needs to be determined for each library. One particularly important consortium for many academic libraries is the Research Libraries Group (RLG, the parent organization of the RLIN database). The RLG includes many of the major libraries in the country, and students and faculty at RLG institutions have the right to use on-site (but not to check out) materials from each other's libraries.

Before making a trip to another library, it is a good idea to know whether that library is likely to have what you are looking for. We have previously mentioned the sources that may be used to locate the periodical holdings of different libraries. Many libraries now have their catalogs available in book form, as we have seen, and these catalogs can be consulted when available. OCLC and RLIN can be checked for holdings of more recent works, although it should always be kept in mind that the older titles of most large research libraries are often not included in these databases. The online catalogs of many academic libraries can also be searched remotely via Internet, a widely used telecommunications network. Where a listing of titles is not available, works exist that describe the general strengths of individual libraries. One such work is Robert Bingham Downs's *American Library Resources: A Bibliographical Guide.*[17] Also important is Lee Ash and William G. Miller's *Subject Collections,*[18] which is organized by subject and lists individual libraries under each subject and describes their collections.

NOTES

1. Eugene P. Sheehy and Rita G. Keckeissen, eds., *Guide to Reference Books*, 10th ed. (Chicago: American Library Association, 1986); Robert Balay, ed. and Eugene P. Sheehy, special editorial advisor, *Guide to Reference Books: Supplement to the Tenth Edition Covering Materials from 1985–1990* (Chicago: American Library Association, 1992). Kept up-to-date with periodic supplements.

2. The history of cataloging is itself a fascinating minor branch of intellectual history, which traces nothing less than humanity's most significant effort to provide order and access to the totality of human knowledge. The standard history of the subject is Dorothy Norris, *A History of Cataloging and Cataloguing Methods 1100–1850: With an Introductory Survey of Ancient Times* (London: Grafton, 1939). This is brought up-to-date by Gertrude London, "The Place and Role of Bibliographic Description in General and Individual Catalogs: A Historical Analysis," *Libri* 30 (October 1980): 253–84. These centuries of thought and effort form the background for contemporary cataloging rules and practices. In English-speaking countries, the current rules are in the *Anglo-American Cataloguing Rules*, 2d ed., ed. Michael Gorman and Paul W. Winkler (Ottawa: Canadian Library Association; London: Library Association Publishing Ltd.; Chicago: American Library Association, 1988).

3. Library of Congress, Subject Cataloging Division, *Library of Congress Subject Headings*, 14th ed. (Washington, D.C.: Library of Congress, 1991). The most recent edition of this publication consists of three massive volumes; a new edition appears every year.

4. University of Texas at Austin, Library, Latin American Collection, *Catalog of the Latin American Collection* (Boston: G.K. Hall, 1969); Sophia Smith Collection, *Catalogs of the Sophia Smith Collection, Women's History Archive, Smith College, Northampton, Massachusetts* (Boston: G.K. Hall, 1975).

5. Alfred W. Pollard, *A Short-Title Catalogue of Books Printed in England, Scotland, & Ireland: And of English Books Printed Abroad 1475–1640*, 2d ed., rev. and enl. begun by W. A. Jackson and F. S. Ferguson, completed by Katharine F. Pantzer (London: The

Bibliographical Society, 1976–); Donald Goddard Wing, *Short-Title Catalogue of Books Printed in England, Scotland, Ireland, Wales and British America, and of English Books Printed in Other Countries, 1641–1700,* 2d ed. (New York: Index Committee of the Modern Language Association of America, 1972–); ESTC is available as a machine-readable file on RLIN, as a microfiche catalog, and as a CD-ROM: *Eighteenth-Century Short-Title Catalogue* (London: The British Library, 1983–   ); *Nineteenth-Century Short-Title Catalogue* (Newcastle-upon-Tyne: Avero, 1984–1985).

6. Charles Evans, *American Bibliography; A Chronological Dictionary of All Books, Pamphlets, and Periodical Publications Printed in the United States of America from the Genesis of Printing in 1639 down to and Including the Year 1820* (New York: P. Smith, 1941–1959).

7. *The National Union Catalog, Pre–1956 Imprints: A Cumulative Author List Representing Library of Congress Printed Cards and Titles Reported by Other American Libraries* (London: Mansell, 1968–1981). This is brought up-to-date by the *National Union Catalog* (New York: Roman and Littlefield, 1963–1983), and by *NUC* (Washington, D.C.: Library of Congress, 1983–), which is issued on microfiche. The latter two publications are largely duplicated by the coverage in OCLC and RLIN (discussed below).

8. For an introduction to MARC cataloging and its history see Henriette D. Avram, "Machine-Readable Cataloging (MARC): 1986," in *Encyclopedia of Library and Information Science*, vol. 43 (1988), 136–60.

9. Joyce Duncan Falk, "OCLC and RLIN—Libraries at the Scholar's Fingertips," *Perspectives* (American Historical Association) 27 (May/June 1989): 1, 1–13, 17.

10. ERIC stands for Educational Resources Information Center. This organization, sponsored by the U.S. Dept. of Education, publishes two major indexes in the field of education: *Resources in Education* (RIE, previously *Research in Education*), and *Current Index to Journals in Education* (CIJE). ERIC also produces a large microfiche collection of materials indexed in RIE. This collection, which is available at most research libraries, includes many unpublished reports and papers. ERIC defines education very broadly, and this microfiche collection includes a large amount of historical material, particularly in the history of education and on the teaching of history.

11. For a brief introduction to CD-ROM and other recent developments in the electronic library see James Rice, "Managing Bibliographic Information with Personal Desktop Technology," *Academe* 75 (July-August 1989): 18–21. This special issue on "The Electronic Library" has several other articles of interest.

12. Little has been written about bibliographic database management programs, but for a discussion of one such program that also mentions several others, see David Y. Allen, "A Look at Notebook II," *Perspectives* (American Historical Association) 29 (May/June 1991): 10–12. See also David L. Clark, "Computer Database Management for Historical Research and Writing," *Perspectives* (American Historical Association) 29 (April 1991): 10–12.

13. Vladimir M. Palic, *Government Publications: A Guide to Bibliographic Tools,* 4th ed. (Washington, D.C.: Library of Congress, 1975).

14. *Guide to Microforms in Print* is an annual publication, issued since 1978 by *Microform Review* (Westport, Conn.); Susanne Gates Dodson, comp., *Microform Research Collections: A Guide* (Westport, Conn.: Meckler, 1984).

15. Two recent works on the interpretation of cartographic materials of particular interest to historians are: Mark S. Monmonier and George A. Schnell, *Map Appreciation* (Englewood Cliffs, N.J.: Prentice-Hall, 1988); David Buisseret, ed., *From Sea Charts*

to Satellite Images: Interpreting North American History through Maps (Chicago: University of Chicago Press, 1990).

16. See David W. Miller and John Modell, "Teaching United States History with the Great American History Machine," *Historical Methods* 21 (Summer 1988): 121–34. For information on the availability of the machine, contact Prof. David Miller, History Dept., Carnegie-Mellon University, Pittsburgh, PA 15213.

17. Robert Bingham Downs, *American Library Resources: A Bibliographical Guide* (Chicago: American Library Association, 1951). Supplements published in 1962, 1972, and 1981.

18. Lee Ash and William G. Miller, *Subject Collections*, 6th ed. (New York: R.R. Bowker, 1985).

6

Using Reference Sources

Charles A. D'Aniello

HOW TO READ A REFERENCE BOOK

A good deal of knowledge is necessary before one can use a reference book well. A reference book will only in a limited way compensate for one's ignorance. In their *How to Read a Book*, Mortimer J. Adler and Charles Van Doren explain that before one can use a reference book well one must:[1]

- have some idea of what one wants to know
- know what type of book is likely to answer the question best; but to do this one must possess a fair idea of all the types of reference books available
- know how to use the book once it is found
- know what is considered knowable

Still very much to the point is Isadore Gilbert Mudge's characterization of a reference book in the sixth edition of *Guide to Reference Books*:[2]

From the point of view of use, books may be divided into two groups: those that are meant to be read through for either information or enjoyment, and those that are meant to be consulted or referred to for some definite piece of information. Books of this second class are called reference books, and are usually comprehensive in scope, condensed in treatment, and arranged on some special plan to facilitate the ready and accurate finding of information. This special arrangement may be alphabetical, as [in] the case of most dictionaries or encyclopedias; chronological, as in historical outlines and similar compends; tabular, as in the case of statistical abstracts; regional, as in atlases; classified or systematic as in the case of some bibliographies, technical handbooks, etc. As such books are used for the finding of single definite facts, some alphabetical arrangement to the fact is usually needed, and if the book is itself arranged alphabetically, it is usually provided with a detailed alphabetical index. Works which follow any of these indicated arrangements are reference books, pure and simple, and are not used for consecutive reading.

There are other books however, which, while intended primarily to be read through for either information or pleasure, are so comprehensive and accurate in their treatment and so well provided with indexes that they serve also as reference books. . . . the treatment of some reference questions will involve first the use of some standard reference book in the reference collection, then reference from that to some book in the stack to which the formal reference book has furnished a clue, or even to some source of information outside the library.

When a historian reviews a reference book what does he or she look for? When the *Journal of American History* began including reviews of research and reference tools in 1987, the section editor, John D. Buenker, listed in the first installment the questions he wanted reviewers to address:

What is the purpose, scope, and content of the work? How clearly does the author state the intended purpose, selection criteria, plan of organization, and instructions for effective use? How faithfully does the work reflect those stated guidelines? Does the work cover the subject matter comprehensively? Are there significant omissions? Is the organization logical and facilitative? Are the finding aids logical and well conceived? Are there valuable appendixes or other supplementary material? What are the major strengths and weaknesses of the work? To whom would the work be most valuable and why?[3]

A case study is illustrative. Conor Cruise O'Brien's review in the *New York Review View of Books* of *A Critical Dictionary of the French Revolution* is a good example.[4] The nature of entries is examined, as is the structure of the index: the former for inclusiveness of coverage and contextual richness; the latter for ease of use. The historiographic orientation of critical entries is noted as is the affiliation of the contributors. Clearly, historians realize that reference tools are value laden and must be used and appreciated as such. Unlike reference sources in the sciences, reference tools in the humanities and social sciences present different interpretations of the same event, and thus, the consultation of overlapping tools is often both useful and necessary. Reference tools are listed and sometimes reviewed in the American Historical Association's *American Historical Review* (1895–   ) and regularly reviewed in the Organization of American Historian's *Journal of American History* (1964–   ). Reference sources on American history are also reviewed periodically in *Reference Services Review* (1973–   ) and, during its years of publication, in *American History: A Bibliographic Review* (1985–1990). Use *American Reference Books Annual* (1970–   ) for international coverage, as well as *Choice* (1964–   ) and *Library Journal* (1976–   ).

Historians ask questions of evidence: Who wrote the document? What does it reveal about the author? Under what conditions was it written? Who was it written to? What does it mean as a whole and in its constituent parts? How much of what was known to the writer can be known to the reader? In the simplest of terms, how closely can we enter the mind of the writer? From what we have before us, how much can we imagine? To enter the mind of the writer, the reader must know what is being said. To do so is often difficult and can lead to serious philosophical discourse but, simply put, without appropriate contextual and background knowledge the reader creates the past totally in his or her own image of it. Reference tools are stores of memories and can be used to answer the myriad basic questions that, when answered, begin to bring a text to life by furnishing the reader—the historian—with necessary contextual and background knowledge.

The various genres or categories of reference sources are described below. Some of these tools provide information, while others direct the user to information sources. Some do both. Different types of tools, alone or in combination, can often answer the same need, giving a date, a name, a location, or an explanation. Historical research is a back-and-forth process, and a researcher may return again and again to reference tools for critical bits of amplification or clarification. The tool that is used is a consequence of the question asked. But before one can begin to use reference works effectively, one must know what types of tools exist.

What follows is not intended as a general guide to history reference sources. Instead, specific tools are listed to show the range and diversity within each of the broad categories listed below, and sources used to complete the exercise that concludes this chapter are included. Standard general as well as historical sources are not necessarily mentioned. It should not be forgotten, as well, that any book can serve a reference function: providing explanation through its text and pointing out additional sources with its footnotes and bibliography, all made accessible by an index and a table of contents. For that matter, a newspaper or periodical run, like a series of almanacs, may serve a reference function through its implicit chronological coverage. Then, of course, whether one is a student or an academic, consulting a colleague or an expert may often be the quickest route to insight and information.

BEGINNINGS, OVERVIEWS, AND CLARIFICATIONS

Manuals. These books explain the craft of historical research. It is customary to include a chapter or two on reference and bibliographic aids in these sources. However, their major function is to explain what to do with historical evidence once it is gathered. Perhaps the most widely used research manual is Jacques Barzun and Henry F. Graff's *The Modern Researcher*, 5th ed. (Fort Worth, Tex.: Harcourt Brace Jovanovich, 1992).

Guides. These are the key to identifying reference materials. They provide access to material through their arrangement (the structure within which information is presented and sources are listed) and their indexing. In fact, the pathfinder exercise described in chapter 4 (see p. 80) is really an exercise in constructing a guide for one's personal use. Refer to pages 347–54 of the concluding bibliography for an annotated listing of general and basic guides useful for students of history and to chapter 7 for guides across the social sciences.

In most library guides one is able to find material either by genre or type of tool and by subject. What is the major historical biographical dictionary for British subjects? What is the most comprehensive historical atlas of the United States? Which indexes cover periodicals published in India? Two comprehensive reference guides designed to answer such questions are generally available in reference collections, the American *Guide to Reference Books*, 10th ed., ed. Eugene P. Sheehy (Chicago: American Library Association, 1986); and the British, *Walford's Guide to Reference Material,* volume 2, *Social and Historical Sciences, Philosophy and Religion*, 5th ed., ed. Alan Day and Joan M. Harvey (London: Library Association, 1989). The latter is part of a multivolume work that is somewhat less carefully produced than its American counterpart but much larger and more international in scope. Both cover sources in all languages. A very useful condensation of bibliographic knowledge is Thomas Mann's *Guide to Library Research Methods* (New York: Oxford University Press, 1987). Guides to historical reference materials include: Ronald H. Fritze, Brian E. Coutts, and Louis A. Vyhnanek, *Reference Sources in History: An Introductory Guide* (Santa Barbara, Calif.: ABC-Clio, 1990); the nationally focused Francis Paul Prucha, *Handbook for Research in American History: A Guide to Bibliographies and Other Reference Works* (Lincoln: University of Nebraska Press, 1987); and a great number of guides to the literature of specific events, topics, and individuals, for instance Sarah Carter and Maureen Ritchie, *Women's Studies: A Guide to Information Sources* (Jefferson, N.C.: McFarland, 1990). The *Harvard Guide to American History*, rev. ed., 2 vols., ed. Frank Freidel, with the assistance of Richard K. Showman (Cambridge: Belknap Press of Harvard University Press, 1974), and the *Guide to Historical Literature,* ed. George Frederich Howe (New York: Macmillan, 1961), are also guides in their bibliographic role of pointing out the most important materials for study and research. General historical guides are described in detail in *A Consumer's Guide to Research Guides for Historical Literature: Antiquity, the Middle Ages, Modern Western Europe, North America, and Latin America*, prepared by the Bibliography and Indexes Committee, History Section, Reference and Adult Services Division, American Library Association (Chicago: Reference and Adult Services Division, American Library Association, 1990). Covering history as well as other social science disciplines, and noting important monographs as well as standard reference works, is the distinguished *Sources of Information in the Social Sciences*, 3d ed., ed. William H. Webb (Chicago: American Library Association, 1986), and the outdated but often insightful *Social Science Research Handbook*, Raymond G. McInnis and James William Scott (New York: Barnes and Noble, 1974; New York: Garland, 1985). Of course, one can also use the subject catalog to identify reference sources.

Dictionaries and encyclopedias. When dealing with scholarly works, dictionaries and encyclopedias often cannot be differentiated, and therefore they are grouped together. Initiate a research project by identifying an appropriate essay or essays in such sources (dictionaries, encyclopedias, biographical dictionaries, reference sets, etc.) that offer bibliographic references for recommended sources.

Even if you have a monograph in hand, these concise overviews may help you to read it more effectively. For a handy list of major historical dictionaries and encyclopedias see *A Consumer's Guide to Ready Reference Sources in History: General, Antiquity, the Middle Ages, Modern Western Europe, the United States, and Latin America*, prepared by the Bibliography and Indexes Committee, History Section, Reference and Adult Services Division, American Library Association (Chicago: Reference and Adult Services Division, American Library Association, 1990). *First Stop: The Master Index to Subject Encyclopedias*, ed. Joe Ryan (Phoenix, Ariz.: Oryx Press, 1989), indexes essays across a wide range of specialized encyclopedias and dictionaries, as well as such reference sets as *The Cambridge Ancient History* and *The Cambridge History of Latin America*. General encyclopedias and single-focus works are excluded.

Dictionaries define words in terms of current and past usage. They may be devoted to general vocabulary (standard usage or slang, jargon, or the language of a particular place or period) or to the vocabulary and concepts of a particular discipline. Examples of the former are the *New Webster's Third International Dictionary of the English Language*, ed. Philip Babcock (Springfield, Mass.: Merriam-Webster, 1986), or the *Oxford English Dictionary*, 2d ed., 20 vols., prepared by J. A. Simpson and E. S. C. Weiner (Oxford: Clarendon Press, 1989). The OED is valuable for its presentation of changing definitions and usage over time, enabling the user to determine the meaning of a word during a particular period.

Examples of disciplinary dictionaries are *A Dictionary of Political Thought*, Roger Scruton (New York: Harper & Row, 1982), and Harry Ritter's *Dictionary of Historical Concepts* (Westport, Conn.: Greenwood Press, 1986). Ritter's work is actually more akin to an encyclopedia in its lengthy historiographic discussions and extensive bibliographies. A dictionary devoted to the terms likely to appear in biblical and theological works is *The Dictionary of Bible and Religion*, William H. Gentz (Nashville, Tenn.: Abingdon, 1986). Definition is the essence of literacy, and dictionaries are the most elemental but essential of handbooks. Whether you are confounded by an old document with unfamiliar words, the concepts of a discipline in which you are untrained, or with words that may have changed their meaning over time, dictionaries offer help.

Encyclopedias, more thoroughly than dictionaries, discuss people, concepts, things, and events, usually giving bibliographic references. Types include: general, *The New Encyclopaedia Britannica*, 15th ed., 30 vols. (Chicago: Encyclopaedia Britannica, 1974); national, *The Great Soviet Encyclopedia*, 31 vols., ed. A. M. Prokhorov (New York: Macmillan, 1973–1983); religious and/or ethnically focused, *Encyclopaedia Judaica*, 16 vols. (New York: Macmillan, 1971–1972); disciplinary or multidisciplinary, *The International Encyclopedia of the Social Sciences*, 18 vols., ed. David L. Sills (New York: Macmillan, 1968); topical, *The Middle Ages: A Concise Encyclopedia*, gen. ed. H. R. Loyn (New York: Thames and Hudson, 1989). It is interesting to note that the *Dictionary of the Middle Ages*, ed. Joseph R. Strayer (New York: Charles

Scribner's Sons, 1982–   ) is in thirteen volumes and much more likely to be thought of as an encyclopedia, and yet it deserves the name *dictionary* because it defines the vocabulary of medieval studies (see p. 168).

Other specialized examples of dictionaries or encyclopedias include: *Handbook of American Women's History*, ed. Angela Howard Zophy (New York: Garland, 1990); *Women's Studies Encyclopedia*, 3 vols., ed. Helen Tierney (Westport, Conn.: Greenwood Press, 1989–1991); *Dictionary of American History*, rev. ed., 7 vols. (New York: Charles Scribner's Sons, 1976); *Dictionary of Afro-American Slavery*, ed. Randall M. Miller and John David Smith (Westport, Conn.: Greenwood Press, 1988); *Afro-American Encyclopedia*, 10 vols., ed. Martin Rywell (North Miami, Fla.: Educational Book Publishers, 1974); *Encyclopedia of American Political History: Studies of the Principal Movements and Ideas*, 3 vols., ed. Jack P. Greene (New York: Scribner, 1984); *The Encyclopedia of Southern History*, ed. David C. Roller and Robert W. Twyman (Baton Rouge: Louisiana State University Press, 1979); and *Encyclopedia of the American Constitution*, 4 vols., ed. Leonard W. Levy (New York: Macmillan, 1986).

Study of the different editions of dictionaries and encyclopedias reveals changing attitudes and orientations across time. And, of course, contemporaneous dictionaries and encyclopedias produced from different orientations delineate opposing or varying viewpoints and perspectives. Thus if you wished a concise statement of the then-Soviet view on a particular topic you might consult the *Great Soviet Encyclopedia* and contrast it with the prevailing western view, presumably presented in *The New Encyclopaedia Britannica*. It is critical, however, to be aware of the dates of publication of the sources used. As well, someone researching the history of France would find more material in *Encyclopedia Universalis*, 20 vols. (Paris: Encyclopedia Universalis France, 1986–1974) and from at least one French perspective, than in a general encyclopedia published in another nation.

Reference sets. The history of the major nations and many historical periods and movements is treated in multivolume sets. Unlike encyclopedias or dictionaries, these sources offer continuity of treatment and provide their authors with the opportunity to explore and interpret the interrelationship and simultaneity of events and ideas. Here are included such standards as: *The Cambridge History of the British Empire*, 8 vols. (Cambridge: Cambridge University Press, 1929–1988); and *The Cambridge History of Japan*, 6 vols. (Cambridge: Cambridge University Press, 1989–1991).

Biographical dictionaries. These volumes vary in the extent of information they provide, from brief sketches to lengthy articles. Scholarly sets generally provide extensive bibliographies. They may be divided into three general, and frequently overlapping, groupings: contemporary, historical, and special interest. The various *Who's Who* dictionaries fall into the first category; the magisterial national sets, *The Dictionary of American Biography*, 20 vols. (New York: C. Scribner, 1928–1937) (United States), and *The Dictionary of*

National Biography, 22 vols., ed. Sir Lesley Stephen and Sir Sidney Lee (1885–1901; London: Smith, Elder, 1908–1909) (United Kingdom) fall into the second; and *Notable American Women, 1607–1950: A Biographical Dictionary*, 3 vols., ed. Janet Wilson James (Cambridge, Mass.: Belknap Press of Harvard University Press, 1971), and *The Dictionary of American Negro Biography*, ed. Rayford W. Logan and Michael R. Winston (New York: W. W. Norton, 1982), fall into the second and third. Other "special interest" sources cover "titled" populations or professions or offices, such as *Burke's Genealogical and Heraldic History of the Peerage, Baronetage, and Knightage* (London: Burke, 1826–   ) and *Dod's Parliamentary Companion* (London: Business Dictionaries, 1832–   ).

Biographical entries are also to be found in general encyclopedias and dictionaries. Among especially useful biographical sources are the volumes of the *Dictionary of Literary Biography* (Detroit: Gale Research Co., 1978–   ) and such sets published by Charles Scribner's Sons as *Ancient Writers: Greece and Rome*, 2 vols., ed. T. James Luce (New York: Charles Scribner's Sons, 1982). Among sources of biographies of historians, we find biographies of famous Americans in vols. 17, 30, and 47 of the *Dictionary of Literary Biography*; many of the world's most important deceased historians are included in the biographical volume of the *International Encyclopedia of the Social Sciences* and *The Blackwell Dictionary of Historians*, ed. John Cannon (Oxford: Blackwell, 1988). For a truly international overview, a publication sponsored by the Commission on the History of Historiography of the International Committee on the Historical Sciences, see *Great Historians from Antiquity to 1800: An International Dictionary* (Westport, Conn.: Greenwood Press, 1989), and *Great Historians of the Modern Age: An International Dictionary* (Westport, Conn.: Greenwood Press, 1991). Entries conclude with bibliographies. Both have been produced under the guidance of Lucian Boia, editor in chief, and associate editors Ellen Nore, Keith Hitchins, and Georg G. Iggers. Like dictionaries and encyclopedias, biographical dictionaries can be studied to reveal perceptions about an individual across time, place, and perspective; and the major national sets capture in time, through their inclusions and exclusions and their interpretations, the mainstream cultural orientation. Another type of source, a reference biography, is composed of interpretive essays, with bibliographies, on aspects of an individual's life, for example: *Thomas Jefferson: A Reference Biography*, ed. Merrill D. Peterson (New York: Charles Scribner's Sons, 1986).

The historian's biographical searching is now vastly facilitated by such major microfiche compilations of biographical dictionaries as the *British Biographical Archive*, managing ed. Laureen Baille, ed. Paul Sieveking (New York: Saur, 1984–   ); the *American Biographical Archive*, managing ed. Laureen Baille, ed. Gerry Easter (New York: Saur, 1986–   ); and *Black Biographical Dictionaries, 1790–1950* (Alexandria, Va.: Chadwyck-Healey, 1987). Also useful is the index to biographical dictionaries *Biography and Genealogy Master Index*, 2d ed. (Detroit: Gale Research Co., 1980–   ).

MISCELLANEOUS READY-REFERENCE AIDS

Abstracts and summaries. These are very helpful, convenient summaries of larger things. Such sources as *Survey of Contemporary Literature: Updated Reprints of 2,300 Essay-Reviews from Masterplots Annuals, 1954–1976*, and *Survey of Contemporary Literature Supplement: With 3,300 Bibliographical Reference Sources*, rev. ed., ed. Frank N. Magill (Englewood Cliffs, N.J.: Salem Press, 1977), obviously do not take the place of reading a book but they are invaluable for awakening old memories and explicating references. Plot synopses can also be found in various handbooks for readers and in such sources as: *The Oxford Companion to American Literature*, 5th ed., ed. James D. Hart (New York: Oxford University Press, 1983), and *The Oxford Companion to English Literature*, 5th ed., ed. Margaret Drabble (Oxford: Oxford University Press, 1985). Although listed here under *Statistical Sources, Historical Statistics of the United States, Colonial Times to 1970*, 2 vols. (Washington, D.C.: Government Printing Office, 1975), and *America Votes: A Handbook of Contemporary American Election Statistics* (New York: Macmillan, 1956–   ), are also digests and handy compilations.

Atlases and gazetteers. The former graphically, and the latter verbally, tell the researcher where a place is and, at least to some extent, what it is like. Historical versions or outdated editions tell one where a place was or what it was like. Among well-known sources are *The Columbia Lippincott Gazetteer of the World*, ed. Leon E. Seltzer (New York: Columbia University Press, 1962), and *Webster's New Geographical Dictionary* (Springfield, Mass.: Merriam-Webster, 1988). Gazetteers also are included in many atlases, and the index to an atlas can serve much the same use. Maps and atlases are not without orientations, and some of these tools have been designed to fulfill propagandistic ends through their creators' use of geographical projections and selection of symbols. More innocently, an atlas published in the United States will obviously deal thoroughly with the geography of the United States, usually covering Canada next in detail, and then the remainder of the globe to a far lesser extent.

There are universal, national, and special-purpose or topical atlases. Examples of historical atlases that go beyond mere maps and present a wealth of topical information in temporal and spatial perspectives are: *Sheperd's Historical Atlas*, 9th rev. ed., W. R. Sheperd (New York: Barnes and Noble, 1980); *Atlas of American History*, K. T. Jackson (New York: Charles Scribner's Sons, 1985); *Battlefield Atlas of the Civil* War, 2d ed., C. L. Symonds (Baltimore: The Nautical and Aviation Publishing Company of America, 1987); *A Historical Atlas of South Asia*, ed. E. Schwartzberg (Chicago: University of Chicago Press, 1976); and *Atlas of Early American History: The Revolutionary Era, 1760–1790*, ed. Lester J. Cappon (Princeton: Published for the Newberry Library and the Institute of Early American History and Culture by the Princeton University Press, 1976).

Commentaries. Such volumes are collections of observations, explanatory notes, or annotations on a text. While the genre is not restricted to religion, large reference collections usually hold several Bible commentaries. Important ones include: *Interpreter's One-Volume Commentary on the Bible: Introduction and Commentary for Each Book of the Bible Including the Apocrypha, with General Articles*, ed. Charles M. Laymon (Nashville, Tenn.: Abingdon Press, 1971); and *Interpreter's Bible: The Holy Scriptures in the King James and Revised Standard Versions with General Articles and Introduction, Exegesis, Exposition for Each Book of the Bible*, 12 vols. (New York: Abingdon Press, 1951–1957).

Chronologies. These volumes often present events by place and topic in a chronological sequence. They are invaluable for illustrating the topical and geographical sequence and simultaneity of events. What was happening in Russia when America declared its independence? What were the major cultural and political events in Europe in 1926? Some chronologies attempt to be universal, while others focus on nations or particular events or topics. Some favor one part of the world over another. Standard chronologies are: *The Encyclopedia of American Facts and Dates*, 8th ed., Gorton Carruth (New York: Harper and Row, 1987); *The Timetables of History: A Horizontal Linkage of People and Events*, B. Grun (New York: Simon and Schuster, 1987); and *Chronology of World History: A Calendar of Principal Events from 3000 BC to AD 1976*, 2d ed., G. S. P. Freeman-Grenville (London: Rex Collings, 1978). *The New York Public Library Book of Chronologies*, ed. Bruce Wetterau (Englewood Cliffs, N.J.: Prentice Hall, 1990) is a rich collection of separate chronologies that are organized under such topical groupings as explorers and exploration, technology, architecture and engineering, accidents and disasters, and science. Useful in identifying a historical figure's contemporaries is *Who Was When? A Dictionary of Contemporaries*, 3d ed., Miriam Allen de Ford and Joan S. Jackson (New York: Wilson, 1976). Chronological and organizational listings of prominent Americans are offered in *Notable Americans: What They Did, From 1620 to the Present*, 4th ed., ed. Linda S. Hubbard (Detroit: Gale Research Co., 1988).

Directories. Within a given population, directories identify individuals, organizations, and things. Directories can be used for purposes of identification or to lead one to additional sources of information, books or periodicals to consult, institutions to visit, or experts to contact. The most widely used association directory is *Encyclopedia of Associations*, 3d ed. (Detroit: Gale Research Co., 1961–   ). It describes each listed organization, giving its principals, publications, membership, and so forth. Learned societies publish directories of their members or of pertinent organizational units; for instance, the American Historical Association publishes *Directory of History Departments and Organizations in the United States* (Washington D.C.: American Historical Association, 1990/91–   ). Historians will also be interested in the *American Library Directory: A Classified List of Libraries in the United States and Canada, with Personnel and Statistical Data* (New York: R.R. Bowker, 1923–   ); *Directory of Historical Organizations in the United States and Canada*, 14th ed. (Nashville, Tenn.: American Association for State and Local History, 1990–   ); and the *Directory of American Scholars: A Biographical Dictionary* (New York: R.R. Bowker, 1942–   ), which includes a volume for historians. Janet Fyfe's *History Journals and Serials: An Analytical Guide* (Westport, Conn.: Greenwood Press, 1986), which treats 689 English-language titles of international reputation, will be of special interest, as will the less-descriptive but comprehensive *Historical Periodicals Directory*, 5 vols., ed. Eric H. Boehm, Barbara H. Pope, and Marie S. Ensign (Santa Barbara, Calif.: ABC-Clio, 1981–1985). There are also directories of directories, such as: *The Directory of Directories: An Annotated Guide to Business and Industrial Directories, Professional and Scientific Rosters, and Other Lists and Guides* (Detroit: Information Enterprises, 1980–   ); and *Guide to American Directories* (New York: McGraw-Hill, 1954–   ).

Quotation dictionaries and concordances. The common expressions of the past—its idioms, proverbs, maxims, and most quoted passages—are often only vaguely identifiable to us. Sometimes, to know what a writer was really thinking we need to know the correct or full reference for his or her quotation or allusion. Furthermore, the nature of quotation engaged in by an author reveals important aspects of his or her personality and intellectual orientation.

Quotation books can serve as indexes to ideas. Important quotation dictionaries include: *Familiar Quotations: A Collection of Passages, Phrases and Proverbs Traced to Their Sources in Ancient and Modern Literatures*, 15th and 125th anniv. ed., rev. and enl., ed. Emily Morison Beck (Boston: Little, Brown, 1980); *The Oxford Dictionary of Quotations*, 3d ed. (Oxford and New York: Oxford University Press, 1979); and *The International Thesaurus of Quotations*, ed. Rhoda Thomas Tripp (New York: Crowell, 1970).

Some dictionaries focus on topics, periods, countries, or persons, examples of which are: women's issues, *The Quotable Woman, 1800–1981*, comp. and ed. Elaine Partnow (New York: Facts on File, 1982); classical studies, *A Book of Latin Quotations with English Translations*, Norbert Guterman (Garden City, N.J.: Anchor Books, 1966); William Shakespeare, *The Quotable Shakespeare: A Topical Dictionary*, comp. Charles DeLoach (Jefferson, N.C.: McFarland and Company, 1988). Many nations have their own quotation dictionaries. It is important to remember that many sources are pruned periodically of quotations judged no longer common, and the historian may well wish to consult previous editions as well as sources that profess a more historical orientation. Dictionaries that focus specifically on history include, for example: *Famous Phrases from History*, C. F. Hemphill (Jefferson, N.C.: McFarland, 1982). Concordances, precise indexes to words and phrases used in a particular text or texts, should also be mentioned: for Shakespeare, *The Harvard Concordance to Shakespeare*, Melvin Spevack (Cambridge, Mass.: The Belknap Press of Harvard University Press, 1973); and for the Bible, *Exhaustive Concordance of the Bible*, James Strong (London: Hodder, 1894; New York: Abingdon, 1963).

Statistical sources. This grouping may include yearbooks, compendiums, or digests. Selective in nature, these aids serve as guides to more detailed statistical information through their footnotes and references as in the *Statistical Abstract of the United States* (Washington, D.C.: Government Printing Office, 1878–   ); or through references and extended discussions, as in *Historical Statistics of the United States, Colonial Times to 1970*, 2 vols. (Washington, D.C.: Government Printing Office, 1975); and *British Historical Statistics*, ed. R. R. Mitchell (Cambridge: Cambridge University Press, 1988). Both officially and commercially produced historical compilations are now common for many nations, and runs of once current statistical abstracts are important sources of historical information. Frequently current sources will also provide some retrospective coverage. Sources such as *America Votes* (New York: Macmillan, 1956–   ) may also be included under this heading.

Yearbooks and almanacs. Within the time frame of a year, these publications abstract a wide range of information. Some are compilations of their regularly issued parts such as *Facts on File: Weekly News Digest with Cumulative Index* (New York: Facts on File, 1940–   ), or are yearbooks published to update encyclopedias, or are annual summaries and analyses like the *Annual Register of World Events: A Review of the Year* (London, 1761–   ). Almanacs also fall into this category and provide a ready annual snapshot of the world; examples are: *Information Please Almanac, Atlas and Yearbook* (New York: Dan Golenpaul Associates, 1947–), and *World Almanac and Book of Facts* (New York: Newspaper Enterprise Association, 1868–   ). Indexes to newspapers such as the abstract-index *The New York Times Index* (New York: New York Times Company, 1913–), which indexes back to 1851, often can serve as a yearbook. Statistical abstracts may also be grouped under this heading.

INDEXES AND ABSTRACTS, BIBLIOGRAPHIES, AND UNION LISTS AND CATALOGS

Indexes and abstracts. Various concerns and disciplines all have their own indexes and abstracts, designed to enable one to identify articles with a high degree of specificity. Others span a wide range of disciplinary and topical concerns. (Abstracts and indexes are discussed in detail in chapter 5, and electronic sources are discussed in chapter 8.) A handy guide to the abstracts and indexes that are useful to historians is *A Consumer's Guide to the Current Bibliography of Historical Literature: Antiquity, the Middle Ages, Modern Western Europe, North America, and Latin America*, prepared by the Bibliography and Indexes Committee, History Section, Reference and Adult Services Division, American Library Association (Chicago: Reference and Adult Services Division, American Library Association, 1988).

Bibliographies, retrospective and recurrent. A bibliography is usually a list of printed material, but there are also filmographies, lists of films, and discographies, lists of recording discs. A bibliography may be descriptive of a physical item; selective, representing only what the compiler feels is most valuable; comprehensive, listing literally everything published on the subject; or descriptively or critically annotated or abstracted. Retrospective bibliographies capture literature on a topic between two points in time, while recurrent bibliographies are published regularly to stay current with a subject. Important retrospective bibliographies include: the Library of Congress's *Guide to the Study of the United States of America: Representative Books Reflecting the Development of American Life and Thought*, prepared under the direction of Roy P. Basler by Donald H. Mugridge and Blanche P. McCrum (Washington, D.C.: Government Printing Office, 1960). Then, of course, there are an endless number of topical bibliographies. The printed book catalogs of special libraries are important retrospective bibliographies because they reflect a focused collecting emphasis. A useful guide to these sources is the helpfully annotated *Guide to Published Library Catalogs*, Bonnie R. Nelson (Metuchen, N.J.: Scarecrow Press, 1982).

Recurrent bibliographies include: *Writings on American History* (Washington, D.C.: American Historical Association, 1902–1990); and *Writings on British History* (1901–1974) and its replacement, the *Annual Bibliography of British and Irish History* (Brighton, Sussex: Harvester Press, Atlantic Highlands, N.J.: Humanities Press for the Royal Historical Society, 1975–   ). Many nations are served by such annual services. Excellent guides to recurrent bibliographies are David Henige's *Serial Bibliographies and Abstracts in History: An Annotated Guide* (Westport, Conn.: Greenwood Press, 1986) and *A Consumer's Guide to the Current Bibliography of Historical Literature: Antiquity, the Middle Ages, Modern Western Europe, North America, and Latin America* (previously cited).

Finally, many events and individuals have been treated in their own bibliographies, and in monographs, dissertations, theses, and serials, which all contain important bibliographies. In addition to the catalog, one should always consult *Bibliographic Index: A Cumulative Bibliography of Bibliographies* (New York: H.W. Wilson, 1937/42–   ), an index to separately published bibliographies and to bibliographies containing more than fifty citations that are included in books and periodicals, many in foreign languages. For a more rigorous search use the sources noted below.

Bibliographies of bibliographies. These works are bibliographies that list bibliographies. They are powerful tools, for one of the first things anyone building a bibliography should do is to determine if a bibliography on the topic already exists. Bibliographies to be consulted, in order of possible consultation, are: *A World Bibliography of Bibliographies and of Bibliographical Catalogues, Calendars, Abstracts, Digests, Indexes, and the Like*, 4th ed., 5 vols., Theodore Besterman (Lausanne: Societas Bibliographica, 1965–1966); *Historical Bibliographies: A Systematic and Annotated Guide*, Edith M. Coulter and Melanie Gerstenfeld (Berkeley: University of California Press, 1935); *World Bibliography of Bibliographies, 1964–1974: A List of Works Represented by Library of Congress Printed Catalog Cards: A Decennial Supplement to Theodore Besterman, A World Bibliography of Bibliographies*, comp. Alice F. Toomey (Totowa, N.J.:

Rowman and Littlefield, 1977); and *Bibliographic Index* (cited in the preceding section), which should always be used to complement and update these sources. Topical bibliographies of bibliographies include *Bibliographies in American History: A Guide to Materials for Research*, 2 vols., Henry Putney Beers (Woodbridge, Conn.: Research Publications, 1982); and *Bibliographies in History: An Index to Bibliographies in History Journals and Dissertations Covering the U.S. and Canada* (Santa Barbara, Calif.: ABC-Clio, 1988).

Current awareness sources. Historians stay current with developments in the profession by reading newsletters, which contain announcements, news, and articles of practical interest, and with the journals that most closely correspond to their interests. Some journals include current bibliographies such as the *Journal of American History*. Until recently the American Historical Association published the bibliography of periodical articles, *Recently Published Articles* (1976–1990, three times a year), and the Institute for Scientific Information publishes and indexes table of contents pages from thousands of journals weekly in such *Current Contents* services as *Current Contents: Arts & Humanities* (Philadelphia: Institute for Scientific Information, 1979–) and *Current Contents: Social & Behavioral Sciences* (Philadelphia: Institute for Scientific Information, 1974–). History is covered most comprehensively in *Current Contents: Arts & Humanities*. These sources may be searched online; they are the final word in updating a bibliography.

Union lists and catalogs. These publications enable one both to identify and to locate a serial, monograph, or other item. For serials, such sources may also give brief but immensely valuable histories of publication. Important standard newspaper aids are: *American Newspapers, 1821–1936: A Union List of Files Available in the United States and Canada*, ed. Winfred Gregory (New York: Wilson, 1937); *History and Bibliography of American Newspapers, 1620–1820*, 2 vols., Clarence S. Brigham (Worcester, Mass.: American Antiquarian Society, 1947); and *Newspapers in Microform: United States, 1948–1983*, 2 vols. (Washington, D.C.: Library of Congress, 1984), which is a union list of microfilmed newspapers published from the colonial period to 1983. For a discussion of union lists and catalogs, see chapter 5.

EVALUATIVE SOURCES

Research reviews and book reviews. Whereas some disciplines publish ''annual reviews'' or ''advances in'' (that particular discipline) to highlight important advances in their disciplines, history is not so served. However, research review articles are becoming increasingly common in historical journals such as the *American Historical Review* and the *Journal of American History*. Review articles may be identified using *Historical Abstracts*, *America: History and Life*, *Bibliographic Index* (articles with over fifty references are often review articles), *Social Sciences Citation Index*, and *Arts and Humanities Citation Index*. As well, doctoral dissertations frequently begin with extensive literature reviews: use

Dissertation Abstracts International (Ann Arbor, Mich.: University Microfilms International, 1938–   ); and *Comprehensive Dissertation Index* (Ann Arbor, Mich.: University Microfilms International, 1973–   ). History journals may be general or specific in their coverage; all devote extensive space to book reviews and notices of books received.

Book reviews sometimes function as miniature literature reviews. Some instructors feel that there is a danger that by reading them students will not think for themselves, but the consultation of these sources opens windows of perception and often creates a context for understanding. Most scholars read the review of a book before actually reading the book. The journals of national historical associations usually provide extensive numbers of reviews and publish letters to the editor. In-depth reviews on works in American history are published in *Reviews in American History* (Westport, Conn.: Redgrave Information Resources, 1973–   ). Not a traditional review service, *Trends in History: A Review of Current Periodical Literature in History* (New York: Institute for Research in History, 1979–1990) was a useful summary and critical assessment of the literature, and was published in topical issues. Issues included: "Sex, History and Culture," "Black History," and "Family History." *Wilson Quarterly* (Washington, D.C.: Woodrow Wilson International Center for Scholars, 1976–   ) publishes review articles on many subjects, including history. Widely used English-language reviews of books published in English and other languages, and vehicles of scholarly conversation across the disciplines, are the *New York Review of Books* (1963–   ), the *Times Literary Supplement* (1902–   ), and, to a lesser extent, the *New York Times Book Review* (1896–   ). In addition to lengthy book reviews, these sources often include articles of general interest to the intellectual community.

Book review indexes. These are index reviews that have appeared in periodicals. Many book review indexes exist, but the most-well-known one is *Book Review Digest* (New York: H.W. Wilson, 1905–   ). Not only does it index reviews, but also it provides brief excerpts from them and gives the length of the total review. This information, combined with the source of the review, readily informs the knowledgeable user of the review's depth and importance. But remember that only seventy journals are indexed for reviews by this source. Among several other major sources, the ones especially useful for the scope and currency of their coverage are: *Social Sciences Citation Index* (Philadelphia: Institute for Scientific Information, 1973–); and *Arts and Humanities Citation Index* (Philadelphia: Institute for Scientific Information, 1976–   ). *America: History and Life* also cites references to book reviews. *Combined Retrospective Index to Book Reviews in Humanities Journals, 1802–1974*, 10 vols., ed. Evan Ira Farber, sen. ed. Stanley Schindler (Woodbridge, Conn.: Research Publications, 1982–1984), and *Combined Retrospective Index to Book Reviews in Scholarly Journals, 1886–1974*, 15 vols., ed. Evan Ira Farber, sr. eds., Ruth Matteson Blackmore, William Scott Buchanan, Frank Wayne Pilk (Arlington, Va.: Carrollton Press, 1979–) are very convenient sources for identifying reviews published in scholarly journals from 1802 to 1974.

PRIMARY SOURCES

Source collections and collected works. Students may be familiar with collections of primary source documents from their classes, and they should be encouraged to think of these sources and collections such as *Documents in American History*, 9th ed., Henry S. Commager (Englewood Cliffs, N.J.: Prentice-Hall, 1973); *Monumenta Germaniae Historica*, ed. Georg H. Pertz et al. (Hanover and Berlin, 1826–); and *New American World: A Documentary History of North America to 1612*, 5 vols., ed. with commentary by David Beers Quinn, with Alison M. Quinn and Susan Hillier (New York: Arno Press, 1979) as reference tools. The collected works of the principals in the area one is working on quickly become a reference source; thus anyone doing serious research on an aspect of Thomas Jefferson's life would require ready access to the most recent edited collection of his papers. This source would enable him or her to search quickly for the verification of information as well as provide essential, and organized, primary source material. Accompanying commentary and notes are invaluable reference aids.

Pictorial works. An illustration or a portrait often gives life and brings understanding to a historical discussion. Common sense will lead one to such sources as encyclopedias, monographs, and newspapers, as well as the collections of major depositories. Among the useful compilations for American history are: *Album of American History*, 5 vols., ed. James T. Adams et al. (New York: Charles Scribner's Sons, 1944–1961); *Dictionary of American Portraits*, Hayward Cirker et al. (New York: Dover, 1967); and *Pageant of America: A Pictorial History*, 15 vols., ed. Ralph H. Gabriel (New Haven, Conn.: Yale University Press, 1925–1929).

Indexes to archival and manuscript material. These are treated in detail in chapter 9.

AN ILLUSTRATION OF USE

William Lloyd Garrison (1805–1879) was a prodigious correspondent. He was widely read and he quoted, paraphrased, and alluded with ease, profusion, and forgivable inaccuracy. He knew many people and traveled extensively.

The exercise that follows illustrates the use of reference sources by employing them to "edit" a letter written by Garrison to Charles Reed in 1870.[5] Many questions are asked to prompt the use of specific types of reference resources and did not, and should not, result in annotations in a scholarly edition. The highest levels of scholarly editing can only take place once one is immersed in the life and times of one's subject. Students should begin by reading the following letter through, and they should be advised that an overview of Garrison's life and of the suffrage movement at the time would be appropriate reading before proceeding with the exercise. Consult monographs, located through the card catalog of the university's library, or the reference tools noted below to find such information or leads to it. *America: History and Life* might also be searched for an appropriate article: see Deborah P. Clifford, ''An Invasion of Strong-Minded Women: The Newspapers and the Woman Suffrage Campaign in Vermont in 1870,'' *Vermont History* 43 (Winter 1975): 1–19, which is cited by the editors (AHL reference 15A: 2312). Or, see the brief discussion and works cited under ''Suffrage'' in the *Encyclopedia of American Political History: Studies of the Principal Movements and Ideas*, elaborated on by appropriate entries in the *Handbook of American Women's History* and the entry ''Woman Suffrage Movement (U.S.),'' as well as the complementary entries on the woman's rights movement and abolitionism in volume three of Helen Tierney's *Women's Studies Encyclopedia*.

One quickly learns that the Vermont meeting was part of the campaign of the American Woman Suffrage Association, many of whose members were former abolitionists. In May 1869, in conflict with Republicans over their insistence that this was the ''Negro's hour'' and that the simultaneous enfranchisement of women would jeopardize the extension of suffrage to black males, the National Woman Suffrage Association (NWSA) was founded by Elizabeth Cady Stanton and Susan B. Anthony. The NWSA linked the demand for suffrage with a wide range of feminist issues. Six months later, Lucy Stone and Henry Blackwell founded the American Woman Suffrage Association (AWSA). The AWSA looked to the Republican party in woman's struggle for suffrage and supported the Fifteenth Amendment even though it did not give the vote to women. In fact, the Fourteenth Amendment, supported by Republican abolitionists, introduced the term ''male'' into the Constitution for the first time. The AWSA worked through the states to secure the vote and equal rights for women, although it supported a federal suffrage amendment. The AWSA hoped that, as women won suffrage in an increasing number of states, passage of a federal amendment would become inevitable. It should be clear that reference tools that cover slavery, women's history, and constitutional history, as well as the suffrage movement in particular, would be useful in understanding the meaning and full context of the letter.

Specific questions are asked of the document and answers are given, along with suggestions for general LC subject headings under which the reference sources used are cataloged. Obviously, for any one question any number of sources might be consulted. The sources listed, however, suggest the types of specialized resources that are available. Once one has determined the type of source likely to answer a question one should consult either the catalog or one of the general or specialized guides to reference materials. The latter choice offers the great advantage of preselection and annotation and is highly recommended.

Guides to reference material make the vast and diverse body of reference literature accessible to their users through their logical arrangement, indexes, and description of sources. They carry researchers beyond the resources of any one institution or the capabilities of its catalog. Early on graduate students should become familiar with the use of the *Guide to Reference Books* (Eugene P. Sheehy, ed. Chicago: American Library Association, 1986) and *Walford's Guide to Reference Material* (Albert John Walford, ed. London: The Library Association, 1989–91.) While smaller guides, mentioned throughout this book, are handy distillations and valuable introductions, they do not match the scope of these works. See section 13 of the concluding bibliography for a listing of research guides and manuals.

This exercise and the preceding discussion may be used as the basis for one or more introductory lectures or as an example of exercises that instructors are encouraged to design for themselves. It is easy to think of any number of additional questions that might be asked to require the use of still other types of sources.

The text of this letter appears as it has been printed in Walter M. Merril and Louis Ruchames, eds., *The Letters of William Lloyd Garrison*, vol. 6, *To Rouse the Slumbering Land, 1868–1879* (Cambridge, Mass.: The Belknap Press of Harvard University Press, 1981), 155–61.[6] The explanatory notes are not reprinted, although they were referred to in the preparation of the answers to the questions posed in this exercise.

All reference works used are noted below. It may be helpful to look under appropriate headings in the preceding discussion, where the works are listed and sometimes briefly discussed.

FROM WILLIAM LLOYD GARRISON[1]
[TO CHARLES REED][2]

Boston, Feb. 1, 1870[3]

To the President of the Convention:—

My disappointment at not being able to take part in the doings of the State Convention to be held to-morrow at Montpelier,[4,5] in behalf of suffrage for the women of Vermont[6] will be quite as great as that as which my absence can possibly create on the part of any who may be in attendance. But I am suddenly detained by a case of bereavement which I feel very tenderly, and by the funeral obsequies connected therewith, which I am pressingly urged to attend, in which, for various considerations, I feel obligated to participate, but which are also to be held to-morrow.[7]

Happily, in itself considered, my presence at the Convention is of the smallest possible consequence, for, with such gifted and persuasive advocates as Mrs. Howe, Mrs. Livermore and Mrs. Stone,[8] (to say nothing of others,) to vindicate the rights of their sex, I know of no man, however able or eloquent, whose voice can add anything to what will fall from their lips in regard to clearness of statement, force of reasoning, or power of speech. Nevertheless, I send my written testimony, which I might considerably expand if I were able to occupy the platform in person.[9,10]

Our Declaration of Independence places the rights of man upon a universal basis, takes them out of the arena of doubt or denial, for "self-evident truths" admit of no skepticism or controversy; stamps them as inalienable; makes their security the primary duty of government; asserts that governments derive their just powers *from the consent of the governed;* and maintains both the right and the duty of the people to alter or abolish any form of government becoming destructive of these ends, "and to institute new government, laying its foundation on such principles, and organizing its powers in such form, as to them shall seem most likely to effect their safety and happiness."[11]

But it is one thing to preach, and another thing to practise. It is easy to enunciate abstract prepositions that lay the ax at the root of all forms of tyranny; but it is not quite so easy to carry them out. The inconsistencies and paradoxes of human nature, in all ages, have been truly astonishing, but these were never so strikingly exemplified than in this instance. At lease one-half of the signers of the Declaration of Independence were the owners of slaves,[12] whose fetters were riveted so tightly that not even revolutionary violence could sunder them. By a singular coincidence, the last surviving signer was Charles Carroll of Carrollton,[13] who completed almost a century, but who clung to his slaves more tenaciously than to life itself, leaving more than a thousand of them to be inherited as so many cattle and swine. Even the author of the Declaration of Independence, Thomas Jefferson, was a slaveholder, and continued such to the end of his days, leaving all his victims in hopeless servitude.[14] Well might he exclaim, "What an incomprehensible machine is man![15] who can endure toil, famine, stripes, imprisonment, and death itself, in vindication of his own liberty; and the next moment be deaf to all those motives whose power supported him through his trial, and inflict on his fellow man a bondage, one hour of which is fraught with more misery than the ages of that which he rose in rebellion to oppose!"[16] At that very time there were in the colonies, chiefly at the South, not less than a half a million bondmen,[17] without any recognized genealogy, or nativity, driven to unrequited toil under the lash, legally held as goods and chattels, and liable to every conceivable indignity, wrong and outrage.

Of course, a people who wage a seven years' war for their own freedom and independence, in utter disregard of the tears and groans of those whom they were holding in an iron thraldom, could not be expected, in accomplishing their object, to form a government under which it would be unlawful to hold slaves;[18] for the first step downward makes the second one comparatively easy. We know what followed, and how it was done. A constitution was adopted; allowing the prosecution of the foreign slave trade indefinitely, providing a three-fifths slave representation in Congress, and the restoration of fugitive slaves to their masters;[19] and throwing a national safeguard around the slave system by pledging the whole naval and military power of the government to suppress domestic insurrection.

In view of such shocking recreancy to the cause of human liberty, and such a mockery of the principles of popular government, well might heaven be indignant and the earth stand aghast. No marvel that, for a period of seventy years, our democratic pretensions were a jest and a by-word throughout all Europe. That was where we stood, as constitutionally organized, from 1787 until the day of our national visitation in 1861, when a just God laid judgement to the line, and righteousness to the plummet; and the hail swept away our refuge of lies, and the waters over-flowed our hiding place.[20] Then the pillars of our so-called temple of liberty, one after another, began to fall; then the union, which had been so constructed as to propitiate an imperious slave oligarchy,[21] was by the same slave oligarchy cloven asunder; then there was "a sound of battle in the land, and of great destruction;"[22] then "Babylon was taken, and Bel confounded, and Merodach broken in pieces, and all their idols confounded."[23,24] Thanks be to God that we have been saved, even as by fire;[25] that under our national banner, instead of millions of slaves crouching in fear, all are personally free; that our union is no longer cemented with innocent blood; the old "covenant with death"[26] has given place to a renovated constitution; and that henceforth we are to advance steadily in the path of liberty and equality; conforming our national practice more and more closely to the principles of our Declaration of Independence.

Since the creation of the world, there has been no diminution of, no addition to, the rights of human nature. They are now precisely what they were from the beginning—primary, inherent, inalienable, equal. How reads the earliest announcement of this sublime postulate? "So God created man in his own image, *male and female created he them.*[27] And God blessed them, and God said unto them, Be fruitful and multiply, and replenish the earth, and subdue it; and have dominion over the fish of the sea, and over the fowl of the air, and over every living thing that moveth upon the face of the earth." Yet it has required six thousand years[28] to get even the rights of man, technically as man, recognized in any part of the world, nor has this yet been fully attained—not even in our own land. By the adoption of the Fifteenth Constitutional Amendment[29] this issue is soon, doubtless, to be disposed of among us, once for all; so that every man, simply by virtue of being of the masculine gender, shall be clothed with all civil and political rights.

Another question, equally far-reaching and important, is now challenging universal consideration, and for the solution of which your Convention is held.

If the only legitimate government is that which is of the people, by the people, and for the people,[30] and if it be true that the consent of the governed[31] confers upon governments their just powers, then the next issue is as to the rights of woman—that is, the rights of one half of the whole people[32]—rights not only hitherto undefined, but in our own, as well as in all other countries, recklessly trodden under foot. I enter into no calculations as to the exact time it will require to settle this issue; but that it will be triumphantly settled, at no distant day, in favor of political equality for women as for men, I entertain not a doubt. For the spirit of the age is increasingly radical and reformative. All the signs of the times are auspicious in this direction. The women not only of the United States, but of Christendom itself, are beginning to move under a common inspirational feeling, with reference to their better development and nobler destiny. On both sides of the Atlantic, their cause to the fullest political extent, is espoused by some of the ablest men in public life. At this very moment of writing, my morning paper announces that a large meeting was recently held in Edinburgh, Scotland,[33] to promote the movement for the enfranchisement of women,[34] at which Mr. Duncan M'Laren, M.P. presided, and Prof. Calderwood, Mr. Jacob Bright, M.P.; Prof. Masson, Dr. Lyon Playfair, M.P., Rev. Dr. Wallace, Sir David Wedderburn, M.P.,[35] and other leading men, took part in the proceedings. In England, France, Germany, Hungary, Italy, Russia, the women are arousing to a sense of their depressed and unnatural condition, and taking the necessary initiatory measures for a redress of their grievances. In this country the movement has already attained colossal proportions. The medical, legal and clerical professions are largely taking stock in it. The Chief-Justice of the United States[36] gives it his approval. Distinguished Senators and Representatives of Congress are marching under its banner. The popular vote of Kansas showed a powerful minority, which at the next trial will in all probability prove a majority,[37] in favor of making womanhood coequal with manhood in the matter of suffrage. This has actually been secured in the territory of Wyoming,[38] where a local government, with legislative powers, is based upon the equal rights of all classes. A resolution is before the legislature of Ohio,[39] looking to an amendment of the State Constitution to the same extent.

Vermont is soon to decide at the polls whether she will so amend her Constitution as to give the ballot to the hand that can hold and the brain that can wield it, without regard to sex. Should she fail (as it is to be hoped that she will not,) at the first trial, to make that atonement which every state is bound to render, it will be no proof that she puts herself intelligently and inexorably in opposition. Her "sober second thought" will quickly come to the rescue, for it is hers to lead, rather than to follow, in the struggle for impartial liberty and equal rights, I cherish a very high appreciation of the intelligence and moral worth of her people;[40] and I shall never forget that it was first on her soil that I began my public advocacy of the cause of the enslaved millions of the South,[41,42] who are now rejoicing in their unconditional emancipation.

As all the objections that were urged against their liberation are now seen to have been frivolous, hollow, absurd, or wicked—so those now urged in opposition to the enfranchisement of women will, in the end, be regarded as equally ridiculous, empty and worthless. In the peace and order of society, in the maintenance of freedom, in the administration of justice, in the protection of life and property, in the welfare and prosperity of the nation, women have as much at stake as men. Why, then, should they not have an equal vote and voice?

Your co-worker,

Wm. Lloyd Garrison[43,44,45,46]

1—Who was William Lloyd Garrison?

Answer: America's most famous abolitionist. Garrison (1805–1879) worked closely with female abolitionists and refused to participate in the World's Anti-Slavery Convention in London in 1840 when he learned that women were excluded. In his old age he "fought unceasingly" for woman suffrage. *Dictionary of American Biography* 4:168–72.

Identification of Sources: An important historical figure, therefore any American biographical source will contain an extensive entry. America's most scholarly collection is the *Dictionary of American Biography*, which indicates his general commitment to women's rights. One will also find numerous entries in the *American Biographical Archive*. Look for suggestions on monographs in the *Harvard Guide to American History* and in the essays of general encyclopedias, or simply consult the catalog. In addition to his name, use LC subject headings: United States—Biography and for the *Harvard Guide*: United States—History—Bibliography; United States—History—Study and Teaching.

2—Who was the president of the convention?

Answer: Charles Reed (1814–1873) was a lawyer with a degree from Harvard who held a variety of public offices. He was interested in temperance, women's rights, and education, and he advocated a woman's suffrage amendment to Vermont's constitution. "Men called the first woman's rights convention, and chose Hon. Charles Reed of Montpelier as its presiding officer, as well as president of the State association." The convention was part of the American Woman Suffrage Association's Vermont campaign in support of a suffrage amendment to be considered by the state's legislature. *History of Woman Suffrage* 3:386.

Identification of Sources: It was necessary for the original editors to determine that Reed was president of the convention since the letter was not addressed to him. They cite

History of Woman Suffrage 3:386. To identify a comprehensive history of the suffrage movement consult the *Harvard Guide to American History*. Search the index under "Women and suffrage movement, 445–46," which leads to section "19.7.2 Feminism" and a citation for *History of Woman Suffrage*, 6 vols., Elizabeth Stanton, Susan B. Anthony, and M. J. Gage (1881–1922), a standard reference source for the topic. The *Handbook of American Women's History* notes that it took ten years to produce the first three volumes, "each one thousand pages long, consisting of letters, speeches, petitions, reminiscences, and convention proceedings—all tied together with a brilliant and passionate radical suffragist analysis. As Stanton predicted, these volumes remain the major source." To find histories of the movement directly use LC subject headings: Women—Suffrage—United States, Women—Suffrage. This information might also be obtained from a Vermont newspaper: consult *American Newspapers, 1821–1936*. The letter was printed in the *Woman's Journal*, then the organ of the American Woman Suffrage Association, on 19 February 1870. Determining this publication's existence would be another approach, and it is excerpted heavily in the *History of Woman Suffrage*. The *Handbook of American Women's History* notes: "As a political arm of suffrage associations . . . reprinted meeting and convention addresses and notes, reported on national and international political and social news." Its report states that Reed was state librarian and president of the State Woman Suffrage Association. Reed is not listed in any of the standard major or even secondary biographical sources. The editor of this letter gives the *Vermont Historical Gazetteer* (Montpelier 1882) 4:322, 325, 513–15, as the source for Reed's biographical sketch. If standard sources fail one should use the evidence provided to decide how to proceed. He is a citizen of Vermont, so anticipate that Reed will appear in biographical sources devoted to that state. If such sources are not available locally, call a major Vermont library or the Vermont Historical Society. (See question 10.)

3—On which day of the week did 1 February fall in 1870?

Answer: In 1870, 1 February fell on a Tuesday. *The World Almanac and Book of Facts: 1991*, 294–95.

Identification of Sources: Perpetual calendars enable one to create calendars for a wide span of years both forward and backward in time. They are regularly found in almanacs. Use LC subject heading: Almanacs, American.

4—What was the population of Montpelier, Vermont, in 1870?

Answer: The population of Montpelier, Vermont, in 1870 was 3,023 people. Use the *Ninth Census of the United States: Statistics of Population, Tables I to VIII Inclusive* (Washington D.C.: Government Printing Office, 1872); see "Table III, Civil Divisions Less Than Counties—State of Vermont," 278. Montpelier is listed under Washington County.

Identification of Sources: Demographic data is needed; however, the standard statistical compilation, *Historical Statistics of the United States, Colonial Times to 1970* does not give the answer, and students should quickly conclude that the census data itself must be consulted. Use LC subject heading: United States—Statistics; United States—Census.

5—Within the state of Vermont, where is Montpelier located?

Answer: It is located in Washington County, central Vermont, on the Winooski River, five miles northwest of Barre; 44°15′ N, 72°34′ W; altitude about 500 feet. *The Columbia Lippincott Gazetteer of the World.*

Identification of Sources: Maps or gazetteers will provide this information. Use LC subject heading: Geography—Dictionaries.

6—What was the female population of Vermont in 1870?

Answer: A total of 165,000 women lived in Vermont in 1870. Use the table "Population of States, by Sex, Race, Urban-Rural Residence, and Age: 1790 to 1970," in *Historical Statistics of the United States, Colonial Times to 1970*, 35. Consultation of the census schedule itself, unnecessary except in the most particular instances, gives slightly different counts—164,830 females and 165,721 males for a total state population of 330,551. Use "Table XXIII—Ages of the Aggregate Population" in *Ninth Census-Volume II: Vital Statistics of the United States: Embracing the Tables of Deaths, Births, Sex, and Age, To Which Are Added the Statistics of the Blind, the Deaf and Dumb, the Insane, and the Idiotic* (Washington, D.C.: Government Printing Office, 1872), 560.

Identification of Sources: Use LC subject headings: United States—Statistics; United States—Census.

7—List some important milestones in the women's suffrage movement that occurred in 1870.

Answer: Lucy Stone founded the *Woman's Journal*, the official organ of the National Woman Suffrage Association; on 1 August women voted for the first time in America in a Utah election. The legislature of Wyoming passed a women's suffrage bill on 12 February. *The Encyclopedia of American Facts and Dates*. Note that the *Woman's Journal* did not become the official publication of the National American Woman Suffrage Association until 1890. Before then it had been the official journal of the American Woman Suffrage Association. *Handbook of American Women's History*, 672.

Identification of Sources: See a chronological listing of important events in American history. Use LC subject heading: United States—History—Chronology.

8—Identify Mrs. Howe, Mrs. Livermore, and Mrs. Stone.

Answer: The essays in the *Dictionary of American Biography* and *Notable American Women* present different perspectives on Julia Ward Howe (1819–1910). The former concentrates on her public life, noting that she worked with her husband, Samuel Gridley Howe, knew "all the prominent Massachusetts intellectuals and reformers of the period," and, because of a host of personal characteristics including "a sense of humor that disarmed irritation," was one of the greatest of woman organizers. She was active in all aspects of the woman's movement: suffrage, peace, woman's clubs, and abolition. In youth she wrote lyrics, but later in life, essays. She is perhaps best known as the author of "The Battle Hymn of the Republic" and as one of the founding members of the American Woman Suffrage Association. The essay in *Notable American Women* explores the tensions that troubled her marriage and interprets much of her early writing in this light. Far more attention is given there to her post–1870 involvements than in the *Dictionary of American Biography*. It is also noted that in 1870 she was a founder of the *Woman's Journal* and in 1898 served on a committee that reunited the suffrage movement. *Dictionary of American Biography* 5:291–92, and *Notable American Women* 2:225–29.

The *Dictionary of American Biography* describes Mary Ashton Rice Livermore (1820–1905) as a reformer, temperance leader, suffragist, and author. The Civil War convinced her that women's suffrage was the most direct route to "curtailing the liquor traffic, improvements in public education, and the alleviation of many problems of poverty." Curiously, her work with the American Woman Suffrage Association is not mentioned.

The entry in *Notable American Women* discusses in detail her extensive work with the Sanitary Commission during the Civil War. She was happily married and, in fact, her husband advocated women's suffrage before she did. As noted in the *Dictionary of American Biography*, however, the Civil War led her to advocate women's suffrage as well. She was a founding member of the American Woman Suffrage Association, which she served as president from 1875 to 1878, and founder of *The Agitator* in 1869, which merged with the *Woman's Journal* in 1870. Essays in each dictionary emphasize her skills as an orator. *Dictionary of American Biography* 6:306–7, and *Notable American Women* 2:410–16.

Lucinda Hinsdale Stone (1814–1900), according to the *Dictionary of American Biography*, possessed "a rare eloquence and a singularly beautiful voice." She was an ardent abolitionist and "uncompromising on the question of woman's rights." She and her husband worked untiringly to have the word "male" struck from the Fourteenth Amendment when it was pending before Congress. She was a founding member of the American Woman Suffrage Association and raised most of the money used to found the *Woman's Journal*. *Notable American Women* covers the same ground in greater and more revealing detail, giving more emphasis to her contributions as an abolitionist and her collaboration with Garrison, her work with the *Woman's Journal*, and the character of her marriage. *Dictionary of American Biography* 9:80–81, and *Notable American Women* 3:387–90.

Identification of Sources: The major biographical set for women in American history is *Notable American Women*. While the above women are included in the *Dictionary of American Biography*, their treatment is less thorough than in the former source. As a rule women are underrepresented in the DAB. For less-scholarly essays, one may also consult the *American Biographical Archive*. Use LC subject headings: Women—United States—Biography; United States—Biography.

9—Identify an account of the proceedings of the convention and determine if Garrison's letter was read before that body.

Answer: Printed in the *Woman's Journal*, the organ of the American Woman Suffrage Association, 19 February 1870: "Great disappointment was felt at the absence of Mr. Garrison, whose attendance had been promised, but whose absence was compelled by the death of a dear friend. Mr. Garrison is one of the idols of Vermont, and if all the other speakers from abroad had remained away, it would have occasioned less regret than was experienced from his non-appearance. Though a grand letter was read to the people, sent by Mr. Garrison, it failed to reconcile them." The *Journal* praises the meeting for dispelling the perception that the Woman Suffrage movement was an anti–man's movement.

Identification of Sources: One would expect the major serial publication of a political movement to report such news, and it did. (See question 2.)

10—Give the address for the Vermont State Historical Society and the addresses for other historical societies or libraries in Montpelier.

Answer: Montpelier Heritage Group, Inc., P.O. Box 671, 05602; Vermont Historical Society, 109 State Street, 05602; and Vermont State Archives, 26 Terrace Street, 05602. Libraries include the Vermont Historical Society Library and the Vermont Department of Libraries, 111 State Street, c/o State Office Building Post Office, 05602. Use the *Directory of Historical Organizations in the United States and Canada* and the *American Library Directory*.

Identification of Sources: There are standard directories for this purpose. In a pinch the appropriate telephone book would also work. Use LC subject headings: Libraries—Directories; Libraries—United States—Directories; History—Societies, etc.—Directories; United States—History—Societies, etc.—Directories.

11—Where in the Declaration of Independence does this passage fall?

Answer:

We hold these truths to be self-evident, that all men are created equal, that they are endowed by their creator with certain inalienable Rights, that among these are Life, Liberty, and the pursuit of Happiness.

That to secure these rights, Governments are instituted among Men, deriving their just powers from the consent of the governed.

That whenever any Form of Government becomes destructive of these ends, it is the Right of the People to alter or to abolish it, and to institute new Government, laying its foundation on such principles and organizing its power in such form, as to them shall seem most likely to effect their Safety and Happiness. Prudence, indeed, will dictate that Governments long established should not be changed for light and transient causes. *Documents of American History.*

Identification of Sources: A copy of the Declaration can be found in just about any American encyclopedia but less common documents, along with common ones, are found in sourcebooks. Use LC subject heading: United States—History—Sources.

12—How many people who held slaves signed the Declaration of Independence, and what were the views of the signers on the issue of slavery?

Answer: Counting John Hancock, fifty-six people signed the Declaration of Independence. Reference books consulted do not provide information on slaveholding. The rough draft of the declaration attacked the king for "captivating and carrying" blacks into slavery, for opposing attempts to end the "excisable commerce," and for "exciting these very people to rise in arms against us and to purchase that liberty of which he has deprived them, by murdering the people on whom he also obtruded them; thus paying off former crimes committed against the liberties of one people, with crimes which he urges them to commit against the lives of another." Representatives from South Carolina and Georgia objected to its inclusion. See the *Afro-American Encyclopedia*, "Declaration of Independence" and "Slavery and the Declaration of Independence." Consulting "Declaration of Independence" in *The Dictionary of Afro-American Slavery*, one finds that "Jefferson argued that it would be both inconsistent and hypocritical to condemn political slavery without denouncing black slavery."

Identification of Sources: A copy of the declaration can be secured from any number of sources. Once a copy of the document is found it is easy to count the number of names. In addition to reference books, collective biographies of signers or monographs on the declaration itself might be consulted. While in such searches basic Boolean logic can work, if you look up the Declaration of Independence in an African-American history source, it does not uncover a count. Nonetheless, entries in reference sources on the relevance of the Declaration for African-Americans are plentiful. Use LC subject headings: Slavery—United States—History—Dictionaries; Afro-Americans—Dictionaries and encyclopedias.

13—Identify Charles Carroll of Carrollton.

Answer: The last surviving signer of the Declaration of Independence (1737–1832). Carroll failed in his efforts to eliminate the slave trade by constitutional provision and to initiate emancipation by law in the 1780s; he was also president of the American Colonization Society. While *The Encyclopedia of Southern History* and the *Afro-American Encyclopedia* entries mention the above, the essay in the *Dictionary of American Biography* 2:522–23, says nothing at all about slavery.

Identification of Sources: This difference in treatment offers an opportunity to point out to students the varying orientations and approaches taken by the authors of reference sources and to explain these variances in terms of time and bias. The *Dictionary of American Biography* would likely be the first place a student would search. Looking in a source focused on slavery or African-American history ensures that if one finds anything it will address this topic. See also the *American Biographical Archive*. Use LC subject headings: United States—Biography—Dictionaries; Afro-Americans—Dictionaries and encyclopedias; Carroll, Charles, 1737–1832.

14—Summarize Thomas Jefferson's attitude toward slavery.

Answer: "There were ambivalences in his attitude toward Negroes as a race and a lack of public support for anti-slavery programs, but his philosophical opposition to slavery as an institution was strong. His overall support of civil liberties, despite some inconsistencies, inspired later democrats" (*Encyclopedia of Southern History*, 647). "Jefferson remained convinced that blacks were equal to whites in one important sphere, the moral sense. Otherwise, Jefferson regarded blacks as mentally inferior to whites, innately so" (*Dictionary of Afro-American Slavery*, 375–76). Jefferson did advance his suspicion that the Negro was inferior to the white in both body and mind. He added, however, that their degree of talent was not a measure of their rights (*Afro-American Encyclopedia* 5:1318). The most sensitive discussion is found in a recent source exclusively devoted to Jefferson: Joseph C. Miller, "Slavery," in *Thomas Jefferson: A Reference Biography*, 417–35.

Identification of Sources: Were one to rely solely on the essay in the *Dictionary of American Biography* one would think that Jefferson had no position on slavery. One discovers only that Jefferson's slaves liked him, because in 1789 he arrived at Monticello and was "welcomed tumultuously by his rejoicing slaves" and that with the Ordinance of 1787 he had attempted to forbid slavery "in all the western territory after 1800." Written by Dumas Malone in the early 1930s, it reflects the thinking of the time during which it was written. Discussions may be found in sources focused on Jefferson, the South, African-American history, or the history of slavery in the United States. Use LC subject headings: Southern States—History—Dictionaries; Presidents—United States—Biography; Slavery—United States—History—Dictionaries; Afro-Americans—Dictionaries and encyclopedias; and, of course, Jefferson, Thomas, 1743–1826.

15—What is the probable literary inspiration for Jefferson's exclamation: "What an incomprehensible machine is man!"?

Answer: Hamlet, 2.2.303: "What a piece of work is man! how noble in reason! how infinite in faculties! in form and moving, how express and admirable! in action, how like an angel! in apprehension, how like a god! the beauty of the world! the paragon of animals! And yet, to me, what is this quintessence of dust?" *The Quotable Shakespeare:*

A Topical Dictionary, *Familiar Quotations*, and, with sufficient patience, *The Harvard Concordance to Shakespeare*.

Identification of Sources: Because this is an adaptation, it is necessary for the researcher to have some familiarity with the same literature that Jefferson was familiar with. One needs to know the phrases that may have rested in his mind. Perhaps this is from Shakespeare. A concordance to his work is the most certain, though not necessarily easiest way to locate a passage. An easier but less comprehensive approach would be to consult a general or specialized dictionary of quotations. Use LC subject headings: Shakespeare, William, 1564–1616—Dictionaries, indexes, etc.; Shakespeare, William, 1564–1616—Quotations; Quotations, English; Shakespeare, William, 1564–1616—Concordances.

16—In which of his works, and in what context, does Thomas Jefferson write: "What an incomprehensible machine is man! who can endure toil, famine, stripes, imprisonment, and death itself, in vindication of his own liberty."?

Answer: Part of a letter to French historian Jean Nicolas Demeunier, 26 June 1786, to correct an essay to appear in *Encyclopédie Méthodique*, a major reference work whose first four volumes had already been published in 1784. A fuller context is as follows:

M. de Meusnier, where he mentions that the slave-law has been passed in Virginia, without the clause of emancipation, is pleased to mention that neither Mr. Wythe nor Mr. Jefferson were present to make the proposition they had mediated; from which people, who do not give themselves the trouble to reflect or enquire, might conclude hastily that their absence was the cause why the proposition was not made; and of course that there were not in the assembly persons of virtue and firmness enough to propose the clause for emancipation. This supposition would not be true. There were persons there who wanted neither the virtue to propose, nor talents to enforce the proposition had they seen that the disposition of the legislature was ripe for it. These worthy characters would feel themselves wounded, degraded, and discouraged by this idea. Mr. Jefferson would therefore be obliged to M. de Meusnier to mention in some such manner as this, "Of the two commissioners who had concerted the amendatory clause for the gradual emancipation of slaves Mr. Wythe could not be present as being a member of judiciary department, and Mr. Jefferson was absent on the legation to France. But there wanted not in that assembly men of virtue enough to propose, and talents to vindicate this clause. But they saw that the moment of doing it with success was not yet arrived, and that an unsuccessful effort, as too often happens, would only rivet still closer the chains of bondage, and retard the moment of delivery to this oppressed description of men. What a stupendous, what an incomprehensible machine is man! *The Papers of Thomas Jefferson, Vol. 10: 22 June to 31 December 1786*, ed. Julian P. Boyd (Princeton: Princeton University Press, 1954), 63.

Identification of Sources: Once quotation dictionaries fail and an individual is not served by a concordance, then there is no choice but to scan through the body of the writer's work. The document from which this quote is taken is found in both *The Papers of Thomas Jefferson*, 24 vols., ed. Julian P. Boyd (Princeton: Princeton University Press, 1950–83), and *The Writings of Thomas Jefferson*, Merrill D. Peterson (New York: Viking Press, 1984). The index to the former has an entry "Slavery—emancipation clause not passed in Va, GA, 10:62–63, and the latter carries the index entry "Slavery, emancipation, 5, 44, 264, 591–92, 799–800, 804–805, 1343–46." A little patience works in both instances. The larger work contains commentary that places the quotation in context. Often a biography, through its index, will help. For instance, see Fawn M. Brodie, *Thomas Jefferson: An Intimate History* (New York: W. W. Norton, 1974), 184, which indexes the passage under "Jefferson, Thomas—Slaves and Slavery, to Demeunier on emancipation, 184." Use LC subject heading: Jefferson, Thomas, 1743–1826.

17—At the beginning of the Revolution, how many slaves lived in the colonies that were to become the original thirteen states?

Answer: This summation is for Negroes, all of whom were not slaves, and is for 1770. New Hampshire–654; Massachusetts–4,754; Rhode Island–3,761; Connecticut–5,698; New York–19,112; New Jersey–8,220; Pennsylvania–5,761; Delaware–1,836; Maryland–63,818; Virginia–187,605; North Carolina–69,600; South Carolina–75,178; Georgia–10,625. Total: 456,622. This is clearly a predictable statistical question; use the table "Estimated Population of American Colonies: 1610 to 1780," in *Historical Statistics of the United States, Colonial Times to 1970*, 1168. Also of interest in the same source is "Population Censuses Taken in the Colonies and States During the Colonial and Pre-Federal Period: 1624–25 to 1786," 1169–71.

Identification of Sources: A common type of statistical question. The first place to consult is always *Historical Statistics of the United States*. Use LC subject headings: United States—Statistics.

18—Briefly explain the struggle among the delegates to the Constitutional Convention over the issue of slavery.

Answer: Division at the convention existed between the slave and free states—not between the small and large states. Southern interests were tied to the continuation of slavery both economically and through fear of "sexually aggressive" free blacks. However, southern delegates did vary and of course, some were idealistic. However, slaves represented a tremendous capital investment for the southern states, and the money was not available to compensate slave owners if their slaves were freed. While the essay consulted (noted below) does not delve into the problem in any depth, the reader is referred in this book's concluding bibliographic essay to: David B. Davis, "American Slavery and the American Revolution," in *Slavery and Freedom in the Age of the American Revolution*, ed. Ira Berlin and Ronald Hoffman (Charlottesville: University of Virginia Press, 1983); David B. Davis, *The Problem of Slavery in Western Culture* (Ithaca, N.Y.: Cornell University Press, 1975); Duncan J. McLeod, *Slavery, Race, and the American Revolution* (New York, 1974); and Donald L. Robinson, *Slavery in the Structure of American Politics, 1765–1820* (New York, 1971). Use Bertram Wyatt-Brown, "Slavery, Sectionalism, and Secession," in *Encyclopedia of American Political History: Studies of the Principal Movements and Ideas* 3:1167–68; and John Hope Franklin, "Slavery and the Constitution," in *Encyclopedia of the American Constitution* 4:1689, which states: "At a time when slavery was waning in the North, the southern states saw in slavery an increasing sense of wealth both in the market value of slaves and in what slaves could produce."

Identification of Sources: Obvious sources to consult would be either an encyclopedia of American political history, an encyclopedia devoted to the Constitution, or one focusing on slavery. Use LC subject headings: United States—Politics and government—Dictionaries; Political Science—United States—History—Dictionaries; United States—Constitutional law—Dictionaries; Slavery—United States—History—Dictionaries.

19—What is Garrison referring to when he writes that a constitution was adopted that returned fugitive slaves to their masters?

Answer: The fugitive slave clause, Art. 4, Sec. 2, 275. "The fugitive slave clause nullified any law or court decision that might have emancipated a runaway slave escaping into a free state. The clause furthermore required that fugitive slaves be 'delivered upon claim' of the owner. The clause failed, however, to indicate how it was to be enforced. In the South it was an important argument for ratification" ("U.S. Constitution, Slavery and The," *Dictionary of Afro-American Slavery*, 755–63). William M. Wiecek, "Fugitive Slavery," in *Encyclopedia of the American Constitution* 2:811–12: "The Constitution contained a clause providing that a 'Person held in service or Labour' shall not be freed when he absconds into another state, 'but shall be delivered up.' "

Identification of Sources: A dictionary or encyclopedia focusing on slavery or the Constitution should be consulted, although any African-American source will contain an entry. Use LC subject headings: Slavery—United States—History—Dictionaries; Afro-Americans—Dictionaries and encyclopedias; United States—Constitutional law—Dictionaries.

20—What is the source of the reference that begins: "when a just God laid judgement to the line . . . "? Briefly explain its biblical meaning.

Answer: Adapted from Isaiah 28:17: "Judgment also will I lay to the line, and righteousness to the plummet: and the hail shall sweep away the refuge of lies, and the waters shall overflow the hiding place" (Strong, *Exhaustive Concordance of the Bible*). "Refuge of Lies" may be a reference "to alien religious practice and trust in alien gods—esp., as has been suggested, a god of the underworld—or to political intrigue" (*Interpreter's One-Volume Commentary on the Bible*, 348).

Identification of Sources: Recognizing that this and the following quotes are biblical, one should turn to a concordance to the King James Version of the Bible. For a useful but not overly cumbersome explicator, select a one-volume Bible commentary. Use LC subject headings: Bible—Concordances; English, Bible—Commentaries.

21—Define the term *oligarchy*.

Answer: Oligarchy: "Government by the few; a form of government in which the power is confined to a few persons or families; also, the body of persons composing such a government" (*Oxford English Dictionary*, 2d ed., vol. 10). "The term 'oligarchy' was also used to refer to the small group of persons who enjoyed a monopoly of political control in the oligarchic governments; the term usually had the added sense that the oligarchy ruled for its own rather than the public interest." The discussion goes on to consider the "inadequacy" of the concept. *International Encyclopedia of the Social Sciences* 11:281–83. From the Greek, oligarchy means rule by a few, but what this means in practice is as difficult to determine as the meaning of "democracy" (*A Dictionary of Political Thought*, 332–33). The three sources consulted offer different perspectives: the *OED* is straightforward, *IESS* explores the term most deeply and concludes with references for further reading, while *A Dictionary of Political Thought* is less methodologically oriented than the *IESS*.

Identification of Sources: Levels of explanation are offered by different sources as illustrated above. The level and type of definition needed will determine the most useful source. Use LC subject headings: English language—Dictionaries; Social sciences—Dictionaries; Political science—Dictionaries.

22—What is the source of the quotation "a sound of battle in the land and of great destruction"? Briefly explain its biblical meaning.

Answer: Adapted from Jeremiah 50:22: "A sound of battle is in the land, and of great destruction." (Strong, *Exhaustive Concordance of the Bible*). An invitation to "all who will to join in the plundering of Babylon, who richly deserves what she will get" (*Interpreter's One-Volume Commentary of the Bible*, 401).

Identification of Sources: (See question 20.)

23—What is the source of the quotation "Babylon was taken, and Bel confounded, and Merodach broken in pieces"? Briefly explain its biblical meaning.

Answer: Adapted from Jeremiah 50:2: "Declare ye among the nations, and publish, and set up a standard; publish, and conceal not: say, Babylon is taken, Bel is confounded, Merodach is broken in pieces; her idols are confounded, her images are broken in pieces" (Strong, *Exhaustive Concordance of the Bible*). A ringing comment on the falsity of the Mesopotamian religion is offered in *Interpreter's One-Volume Commentary on the Bible*, 401.

Identification of Sources: (See question 20.)

24—Identify "Bel," "Merodach," and "Babylon."

Answer: Bel is a designation for the chief god of Babylon and Babylonia, Marduk. Merodach is not found in this form, only as Merodach-Baladan, a Chaldean prince who was a thorn in the side of Assyrian kings. Babylon was a tyrannical military empire that threatened Israel and Judah on several occasions. In 586 B.C. the upper classes of Judah were taken into exile in Babylon. The customary New Testament usage is in reference to tyranny and contemporary opposition to God. *The Dictionary of Bible and Religion*, 115, 680, 99.

Identification of Sources: While any major dictionary or encyclopedia will do, one devoted to the Bible is most appropriate. Use LC subject headings: Theology—Dictionaries; Bible—Dictionaries; Religion—Dictionaries; Religions—Dictionaries.

25—What is the source of the reference "Thanks be to God that we have been saved"? Briefly explain its biblical meaning.

Answer: Adapted from 1 Corinthians 3:15: "If any man's work shall be burned, he shall suffer loss; but he himself shall be saved; yet so as by fire" (Strong, *Exhaustive Concordance of the Bible*). Of the apostle's work: "Good workmanship will endure, but the fires of judgement will destroy the worthless products of any man's labor." Any man's salvation depends on God's grace, and "what matters most is not the primacy but the quality of one's work" (*Interpreter's One-Volume Commentary on the Bible*, 798).

Identification of Sources: (See question 20.)

26—What is the source of the phrase "covenant with death"? Briefly explain its biblical meaning.

Answer: Taken from Isaiah 28:15: "Because ye have said, We have made a covenant with death, and with hell are we in agreement; when the overflowing scourge shall pass through, it shall not come unto us: for we have made lies our refuge, and under falsehood have we hid ourselves" (Strong, *Exhaustive Concordance of the Bible*). "The rulers of Jerusalem live in false security, unafraid of the threatened disaster. The prophet mockingly puts into their mouths words descriptive of their real position" (*Interpreter's One-Volume Commentary on the Bible*, 348).

Identification of Sources: (See question 20.)

27—What is the source of the quotation "So God created man in his own image"? Briefly explain its biblical meaning.

Answer: Genesis 1:27: "So God created man in his own image, in the image of God created he him; male and female created he them" (Strong, *Exhaustive Concordance of the Bible*). "God's creation embraces mankind as a whole" (*Interpreter's One-Volume Commentary on the Bible*, 4).

Identification of Sources: (See question 20.)

28—Confirm the accuracy of six thousand years of human evolution.
Answer: The earliest cities in Mesopotamia have been carbon-dated and are between seven thousand and six thousand years old. Between 2000 B.C. and 1500 B.C. Hammurabi, king of Babylon, provided the first of all legal systems. *The Timetables of History,* 2–3. During the late 19th century, 4,000 years was seen as the "limit of genuine history," that is, "beginning . . . with the historical books of the Old Testament." "History," *Encyclopaedia Britannica* (1881), 12:22.

Identification of Sources: Consult a general chronology of world history. Use LC subject heading: Chronology, Historical—Tables.

29—Provide the text of the Fifteenth Amendment, a brief history of its adoption, and the Supreme Court's early interpretation of it.

Answer: "Section 1. The right of the citizens of the United States to vote shall not be denied or abridged by the United States or by any State on account of race, color, or previous condition of servitude. Section 2. The Congress shall have the power to enforce this article by appropriate legislation." The text can be obtained from an encyclopedia or documentary sourcebook. A brief history of its adoption, which says nothing about the hopes that women had about it, is found in William Gillette, "Fifteenth Amendment (Framing and Ratification)" and Ward E. Y. Elliott, "Fifteenth Amendment (Judicial Interpretation)" in *Encyclopedia of the American Constitution* 2:725–27, 727–28. Republicanism brought idealism and pragmatism together for the amendment's passage. It moved forward because Grant nearly lost the election of 1868, and it was advisable to augment Republican strength with black voters. Ratification was uncertain until the very end. Upon ratification Congress quickly passed three Force Acts forbidding both public and private interference with voting on the basis of race or color, but by 1875 the Court would not uphold convictions for private interference with voting rights in state or local elections. Another useful source is *The Constitution of the United States of America: Analysis and Interpretation: Annotations of Cases Decided by the Supreme Court of the United States to July 2 1982*, rev. and annotated, ed. Johnny H. Killian, assoc. ed. Leland E. Beck (Washington, D.C.: Government Printing Office, 1987).

Identification of Sources: Encyclopedia articles or references complemented by an annotated version of the Constitution would be useful. Use LC subject headings: United States—Constitutional law—Dictionaries; United States—Constitution.

30—Identify the origin of the phrase "of the people, by the people, for the people."

Answer: The reference is to Lincoln's Gettysburg address (1863): "and that government of the people, by the people, for the people, shall not perish from the earth." The framing of the idea was not unique to Lincoln, however. John Wycliffe (1382): "This Bible is for the government of the People, by the People, and for the People." Benjamin Disraeli

(1826): "from the people, and for the people, all springs, and all must exist." Theodore Parker (1850): "A democracy—that is a government of all the people, for all the people." *Familiar Quotations*, 523.

Identification of Sources: One should always try *Familiar Quotations* first if the quote is by an American. The evolution of a "quotation" may be traced through footnotes and the index. Use LC subject heading: Quotations, English.

31—Identify the origin of the statement "if it be true that the consent of the governed confers upon governments their just powers . . . "

Answer: The Declaration of Independence states: "governments are instituted among men, deriving their just powers from the consent of the governed." Once again, the expression of the idea has a genealogy. Giovanni Battista [Gambattista] Vico (1725): "Governments must be comfortable to the nature of the governed; governments are even a result of that nature." John Adams (1774): "they will never find any other moral principle or foundation of rule or obedience, than the consent of governors and governed." *Familiar Quotations*, 387.

Identification of Sources: (See question 30.)

32—What was the female population of the United States in 1870, and what percentage did it constitute of the nation's total population?

Answer: In 1870 there were 19,064,806 females and 19,493,565 males, for a total population of 38,558,371. While the percentage is not given it is easily calculated; females constituted 49.44 percent of the total population. Found in the table "Population, by Age, Sex, Race, and Nativity: 1790 to 1970," in *Historical Statistics of the United States, Colonial Times to 1970*, 15.

Identification of Sources: A standard statistical question. Certain problems with these figures are explained in the footnotes to the table. Sources for all figures are listed on p. 4. Use LC subject heading: United States—Statistics.

33—Identify the newspaper in which the account of the Edinburgh, Scotland, convention Garrison refers to probably appeared.

Answer: Among newspapers published in Boston at the time were: the *Boston Daily Advertiser*, *Boston Herald*, *Boston Daily Journal*, *Boston Post*, and *Boston Traveller*. Morning newspapers or editions included: the *Boston Journal*, *Boston Post*, and *Boston Traveller*. See *American Newspapers, 1821–1936: A Union List of Files Available in the United States and Canada*, ed. Winfred Gregory (New York: Bibliographical Society of America, 1937) and *Newspapers in Microform: United States, 1948–1983*, 2 vols. (Washington, D.C.: Library of Congress, 1984).

Identification of Sources: To identify newspapers published during the period see bibliographies and union lists. Use LC subject headings: American newspapers—Bibliography, Newspapers—Bibliography—Union lists.

34—What was the combined female population of England, Wales, Scotland, and Ireland in 1870, and what percentage did it constitute of the total population?

Answer: England and Wales: males–10,956,000 and females–11,545,000; total: 22,501,000. Scotland: males–1,591,000 and females–1,746,000; total: 3,337,000. Ireland: males–2,642,000 and females–2,777,000; total: 5,419,000. Percentages can be easily computed from these figures: England and Wales, 49 percent male and 51 percent female; Scotland, 48 percent male and 52 percent female; Ireland, 49 percent male and

51 percent female. Total: 48.6 percent male and 51.4 percent female. *British Historical Statistics*, 11–14.

Identification of Sources: Just as there are compilations of historical statistics for the United States, there are similar sources for other nations. Use LC subject headings: Great Britain—Statistics—History.

35—Identify Duncan M'Laren, Prof. Calderwood, Jacob Bright, Prof. Masson, Dr. Lyon Playfair, Rev. Dr. Wallace, and Sir David Wedderburn.

Answer: Duncan M'Laren (1800–1886) was an Edinburgh draper who was active in city government and tax and educational reform. He served in Parliament for many years (1865–1881) with such authority on Scottish matters that he was called "the member for Scotland." *Dictionary of National Biography* 12:638–39.

Henry Calderwood (1830–1897) was a widely published minister and professor at the University of Edinburgh. He held modified Darwinian views and espoused many reform causes, including woman suffrage and temperance. In 1870 he was elected a ruling elder in the Morningside United Presbyterian Church, Edinburgh. *Dictionary of National Biography*, Supplement, 22:373–74.

Jacob Bright (1821–1899), younger brother of John Bright (1811–1889), who was an important reform politican and orator who advocated free trade, peace, and parliamentary reform. Jacob Bright represented Manchester in Parliament between 1867 and 1895, except for two years, and in 1869 succeeded in securing the municipal vote for women. *Dictionary of National Biography* (found using the index), Supplement, 22:291.

George Joseph Gustave Masson (1819–1888) translated many works about French literature and edited the French classics for English students. He was born in England, although his father was born in France. *Dictionary of National Biography* 13:16–17.

Lyon Playfair (1818–1898), first Baron Playfair of St. Andrews. He served in Parliament between 1868 and 1892. He was active on many government committees and commissions, serving as a member of the executive committee of the Great Exhibition of 1851. He was intensely interested in the application of science to industry and was a chemist and professor at the Royal College of Science and at Edinburgh University. *Dictionary of National Biography*, Supplement, 22:1142–44.

Robert Wallace (1831–1899), a famous Scottish minister who, in 1872, was appointed to the chair of church history at Edinburgh University, which he left in 1876. Prior to appointment he had been impeached for heresy. In 1886 he became a radical member of Parliament. *Dictionary of National Biography*, Supplement, 22:1376.

Sir David Wedderburn (1835–1882) was born in Bombay and educated at Trinity College. He was a Liberal serving terms in Parliament between 1868 and 1874 and 1879 and 1882. *Burke's Peerage* (1938), 2538, and *Dod's Parliamentary Companion* (1869), 316.

Identification of Sources: Use *The British Biographical Archive, 17th–19th Centuries* to find copies of entries from a number of nineteenth- and early twentieth-century biographical sources. Being sensitive to the dates involved one can usually differentiate easily between individuals with the same name: brothers, sisters, mother, father, sons, daughters, and other relations. But the first source to consult for British individuals remains the *Dictionary of National Biography;* for a peer, *Burke's Genealogical and Heraldic History of the Peerage, Baronetage, and Knightage*; and for a member of Parliament, *Dod's Parliamentary Companion*. Use LC subject headings: Great Britain—Biography, Great Britain—Bio-bibliography.

36—Who was chief justice of the United States Supreme Court in 1870, and what was his position on women's suffrage?

Answer: Salmon P. Chase (1808–1873) was chief justice. He was appointed by President Lincoln in 1864 and served until his death in 1873. *Notable Americans: What They Did, from 1620 to the Present*; see the table of contents under "V. U.S. Government Judicial Branch: Justices of the Supreme Court of the United States." "The last category of major Chase court cases dealt with the scope of the Reconstruction amendments and the extent to which they would alter the prewar balances of the federal system." In an 1867 case Chase ruled broadly, but in the 1873 Slaughterhouse cases, Justice Miller, for the majority, held that the Reconstruction amendments were strictly interpreted to ensure the liberation of blacks, "not an extension of the rights and privileges of whites." Chase dissented in 1873 when Justice Miller refused to overturn the Illinois Supreme Court's decision to deny a woman's admission to that state's bar solely on the basis of gender. Miller wrote, "The paramount mission and destiny of woman are to fulfill the noble and benign offices of wife and mother" (William M. Wiecek, "The Chase Court," *Encyclopedia of the American Constitution* 1:238).

Identification of Sources: Use a table of appointed or elected federal officials to determine who was chief justice. For an overview of Chase's opinions consult an appropriate encyclopedia. Use LC subject headings: United States—Constitutional law—Dictionaries.

37—Explain Garrison's reference to the popular vote of Kansas.

Answer: In 1867 amendments were considered to the state's constitution that would have given suffrage to both blacks and women. Women reformers had believed that fellow abolitionists and Republicans would support their cause, but they were told this was the "Negro's hour" and that their agitation would endanger the cause of Negro suffrage. Such outspoken reformers as Gerrit Smith, Frederick Douglass, as well as William Lloyd Garrison, were indifferent. And Kansas Republicans were told by representatives of the national party that Negro suffrage was a national issue. Nonetheless, while both amendments were defeated there were nearly as many votes for woman suffrage (9,070) as for Negro suffrage (10,843). *History of Woman Suffrage* 2:229–68.

Identification of Sources: While the answers to this and the other highly focused suffrage questions are not provided by J. Morgan Kousser in her essay "Suffrage" in *The Encyclopedia of American Political History: Studies of the Principal Movements and Ideas*, 1242, important bibliographic references are given (see p. 1257). Offering promise are: Eleanor Flexner, *Century of Struggle: The Women's Rights Movement in the United States* (New York, 1972); and Anne F. and Andrew M. Scott's *One Half of the People: The Fight Over Women Suffrage* (Philadelphia, 1975). One may also consult the *Harvard Guide to American History*. Search the index under "Women and suffrage movement, 445–446," which will lead to section 19.7.2 "Feminism" and a citation for *History of Woman Suffrage*, 6 vols., Elizabeth Stanton, Susan B. Anthony, and M. J. Gage (1881–1922). This set is a standard reference source for the topic. To approach the topic directly, use LC subject headings: Women—Suffrage—United States, Women—Suffrage. Indirectly, use: United States—Politics and government—Dictionaries; Political science—United States—History—Dictionaries; United States—History—Bibliography; United States—History—Study and teaching.

38—Explain Garrison's reference to the territory of Wyoming.

Answer: In May 1869 Wyoming was organized as a territory. Its Democratic legislature passed a women's suffrage bill in 1870 with the approval of its Republican governor. A combination of pressure from the wives of key Democratic politicians and a desire to secure advantages in future elections for the Democrats had led to the initiative. At first Governor Campbell had been inclined to veto it, but he did not want to place the Republican party "in open hostility to a measure which he saw might become of political force and importance." However, many Democrats who had put the bill forward had been convinced that Governor Campbell would veto it. Shortly after the bill passed in 1870, women began to be appointed jurors and justices of the peace. In 1871 "many Democrats were found to be bitterly opposed to woman suffrage" and "they said it was evident that they were losing ground" to the Republicans because of it. The legislature attempted to repeal the measure in 1871 but Campbell vetoed the attempt. He wrote in a long message: "The law granting to women the right to vote and to hold office in this territory was a natural and logical sequence to the other laws upon our statute-book." *History of Woman Suffrage* 3:726–48.

Identification of Sources: (See question 37.)

39—Explain Garrison's reference to Ohio.

Answer: In 1869 a resolution was before the Ohio legislature "to amend the constitution so as to strike out the word male, proposing that at the October election, 'in all precincts in the State, there shall be a separate poll, at which all white women over 21 years of age shall be permitted to vote, and if the votes cast be a majority of all the white women, the constitution shall be amended.'" The means by which the end was to be achieved was controversial among Ohio women. *History of Woman Suffrage* 3:492–93.

Identification of Sources: (See question 37.)

40—What ultimately happened concerning Vermont's constitutional amendment for women's suffrage?

Answer: Suffrage was defeated at the Vermont constitutional convention in June of 1870. Mary A. Livermore wrote: "The Vermont constitutional convention has rejected a proposition to give the ballot to woman, by a vote of 231 to 1. It flouted all discussion of the question, and voted it down with the utmost alacrity." Reprinted from the *Woman's Journal* in *History of Woman Suffrage* 3:388.

Identification of Sources: (See question 37.)

41—Explain Garrison's statement, "I shall never forget that it was first on her soil that I began my public advocacy."

Answer: In 1828 Garrison met Benjamin Lundy. Lundy alerted him to the evils of slavery. Shortly after meeting Lundy Garrison moved to Bennington, Vermont, to coedit *Journal of the Times*, an anti-Jackson paper. His first speech against slavery was made in Boston in March of 1829. The proximity of dates makes it relatively certain that Garrison did, indeed, say something against slavery first in Vermont. *The Dictionary of American Biography* 4:168–72.

Identification of Sources: Use a standard biographical dictionary or consult a standard Garrison biography. Use LC subject heading: United States—Biography—Dictionaries.

42—How many slaves were there in the states and territories of the United States in 1860?

Answer: There were 1,982,625 male slaves and 1,971,135 female slaves, which totals

3,953,760. Found in the table: "Population by Age, Sex, Race, and Nativity: 1790 to 1970," in *Historical Statistics of the United States, Colonial Times to 1970.* A consultation of the 1860 census volume, referred to below, indicates: seventeen states reporting slaves—3,950,531, and three territories—3,229, for a total slave population of 3,953,760. "Recapitulation, Slave Population by Age and Sex," in *Population of the United States in 1860, Compiled from the Original Returns of the Eighth Census* (Washington D.C.: Government Printing Office, 1864), 594–95.

Identification of Sources: (See question 6.)

43—How old was Garrison at the writing of this letter?

Answer: Garrison was born 10 December 1805. He died 24 May 1879. Therefore he was 64 years, 2 months old when he wrote this letter, and he was to die 9 years, 4 months after writing it. Any encyclopedia would provide the necessary information to answer this question. However, the most authoritative source of biographical information for historical American figures is *Dictionary of American Biography* 4:168–72.

Identification of Sources: (See question 1.)

44—Identify two manuscript collections of papers by or relevant to Garrison.

Answer: Consultation of the indexes to the *National Union Catalog of Manuscript Collections* identifies, among many entries: (1) Garrison, William Lloyd, 1805–1879. Eunice McIntosh Merrill Collection of William Lloyd Garrison Papers, 1814–1879. 4 ft. In Wichita State University Library (Kan.). MS 83–663. (2) Garrison Family Papers, 1801–1938. Ca. 5,000 items, 9 boxes, and 41 folders. In Harvard University, Houghton Library (Cambridge, Mass.). MS 82–626.

Identification of Sources: Use the nation's major guide to manuscript collections, the *National Union Catalog of Manuscript Collections* (NUCMC). A search of *Index to Personal Names in the National Union Catalog of Manuscript Collections, 1959–1984*, 2 vols. (Alexandria, Va.: Chadwyck-Healey, 1988) finds many entries. Complementing a search of NUCMC would be consultation of the *National Inventory of Documentary Sources in the United States*, Part 1, *Federal Records*; Part 2, *Manuscript Division, Library of Congress*; and Part 3, *State Archives, State Libraries, State Historical Societies, Academic Libraries and Other Repositories* (Alexandria, Va.: Chadwyck-Healey, 1985–). This source provides microfiche copies of finding aids: calendars, inventories, and so forth. Also to be searched is the Archives and Manuscripts Control file (AMC) of the Research Libraries Group's Research Libraries Information Network (RLIN). In addition, consultation of major biographies and collections of letters and other writings will normally lead one to this type of information. Use LC subject headings: United States—Catalogs; United States—History—Sources—Bibliography.

45—Identify the collected scholarly editions of Garrison's writings.

Answer: Garrison, Francis J., and W. P. Garrison, *William Lloyd Garrison, 1805–1879*, 4 vols. (1885–1889); Garrison, William Lloyd, *The Garrison Letters*, vol. 1, *I Will Be Heard, 1822–1835*, ed. Walter M. Merrill; vol. 2, *A House Dividing Against Itself, 1836–1840*, ed. Louis Ruchames (1971). Consult *The Harvard Guide to American History*, either the table of contents under "Individual Biography and Selected Writings" or the index in vol. 2, under "Garrison, William Lloyd." References are on p. 195.

Identification of Sources: When selecting an individual's collected works for use, give special attention to publisher and date of publication. Choices can be made without the help of a selective list, but for an indication of the most important works, consult the *Harvard Guide*. The *Harvard Guide* indicates that *The Garrison Letters* is an open set, but it was completed in 1981 in six volumes. The correct citation is *The Letters of William Lloyd Garrison*, 6 vols., ed. Walter M. Merrill (vols. 2 and 4, ed. Louis Ruchames; vol. 6, ed. Walter M. Merrill and Louis Ruchames (Cambridge, Mass.: Belknap Press of Harvard University Press, 1971–1981). The *Harvard Guide* (1974) is outdated and often imprecise in its citations; these factors must always be considered. Use LC subject headings: United States—History—Bibliography; United States—History—Study and teaching.

46—Garrison quoted profusely and passionately and tried to be "as harsh as truth and as uncompromising as justice." In what context did he write this phrase?

Answer: *The Liberator*, no. 1 (1 January 1831). "I will be as harsh as truth and as uncompromising as justice. On this subject I do not wish to think, or speak, or write, with moderation. No. No! Tell a man whose house is on fire to give a moderate alarm; tell him to moderately rescue his wife from the hands of the ravisher; tell the mother to gradually extricate her babe from the fire into which it has fallen; but urge me not to use moderation." *Familiar Quotations*, 505.

Identification of Sources: For a major American figure, a major American quotation dictionary should be used. Perhaps Garrison was inspired by Thomas Paine; a reference after his quote is provided to Paine's *Rights of Man*: "A thing moderately good is not so good as it ought to be. Moderation in temper is always a virtue; but moderation in principle is always a vice" (*Familiar Quotations*, 385). Use LC subject headings: Quotations, English.

NOTES

1. Mortimer J. Adler, and Charles Van Doren, *How to Read a Book*, rev. ed. (New York: Simon and Schuster, 1972), 168–88.

2. *Guide to Reference Books*, 9th ed., ed. Eugene P. Sheehy (Chicago: American Library Association, 1986), xiv.

3. John D. Buenker, "Research and Reference Tools Reviews," *Journal of American History* 73, no. 4 (March 1987): 1097. On reviewing reference works in general, citing the work of other librarians, see Deborah Fink, *Process and Politics in Library Research: A Model for Course Design* (Chicago: American Library Association, 1989), 32–35. For thoughts on reviewing historical monographs, see the associate editor of the *Journal of American History*, Steven Stowe, "Thinking About Reviews," *Journal of American History* 78, no. 2 (September 1991): 591–95. Assessment of a survey indicates that reviews are the *Journal*'s most-used feature. Readers favor a straightforward account of what the book is about, an assessment of its scholarly soundness, and an attempt to place it within its historiographical context.

4. *A Critical Dictionary of the French Revolution*, ed. François Furet and Mona Ozouf, trans. Arthur Goldhammer (Cambridge, Mass.: Belknap Press of Harvard University Press, 1989); Conor Cruise O'Brien, "The Decline and Fall of the French Revolution," *New York Review of Books* 37, no. 2 (15 February 1990): 46–51.

5. For a comprehensive guide to publications on the aspects and issues of scholarly editing, see Beth Luey, with the assistance of Kathleen Gorman, *Editing Documents and Texts: An Annotated Bibliography* (Madison, Wisc.: Madison House, 1990).

6. Reprinted by permission of Harvard University Press.

7

Sources for Interdisciplinary Research

Raymond G. McInnis

The materials described below are selected from numerous sources of potential research on topics in interdisciplinary history. Space limitations restrict discussion to only the more important sources, however. This guide is suggestive, then, not comprehensive. For a more extensive review of available resources, consult the recommended research guides to the disciplines relevant to your topic. Space constraints also limit the number of times important, larger, general cross-disciplinary sources can be repeated in the sections on individual disciplines. To remind you that some general sources may also be worth consulting, a "see also" set of directions is often given at the beginning of each disciplinary section.

In general, under each discipline that is covered in this chapter, materials are arranged in the following order:

1. Research Guides
2. Substantive Information Sources
3. Substantive-Bibliographic Information Sources
4. Bibliographic Information Sources

In this research guide, "substantive information" refers to the subject matter—the textual material—of the published literature of a particular research topic. "Bibliographic information," through a convention known as the bibliographic citation, provides the key to locating substantive information. Research guides

Keep Harry Ritter's discussion of interdisciplinary historical research in mind when reading and using the following guide, which focuses on the reference aids that provide access to the concepts and/or methods of several fields other than history.

are essentially annotated bibliographies, aids to locating information sources (bibliographies, reviews of research, and the like) in libraries.

"Substantive information sources" refers to those reference sources designed primarily to provide special formulations of the subject matter associated with a particular research topic and, for the most part, presented in a distilled, synthesized format. Primary among examples of this genre are the specialized dictionaries that define and briefly explain the "prescribed" meanings of terms specific to a field of inquiry. Normally little emphasis is given to naming scholars who contributed to the development of specific fields of knowledge. An example is John W. Smith and John S. Klemanski's *Urban Politics Dictionary*.

However, in "substantive-bibliographic information sources," considerable attention is given to both the bibliographic and the substantive aspects of a specific research topic. Examples of substantive-bibliographic sources are the comprehensive encyclopedias (with extensive bibliographies provided at the end of articles) and reviews of research. The preeminent example of a comprehensive encyclopedia is the *International Encyclopedia of the Social Sciences*. Its articles are concerned with both substantive and bibliographic components of social-scientific terms. Serving a function similar to encyclopedias, reviews of research provide authoritative appraisals of research advances in a given field. They also function, however, as bibliographies, as sources of definitions of concepts, and as a means of identifying key people. The practice seems to be to call recurrent review publications either *Annual Review of*— or *Advances in*—, while single volumes or multiple-volume sets are most often entitled *Handbook of*—. In addition, there are periodicals that devote all or a great proportion of their pages to review articles, and it is not uncommon for individual scholarly journals to contain occasional review articles. Characteristically, comprehensive encyclopedias stress theoretical aspects of the topic being considered, while reviews of research usually give greater emphasis to the empirical aspects of these same topics. Thus, it is often useful to make joint use of these two different sources.

"Bibliographic information sources" refers to those reference sources designed to provide almost exclusively bibliographic information for the individual publications associated with a particular research topic. In contrast to the distilled, synthesized treatments of a literature's subject matter in substantive information sources, bibliographic information sources treat the subject matter of the same literature according to its more discrete, analytical characteristics. Primary among examples in this category are the periodical index, the abstract journal, and the retrospective bibliographies dedicated to specific areas of inquiry.

Outline of Chapter

Quantitative Methods

General and Area Studies

Social Sciences

    Anthropology

Business and Labor
Communication, Mass Media, and Journalism
Demography
Economics and Economic Thought
Education
Political Science
Psychology
Sociology
Women's Studies
Humanities
Fine and Applied Arts
Language and Literature
Philosophy and Religion
History of Science and Technology

QUANTITATIVE METHODS

Research Guides

The following serve as guides to appropriate material as well as introductions to the methods of quantitative historical research. See also the Watson bibliography at the end of the next section.

Dollar, Charles N. and Richard J. Jensen. *Historian's Guide to Statistics*. New York: Holt, Rhinehart, and Winston, 1971.

Floud, Roderick, ed. *An Introduction to Quantitative Methods for Historians* 2nd ed. London: Methuen, 1979.

Haskins, Loren, and Kirk Jeffrey. *Understanding Quantitative History*. Cambridge, Mass.: MIT Press, 1990.

Jarausch, Konrad Hugo, and Kenneth A. Hardy. *Quantitative Methods for Historians: A Guide to Research, Data, and Statistics* Chapel Hill: University of North Carolina Press, 1991.

Substantive-Bibliographic Information Sources

The following works offer valuable substantive and bibliographic information and are by major figures in the application of this methodology.

Kruskal, William H., and Judith M. Tanur, eds. *International Encyclopedia of Statistics*. 2 vols. New York: Macmillan, 1978.

The *International Encyclopedia of Statistics* contains over seventy articles on statistics and about forty-five biographies of statisticians and others important in the development of statistics. Articles, selected from the *International Encyclopedia of the Social Sciences* (next section), are revisions of the originals. In addition, five new articles and twelve additional biographies are included. Each author of an *IESS* article was asked to prepare a postscript covering recent advances and second thoughts, to supply emendations, and to add an updated bibliography. On pages vii–ix of volume 1, articles are listed alphabetically.

Aydelotte, W. O., et al., eds. *The Dimensions of Quantitative Research in History*. Princeton, N.J.: Princeton University Press, 1973.

Nine contributors discuss applications of quantification to research in French, British, and American history from the sixteenth to the twentieth centuries. They employ a range of statistical techniques and models. In broad and general terms the introduction sets each essay in historiographic context.

Aydelotte, W. O., ed. *Quantification in History*. Reading, Mass.: Addison-Wesley, 1971.

Reprints four articles published between 1954 and 1970, including Jerome Clubb's seminal article, "The Problems of Historical Generalization." According to Theodore Rabb (below), this is the first "substantial assessment of the potential of quantification in history" (p. 592).

Barraclough, Geoffrey. "History." In *Main Trends of Research in the Social and Human Sciences*, ed. Jacques Havet. The Hague: Mouton Publishers/UNESCO, 1973. Part 2, vol. 1: 229–487.

Part of this 258-page chapter, pp. 312–17, focuses on trends and developments for "quantification in history," and discusses twenty-nine studies. See next section for further discussion of this important study.

Benson, Lee. *Toward the Scientific Study of History: Selected Essays*. Philadelphia: J. B. Lippincott, 1972.

Reprints Benson's essays on quantification, including the noted 1957 paper "Research Problems in American Political History." Benson is "committed to a view of history as a social science and of scientific history as the foundation of all other social sciences."

Bogue, Allan G. "The Historian and Social Science Data Archives in the United States." *American Behavioral Scientist* 19 (March/April 1976): 137–75.

Bogue claims that quantification includes "the identification, processing, and administrative control of quantitative historical evidence in the form of machine-readable data, the conceptual framework and research designs in which quantitative research is developed and presented." To Bogue, quantification in history has its roots in the behavioral transformation in the social sciences of the 1950s. This article discusses 116 studies.

Bonnell, Victoria E. "The Uses of Theory, Concepts and Comparison in Historical Sociology." *Comparative Studies of Society and History* 22 (1980): 156–73.

Bonnell discusses fifty-eight studies that explore issues relating to the sociological study of history, especially new methodological approaches and problems that she believes have not received the attention they deserve. Beginning with a brief consideration of the contrasting methodological perspectives in the two disciplines, she argues "that the methodological foundations of historical-sociological research must be sought, first, in the way theories and concepts are formulated and applied to historical problems." She discusses two types of research strategy "involving the mediation of history by theory and the mediation of history by concepts." The use of comparison is a "related and equally important methodological component of historical-sociological research." Here, Bonnell also discerns "a binary division between 'illustrative' and 'analytical' forms of comparative study."

Clubb, Jerome M., and Erwin K. Scheuch, eds. *Historical Social Research: The Use of Historical and Process-Produced Data*. Vol. 6. Stuttgart: Klett-Cotta, Historisch Socialwissenschaftliche Forschungen, 1980.

The chapters, which vary both in analytical level and in purpose, are loosely organized into sections: on types of data (including administrative and census data); on life histories; and on content and document analysis. Other chapters look at time series, networks, and problems of generating and handling complex data files.

Lorwin, Val R., and Jacob M. Price, eds. *The Dimensions of the Past: Materials, Problems, and Opportunities for Quantitative Work in History.* New Haven, Conn.: Yale University Press, 1972.
Surveys of sources, bibliographies, and reviews of quantitative work in various nations, including: medieval Europe; Britain from 1650 to 1830; France since 1789; Germany in the nineteenth and twentieth centuries; the Nordic countries since the late seventeenth century; five centuries of Spanish history; Russia from the sixteenth to nineteenth centuries and the Soviet period; Latin America in colonial times and in the nineteenth and twentieth centuries; Japan since 1600; and India since 1500.

Rabb, Theodore K. "The Development of Quantification in Historical Research." *Journal of Interdisciplinary History* 13 (Spring 1983): 591–601.
Rabb, confident that "quantification will remain a powerful force" in historical explanation, discusses nearly twenty theoretical studies or empirical applications, several of which are also published in this issue.

Swierenga, Robert P. "Computers and American History: The Impact of the 'New' Generation." *The Journal of American History* 60 (1974): 1045–70.
Surveys applications in quantitative history and evaluates guides on how to do it. Swierenga mentions over two hundred publications.

Wrigley, E. A., ed. *Nineteenth Century Society: Essays in the Use of Quantitative Methods for the Study of Social Data.* New York: Cambridge University Press, 1972.
Contains chapters by British historians designed to assist research utilizing British censuses of 1841, 1851, and 1861.

Bibliographic Information Sources

Stephen R. Grossbart, "Quantitative and Social Science Methods for Historians: An Annotated Bibliography of Selected Books and Articles," published in 1992 in *Historical Methods*, is a revision of Nancy Fitch's 1980 *Historical Methods* bibliographical article, "Statistical and Mathematical Methods for Historians." It is a partially annotated listing organized under fifteen headings; topics covered include multivariate analysis, econometrics, general linear models, causal models, models for contingency tables, exploratory analysis and graphical techniques, longitudinal analysis and panel analysis, Markov processes, political analysis, and simulation.

Appropriate sections of Susan K. Kinnell's *Historiography: An Annotated Bibliography of Journal Articles, Books and Dissertations* are useful. Annotated citations are drawn from the database of ABC-Clio, producer of *America: History and Life* and *Historical Abstracts*. It contains more than eight thousand citations for historiographic studies published between 1970 and 1985. Entries are classified in a thematic–geographic scheme of fourteen categories. A subdivision of the category Methodology and Schools of Historiography, "Quantitative Method and the Statistical Approach," contains ninety-five annotated entries. Additional studies of quantitative method for individual countries are accessible through the index.

Stephen R. Grossbart. "Quantitative and Social Science Methods for Historians: An Annotated Bibliography of Selected Books and Articles." *Historical Methods* 25, no. 3 (Summer 1992): 100–120.

Kinnell, Susan K. *Historiography: An Annotated Bibliography of Journal Articles, Books and Dissertations.* 2 vols. Santa Barbara, Calif.: ABC–Clio, 1987.

GENERAL AND AREA STUDIES

Research Guides and Bibliographies of Reference Works

Now in a tenth edition, the basic volume of Sheehy's *Guide to Reference Books* is updated by a supplement published in 1992. In the basic volume, over fifteen hundred reference works and related publications issued as late as 1984 are arranged by broad subject and then further subdivided into: guides and manuals; bibliographies; indexes and abstracts; encyclopedias; dictionaries of special terms; handbooks; annuals and directories; histories; biographical works; atlases; and serial publications. Annotations are carefully written but uncritical, and there is an excellent index. *Walford's Guide to Reference Material* is a British research guide similar in intent and format to Sheehy, but with more comprehensive coverage for the sciences and materials published in or about European countries.

Webb's *Sources of Information in the Social Sciences* is in a third edition. It presents the collective wisdom of nineteen individuals with expert knowledge about both the substantive and the bibliographic aspects of the whole range of social science topics. Besides history itself, chapters explore the substantive literature and reference materials of geography, economics and business, sociology, anthropology, psychology, education, and political science. An introductory chapter, "Social Science Literature," offers an analytical framework for these chapters. Excluding materials in the history chapter, over 6,300 items are cited.

Nancy L. Herron and others have written *The Social Sciences: A Cross-Disciplinary Guide to Selected Sources.* Over 790 critically annotated citations are contained in twelve chapters arranged in four parts: a general section composed of reference sources applicable across all disciplines; disciplines firmly established by scholarly tradition among the social sciences: political science, economics and business, history, law and legal issues, anthropology, and sociology; disciplines defined as "emerging" from roots in the humanities or pure sciences into the areas of the social science disciplines: education, psychology, and communication; and disciplines related to the social implications for the other disciplines mentioned above: geography and statistics and demographics.

Chapters consist of two sections: "a treatise on the discipline including a description of its reference environment and any unique aspects of the literature related to that discipline," and an annotated listing of selected titles arranged from the general to the specific.

Update these research guides with the *American Reference Books Annual.* Each annual volume provides reviews of reference books published in the United States during the previous year. Reviews, arranged in over forty subject categories, are further subdivided by type: bibliographies, encyclopedias, directories, handbooks and yearbooks, and indexes.

American Reference Books Annual. Littleton, Colo.: Libraries Unlimited, 1970–

Herron, Nancy L., ed. *The Social Sciences: A Cross-disciplinary Guide to Selected Sources.* Englewood, Colo.: Libraries Unlimited, 1989.

Sheehy, Eugene P., ed. *Guide to Reference Books.* 10th ed. Chicago: American Library Association, 1986. Supplemented by Balay, Robert, ed. *Guide to Reference Books, Covering Materials from 1985–1990.* Supplement to the Tenth Edition. Chicago: American Library Association, 1992.

Walford, Albert J., ed. *Walford's Guide to Reference Material.* 3 vols. 5th ed. London: Library Association, 1989–1991.

Webb, William H., et al. *Sources of Information in the Social Sciences.* 3d ed. Chicago: American Library Association, 1986.

Substantive Information Sources

Designed primarily for undergraduates, Jack C. Plano's *Dictionary of Political Analysis* attempts to foster an awareness of the need for precise definitions and to encourage greater command of the vocabulary. Stressing the behavioral approach to inquiry, concern is for key analytical concepts, theories, methods of inquiry, and research techniques. Entries are in two parts: the first defines the meaning of a term, and the second explains its significance. Names of institutions, agencies, and people are included. A selected bibliography of sources of additional information is given at the end, but no attempt is made to connect individual terms with these titles.

Plano, Jack C., et al. *Dictionary of Political Analysis.* 2d ed. Santa Barbara, Calif.: ABC-Clio, 1982.

Substantive-Bibliographic Information Sources

Subtitled "The Master Index to Subject Encyclopedias," Joe Ryan's *First Stop* creates a wealth of opportunities for interdisciplinary research by indicating the locations of discussions of concepts, methods, and names of key people. It is a "keyword" and "broad subject index" to nearly forty thousand topics in 430 English-language subject encyclopedias, dictionaries, handbooks, comprehensive textbooks, and other standard reference sources. Criteria used to select articles in the sources included length (250 words or more per entry) and if it has a bibliography. Many encyclopedias and dictionaries discussed in this section are indexed in *First Stop*.

Ryan, Joe, ed. *First Stop: The Master Index to Subject Encyclopedias*. Phoenix, Ariz.: Oryx Press, 1989.

Single-volume dictionaries. Several excellent specialized dictionaries focus on concepts, terms, methods, and so forth in a variety of areas of interest for interdisciplinary history projects.

In *Dictionary of Modern Thought*, editors Alan Bullock and Oliver Stallybrass steer "a middle course between an ordinary dictionary and an encyclopedia: in an alphabetical arrangement, over one hundred contributors set forth some four thousand key names and terms from across the whole range of modern thought." Terms are explained briefly and authoritatively in entries from ten to a thousand words "in a language as simple as can be used without *over*-simplification." To the editors, "modern" means the twentieth century, with particular emphasis upon new or recent words and phrases and on familiar words that have acquired special meanings.

One of several uniform volumes in Greenwood's "Reference Sources for the Social Sciences and Humanities" series, Harry Ritter's *Dictionary of Concepts in History* makes accessible brief, substantive discussions (occupying from one to two-and-a-half pages of text) of the etymology and contemporary use of close to one hundred concepts in history. Each article consists of four parts: brief statements of the concept's current meaning; paragraphs that trace the concept's origins and connotative development; bibliographical notes, listing and briefly discussing sources mentioned in the article; and sources of additional information. In addition, there is an index of names and subjects.

In the same series as Ritter, and also useful for interdisciplinary studies, Paul Durbin's *Dictionary of Concepts in the Philosophy of Science* discusses one hundred concepts in the broad area "philosophy of science." Beginning with "Analogy," and in the same format as Ritter, he treats such concepts as: analysis, and analytical-synthetic distinction; behaviorism; causality; concept; covering law model; determinism; dialectical materialism; empiricism; explanation; functionalism; hypothetico-deductive method; idealism; induction; laws and science; logical positivism; materialism; methodology; methods, mathematical and statistical; mind-body problem; observation; paradigm; perception; reduction and reductionism; scientific method; scientific progress; social science; structuralism; system; and theory.

An older but still useful work, the *Dictionary of the Social Sciences* contains discursive entries that define and explain more than one thousand terms from anthropology, economics, political science, and sociology, but those relating to the last two disciplines predominate. Included concepts range from abnormal (also normal) and acceleration principle through idealism and ideology to working class and zonal hypothesis. With few exceptions, entries by two hundred American and British social scientists are arranged as follows: (a) the generally accepted meaning of the term; (b) its historical background or a more extensive explanation; and (c,d, e) and so on are where "controversies and divergencies of meaning have been explored and an attempt made to place them in their perspective." Many definitions are illustrated with quotes from authorities.

Major encyclopedias. The two most prominent multivolume encyclopedias in the social sciences are the fifteen-volume *Encyclopedia of the Social Sciences (ESS)* and the seventeen-volume *International Encyclopedia of the Social Sciences (IESS)*. The editorial policy on the latter work was to complement rather than supersede the original. Together they represent excellent sources of information on a wide range of subjects within and related to disciplines in the social sciences.

The *ESS* includes articles on all major topics in politics, economics, law, sociology, and social work, with some attention directed toward what in the 1930s were considered peripheral subjects: ethics, education, philosophy, psychology, and geography. There are some four thousand biographies of persons deceased when the *ESS* was published. Articles are of varying lengths, signed by their authors, and arranged alphabetically. Cross-references to related articles are provided, and the final volume has a comprehensive index and a classification of the articles in subject and biography groups. Most articles have brief bibliographies.

Although the *IESS* has some differences in scope and format, a marked resemblance to the original still exists. Along with anthropology, there are extensive articles on the concepts, theories, and methods of economics, geography, history, law, political science, psychology, and sociology. Articles on disciplines have cross-references to the related topical and biographical articles. Excellent— often extensive—bibliographies accompany each article. Articles emphasize analytical and comparative aspects of topics, with historical and descriptive material added to illustrate concepts and theories.

Among the several articles in the "history" entry in *IESS* are ethno-history and culture history. The *IESS* has only six hundred biographies, compared with over four thousand in *ESS*, but the articles are longer and emphasize individuals not included in the first work, including prominent social scientists who had died since the preparation of the original volumes or who had been born no later than December 31, 1908. The *International Encyclopedia of the Social Sciences: Biographical Supplement* makes available over two hundred additional biographies. Two bibliographies follow most entries: one of the subject's own works, and the other of works related to the subject.

Other encyclopedic sources. Adam Kuper and Jessica Kuper have edited the single-volume *Social Science Encyclopedia*. International in scope, over seven hundred entries by recognized authorities deal with theories, issues, and methods, and the life and work of individual scholars whose contributions are exceptional. Anthropology, economics, political science and political theory, psychology, and sociology are treated in one (or more) master entries. Other entries cover subfields in these disciplines, and also particular theories and problem areas.

Other disciplines, not considered mainstream social sciences, are dealt with in less complete fashion. These include demography, development studies, linguistics and semiotics, and psychiatry. Other intellectual traditions, professions, and problem areas are examined, notably the biological dimension of the social sciences, business studies, industrial relations communication and media studies, education, geography, history, law, Marxism, medicine, and women's studies. Special emphasis is given to methods and to relevant issues in philosophy. The *Encyclopedia* also deals with applications of the social sciences in market research and opinion polls, in therapy, in aptitude testing and the measurement of intelligence, in industrial relations and in management, in economic and financial analysis and planning, in social work, in criminology and penology. All entries include at least one reference, and while there is no general index, at the close of the volume is a list of entries.

An ambitious UNESCO-sponsored project, the three-volume *Main Trends of Research in the Social and Human Sciences* is the work of internationally recognized scholars. Stressing interdisciplinary approaches to these disciplines, the project focuses "on the main trends in research, not on results achieved by research or even on the status of current research." Thus the project seeks not to draw up a balance sheet of contemporary research and its results, but to diagnose and describe key tendencies in the social and human sciences. To predict future directions of scholarly activity, then, is the project's aim. The scope is toward current research orientations throughout the world, taking into account as fully as possible the diversity of social and cultural contexts, and of schools thought and doctrinal, ideological, and methodological standpoints. Throughout the set, chapters are extensive, several over one hundred pages, all richly documented.

Volume 1 covers major "law-seeking" disciplines such as sociology, political science, psychology, economics, demography, and linguistics. Consideration is given to the interdisciplinary dimensions of research: "common mechanisms, mathematical models, problem-focused research, cross-cultural research." The second part of the project, that is, volumes 1 and 2 of part 2, identifies "the principal research trends in the legal sciences, the historical sciences, social and cultural anthropology, archaeology and prehistory, language, the study of forms of artistic and literary expression, and philosophy, Eastern and Western humanism, and philosophy of religion."

To a certain extent, *Main Trends* is updated in the quarterly *Social Science Information*. Its articles focus on progress in teaching and scholarship in the social sciences and frequently present extensive reviews of work in interdisciplinary fields. From 1962 until the late 1970s, it also published annual or biennial bibliographies. One, "Social Science Methodology," arranged in a detailed classification scheme, lists consecutively, from issue to issue, articles and books in all languages. Among the main headings are general studies, basic orientations, observation–data collection, types of analysis, analytical tools, decisions analysis, and forecasting methods. Other regular bibliographical listings are under the following headings: interdisciplinary relations in the social sciences, surveys of research in social science, studies concerning concepts in the social sciences, and the sociology of the social sciences (an international bibliography). Coverage is international, items are arranged according to detailed classification schemes, and there are some annotations. For interdisciplinary projects especially, these bibliographies are very promising sources of references for studies on methods and concepts, or they may otherwise be used simply to generate ideas. We can only regret they are no longer published.

C. D. Kernig's *Marxism, Communism and Western Society* is the first work of such magnitude to attempt a comparative analysis of "Western thought and the ideological concepts and doctrines as represented in the major writings of Soviet, Chinese, and Yugoslavian authors." The set contains over four hundred articles ranging from politics, economics, and education to psychology, sociology, and literature; and with the collapse of communist regimes in Eastern Europe, it becomes even more valuable for historical and interdisciplinary research. Most articles consist of three parts: western aspects, Soviet and Marxist aspects, and a critical comparison. A bibliography, including Soviet works, concludes each article.

Subtitled "Studies of Selected Pivotal Ideas," Philip Wiener's *Dictionary of the History of Ideas* contains approximately three hundred extensive articles by specialists, ranging in title from "Crisis in History" and "Progress in the Modern Era" to "Psychological Schools in European Thought," and "Psychological Schools in American Thought" to "Nationalism" and "Protest Movements." Although stress is given to interdisciplinary, cross-cultural relations, such emphasis is not "intended as a substitute for the specialized histories of the various disciplines, but rather serves to indicate actual and possible interrelations." The articles focus on the external order of nature; human nature in anthropology, psychology, religion, and philosophy; the historical development of economic, legal, and political ideas and institutions, ideologies, and movements; and formal mathematical, logical, linguistic, and methodological concepts. Each article is accompanied by a list of books and articles recommended as sources of additional information. The set's fifth volume is the index. Volume 1 presents a list of articles and an analytical table of contents.

In Jeremy L. Tobey's *History of Ideas: A Bibliographical Introduction*, extensive critical bibliographical essays complement the *Dictionary of the History of Ideas*. Volume 1 deals with classical antiquity, volume 2, medieval and early modern Europe (that is, 1727, the date of Isaac Newton's death). "In this bibliography," the author notes, "the history of ideas means the study of the ideas used by educated people in each era to comprehend the universe and rationalize their social institutions, arts, and religions." Over a third of each volume concerns philosophical materials. Areas of scholarship also covered are the history of science, literature, and such humanistic issues as architecture, fine art, and classical music. References are given in two ways: briefly in the text and fully in the alphabetical author index that serves each volume as an index of authors of works discussed.

Barraclough, Geoffrey. "History." In *Main Trends of Research in the Social and Human Sciences*. Part 2, vol. 1. Ed. Jacques Havet. The Hague: Mouton Publishers/ UNESCO, 1973.

Bullock, Alan, and Oliver Stallybrass, eds. *Dictionary of Modern Thought*. New York: Harper and Row, 1977.

Durbin, Paul T. *Dictionary of Concepts in the Philosophy of Science*. Westport, Conn.: Greenwood Press, 1988.

Gould, Julius, and William L. Kolb, eds. *Dictionary of the Social Sciences*. New York: Free Press, 1964.

Kernig, C. D., ed. *Marxism, Communism and Western Society: A Comparative Encyclopedia*. 8 vols. New York: Herder and Herder, 1972–1973.

Kuper, Adam, and Jessica Kuper. *The Social Science Encyclopedia*. London: Routledge and Kegan Paul, 1985.

Main Trends of Research in the Social and Human Sciences. Ed. Jacques Havet. 2 parts in 3 vols. The Hague: Mouton Publishers/UNESCO, 1973.

Ritter, Harry. *Dictionary of Concepts in History*. Westport, Conn.: Greenwood Press, 1987.

Seligman, E. R. A., ed. *Encyclopedia of the Social Sciences*. 15 vols. New York: Macmillan Co., 1930–1935.

Sills, David, ed. *International Encyclopedia of the Social Sciences*. 17 vols. New York: Macmillan and Free Press, 1968.

Social Science Information. London: Sage, 1962–.

Tobey, Jeremy L. *The History of Ideas: A Bibliographical Introduction*. 2 vols. Ed. Philip Wiener. Santa Barbara, Calif.: ABC-Clio Press, 1975–1977.

Wiener, Philip, ed. *Dictionary of the History of Ideas: Studies of Selected Pivotal Ideas*. 5 vols. New York: Charles Scribner's Sons, 1973–1974.

Bibliographic Information Sources

Theodore Besterman's *A World Bibliography of Bibliographies* is a massive five-volume set listing all known bibliographies published as individual books (117,000) up to 1963, covering all subjects, periods, and languages, and giving the number of items in each bibliography. (Bibliographies published as sections of books or in periodicals are not included.) The set is arranged alphabetically by subject and has an author index. Several new editions, narrowly focused on particular geographical regions, have appeared since 1965 (for example, Africa, Asia).

Perhaps the most useful publication designed to list bibliographies and literature reviews by subject is *Bibliographic Index*. Two issues appear each year, with annual and subsequent cumulations covering intervals of four or five years. The *Index* includes bibliographies and literature reviews published separately as well as in books or in periodicals. About fifteen hundred periodicals are examined regularly.

The following bibliographical sources for American studies are examples of bibliographies devoted to a specific geographical area. Their counterparts for Eastern Europe, Latin America, Asia, and so on can be identified in the research guides in this section.

Since 1955, *American Quarterly* has published a selected, briefly annotated bibliography of about seven hundred articles, which has appeared in the summer issue. Truly interdisciplinary in purpose, the "criterion for listing an article is the extent to which it manifests a relationship between two or more aspects of American Civilization." Articles are arranged under the following subjects: art and architecture, economics, education, folklore, history, language, law, literature and drama, mass culture, music, political science, psychiatry and psychology, public address, religion, science and technology, and sociology and anthropology. Interdisciplinary relevance is further indicated with letter symbols. In 1972 Pierian Press published in two volumes *Articles in American Studies, 1954–1968*, a cumulation of the annual bibliographies from *American Quarterly*.

A more ambitious project, Jack Salzman's *American Studies: An Annotated Bibliography*, a three-volume set, annotates books written in the twentieth century (to 1983) in eleven distinct fields of American studies: anthropology and folklore; art and architecture; history; literature; music; political science; popular culture; psychology; religion; science, technology and medicine; and sociology. The 7,634 entries constitute a reasonably comprehensive and authoritative list of sources of information concerning this country. Arrangement within sections is alphabetical by author's name, then by title. Most sections are subdivided; for example, popular culture is grouped into such categories as literature, comics, film, and material culture. An update volume to cover the publications of 1984–1988 was published in 1990.

At the beginning of each of the sections is a preface designed to "introduce the reader to the basic bibliographic resources necessary to doing research in that particular discipline." Not always, however, are these as complete as one would desire. A table of contents lists the eleven major sections and the index volume contains author, title, and subject sections. The 1990 update volume is organized slightly differently.

Scattered among the 158 references in the "Research Methods in History" chapter in Alexander S. Birkos and Lewis A. Tamb's *Historiography, Method, History Teaching: A Bibliography of Books and Articles, 1965–1972* are numerous studies that address interdisciplinary issues. See, in addition, Kinnell's *Historiography: An Annotated Bibliography of Journal Articles, Books and Dissertations*, described in this section.

As of June 1974, the *Humanities Index* and *Social Science Index* are two quarterly indexes superseding the *Social Sciences and Humanities Index*. Together they index over seven hundred periodicals. The main body of each consists of author and subject entries in a single sequence that refers to periodical articles in the fields of archaeology and classical studies, area studies, folklore, history, language and literature, literary and political criticism, performing arts, philosophy, religion and theology, as well as related subjects. There is, following the main body of the index, an author listing of citations to book reviews.

History, sociology, economics, archaeology, and related subjects are indexed by subject in the quarterly *British Humanities Index*. With annual cumulations, it includes an index to authors. About three hundred periodicals are researched regularly. From 1915 to 1961, it was known as the *Subject Index to Periodicals*.

Robert Irving Watson's retrospective bibliography, *The History of Psychology and the Behavioral Sciences*, is an intelligently produced source for interdisciplinary topics in such fields as psychology, science, philosophy, psychiatry and psychoanalysis, biology, medicine, anthropology, sociology, and education. In addition, the well-annotated volume of over eight hundred mostly English-language entries presents sections on: general resources, including guides to the literature; encyclopedias; bibliographies of books, articles, and retrieval systems; biographical collections; dictionaries; archives and manuscript collections, including oral histories; and journal bibliographies; methods of historical research, including "Critical Analysis: Narrative Methods"; "Biography as Narrative"; "The Narrative and *Verstehen*"; "Methodological Objectivity, and the Presentist and Historicist Attitudes in Writing the Narrative"; "Quantitative Methods in General"; "Content Analysis"; "Citation Indexes"; and "Illustrations of Applications of Other Quantitative Techniques"; historiographic fields, including "General History"; "Psychology"; "Behavioral Science"; "Science and the Philosophy of Science"; "Philosophy"; "Psychiatry"; "Psychoanalysis and Psychohistory"; "Biology, Physiology, and Medicine"; "Sociology and the Social Sciences"; "Education"; "Intellectual History"; and historiographic theories, including "General Theoretical Statements"; "Speculative Theories of History and the Nineteenth- and Twentieth-Century Reactions from Historians"; "Contemporary Pluralistic Emphases on the Dynamics of Historical Change"; "Methodological Individualism–Holism and Psychologism as Problems in Dynamics"; and "Explanation and Related Problems."

Modernization, as a concept in the social sciences, comes from post–1945 American social theory. John Brode's *Process of Modernization: An Annotated Bibliography on the Sociocultural Aspects of Development* lists and selectively annotates over twelve thousand writings that focus on economic development and social change in four categories: general, industrialization, urbanization, and rural modernization. Each of these four categories is, in turn, broken down into narrower divisions. "Industrialization" and "Urbanization," for example, include such divisions as "annotated case studies" of the industrial worker, the impact of industry, urban problems, and urban families. Indexes for authors and area are provided.

Citation indexes. Truly interdisciplinary, the *Arts and Humanities Citation Index* (*AHCI*) and *Social Sciences Citation Index* (*SSCI*) bibliographic sources are the most efficient ones available for tracing both the historical record and the most recent research on a particular topic in the broad areas of the social sciences and the humanities. (Although not described in detail here, most of what is said of the *AHCI* and *SSCI* is also true for *Science Citation Index*, an indispensable bibliographic source for interdisciplinary topics in the sciences and history of science and technology.)

Unfortunately, first attempts to use the indexes often result in frustration, but with patience their payoff is worth the effort. Each of these citation indexes is issued three times a year, with the final number of all titles being a cumulation of the whole year. In addition, cumulative indexes covering periods of five to ten years have been published.

In general, citation indexes are most useful for tracing the trends and developments that result from the publication of particular research reports. In scholarship one soon learns that the names of people can be substituted for the subjects with which they are associated. Thus citation indexes provide the opportunity of advancing from earlier research to more recent studies on the same topic.

These indexes consist of three separate but related indexes: the *Source Index*, the *Citation Index*, and the *Permuterm Subject Index*. Of the three, the *Citation Index* is the largest and most useful, but for a clear understanding, it is better to describe first the *Source Index*. (In most cases, using citation indexes is a two-step operation.)

The *Source Index* lists articles and related materials such as opinion papers, editorials, book reviews, literature reviews, bibliographies, and letters published in a given year in each indexed periodical. The arrangement is alphabetical by author's name. (The *SSCI* indexes about two thousand periodicals, and the *AHCI* about nine hundred, and for an interval in the late 1970s until the early 1980s, multiauthored books were indexed as well.) Along with author's name, the information given includes title of article, abbreviated title of periodical in which the article is published, volume, date, pages of issue, and number of references cited.

Beginning with the 1974 cumulation of *SSCI*, abbreviated references of all citations contained in each listed article have actually been given in the *Source Index*. Three cumulative sets of volumes, retrospectively extending *SSCI*'s coverage to 1956, are available. Characteristic of volumes published since 1974, these cumulative volumes feature the *Source Index* display of citations in each entry. This display of citations has been included in *AHCI* from the beginning.

In addition, when an article is not specifically a report of empirical research or a similar scientific communication (for example, a book review, a letter, a literature review, or a bibliography), letter symbols are used to indicate the type of information it contains. For example, an *R* symbol indicates the location of a review of a body of research literature on a topic, a *B* symbol, a book review, and so on. The table of symbols employed is part of the illustrated instructions for using these two indexes inside the cover of each volume.

The *Citation Index*, also arranged alphabetically by author's name, lists articles cited by authors listed in the *Source Index*. Information given for entries in the *Citation Index* includes brief bibliographical data on where the publication is located. Below each entry in the *Citation Index* are the names of authors and brief bibliographical data for articles in the *Source Index* in which their work is cited. Significantly, when appropriate the letter symbol given in the *Source Index* indicating a cited work's special type is repeated in the *Citation Index*. For example, an *R*, the symbol for review, would indicate that Smith's article on ethnic stereotypes is one of several discussed in a review of the literature on the study of ethnic stereotypes.

Because authors of articles in the *Source Index* ordinarily cite numerous publications, the *Citation Indexes* of both the *SSCI* and the *AHCI* are several times larger than the corresponding *Source Index*. (About 100,000 citations appear in each annual set of the *SSCI*, about 90,000 in *AHCI*.)

Although not as efficient a device for research, the *Permuterm Subject Index* serves when researchers do not know a specific author concerned with a topic for which information is required. In the *Permuterm Subject Index* words derived from the titles of articles listed in the *Source Index* are paired in columns, thus suggesting the subject treated in the *Source Index* article. Because generally titles of articles reflect the subjects they cover, this "natural-language" source is perhaps most useful for capturing topics that are rapidly changing.

American Quarterly. Philadelphia: American Studies Association, 1949–.

Articles in American Studies, 1954–1968. 2 vols. Ann Arbor, Mich.: Pierian Press, 1972.

Arts and Humanities Citation Index. Philadelphia: Institute for Scientific Information, 1978–.

Besterman, Theodore. *A World Bibliography of Bibliographies*. 5 vols. Geneva: Societas Bibliographica, 1965.

Bibliographic Index. New York: Wilson, 1938–. (Computer searchable, November 1984–.)

Birkos, Alexander S., and Lewis A. Tambs. *Historiography, Method, History Teaching: A Bibliography of Books and Articles, 1965–1972*. Hamden, Conn.: Linnet, 1975.

British Humanities Index. London: Library Association, 1915–.

Brode, John. *The Process of Modernization; an Annotated Bibliography on the Sociocultural Aspects of Development*. Cambridge, Mass.: Harvard University Press, 1969.

Humanities Index. New York: H.W. Wilson, 1974–. (Computer searchable, 1981–.)

Kinnell, Susan K. *Historiography: An Annotated Bibliography of Journal Articles, Books and Dissertations*. 2 vols. Santa Barbara, Calif.: ABC-Clio, 1987.

Salzman, Jack, ed. *American Studies: An Annotated Bibliography*. 3 vols. Cambridge: Cambridge University Press, 1986.

———. *American Studies: An Annotated Bibliography, 1984–1988*. Cambridge: Cambridge University Press, 1990.

Social Sciences Citation Index. Philadelphia: Institute for Scientific Information, 1956–.

Social Sciences Index. New York: H.W. Wilson, 1974–. (Computer searchable, 1981–).

Watson, Robert Irving. *The History of Psychology and the Behavioral Sciences*. New York: Springer Publishing Company, 1978.

SOCIAL SCIENCES: ANTHROPOLOGY

Research Guides

John M. Weeks's *Introduction to Library Research in Anthropology* is broad in coverage and foreign materials are well represented, but annotations are brief. Separate chapters cover online databases, government documents, and the Human Relations Area Files; appendices provide sketches of the *Outline of Cultural Materials* and the *Outline of World Cultures* as well as the Library of Congress classification schedules for anthropology and related subjects.

Josephine Z. Kibbee's *Cultural Anthropology: A Guide to Reference and Information Sources* is an expertly annotated and intelligently classified and indexed guide to a diversity of primarily English-language reference sources. Subfields of anthropological study receive special attention, such as linguistics, medicine, psychology, economics, urban concerns, and women.

Kibbee, Josephine Z. *Cultural Anthropology: A Guide to Reference and Information Sources.* Englewood, Colo.: Libraries Unlimited, 1991.
Weeks, John M. *Introduction to Library Research In Anthropology.* Boulder, Colo.: Westview Press, 1991.

Substantive-Bibliographic Information Sources

Consult also Ryan, Durbin, Webb, Sills, and others in the second section. In the same series and format as Ritter (second section), Joan Stevenson's *Dictionary of Concepts in Physical Anthropology* and Robert Winthrop's *Dictionary of Concepts in Cultural Anthropology* each treat one hundred major concepts in their respective fields. These works are unique to their respective areas and do much to sort out some of the confusion or misunderstanding in the scholarship that has built up over the years about any of the two hundred core concepts they treat.

Similar in purpose to the Stevenson and Winthrop volumes, but now somewhat dated, Ake Hultkrantz's *General Ethnological Concepts* deals with general concepts, schools, and methods in ethnology (and, to a certain extent, in folklore) in the fields of European regional ethnology, European general ethnology, and Anglo-American ethnology and anthropology. Except for tracing a chain of ideas in the context of a definition, no attempt is made to give the historical development of concepts. It gives "preference . . . to the terms created by European regional ethnologists, and the space devoted to their definitions is relatively larger than that reserved for those of their American colleagues." The more functionally inclined British and American anthropology, particularly after 1945, has created a mass of new and often clearly delimited concepts. In this area, the contributions of the Anglo-Americans predominate, "as they are much more concerned with problems of definition." In general, after a short definition, each article has an account, with quotations, of how authorities have treated the term. Authorities are listed for each of the four hundred-odd definitions, and at the end there is a list of the approximately five hundred works consulted. For example, the definition of *acculturation* consists of seven pages of text, including its etymology; French, Spanish, German, and Swedish equivalents; and a brief definition. The bulk of the article, however, comprises a discussion of the use of the term by thirty-five authorities.

John Joseph Honigmann's *Handbook of Social and Cultural Anthropology* is the first major assessment of what is known in social and cultural anthropology since Kroeber's *Anthropology Today*. In twenty-eight chapters, authorities present a review of literature, "including where relevant a history of what has been accomplished, major subdivisions or lines of work, unresolved issues, and future prospects." The works of some 2,400 anthropologists and others in related disciplines are discussed. Author and subject indexes give access to the whole volume.

Including social as well as cultural anthropology, Raoul Naroll and Ronald Cohen's *Handbook of Method in Cultural Anthropology* is oriented "toward theory—testing and theory—construction, rather than the analysis and presentation of ethnographic facts." This approach implies "a concern with problems that tend to promote explanation applicable across cultures." The volume is arranged in seven parts: general introduction, general problems, the fieldwork process, models of ethnographic analysis, comparative approaches, problems of categorization, and special problems of comparative method. Specialists cover the various kinds of methodological problems considered most important in cross-cultural research. Chapters end with a bibliography of the works discussed, and there are indexes of names and subjects. Besides a subject index, each volume of William Wilson Lambert Triandis's *Handbook of Cross-Cultural Psychology* contains an index of one thousand to fifteen hundred names of people whose works are discussed. More information about this source is given on p. 204.

The *Encyclopedia of World Cultures*, edited by David Levinson, provides a wide range of demographic, historical, social, economic, political, and religious information for each of the cultures for which it has an entry. All entries are signed and conclude with bibliographical references. Volumes are devoted to specific geographic designations, and each volume concludes with a glossary, a filmography, and an ethnonym index (an ethnonym is an alternative name for a culture). A more complete bibliography will be published in the tenth and final volume.

Honigmann, John Joseph, ed. *Handbook of Social and Cultural Anthropology*. Chicago: Rand McNally, 1973.

Hultkrantz, Ake. *General Ethnological Concepts*. Copenhagen: Rosenkilde and Bagger, 1960. (*International Dictionary of Regional European Ethnology and Folklore*, vol. 1.)

Levinson, David, ed. *Encyclopedia of World Cultures*. Boston, Mass.: G. K. Hall, 1991– .
Naroll, Raoul, and Ronald Cohen, eds. *Handbook of Method in Cultural Anthropology*. Garden City, N.Y.: Natural History Press for the American Museum of Natural History, 1970.
Stevenson, Joan. *Dictionary of Concepts in Physical Anthropology*. Westport, Conn.: Greenwood Press, 1990.
Triandis, William Wilson Lambert, et al., ed. *Handbook of Cross-Cultural Psychology*. 6 vols. Boston: Allyn and Bacon, 1980.
Winthrop, Robert. *Dictionary of Concepts in Cultural Anthropology*. Westport, Conn.: Greenwood Press, 1991.

Bibliographic Information Sources

Margo L. Smith and Yvonne N. Damien's *Anthropological Bibliographies: A Selected Guide* arranges more than 3,200 bibliographies, filmographies, and discographies first by major geographical region then into smaller geographic or national units. A separate section lists topical bibliographies that treat more than one geographic area or a specific subject. There is an author, title, and subject index.

A listing of articles and books by author and subject, the fifty-two-volume *Catalogue* of the Tozzer Library in Harvard University's Peabody Museum of Archaeology and Ethnology is the most important retrospective bibliography in anthropology. The microfiche edition of the catalog, issued in 1988 and current through 1986, contains more than 50 percent additional material than the original. While the entire world is represented, the Peabody Museum, and thus its library, is particularly strong in material on Central America and Mexico.

In the quarterly *Abstracts in Anthropology* about four thousand abstracts of books, conference papers, and articles from some two hundred periodicals are annually arranged first in four categories, then appropriately subdivided: archaeology; linguistics; physical anthropology; and cultural anthropology. Issues include author and subject indexes. One of the most complete current indexes to journal literature in anthropology, the quarterly *Anthropological Index to Current Periodicals in the Museum of Mankind Library* presents a general section first and then five sections devoted to a geographical area. No subject indexing, but an author index is published annually. A third quarterly, *Anthropological Literature*, publishes the indexing of Harvard University's Tozzer Library in the Peabody Museum of Archaeology and Ethnology. International in scope, it arranges entries by author in five sections: Archaeology; Biological/Physical Anthropology; Cultural/Social Anthropology; Linguistics; and Research in Related Fields/Topics of General Interest. In addition, it publishes quarterly and annual indexes of authors, archaeological sites, culture, ethnic and linguistic groups, and geographic area.

An annual, the UNESCO-sponsored *International Bibliography of Social and Cultural Anthropology* presents five thousand citations for selected books and articles published throughout the world on ethnology, archaeology, linguistics, folklore, and applied anthropology, as well as related historical and geographical materials. A section on methodological issues is included. Each volume has author and subject indexes.

Abstracts in Anthropology. Westport, Conn.: Greenwood Periodicals, 1970–

Anthropological Index to Current Periodicals in the Museum of Mankind Library. London, 1963– .

Anthropological Literature: An Index to Periodical Articles and Essays. Pleasantville, N.Y.: Redgrave, 1979–   ; for Tozzer Library, Peabody Museum of Archaeology and Ethnology.

Harvard University. Peabody Museum of Archaeology and Ethnology. Tozzer Library. *Catalogue.* 52 vols. Boston: G.K. Hall, 1961; Tozzer Library. *Author and Subject Catalogues of the Tozzer Library* (formerly the Library of the Peabody Museum of Archaeology and Ethnology). 2d. enl. ed. Boston: G. K. Hall, 1988. 1,122 fiche in 8 binders.

International Bibliography of Social and Cultural Anthropology. Paris: UNESCO, 1955–

Smith, Margo L., and Yvonne N. Damien, eds. *Anthropological Bibliographies: A Selected Guide.* South Salem, N.Y.: Redgrave, 1981.

BUSINESS AND LABOR

Research Guides

The best source for information about publications for all aspects of American business, Lorna Daniells's *Business Information Sources* is arranged first by type (that is, bibliographies, indexes, dictionaries, and so forth), then by narrow fields such as accounting, marketing, and personnel management. "Business History," for example, is a subsection of chapter 9, "Business in American Society." Detailed author and subject indexes are included.

The approach of Diane Wheeler Strauss's *Handbook of Business Information* is different than that of Daniells, with more deliberate concern for giving researchers "a grounding in business basics, and to identify, describe, and in many instances illustrate the use of key information sources." The eighteen chapters in this elaborate guide begin with "business fundamentals, introducing basic concepts and vocabulary" that helps researchers comprehend and use more effectively the myriad business information sources available. Following this discussion, key reference works are discussed. However, the focus is almost entirely directed at current matters, with seeming little regard for historical issues.

Michael R. Lavin's *Business Information: How to Find It, How to Use It* is now in its second edition. Business concepts are discussed in considerable detail and, within this context, the publications and databases valuable to business researchers are considered in chapters focusing on such topics as public and private corporate finances, the census of population and housing, general economic statistics, and industry statistics.

Along with Daniells, Lavin, and Strauss consult the previous section's research guides, like the economics and business chapter in Herron and, for some topics, perhaps, research guides listed under "Economics and Economic Thought."

Daniells, Lorna. *Business Information Sources*. Berkeley: University of California Press, 1984.

Lavin, Michael R. *Business Information: How to Find It, How to Use It*. 2d ed. Phoenix, Ariz.: Oryx Press, 1992.

Strauss, Diane Wheeler. *Handbook of Business Information*. Englewood, Colo.: Libraries Unlimited, 1988.

Substantive-Bibliographic Information Sources

An example of an excellent encyclopedia devoted to a specific geographical area, Glenn Porter's three-volume *Encyclopedia of American Economic History* is the work of economists and business historians on U.S. economic history from the seventeenth century to the mid-twentieth century. Its subtitle, "Studies of the Principal Movements and Ideas," indicates something of its depth and scope. The following major divisions are further broken down in long, discursive articles, each with extensive bibliographies: historiography of American economic history, the chronology of American economic history, the framework of American economic growth, the institutional framework, and the social framework. The last division, for example, consists of nineteen chapters on such topics as imperialism, bureaucracy, military-industrial complex, work, family, women, immigration, social mobility, and poverty. Also consult Ryan, Webb, Sills, and other sources in the previous section or, as mentioned above, research guides under "Economics and Economic Thought."

Porter, Glenn, ed. *Encyclopedia of American Economic History: Studies of the Principal Movements and Ideas*. 3 vols. New York: Charles Scribner's Sons, 1980.

Bibliographic Information Sources

Supplement the following retrospective and recurrent bibliographic sources with items such as *Bibliographic Index* or Webb, mentioned in the previous section, or the bibliographic portion of "Economics and Economic Thought."

A selective, unannotated listing, Maurice F. Neufeld's *American Working Class History* comprises over seven thousand references, including films, dissertations, periodical articles, government documents, and novels. Published materials range from the early 1800s to 1982 and come from the popular press as well as scholarly sources. Entries are organized into thirteen major classifications, some of which are subdivided. Categories cover subjects such as periods of labor development, women, strikes and strike legislation, leadership, and labor activities within individual occupations. The index lists authors' names but only titles of works for which no authors' names are available.

In *Business Periodicals Index*, U.S. titles predominate among the almost two hundred periodicals indexed by subject. The range of subjects is indicated by the subtitle: "A Cumulative Subject Index to Periodicals in the Fields of Accounting, Advertising, Banking and Finance, General Business, Insurance, Labor and Management, Public Administration, Taxation, Specific Businesses, Industries and Trades."

Since 1965, but with some exceptions, each fall issue of the quarterly *Labor History* contains an "annual bibliography of periodical articles and dissertations on American labor history." The 150-odd articles and dissertations are classified according to categories such as General History; American Labor Movements Before the Knights of Labor; Communitarian Movements; Upheaval and the Growth of the Knights of Labor; Triumph of the American Federation of Labor; The I.W.W.; Socialism; Women; Child Labor; Communism; New Deal and the Rise of the C.I.O.; Blacks and other Minority Groups; American Labor and International Affairs; and the last section, Individual Trades, Occupation, and Industries, is subdivided by topic.

Business Periodicals Index. New York: Wilson, 1958–   . (Computer searchable, 1982–.)
Labor History. New York: Tamiment Institute, 1965–   .
Neufeld, Maurice F. *American Working Class History.* New York: R.R. Bowker, 1983.

COMMUNICATION, MASS MEDIA, AND JOURNALISM

Research Guides

Jo A. Cates's *Journalism: A Guide to the Reference Literature*, is an annotated bibliography and guide to the reference literature of print and broadcast journalism. It discusses nearly one thousand items. It includes entries for material important to the practicing journalist as well as entries for catalogs, directories, and special collections invaluable to the historian.

Somewhat dated, A. George Gitter and Robert Grunin's *Communication: A Guide to Information Sources* remains useful for topics in interdisciplinary history. It annotates in seven chapters over seven hundred books and articles on aspects of communication: communication research, interpersonal communication, international communication, political communication, attitude change, mass communication, and reference works.

Cates, Jo A. *Journalism: A Guide to the Reference Literature.* Englewood, Colo.: Libraries Unlimited, 1990.
Gitter, A. George, and Robert Grunin. *Communication: A Guide to Information Sources.* Detroit: Gale Research, 1980.

Substantive-Bibliographic Information Sources

As well as the chapter on communication in Herron, consult Ryan, Durbin, Webb, Sills, and others in the previous section. A major work, Erik Barnouw's

International Encyclopedia of Communications contains over five hundred authoritative articles replete with bibliographies on topics in such fields as: advertising and public relations, ancient world, middle ages, motion pictures, music, political communication, religion, television, theater, theories of communication, and theorists. Volume 4 includes an extensive index.

The work of over thirty scholars, Ithiel Pool and Wilbur Schramm's *Handbook of Communication* attempts to distill and synthesize the diverse and diffused research literature of communication. Thirty-one chapters are arranged in three parts. Part 1, "The Communication Process," contains eleven chapters on such topics as communication systems; problems of meaning in natural languages; sociolinguistics; nonverbal communication; communication and learning; communication and children; persuasion, resistance, and attitude change; and mass media and interpersonal communication. The bulk of the volume is taken up by the eighteen chapters in part 2, "Communication Settings," including topics such as the press as a communication system; broadcasting, technological change, and the mass media; communication in small groups; consumer and advertising research; public opinion; and bargaining and communication. Finally, in part 3, two chapters survey topics in communication research: "Aggregate Data," and "Experiments on Communication Effects." In addition to a subject index, there is an index of the names of approximately 2,500 researchers whose works are discussed.

Truly interdisciplinary, semiotics is the study of patterned human behavior in communication in all modes. In Thomas A. Sebeok's three-volume *Encyclopedic Dictionary of Semiotics*, over 230 international authorities contribute entries covering most of the major academic disciplines and interdisciplinary areas in the natural and social sciences and humanities. The set comprises three sorts of entries: (1) entries tracing the historical background and range of the present usage of terms—*seme*, for instance—with recommendations, where appropriate, for standardizing current convention; (2) evaluative biographical sketches of leading figures in semiotic studies, such as Charles Morris; and assessments of aspects of the work of others, such as Aristotle, who have made pivotal contributions to semiotic studies, yet are not commonly thought of in this context; (3) expositions of the impact of semiotics on various traditional arts and sciences, say, architecture, mathematics, music, and the like; and of the penetration of semiotic methods of inquiry into the study of established academic fields of study, such as the philosophy of language, logic, and the like. Volume 3, the bibliography, cites all references mentioned in entries.

Barnouw, Erik, ed. *International Encyclopedia of Communications*. 4 vols. New York: Oxford University Press, 1989.

Pool, Ithiel, and Wilbur Schramm, eds. *Handbook of Communication*. Chicago: Rand McNally, 1973.

Sebeok, Thomas A., ed. *Encyclopedic Dictionary of Semiotics*. 3 vols. Berlin: Mouton de Gruyter, 1986.

Bibliographic Information Sources

Mass Communication: A Research Bibliography, by Donald A. Hansen and J. H. Parsons, is a selected list of some three thousand books, articles, and reports published since World War II. Arranged in a classified order, this compilation focuses on issues such as the media, programming, content, audiences, and the media's impact on society. There is an author index. Update this with the quarterly listing of "Articles on Mass Communications in US and Foreign Journals" in each issue of the *Journalism Quarterly*. An extensive bibliography, briefly annotated, Bruce L. and Chitra H. Smith's *International Communication and Political Opinion* emphasizes works on propaganda and public opinion. To a certain extent updated by the quarterly listings in "Articles on Mass Communications in American and Foreign Journals" in the *Journalism Quarterly*.

Hansen, Donald A., and J. H. Parsons. *Mass Communication: A Research Bibliography*. Berkeley, Calif. Glendessary, 1968.

Journalism Quarterly. Minneapolis: Association for Education in Journalism and Mass Communication, 1928– .

Smith, Bruce L., and Chitra H. Smith. *International Communication and Political Opinion: A Guide to the Literature*. Princeton, N.J.: Princeton University Press, 1956.

DEMOGRAPHY

Research Guides

Begin your research with Nancy Herron's chapter on demography in her *Social Sciences: A Cross-Disciplinary Guide* (previous section). Curiously, not mentioned by Herron is *The Methods and Materials of Demography*, acknowledged as systematic and comprehensive, with illustrations and extensive bibliographies, and giving current methods for dealing with demographic data: how data on population is gathered, classified, and treated to yield tabulations and various summarizing measures that reveal significant aspects of the composition and dynamics of populations. For countries with incomplete statistical series considerable attention is given to the kinds of data that are available and their quality, and to special methods worked out for handling incomplete and defective data. Each volume contains author and subject indexes.

U.S. Bureau of the Census. *The Methods and Materials of Demography*. By Henry S. Shryrock, et al. 2 vols. Washington, D.C.: Government Printing Office, 1971. (A condensed version, by Edward G. Stockwell, was published by Academic Press in 1976.)

Substantive-Bibliographic Information Sources

In William and Renee Petersen's *Dictionary of Demography: Terms, Concepts, and Institutions*, demography as a discipline is the focus for over fourteen hundred entries on vocabulary, institutions, and nations. Arranged in alphabetical order, entries vary from a line or two to "essays of some depth." When appropriate, entries include sources of additional information. The difficulties the authors encountered in compiling this work, especially with issues that relate to the prescriptive nature of the special meanings attached to terms in demography, are detailed in the introduction. There is a one-hundred-page index; to use it properly, you should read first the brief introduction on p. 1059. Although designed as an independent set, these two volumes are also part of a five-volume work that includes biographies of prominent demographers and multilingual equivalents of demographic terms.

In John A. Ross's *International Encyclopedia of Population*, over 150 internationally recognized scholars contribute 129 articles that discuss what is known on issues in the study of population. Articles, which include bibliographies, are arranged alphabetically. The article "Historical Demography" covers its scope, development, sources of data, methods of data treatment, topics of analysis, and major contributions. The bibliography lists fourteen sources.

An example of an increasing number of statistically oriented sources in demography that also include substantive discussion and bibliographic information is *International Mortality Statistics*. Michael Alderson, professor of epidemiology at the Institute of Cancer Research in the United Kingdom, presents mortality statistics for thirty-one countries, with breakdowns by sex, calendar period, and 178 causes of death. Coverage is between 1901 and 1975; the geographic areas covered are Europe (including Scandinavia), Australia, Canada, Chile, Iceland, Japan, New Zealand, Turkey, and the United States. It also provides methodological and evaluative information on the statistics and special influences on mortality such as the effects of wars and migration. Sections on method discuss the validity of existing mortality data, the use of the International Classification of Diseases, the development of national mortality registration systems, indicators of the quality of the data, and available analyses of mortality trends. A separate chapter is devoted to statistical methodology.

Consult also Ryan, Durbin, Webb, Sills, and others in the previous section.

Alderson, Michael. *International Mortality Statistics*. New York: Facts on File, 1981.
Petersen, William, and Renee Petersen. *Dictionary of Demography: Terms, Concepts, and Institutions*. 2 vols. Westport, Conn.: Greenwood Press, 1986.
Ross, John A., ed. *International Encyclopedia of Population*. 3 vols. New York: Free Press, 1982.

Bibliographic Information Sources

Worldwide in coverage, the quarterly *Population Index* briefly annotates all entries: books, articles, and official reports. The arrangement is topical, and the nineteen sections range from general population studies and theory through such subjects as mortality and international migration to official statistical publications. Of particular interest for interdisciplinary history topics are the two subdivisions of "Historical Demography and Demographic History": general historical demography and methods of historical demography. A nine-volume cumulation covering 1935 to 1968, with cumulative author and geographic indexes, was issued in 1971.

Quarterly journals, both *International Migration* and *International Migration Review* publish in selected issues references (often annotated) to some five hundred articles, books, and related reports on interdisciplinary studies of sociological, demographic, and historical aspects of migration movements.

A retrospective bibliography, J. J. Mangalam and Cornelia Morgan's *Human Migration Literature in English, 1955–62* arranges more than two thousand items in three sections: articles and chapters, books and reports, and material listed in the recurrent publications *Industry and Labor*, *International Labor Review*, and *Population Index*. The Population Research Center at the University of Texas has published the seven-volume *International Population Census Bibliography*. Six volumes cover major world regions: Latin America and the Caribbean, Africa, Oceania, North America, Asia, and Europe; the seventh is a supplement for 1968. The work is limited to population censuses, including census data on housing and education. Also useful, the dated *Bibliographic Guide to Population Geography* by Wilbur Zelinsky lists some 2,500 items, more than 2,200 of which deal with major regions and countries of the world from the late-nineteenth century to the early 1960s.

International Migration. Geneva: Intergovernmental Committee for European Migration and Research Group for European Migration Problems, 1961–   .
International Migration Review. New York: Center for Migration Studies, 1964–.
Mangalam, J. J., and Cornelia Morgan. *Human Migration Literature in English, 1955–62*. Lexington: University of Kentucky Press, 1968.
Population Index. Princeton. Office of Population Research, Princeton University, and the Population Association of America. Princeton, N. J., 1935–.
University of Texas. Population Research Center. *International Population Census Bibliography*. 7 vols. Austin: University of Texas, Bureau of Business Research, 1965–1968.
Zelinsky, Wilbur. *A Bibliographic Guide to Population Geography*. Chicago: Department of Geography, University of Chicago, 1962.

ECONOMICS AND ECONOMIC THOUGHT

Research Guides

In John Fletcher's *Information Sources in Economics*, twenty-two British librarians and economists contribute twenty-four chapters that range from "Libraries and Making a Literature Search" to "History of Economic Thought" and "Economic History" to "Social Economics." The volume's purpose is to indicate: "(1) what material there is on the various branches of the subject, what is important and valuable, and what level it best serves, (2) what tools are available to assist the researcher to make a more extensive and intensive survey of the literature of his specialized field, and (3) where the material can be found.'' There is a general index.

Chapter by chapter, William K. Hutchinson's *History of Economic Analysis: A Guide to Information Sources* surveys primary and secondary literature devoted to schools of thought, 1600 to 1940: the forerunners of classical economics, inductivists, marginalists, American economists, and twentieth-century British economic thought. Chapters consist of an introduction, major contributions, and commentaries on the major contributions. The book lists relevant journals and organizations and includes author, title, and subject indexes.

An example of a research guide dedicated to a specific country, Robert W. Lovett's *American Economic and Business History Information Sources* is a large, well-annotated bibliography of books and other information sources on all phases of economic history. Chapters present materials for economic history, business history, agricultural history, labor history, and the history of science and technology. Four appendixes list and very briefly describe articles and books on the historiography and methodology of economic and business history, as well as organizations and journals concerned with those disciplines. The index combines names, titles, and subjects.

Fletcher, John. *Information Sources in Economics.* London: Butterworths, 1984.
Hutchinson, William K. *History of Economic Analysis: A Guide to Information Sources.* Detroit: Gale Research, 1976.
Lovett, Robert W. *American Economic and Business History Information Sources.* Detroit: Gale Research, 1971.

Substantive-Bibliographic Information Sources

Edited by John Eatwell et al., *The New Palgrave: A Dictionary of Economics* is an impressive four-volume set designed to update the venerable *Dictionary of Political Economy* (1894–1899). About one hundred prominent economists contributed to the work. The articles, which range from about one page to several pages, almost always include extensive bibliographies. The index is confined to references for significant discussions of key subjects. If you do not find your topic in the index, consult the introductory notes in volume 1.

An example of a single-volume dictionary dedicated to economics is *The McGraw-Hill Dictionary of Modern Economics.* Subtitled ''A Handbook of Terms and Organizations,'' it includes about thirteen hundred terms and descriptions of some two hundred private, public, and nonprofit organizations and institutions; tables and graphic representations; and references to other sources such as economic texts and significant articles. Terms and organizations are arranged alphabetically in two parts. The suggested sources for more information on each term and organization make this the most useful dictionary of economics.

A critical survey and bibliography of economic thought, O. Popescu's ''On the Historiography of Economic Thought'' is arranged in the following parts: ''Introduction''; ''General History of Economic Thought''; ''Stages of the History of Economic Thought''; and ''Critical Guide for a History of Economics, 1768–1963.'' In the bibliography, over 170 titles are covered, most of them extensively annotated; the contributions of Planqui, MacCulloch, Twiss, Cossa, Whittaker, Oser, and Schumpeter are given special attention.

Sponsored by the American Economic Association, the three-volume *Surveys of Economic Theory* features extensive review articles by specialists analyzing the theoretical literature on such issues in economic research as money, interest, and welfare; growth and development; and resource allocation.

Consult also Herron, Ryan, Durbin, Webb, Sills, and others in the previous section.

American Economic Association. *Surveys of Economic Theory*. 3 vols. London: Macmillan, 1965–1966.
Eatwell, John, et al., eds. *The New Palgrave: A Dictionary of Economics*. 4 vols. New York: Stockton Press, 1987.
The McGraw-Hill Dictionary of Modern Economics: A Handbook of Terms and Organizations. 3d ed. New York: McGraw-Hill, 1983.
Popescu, O. ''On the Historiography of Economic Thought: A Bibliographic Survey.'' *Cahiers d'histoire mondiale* [Journal of world history] 64, no. 8 (1964): 168–209.

Bibliographic Information Sources

An annual since 1966, the American Economic Association's *Index of Economic Articles in Journals and Collective Volumes* provides in a classified arrangement an uninterrupted account of the development of the discipline since 1866. (An illustration of the scheme is provided in the economics and business chapter in Herron, described in the previous section.) Each volume is in two parts. Part 1 arranges materials by subject according to a special classification scheme consisting of twenty-three main classes with nearly seven hundred subclasses. Part 2 lists articles alphabetically by author, then chronologically. Either part makes possible tracing articles by a particular economist or on a particular topic over a great many years. The *Index* includes a methods article, chapters of books, readings in special fields, and even testimony given by economists for congressional committees.

A second annual, the UNESCO-sponsored *International Bibliography of Economics* lists approximately eight thousand items each year from about fifteen hundred international journals. Topics covered in pure and applied economics include methods, history of economic thought, economic history, and so forth. Volumes include author and subject indexes.

Using a classification scheme similar to *Index to Economic Articles*, the American Economic Association's *Journal of Economic Literature* lists and abstracts articles from journals and chapters from books. In addition each issue begins with an extensive review of literature on a topic of current interest in economics.

There are author indexes, issue by issue, and with the final issue in a volume, a cumulative index is published.

For other recommended bibliographic sources, see Herron, previous section.

American Economic Association. *Index of Economic Articles in Journals and Collective Volumes*. Homewood, Ill.: R.D. Irwin, 1886– . *International Bibliography of Economics*. Chicago, Ill.: Aldine, 1955– . *Journal of Economic Literature*. Nashville, Tenn.: American Economic Association, 1963–

EDUCATION

Research Guides

In *Education: A Guide to Reference and Information Sources*, Lois Buttlar describes over nine hundred sources for education and fields related to it, including encyclopedias, dictionaries, guides, bibliographies, indexes, abstracts, and other reference sources. The guide also indicates databases that can be searched online and major research centers and organizations.

By Marda Woodbury, *A Guide to Sources of Educational Information* presents in part 1 suggestions for effective research in education and then annotates seven hundred items in three parts. Part 2 covers general reference sources; part 3, sources limited to a particular subject (e.g., special education); part 4, computer-searchable databases, assessment instruments, library services, and other non-print information sources.

Edited by Deborah Brewer, the *ARBA Guide to Education* reprints from *American Reference Books Annual*, with some revisions and editions to reflect changes, about 450 reference sources in education published between 1970 and 1985. The guide is in three parts: part 1, ''Sources of Bibliographic Information''; part 2, ''Sources of Factual Information''; and part 3, ''Special Topics.'' Arrangement in parts 1 and 2 is by type of source (e.g., indexes, dictionaries, and encyclopedias). Part 3's special topics include bilingual and minority education, instructional media, reading, and special education. The book is indexed by author/title and subject.

Brewer, Deborah J., ed. *ARBA Guide to Education*. Littleton, Colo.: Libraries Unlimited, 1985.
Buttlar, Lois J. *Education: A Guide to Reference and Information Sources*. Englewood, Colo.: Libraries Unlimited, 1989.
Woodbury, Marda. *A Guide to Sources of Educational Information*. 2d rev. ed. Arlington, Va.: Information Resources, 1982.

Substantive-Bibliographic Information Sources

Major encyclopedias. Numerous encyclopedias and dictionaries exist for education, but here only a handful are discussed. Because of either their international scope or their orientation toward matters in education history, three ten-volume sets stand out: Lee C. Deighton's *Encyclopedia of Education*, Asa S. Knowles's *International Encyclopedia of Higher Education*, and Torsten Husen and T. Neville Postlethwaite's *International Encyclopedia of Education: Research and Studies*. Each set includes an index volume.

The work of over eleven hundred authorities, *The Encyclopedia of Education* attempts to give in a distilled format a fairly comprehensive view of what is known in a broad range of educational fields. Over one thousand lengthy articles examine institutions, processes, and products in educational practice, including history, theory, research, philosophy, and the general structure and fabric of this broad and diffuse discipline. Among these three areas of emphasis, articles on "process" will probably most interest researchers concerned with topics in interdisciplinary history. (In the *Encyclopedia of Education*, education as "product" is viewed as the outcome of the education "process.") In the "Guide to Articles" portion of the index volume, for example, pages 168–69 list almost one hundred articles on historical topics. Given the often rapid shifts or changes in what a scholarly community considers valid knowledge about a specific research topic, not unexpectedly a certain amount of caution must be exercised when dealing with articles such as Arthur R. Jensen's "Heredity, Environment, and Intelligence." Most articles include a bibliography of up to fifty entries or more of publications discussed and sources to consult for additional information.

Broad in scope, Knowles's *International Encyclopedia of Higher Education* contains over thirteen hundred descriptive and interpretive articles by some 580 authorities on a broad range of topics in higher education. Besides giving historical and current information on scores of issues related to higher education, most articles include extensive bibliographic references directing users to five categories of sources where additional information can be obtained: general references; current bibliographies; periodicals; encyclopedias, dictionaries, handbooks; and directories.

The topics of articles fall into the following categories: articles on national systems of higher education in almost two hundred countries and territories; topical essays focusing on over 280 economic, political, administrative, social, scientific, historical, and current concerns of higher education (e.g., adult education; career, vocational, and technical education; counselor education; criminology; early childhood education, teacher training for; health foods; instructional technology; occupational therapy; psychology; public health; and special education); articles on over 140 fields of study or academic disciplines that are currently part of institutions of higher education; descriptions of over three hundred national, international, and regional educational associations; facts about over ninety centers of higher education research; summaries of internationally influential reports on higher education; and descriptions of over two hundred documentation and information centers.

The *International Encyclopedia of Education: Research and Studies*, edited by Husen and Postlethwaite, emphasizes six themes: human development, educational policy, curriculum and educational levels, evaluation and research, educational systems, and disciplines related to education. This encyclopedia concentrates more on primary and secondary education than on postsecondary education. The set arranges fourteen hundred articles by thirteen hundred authorities from over one hundred countries in twenty-five broad categories (listed in groups in the index volume), and includes topics in administration; adult education; comparative and international education; counseling; curriculum; developing countries; discipline; early childhood; economics; educational institutes, organizations, and societies; policy and planning; higher education; educational technology; evaluation; human development; motivation; national systems; research; sex roles; social stratification; special education; teacher education; vocational education; and women in education. Systems of education in 160 countries are discussed along with demographic data provided in charts and tabular form.

For additional references, consult Herron, Ryan, Durbin, Webb, Sills, and others in the previous section.

Deighton, Lee C., ed. *The Encyclopedia of Education*. 10 vols. New York: Macmillan, 1971.

Husen, Torsten, and T. Neville Postlethwaite, eds. *The International Encyclopedia of Education: Research and Studies*. 10 vols. Oxford: Pergamon, 1985.

Knowles, Asa S., ed. *International Encyclopedia of Higher Education*. 10 vols. San Francisco: Jossey-Bass, 1977.

Bibliographic Information Sources

Recurrent bibliographic sources. International in scope, the monthly *Research in Education* lists and abstracts about twelve hundred publications added to the Educational Resources Information Center (ERIC) system, which in 1989 held approximately 275,000 publications. Arranged in a classification scheme consisting of seventeen categories, entries are indexed by subject, author, sponsoring institution, and "publication type." Begun in July 1979, the publication type index identifies the *form* or *organization* of a publication, as contrasted to its subject matter. Examples of what is meant by form are "Bibliographies," "Dissertations," "Directories," "State of the Art Reviews," and "Tests, Questionnaires, Evaluation Instruments." Cumulative indexes for *RIE* are published in both paper and microfiche. On a monthly basis, with annual cumulations, *Current Index to Journals in Education* indexes by subject and author some sixteen thousand articles in seven hundred journals each year. Articles are briefly annotated. *Education Index*, a subject index of education literature from about 250 journals, also includes selected pamphlets, yearbooks, and special reports.

Current Index to Journals in Education. Phoenix, Ariz.: Oryx, 1964–. (Computer searchable as part of ERIC system, 1969–.)

Education Index. New York: Wilson, 1929–. (Computer searchable, 1984–.)

Research in Education. Washington, D.C.: Government Printing Office, 1956–. (Computer searchable as part of ERIC system, 1966–.)

Retrospective bibliographies. For topics in the history of American education, consult Michael W. Sedlak and Timothy Walch's *American Educational History: A Guide to Information Sources*, and Francesco Cordasco, et al., *The History of American Education*. The first arranges entries in nine sections: "American Educational Development (1632–1965)," "Pedagogy," "Higher Education," "Outsiders," "Race and Education," "Families and Delinquents," "Cities," "Schooling and the Workplace," and "Guides to Further Research." Brief historiographic essays introduce chapters. Entries are briefly annotated, and access to titles is provided in both subject and author indexes. The compilers were selective in choosing materials, with preference given to literature in books and periodicals of "enduring value" not cited in other bibliographies, with emphasis on materials about American educational history published since 1965. Minor attention is given to Canadian sources.

Cordasco's volume cites almost 2,500 mostly unannotated reference works and primary and secondary sources. Among the eleven chapters are "Historiography of American Education"; "Source Collections"; "The American College and University"; and "Teachers, Teaching, Textbooks, and Curriculum." Indexes of authors, titles, and subject complete the volume.

Cordasco, Francesco, et al. *The History of American Education*. Detroit: Gale Research, 1979.
Sedlak, Michael W., and Timothy Walch, eds. *American Educational History: A Guide to Information Sources*. Detroit: Gale Research, 1981.

POLITICAL SCIENCE

Research Guides

Now in a fourth edition, Frederick L. Holler's *Information Sources of Political Science* is a massive research guide of over 2,400 entries, with much material useful for interdisciplinary research topics. After an introductory section discussing political reference theory, Holler presents seven chapters devoted to: general reference sources; social sciences; American government, politics, and public law; international relations; comparative and area studies of politics and govenment; political theory; and public administration. Each chapter is appropriately subdivided. The "social sciences" chapter, for example, is broken down into anthropology, economics, education, and geography. There are author, title, and subject indexes.

Subtitled "A Guide to Reference and Information Sources," Henry E. York's *Political Science* describes over seven hundred major resources designed for political science and its subdisciplines and related social science fields. Printed reference sources, mostly in English and published between 1980 and 1987 are covered, although a few older works are included. Since chapter titles suggest an organizational approach that follows Holler's, evidently this research guide is seen as an update of Holler. One chapter, however, treats online and CD-ROM databases.

Holler, Frederick L. *Information Sources of Political Science*. 4th ed. Santa Barbara,
    Calif.: ABC-Clio, 1986.
York, Henry E. *Political Science: A Guide to Reference and Information Sources*. En-
    glewood, Colo.: Libraries Unlimited, 1990.

Substantive Information Sources

No other discipline is blessed with the same quantity of specialized dictionaries as political science. Each of the dictionaries in the ABC-Clio series on dictionaries in political science focuses on a particular area of study, such as local government, Latin American politics, or international law. Designed for easy access to both the definition and the significance of terms, these dictionaries treat each entry according to a uniform format that helps one obtain a broader understanding of concepts in both their historical and their contemporary contexts. Entries have two parts: the first defines the meaning of the term, the second explains its importance. A selected bibliography of sources of additional information is given at the end, but no attempt is made to connect individual terms with these titles. Because entries are grouped according to the topic they cover, the index should be consulted.

Ali, Sheikh R. *International Organizations and World Order Dictionary*. Santa Barbara,
    Calif.: ABC-Clio, 1991.
———. *The Peace and Nuclear War Dictionary*. Santa Barbara, Calif.: ABC-Clio, 1989.
Bledsoe, Robert L., and Boleslaw A. Boczek. *The International Law Dictionary*. Santa
    Barbara, Calif.: ABC-Clio, 1987.
Chandler, Ralph C., et al. *The Constitutional Law Dictionary*. Volume 1. *Individual
    Rights*. Volume 2. *Governmental Powers*. Santa Barbara, Calif.: ABC-Clio, 1985.
Chandler, Ralph C., and Jack C. Plano. *The Public Administration Dictionary*. Santa
    Barbara, Calif.: ABC-Clio, 1988.
Elliot, Jeffrey M., and Sheikh R. Ali. *The Presidential-Congressional Political
    Dictionary*. Santa Barbara, Calif.: ABC-Clio, 1984.
———. *The State and Local Government Political Dictionary*. Santa Barbara, Calif.:
    ABC-Clio, 1988.
Elliot, Jeffrey M., and Robert Reginald. *The Arms Control, Disarmament, and Military
    Security Dictionary*. Santa Barbara, Calif.: ABC-Clio, 1989.
Fry, Gerald W., and Galen R. Martin. *The International Development Dictionary*. Santa
    Barbara, Calif.: ABC-Clio, 1991.
Kruschke, Earl R. *The Public Policy Dictionary*. Santa Barbara, Calif.: ABC-Clio, 1987.
McCrea, Barbara P., et al. *The Soviet and East European Political Dictionary*. Santa
    Barbara, Calif.: ABC-Clio, 1984.
Phillips, Claude S. *The African Political Dictionary*. Santa Barbara, Calif.: ABC-Clio,
    1984.

Plano, Jack C. *The American Political Dictionary*. 7th ed. Santa Barbara, Calif.: ABC-Clio, 1985.

Plano, Jack C., and Roy Olton. *The International Relations Dictionary*. 4th ed. Santa Barbara, Calif.: ABC-Clio, 1988.

Plano, Jack C., et al. *Political Science Dictionary*. Hinsdale, Ill.: Dryden Press, 1973.

Renstrom, Peter G. *The American Law Dictionary*. Santa Barbara, Calif.: ABC-Clio, 1990.

Renstrom, Peter G., and Chester B. Rogers. *The Electoral Politics Dictionary*. Santa Barbara, Calif.: ABC-Clio, 1987.

Rossi, Ernest E., and Barbara P. McCrea. *The European Political Dictionary*. Santa Barbara, Calif.: ABC-Clio, 1985.

Rossi, Ernest E., and Jack C. Plano. *The Latin American Political Dictionary*. Santa Barbara, Calif.: ABC-Clio, 1980.

Smith, John W., and John S. Klemanski. *The Urban Politics Dictionary*. Santa Barbara, Calif.: ABC-Clio, 1990.

Ziring, Lawrence. *The Middle East Political Dictionary*. Santa Barbara, Calif.: ABC-Clio, 1984.

Ziring, Lawrence, and C. I. Eugene Kim. *The Asian Political Dictionary*. Santa Barbara, Calif.: ABC-Clio, 1985.

Substantive-Bibliographic Information Sources

Fred I. Greenstein and Nelson W. Polsby edited the multivolume *Handbook of Political Science*, a distillation and synthesis of what is currently known about political institutions, organizations, and behavior. As a measure of the significance attached to it, each volume was reviewed separately in the *American Political Science Review* 77 (1977): 1621–36. Fifty-seven authorities have contributed thirty-eight chapters. Over five thousand studies are discussed.

Volume 1, *Political Science: Scope and Theory*, covers in five chapters: historical perspectives, explanation and interpretation, relevance of the classics of political philosophy, central concepts and their application, and problems of political evaluation. *Micropolitical Theory*, volume 2, is also in five chapters: personality and politics, socialization, recruitment, groups theories, and organization theory. The six chapters of volume 3, *Macropolitical Theory*, are: political development, governments and political oppositions, totalitarian and authoritarian regimes, theory of collective choice, revolutions and collective violence, and social structure and politics. Volume 4, *Nongovernmental Politics*, covers: political participation, public opinion and voting behavior, interest groups, and political parties. Volume 5, *Governmental Institutions and Processes*, discusses: constitutionalism, federalism, executives, legislatures, courts, and bureaucracies. Similarly structured volumes are devoted to: *Policies and Policymaking*; *Strategies of Inquiry*; and *International Politics*. The last volume indexes the set.

According to editor David Miller, the *Blackwell Encyclopedia of Political Thought* attempts to be a guide to the major ideas and doctrines that influence the contemporary world, outlines the thought of leading political theorists, past and present, and considers the ways in which thinking about politics has evolved historically. The work of over one hundred internationally known political scientists, the volume gives attention largely to the western tradition of political thought. Designed to introduce certain nonwestern traditions, however, survey articles on such nonwestern topics as Chinese, Hindu, and Islamic political thought are included. Philosophers, historians, lawyers, economists, and sociologists are included only when they have made some direct contribution to political debate. A reading list that includes modern English-language editions (where these exist) of the primary literature referred to, as well as relevant secondary literature, closes each entry. The volume includes a fifteen-page index.

A companion to Miller's *Blackwell Encyclopedia of Political Thought*, Vernon Bogdanor's *Blackwell Encyclopedia of Political Institutions* contains extensive entries on the central concepts used in the study of the political institutions of advanced industrial societies, the principal political organizations and movements in these societies, the main types of political community, and the leading political scientists of the past, but excludes political scientists still living and selected "culture-specific terms that have either passed into general use, or whose use is confined to Britain, the United States and Western Europe."

Dan Nimmo and Keith R. Sanders edited *The Handbook of Political Communication*, a volume of twenty-two chapters arranged in four major areas of research: part 1, "Contemporary Theoretical Approaches"; part 2, "Modes and Means of Persuasive Communication in Politics"; part 3, "Political Communication Settings"; and part 4, "Methods of Study." Each chapter is heavily documented. In addition, for historians wanting to research interdisciplinary topics in political communication, the two appendixes are also promising as sources of information: Appendix A, European Research, and Appendix B, Guide to the Literature. The latter, for example, critically discusses bibliographies, scholarly journals, professional and popular publications, books, dissertations and theses, indexes and indexing services, professional associations and conventions, and nonprint sources.

Bogdanor, Vernon, ed. *Blackwell Encyclopedia of Political Institutions*. New York: Blackwell, 1987.
Greenstein, Fred I., and Nelson W. Polsby, eds. *Handbook of Political Science*. 9 vols. Reading, Mass.: Addison-Wesley, 1975.
Miller, David, ed. *Blackwell Encyclopedia of Political Thought*. New York: Blackwell, 1987.
Nimmo, Dan, and Keith R. Sanders, eds. *The Handbook of Political Communication*. Beverly Hills, Calif.: Sage Publications, 1981.

Bibliographic Information Sources

One of several recurrent bibliographical publications in political science, the UNESCO-sponsored *International Bibliography of Political Science* includes much material that discusses concepts and/or methods in the discipline. An annual containing about five thousand entries for articles and monographs, it claims that only works "of true scientific character" are selected for inclusion; journalistic or polemical items are excluded. Each volume is arranged according to a detailed classification scheme of six broad categories: general political science, political thought, government and public administration, governmental process, international relations, and area studies. There are author and subject indexes.

International Political Science Abstracts is more selective than the *International Bibliography of Political Science*, being limited to 150 periodicals. It arranges entries according to the same classification, however; each issue has a subject index, and each volume has cumulative subject and author indexes.

Other recommended recurrent bibliographical sources include *ABC POL SCI: Advance Bibliography of Contents*, which reproduces in advance of their publication the tables of contents of 260 journals in political science, public administration, law, and related fields. There is an author index (cumulated twice yearly) and an annual subject index.

United States Political Science Documents, an annual computer-produced abstract journal, contains 2,500-odd abstracts from about 120 journals, mostly published in the United States. In two volumes, the smaller consists of the "Document Descriptions Listing" where each entry contains: (1) an accession number (entries are listed in numerical order); (2) bibliographical information; (3) an abstract of the article; (4) special features (the titles of all tables, charts, figures, maps, and the like); and (5) the subject headings (descriptors) under which the article is listed in the various indexes. The second volume has five indexes: Author/Contributor; Subject; Geographic Area; Proper Name; and Journal Title.

ABC POL SCI: Advance Bibliography of Contents: Political Science and Government. Santa Barbara, Calif.: ABC-Clio, 1969–.
International Bibliography of Political Science. Chicago: Aldine, 1954–.
International Political Science Abstracts. Paris: UNESCO, 1951–.
United States Political Science Documents. Pittsburgh: University Center for International Studies, University of Pittsburgh, 1975–. (Computer searchable, 1975–.)

PSYCHOLOGY

Research Guides

Raymond G. McInnis's *Research Guide for Psychology* is arranged according to the classification schedule employed by *Psychological Abstracts*. This guide describes over twelve hundred reference and related materials in psychology and related areas such as cross-cultural psychology, sociology, and anthropology. As well as recommending appropriate search strategies, special attention is given those materials designed to reveal the substantive literature of topics, for example, literature reviews, handbooks, and the like. Critically annotated, users are generally furnished with enough information about a source to go straight to the library's shelves and begin using it. There is an index of authors, titles, and subjects.

Designed primarily for undergraduate use, Jeffrey G. Reed and Pam M. Baxter's *Library Use: A Handbook for Psychology* in its chapters provides information on selecting a topic, locating books and book reviews, using indexes and abstracts to find articles, computerized literature searches, materials on tests and measurements, and biographical sources.

Henry Lawton's *Psychohistorian's Handbook* is made up of chapters that present overviews of psychohistory as a discipline and its various methodologies and approaches. Extensive bibliographies with some brief annotations are provided throughout. A brief and sketchy chapter is devoted to library resources. Interesting features include chapters on getting published, the emotional and intellectual traits of a psychohistorian, and a bibliography of notable psychohistorical works.

Although outdated, Lloyd DeMause's unannotated *Bibliography of Psychohistory* remains of some use. It is unconstrained by language of publication, and it is organized into sections for: Asia; history of childhood; medieval and Renaissance history; methodology; and modern history. However, it is most valuable for its reprinting of Manuel D. Lopez's "A Guide to the Interdisciplinary Literature of the History of Childhood." In this guide, well-annotated entries for a variety of reference tools are organized under sections, some of which cover: autobiographies and biographies; bibliographies; character-books, courtesy books and etiquette books; diaries and letters; and the history of pediatrics.

DeMause, Lloyd, ed. *A Bibliography of Psychohistory*. New York: Garland Press, 1975.
Lawton, Henry. *The Psychohistorian's Handbook*. New York: Psychohistory Press, 1988.
McInnis, Raymond G. *Research Guide for Psychology*. Westport, Conn.: Greenwood Press, 1982.
Reed, Jeffrey G., and Pam M. Baxter. *Library Use: A Handbook for Psychology*. Washington, D.C.: American Psychological Association, 1983.

Substantive-Bibliographic Information Sources

Benjamin B. Wolman's *International Encyclopedia of Psychiatry, Psychology, Psychoanalysis and Neurology* is a work of some two thousand contributors. It seeks to cover "the various branches of science dealing with human nature, its deficiencies, and their treatment." Over nineteen hundred highly compressed, interpretive articles examine and assess the theory and research of narrow topics within areas of psychology such as experimental (human and animal), physiological, developmental, social, educational, applied, and industrial. In addition, articles treat topics in personality, communication and psycholinguistics, psychological measurement and methodology, psychohistory, biochemistry, genetics, and psychosomatic medicine. Psychohistory, for example, receives four pages of discussion and recommends nine sources of additional information.

Cross-references lead you to the articles "History and Psychoanalysis" and "History and Psychology." When not certain about what article to consult, the name and subject indexes in volume 12, the index volume, and the cross-references should be used.

John Popplestone and Mary McPherson White's *Dictionary of Concepts in General Psychology* is in the same series and format as the Ritter volume (previous section), and is an excellent place to locate the evolution of the meanings of about one hundred concepts in general psychology as well as important contributors to the discussion.

William Wilson Lambert Triandis's six-volume *Handbook of Cross-Cultural Psychology*, an elaborate treatise of cross-cultural scholarship, is described in greater detail in McInnis's *Research Guide for Psychology*. In over forty chapters by recognized authorities, the set examines a broad range of topics that currently concern this emergent subdiscipline. In contrast to more traditional psychologists, the editors note, "cross-cultural psychologists try to discover laws that will be stable over time and across cultures," a task made difficult when the existing "data excludes the great majority of mankind who live in Asia and the Southern Hemisphere." Besides a subject index, each volume contains an index of one thousand to fifteen hundred names of people whose works are discussed. The individual works mentioned are cited at the end of chapters.

See also Lawton, described in the previous section (Research Guides).

Popplestone, John, and Mary McPherson White. *Dictionary of Concepts in General Psychology*. Westport, Conn.: Greenwood Press, 1988.
Triandis, William Wilson Lambert, et al., ed. *Handbook of Cross-Cultural Psychology*. 6 vols. Boston: Allyn and Bacon, 1980.
Wolman, Benjamin B. *International Encyclopedia of Psychiatry, Psychology, Psychoanalysis and Neurology*. 12 vols., and "Progress" volume. New York: Van Nostrand Reinhold, 1977.

Bibliographic Information Sources

The monthly *Psychological Abstracts*, generally recognized as a model of an abstract journal, annually contains over twenty thousand entries for doctoral dissertations and articles in periodicals published around the world. (Currently 25 percent more entries are contained in the computerized database, including doctoral dissertations since 1980.) Materials are arranged in a classified scheme composed of eighty-odd subdivisions. Basic to understanding the indexing employed by *Psychological Abstracts* is familiarity with the *Thesaurus of Psychological Index Terms*. Containing over four thousand terms, it leads one to the appropriate descriptors (subject headings) to use when looking for literature on a topic. Each issue of *Psychological Abstracts* includes an author index and a "brief subject" index, and cumulative author and subject indexes are currently published annually.

Psychological Abstracts. Washington, D.C.: American Psychological Association, 1927–. (Computer searchable, 1967–.)

Retrospective bibliographies. A rapidly growing field, the history of psychology has several bibliographies. Indispensable for the intellectual history of psychology and related disciplines, Robert I. Watson's *Eminent Contributors to Psychology* is an elaborate listing in two volumes of both primary and secondary sources for some five hundred individuals who lived between 1600 and 1967 and who made an important contribution to the development of psychological literature. (For a detailed description of organization and use of Watson, see McInnis above.) Smaller in scope, both Wayne Viney's *History of Psychology* and Watson's own *History of Psychology and the Behavioral Sciences* (previous section) complement Watson's *Eminent Contributors to Psychology.*

Viney, Wayne, et al. *History of Psychology: A Guide to Information Sources.* Detroit: Gale Research, 1979.

Watson, Robert I. *Eminent Contributors to Psychology.* 2 vols. New York: Springer Publishing, 1975–1976.

SOCIOLOGY

Research Guides

Stephen H. Aby's *Sociology: A Guide to Reference and Information Sources* is arranged in three sections: part 1, general social science; part 2, individual disciplines, such as education, economics, psychology, social work, anthropology, and history; and part 3, the largest section, general reference sources in sociology and in twenty-three subdivisions. The guide covers over eight hundred guides, bibliographies, indexes and abstracts, handbooks and yearbooks, dictionaries and encyclopedias, statistics sources, directories, and biographies.

Consult also Herron, Ryan, Durbin, Webb, Sills, and others in the previous section.

Aby, Stephen H. *Sociology: A Guide to Reference and Information Sources.* Littleton, Colo.: Libraries Unlimited, 1987.

Substantive-Bibliographic Information Sources

The sources below can only suggest the richness of the literature on interdisciplinary combinations of history and sociology.

To demonstrate how sociology can contribute to historical research, in *Sociology and History* Peter Burke, himself a historian, applies sociological concepts and methods to historical events, mostly eighteenth-century Europe. His first chapter highlights the development of social history, with particular attention given the contributions of Karl Lamprecht, Lucien Febvre, Marc Bloch, and Fernand Braudel. Then Burke explores social structure, including models, sampling, systems, functions, social role, kinship, socialization, class, bureaucracy, myths, rituals, and so on, all of which, he argues, can be useful to historians.

Finally, Burke analyzes the work of four historians who explain historical events with interdisciplinary methods: Braudel, who focuses on the concept of time in his studies of the Mediterranean; William McNeill, who considers the impact of the frontier in the Ottoman Empire; Le Roy Ladurie, who emphasizes population in his Languedoc study; and Nathan Wachtel, who looks at acculturation in Spanish Peru.

The Handbook of Sociology, edited by Neil J. Smelser, while not covering the entire landscape of the discipline, seeks to incorporate most of what sociologists consider the purview of its main subfields. Twenty-two chapters fall in four broad parts. Part 1 deals with theoretical and methodological issues. Chapters focus on these themes as opposed to representations of the knowledge in sociology as a social science; how the central concept in sociology, social structure, has been employed at both macroscopic and microscopic levels of analysis; the methodological status of data and its measurement; and the problem of inferring causal relationships.

Part 2, which concentrates on inequality, another central conceptual framework in sociology, is organized according to the major bases of inequality in society: economic; racial and ethnic; age; and gender and sex. Major social institutions are the focus of part 3: political and economic institutions and other institutions that have a primary emphasis on socialization such as: family, education, culture, the mass media, science, and medicine. Finally, the four chapters in part 4 examine social processes and social change: the organization of social processes around the dimension of space; deviance and social control; the dynamics of social movements; and international economic arrangements and their impact on developmental processes within nations. The scope of this work, which has both author and subject indexes, is perhaps best made evident by counting the authors listed in the name index—approximately 2,700.

The *Encyclopedia of Sociology*, edited by Edgar F. Borgatta, is composed of lengthy signed entries, with extensive bibliographies, that discuss such subjects as African Studies, African-American Studies, popular culture, and historical sociology. More conceptual subjects represented include alienation, courtship, and social humor.

Successive editions of the *Encyclopedia of Social Work* are excellent for tracing the development of social work, especially in the United States. Volumes cover current developments and trends of social work, social security, and related matters. Over two hundred authoritative articles by specialists survey the literature of a broad range of topics. The article "History of Social Welfare," for example, considers the general course of development of social welfare and social work in the United States. It outlines the ideas and institutions brought by European colonists, the relation between nineteenth-century charities and twentieth-century social welfare, the changing scope of social welfare, and the origin and growth of professional social work. In addition, articles are heavily documented, and their bibliographies are often miniature guides to research on the topic. Finally the set contains a directory of international, governmental, and volunteer social work organizations, statistics on U.S. social welfare and demographic conditions, and biographies of prominent people in the field.

The primary focus of the British publication *A New Dictionary of the Social Sciences*, edited by Geoffrey Duncan Mitchell, is sociology. Among the 350-odd articles are numerous biographical sketches of prominent sociologists. Selected entries contain references to additional sources of information.

Borgatta, Edgar F., ed. *Encyclopedia of Sociology*. 4 vols. New York: Macmillan, 1992.

Burke, Peter. *Sociology and History*. Winchester, Mass.: Allen and Unwin, 1980.

Encyclopedia of Social Work. 18th ed. 2 vols. Silver Springs, Md.: National Association of Social Workers, 1987.

Mitchell, G. Duncan, ed. *A New Dictionary of the Social Sciences*. New York: Aldine, 1979.

Smelser, Neil J., ed. *The Handbook of Sociology*. Beverly Hills, Calif.: Sage Publications, 1988.

History of the family. Over 120 items are discussed in the two evaluative studies that follow. In her article, "The History of the Family as an Interdisciplinary Field," social historian Tamara K. Hareven argues that historians studying the family have tended to borrow from a narrow range of models and theories in the social sciences and to overlook possible alternative approaches. As an interdisciplinary field, Hareven states, the history of the family "utilizes the tools of demography and the conceptual models of anthropology, psychology, and sociology." She divides her article into the following sections: the anthropological perspective; demography; the psychological impact: a developmental approach; the sociological dimension; the family and social change: the problem of interaction; and prospects.

In her article, "The Family Revisited: Themes in Recent Social Science Research," Arlene Skolnick extends Hareven's discussion. She notes that new approaches to the family seem to close some of the gaps that have separated the work of historians and social scientists. New research in particular has introduced concepts that historians "may find useful." Finally, she argues that many of the questions raised by social scientists but still not yet adequately answered by them, "can be answered only by historical research."

Hareven, Tamara K. "The History of the Family as an Interdisciplinary Field." *Journal of Interdisciplinary History* 2 (1971–1972): 399–414.

Skolnick, Arlene. "The Family Revisited: Themes in Recent Social Science Research." *Journal of Interdisciplinary History* 5 (Spring 1975): 703–19.

Bibliographic Information Sources

Using an interdisciplinary approach, the UNESCO-sponsored *International Bibliography of Sociology* annually includes over five thousand citations of articles, books, and related works considered important, regardless of the country of origin or the language in which they are drafted. Volumes 1–4 appeared in *Current Sociology* (1951–1954). Items are arranged according to an elaborate classification scheme. Section A, "History and Organization of Social Studies," includes historical developments, current trends, reference works, and bibliographies. Section B, "Theories and Methods of Sociology," has subdivisions on definitions and fundamental problems, scope, methodology, general theoretical systems, and analysis of basic sociological concepts. The subdivision on methodology is further divided into such categories as historical methods, statistical methods, sampling techniques in fieldwork, and test models and scales. Section C, "Social Structure," contains such subdivisions as demography, age groups, geographical and ecological factors, culture and personality, social complexes and social groups, social stratification (and social mobility), marriage and family, ethnic groups, economic institutions, labor organizations, and political and religious institutions. Among the subdivisions of section D, "Social Control and Communication," are customs; morals; religion; mythology; law, opinion, and attitudes; ideologies; language; mass media; and education. "Social Change," section E, focuses on issues such as the influence of technology on social change, social factors of economic development, and the history of human societies. Section F, "Social Problems and Social Policy," lists studies of the practical application of research findings in determining the roots of problems and in providing remedies. Among the subdivisions on social problems are poverty and unemployment, sexual abnormalities, drug addiction and alcoholism, crime and delinquency, and punishment and penal institutions; the subsection on social policy contains such topics on the family as: protection, health insurance, social service, and community organizations and services. About fifteen hundred international journals are searched. There are author and subject indexes.

The eight issues of each annual volume of *Sociological Abstracts* contain over five thousand abstracts of books, sections of books, and articles. Among the twenty-one divisions and fifty-one subdivisions of the elaborate classification scheme are methodology and research technology, history, theory and the sociology of knowledge, social psychology, culture and social structure, social change and economic development, mass phenomena, political interactions, social differentiation, urban sociology, sociology of religion, demography and human biology, the family and socialization, sociology of health and medicine, and social problems and welfare. The indexing, by subject and author, can be confusing. There are indexes for each issue, annual indexes, and cumulative indexes covering five-year periods. Now available in CD-ROM format, the confusing problems inherent in the paper-copy indexing are eliminated.

International Bibliography of Sociology. London: Tavistock, 1952–
Sociological Abstracts. San Diego, Calif.: Sociological Abstracts, 1952–. (Computer
     searchable, 1963– .)

Social stratification and mobility. Subtitled "A Research Bibliography," Norval D. Glenn's *Social Stratification* lists books and articles published in English primarily between 1940 and 1968. Indexed by author only, the unannotated entries are arranged under such topics as class conflict, income distribution, role of minorities, characteristics of lower, middle, and upper strata, and so forth. About thirty-five bibliographies on social stratification or related topics are also included.

Glenn, Norval D., et al. *Social Stratification: A Research Bibliography*. Berkeley, Calif.: Glendessary Press, 1970.

Marriage and the family. Joan Aldous has edited the two-volume basic set to research on marriage and family topics: Volume 1, *International Bibliography of Research in Marriage and the Family, 1900–1964*, an extensive bibliography of over twelve thousand research studies, is arranged in five sections: a "key-word-in-context" or KWIC index, a subject index, a "complete reference list," an author list, and a list of periodicals. A code combining letters and numbers directs users from entries in other sections to the "complete reference list." In the subject index, items are classified in twelve divisions and 131 subdivisions, including such headings as macroscopic studies of marriage and family as an institution, family transactions with groups, mate selection, marriage and divorce, reproductive behavior, family and sex, special problems (disorganization, economic stress, mentally ill, juvenile delinquency, mobility, and so on), applied fields (education for marriage and parenthood, sex education, marriage counseling, therapy), subcultural group membership and the family (ethnic groups in the United States, family and social class, and trends in marriage, fertility, and divorce rates). An "Aids for Research" section lists family research methodologies, critiques and analyses of research literature, and bibliographies. Volume 2 contains about twice as many entries published between 1965 and 1970.

An updating of Aldous, David H. L. Olsen's *Inventory of Marriage and Family Literature* is now issued annually. According to the editors, coverage is expanded from earlier volumes (where only research and theory articles were included), but entries are limited to articles from English-language periodicals. The same three types of indexes are modified to facilitate use. The subject index has been expanded to provide broader coverage and a more detailed breakdown of topics of growing interest such as: alternative life-styles, futuristic studies of the family, day care, foster care, family of the physically ill, employment and the family, father-child relationships, specific stages of family life cycle, pregnancy, abortion, premarital sex, marital sex, extramarital sex, child abuse, drug abuse, runaways, suicide and the family, bereavement and the family, sex education, and social mobility and the family. In the classified subject index, two subdivisions, "critiques of the literature," and "classified bibliography," usefully draw together all articles that give assessments or a synthesis of recent work. For example, the 1985 volume lists E. Zaretsky's bibliography, "New Work on the History of the Family," *Theory and Society* 14 (1985): 371–80.

Two retrospective bibliographies on topics in the history of the family complement Hareven and Skolnick (above): James Wallace Milden's *The Family in*

Past Time annotates over thirteen hundred entries organized topically into such categories as methodology and theory; the family in European history; American family history; Latin American, African, and Asian family history; and family history projects. Gerald L. Soliday's *History of the Family and Kinship* covers the literature more comprehensively than Milden. It includes current as well as historical material. The 6,200 entries are arranged first according to geographical and/or national divisions and then chronologically. Entries include books, chapters of books, articles, and government publications (for example, Daniel P. Moynihan's 1965 report, *The Negro Family in America*). There are no annotations but there is an author index.

Aldous, Joan. *International Bibliography of Research in Marriage and the Family, 1900–1964*. 2 vols. Minneapolis: Minnesota Family Life Study Center and the Institute of Life Insurance, 1967–1974.

Milden, James Wallace. *The Family in Past Time: A Guide to the Literature*. New York: Garland, 1977.

Olsen, David H. L., et al. *Inventory of Marriage and Family Literature*. St. Paul, Minn.: Family Social Science, University of Minnesota, 1975–   .

Soliday, Gerald L., ed. *History of the Family and Kinship: A Select International Bibliography*. Millwood, N.Y.: Kraus International Publications, 1980.

WOMEN'S STUDIES

Research Guides

Susan E. Searing's *Introduction to Library Research in Women's Studies* introduces reference works and library services useful in investigating topics related to women. The bulk of the materials described are selected bibliographies, indexes, catalogs, handbooks, directories, and biographical dictionaries. In part 1, five chapters discuss "What Is Women's Studies?" developing research strategy, the library card catalog, going beyond the card catalog, and interlibrary loan services. Part 2, "The Tools of Research," is divided into eleven chapters: guides to women's studies research and bibliographies of reference sources, general women's studies bibliographies, multidisciplinary bibliographies and indexes, indexes in special fields, library catalogs and guides to special collections of books and archives, biographical sources, directories of organizations and services, microform services, online services, periodicals, and miscellaneous guides and handbooks. Chapters 3 and 4 are further subdivided. For example, the chapter on bibliographies and indexes falls into seventeen subdivisions, from anthropology and the arts through minority studies and political science to religion and sociology. The works of over four hundred authors are discussed. There are author, title, and subject indexes.

Women's Studies: A Guide to Information Sources, by British librarians Sarah Carter and Maureen Ritchie, critically annotates about one thousand of the most important printed and organizational sources in women's studies published throughout the world. Part 1 focuses on general reference sources. Part 2, "Women in the World," considers the international perspectives on women, including materials designed for specific geographical areas: Africa; Asia and the Pacific; Australia and New Zealand; Europe; Latin America and the Caribbean; The Middle East; and North America. Part 3 treats special subjects such as the arts and media; black women; education; history; law and politics; lesbians; literature and language; mind and body; science, mathematics and science; technology; society and the environment; spirituality, mythology, and religion; travel, leisure, sport; and women in the labor force. The volume's last section is a post-script section, "Men's Studies."

Carter, Sarah, and Maureen Ritchie. *Women's Studies: A Guide to Information Sources.* London: Mansell, 1990.
Searing, Susan E. *Introduction to Library Research in Women's Studies.* Boulder, Colo.: Westview Press, 1985.

Substantive-Bibliographic Information Sources

The first encyclopedic set in women's studies is Helen Tierney's three-volume *Women's Studies Encyclopedia.* The first volume, *Views from the Sciences,* is "limited to subjects from fields that can be considered, in some sense, as 'science': natural, behavioral, and social sciences, health and medicine, economics."

Because of space limitations, Tierney notes in the Introduction that volume 1 "is, necessarily, partial and incomplete in its coverage: the volume of scholarship on topics related to and affecting women is so enormous, the research fields, subfields, and specialties so prolific, that one volume could scarcely scratch the surface of a single discipline, let alone of all the sciences." Volume 1 contains a fourteen-page index.

In volume 1 over one hundred specialists, men and women, contribute articles, mostly in the 750- to 1,500-word range, a factor Tierney claims limited the topics that could be treated. In general, says Tierney, articles on health and medicine are limited to women's most common problems (e.g., cystitis, vaginitis) or problems that affect women much more than men (e.g., depression, agoraphobia); articles on women's employment are limited to fields in which women predominate (e.g., health professions, teaching, librarianship, clerical occupations). A few topics of major importance to women (e.g., the family, socialization) are treated in more than one article, from different disciplinary perspectives.

The volume's major focus, notes Tierney, also dictated by space limitations, is on the American experience. Most articles are limited just to the United States. Some include the wider compass of the industrialized West, but very few include nonindustrial cultures. Further, "no single feminist perspective" prevails throughout the set: "all shades of opinion, from those so conservative that some will deny they are feminist to the most radical, are represented."

Although entries in volume 1 are authoritative, they "are meant to convey information to an educated audience without expertise in the subject area of the individual entry," a factor that Tierney says limits "the bibliographic apparatus. The few references included at the end of some articles are meant primarily to direct readers to works from which they may obtain a fuller explanation or more detailed information on the subject."

Entries in the latter two volumes are more widely dispersed by chronology, geography, and ethnicity than was the first volume. Volume 2, *Literature, Arts, and Learning*, includes among its entries national groupings of writers and genres, concepts, and art forms. The third volume, *History, Philosophy, and Religion*, includes entries for the women's liberation movement in various countries; women in the American labor movement; the history of abortion in the United States; and a diversity of historical, religious and philosophical concepts and topics. The introductions to each of these two volumes indicate the characteristics and limitations of the coverage of each.

According to Maggie Humm, *The Dictionary of Feminist Theory* is "a broad, cross-cultural and international account of contemporary feminist thought," but most attention is given to Anglo-American and French theory. Her "goal is to show how feminist theory both challenges, and is shaded by, the academy and society; to present feminist theory as a body of research in its own right and to explore the nature of feminist theory for the future of feminism." The format of entries follows several conventions:

1. An entry ending with a reference indicates a summary of that writer's ideas. Verbatim quotations are followed by their references.
2. Entries are arranged in chronological order of the term's development.
3. Where appropriate, entries indicate the contributions of lesbian, heterosexual, black, white, radical, or liberal women.
4. Entries are under both the names of particular writers and the ideas they have produced.

All entries have at least one reference, and the bibliography occupies twenty-five pages of text. A second, earlier feminist dictionary, Cheris Kramarae and Paula A. Treichler's *Feminist Dictionary*, is described as an attempt to correct what these feminist authors believe is an imbalance favoring masculine meanings in many words in today's vocabulary. The entries vary in length from one sentence to several pages and frequently include quotations and/or references to sources of additional information. A bibliography of seventy-odd pages provides complete citations for references in the text.

In Joyce McCarly Nielsen's *Feminist Research Methods: Exemplary Readings in the Social Sciences*, feminist research techniques in sociology, history, and anthropology reveal consistent approaches on how to study women. In all three disciplines, the contributors argue, feminist methodology reveals a pervasive lack of information about women's worlds, a bias in the underrepresentation of women researchers, a need to reconceptualize previously investigated phenomena to include women's experiences, and biases in the kind of research questions asked. To resolve these omissions and biases, feminist scholars take techniques in one discipline and apply them to the subject matter of another in order to avoid sexist assumptions about their own field's methods. Examples are the use of linguistic methodologies in sociology, archaeological and ethnohistorical techniques in anthropology, and demographic analysis in history research. Also, feminist methodology duplicates earlier research to evaluate its analysis and explanation (or lack of analysis and explanation) for gender inequality. Finally, feminist research in all three disciplines involves the development and refinement of new methods of data collection. Nontraditional sources, such as women's medical and church records, minutes of women's clubs and voluntary societies, and refined essay questionnaires, are used. In these ways, feminist methodology unveils the distortions of a sexist society while working toward a transformation of the future.

In the first part of her introduction, Nielsen describes scientific method as it is usually presented and shows that, at first glance, it does seem contradictory to feminist-based inquiry. The second section demonstrates that an identifiable feminist approach to research exists, grounded both "in an older positivist-empirical tradition and in a newer postempirical one." The book contains eleven richly documented chapters by authors from various social science disciplines (sociology, history, anthropology, and political science). In part 1, chapters focus on themes discussed in the Introduction, including an explanation for the masculine character of science, feminist criticism of the social sciences, and feminist methodologies. The last chapter, on oral history, sets the stage for part 2. Chapters in part 2 explore feminist inquiry through approaches such as "a combination of anthropological fieldwork and feminist literary analysis," "survey and interview work with women workers," "reanalyzing and reinterpreting data on sex differences in suicide rates," "challenging arguments for sex differences in cognitive abilities with a reanalysis of quantitative data," and "two kinds of linguistic analysis."

Humm, Maggie. *The Dictionary of Feminist Theory*. Columbus: Ohio State University Press, 1990.

Kramarae, Cheris, and Paula A. Treichler. *A Feminist Dictionary*. Boston: Pandora Press, 1985.

Nielsen, Joyce McCarly, ed. *Feminist Research Methods: Exemplary Readings in the Social Sciences*. Boulder, Colo.: Westview Press, 1990.

Tierney, Helen, ed. *Women's Studies Encyclopedia*. 3 vols. Westport, Conn.: Greenwood Press, 1989–1991.

Bibliographic Information Sources

Now in a second edition, Patricia K. Ballou's *Women: A Bibliography of Bibliographies* critically assesses bibliographical publications, including individually published volumes, abstract journals, and periodical articles that treat women's studies literature. Arranged by subject, there is an author index.

A quarterly, *Women Studies Abstracts* indexes journal articles, books, and reports. Special issues of journals and reports and special publications are identified and annotated. The materials are arranged by broad subject areas. Each issue is indexed, and there are cumulative annual indexes.

Maggie Humm's *Annotated Critical Bibliography of Feminist Criticism* is a guide to feminist writings in every discipline. The entries, dating from 1950, are arranged chronologically within subject categories and include over nine hundred books and articles in English. There are indexes of authors and subjects.

Ballou, Patricia K. *Women: A Bibliography of Bibliographies.* 2d ed. Boston: G.K. Hall, 1986.

Humm, Maggie. *An Annotated Critical Bibliography of Feminist Criticism.* Boston: G.K. Hall, 1987.

Women Studies Abstracts. Rush, N.Y.: Rush Publishing Co., 1972–.

HUMANITIES: FINE AND APPLIED ARTS

Research Guides

Several recommended research guides exist for various specialities in fine and applied arts. The primary research guide for philosophy, religion and mythology, the visual arts, the performing arts, and language and religion, Ron Blazek and Elizabeth Aversa's *Humanities: A Selective Guide to Information Sources* introduces twelve hundred reference works. Now in a third edition, this guide to almost one thousand annotated sources also features "accessing" chapters for each of the humanities treated as separate chapters. As well as a chapter for general humanities reference materials, these include: philosophy, religion, the visual arts, performing arts, language and literature. Pretty consistently, the accessing chapters contain the following subdivisions: working definitions of . . . ; major divisions of the field; use and users of information in . . . ; computers in . . . ; and major organizations, information centers, and special collections. The guide includes an author and title index and a subject index.

In art history, Etta Arntzen and Robert Rainwater's *Guide to the Literature of Art History* annotates over four thousand reference and related publications. Entries are arranged first in four broad categories and then are appropriately broken down into narrower divisions, including general reference sources, and specific arts such as painting, sculpture, architecture, prints, drawings, photography, the decorative arts, and serials. Selective treatment is given to archaeology, aesthetics, philosophy of art, and art criticism. There are author/title and subject indexes. Limited to architecture, sculpture, and painting, Donald L. Ehresmann's *Fine Arts: A Bibliographic Guide to Basic Reference Works, Histories, and Handbooks* annotates some two thousand reference books in western European languages in two broad sections: reference works are arranged under categories such as bibliographies, dictionaries, indexes, iconographies, and so forth; and histories and handbooks by specific periods or geographical areas.

There are author and subject indexes. The publisher claims a separate volume on sculpture and painting is in preparation and that the series, "when complete ... will comprise the most comprehensive bibliography of books on art history available."

Lois Jones arranges her *Art Research Methods and Resources: A Guide to Finding Art Information* first in four broad parts, according to categories composed of approaches to materials (for example, general reference, specialized publications, and so on). The four parts are: "Before research begins," which is designed to develop research strategies; "Art research methods," which specifies recommended strategies; "Art research resources," which annotates over fifteen hundred publications; and "Deciphering and obtaining the needed material," which guides the reader through the intricacies of large research libraries and interlibrary loan policies. Indexes to publications are by titles and authors and institutions to subjects, terms, and professions. Gerd Muesham's *Guide to Basic Information Sources in the Visual Arts* is designed to help develop research strategies and introduce specialized reference materials in art and sources of information about individual artists.

Donald L. Ehresmann's *Applied and Decorative Arts: A Bibliographic Guide to Basic Reference Works, Histories, and Handbooks* annotates in a classified arrangement over twelve hundred publications of the last one hundred years in western European languages. Topics covered include folk art, arms and armor, ceramics, clocks, watches and related devices, costume, decorative art such as furniture, musical instruments, textiles, toys and dolls, or all arts and crafts that fall under the rubric "applied and decorative arts." There are author and subject indexes.

By British librarian David F. Cheshire, *Theatre: History, Criticism and Reference* is an extensive paragraph-by-paragraph discussion of general reference works, histories, dramatic criticism, biographies and autobiographies, theory, and theater serials. It is indexed by author, title, and subject.

Indispensable for research on topics in music, Vincent Duckles's *Music Reference and Research Materials* annotates almost two thousand dictionaries, encyclopedias, catalogs, histories, and related materials written to aid in the study of music. Designed to extend Duckles, the ambitious project by Guy A. Marco and Sharon Paugh Ferris, *Information on Music: A Handbook of Reference Sources in European Languages*, is intended to have eight volumes. The set's three published volumes cover (1) basic and universal sources, (2) the Americas, and (3) Europe. Other volumes propose to cover sources on individual musicians and musical editions. Each volume has its own author, title, and subject indexes.

Arntzen, Etta, and Robert Rainwater. *Guide to the Literature of Art History*. Chicago: American Library Association, 1979.
Blazek, Ron, and Elizabeth Aversa. *The Humanities: A Selective Guide to Information Sources*. 3d ed. Littleton, Colo.: Libraries Unlimited, 1988.
Cheshire, David F. *Theatre: History, Criticism and Reference*. Hamden, Conn.: Archon Books, 1967.

Duckles, Vincent. *Music Reference and Research Materials*. 4th ed. New York: Schirmer Books, 1988.

Ehresmann, Donald L. *Applied and Decorative Arts: A Bibliographic Guide to Basic Reference Works, Histories, and Handbooks*. Littleton, Colo.: Libraries Unlimited, 1977.

———. *Fine Arts: A Bibliographic Guide to Basic Reference Works, Histories, and Handbooks*. 3d ed. Littleton, Colo.: Libraries Unlimited, 1990.

Jones, Lois Swan. *Art Research Methods and Resources: A Guide to Finding Art Information*. 2d ed. Dubuque, Iowa: Kendall/Hunt, 1984.

Marco, Guy A., and Sharon Paugh Ferris. *Information on Music: A Handbook of Reference Sources in European Languages*. 3 vols. Littleton, Colo.: Libraries Unlimited, 1975.

Muesham, Gerd. *Guide to Basic Information Sources in the Visual Arts*. Santa Barbara, Calif.: ABC-Clio, 1978.

Substantive-Bibliographic Information Sources

Departing from traditions in earlier editions under Stanley Sadie, the current edition of *The New Grove Dictionary of Music and Musicians* "seeks to discuss everything that can be reckoned to bear on music in history and on present-day musical life." Although the bulk of articles cover composers, the set also includes: (1) performers, scholars, theorists, patrons and music publishers, or other people whose work is significant in music history; (2) terminology, musical genres, and concepts; and (3) institutions, orchestras, and societies, and cities and towns with significant musical traditions. In this work of 2,500 contributors, the biggest departure in tradition, however, is the "treatment of non-Western and folk music, far more extensive and more methodical than anything of the kind attempted before." Also new to this edition, and of interest for interdisciplinary history, are the articles about aesthetics, analysis, computers, electronic music, ethnomusicology, historiography, iconography, popular music, psychology, and sociology and theory. The set includes extensive bibliographies for articles and an elaborate index.

The only work in English providing extensive coverage of all countries and all periods, the *Encyclopedia of World Art* contains lengthy articles by scholars on related topics such as architecture and "primitive" art (that is, art of non-western peoples) and, the preface states, "every other man-made object that, regardless of its purpose or technique, enters the field of aesthetic judgment because of its form or decoration." Articles include extensive bibliographies, excellent black-and-white and colored plates, and detailed indexes.

Encyclopedia of World Art. 17 vols. New York: McGraw-Hill, 1959–1987.

Sadie, Stanley, ed. *The New Grove Dictionary of Music and Musicians*. 6th ed. 20 vols. London: Macmillan, 1980.

Bibliographic Information Sources

Dating back to 1929, *Art Index* provides coverage of articles for about 140 American and foreign periodicals for art and related topics, listing entries by author as well as subject. A major semiannual bibliography, *RILA, International Repertory of the Literature of Art* cites a wide array of documents including: books, collected essays, festschriften, conference proceedings, museum publications, exhibition catalogs, dissertations, and periodical articles—or over 100,000 entries as of 1988. Book and exhibition reviews, obituaries, interviews, and published lectures are included. Individual essays are included as separate abstracts.

Music Index is an index by author and subject for articles published in some 350 periodicals. A policy of interpreting music very broadly means coverage ranges from musicology to the current music publishing and recording scene. *RILM Abstracts of Music Literature* abstracts and indexes periodical articles, reviews, books, dissertations, and other appropriate publications in music studies. By mid–1989, it claimed over eighty thousand entries. It arranges entries in a classification scheme consisting of nine main divisions: reference and research materials; collected writings; historical musicology; ethnomusicology; instruments and voice; performance practice and notation; theory and analysis; pedagogy; music and other disciplines. The fourth issue of each volume is a cumulative author-subject index.

Art Index. New York: Wilson, 1929–. (Computer searchable, 1985–.)
Music Index. Detroit: Information Service, 1950–.
RILM Abstracts of Music Literature. Flushing, N.Y.: International Repertory of Music
    Literature, 1967–. (Computer searchable, 1972–.)
RILA, International Repertory of the Literature of Art. New York: College Art Association
    of America, 1975–. (Computer searchable, 1973–.)

LANGUAGE AND LITERATURE

Recent experience with research on topics in both language and literature suggests that some of the older, traditional sources are not as central as they were, say, a decade ago. In today's research "vocabulary" (*vocabularies* might be an even more precise term), terms for methods and concepts have often been appropriated from scholarly communities whose members employ approaches to critical analysis developed in movements such as feminist criticism and post-structuralism. When this situation seems to prevail with a research topic associated to language or literature, perhaps by exploring appropriate volumes in other sections of this guide (for example, "Women's Studies") the needed information will be located. Below are listed mostly older reference works that have proved their worth over the years, but sometimes do not contain the information that reflects more recent scholarly approaches.

Research Guides

Anna L. DeMiller's *Linguistics: A Guide to the Reference Literature* is a critically annotated guide to reference sources in linguistics published primarily in the last three decades. In addition to reference works in the traditional areas of historical and comparative linguistics, morphology, phonetics, phonology, semantics, and syntax, it covers anthropological linguistics, applied linguistics, mathematical and computational linguistics, psycholinguistics, semiotics, and sociolinguistics. The concluding part discusses reference sources for specific families of languages, such as Indo-European, Sino-Tibetan, Pidgin, and Creole. Most references are in English, with selected treatment of material in other languages, primarily French and German.

Indispensable for research on most English or American literature topics, Richard Daniel Altick and Andrew Wright's *Selective Bibliography for the Study of English and American Literature* is a venerable guide to what the authors consider the most important works in the field. It briefly annotates over nine hundred items under such headings as literary encyclopedias and handbooks, guides to libraries, bibliographies of literature, general reference guides, bibliographies of bibliographies, author bibliographies, subject catalogs, indexes to composite books, guides to anonymous and pseudonymous literature, encyclopedias, and dictionaries. Also recommended is Margaret C. Patterson, *Literary Research Guide*. Broader in scope than Altick and Wright, its long subtitle explains its contents: "An evaluative, annotated bibliography of [almost 2,000] important reference books and periodicals on English, Irish, Scottish, Welsh, Commonwealth, American, Afro-American, American Indian, continental, classical, and world literatures, and sixty literature-related subject areas including bibliography, biography, book collecting, film, folklore, linguistics, little magazines, prosody, reviews, teaching resources, textual criticism, women's studies." Thoughtfully indexed, entries are given for titles of reference books and periodicals, editors, criticism, national literatures, chronological periods, genres, subjects, series, and a few authors, such as Wordsworth, Steinbeck, and Goethe, who have had serial publications dedicated to their life and works. Equally thoughtful are the two examples in the introduction of recommended search strategies for research projects associated with topics on Flannery O'Connor and Lord Byron.

James L. Harner's *Literary Research Guide: A Guide to Reference Sources for the Study of Literature*, intended to replace Patterson's *Literary Research Guide*, is an extensive and critically annotated tool that is focused on U.S. and British literature but that also treats Irish, Scottish, and Welsh literature and, in less depth, the literatures of Africa, Australia, Canada, the Caribbean, India, and New Zealand. The intersection of literary study with other disciplines is recognized in sections for composition and rhetoric, computers and the humanities, film and literature, folklore and literature, history and literature, political science and literature, and women and literature. The full range of reference materials is covered and access is provided by a table of contents, chapter outlines, and separate indexes for names, titles, and subjects.

Also important is James F. Bracken's *Reference Works in British and American Literature: English and American Literature* and its companion volume, *English and American Writers*. The former contains 512 entries. Annotations are lengthy and often critically comparative, and numerous cross references provide access to the full range of literary reference material. The second volume covers more than 650 writers; for each Bracken lists annotated entries for any reference material specifically devoted to that individual.

For other sources, consult Sheehy and Walford in the second section and Blazek and Aversa under "Fine and Applied Arts."

Altick, Richard Daniel, and Andrew Wright. *Selective Bibliography for the Study of English and American Literature*. 6th ed. New York: Macmillan, 1979.

Bracken, James K. *Reference Works in British and American Literature*. Englewood, Colo.: Libraries Unlimited, 1990.

———. *English and American Writers*. Englewood, Colo.: Libraries Unlimited, 1991.

DeMiller, Anna L. *Linguistics: A Guide to the Reference Literature*. Englewood, Colo.: Libraries Unlimited, 1991.

Harner, James L. *Literary Research Guide: A Guide to Reference Sources for the Study of Literatures in English and Related Topics*. New York: Modern Language Association of America, 1989.

Patterson, Margaret C. *Literary Research Guide*. 2d ed. New York: Modern Language Association of America, 1983.

Substantive Information Sources

Perhaps most useful for brief definitions of specialized literary terms is Clarence Hugh Holman's *Handbook of Literature*, a dictionary of approximately fourteen hundred entries. Although it lacks a bibliography, it is especially good as a source of brief information on concepts, literary schools, genres, movements, and literary devices (for example, allegory, kenning, and metaphor).

Holman, Clarence Hugh. *A Handbook to Literature*. 5th ed. New York: Macmillan, 1986.

Substantive-Bibliographic Information Sources

Designed to support interdisciplinary research, David Crystal's *Cambridge Encyclopedia of Language* is organized first into eleven parts, then into sixty-five thematic sections. Each section is a self-contained presentation of a major theme in language study, with cross-references included to related sections and topics. Among the eleven main parts are language and identity, structure of language, languages of the world, and language in the world. Many of the book's subsections are potentially useful for research on interdisciplinary topics in history. For example, the parts on languages of the world and language in the world contain subsections that explore such linguistic concerns as "how many languages?" "how many speakers?" and "families of languages." The part on language and identity examines identity from several perspectives, including psychological, geographical, ethnic and national, and social ones. The book's bibliographical apparatus works on two levels: first, publications mentioned in the text are cited in full in the bibliography at the end of the volume; in addition, preceding this bibliography is an extensive eleven-part discussion of "further reading," corresponding to the book's eleven parts. An elaborate, three-part index lists languages, families, dialects, scripts, authors, personalities, and topics. Described above under "Communication, Mass Media, Journalism," Erik Barnouw's *International Encyclopedia of Communications* contains a section on language and linguistics.

Wolfgang Bernard Fleischmann's *Encyclopedia of World Literature in the 20th Century* is the only recent, major encyclopedic-type publication in English that attempts to explore the corpus of the world's literature. Earlier works, still recommended, whose scope is worldwide include the four-volume *Penguin Companion to World Literature* and S. H. Steinberg's two-volume *Cassell's Encyclopedia of Literature*. Containing over seventeen hundred entries, Fleischmann's set surveys the work and reputation of the century's major authors, literary movements, national literatures, movements in ideas, literary criticism, and literary genres (the essay). Biographical entries on authors include portraits and bibliographies. In the current edition, a particular effort was made to include surveys of national literatures; for example, in extensive articles with bibliographies, authorities survey some eighty-five Asian and African literatures, including those of the Asian "republics" and autonomous regions of the former Soviet Union.

Each of the four volumes of the *Penguin Companion to World Literature* is devoted to specific literatures: volume 1, English; volume 2, European; volume 3, American; volume 4, classical and Byzantine, Oriental and African. The main purpose of the set is "to provide a handy and readable 'Who's Who' of the most significant writers, from ancient times to the present day." Each brief entry includes important facts of the author's life and a concise guide to outstanding works and significant critical studies. The volume on American literature includes a section on Latin America. The primary focus of Cassell's *Encyclopedia of Literature* is Europe, but it pays attention to other literatures. The first volume contains histories of the literatures of the world, literary genres and rhetorical conventions, and biographies of authors who died before 1914; the second includes biographies of authors living in 1914 or born after that date. Articles, including biographies, are written by authorities, and bibliographies are included.

Crystal, David. *The Cambridge Encyclopedia of Language*. Cambridge: Cambridge University Press, 1987.

Fleischmann, Wolfgang Bernard, ed. *Encyclopedia of World Literature in the 20th Century*. 4 vols. New York: Ungar, 1967–1975.

Penguin Companion to World Literature. 4 vols. New York: McGraw-Hill, 1971.

Steinberg, S. H., ed. *Cassell's Encyclopedia of Literature*. 2 vols. New York: Funk and
    Wagnalls, 1953.

Bibliographic Information Sources

Indispensable since 1921, *MLA International Bibliography* is the standard
guide to criticism for the world's languages, literatures, psycholinguistics, and
folklore. It indexes dissertations, books, chapters of books, articles, and audio
and video materials. Citations to books and articles in all languages are arranged
by linguistic type, and then by subdivision, with authors' names indexed. Festschriften and other collections are listed in separate sections. A special symbol
in brackets following a title refers to these items. There are no annotations, but
the bibliography is noted for the small time lag between publication and listing
of items, and—with computer-assisted online searching or the CD-ROM setup—
it is a powerful tool for retrieving "cutting-edge" criticism.

Linguistics and Language Behavior Abstracts attempts to meet the needs of
"all researchers and practitioners in the various disciplines concerned with the
nature and use of language." The classification scheme includes twenty-five
disciplines under which materials are listed. Each monthly issue contains author,
subject, book review, and source publication indexes, and there are annual
cumulative indexes.

Linguistics and Language Behavior Abstracts. San Diego, Calif.: Sociological Abstracts,
    1967– . (Computer searchable, 1973– .)
MLA International Bibliography. New York: Modern Language Association, 1921–.
    (Computer searchable, 1965– .)

PHILOSOPHY AND RELIGION

Research Guides

In *The Philosopher's Guide to Sources, Research Tools, Professional Life,
and Related Fields*, Richard T. DeGeorge divides the discipline broadly into
twenty-two chapters grouped in three sections: philosophy, general research
tools, and related fields. About eight hundred titles are cited. There is a general
index. More discursive in approach than DeGeorge, Terrence N. Tice and
Thomas P. Slavens's *Research Guide to Philosophy* comprises thirty chapters
grouped under "History of Philosophy" and "Areas of Philosophy." Tice critically reviews modern studies of philosophy's development from ancient times
through the latter part of the twentieth century. His focus includes literature on
the major contributors and on the discipline's major subdivisions (including
"philosophy of history"). Over three thousand works are discussed. In eleven
pages, Slavens annotates almost fifty reference works. There are author-title and
subject indexes.

Hans E. Bynagle's *Philosophy: A Guide to the Reference Literature* lists and critically discusses over four hundred general bibliographic and research guides, dictionaries, encyclopedias, and handbooks, and specialized dictionaries, encyclopedias, and handbooks; general indexes, abstracts, reviewing journals, and retrospective and serial bibliographies; specialized bibliographies: branches, schools, and periods; specialized bibliographies: countries, regions, and special classes of materials; specialized bibliographies: bibliographies on individuals; directories and biographical sources; concordances and indexes to individual philosophers; and miscellaneous other reference works.

John F. Wilson and Thomas P. Slavens's *Research Guide to Religious Studies* is in two parts. The first, "Introduction to Religious Scholarship," discusses book-length studies of religions, the history of religions, religious traditions in the West, and religious thought and ethics. Part 2 introduces fifty pages of major reference works designed to aid research on religious topics.

Bynagle, Hans E. *Philosophy: A Guide to the Reference Literature*. Littleton, Colo.: Libraries Unlimited, 1986.
DeGeorge, Richard T. *The Philosopher's Guide to Sources, Research Tools, Professional Life, and Related Fields*. Lawrence, Kans.: The Regents Press of Kansas, 1980.
Tice, Terrence N., and Thomas P. Slavens, *Research Guide to Philosophy*. Chicago: American Library Association, 1983.
Wilson, John F., and Thomas P. Slavens. *Research Guide to Religious Studies*. Chicago: American Library Association, 1982.

Substantive-Bibliographic Information Sources

Edited by Paul Edwards, the *Encyclopedia of Philosophy* features long articles on major philosophical issues and philosophers of the world. Written by specialists, articles include extensive bibliographies. The fifteen hundred contributors, including mathematicians, physicists, biologists, psychologists, and sociologists, come from twenty-four nations and represent many schools of philosophy. Although analytical, empirical, and linguistic approaches predominate, the set is truly international in scope and deals with the major philosophical problems and philosophers of the world. Volume 8 is a detailed index.

The work of many hands, Mircea Eliade's long-needed and long-awaited *Encyclopedia of Religion* surveys many topics in the broad area of religious studies throughout the world. To help understand and explain religious phenomena, religious scholars today draw upon knowledge from a wide range of disciplines. These include the social, physical, and biological sciences, the law, and humanistic disciplines, especially the arts, literature, and philosophy, as well as religion itself. Religious scholars also claim that religion has three "expressions" or dimensions: (1) the theoretical (for example, doctrines, dogmas, myths, theologies, ethics); (2) the practical (for example, cults, sacraments, meditations); and (3) the sociological (for example, religious groupings, ecclesiastical forms). This set attempts to incorporate explanations of these three forms of religions. And to help achieve these goals, it draws from a large number of contributors from the nonwestern world. Articles are accompanied by bibliographies, which list the most useful publications on the topics discussed and which recommend further reading. Volume 16 presents a synoptic outline and a comprehensive index of the set. For a discussion of the multitude of other encyclopedic or dictionary-type works in religion, see Wilson and Slavens above.

Edwards, Paul, ed. *Encyclopedia of Philosophy*. 8 vols. New York: Macmillan, 1967.
Eliade, Mircea, ed. *Encyclopedia of Religion*. 15 vols. New York: Macmillan, 1987.

Bibliographic Information Sources

Cumulated annually, the quarterly *Philosopher's Index* gives access by author and subject to articles published in three hundred-odd periodicals in western European languages. Books were added in 1984. Issues contain: subject index, annotated author index, book review index, philosophy research archives, and translations in progress. Over fifteen thousand books published between 1940 and 1976 are indexed in the two-volume *Philosopher's Index: Retrospective Index to U.S. Publications from 1940*.

Beginning with volume 17, number 3 (1976), issues of *Review of Religious Research* abstract about thirty to forty articles, books, and dissertations on social scientific studies of religion. It is published three times a year and is indexed in *Religion Index One: Periodicals*. Formerly entitled *Index to Religious Periodical Literature*, *Religion Index One* is a subject index to over one hundred religious periodicals. *Religion Index Two: Multi-Author Works* is an attempt to analyze the contents of separately published volumes containing chapters by more than one author. Scholarly works with a religious or theological focus are included in the over two hundred books indexed annually. Access to entries is given by author and subject. Coverage in *Religion Index Two: Multi-Author Works* begins in 1970, but the single-volume *Religion Index Two: Festschriften, 1960–1969* retrospectively takes coverage back one decade.

Founded in 1958 by J. D. Pearson, *Index Islamicus* in book form covers 1906 to 1980 and, in periodical form from 1976, covers the entire field of publications in Islamic studies. With over 26,000 entries in the main work, this source organizes entries in a classified arrangement with author indexes. For literature on Catholic topics, *Guide to Catholic Literature, 1888–1940* is a retrospective single volume. This is continued and supplemented first by *Catholic Periodical Index; A Cumulative Author and Subject Index to a Selected List of Catholic Periodicals, 1930–1966*, a quarterly with biennial cumulations; then by *Catholic Periodical and Literature Index*, issued six times per year, with biennial cumulations. For a discussion of other bibliographic works in religion, see Wilson and Slavens above.

Catholic Periodical and Literature Index. Haverford, Pa.: Catholic Library Association, 1968–.
Catholic Periodical Index; A Cumulative Author and Subject Index to a Selected List of

Catholic Periodicals, 1930–1966. New York: Catholic Library Association, 1939–1967.

Guide to Catholic Literature, 1888–1940. Detroit: Romig, 1940.

Pearson, J. D., comp. *Index Islamicus, 1906–1955: A Catalogue of Articles on Islamic Subjects in Periodicals and Other Collective Publications.* London: Heffer, 1958. Supplements published since 1961 by Mansell, London.

Philosopher's Index. Bowling Green, Ohio: Philosophy Documentation Center, Bowling Green University, 1967–. (Computer searchable, 1940–.)

The Philosopher's Index: Retrospective Index to U.S. Publications from 1940. 2 vols. Bowling Green, Ohio: Philosophy Documentation Center, Bowling Green University, 1978.

Religion Index One: Periodicals. Chicago: American Theological Librarians Association, 1949/1953–. (Computer searchable, 1949–1959, 1975–.)

Religion Index Two: Festschriften, 1960–1969. Chicago: American Theological Association, 1980–.

Religion Index Two: Multi-Author Works. Chicago: American Theological Association, 1978–. (Computer searchable, 1960–.)

Review of Religious Research. North Newton, Kans.: Religious Research Association, 1976–.

HISTORY OF SCIENCE AND TECHNOLOGY

Research Guides

In Paul Durbin's *Guide to the Culture of Science, Technology and Medicine*, nine chapters are arranged in four broad areas. Of most interest for historical research are the three chapters on the history of science, technology, and medicine. Each chapter is broken down further into narrow topics, which are listed in the analytical table of contents. In each chapter an authority assesses the historical literature, about four hundred titles in all. In addition, chapters list the principal archives, bibliographies, dictionaries, texts, classics, historiographic discussions, and so forth. There is a general author and subject index for the entire volume.

Kathleen J. Haselbauer's *Research Guide to the Health Sciences: Medical, Nutritional, and Environmental* is a large, thoughtfully produced guide to reference and related materials. Haselbauer arranges over two thousand entries in forty-four chapters. Chapters 1 to 10 cover general categories such as bibliographies, indexes, encyclopedias, dictionaries, statistics sources, and online computerized databases, which cover all or most of the volume's subjects. Scattered throughout the other chapters, which focus on specialties within these broad areas, are materials on the history of: human genetics, bioethics, legal medicine, hospitals and hospital statistics, aging, nutrition, pediatrics, and psychiatry. The index contains authors, titles, and subjects.

Durbin, Paul T., ed. *Guide to the Culture of Science, Technology and Medicine.* New York: Free Press, 1980.

Haselbauer, Kathleen J. *A Research Guide to the Health Sciences: Medical, Nutritional, and Environmental*. Westport, Conn.: Greenwood Press, 1987.

Substantive-Bibliographic Information Sources

Promising to become indispensable as a source for any aspect of the history of science, R. C. Olby's *Companion to the History of Modern Science* is a massive compendium of scholarship arranged first in two broad sections, and then into three narrower categories, which in turn are divided into sixty-seven chapters. In part 1, "The Study of the History of Science," are: history of science in relation to neighboring disciplines; analytical perspectives; and philosophical problems. Part 2, "Selected Writings in the History of Science," contains: turning points; topics and interpretations; and themes. The work of over sixty acknowledged authorities, its "principal aim," according to the Introduction, "is to introduce the reader to the historical development of modern Western science itself and to the extensive scholarly literature that has been written about it. Modern science is here defined as science, excluding medicine and technology from the sixteenth century to the present." The Introduction states further that in genre, it is most closely patterned on the *Dictionary of the History of Ideas* or the *Encyclopedia of Philosophy*. Indexes of names and subjects are provided.

More modest in scope but equally authoritative is W. F. Bynum's *Dictionary of the History of Science*. The work of about forty authorities, this dictionary defines in extensive entries seven hundred terms from the history of the sciences. A large biographical index helps to identify names mentioned in the text. As well as brief bibliographies included with most entries, a bibliography of suggested sources of additional information is at the front of the text.

Indispensable for research on topics in scientific history, Charles C. Gillispie's *Dictionary of Scientific Biography* presents five thousand accounts of the life and work of famous deceased scientists of all periods and all nations. Extensive bibliographies of primary and secondary source materials are included for each entry.

George Sarton, a pioneer in the history of science as a discipline, is the author of *Introduction to the History of Science*, a dated but still valuable scholarly work. This set is characterized more as an encyclopedia than a history. "Indispensable for the period from classical times to the beginning of the fourteenth century," it is, notes the American Historical Association's *Guide to Historical Literature*, "unsurpassed for biographic and bibliographical data."

A more recent work with intent similar to Sarton's is Stephen G. Brush's *History of Modern Science*. Subtitled "A Guide to the Second Scientific Revolution, 1800–1950," it is designed to "introduce the literature for advanced students, scientists, historians, and others who want to learn about the subject on their own." Following an overview of the subject and a survey of textbooks and research publications, the book is organized first as a series of thirteen chapters covering selected major developments in biology, anthropology, psychology, physics, mathematics, and astronomy between 1800 and 1950, along with philosophical and sociological approaches to these developments.

The thirteen chapters are further divided into sixty-eight sections consisting of: an outline of topics with brief expository essays, suggestions about materials for reading, and references to major sources and recent scholarly analyses. Bibliographies at the end of the sections in general include only works published within the last ten years, along with standard editions of primary sources, autobiographies, bibliographies, and appropriate articles in the *Dictionary of Scientific Biography*.

For technology, the seven-volume *History of Technology* by Charles Singer and others is the standard work on technology from its beginnings to 1950 (although coverage is generally confined to the Middle East, Europe, and the United States). Chapters include bibliographies for tracing topics more extensively. An eighth volume is a "consolidated index" in several "parts." Part 1, for example, summarizes the lists of contents for all seven volumes of the text and is useful for tracing the development of main subject areas through the ages.

Brush, Stephen G. *The History of Modern Science: A Guide to the Second Scientific Revolution, 1800–1950*. Ames, Iowa: Iowa State University Press, 1988.

Bynum, W. F., et al., eds. *Dictionary of the History of Science*. Princeton, N.J.: Princeton University Press, 1981.

Gillispie, Charles C., ed. *Dictionary of Scientific Biography*. 16 vols. New York: Charles Scribner's Sons, 1970–1980.

Olby, R. C., et al., eds. *Companion to the History of Modern Science*. London: Routledge, 1990.

Sarton, George. *Introduction to the History of Science*. 5 vols. Baltimore: William and Wilkins, 1927–1948.

Singer, Charles, et al. *A History of Technology*. 5 vols. Oxford: Clarendon, 1956–1964.

Bibliographic Information Sources

The quarterly periodical *Isis*, devoted to the history of science and its influences, includes a lengthy annual bibliography. Various historical, philosophical, literary, and medical journals are searched for appropriate articles, and important books are also included. Many entries are annotated, and the existence of book reviews is noted. Arranged in four main parts, the bulk of the entries fall under "Histories of the Special Sciences" and "Chronological Classifications." Historiographic and methodological material is included. The 1986 volume lists over three thousand new books and articles. The *Isis Cumulative Bibliography* cumulates annual bibliographies from 1913 to 1965. Edited by Magda Whitrow, this is a massive six-volume compilation. Volume 6, the author index, contains 75,000 entries.

Similar to *Isis*, an annual bibliography in the history of technology has been published in *Technology and Culture* since 1964. The classification scheme incorporates sixteen categories and six chronological divisions. The annotations are informative, and along with scope and contents, the existence of bibliographies is noted. Issues have author indexes.

Isis. Baltimore: Johns Hopkins University, 1950– .

Technology and Culture. Detroit: Society for the History of Technology, 1959– . *Current Bibliography in the History of Technology*, computer searchable on RLIN, 1987– .

Whitrow, Magda, ed. *Isis Cumulative Bibliography*. 6 vols. London: Mansell Publishing, 1971–1984.

8

Using Electronic Information Sources

Joyce Duncan Falk

Electronic information retrieval is now a standard feature of academic and public libraries. Many serial bibliographies in the humanities and social sciences, as well as some reference books and texts, are available in electronic form and may be used in the library along with those in printed-paper format. The ability to use such resources has become imperative for today's teachers and students. Once considered appropriate only for advanced research and writing projects, electronic databases are now available in a variety of formats for use by undergraduates as well as by faculty members and graduate students. As part of the general shift in role among academic libraries from being passive storehouses to active information providers, most library instruction programs include instruction for students and faculty in electronic resources. In addition to library instructors, history professors, too, in fulfillment of their responsibilities to include research skills in their teaching, must inform students of the availability of electronic information services, their scope, advantages, limitations, procedures, and costs.

The basic premise of instruction in electronic information retrieval is that it be fully integrated into the teaching of bibliographic skills and research methods in history and that use of electronic databases be presented as one part of the complex process of research—a powerful aid to be used in conjunction with other methods. A corollary is that computer-assisted or electronic information retrieval should not be presented as a linear process or mechanical procedure. It still depends upon the ability of the historian, librarian, and student to exploit it skillfully, critically, and imaginatively. A third general point is that instruction should emphasize general principles applicable across the various types of electronic information retrieval and leave the mechanics of a system to individual or second-level instruction.[1] Finally, the most important technique in teaching electronic information retrieval is to use live demonstrations.

This chapter first introduces a few terms used in discussions of electronic information retrieval, the kinds of systems in use, and the types of databases, with examples of databases of interest to historians. A section on the search process explains the advantages of electronic database searching, outlines its basic operations, and suggests why and when to use it. Some points of concern for searching in history—logical context, geographic setting, and historical time period—are discussed in greater detail. The mechanics of obtaining a search, either by doing it oneself or by using the library, are described. The conclusion emphasizes the potential value of electronic database searching as both highly rational and creative. Databases, directories, and database systems are listed in the appendix.

DEFINITIONS

An introduction to the terminology of electronic information retrieval will facilitate reading this chapter as well as other literature on the subject.[2]

A *database* is a collection of bits of information in electronic, machine-readable form, organized and labeled so the data can be processed by a computer, and usually stored on magnetic tapes or disks. A typical example is a bibliography or index—the type of database that is the primary concern in this chapter.

An *online information retrieval system* is the entire apparatus for storing the database, searching and retrieving the data, and distributing the data to the user. Information retrieval systems are developed and marketed by companies or other organizations like Dialog Information Services, BRS Information Technologies, and the Research Libraries Group.

The *search analyst* is the trained intermediary, usually a librarian, who plans the search strategy and operates the equipment to manipulate a database in order to select and retrieve data for the user.

The *user* or *end user* is the student, professor, researcher, or other person for whom the data is retrieved. When the user does his or her own searching rather than employing an intermediary search analyst, the activity is called *end-user searching*.

A database that is available for direct, immediate, and interactive searching is said to be *online*. Online access allows the searcher to send requests to a computer, get results within seconds, and request additional data based on the results just received. Access is achieved through an electronic data terminal or a computer, usually a microcomputer, connected via telephone to an information retrieval system's large, mainframe computer where the databases are stored. Access can also be via direct wire or via telecommunications satellite. Another variety of online access to electronic databases is through the local online public access catalog (OPAC). Periodical index databases can be added to a library's online catalog and accessed using the same search system. For example, tapes of the Wilson Company indexes are available for lease to libraries and the University of California's Melvyl catalog offers access to *Medline* and *Current Contents*.

A database may also be stored locally on a laser video disk or compact disk read-only memory (CD-ROM), directly accessed by a personal computer. Although they are not considered "online," CD-ROM systems perform logical operations similar to online systems, are attached to printers, and all have their own search systems. The databases are usually updated monthly or quarterly.

An individual database may be available in any one or in all three of the following means of access: via an online information retrieval system, an online library catalog, or a CD-ROM. As new methods of electronic storage and retrieval are developed, instructors will have to learn their features and be able to compare them to both printed publications and the online database searching emphasized in this chapter.[3]

In electronic searching jargon, a *source document* or an *original document* is not necessarily either a document or a primary source in the historian's sense. Rather, it is the article, book, dissertation, government document, speech text, manuscript, film, or other item represented by a record, most often a bibliographic record, in a database; that is, it is the source of the data recorded in a particular piece or record of the database.

DATABASES

Types of Databases

The type of database of primary concern here is the familiar bibliographic one. Bibliographic databases contain records that refer to sources of information, mostly secondary literature. These databases frequently have a printed paper or microform counterpart; that is, a bibliography, index, or abstracts publication, such as *Historical Abstracts* or *Dissertation Abstracts International*. Notable examples of bibliographic databases with no printed counterpart of the entire database are the catalog databases of the Online Computer Library Center (OCLC) and the Research Libraries Group (RLG). Originally developed for library cataloging purposes, these databases are now valuable reference bibliographies.

Another common type of database is the directory, which provides lists of names, addresses, and various other data. Examples are the *Encyclopedia of Associations*, *Dun's Electronic Yellow Pages*, and *American Men and Women of Science*.

A few numeric databases are available, particularly collections of economic and demographic data, including statistics on population, prices, employment, earnings, and interest rates, among others.[4] Examples of online databases are the U.S. Bureau of the Census's *Cendata*, *Donnelly Demographics*, and *Chase Econometrics*. The degree to which statistical analyses can be performed on any of these varies with the database, the information retrieval system, and the searcher's own software.

A type of database that promises to be more popular as storage capacity of systems increases and becomes less expensive is the full-text database. Full text means that the entire texts of the source document, not just the bibliographic references, are in the database and may be retrieved online or at the CD-ROM work station. Full-text databases exist for encyclopedias; U.S. government and United Nations documents; newsletters and newspapers; individual publications, for example, *Harvard Business Review* and the Bible; collections of textbooks, article excerpts, photographs, and maps; and collections of popular and business periodicals. Full-text databases of interest to the historian, but not now online, include the machine-readable data files of the Interuniversity Consortium for Political and Social Research (ICPSR), the *American and French Research on the Treasury of the French Language* (ARTFL) at the University of Chicago, and *The London Stage, 1660–1800* at Lawrence University. The *Thesaurus Linguae Graecae* (TLG), a database of all ancient Greek texts extant, is available on CD-ROM, as is a collection of history books and images called *U.S. History on CD-ROM.*[5]

Critical Evaluation of Databases for History Topics

Effective exploitation of electronic information retrieval requires the researcher to make the same critical analyses of databases as of other sources of information. Databases, like printed publications, have parameters of subject scope, number and type of source documents indexed, languages of source documents, publication dates or number of years of coverage, type of records (i.e., type and amount of data in each record), quality of subject indexing, currency and consistency of coverage, and accuracy of data. They also have points of view, which are expressed in selection practices.

The historian must first of all determine to what extent the field or subfield under study is served by electronic databases. For example, twentieth-century U.S. history is well covered by *America: History and Life*, supplemented, if desired, by general social science and humanities databases. For ancient Greek history, however, one has to consider whether the less extensive coverage of *Arts and Humanities Search* and the databases less specifically for history— *Philosopher's Index, Religion Index*, or the *French Retrieval Automated Network for Current Information in Social and Human Sciences* (FRANCIS)—are worth using. Selected databases for work in history are briefly discussed in this chapter, and more are listed at the end. Current complete lists of databases are available from the information retrieval systems and in database directories, noted following the list of databases at the end of the chapter.

Researchers must be especially aware of the fact that electronic databases, by and large, include only material published in the past fifteen to twenty years whereas the historian frequently needs material from earlier years as well. *America: History and Life*, which includes literature since 1963, is one of the oldest of the social science and humanities databases, and *Philosopher's Index* has some material dating back to 1940; but most others begin in the 1970s. Databases of books, which do include older publications, are the Library of Congress collections for which there is machine-readable cataloging (databases called LC MARC and REMARC on the Dialog Information Retrieval Service) and the OCLC and RLIN catalog databases.

Another limitation of electronic databases for the historian's use is that they do not usually include primary sources. Neither full-text primary sources themselves nor indexes to them exist in electronic databases. Exceptions to this generalization are TLG, ARTFL, RLIN's *Eighteenth-Century Short Title Catalogue*, the catalog databases noted in the previous paragraph, and full-text databases of newspaper and magazine articles—to the extent that older books and current reports and essays may be considered primary sources.

The differences between an electronic database and its print counterpart or between an online database and its CD-ROM version should also be noted. Because databases in the social sciences and humanities were developed from and continue to be based on the storage media that are used to typeset the printed publications, these differences are minimal. But it is helpful to understand that some of the awkward and inefficient situations that occur in online searching are a result of the databases having been designed originally to produce printed publications and not computer-searchable databases.

Points to consider in comparing online and CD-ROM versions of a database are convenience, costs, content, intended use of the search results, and search system capabilities. CD-ROMs usually employ a "user-friendly" menu system in which sophisticated capabilities are sacrificed to ease of use; some CD-ROMs, such as PAIS, offer different levels or modes of searching from simplest to more sophisticated. Despite their purported ease of use, the consensus is that CD-ROM databases require more training than is at first assumed and than is indicated by the database producers.[6] It is possible that a newly designed CD-ROM version of a database will avoid the problems in the existing online version—that database producers and online information retrieval systems have been reluctant to fix—and offer an improved database and more trouble-free searching.

One advantage of online databases is their more frequent updating and greater currency than the printed versions and the CD-ROM versions, but in the social sciences and humanities the online database is sometimes no more current than the printed publication. A few databases offer the option of searching the CD-ROM version then switching to the online system for a search of the most recent data.

In a few cases the data may differ between the print, online, and CD-ROM publications. For example, the online database *PsycInfo* includes citations to dissertations not indexed by the printed *Psychological Abstracts*. The CD-ROM *Social Sciences Citation Index* permits searching for related records, a feature not present in the printed or online versions. In the printed *America: History and Life* (AHL) and *Historical Abstracts* (HA), classification section headings are visible and provide subject and geographic information, especially in the older volumes; but these section headings are not present in the online databases.

In these same history databases corrections and improvements to the annual subject indexes are not transferred to the online databases. On the other hand, the database records display the index terms right with the bibliographic data, whereas in the printed version the index terms appear only in the index. The CD-ROM versions of AHL and HA differ from both the printed publications and the online versions, and the CD-ROM search system differs from the online versions as well as from other CD-ROM systems.

Experience with searching full-fledged online databases by a skilled intermediary can help prepare students and researchers to compare the various types of access to data—printed-paper copy, online database, and CD-ROM or other computerized system—and choose the ones that suit their needs.

Examples of Databases for History Topics

The bibliographic databases of interest to the historian may be grouped into five categories: history, multidisciplinary humanities and social sciences, specific subjects, general reference, and current affairs. The comments on the advantages, limitations, and other aspects of the databases discussed here can be used to help evaluate additional databases, both online and CD-ROM.[7]

Historical Abstracts (HA) and *America: History and Life* (AHL) interpret history broadly and include references to source documents in the social sciences, literature, and the arts, as well as history itself. The list of journals surveyed has varied as journals began and ceased publication and as the total number of journals covered gradually expanded to about two thousand. Because securing, editing, and indexing abstracts is labor-intensive and time-consuming, the lag time between publication of an article and indexing it in HA or AHL is at least a year and often longer, and journal issues are not always indexed in the order in which they are published.

The HA online database, which begins with volume 19 (1973), indexes international scholarly literature on world history of the period between 1450 and the present, excluding the United States and Canada. Because of the vagaries of publishing in some parts of the world and the difficulty of obtaining personnel with expertise in certain languages, more publications of the western world are indexed than of nonwestern areas, and Europe is better covered than Latin America.

Originally HA abstracted and indexed only journal articles. Additional types of source documents and indexing features were added at various times, such as indexing descriptors in 1975 and books and dissertations in 1980. The addition of five volumes of article entries left out of the 1955–1978 volumes of HA causes retrieval of some references with publication dates earlier than the official beginning date (1972) for the material in the online file; thus a 1965 article record may be retrieved but consistent coverage of articles begins with 1972. An online search retrieves records for articles dated primarily 1972 and later, plus books and dissertations dated 1979 and later. For details of HA coverage and record types, it is imperative to consult the publisher's searching manual.[8]

HA online merges the two parts of the printed HA into a single file so that both parts are searched simultaneously. Also, occasionally duplicate records may be retrieved for items that span the 1914 dividing line and are printed in both *Part A—1450–1914* and *Part B—1914–Present.*

The strengths of the HA database are that it indexes more history journals than any other database; covers journals from all over the world, regardless of language; gives the original language titles and their English translations; provides detailed subject indexing; assigns historical period or specific date indexing to every record (since 1975); and includes abstracts or annotations for each article record. The last three points are especially important in electronic searching because they make possible both greater comprehensiveness and greater precision in a search.

AHL, the companion history database to HA, covers United States and Canadian history and culture of all periods, beginning with 1963 publications. (Some 6,000 entries from 1954 to 1963 on the limited historical period of 1775 to 1945 are best ignored in describing the coverage.) AHL is more inclusive than HA in the areas of folklore, archaeology, popular culture, and contemporary social and political issues. With the 1974 volume major changes were made to AHL: coverage was extended to include 1973-and-later books, book reviews, and dissertations; and index descriptors were introduced. Journal profiles, added in 1973, have been discontinued, as has coverage of collections of essays. These changes, and others as they occur, must be kept in mind by the researcher and the search analyst in both planning the search and evaluating the results.

The strengths of AHL are similar to those of HA: coverage of more history journals than any other database, including U.S. local and regional journals and foreign ones, plus journals in related fields; English translations of all foreign-language titles; book review citations with book titles; detailed indexing of records in the majority of the file, not only of articles but also of books and dissertations; historical period or date indexing for all records beginning with volume 10 (1974); abstracts and annotations. The presence of indexing and abstracts significantly enhances the potential for an effective search. Highly specific indexing of the subject/time period of each source document is unique to AHL and HA.

Among the multidisciplinary humanities and social sciences databases are the next most generally useful databases for history, the citation indexes *Arts & Humanities Search* (A&HS) and *Social Scisearch.* The outstanding features of these databases are: the breadth and number of journals indexed; identification of journals that are indexed cover-to-cover rather than selectively; rapid indexing of the journals and weekly updating of the online file; and citation indexing.

Beginning in 1980 A&HS indexes some thirteen hundred journals of which about two hundred are history or general humanities journals. Source documents include articles, book reviews, creative works (stories, poems, etc.), editorials, and letters; selected articles from social science journals are also listed. *Social Scisearch* is considerably older, dating back to 1972. It indexes all substantive items in about fifteen hundred social science journals, about eighty of which are history or area studies titles. Thus these two databases are broader in subject scope and types of source documents than the other databases discussed here.

Citation indexing, which enables one to find all papers that have cited a particular previous work (provided certain identifying data is known), is a unique feature of these two files and their cousin, *Scisearch*. The A&HS file, however, has more data per record and more data provided by human editors than the other citation indexes: more supplementary words added to titles to enhance their meaning; titles of cited references in addition to publication data; implicit references from the body of a text as well as from footnotes and bibliographic lists; and a cross-reference index of cited authors that indicates which form of a name to use, for example, "Leonardo" or "da Vinci." Searchers are urged to study carefully the instructions for searching this database.[9]

The limitations of A&HS and *Social Scisearch* center on the lack of a subject index and the absence of annotations (except the addition of meaningful words to titles); thus a search depends on words in article titles and on the use of citation indexing. The only control or standardization applied to words on which one must search is the use of preferred spellings and the use of a single form of the name for frequently cited authors and artists. As a consequence of this almost completely nonstandardized, title-word-dependent search vocabulary, a search for a particular historical period is virtually impossible. A search for another crucial facet of many history topics, the geographic area, is very unreliable. Neither geographic terms nor dates appear consistently in titles of articles; and no indexing is imposed upon the titles in these two databases.

Another characteristic of these databases is that the article titles on the records are sometimes inexact or incomplete—spellings are changed, words are omitted, other words are added, and only the English translations of foreign-language titles are given (except titles of creative works, e.g., *Le Rouge et le Noir*, but these titles also vary!). Thus records in the databases cannot be depended upon for accurate titles.

While the inclusion of book reviews and other types of reviews in A&HS is an advantage in that it extends retrieval to books and to criticism, the number of reviews in A&HS and *Social Scisearch* is so great that it is often desirable to exclude them from the search results.

Other general humanities and social sciences databases are *PAIS International* (PAIS) and the H. W. Wilson indexes *Humanities Index* and *Social Sciences Index*. PAIS is important for its coverage of contemporary political, social, and economic affairs through indexing of journal articles, books, government publications, agency reports, pamphlets, and other publications. The electronic database merges the two printed publications *Public Affairs Information Service Bulletin* (beginning in 1972) and the *Foreign Language Index* (French, German,

Italian, Spanish, and Portuguese publications, beginning in 1976), which are now printed together. The database has a controlled indexing scheme of headings and subheadings and occasional notes to amplify the meaning of vague titles. Unfortunately there is no means to focus a search on any historical period, except when the subject is by definition confined to certain years: for example, Watergate Incident, 1972, or Vietnamese Conflict, 1961–1975.

Humanities Index and *Social Sciences Index*, beginning in 1984 and 1983 respectively, are suitable for searches on almost any history topic, regardless of the period, for undergraduates or the general public who need some quality articles from leading, easily obtained, English-language journals. The bibliographic citations are not annotated, but a carefully controlled indexing vocabulary based on the familiar Library of Congress subject headings and an online cross-reference system facilitate use of the databases. Like PAIS, there is no historical period or date indexing but only those index terms with inherent dates (e.g., Reformation or Enlightenment) or with dates as part of the subject heading (e.g., World War, 1914–1918, or Philip II, King of Spain, 1527–1598).

The historian may choose from among a wide array of subject-specific databases those that are directly related to the topic of research. Major subject databases in the humanities and social sciences are listed in the appendix to this chapter.

Beyond the social sciences and humanities, databases abound. The historian working on American rural life or the farm economy might check *Agricola*, produced by the National Agricultural Library. For any topic in the history of medicine or public health, the National Library of Medicine's *Medline* and *Histline* should be considered. For the many possibilities in corporate and business history, *ABI/Inform* is a likely prospect to supplement the history and social science databases. And any subject even remotely concerned with education may be found in ERIC, including online searching, teaching of history, books and publishing, literacy and reading habits, and the history of education. It offers inexpensive access to a large amount of data useful for both simple undergraduate papers and more rigorous research.[10]

Examples of reference or general databases frequently of use to historians are *Dissertation Abstracts* (DA), *Books in Print*, LC MARC, and the RLIN catalog. By combining information printed in *Dissertation Abstracts International* and other indexes, DA lists practically every doctoral dissertation accepted by accredited North American universities since 1861. Searching the database is complicated by inadequate subject indexing and by the presence of lengthy abstracts on records since 1980. Because of the unusually long abstracts, searching DA often requires two different search strategies, one for the part of the file without abstracts and one for the part with abstracts. Searchers are reminded that recent dissertations are also included in other databases that have better indexing, for example, in AHL beginning in 1974 and HA beginning in 1975.

Current affairs, the final category of databases for history topics, includes both bibliographic and full-text ones. They cover mostly general magazines and newspapers, although PAIS and *Mideast File* from the subject-specific category could also be considered current affairs databases. *Magazine Index* indexes about 240 popular magazines beginning in 1959 and now approximately 500 such magazines. A subject indexing scheme is used, and there is a published subject heading list, but reviewers have noted that quality control of the indexing is lax. Indexing is accomplished within hours or a few days of receipt of a magazine so that the data can be entered into *Newsearch*, the database of the current month's magazine and newspaper indexing. The full text of about 120 of the magazines is available in the online database *Magazine ASAP*. Obviously *Magazine Index* and the other magazine and newspaper databases are useful for news of today and last year, but *Magazine Index*'s coverage dating back to 1959 makes it useful for work on recent American history and the society, politics, and culture of the 1960s and 1970s.

In addition to the brief introduction here and the list of databases in the appendix, guidance in selecting the appropriate databases for a particular topic and in choosing online or CD-ROM systems can be obtained from an experienced search analyst, from catalogs and directories of databases, and from online multidisciplinary indexes like Dialog's *Dialindex* and BRS's CROSS.

THE SEARCH PROCESS

Once the historian has determined that one or more electronic databases are likely to contain references on the topic of inquiry, the search process can be addressed. Crucial to an understanding of the use of CD-ROM systems as well as of online searching is instruction in question analysis, selection of search terms, and development of the search strategy.[11]

A review of the advantages of *online* database searching is a useful introduction to electronic information retrieval in general, how it works, and when it is appropriate to use it. Certain characteristics of searching for history topics require additional attention.

Advantages of Online Searching and How It Functions

Speed. An introduction to the capabilities and advantages of online—or any electronic—searching begins with the most obvious and possibly the most attractive feature, speed. The computer can search all volumes and issues of an index or abstracts publication and print a bibliography in a matter of minutes, saving the researcher several hours or even days of manual searching. Moreover, several databases can be searched in the same location at the same search session, if desired. The need for an appointment with a search analyst, who must juggle a busy schedule and equipment availability, occasionally negates the time-saving advantage, at least when the user wants the results on the spur of the moment. In most cases, however, the ability to search massive amounts of data quickly, once the preliminary planning has been done, is a decided advantage. End-user searching of simplified online systems (Knowledge Index, BRS/After Dark) or CD-ROM databases may be more convenient, depending on the particular local facilities.

Convenience. An additional convenience of both online and CD-ROM searching is that they save time and eliminate copying errors by providing a neatly typed bibliography with or without annotations and index terms, depending on the preference of the researcher. The bibliography may be printed at the terminal at the time of the search or printed offline and sent to the user in a few days. Many libraries can also transfer search results to a floppy disk or to the user's own computer, bypassing the printed stage. The user can then select, sort, and edit the bibliography on the microcomputer and print whatever is needed.

Flexibility. Although not as immediately recognized as speed and convenience, the defining characteristic of online searching that makes speed and convenience possible is its interactive nature. The flexibility achieved by immediate interaction with the online database makes searches faster and more accurate. The searcher can send a request, get a response instantly, evaluate that response, and proceed with the search based on the evaluation of the initial response. At any time during the search the searcher can ask to see some sample records and can change the search terms or the strategy if desired. CD-ROM systems share this characteristic to varying degrees.

Comprehensiveness. Another advantage of online searching is the ability to conduct a more thorough and comprehensive search than is possible in printed volumes of the same database. The search through many volumes and several databases at once is not only fast, it is thorough, which is especially helpful for multidisciplinary topics. A researcher using a good printed bibliography has a subject and author index and possibly some classification headings with which to work, but the computer can search for subject words in the titles and abstracts or annotations as well as in the subject index. The online database search can be done using the indexing vocabulary of the particular database, the natural language of the researcher, or both. This comprehensive searching of all significant words in the online record is especially valuable when looking for new, unusual, or obscure words, or for proper names that have not been included in the subject index. CD-ROM searching is similar but, depending on both the particular database and the CD-ROM system, may not include as many volumes of a database and does not have as many databases available at once as online systems have.

Precision (coordination). Online database searching is characterized by both greater access and better focus than printed indexes. Online databases typically have more types of indexes or access points than their print counterparts. Besides being able to search all words in the titles, annotations, and subject index, the computer can be instructed to search such additional indexes as author, journal name, date of publication, type of source document, and original language. The computer can focus the search by coordinating these types of data with the subject search to produce very specifically tailored bibliographies, such as one of post–1980 items in English about revolutions in France. An online search can also be used to find bibliographic citations for which only some of the data is known, for example, an article by Scott in the *Journal of Library History* having to do with women.

Expanding a search to numerous words and indexes and focusing a search on a certain combination of terms is achieved through the use of the information retrieval system's logical operators **AND, OR,** and **NOT** (called Boolean logic). For example, in a search on woman suffrage the use of **OR** to link synonyms or related terms expands a search: the computer is instructed to search for the words *woman* **OR** *female* and to set aside all the records that contain either one or both of the words. Another subject set is similarly developed: *suffrage* **OR** *franchise* **OR** *right to vote*. The **AND** operator narrows a search by requiring both words or subject sets to be present in a record, for example, the word *woman* **AND** the word *suffrage*.

Because of the ambiguity of ''and'' and ''or'' in everyday usage, the explanation of the logic of online searching should be illustrated with Venn diagrams:

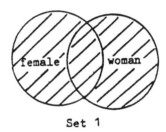

Set 1

WOMAN **OR** FEMALE retrieves all records that contain one or both words. We call it set 1.

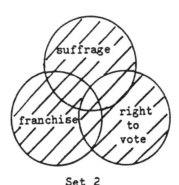

Set 2

SUFFRAGE **OR** FRANCHISE **OR** RIGHT TO VOTE retrieves all records containing one or more of the words. We call it set 2.

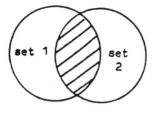

Set 3

SET 1 **AND** SET 2 retrieves only those records that have at least one of the words from set 1 (*woman* or *female*) **AND** one of the words from set 2 (*suffrage* or *franchise* or *right to vote*). The result is called set 3.

When the computer reports the number of records that have been found in set 3, the searcher may decide to limit the search further by requiring the presence of another subject (e.g., **AND** SOCIALISM), by restricting the search to a geographical area (e.g., **AND** FRANCE), by excluding a subject or type of source document (e.g., **NOT** DISSER-TATION), or by any combination of these options.

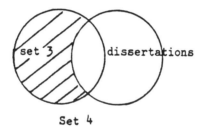

Set 4

SET 3 **NOT** DISSERTATION removes dissertation records from the results and creates a new set, set 4.

Once the basic logic has been grasped, a sample search can be illustrated that includes the use of truncation, word linking, and searching selected parts of the record, such as titles or index terms. A *truncation* symbol is a dummy or universal character that allows for the addition or substitution of letters in order to retrieve all variants of a word. Word-linking symbols, called word proximity operators, enable the computer to search for two or more words adjacent to or within a few words of each other. Each retrieval system uses its own symbols for truncation, word proximity, and restriction of the search to certain parts of the record (e.g., titles); they are explained in the manuals of the respective information retrieval services and in the guides that are provided with CD-ROMs—but the principles are the same. The illustrations here show the Dialog symbols and format.

Sample search in historical abstracts on Dialog. Planning a search strategy begins with an analysis of the search question. The instructor should illustrate, using visual aids, at least a couple of examples of breaking down a question into its component concepts and other parameters. Although scholars may do this instinctively when using traditional resources, the searcher—student, professor, or search analyst—using an electronic database must do it deliberately.

The student planning a term paper may know only that he or she wants to write on something about women's voting rights in Europe; the scholar may wonder if a certain political faction or individual influenced the campaign for woman suffrage in France. In either case the researcher must consciously analyze the topic; note the concepts, which in this instance are women, suffrage, Europe or France; write down a list of synonyms or related terms for each main concept; and note additional parameters such as language and publication dates of the material desired or particular types of material (articles, books, dissertations).

The following sample search illustrates grouping synonyms, searching first for the main concepts, pausing to check the number of entries found, continuing with the search for an additional concept, and then typing five sample records to determine if they are indeed on the topic as the researcher views it. Sampling the results may also suggest additional search terms or other directions for research. The Dialog format shown uses the *?* as a truncation symbol, the *(w)* and *(2w)* as word linking operators, and the */ti,de* to restrict the search for the word *french* to the titles and index descriptors. The bracketed words are explanatory, not part of the search. The actual appearance of the screen and/or printout will vary slightly depending on equipment and initial search software settings. The objective is to understand the principles of online searching, not the mechanics of a particular system.

Woman Suffrage, Subsequently Focused on France

[searcher] select wom?n? or female? or femini?

[response] 7647 wom?n?

          1386 female?

          1397 femini?

      s1 8375 wom?n? or female? or femini?
[searcher] select suffrag? or franchise or right?(2w)vote or voting(w)right?

[response]   488 suffrag?

           142 franchise

          8784 right?

           700 vote

            49 right?(2w)vote

          1174 voting

          8784 right?

            53 voting(w)right?

       s2   662 suffrag? or franchise or right?(2w)vote or voting(w)right?

[searcher] select s1 and s2

[response] 8375 s1

      662 s2

   s3   216 s1 and s2

[Pause to decide to narrow the search by another concept, *France*. In the following statement the search for the word *french* is limited to words in the titles and index terms.]

[searcher] select france or french/ti,de

[response] 25580 france

      6831 french/ti,de

   s4 27965 france or french/ti,de

[searcher] select s3 and s4

 [response] 216   s3

    27965   s4

   s5 21 s3 and s4

[To sample the resulting retrieval, request that five records be printed in the format that includes abstracts (only the first record is shown here).]

[searcher] type s5/5/1–5

[response]

  5/5/1

1214554 38A–02139

Citizeness of the Republic: Class and Sex Identity in the Feminist Career of Hubertine Auclert, 1848–1914.

Hause, Steven C.; McBride, Theresa

Proceedings of the Annual Meeting of the Western Society for French History 1984 12: 235–242.

NOTE: Comments, pp. 257–259. Based on documents in the departmental archives of the Allier and in the Parisian Prefecture of Police; 21 notes.

DOCUMENT TYPE: ARTICLE

ABSTRACT: Hubertine Auclert (1848–1914) was the founder of the women's suffrage movement in France. She worked indefatigably for that cause beginning in the 1870's. Her career demonstrates that she combined an interest in women's rights with a concern for the rights of the working class. Although at different times she worked with various republican or socialist groups, she never felt comfortable with any of them. (T. J. Schaeper)

DESCRIPTORS: Women's Liberation Movement; 1870's–1914; Auclert, Hubertine; Suffrage; France; Working class

HISTORICAL PERIOD: 1870D 1880D 1890D 1900D 1910D 1800H 1900H

HISTORICAL PERIOD (STARTING): 1870's

HISTORICAL PERIOD (ENDING): 1914

5/5/2

[etc.]

Information retrieval systems offer many additional features and search techniques so experienced search analysts may take shortcuts not shown above, and CD-ROM systems may allow the searcher to combine steps. For purposes of

Special Topics

both classroom and individual instruction, however, it is clearer to develop the sets one at a time and then combine the sets, step-by-step, as in the above example.

When to Use Electronic Database Searching

Suggestions for when to use online searching derive from the advantages outlined above. Most, but not all, also apply to the use of CD-ROMs. Provided the subject is represented in one or more databases, an electronic database search is appropriate in the following situations:

- Complex topics: two or more concepts or other variables are to be combined, for example, finding review articles published after 1979 on studies of the U.S. Constitution.
- The search is for a single concept, but one on which there is not much literature and there are many printed volumes to look through, for example, William F. (Buffalo Bill) Cody in AHL.
- Both or all concepts in a query have many references in the printed index, for example, women and the labor movement, so that it would be tedious to sort through either one of the index terms.
- A thorough, extensive search is needed for all possible occurrences of a word or a name in titles and abstracts as well as in index terms.
- The search involves obscure, unusual, or very recent terminology that is not used as index terms but is present in titles and abstracts; these topics are not searchable in the printed indexes because index terms do not exist.
- A thorough, extensive search of several bibliographies is desired, especially for an interdisciplinary topic. CD-ROMs are much more limited than online systems in the number of databases they can access.
- The printed index or bibliography is not available.
- A person wants the convenience of a quick search that produces a printed bibliography, even if the topic is relatively easily searched by hand.
- The complete bibliographic data is needed to verify a citation.
- A researcher wishes to take advantage of the dynamic nature of online searching to explore a subject or a line of inquiry not yet fully defined.

When Not to Use Electronic Database Searching

As electronic information retrieval has become a standard feature of the library scene, as databases and retrieval systems have proliferated, including a multitude of end-user ones, as search analysts have become more skilled, and as students and other users have become more familiar with computers, the instances in which an electronic search is considered inappropriate have become fewer and fewer. They involve primarily inadequate topic definition.

Among the situations in which an *online* search is not suitable are broad topics not yet sufficiently focused by the student, such as segregation, women, World War II, or American foreign policy. In these cases it is useful first to discuss the topic with the professor or librarian and peruse some printed works like textbooks, indexes, and review articles to narrow the topic to more feasible bounds. A CD-ROM search that produces thousands of "hits" can demonstrate the necessity for better topic definition.

A related type of query for which an electronic search is not satisfactory is one that involves a vague concept that cannot be clearly stated in words that are present in the literature, or a complex and ill-defined concept that must be expressed in numerous synonyms or indirectly related terms. For example, in a search on the question of whether Spain declined or faced a crisis in the seventeenth century, the expression of the idea of decline and of the pros and cons of the argument is difficult to capture.

This stricture against searching on vague and multidimensional concepts applies to searches for undergraduates, but more advanced researchers can benefit decidedly from such a search. One real search that this author worked on was related to the use and characteristics of public space in certain epochs of American history. The concept of public space was not then established; it was not clearly represented in the existing literature, nor could it be defined in a few words; it was vague and required several dozen terms to express it. Through the process of a few online searches, trying new terms and combinations and eliminating others, the subject took shape. This was an excellent example of using interactive, trial-and-error searching to contribute to the research process. Another actual search was on the notion of night in Japan for a yet-undefined research project. Instead of pursuing all the expressions the researcher and search analyst could think of for nighttime phenomena and activities, such as nightclubs, night life, or after dark, the researcher chose to sample entries about Japan that contained the word *night* regardless of its context. As a preliminary exploration of current literature and as a stimulus to possible directions of research, the search was useful.

A third situation in which electronic searching may not be as helpful as expected is when the search question contains facets that are ambiguous in the database because relationships are not expressed in computer-searchable terms. For example, in a search for publications about nineteenth-century French historiography on the Italian Renaissance, the database and retrieval systems cannot match each time period with the right country; or, in a search for discussions of Voltaire's views about England, the electronic search will retrieve references on the reception of Voltaire's writings in England. Some databases, such as PAIS, try to overcome this problem by linked headings and subheadings that distinguish relationships like U.S. foreign policy toward the USSR from the USSR's foreign policy toward the United States, but these devices do not always work satisfactorily and must be used with caution. This inability to distinguish relationships seldom causes a problem; but the user should understand why it happens and not be unduly disappointed.

Finally, whenever the use of printed indexes or a CD-ROM database is more convenient, easier, or faster, those resources should be used instead of the online search. Students often need only a very few references on uncomplicated subjects or current affairs, which are easily found in readily available printed indexes; for example, topics like the California gold rush, Daniel Boone, Geraldine Ferraro, Watergate, or teenage pregnancy. In the past there was a tendency to discourage the use of online searching merely for convenience, and searches for undergraduates were often considered inappropriate and too costly; but because undergraduates rely more heavily on secondary sources than on primary ones, an online search service is appropriate for them. Furthermore, it is a mistake to assume that all undergraduate work is at an elementary level; topics are not always simple and easily searched in printed indexes.[12] With the widespread introduction of end-user online systems and CD-ROMs, electronic database searching for and by undergraduates is not only accepted but also recognized as contributing to the learning process.[13]

Additional Points to Consider

Certain characteristics of research and writing in the humanities, including history, require special attention when searching electronic databases, namely the language used to express subject matter, geographic boundaries, and dates or time periods. All terminology must be matched to the words in the database. Recognition at the outset of some limitations and possible problems avoids surprises and disappointments for the student or other occasional user and prepares the user to deal with them.

Conscious consideration of the relationship of the search question to titles of existing literature is more necessary in planning an electronic search than in scanning printed bibliographies because information retrieval systems are, for the most part, literal. For the computer to retrieve any entry there must be an exact match between the words requested and the words in the database. The computer leaves the thinking to the database designer and the searcher. Databases whose records have no annotations and little or no indexing are particularly problematic because in the fields of history and the humanities title words alone yield a low percentage of relevant entries. In addition there is no way for the computer to discern relationships between broader and narrower aspects of a subject. A broad topic may occur in more narrow articles; for example, information on the economic development of mid-nineteenth-century France is found in works on the railway industry in Lyon, and the status of eighteenth-century European women in publications about nuns, actresses, prostitutes, and witches.[14] The opposite relationship also exists: a narrow topic may be covered in more general works, such as Rousseau's concept of the state in articles on the political ideas of the *philosophes* or lesbianism in works on women and gender. Therefore the researcher must consider searching on a broader basis than the specific idea, event, person, or other focus of the investigation and, conversely, on more detailed components of it.

Historians are accustomed to working with these relationships, but in online searching one makes decisions about the boundaries of the search more deliberately and, at least tentatively, at the outset. Whether to begin the search broadly or more narrowly depends upon the degree of comprehensiveness desired, the amount of literature assumed to exist on a topic, and the stage of the researcher's work; that is, exploration of the topic, preliminary bibliography, or focusing on a well-defined detail.

Regardless of how the search is initially conceived, two important points are to be kept in mind: First, the search strategy is checked all along the way; sample entries may be viewed; and the search strategy can be modified to produce results that are most satisfactory for the researcher's interpretation of the topic. Second, the final evaluation and selection of bibliographic references are still made by the *human* researcher. The user discards less-relevant items (and the occasional "false drop"), just as they are seen and passed over when looking at traditional printed bibliographies; the computer search simply makes this process more obvious. Sometimes the speed and apparent ease with which electronic searching, especially end-user searching, produces a printed bibliography misleads the user about the results; so instructors should emphasize that the computer makes no judgments; the user must still evaluate the references for quality and relevance.[15]

The geographic focus and the historical time period of a search question especially require a consideration of the broader and narrower confines of the concept. For topics on which not a great deal of material has been published or when focus on a single country or smaller area is new, a broader geographic scope may be necessary. For a study of women in prerevolutionary France the researcher has to decide whether to search on Europe as well as France (i.e., select Europe **OR** France) in order to retrieve citations of works on Europe that, most likely, make significant references to France.

To search accurately for geographic elements the researcher or search analyst must have two kinds of information: (1) the various names by which the area is referred to, variant spellings of names, the larger geographic or political units to which the area belongs and has belonged (e.g., Rumania, Romania; Austria-Hungary, Austro-Hungarian, Hapsburg, or Habsburg Empire; Eastern Europe, Warsaw Pact, Soviet Bloc, etc.), and if it is a large area, its component parts (e.g., all the countries that constitute South America); and (2) the index terms and structure used in the selected database.

Any one geographic area may have a variety of names in a database. Names of places change over time as a result of changing boundaries, sovereignty, politics, or cultural sentiment (e.g., Stettin to Szczecin, Persia to Iran, or Rumania to Romania). Names may vary depending on the language used (Firenze or Florence, Sevilla or Seville) and, although each database has rules about which form of a name to use, there are inconsistencies. Imprecise and unofficial names for areas are also used, like the Sun Belt, the Pacific Rim, or the Third World. HA and AHL attempt to use as index terms the names of countries that are historically correct for the period under discussion (England or Great Britain, Russia or USSR), but this practice does not alleviate the problem of varying names. The appropriate name cannot always be determined from the source document, or the document may cover a period in which the country had more than one name. Databases that use the name in vogue at the time of indexing also end up with various names for a single country as countries continue to change their names. At this time it is not economically feasible for database producers to update the geographic index terms throughout the entire database every time a change occurs. Databases lack complete cross-reference structures, so it is up to the researcher to supply the synonyms and variations of the geographic terms to be used in a search.

In planning an online or CD-ROM search, the researcher should check the indexing used in the database to be searched, not only for the geographic terms but also for the hierarchical structure of the index. For example, to search for references on South America, must one list all the countries? Will a search on France retrieve all items about individual cities in France? Most databases provide very little hierarchical arrangement or grouping of related geographic terms. AHL gives in the index the state name along with the town, county, or other local unit so that a search on California retrieves all references to cities, towns, and other smaller entities in the state. In HA the country name is shown in the index followed by the name of the smaller geographic unit such as town or province, for example, France–Paris or France–Loire Valley. Thus one does not have to use both the town name and the state in AHL or the town and the country in HA unless there are two towns with the same name. But what the database indexers consider to be a country—that is, the main index term—is not always obvious and must be determined before the search is conducted. For example, in HA Wales is indexed as a country—a leading index term—rather than as a subdivision of Great Britain. A search on the term *Great Britain* will not retrieve a record about Wales unless that record is about both the larger political entity (Great Britain) and Wales, in which case the record is indexed with both terms, *Great Britain* and *Wales*.

The other major defining element in many history topics is the time period. Here, too, researchers must be sensitive to broadening their search to take into account the existing literature and to adapting a search to the way it is represented in the database. There are no standard terms for historical periods either in the literature or in the databases. Only HA and AHL provide historical period index terms (dates) for every record for which there is indexing. The date index terms reflect exactly the period covered by the source document, which may be a single year, a range of years, a century, or several centuries. Other databases, such as *MLA Bibliography*, *Philosopher's Index*, *Religion Index*, and *Histline*, offer historical period indexing on some but not all of the records, and the index terms are for broad periods and traditional eras like centuries (1600–1699), Renaissance, ancient, 1517–1648, and 1789–1815.

Basic guidelines for historical period searching are: (1) do not search for dates or historical periods unless necessary—subject terms alone are often sufficient, such as Martin Luther, French Revolution, Boston Tea Party, Watergate; (2) use subject terms and synonyms to supplement dates, such as Louis Philippe **OR** July Monarchy **OR** 1830–1848; and (3) check the database to be searched to see what kind of indexing is available and adapt the search strategy to it.

In searching the history databases HA and AHL, the researcher is cautioned against defining the historical period too strictly and thereby missing relevant records. For example, the search on women in prerevolutionary eighteenth-century France, given the small amount of material on that specific topic, might be extended to the sixteenth and seventeenth centuries to pick up more general works that span the early modern period. A search on American reform movements of the 1890s should allow some leeway on either side of the decade, such as 1885–1900 or 1875–1910, depending on the researcher's interest and the estimated amount of literature.

Because the effective use of historical period indexing in HA and AHL is not immediately obvious to users and some published materials are incorrect on this point, the search analyst and the researcher doing his or her own searching should consult the AHL-HA searching manual.[16]

Other possible problems of electronic information retrieval that need to be explained include the retrieval of duplicate citations and irrelevant references. The latter, called ''false drops,'' occur when a search word has more than one meaning and the various meanings are not distinguishable by the computer. For example, a search on theater, a dramatic production, may retrieve entries on a military campaign like the Pacific Theater of World War II.

Students, or those whose belief in the magic of the computer is untempered by experience, are sometimes disappointed that the search results are not limited to the holdings of their own library or to English-language references. The ability to match search results against a library's collection is not yet widely available, but one such system is the NOTIS Multiple Database Access System, which displays the local library's call number along with the database record. Limitation to English-language references is possible in many databases. Researchers who object to getting references not locally obtainable or in foreign languages should be reminded of the broader view required in research: Even if one cannot use all the sources and literature discovered about a topic, one should have a command of the existing literature to be able to gauge the limits of one's investigation and to place one's own work in the context of the body of scholarship. An undergraduate can write a term paper on the International Brigade in the Spanish Civil War using English-language materials but needs to know the scope and type of additional literature on the subject.

A factor that sometimes discourages the use of online searching and hampers exploiting it to its fullest advantage is that its cost is so immediately stated in dollars and cents, as opposed to the cost of a researcher's time or the "cost" of missing data; many libraries charge the user for online searching. More and more libraries, however, have accepted the fact that electronic database searching must be provided as part of their regular reference and information services.[17] The advent of less-expensive end-user online systems and CD-ROM databases has enabled libraries to offer more electronic information services without direct cost to the user. The costs of online searching are discussed below.

HOW TO OBTAIN AN ELECTRONIC DATABASE SEARCH

Access to electronic databases is available in two basic ways: through the computer-assisted reference service of a library, where an experienced search analyst plans and executes the search, called intermediary searching, or by doing one's own search using one's own personal computer or equipment provided by the library. The policies and procedures of electronic information retrieval services vary among libraries, so it is important for the teacher or the researcher to determine in advance what services are available, what philosophy and policies are in force, and what the costs are at a particular institution.

End-user searching of CD-ROMs and simplified online systems have quickly eclipsed mediated online searching by search analysts. The value of these approaches is still primarily for conducting comparatively simple and nonextensive searches, for initial exploration of a topic, and for gaining experience with computerized information retrieval systems that will be helpful when using more sophisticated ones.

The most popular form of electronic information retrieval is the library microcomputer search station equipped with CD-ROMs or other electronic forms of databases. Some of these are merely fast, mechanized indexes while others have the interactive and logical operations of online searching without the telephone and time charges. Both Dialog and the H. W. Wilson Company also offer a combination online and CD-ROM search station that allows users to switch from a CD-ROM database to its online version.[18] Instructions for using these systems are usually provided right on the screen and in printed guides prepared by the database producer or the local library. Libraries may also offer instructional sessions on the specific CD-ROM systems. In a general bibliographic instruction session or one intended to introduce users to electronic information retrieval, however, instructors are cautioned against teaching mechanical details; these are best treated in separate specialized sessions or in individual instruction.[19]

Library users can also do their own end-user searching of electronic databases mounted on an online public access catalog. They can use the catalog at the library from home or office through a microcomputer and modem, and they can use the same search system to locate periodical articles as that used to locate books and journal titles as noted above under "Definitions."

A third type of end-user searching is that available on simplified versions of the online retrieval systems, designed specifically for the end user or the occasional searcher. These "user-friendly" systems, such as Dialog's Knowledge Index, BRS's BRS/After Dark, and Information Access Corporation's Search Helper, may be subscribed to directly by the individual or used in libraries that offer the service. The searching language and routines of these systems are easier to use, but the systems have less sophisticated search capabilities and fewer databases than the parent information retrieval systems. They do require some training, and those libraries that offer this service usually provide at least minimal training.

An individual may subscribe to an online information retrieval system like Dialog or BRS, as libraries do, and use his or her own microcomputer and modem to access the system, but it is usually neither cost-effective nor a sound research method to do one's own *online* database searching. Full-scale online information retrieval systems require training and constant practice to operate them effectively; the databases are complex, and each one has a different structure and features. The historian is not likely to need online searches frequently enough to maintain the skills required for effective searching.[20]

Still the most effective method of searching electronic databases is to take advantage of the library's experienced staff for an online search. The description here of online search service is what a researcher can expect of the best library services. Although some reservations have been expressed about the skills and subject knowledge of intermediary search analysts,[21] ideally the historian complements the work of the search analyst to achieve optimum results. The most important assistance the historian can give the search analyst is a thoughtful explanation of the research question and appropriate synonyms and related terms on which to search, including names and dates of historical events, periods, and people involved in the topic.

It is vital to the success of a mediated online search and to the historian's understanding of the results that he or she actively participate in the planning and execution of the search. In fact, historians should avoid organizations that simply take a search request and deliver the results. Such services may be acceptable when performed by trained specialists in medicine, science, or technology, or when the requested search is simple, but they are not adequate for serious researchers in the social sciences and humanities.

1. The search begins with the researcher having done enough preliminary work on the topic to be able to explain it to the search analyst and to supply correct nomenclature (names of people, places, events, subjects), dates, and synonyms or related terms that appear in the literature on the subject. The experienced scholar already knows the subject, so it is a matter of articulating the details and deciding which terms are most relevant to his or her view of the question. The researcher who is less familiar with a topic, including most undergraduates, will have to consult textbooks, subject handbooks or encyclopedias, and current indexes or abstracts to determine recent research trends and terminology in order to define the search question. In either case, the viewpoint and emphasis of the individual is needed to develop a search strategy that will produce the most satisfactory results.

2. Most library search services require a written statement of the search question, usually on a printed form that also requests information about the purpose of the bibliography, such as for an undergraduate term paper, a class reading list, exploration of a dissertation topic, or a grant proposal. Keywords may be listed to supplement but not substitute for the narrative statement. The written request forces the researcher to articulate the question, which helps define and clarify it; it also gives the search analyst a concrete statement from which to plan the search. The search request form often becomes a worksheet for the search analyst.

3. The next step is the informational or reference interview in which the search analyst and the historian discuss the topic and decide, at least tentatively, on certain parameters like types of source documents and publication dates desired, language limitations, whether or not abstracts will be printed, and the costs. This interview may be held either when the written request is completed or just prior to performing the search, which is usually done on an appointment basis. In most cases some time must be allowed between the submission of the search request and the actual search, partly because of the necessity to schedule the equipment and the analyst's time, and partly because the analyst needs time to consult manuals and reference books and to plan at least a preliminary search strategy. Searches that are done on the spur of the moment do not represent the best service and should never be depended upon for advanced research.

4. During the interview or at the time of the search, the search analyst, in consultation with the historian, selects the databases to be searched.

5. Next, search strategies for the particular databases are sketched—beware of search analysts who think they know the system and databases so well that they do not have to write down the strategy! Choose the vocabulary to search; decide whether to search for the terms as index descriptors, title words, words in abstracts, or all three; outline the plan for using the computer's logic to combine terms to achieve the desired breadth or focus, including alternate strategies; note the techniques for limiting retrieval to certain languages, publication dates, and types of sources.

6. The preliminary search strategy is typed in and the results are checked by noting the number of times each search term was found and by sampling some of the retrieved records. If the results are not satisfactory or if they stimulate ideas for different search terms or operations, the strategy can be modified before the results are printed. The search analyst must be skilled and flexible enough to take advantage of the trial run to try new approaches. This dynamic characteristic of online searching should be used to the fullest, both to improve and refine the planned search and to open up new lines of research.

7. The online search session concludes with a postsearch review in which the search analyst explains the process and the results, including the parts of the records printed. If the bibliography is printed offline and sent to the user later, this explanation is given on the sample results supplemented by a written explanation attached to the prints.

Costs

Costs of electronic database searching vary by the type of services and policies at the host institution, so this information should be gathered locally and clearly explained. Libraries usually do not impose any charge for using CD-ROMs. End-user searching of online systems like BRS/After Dark may be free or may carry a modest charge. There are frequently limits, however, on the amount of time, search questions, or search results per user. Searching the online public catalog at the library is free; remote access and access to the periodical indexes may be limited to those affiliated with the home institution and/or may require arranging for a means of payment.

At the present time many libraries charge some kind of fee for online searching performed by a search analyst. This may be a flat charge per search; it may be based on what the information retrieval system charges the library; or it may be a combination of the two. Information retrieval service charges vary among companies and among databases; in addition they depend on the number of databases used, on the amount of time online (which is directly related to the complexity of the search), and on the number of items printed as a result of the search. There may be a difference in costs depending on whether the results are printed online at the time of the search or are printed offline and sent to the user in five to seven days. These cost factors must be considered for each search. It is difficult to estimate search costs, but analysts will try to give some idea of what to expect. An average online search cost is misleading because of the enormous range in the complexity of search questions and the number of factors on which charges are based. Searches on history topics may range from $10 to $100, with the majority of searches for undergraduate projects in history costing $20 to $50 for the online searching time and results (i.e., information retrieval service charges), exclusive of any additional charges levied by the library. These costs are usually reviewed by the search analyst with each person who requests a search. College and university libraries have a wide variety of policies to provide online searching service at no cost or at a reduced cost to students, professors, and other members of the academic community. Special arrangements may also be offered in conjunction with the library's bibliographic instruction program.

ELECTRONIC SEARCHING, BIBLIOGRAPHIC INSTRUCTION, AND THE RESEARCH PROCESS

Electronic information retrieval has faced criticism for the lack of comprehensiveness of the databases and the difficulty of matching a researcher's statement of a question to the language and logic of the computer system, but early skepticism about the role of online database searching in education and research has been replaced by concern that electronic information retrieval be integrated into the total research process and not be represented as a mechanical operation. With the proliferation of user-friendly menu-driven systems, the challenge to instructors to convey the potential and the limitations of electronic information retrieval is even greater than when they were dealing solely with mediated online searching. ''Without instruction in methods for using the power of the system and advice about the designed-in limitations of the user-friendly menus, many users may never know what the real potential and value of the system may be. . . . Users may lose contact with the overall information-searching process. . . . Perhaps more insidious is the fact that such systems encourage users to think of information-seeking according to an inflexible, linear pattern.''[22] The speed and ease of obtaining a list of references may mislead students about the need to use other resources in printed form or about the necessity to pursue other steps in the research process, such as critically evaluating the sources, selecting and organizing the information, and presenting the results in an interesting and intelligible manner.[23]

Other reservations about the use of electronic database searching have been based on representing them as static, mechanical collections of bibliographic references unresponsive to human thought processes and alien to the imaginative, critical pursuit of a research question. Librarians' emphasis on rational, highly organized search strategies, both in bibliographic instruction in general and in online searching, has tended to portray the research process more narrowly than it is in fact. Contemporary trends in bibliographic instruction present more sophisticated and more flexible views of both the research process and electronic database searching than those cited by the critics.[24] There are three major aspects to the current status of bibliographic instruction in electronic information retrieval:

1. Electronic database searching is an integral part of library use and bibliographic instruction. Databases have their strengths and limitations and, like other reference sources, must be examined, evaluated, and used judiciously. The task of the instructor is to present electronic searching in the context of what is needed for a particular research project.

2. Research is recognized as an organic process; a problem-solving activity, not merely a rational and linear movement through a stipulated set of steps. The gathering of bibliographic data is only part of the process, a process that requires imagination and critical thinking. Librarians need to balance the explanation of rational search strategies (especially useful for undergraduates) with an ability to admit and work with the illogical information-seeking habits of researchers.

3. Electronic database searching, which is the epitome of logic and rationality, is not necessarily the straitjacket process that has sometimes been depicted; it can be a generative and creative process. The limitations cited—the inability to browse, to see entries in a larger context, to see an interesting item on an adjacent page; the difficulty of expressing a question in words usable in the database—are in part vestiges of users' long familiarity with the printed page in a book, lack of adaptation to the techniques of using computers and databases, and sometimes an excuse for lack of effort in analyzing and expressing the question. It is not true that electronic databases cannot be browsed. And the fear that students' use of electronic searching may deprive them of some "enriching educational experience of browsing through bibliographies, footnotes, printed indexes, and library stacks" is outdated, to say the least.[25] The potential of online searching for interactive, trial-and-error information retrieval, which con-

tributes to the research process by simulating the reformulation of questions—not just by producing the bibliography product—has always been used by knowledgeable search analysts. This potential has been clearly and forcefully articulated by librarians and by nonlibrarian instructors who have discovered that learning to use an electronic database can teach students and instructors alike to think more clearly and consciously about their research topics.[26]

Electronic database searching, either mediated online searching or end-user searching based on adequate training, can assist the researcher's creativity in two ways: On the one hand it fosters the creative, generative process of research when used imaginatively by researcher and search analyst, as noted above. On the other hand, requiring the researcher to analyze the question so it can be handled by the computer's logic forces her or him to give deliberate attention to boundaries of the question and to possible alternate parameters, to think about the implications of each decision, and either to clarify the question or to recognize that clarity and definition are not yet possible or desirable. Furthermore, it forces the researcher to make decisions *consciously* and consistently that otherwise are sometimes made randomly and without fully articulating them. The pursuit of logic and rationality is not necessarily anticreative; it stimulates new ideas as well as clarifies existing ones.

The objective of bibliographic instruction in electronic information retrieval in the field of history is to introduce researchers at all levels to this technology and to some of the basic facts about its use, without getting bogged down in arcane details of particular systems. Bibliographic instruction should explicitly consider the place of information gathering in the research process, explain the relationship between existing sources regardless of format, and recognize the potential of online searching to contribute to research through both its demand for logic and its interactive dynamism.

NOTES

1. Experienced instructors present these points in a variety of guises. See esp. David N. King with Betsy Baker, "Teaching End-Users to Search: Issues and Problems," in *Bibliographic Instruction and Computer Database Searching* [LOEX 86], ed. Teresa B. Mensching and Keith J. Stanger (Ann Arbor, Mich.: Pierian Press, 1988), 27–33; Nancy Taylor and Sara Penhale, "End-User Searching and Bibliographic Instruction," ibid., 57–60; and Connie Miller and Patricia Tegler, "Online Searching and the Research Process," *College & Research Libraries* 47 (July 1986): 370–73.

2. Additional suggestions are in Bonnie Snow, "What Jargon Is Really Necessary When Teaching (and Learning) Online Skills?" *Online* 10 (July 1986): 100–107.

3. A good overview of CD-ROM issues is in Stephen P. Harter and Susan M. Jackson, "Optical Disc Systems in Libraries: Problems and Issues," *RQ* 27 (Summer 1988): 516–27.

4. Patricia Suozzi, "By the Numbers: An Introduction to Numeric Databases," *Database* 10 (February 1987): 15–22.

5. A broader discussion is in Joyce Duncan Falk, "Databases for Historical Research:

Overview and Implications,'' *American History: A Bibliographic Review* 4 (1988): 1–13.

6. Rebecca Bostian and Anne Robbins, ''Effective Instruction for Searching CD-ROM Indexes,'' *Laserdisk Professional* 3 (January 1990): 14–17; Gillian Allen, ''CD-ROM Training: What Do the Patrons Want?'' *RQ* 30 (Fall 1990): 88–93; Loretta Caren, ''New Bibliographic Instruction for New Technology,'' *Library Trends* 37 (Winter 1989): 366–73; Susan K. Charles and Katharine E. Clark, ''Enhancing CD-ROM Searches with Online Updates,'' *College & Research Libraries* 51 (July 1990): 321–28; John G. Jaffe, ''For Undergrads: InfoTrac Magazine Index Plus or Wilsondisc with *Readers' Guide* and *Humanities Index*?'' *American Libraries* (October 1988): 759–61; Lucy Anne Wozny, ''College Students as End User Searchers: One University's Experience,'' *RQ* 28 (Fall 1988): 54–61; Harter and Jackson, ''Optical Disc Systems''; King and Baker, ''Teaching End-Users to Search.''

7. An extensive analysis of sixteen humanities databases that details their strengths and weaknesses, directly relevant to history, is Joyce Duncan Falk, ''Humanities,'' in *Women Online: Research in Women's Studies Using Online Databases*, ed. Steven D. Atkinson and Judith Hudson (New York: Haworth Press, 1990), 7–72.

8. Joyce Duncan Falk and Susan K. Kinnell, *Searching America: History and Life (AHL) and Historical Abstracts (HA) on Dialog* (Santa Barbara, Calif.: ABC-Clio, 1987). An explanation of the addition of retrospective volumes is in Joyce Duncan Falk, ''Introduction,'' *Historical Abstracts Part A* 31 (1980): v. A brief preliminary review of the HA and AHL CD-ROMs is in *College & Research Libraries* 53 (March 1992): 170–71, and a more detailed review is in *CD-ROM Professional* 5, no. 3 (May 1992): 83–86.

9. *User Guide Arts & Humanities Search* (Philadelphia: Institute for Scientific Information, 1988). Joyce Duncan Falk, ''Database Characteristics and Search Problems in the Humanities,'' *Online '85 Conference Proceedings* (Weston, Conn.: Online, 1985), 102–6.

10. A few articles on multidisciplinary searching related to history are: Suzanne Hildenbrand, ''Women's Studies Online: Promoting Visibility,'' *RQ* 26 (Fall 1986): 63–74; Jo Kibbee, ''Tradition Meets Technology: Searching Folklore Online,'' *Database* 10 (February 1987): 24–26; Robert E. Skinner, ''Searching the History of Science Online,'' *Database* 6 (June 1983): 54–61, but beware of erroneous suggestions on historical period searching in HA and AHL; Robert E. Skinner, ''Searching the History of the Social Sciences Online,'' *Database* 8 (February 1985): 28–34; Falk, ''Humanities,'' in *Women Online*.

11. Recent literature on end-user CD-ROM training emphasizes the need for understanding basic concepts and development of search strategy. Bostian and Robbins, ''Effective Instruction,'' 16; Charles and Clark, ''Enhancing CD-ROM Searches,'' 324; Harter and Jackson, ''Optical Disc Systems,'' 519; King and Baker, ''Teaching End Users to Search,'' 29; Rudy Widman and Jimmie Anne Nourse, ''Delivering Hi-Tech Library Instruction,'' *Laserdisk Professional* 2 (November 1989): 50–54.

12. Evelyn-Margaret Kiresen and Simone Klugman, ''The Use of Online Databases for Historical Research,'' *RQ* 21 (Summer 1982): 344. Linda L. Phillips and Rita H. Smith, ''Online Searching for Undergraduates,'' in *Academic Libraries: Myths and Realities, Proceedings of the Third National Conference of the Association of College and Research Libraries* (Chicago: Association of College and Research Libraries, 1984), 395–99.

13. Sara J. Penhale and Nancy Taylor, ''Integrating End-User Searching into a Bib-

liographic Instruction Program,'' *RQ* 26 (Winter 1986): 212–20; Taylor and Penhale, ''End-User Searching''; Scott Stebelman, ''Integrating Online Searching into Traditional Bibliographic Instruction,'' in *Bibliographic Instruction and Computer Database Searching* [LOEX 86], Mensching and Stanger, 23–26. Harold H. Kollmeier and Kathleen Henderson Staudt, ''Composition Students Online: Database Searching in the Undergraduate Research Paper Course,'' *Computers and the Humanities* 21 (July-September 1987): 147–55, discovered that learning to use a computerized database helped teach students to think more clearly about refining their research topics and seeing their topics in broader scholarly contexts.

14. On searching women's history topics see Joyce Duncan Falk, ''The New Technology for Research in European Women's History: 'Online' Bibliographies,'' *Signs* 9 (Fall 1983): 120–33; and Falk, ''Humanities,'' in *Women Online*.

15. This point is stressed by, among others, Penhale and Taylor, ''Integrating End-User Searching,'' 214; Charles and Clark, ''Enhancing CD-ROM Searches,'' 327.

16. Falk and Kinnell, *Searching*. A simpler strategy for historical period searching is shown in Falk, ''Humanities,'' in *Women Online*, 37–39.

17. The trend toward eliminating fees is illustrated by two reports: Virgil Diodato, ''Eliminating Fees for Online Search Services in a University Library,'' *Online* 10 (November 1986): 44–50; Jay Martin Poole and Gloriana St. Clair, ''Funding Online Services from the Materials Budget,'' *College & Research Libraries* 47 (May 1986): 225–37.

18. Cynthia Hall, Harriet Talan, and Barbara Pease, ''InfoTrac in Academic Libraries: What's Missing in the New Technology?'' *Database* 10 (February 1987): 52–56; Charles and Clark, ''Enhancing CD-ROM Searches.''

19. Taylor and Penhale, ''End-User Searching,'' 60; King and Baker, ''Teaching End-Users to Search,'' 29; Wozny, ''College Students as End User Searchers,'' 60–61.

20. David Y. Allen, ''Computerized Literature Searching, A Do-It-Yourself Activity?'' *Perspectives* 23 (February 1985): 23–24, and Joyce Duncan Falk, ''Bringing the Library Home in a Microcomputer,'' *Proceedings of the Annual Meeting of the Western Society for French History* 12 (1984), 260–68, both of whom are historians and trained search analysts, are more cautious about end-user searching than Don Karl Rowney, ''The Microcomputer in Historical Research: Accessing Commercial Databases,'' *History Teacher* 18 (Fall 1985): 227–42, who makes some mistakes in discussing the indexing of HA.

21. Online search service coordinators do not consider lack of experience in searching the humanities databases important, which differs from this author's observations; see Joyce Duncan Falk, ''Survey of Online Searching in the Humanities in Four-Year College and University Libraries,'' ERIC ED 261 687 (Arlington, Va.: ERIC Document Reproduction Service, 1986): 22. Fred Batt, ''The Online Search Request: When and How to Say No,'' in *The International Conference on Databases in the Humanities and Social Sciences 1983*, ed. Robert F. Allen (Osprey, Fla.: Paradigm Press, 1985), 277, notes that patrons are at the mercy of searchers whose skills vary widely and who have other concerns at hand; Kiresen and Klugman, ''The Use of Online Databases for Historical Research,'' 347, mention one instance of dissatisfaction with the searcher in the evaluation of their project; and Stephen K. Stoan, ''Computer Searching: A Primer for the Uninformed Scholar,'' *Academe* 68 (November-December 1982): 10–15, cites librarians' limited knowledge of a discipline as an obstacle.

22. King and Baker, ''Teaching End-Users to Search,'' 31.

23. The earlier ''knee-jerk'' reactions about computers doing the students' work for

them or defeating the purpose of an assignment in information sources have generally given way to more thoughtful criticisms, but one report cites an instance of a faculty member who still believes that students "should do their own research and, therefore, use printed indexes" (Juleigh Muirhead Clark and Susan Silverman, "What Are Students Hearing about Online Searching? A Survey of Faculty," *RQ* 29 (Winter 1989): 230–38). Stebelman explains librarians' old view that online searching is students paying librarians to find their term paper material as a conflict of values: the conviction that students need to know about the latest information technology versus the belief that they need to become self-reliant library users ("Integrating Online Searching," 24). Connie Miller and Patricia Tegler attack librarians' overemphasis on teaching patrons to be independent users, "In Pursuit of Windmills: Librarians and the Determination to Instruct," *The Reference Librarian* 18 (Summer 1987): 119–34.

24. C. Paul Vincent, "Bibliographic Instruction in the Humanities: The Need to Stress Imagination," *Research Strategies* 2 (Fall 1984): 179–84; Constance A. Mellon, "Process Not Product in Course Integrated Instruction: A Generic Model of Library Research," *College & Research Libraries* 45 (November 1984): 471–78; the several respondents in the column edited by Carolyn Kirkendall, "Dialogue and Debate . . . ," *Research Strategies* 3 (Winter 1985): 40–43, and 3 (Spring 1985): 93–94; Ruth Friedman, "Computer Comments" [letter in reply to Stephen K. Stoan], *Academe* 69, no. 1 (1983): 40; literature cited in notes 6 and 13 above; and the extensive article on the library's mission to provide bibliographic instruction by Harold B. Shill, "Bibliographic Instruction: Planning for the Electronic Information Environment," *College & Research Libraries* 48 (September 1987): 433–53.

25. Shill, "Bibliographic Instruction," 446. He adds that the "idea generating potential of online searching is far greater than that of print indexes without any real sacrifice of the potential for serendipitous discovery," 447.

26. Miller and Tegler, "Online Searching and the Research Process"; Kollmeier and Staudt, "Composition Students," 148, 155. Unfortunately while extolling the virtues of end-user searching, Kollmeier and Staudt, 149–50, misrepresent the presearch interview for a mediated online search as static and final. They ignore the interactiveness of a properly conducted mediated search and do not appear to know that search results are sampled while online, and the search strategy is further refined.

APPENDIX

Databases

Following is a selection of electronic databases relevant to historical research together with the major information retrieval systems on which each is offered, the subject scope, type of source documents, and beginning date of the online file. These data change frequently; current information on databases and their various electronic formats may be found in the directories listed following the database listings.

History

America: History and Life (AHL), Dialog, Knowledge Index; *America: History and Life on Disc* (1982–   )

Subject: History and culture of the United States and Canada, prehistory to the present. *Sources*: Articles from approximately 2,100 journals in history, social sciences, and humanities, and from selected collections, 1964– ; books, book reviews, and dissertations, 1973– ; historical film and video reviews, 1989– .

Historical Abstracts (HA), Dialog, Knowledge Index; *Historical Abstracts on Disc* (1982–)
Subject: World history, broadly defined (excluding U.S.A. and Canada), 1450-present. *Sources*: Articles from about 2,100 journals in history, social sciences, and humanities, 1973– ; books and dissertations, 1979– .

Social Sciences and Humanities—Multidisciplinary

Arts & Humanities Search (A&HS), BRS, BRS/After Dark, Dialog; ISI CD-ROM
Subject: Humanities, archaeology, architecture, art, classics, dance, film, folklore, history, literature, music, philosophy, theater, religion, and others. *Sources*: Articles, editorials, letters, poems, short stories, plays, music scores, and reviews from 1,400 journals (about 200 history and general humanities titles); additional articles from social science and science journals, 1980– .

FRANCIS (French Retrieval Automated Network for Current Information in Social and Human Sciences), Télésystèmes-Questel
Subject: Combined 19 databases including Art and Archaeology (Near East, Asia, America), Répertoire d'Art et d'Archéologie, History of Science, History and Science of Religions, History of Science and Techniques, Linguistics, Philosophy, and Pre-history and Protohistory. *Sources*: Primarily articles from 4,500 journals; books, theses, government documents, 1972– .

Humanities Index, OCLC: EPIC/FirstSearch, Wilsonline, Wilsontape; Wilsondisc CD-ROM
Subject: Humanities, language, linguistics, literature, history, philosophy, theology, journalism. *Sources*: Every article in about 295 English-language periodicals, 1984– .

PAIS International, Dialog, Knowledge Index, BRS, BRS/After Dark, OCLC: EPIC/FirstSearch, RLIN: CitaDel, Data-Star; PAIS-on-CD-ROM, SilverPlatter CD-ROM
Subject: Current political, social, and economic affairs, international relations, public administration, public policy, social welfare, sociology. *Sources*: Combines records from *Public Affairs Information Service Bulletin* and *Foreign Language Index*, which index about 1,200 journals and 8,000 books, pamphlets, government publications, and other items per year, 1972– .

Social Sciences Index, OCLC: EPIC/FirstSearch, Wilsonline, Wilsontape; Wilsondisc CD-ROM
Subject: All the social sciences, including environmental sciences, public administration, education. *Sources*: Articles and book reviews from a little over 300 English-language periodicals, 1983– .

Social Scisearch, Dialog, Knowledge Index, BRS, BRS/After Dark, Data-Star; ISI CD-ROM
Subject: All the social sciences, including information science and education. *Sources*: Electronic version of *Social Sciences Citation Index*; articles, reviews, editorials, other

substantive items from about 1,500 social science journals (about 45 are history titles and 35 area studies journals), plus social science articles from more than 3,300 science journals, 1972– .

Social Sciences and Humanities—Subject Specific

Art Index, OCLC: EPIC/First Search, Wilsonline, Wilsontape; Wilsondisc CD-ROM
    Subject: Art, design, architecture, photography, urban planning, film, television, crafts, industrial design. *Sources*: Articles from 240 domestic and foreign periodicals, yearbooks, and museum bulletins, October 1984– .

Art Literature International (RILA), Dialog, FRANCIS, Knowledge Index
    Subject: Western art from the fourth century to the present (i.e., postclassical European and postdiscovery American art), theory and criticism. *Sources*: Articles from 400 journals, books, exhibition catalogs, dissertations, collections of essays, 1973– .

Artbibliographies Modern, Dialog, Knowledge Index
    Subject: Nineteenth- and twentieth-century art and design, architecture, folk art, town and country planning, scenic design, art history, photography, film. *Sources*: Exhibition catalogs, dissertations, books, and articles from about 500 core journals and 200 journals in the humanities and social sciences, 1974– .

Avery Index to Architectural Periodicals, RLIN, Dialog
    Subject: Architecture, urban planning, environment, landscape architecture. *Sources*: About 700 architecture periodicals, 1979– .

Economic Literature Index, Dialog, Knowledge Index; SilverPlatter CD-ROM
    Subject: Economics worldwide, historical and contemporary.
    Sources: Corresponds to the index of the *Journal of Economic Literature* and *Index of Economic Articles*; articles and book reviews from 285 journals and about 200 books per year, 1969– .

ERIC, BRS, BRS/After Dark, Dialog, Knowledge Index, OCLC: EPIC/FirstSearch, Orbit; Dialog OnDisc, SilverPlatter, and OCLC CD-ROMs
    Subject: Education and related subjects. *Sources*: Combines *Resources in Education* (unpublished research reports, the ERIC microfiche collection) and *Current Index to Journals in Education*, 775 periodicals, 1966– .

Histline, U.S. National Library of Medicine's MEDLARS
    Subject: History of medicine. *Sources*: Journal articles, monographs, others, 1970– .

Mideast File, Dialog
    Subject: Contemporary life and work in the Middle East.
    Sources: Originally 350, now about 1,200 journals plus research reports, gazettes, government publications, broadcasts, books, book reviews, dissertations (approximately 50 percent from Arabic sources), 1979– .

MLA International Bibliography, Dialog, Knowledge Index, Wilsonline; Wilsondisc and SilverPlatter CD-ROMs
    Subject: Literature, languages, linguistics, folklore; medieval to contemporary. *Sources*: Books, dissertations, and articles from approximately 3,000 journals and series and 700 collections per year, 1964– .

Philosopher's Index, Dialog; Dialog OnDisc

Subject: Philosophy and related interdisciplinary fields, philosophy of various disciplines, history of philosophy. *Sources*: Articles from 300 journals, books, dissertations, 1940– (some gaps).

Religion Index, BRS, BRS/After Dark, Dialog; Wilsondisc CD-ROM
  Subject: Church history, history of religions, theology, biblical literature, and related areas in the humanities and current affairs. *Sources*: Articles and book reviews from 400 journals and 350 collections, proceedings, and series, dissertations; collections 1960– , periodicals 1975– , theses 1981– .

RILM Abstracts, Dialog; CD-ROM
  Subject: Music, historical musicology, ethnomusicology, instruments, performance, theory, and music related to other disciplines. *Sources*: Articles from about 300 journals, books, reviews, dissertations, recordings, catalogs, 1971– .

Sociological Abstracts, BRS, BRS/After Dark, Dialog, Knowledge Index, Data-Star, OCLC: EPIC/FirstSearch; SilverPlatter CD-ROM
  Subject: Sociology and related social and behavioral sciences worldwide, including family studies, gerontology, policy sciences, urban and rural sociology, and feminist studies. *Sources*: Book chapters and articles, reviews, research reports, conference papers, and case studies from about 1,500 journals and other serial publications, 1963– .

U.S. Political Science Documents, Dialog
  Subject: Political science, including theory and methodology, foreign policy, international relations, world politics, economics, public administration. *Sources*: Articles in 150 U.S. scholarly journals, 1975– .

General and Reference

Bible, King James Version, Dialog; Compton's CD-ROM
  Full text of the 1769 edition as edited by Thomas Nelson Publishers.

Dissertation Abstracts Online, BRS, BRS/After Dark, Dialog, OCLC: EPIC; UMI CD-ROM, SilverPlatter CD-ROM
  Combines *Comprehensive Dissertation Index*, *American Doctoral Dissertations*, *Dissertation Abstracts International*, and *Masters Abstracts International*; beginning 1980 includes abstracts when submitted by the author, 1861–.

Eighteenth-Century Short Title Catalogue (ESTC), RLIN, Blaise-line (U.K.); CD-ROM
  Subject: Publications of the eighteenth century, useful for history, literature, art, history of publishing. *Sources*: Bibliographic records and locations for all items published in Great Britain or British territories and items in English published anywhere.

GPO Monthly Catalog, BRS, BRS/After Dark, Dialog, OCLC: EPIC/FirstSearch, Wilsonline; U.S. Government Printing Office, Wilsondisc CD-ROMs
  List of publications of the federal government, including Congress and all Senate and House hearings, on a vast range of topics, 1976–.

LC MARC, Dialog, Blaise-line (U.K.), Wilsonline (as LC/Foreign MARC and LC MARC)
  Bibliographic records for all books cataloged by the Library of Congress since 1968; see REMARC.

OCLC Online Union Catalog, OCLC: EPIC/FirstSearch; BRS and BRS/After Dark as OCLC EASI Reference; OCLC CD-ROM

Cataloging and library locations for books, serials, manuscripts, audiovisual materials, maps, and music scores; OCLC EASI Reference on BRS, the four most recent years or the most recent one million records.

REMARC, Dialog
Bibliographic records for Library of Congress, 1897–1980 (English-language works prior to 1968 and other languages up to the date they are entered in LC MARC).

Research in Progress Database, RLIN
Records for articles accepted for publication by selected journals, grants from NEH, and other works in progress reported to the National Council for Research on Women, 1988– .

RLIN Catalog, RLIN
Bibliographic records from Library of Congress (since 1968) and from libraries that are members of the Research Libraries Group, mostly large research libraries and special law and art libraries.

Current Affairs

Academic Index, IAC CD-ROM
Subject: Current affairs, all topics of popular interest. *Sources*: Articles from 385 scholarly and general interest journals, 1985– .

Magazine ASAP, BRS, Dialog
Subject: Same as *Magazine Index*. *Sources*: Full text of articles in more than 100 of the magazines indexed in *Magazine Index*, 1983– .

Magazine Index, BRS, BRS/After Dark, Dialog, Knowledge Index; IAC CD-ROM
Subject: General, scholarly to lighthearted, current affairs, performing arts, business, sports, travel. *Sources*: Articles, and so forth, from some 240 popular magazines, 1959–1969 and 1973–1976, from about 435 magazines, 1977– .

National Newspaper Index, BRS, BRS/After Dark, Dialog, Knowledge Index
Subject: General news, reviews, editorials, poetry, cartoons, obituaries. *Sources*: *Christian Science Monitor*, *New York Times*, *Wall Street Journal*, 1979– ; *Los Angeles Times*, *Washington Post*, both selectively, 1982– .

Newspaper Abstracts, Dialog, OCLC: EPIC/FirstSearch, RLIN: CitaDel; *Newspaper Abstracts Ondisc* (1985–)
Subject: General news, reviews, editorials, obituaries. *Sources:* More than twenty-five national and regional newspapers are covered beginning with January 1, 1989. Papers include: the *Atlanta Constitution*, *Boston Globe*, *Christian Science Monitor*, *Los Angeles Times*, *Wall Street Journal*, *New York Times*, and *Washington Post*.

Newsearch, BRS, BRS/After Dark, Dialog, Knowledge Index
Subject: General news, current events, book and theater reviews, virtually all subjects. *Sources*: Articles and reviews from some 2,000 magazines, newspapers, and books indexed for other Information Access Company databases such as *Magazine Index* and *National Newspaper Index*; most recent two to six weeks.

Readers' Guide to Periodical Literature, OCLC: EPIC/FirstSearch, and *Readers' Guide Abstracts*, Wilsonline, Wilsontape; Wilsondisc CD-ROM

Subject: General information, current events. *Sources*: More than 180 popular, English-language, general interest magazines from the United States and Canada, 1983– . *Readers' Guide Abstracts*, 1984– .

Directories of Databases (Selected)

BRS/Search Service Database Catalog, current edition (Latham, N.Y.: BRS Information
    Technologies).
CD-ROMs In Print (Westport, Conn.: Meckler, 1987–) annual.
Computer-Readable Databases (Detroit: Gale Research, 1991–), annual.
Dialog Database Catalog, current edition (Palo Alto, Calif.: Dialog Information Services,
    Inc.).
Directory of Online Databases (New York: Cuadra/Elsevier, 1979–), quarterly.
Directory of Portable Databases (New York: Cuadra/Elsevier, 1990–), semiannual.
Fulltext Sources Online (Needham, Mass.: BiblioData, 1988–), semiannual.

Major Information Retrieval Systems with Databases of Interest to Historians

BRS/Search Service (BRS Information Technologies, 1200 Route 7, Latham, NY 12110;
    tel. 800–468–0908)
    Offers more than 125 databases in all fields: medicine, science, business, social sciences, and general reference. In addition to the full-scale service, there is an evening service for end users, BRS/After Dark, which includes several useful files.

Dialog Information Retrieval Service (Dialog Information Services, Inc., 3460 Hillview
    Ave., Palo Alto, CA 94304; tel. 800–334–2564)
    A multidisciplinary service with more than 350 databases including the U.S.-produced history and humanities ones. The simplified system for the end user, called Knowledge Index, includes the history databases AHL and HA, *Artbibliographies Modern*, the *Bible*, *MLA Bibliography*, PAIS, *Sociological Abstracts*, and others.

Nexis (Lexis/Nexis) (Mead Data Central, Inc., 9443 Springboro Pike, P.O. Box 933,
    Dayton, OH 45401–9964; tel. 800–227–4908)
    Full-text access to news, trade, and professional publications; wire services; broadcast transcripts; and domestic and foreign newspapers. Wire services covered include the Associated Press, Asahi News Services, Reuters, Tass, United Press International, and Xinhua (China). Broadcast transcripts covered include *ABC News Transcripts*, *BBC Summary of World Broadcasts*, and *MacNeil/Lehrer News Hour*. Domestic newspapers include the *Chicago Tribune* (November 1988–), *Los Angeles Times* (January 1985–), and the *Washington Post* (January 1977–). The Lexis service provides access to state and federal legal codes and law reports and reviews, to a wide range of state and national legal and legislative services, and to legal information from the United Kingdom and Commonwealth countries and France.

OCLC (OCLC Online Computer Library Center, Inc., 6565 Frantz Road, Dublin, OH
    43107–3395; tel. 800–818–5878)

EPIC is a full-featured search system designed for the expert searcher. FirstSearch is a system specifically designed for library patrons. In addition to the OCLC Online Union Catalog, these services include among their databases: ERIC, *GPO Monthly Catalog*, *Newspaper Abstracts, Readers' Guide to Periodical Literature, Business Periodicals Index, Humanities Index, Biography Index, Sociological Abstracts*, and *Social Sciences Index*.

Research Libraries Information Network (RLIN) (Research Libraries Group, 1200 Villa
 St., Mountain View, CA 94041–1100, tel. 415–962–9951)

In addition to the bibliographic database based on Library of Congress cataloging since 1968 and the holdings of more than 25 large research libraries, RLIN has the special databases *Avery Index, Eighteenth-Century Short Title Catalogue, Research in Progress Database*, and others. The CitaDel service includes a number of scholarly databases: *ABI/INFORM, Periodical Abstracts, Dissertation Abstracts, Newspaper Abstracts, PAIS '80 +, Isis Current Bibliography of the History of Science, Current Bibliography of the History of Technology*, and *Hispanic American Periodicals Index*.

Télésystèmes-Questel (Questel, Inc., 5201 Leesburg Pike, Suite 603, Falls Church, VA
 22041; tel. 800–424–9600)

Offers a group of French humanities and social science bibliographies combined into the FRANCIS database.

VU/TEXT Information Services (VU/TEXT Information Services, 325 Chestnut Street,
 Suite 1300, Philadelphia PA 19106; tel. 800–258–8080)

Full-text access to over forty U.S. daily newspapers, including most Knight-Ridder papers. Among newspapers covered are the *Boston Globe, Chicago Tribune, Los Angeles Times, Philadelphia Inquirer*, and *Washington Post*. Other publications covered include *Life, People*, and *USA Today*.

Wilsonline (The H. W. Wilson Company, 950 University Ave., Bronx, NY 10452; tel.
 800–367–6770, in New York State 800–462–6060)

Includes the Wilson indexes, for example, *Humanities Index* and *Social Sciences Index*. The databases are also available for end-user searching on Wilsearch, on the Wilsondisc CD-ROM system, and for lease to libraries for mounting on their online catalogs.

Instructional Materials

Each information retrieval service publishes a thorough manual explaining how to use the system. Many database producers publish manuals for the individual databases; their names and addresses are given in the directories of databases listed above. The most important ones for history are the following:

ABC-Clio Online. ABC-Clio, P. O. Box 1911, Santa Barbara, CA 93116–1911; tel. 805–
 968–1911, 800–422–2546
User Guide Arts & Humanities Search. Institute for Scientific Information, 3501 Market
 St., Philadelphia, PA 19104; tel. 800–523–1850, 800–336–4474

Using the Finding Aids to Archive and Manuscript Collections

Trudy Huskamp Peterson

"No history," wrote Fernand Braudel, "can be written without precise knowledge of the vast resources of its archives. . . . To prospect and catalogue . . . these mines of the purest historical gold, would take not one lifetime but at least twenty."[1] Prospecting and cataloging are indeed slow processes. They can be speeded considerably, however, if the researcher has a working knowledge of the principles used to administer primary sources and of the finding aids that describe the source materials.

A source is a person, document, or object from which information is derived. A source that provides direct and immediate access to the information is a primary source; a source that provides indirect exposure to the information is a secondary source. For example, a person explaining his experience during the Vietnam War is a primary source, while if one of his listeners later recounts the explanation, that secondhand recitation is a secondary source. Similarly, a document from the files of the Federal Bureau of Investigation about Martin Luther King, Jr., is a primary source for understanding the bureau's relationship to King, while a book written about the bureau and King is a secondary source.

Often primary and secondary sources are discussed as if people, documents, and books are the totality of sources available for the study of the past. Yet a great deal of historical research can be completed through the use of the built environment (roads, houses, monuments, for example) and objects of material culture (cooking utensils, farm tools, manufacturing equipment) as primary sources. These nonverbal primary sources provide the same immediacy of experience as verbal sources, but their analysis requires different skills.[2] While recognizing the growing importance of these nonverbal items for historical re-

The opinions expressed are those of the author and do not necessarily represent those of the Federal agency with which she is associated.

construction, this chapter will focus on primary sources that are verbal, particularly those sources found in archives, manuscript repositories, and libraries.

Primary sources may be published or unpublished. A book by Ernest Hemingway and a newspaper review of Hemingway's book are both published, but the former is a primary source and the latter is a secondary one. Alternatively, however, if researching how the critics received Hemingway's works, the newspaper review would be a primary source for that investigation. Newspapers, magazines, mail-order catalogs, government publications, corporate annual reports, and a host of other published items are primary sources of great significance. Normally a researcher locates published materials through one system of finding aids and unpublished materials through a separate system. This chapter focuses on strategies for locating unpublished sources, primarily those in the United States.

PUBLISHED PRIMARY AND SECONDARY SOURCES

The relationship of secondary to primary sources, of published to unpublished primary sources, and of the finding aids to them suggests a logical research strategy. A thorough mastery of published secondary and primary sources is the most important preparation a researcher can have for using unpublished sources.

Published secondary sources are usually easier to locate than either published or unpublished primary sources, may exist in multiple copies in many libraries, and will probably provide a broad background to a research topic. They need to be thoroughly exploited by the researcher before turning to primary sources. A researcher interested in the New Deal, for instance, might begin by reading Ellis W. Hawley's *New Deal and the Problem of Monopoly* (1966), not only for its content but also for the leads to sources that can be derived from the citations in Hawley's footnotes. Secondary sources provide the grounding necessary to understand the detailed primary sources and to move swiftly through them, selecting items central to the research interest.

Published primary sources exist in multiple copies and are often more easily accessible than unpublished ones. It is good research strategy to read the Department of State *Bulletin* (a primary source) for the period of the Suez Crisis before attempting to use Eisenhower's presidential papers from the period, for example. Not only will the published primary source often provide the official interpretation of an event, but it may also give the researcher valuable references to unpublished items and provide a chronological outline of events.

The archives of an institution or organization will normally include a set of all publications of the parent body. These are often called the "record set" of publications or the "printed archives" of the organization. While a researcher can use the publications at the archives, it is usually more profitable to read them elsewhere if possible before making a research visit.

Having reviewed the published literature, the researcher is now ready to turn to the unpublished sources. He or she will quickly learn that it is important to understand the jargon that archivists and manuscript curators use. Next the researcher will need to understand the organization of archival institutions and the sources they hold. Locating and understanding the finding aids is the next problem, followed by locating the sources identified by the finding aids. Finally the researcher is ready to work with the staff of the archival institution to obtain the sources sought. The remainder of this chapter will address these issues.

UNPUBLISHED SOURCES

Defining Terms

All archival definitions begin with the *document*. A document is recorded information regardless of medium or characteristics and has three components: a physical base (clay tablets, papyrus, wood, parchment, paper, film, computer tape, laser disks); an impression on the physical base, made by either manual or mechanical means (such as a pen on paper or an electrical impulse on computer tape); and information conveyed by the impression upon the base. *Document* is the usual archival term for a single item.

Not all documents are records, but all *records* are documents. Records are all documentary material, regardless of physical form or characteristics, made or received and maintained by an institution or organization in pursuance of its legal obligations or in the transaction of its business. Records are one-of-a-kind. Thus, for example, the local Congregational church has only one set of baptismal records, and a university has only one series of minutes of the faculty council meetings. Records grow naturally out of the activities of the institution (archivists often say that records are ''organic'').

Just as all records are documents but not all documents are records, so all *archives* are records but not all records are archives. Archives are the records of an institution or organization that are determined to have permanent value either as evidence of the operation of that institution or because they provide important information about people, places, events, or phenomena. In addition, the word *archives* can also mean the administrative unit responsible for the permanent records or the building in which such records are housed. Archives, in the purest sense, maintain the permanently valuable records of the organization of which the archives are a part: the National Archives holds records of the United States government and is a part of the government; the Emory University Archives holds the records of the university and is a part of the university; the archives of Chase Manhattan Bank holds the records of and is a part of the bank.

Personal papers are documents, just as records are, but, unlike records that by definition originate in an institution or organization, personal papers are the private documents accumulated by an individual, belonging to him or her and subject to his or her disposition. Like records, personal papers have an organic unity, for a body of personal papers is formed naturally over the course of a person's life (a marriage license or two, income tax forms, personal letters, photographs).

Other documents are formed into *artificial collections*. These are accumulations brought together from various sources, usually to illustrate an event (e.g., the dedication of the Statue of Liberty), a person (anything related to Charles Lindbergh), or a set of something (the autographs of all the signers of the Declaration of Independence). These collections are the product of a purposeful collecting activity by an individual or institution, which may include purchase. Such collections differ from both records and personal papers, each of which is the natural product of business or personal life and has an organic unity.

The term *manuscript* (deriving from the twin roots *manu* "hand" and *script* "writing") originally referred simply to handwritten items. In the nineteenth century "manuscript collections" were groups of handwritten materials, whether records of an institution, personal papers, or artificial collections. During this century the definition of manuscript has shifted. Now manuscript refers to a body of records or personal papers or an artificial collection with historical value held by an institution or individual other than the creator. An institution that has as its purpose the collection and maintenance of documents donated to it by sources outside the institution is a *manuscript repository*.

The difference between an archives and a manuscript collection is the difference between the Archives of the City of New York, which is a part of and maintains the records of the government of the city, and the New-York Historical Society, which maintains personal papers and records that have been donated to it by individuals and institutions in New York. Similarly, the National Archives is a part of and holds the records of the U.S. government while the Manuscript Division of the Library of Congress, although part of the U.S. government, holds personal papers, records, and artificial collections that have been donated to it by individuals and nongovernmental institutions.

Understanding the Institutions

All archives and manuscript collections have to solve three basic problems: acquiring source materials, organizing them, and providing access to the materials for the user. While there are some basic concepts common to both archives and manuscript repositories, in each of these three areas there are also significant differences in the solutions available.

Acquisition. Obtaining source materials in a manuscript collection is a matter of deciding what types of records, personal papers, and artificial collections the institution wants to obtain and then either soliciting their donation or purchasing them. Manuscript curators spend a good deal of effort defining the collection development policy of the institution. They have to make decisions such as whether to concentrate on obtaining papers of twentieth-century authors, obtaining records of businesses in a particular geographic region, or collecting documents from a particular time period irrespective of source. In addition, all manuscript repositories are offered items by potential donors that may not fall within the collection parameters. Whether the institution accepts them or not depends on a variety of factors, from the space available in the repository, to how divergent the subject content is, to the identity of the donor. This means that a manuscript repository contains a central core of holdings relating to the basic collecting thrust of the repository but will also have some very heterogeneous collections.

Obtaining source materials in an archives is very different. The role of the archives is to document the organization of which it is a part. The archivist cannot independently develop a collecting policy, because the policy must reflect the direction that the parent organization takes. For example, if a university decides to establish a school of forestry, the university archives will receive and must maintain the documents relating to the school of forestry, regardless of whether there is any interest in forestry by the archives or any materials already in the archives relating to trees. Similarly a corporation may suddenly acquire a new company or divest itself of one, and the archives will reflect that; or a government may decide to establish a new agency, and the archives will suddenly receive records from that agency which may be wholly unlike any records it already has.

The power that an archives has in obtaining materials is in selecting what it wants to maintain of the body of record material created by the parent institution. Here the difference between records and personal papers is striking. If a manuscript repository solicits and receives a set of personal papers, it is likely to keep 90 percent of the donation. If a body of records is available for transfer to an archives, the archivist may keep a tenth and throw away 90 percent—the reverse of the situation with personal papers. The reason for this difference is simple: institutions create a lot of paper that has marginal long-term value, such as employee time cards, records of purchases of pencils and paper clips, contracts for janitorial services, and the like. Institutions also create record series that are so voluminous that they cannot practically be maintained in toto by the archives, such as records of all local police investigations or all applications for housing assistance. The archivist (and the manuscript curator who solicits the donation of records) determines whether to save a series of records in whole or in part, or to destroy it. Because records are unique, this is a substantial responsibility.

No archives can save everything, so it is important that the researcher understand how the institution decides what to accession and what to destroy, since that determines the documentary resources available for research use. Appraisal decisions and solicitations of donations are documented in dossiers. These files are usually available for review by researchers.[3]

Organization. Once the materials are selected, the repository must organize and make sense of them. Again, important distinctions emerge between the handling of personal papers and the handling of institutional records. Often when personal papers arrive at a repository the entire accumulation comes at once. This means the curator working on the collection knows from the very beginning the collection's size, subject, and chronological coverage. A comprehensive finding aid can be developed immediately. With records, unless they are from a defunct organization, everything is different. The records transferred are only part of the total picture. More records will inevitably arrive, and the archivist may not know when. Any finding aid that is created is partial and will be out-of-date as soon as the next accretion of records arrives. A researcher should always look at the date on a published finding aid for records before concluding that the repository does not contain the records desired; if the date is more than a few years old, the researcher should contact the repository to find out if any further accretions have arrived since the finding aid was published.

To organize the holdings of a repository, archivists and curators follow the principle of provenance. This concept holds that since the archives of a given organization belong to and constitute an organic whole, they must not be inter-mingled with those of any other organization; similarly, the papers of one in-dividual reflect his or her life and work and should not be intermingled with those of other individuals.

Archivists worldwide have adopted the principle of provenance for several important reasons. First, it protects the integrity of the records because their origins can quickly be determined. Second, it helps to reveal the significance of the records, for the subject matter of individual documents can be fully understood only in the context of related documents from the same source. Third, it is a workable and economical method of arranging, describing, and providing ref-erence service, often enabling the archivist and the researcher to utilize finding aids prepared in the office that created the records.

Let us look at an example of why provenance is so important. In 1970 the United States conducted an "incursion" into Cambodia. The records of that event are scattered among the various agencies that had a part in the event. They could, of course, be brought together and put in simple chronological order or classified in some subject categories. But think of the questions that could not be answered if the records were combined: Was the State Department fully informed in advance? Did the information developed by the National Security Agency get to the army command or was it held in the Department of Defense? Which items originated in the National Security Council but went out over the signature of the Secretary of Defense? What information simply was not shared? There are many more questions. This means that a researcher has to think in terms of organizational structure when working with archival materials and must plan to look in a variety of record groups in order to understand the full story.

A second organizing principle, very widely observed by archivists but less universal among manuscript curators handling personal papers, is the concept of original order. This principle dictates that the archives of an organization should be maintained in their original filing arrangement. The reasons that ar-chivists use original order are the same as those for adopting the principle of provenance: it protects integrity, reveals significance, and remains economical. The reason the principle of original order is less closely followed when dealing with personal papers is simple: Not all individuals have a formal filing system, whereas every office does. If an individual did have a clear filing system, curators usually maintain it when the papers are donated to a manuscript repository. If there is no discernible system, however, curators impose one, often starting with the most personal items, such as diaries, and ending with the least personal, such as clippings.

Access. A third major issue in administering archives and manuscript collections is determining when the documents can be released for research use. Here the differences between donated materials and records that remain within the creating institution are the sharpest. When items are donated to a repository the transfer is documented in writing, sometimes by an exchange of letters, sometimes by a will, sometimes by a deed of gift or a deposit agreement. In this instrument of transfer the conditions for access are normally enumerated. Sometimes the donor specifies that the entire collection be closed for a period of years or until a certain event has occurred (the death of a spouse, for example); sometimes the donor establishes general guidelines (for example, restricting access to ''documents that would invade the privacy of living individuals'') and turns over to the repository the responsibility for identifying and withholding those particular items. Most repositories accept donations with restrictions, so long as it is agreed that at some time the materials will be wholly open for research use. Repositories must be scrupulous in living up to their donor agreements; the success of future collecting depends upon it. Researchers may be able to ask the repository to review the items that have been withheld to see whether enough time has passed so that the documents can be released, but it is unlikely that a researcher could successfully challenge restrictions in a legally completed donation.

With records that stay within the creating institution, the situation is rather different; here the distinction between public and private archives becomes important. Public archives are governmental archives—municipal, county, state, national. Normally there are laws governing access to the records of government.[4] It is the responsibility of the archivist to look at the records in a public archives and apply to them the statutory provisions. In the federal government, for example, there are dozens of laws that pertain to access to information, and records of each of the three branches of government are covered by different provisions.

With records of a private business or organization, on the other hand, no laws normally intrude. A private organization, such as a business or a church, may or may not grant access to its records. And while archivists subscribe to the principle of equal access for all users, a private organization can and sometimes does allow an official historian to use records that are denied to other researchers. Legal challenges for access to the records of private institutions are unlikely to succeed because records are the property of the institution that created them, and absent a particular statutory requirement the property can be preserved, disposed, and dispensed of as the organization chooses.

Figure 9.1
Levels of Arrangement and Description

I.	Repository	Guide
II.	Record Group	Inventory
	Personal Papers	Register
III.	Series	Series Description
IV.	Filing Unit	Folder-Title List
V.	Item	Calendar
		Special List

Finding the Finding Aids

Archival and manuscript repositories describe documents in a wide variety of finding aids, both published and unpublished. The principal characteristic of archival description is that it is a collective description rather than an item description. With large modern series of records or personal papers, it is impossible for archivists to list every sheet of paper in the holdings. Archivists of necessity opt to describe documents in blocks.

Each type of finding aid that a repository creates relates to a particular level of arrangement of the holdings. Modern archival theory suggests that there are five levels of arrangement: repository, record group or collection, series, filing unit, and item. Specific finding aids are associated with each level. (See figure 9.1.)

At any one of these levels the finding aids may be provenance-based or pertinence-based. A provenance-based finding aid is one that discusses the holdings in terms of the organization that created the records. For example, a provenance-based finding aid to the records within a state archives would have as major topics "Records of the Governor," "Records of the Legislature," "Records of the Department of Agriculture," and "Records of the Attorney General."

A pertinence-based finding aid is confined to a particular topic, irrespective of where the source materials are located. Nationally there have been publications of sources for women's history, sources relating to the history of particular countries, sources for the study of American foreign relations, and many more.[5] An institution sometimes also publishes subject-oriented finding aids, such as the National Archives's guides to sources for black history, American Indian history, and Alaskan history.[6]

Repository. The first level of description includes both multi-institutional and comprehensive, single-institution finding aids. The earliest of the multi-institutional finding aids was the National Union Catalog of Manuscript Collections, known as NUCMC. The catalog, as its name implies, is selective: It covers only materials that are donated to a repository. The compilers reasoned that if someone wanted to see the records of Kraft, Inc., the person would write to Kraft, but if the Kraft records had been donated to a university the researcher would have difficulty finding them. Therefore, all archival records that stay within the creating institution—including all the records of government—are omitted. In other words, NUCMC covers manuscript repositories but not archives.

The first attempt at a comprehensive directory of all repositories, both archival and manuscript, was published in 1961 by the National Historical Publications and Records Commission. It has been updated twice, in 1978 and 1988.[7] The directory provides the name, address, and general nature of the holdings of all repositories in the United States. It is the place for the researcher to begin a search. (See figure 9.2.) If the researcher does not find a church or business or organization listed in the directory as maintaining its own archives, the next step is to search in NUCMC to see if the church or business or organization has donated its records to a manuscript repository. For example, a check of the directory reveals no entry for an archives maintained by the National Association for the Advancement of Colored People (NAACP); a check of NUCMC reveals that the NAACP records are at the Library of Congress's Manuscript Division. If the researcher wants to locate personal papers, NUCMC is the best place to begin.[8] (See figure 9.3.)

Many multi-institutional guides cover particular types of repositories or repositories in a geographic area. Some of these are produced by consortia of institutions. Others, such as the guide to the holdings of the presidential libraries, are produced by commercial firms. In one recent case, a single repository produced a pertinence-based guide covering both its holdings on immigration and related holdings in European repositories.[9]

The goal of most archival and manuscript repositories is to publish a guide to their total holdings, and many of them have done so. The guide to a repository gives the prospective user an overview of what materials are available there; it usually also provides information on rules of access and specialized finding aids for particular parts of the holdings. Often an index provides some subject access to the descriptions in the guide. (See figure 9.4.)

For example, consider a researcher who is interested in issues relating to water rights in the dry states of the American West. In the *Guide to the National Archives of the United States* the index has an entry for water rights that will lead him or her, among other places, to an entry for the records of the Bureau of Reclamation in the Department of the Interior. This entry gives a capsule history of the establishment and legal jurisdiction of the bureau, a statement of the volume of its records held in the National Archives, the chronological coverage of the records, an indication of the types of subjects found in the records, a sketch of available cartographic and audiovisual records, a reference to the portion of the records that have been microfilmed and can be purchased from

Figure 9.2
Extract from the *Directory of Archives and Manuscript Repositories in the United States*

STONINGTON

CT772-720
Stonington Historical Society
Library
Whitehall Mansion
Whitehall Avenue
Stonington CT

MAILING ADDRESS:
P.O. Box 103
Stonington CT 06378

(203) 536-2428

OPEN: Th 2-4 or by appointment
COPYING FACILITIES: no
MATERIALS SOLICITED: Stonington's history, including records of early families, of whaling, sealing, and ocean shipping voyages, and of land warfare. Will also accept similar materials regarding adjacent areas, such as Waverly, RI, and New London, Mystic, and Groton, Ct.

HOLDINGS:
Total volume: 700 items
Inclusive dates: 1672 - 1902
Description: Letters, diaries, records, and accounts pertaining to the history of Stonington and the families of the first settlers, Miner, Stanton, Trumbull, Palmer, Williams, and Chesebrough. Other materials related to Stonington include ships' logs and other records of whaling, sealing, exploration, and merchant shipping, including the China trade.

SEE: NUCMC, 1962.

SEE: Ingram.

SEE ALSO: Walter Schatz, ed., *Directory of Afro-American Resources* (Bowker, 1970).

Source: *Directory of Archives and Manuscript Repositories in the United States.* 2nd ed. Phoenix, Ariz.: Oryx Press, 1988.

the National Archives as a microfilm publication (thereby saving an expensive trip to Washington), and a cross-reference to the detailed finding aid (called an inventory) for the records of the Bureau of Reclamation—all in less than two pages.

Record group and manuscript collection. After the researcher has identified

Figure 9.3
Extract from *National Union Catalog of Manuscript Collections*

MS 77-1015

Ballantine, Joseph William, 1888-1973.
  Papers, 1909-70. ca. 1 ft.
  In Hoover Institution on War, Revolution and Peace,
Stanford University (Calif.)
  In part, photocopies.
  Foreign Service officer, State Dept. official, and
political scientist. Unpublished autobiography; content
analysis of selected writings of Owen Lattimore; and
miscellaneous notes, reports, articles, printed mat-
ter, and other papers.
  Unpublished preliminary inventory in the repository.
  Gift of Mrs. Leslie Foster Ballantine, 1973.

MS 77-1016

Belgium (Territory under German Occupation, 1914-
  1918)
  German Military Government in Belgium collection,
1914-18. ca. 16 ft.
  In Hoover Institution on War, Revolution and Peace,
Stanford University (Calif.)
  Public proclamations and announcements issued by
the German Military Government of Belgium during
World War I. In German, French, and Flemish.
  Most have been published in Les avis, proclamations
et nouvelles de guerre allemandes affichés à Bruxelles
pendant l'occupation (1915-18).
  Gift of Grace Davis Booth.

Source: *National Union Catalog of Manuscript Collections*. Washington, D.C.: Library of Congress,
  1962–

the repository that holds the material sought and has used the institution's guide,
he or she is ready to turn to the second level of description: that of a particular
body of materials within the repository. In archives this body is the record group,
in manuscript repositories it is the collection.

A record group is a body of records deriving from the same source that is
managed as an entity. Records in a repository can belong to one and only one
record group, for provenance is the determining factor (only one body of records
exists for the Bureau of Reclamation, for example). For records, the finding aid
for describing all the records within each record group is the inventory; for
personal papers, the finding aid is called the register.[10]

An inventory and a register have many features in common. Both begin with
an introduction that defines the limits of the record group or the set of personal
papers and provides a basic history of the agency and its records or gives a brief
biographical sketch of the person's life. Next, they provide a brief description
of the series within the record group or set of papers. Both inventories and
registers frequently include appendixes that provide supplemental information.
A few repositories publish their inventories or registers. Most, however, provide

Figure 9.4
Example of a Guide Entry

RECORDS OF THE BUREAU OF RECLAMATION
(RECORD GROUP 115)

The Bureau of Reclamation, first known as the Reclamation Service, was created under the Reclamation or Newlands Act of June 17, 1902, which established a reclamation fund from the sale of public lands to finance the location, construction, and maintenance of irrigation works that would store, divert, and develop waters for reclaiming arid and semiarid lands in the States and territories. The act gave responsibility for administering the fund to the Secretary of the Interior, who established the Reclamation Service to exercise that function under the jurisdiction of, but not as a part of, the Geological Survey. On March 9, 1907, the Service was separated from the Survey and was made directly responsible to the Secretary. It was renamed the Bureau of Reclamation on June 20, 1923. The Bureau plans, constructs, and operates irrigation works in 17 contiguous Western States and Hawaii; builds and operates hydroelectric powerplants; and distributes electric power and energy generated at certain powerplants, reservoirs, projects, and dams.

See Institute for Government Research, *The U.S. Reclamation Service* (New York, 1919).

There are 2,418 cubic feet of records dated between 1891 and 1963 in this record group.

GENERAL RECORDS. 1891-1960. 2,431 lin. ft.

These consist of general administrative and project correspondence, with indexes, 1902-45; accident and injury reports, 1902-29; project and feature histories, reports of engineering boards, reports to the Board of Army Engineers, project operation and maintenance reports, and other special reports, 1902-60; summary cost reports and narrative statements concerning construction at reclamation projects, 1916-49; Service and Bureau specifications for reclamation projects, 1902-55 (in WNRC); public land withdrawal and restoration files, 1891-1945; a personnel correspondence file, 1902-40; and records relating to Bureau administration of Civilian Conservation Corps activities, 1934-43.

RECORDS OF THE COMMITTEE OF SPECIAL ADVISERS ON RECLAMATION. 1923-24. 13 lin. ft.

The Secretary of the Interior appointed this factfinding committee in September 1923 to study Federal methods for reclaiming land through irrigation. On April 10, 1924, it submitted its report, which was published as Senate Document 92, 68th Congress, 1st session. Committee records include reports, correspondence, and exhibits accompanying the final report.

RECORDS OF ORGANIZATIONS CONCERNED WITH RECLAMATION. 1899-1934. 43 lin. ft.

The Bureau acquired the records of several private organizations interested in reclamation. Included are records of the National Irrigation Association, including clippings about irrigation, 1899-1906, land law repeal, 1903, and agriculture, 1905-10; press releases, 1903-6; drafts of legislation relating to river control, 1911; and records of the Mitchell News Bureau, 1902-3. Records of the National Reclamation Association consist of general correspondence, 1911-34, correspondence with Government officials, 1914-18, miscellaneous records and correspondence, 1912-14 and 1918-33, George H. Maxwell's scrapbooks relating to Association activities, 1912, court decrees and claims for water rights in Utah and Wyoming, 1904-16,

Source: *Guide to the National Archives of the United States*. Washington, D.C.: National Archives and Records Administration, 1987.

Figure 9.5
Example of an Inventory

Preliminary Inventory of the General Records of the Department of Justice

Contents

	Entries	Page
Introduction		1
Part I. Records of the Attorney General's Office		5
General Records		5
Opinions, 1790-1870	1-5	5
Letters Received, 1809-70	6-9	6
Letters Sent, 1793; 1818-70	10-15	7
Miscellaneous Records	16-23	
Records Relating to California Land Claims	24-31	
Records of the Solicitor of the Court of Claims		
Personal Papers of the Attorney General		

GENERAL RECORDS OF THE DEPARTMENT OF JUSTICE

Records of the Lands Division, 1917-26; 1936-40

The Lands Division, now called the Land and Natural Resources Division, handled legal matters, with the exception of crimes, pertaining to the public domain, condemnation of lands, titles to lands, forest reserves, reclamation and irrigation projects, conservation of natural resources, and Indian lands and property (including Indian tribal suits in the Court of Claims). It also had charge of similar legal matters affecting insular and Territorial affairs, Federal reservations, public works projects, and boundary disputes (international, interstate, and between States and the United States).

Records of the Birmingham, Ala., Field Office, 1936-40.

265. GENERAL ADMINISTRATION FILE. 1936-40. 1 ft.

ment of Agriculture, particularly the Farm Security Administration (formerly the Resettlement Administration). Much of the correspondence and telegrams was exchanged with the Montgomery, Ala., office of the Land Utilization Division of the Farm Security Administration.

269. ATTORNEYS' FILE. 1936-40. 4 ft.

Arranged alphabetically by surname of attorney and thereunder alphabetically by subject.

Files for A. R. Brindley and Charles B. Verner, Special Assistants to the Attorney General, and Mac Beatty, Judge Virginia H. Mayfield, and Travis Williams, Special Attorneys, consisting of correspondence with the Department of Justice, other agencies, and landowners; memorandums, including "curative" memorandums concerning work to cure apparent

Source: *Preliminary Inventory of the General Records of the Department of Justice.* Washington, D.C.: National Archives and Records Administration.

them to the researcher visiting the institution and make copies of the unpublished finding aid on demand. (See figures 9.5 and 9.6.)

The principal difference between the inventory and the register is that the register normally includes a listing of the file units making up the series (at least for the principal series) while the inventory does not. In part this difference reflects a difference in the character of the materials described: Personal papers are by nature heterogeneous while records are more homogeneous. It is difficult to understand what might be contained in personal papers without a filing unit description (usually called a *folder–title list*), while a collective description of a series or records (e.g., ''Proceedings of the 38th Annual Convention'') may be adequate. In part, however, the difference is a function of the size of the de-

Figure 9.6
Example of a Register

LIBRARY OF CONGRESS
MANUSCRIPT DIVISION

The Papers of

HARLAN FISKE STONE

The papers of Harlan Fiske Stone (1872-1946), U.S. Attorney General, Associate Justice of the Supreme Court, and Chief Justice of the United States, were given to the Library of Congress in 1949 by Agnes H. (Mrs. Harlan Fiske) Stone.

In 1957 Russell M. Smith processed the Stone papers
guide. In 1975 the collection was reorganized and
Nolen and Joseph F. McKeever.

Lit

Biographical Note

1872, Oct. 11	Born, Chesterfield, N.H.
1888-90	Student, Massachusetts Agricultural College
1894	B.S., Amherst College
1894-95	Teacher, Newburyport (Mass.) High School
1895-96	Teacher (part-time), Adelphi Acade
1898	LL.B., Columbia Uni
	Admitted to
1898-99	

Scope and Content Note

The Harlan Fiske Stone papers span the period 1889 to 1953, but most of the papers are dated in the years 1925 to 1946 when Stone served on the Supreme Court of the United States. The collection consists of family, general, and special correspondence, subject files, Supreme Court files, and miscellany.

Stone's family correspondence consists chiefly of letters exchanged between Stone and his brother Lauson, sister Helen, and sons Marshall and Lauson. Very few letters in the collection are between Stone and his wife, Agnes. Although Stone occasionally mentioned the Court or other issues of the day, the letters in this series are mainly concerned with personal and family matters.

Source: *The Papers of Harlan Fiske Stone*. Washington, D.C.: Library of Congress, Manuscript Division.

Figure 9.7
A Series Entry

> **191. RECORDS OF THE COMMITTEE ON FIRE**
> **AND EXPLOSION RISKS. 1921. 3 in.**
> Arranged chronologically.
> Chiefly reports of a survey of all buildings
> occupied by the Department with a view to taking
> steps necessary to guard against explosions and fires.
> Chairman of the Committee W. W. Stockberger was
> appointed by the Secretary.

Source: Helen Finnerman Ulibarri, comp. *Preliminary Inventory of the Records of the Office of the Secretary of Agriculture*. Washington, D.C.: National Archives and Records Administration.

scription problem: Records series can run to hundreds of feet of paper in even moderate-sized archives, while in governmental archives they run to the thousands. To list every folder title in a series of five thousand feet is usually an insuperable task.

A commercial firm has microfilmed the inventories of a number of repositories, including the Manuscript Division of the Library of Congress and the National Archives. This microfilm production, sold as the *National Inventory of Documentary Sources*, pulls together a good deal of informative material. Because it publishes only those finding aids the firm selects of those that the repository is willing to have reproduced, the "National Inventory" gives only a partial view of the complete holdings of a repository.[11]

Series. The third level of description is the series. Series are bodies of records that have an internal unity because they share a common filing order (e.g., alphabetic, numeric), a common physical form (correspondence, maps), a common subject, or all three. (See figure 9.7.) Series are the foundation of the arrangement of records, and series descriptions are the building blocks of inventories. A series description has three parts: a title line (consisting of the name of the series, its chronological coverage, and physical volume), an arrangement statement, and a subject-matter description. With textual records this is often the most refined level of description that an archives will achieve.

Filing unit. The fourth level of arrangement is the filing unit. A filing unit may be a bound volume, a manila folder of loose documents, or any other small group of documents handled as a single entity by the *creator* of the documents. These are most often described by lists, either by the title on the filing unit (called a folder–title list) or by the title of the first and last folders in each storage box (a box list). (See figure 9.8.) Folder–title lists are used when the filing units are extremely varied; box lists when they fall into a pattern (chronological or alphabetical, for instance).

Figure 9.8
Example of a Folder–Title List

ARRANGEMENT AND DESCRIPTION

Syracuse University Archives
SAWYER FALK PAPERS
General Files   1919-61

Series 3

Box Number	Folder Number	Contents	
1	1	A correspondence	1944-45 to 1961
	2	American Academy of Dramatic Art - Notes	
	3	American Theatre Council 1937	
	4	Arena Guild	1952-53
	5	Arts Council of New York State	1955-58
	6	"Alcestes" speech	1960-61
	7	B correspondence	1944-45 to 61
	8	Bacon, Ernst	1946-48
	9	Baker, Paul	1946-56
	10	Barrow, Bernard	1948-61
	11	Barter Theatre	1949-50
	12	Berkeley, California - correspondence 1942	
	13	Binns, Graham	1949-50
	14	Bolam, Elsa	1958-60
	15	Bowles, Kenneth	1951
	16	Breen, Robert	1946-59
2	1	Bricker, Herschel	1945-52
	2	Broder, I. Robert	1948-58
	3	C correspondence	1944-45 to 1961
	4	Censorship	1939
	5	Chrow, Lawrence	1946-47
	6	Cisney, Marcella	1942-58
	7	Clark, Barrett H.	
	8	Committee on International Exchange of Persons	1950
	9	Committee on International Exchange of Persons	1953-54
	10	Committee on International Exchange of Persons	1955-56
	11	Committee on Labor Relations 1936	
	12	Conferences on Art, Music and Dramatic Art	1936
	13	Congressional Bills	1937
	14	Congressional Bills	1951
	15	Congressional Bills	1952-53
	16	Congressional Bills	1953-54

Source: David C. Maslyn and Judy Woolcock, comps. *Sawyer Falk: A Register of His Papers in the Syracuse University Library* (Syracuse, N.Y.: Syracuse University Archives, 1965), 20.

Filing unit lists are particularly common in descriptions of personal papers. They are also developed when such a large number of researchers wants the same information that it is easiest to produce a specialized finding aid to answer repeat requests.

Item. This, the most detailed level of arrangement and description, was the standard level of description in the nineteenth century. Item descriptions included the names of the correspondents and a brief abstract of the subject matter of the

Figure 9.9
Example of a Calendar Item List

Israel Shreve Papers

1. SCHUYLER, General Philip. ALS. 1p. fol. Albany, April 5, 1776. To Lieutenant-Colonel Shreve.

2. TILGHMAN, Colonel Tench. Aide to General Washington. ALS. 1p. 4to, no date. Torn. To Colonel Alexander Scammell.

3. PUTNAM, Major-General Israel. LS, 1p. sm. 4to. Princeton, April 5, 1777. To Colonel Shreve.

4. MAXWELL, Brigadier-General William. ALS. 1p. fol. Westfield, April 11, 1777. To Colonel Shreve.

5. SHREVE, Colonel Israel. Autograph Manuscript, 1½pp. fol., Chimney Rock, opposite Crown Point, New York, Monday, Aug. 4. [1777]

6. PICKERING, Colonel Timothy. ADS, 1p. 4to, in camp, August 10, 1777. To Major-General Lord Sterling, or, in his absence, to Brigadier-General William Maxwell.

7. GENERAL STAFF OF THE ARMY AS OF NOV. 1, 1777. Autograph Manuscript, 1p. fol., Nov. 2, 1777. In unknown handwriting.

8. LIVINGSTON, General William. ALS, 1p. fol., Trenton, March 23, 1778. To Colonel Shreve.

9. FORMAN, General David. Chief of Washington's Secret Service in New Jersey. ALS, 1¼pp. fol., Barnegat, April 7, 1778. To Colonel Shreve.

10. SHREVE, Colonel Israel. Draft of his ALS, 1½pp. fol., Mt. Holly, April 9, 1778. To General Washington.

11. RHEA, Lieutenant-Colonel David. ALS, 1p. fol., Freehold, April 17, 1778. To Colonel Shreve.

12. DICKINSON, Major-General Philemon. ALS, 1p. fol., Trenton, May 25, 1778. To Colonel Shreve. With franked address on verso.

Source: *The Shreve Papers* (Houston: University of Houston Libraries, 1967).

document. Because the items were usually listed chronologically in the finding aid, the lists were called "calendars."

Item-level finding aids provide detailed descriptions, therefore they are both exceptionally useful and exceptionally expensive to produce. Repositories generally compile them only when the documents are of unusual value or when access is extremely difficult without a list. (See figure 9.9.)

Item lists are quite common for nontextual records. For motion pictures, cartography, architectural and engineering drawings, sound recordings, and machine-readable records, item-level description is the norm because technical information on each item is required if it is to be used successfully (scale of the map or drawing, size and speed of the motion or sound recording, density of the computer tape, and so forth). Few of these item lists are published, but repositories make them available to users.

Accessioned finding aids. Not all finding aids are created by the archives or manuscript repository. Many finding aids, such as indexes, were created by the originator of the documents and transferred to the archives or manuscript collection with the materials. These are very common accompaniments to textual materials in the nineteenth century, when it was standard office practice to register every piece of mail that arrived and every piece that went out. Indexes, sometimes in bound volumes and sometimes on cards, were prepared for these registers, which themselves led to the correspondence (in other words, a three-step process of index, register, and correspondence). The process was discontinued with the advent of self-indexing filing systems in the twentieth century, and file folders and alphabetic or numeric filing took its place.

Nontextual records, however, continue to be controlled on an item level in many offices. Every photographic negative has a number, every map has a number, and every videotape has a file card describing it. When nontextual materials are turned over to a repository, the archivists make every effort to obtain these item-level finding aids, which in turn become the basis for archival control of the nontextual holdings. Again, these are normally unpublished but available to researchers at the repository.

Automated finding aids. Automation is altering the world of finding aids. Unlike the library world, where many institutions hold identical books and therefore can attain real cost savings by sharing cataloging, archives and manuscript repositories by definition hold distinct, unique materials. The benefits of sharing information about the holdings are much more elusive: to enable repositories to understand what others have collected, to enable them to refer researchers to one another, to help researchers find out what is in the repository without having to travel there. None of these promises the cost savings that helps persuade library administrators to share systems.

Nevertheless, a number of shared databases are emerging. Inevitably, perhaps, the first one emerged out of the manuscript collections held by major research libraries that are members of the Research Libraries Group (RLG). Using the Research Libraries Information Network (RLIN), the bibliographic utility of RLG, several of these libraries began to put information on their major manuscript collections into a shared database.

At about the same time as it became possible to employ internal automated systems for archives and manuscripts, archivists and manuscript curators began to look for a common format to describe their holdings in automated databases. Early experiments quickly convinced them that the library world's standard MARC format was not adequate for handling manuscript collections and archival records, and demands for an archival format arose. The Society of American

Archivists obtained a grant to develop a format acceptable to the profession, and a National Information Systems Task Force was established, which included MARC format specialists from the Library of Congress. The result was the development of a specialized version of MARC for Archives and Manuscript Control known as the MARC/AMC format.

In June 1990, RLG announced that more than 250,000 descriptions of personal papers and records of businesses, organizations, and government agencies were now in RLIN's MARC/AMC file. The majority of these, more than 180,000 entries, were from nongovernmental archives and manuscript repositories. Thirteen state archives contribute to RLIN, and one—New York—announced in 1990 that all its series descriptions are now entered. Two municipal archives, New York City and Washington, D.C., also enter data, and the National Archives has entered selective data.[12] (See figure 9.10.)

It seems clear that the MARC/AMC format will be the exchange format for the foreseeable future. It is less clear that RLIN will be the only bibliographic utility used to exchange MARC-formatted data. It is also not clear that all archival institutions will adopt the MARC/AMC format for internal automation, even though they may rely upon it as an exchange format.

While the MARC/AMC format can be used to describe nontextual materials, variations in the MARC format have been devised for particular media. The MARC/VM (visual materials) format is of particular utility when describing motion pictures, for example; other format variations are available for maps, music, and computer files. Discussions are now under way about the possibility of integrating all specialized format descriptions into one giant MARC. At present a user must search under each format; for example, if seeking a motion picture a user would be wise to look under both MARC/VM and MARC/AMC to make sure all descriptions are retrieved. A unified MARC would eliminate this necessity. Another possibility is that databases specializing in a particular type of media may emerge. Recently a pilot project tested the feasibility of an international database for description of architectural drawings; databases for moving images have also been discussed. Such initiatives may multiply as automated systems become readily available to all repositories and exchange formats are adopted.

Many archives and manuscript repositories are now automating internal finding aids. Sometimes this means simply that word-processing equipment is used to produce traditional paper finding aids, but in other cases it means converting card files into databases or even creating whole new control systems. Because of the size and geographic diversity of its holdings, the National Archives is developing several national automated systems for control of its holdings. While intended primarily to meet the administrative needs of the Archives, these systems have records description components that will ultimately be accessible to researchers. At present the most fully developed is the control system for the holdings of the presidential libraries, called PRESNET. A system for federal records held by the National Archives is under development, as is a system to

Figure 9.10

A MARC/Archives and Manuscripts Control (AMC) Record from the RLIN Database

DCNV89-A159

United States. Bureau of the Census.
   Agriculture, industry, social statistics, manufactures, and
supplemental schedules for Tennessee, 1850-1880.
   39 microfilm reels.

   Organization: Arranged chronologically by year of census and
thereunder by type of schedule and thereunder alphabetically by
county.
   Summary: Series includes agriculture, industry (manufactures),
and social statistics schedules (supplemental schedules) for
1850, 1860, 1870, and 1880.
   The 1850 and 1860 agriculture schedules show the owner, agent,
or tenant of farms with annual produce worth $100 or more.
Information about the kind and value of acreage, livestock,
machinery, and produce is also recorded. The 1870 and 1880
schedules record the same information as the earlier schedules
but only for farms of three acres or more or for farms with an
annual produce worth at least $500. The 1880 schedule is
supplemented by special schedules which relate to specific
phases of agriculture.
   The 1850, 1860 and 1870 industry schedules all record
information relating to industry on a schedule entitled
"Products of Industry." These schedules record information on
every manufacturing, mining, fisheries, mercantile, commercial,
and trading business with an annual gross product of $500 or
more. They call for the name of each company or product; amount
of capital invested; quantity, kind and value of raw material
used; kind of machinery; number of employees and amount of
wages; and quantity, kind, and value of annual output.
   The 1880 industry census uses a general schedule relating to
manufacturing, which is supplemented by twelve special schedules
for separate industries. Special agents, rather than the
regular enumerators, collected statistics for certain industries
and for industries in 279 cities of more than 8,000 inhabitants.
The type of information collected was the same as that collected
in the previous schedules.
   The social statistic schedules for 1850-1870 requested
information on churches, schools, libraries, newspapers, taxes,
wealth, the public debt, wages, paupers, and criminals. In 1880
the social statistic schedules were withdrawn from the regular
enumerators and special agents were appointed to collect the
information. Suppplemental schedules were printed and
distributed to the regular enumerators. These schedules were
designed to collect information on the defective, dependent, and
delinquent classes: insane inhabitants, idiots, deaf-mutes,
blind inhabitants, homeless children, inhabitants in prison, and
pauper and indigent inhabitants.
   Cite as: Non-Population Schedules, 1850-80, Tennnessee,
Microfilm Publication, T1135. Available from the Publications
Services Branch (NEPS), National Archives, Washington, DC 20408.
   Originals at Duke University, Perkins Library, Manuscript
   Dept. Durham, NC.
   Finding aids: 1989 Edition of the NARS A-1 Descriptive
Database; Federal Census Schedules, 1850-80: Primary Sources for
Historical Research, Reference Information Paper No. 67; and
Preliminary Inventory of the Records of the Bureau of the

Figure 9.10 (continued)

```
Census, PI 161 available at the National Archives and Records
Administration, Washington, DC.
   In Related Rec. ID: (CStRLIN)DCNV89-A125 may be found an
agency history record related to this records unit description.
   Location: National Archives and Records Administration, 8th
and Pennsylvania Ave., NW, Washington, DC.
   1.  United States. Bureau of the Census.  2.  United States.
Census Office.  3.  United States.  Dept. of the Interior.  4.
United States.  Dept. of Commerce.  5.  United States--Census,
7th, 1850.  6.  United States--Census, 10th, 1880.  9.  Vital
statistics.  10.  Census.  11.  Federal government records.  12.
Demography.  13.  Statistics.  14.  Tennessee--Census.  15.
Agriculture--Statistics.  16.  Agriculture.  17.  Farms.  18.
Farm equipment.  19.  Farm produce.  20.  Livestock.  21.
Industry--Statistics.  22.  Industry.  23.  Industrial
equipment.  24.  Wages.  25.  Manufactures.  26.  Commercial
products.  27.  Churches.  28.  Schools.  29.  Libraries.  30.
Newspapers.  31.  Taxation.  32.  Debts, Public.  33.  Poor.
34.  Criminal statistics.  35.  Mentally handicapped.  36.
Mentally ill.  37.  Deaf.  38.  Blind.  39.  Homeless youth.
40.  Prisoners.  41.  Agricultural census.  42.  Social
statistics census.  43.  Industrial census.  44.  Tennessee.

   035:  NARS A-1 Microfiche edition:  A-29, B-30, C-30, Series
   23
   RGPN:  29.  Record group.
   ID:  DCNV89-A159                    CC:  9554
   DCF:  a
```

Source: Reprinted courtesy of The Research Libraries Group, Inc.

be used in identifying records still held by federal agencies but destined to come into the National Archives. Full development of these linked, searchable databases is a decade away.

Automating the Documents

The automation described above is automation of finding aids, of information *about* holdings. But what of automating the holdings themselves? What of the day when, with a personal computer and a modem, the papers of Felix Frankfurter or the records of the World War II War Crimes Trials can be read in the researcher's living room?

Archivists and manuscript curators frequently publish documents in letterpress transcript, in facsimile editions, on microfilm and microfiche. Sometimes the documents are copied at a number of different institutions, and a team of editors, usually based in an academic institution, produces a scholarly edition. Increasingly, however, the cost of printing leads the editors to microfilm the majority of documents and create a small printed volume of the most significant ones.

Archives and manuscript collections have long preserved paper items by providing microforms for everyday use. In addition, microform duplication allows copies of the items to be obtained anywhere in the world for the cost of a roll of film or a piece of microfiche. Sometimes, too, an archives films items that will inevitably deteriorate, and the film becomes the only extant copy. Many states have filmed local newspapers as a way of preserving them beyond the life of the newsprint. Commercial microfilming companies are also active in archives and manuscript repositories, selecting bodies of material to film and market while leaving the original documents in the care of the repository. Finally, some records are on microfilm when received by the repository; offices that want to save space frequently film records and dispose of bulky paper. In those instances, the archives may produce a finding aid to the accessioned film and turn it into a documentary microfilm publication; in other cases the film will merely be duplicated for local use in the repository.

At present microfilming is still a widely used technique in archives and manuscript repositories. Increasingly, however, these institutions are investigating technologically advanced formats, often with associated automated indexing, to provide reference copies for users. For several years the Library of Congress has been putting still photographs on video disks, which are searched with an automated index; the Air and Space Museum has an ongoing program for reproducing engineering and aeronautical drawings on optical disks with automated indexes; and the National Archives conducted an experiment to put nineteenth-century Civil War military service records (a major resource for genealogists) on optical disks with associated automated indexing. It is clear that significant changes in access are possible through the use of these new systems. They are very costly, however, limiting their present availability to only the largest institutions.

For nearly two decades some documents have been arriving at repositories already automated. Most major archives now have some computer tapes; by the end of the century all will have them. The fragility of the tapes is well known, and archives continue to look for alternatives for storing machine-readable records (as computer tapes are usually called in the jargon of the archival profession). Researcher use of computer tapes in archives has as yet been relatively slight. Archives normally provide a user with a duplicate copy of the tape or a printout of a portion of it, but archives do not yet have computer rooms where a user can sit at a terminal and manipulate data, or call-in facilities that allow a researcher to request that a tape be mounted to be used over a remote terminal via a telephone line. Changes will be apparent by the end of the century, but unless a particular tape contains information of very active interest to researchers, it is unlikely that machine-readable records will be maintained online. It is more likely that machine-readable records will be downloaded from computer tapes to floppy disks; the disks can be purchased or used in research rooms.

Another type of automated record is the automated index that comes to the archives from the creating agency with the associated paper or film records.

Automated indexes are already quite common as technology shifts from a wholly paper office to a mixed-media one. At present archives usually choose to access the automated index, print it out, and use the paper for daily reference purposes while preserving the index on tape. Within a few years, however, archives will surely use the index in automated form, probably with copies that can run on personal computers located in the research areas.

Working with an Archivist

No archives or manuscript repository ever has all its holdings described in finding aids; no repository exists that does not have a backlog of work. This means that no matter how extensive a literature search the researcher has completed in advance, the archivist in the repository will have important pieces of unpublished information that will assist the user.

There are several things a researcher can do to make his or her time—and the archivist's—more productive. The first step is to define the research question carefully. Is the question, What caused the Great Depression? or is it, What was the relationship between the information the federal government had about economic conditions in the Midwest in 1935–37 and the statutory remedies that were proposed? Once the basic outlines of the inquiry are clear, and if there is not a published finding aid that specifically outlines repository holdings that pertain to the topic, the researcher should start to think in terms of organizations. What institution or organization would have been involved in this issue? What level of government: federal, state, or local? If the government is involved, which branch? Are there relevant legislative records because legislation was involved? Are there court records because the legislation was challenged or someone was prosecuted? Were one or more executive branch agencies involved? Were prominent individuals involved, and if so, did they donate their papers to a manuscript repository? Did someone complete an oral history project that touched on the topic, and, if so, are the oral history interviews available in some institution? At that point the researcher is ready to write to the repositories.

Archivists talk about five parts of reference service: providing information about the institution and its records; providing information from the records; providing the physical items; providing copies of the records; and loaning the records, usually for exhibition. All repositories handle these functions, but researchers who visit more than one repository in the course of their work will notice distinct variations among them. A manuscript collection usually has scholarly researchers as its principal clientele, and the research regulations are geared to those users. Archivists in private institutions often find that the majority of their users are from the institution itself: The alumni office uses the university archives, the public relations office uses the corporate archives. Government archives are used extensively by genealogists, with an additional clientele of government and academic researchers. Some institutions serve all physical types of materials in one research room; others have separate rooms for papers, photographs, microfilm, and so on.

The researcher's first letter usually is handled by a staff professional. The reply provides information about the nature and extent of the pertinent holdings, requirements for use, and basic institutional routines, such as the operating hours. If the records are available on microfilm or in a publication, the researcher will be directed to those sources. If the researcher's question can be answered through commonly available library materials, the user is referred to a local library. If only a few pages or a photograph or two are involved, the archivist may suggest that the items can be duplicated and mailed to the researcher for a specified fee. Sometimes if a number of photographs are identified as pertinent the archives will send the researcher a selection of electrostatic copies and suggest that the researcher identify the ones to be reproduced.

Most often, however, a scholar wants to visit the repository and review the materials. Some repositories require the researcher to make an appointment for an initial visit; most do not, but all want to know when to expect the researcher to arrive. If the researcher plans to use records that require special equipment, such as motion picture projectors or oversize tables for maps, appointments are advisable. Sometimes the correspondence is specific enough to permit the archive's staff to identify and send some items to the research room in preparation for the visit; most of the time, however, archivists wait to talk to the researcher in person before selecting records for use.

The first time a researcher comes to the repository he or she is interviewed and asked to complete some forms and provide some identification, after which he or she will be issued a research card. Then the research-room regulations are briefly explained, usually supplemented by a printed copy for the researcher's retention, and the aim of the research is discussed. Some researchers are reluctant to be entirely candid with an archivist, fearing that the archivist will reveal details of their research interests to others working on similar topics. These fears are almost always unfounded: The code of ethics to which archivists and manuscript curators subscribe requires that one user's interests will not be discussed with another researcher unless the first user explicitly permits such discussion. The archivist can help the researcher only to the extent that the archivist understands the research project. On the other hand, the researcher should not expect the archivist to interpret the records. Archivists normally will answer questions about what bodies of documents contain information relevant to the research topic, how the documents came to the repository, how they are organized, and what subjects are covered in them. They usually do not answer questions such as, Why did the president *really* send the National Guard to Kent State?

The initial interview is the time to clarify with the archivist whether any portion of the records or personal papers are restricted from research use. If items are restricted, the researcher will want to inquire about possible avenues for review of the closed items or persons from whom permission for access must be sought. In addition, particularly if using nontextual materials or the papers of literary figures, the researcher should ask whether copyright provisions cover any of the items. Finally, copying services and associated charges should be discussed.

Research room rules vary enormously from institution to institution. Some institutions, such as the Manuscript Division of the Library of Congress and the Washington reading rooms of the National Archives, strictly limit the items a researcher can bring into their reading rooms; these institutions provide free paper and note cards. Some institutions allow researchers to bring in electronic typewriters and personal computers; others do not have enough electrical outlets to handle these items. Sometimes researchers can use hand-held cameras, microfilm cameras, or personal copying machines. Before a researcher makes an expensive purchase or drags equipment halfway across the country, he or she should check with the repository to see exactly what will be permitted in the research rooms.

Researchers usually are asked to sign in and out of the research room on a daily basis and to sign for items provided to them. The staff of archives and manuscript repositories want to know who is in the reading rooms and how many items are used for a wide variety of reasons—but foremost among them is a record for security purposes. Enough thefts from archives and manuscript collections have occurred that archivists are conscious of the need to know precisely who had access to what items and when.

A range of copying services may be provided, from self-service copiers to duplication of computer tapes. Only a specific inquiry to the institution will clarify the types of and fees for these services.

Sometimes a researcher cannot visit a repository but can refine an inquiry sufficiently so that it can be answered by a factual response. Normally an inquiry such as, Can you select and copy several letters for me from the personal papers of Henry Cabot Lodge that show his attitudes toward immigrants? will be answered with a suggestion that the researcher come into the archives and review the materials. But some archives (though not all) will answer questions such as, When was the bridge over the South River built? or, When did my grandfather join the Illinois militia? Whether or not the archives will provide this service and whether or not it is provided free of charge is a decision made by the archival institution. Occasionally researchers ask a repository to transfer records for their use through interlibrary loan to a more conveniently located repository. Archives and manuscript repositories almost never agree to such requests.

Occasionally, too, a user asks to see original records that have been published in books or on microfilm. The archives or manuscript repository will probably refuse the request unless the user demonstrates that the film is inadequate to meet his or her particular research needs.

Many researchers and archivists strike up friendships that continue all their working lives. Archivists and manuscript curators take special pride in appearing in the acknowledgments in book prefaces, as well as meeting new researchers who have been referred by a previous satisfied patron.

Searching for Other Sources

The preceding discussion has been based on research within an archives or manuscript repository in the United States. There are at least two other possible locations for primary sources, however: in the hands of the creator or the creator's heirs, or in a foreign country.

Every experienced researcher has tales of working in sources outside an archival institution. "Did I tell you about the time I found the personal papers on the front porch being used as a bed for nine cats?" one will ask. "Yes," another replies, "but that is not nearly so bad as spending days in August in the attic of the courthouse looking at ancient land records." Finding such sources is a matter of both common sense and luck. If the records are from a local government and do not seem to be in the state archives, and if the local government officials have no memory of them, it still may be wise to ask the state archivist where they may be located. There is at least a possibility that he or she knows where they are; if not, the archivist may be interested in finding them, too. And things do turn up: Some early records of the city of Chicago, thought to be lost forever, appeared during a survey several years ago. If the records are nongovernmental and are not in an archives or manuscript repository, the best leads may come from retired members of the organization who once had responsibility for the program or for its records.

Personal papers are another matter entirely. If the person is living, it may be a simple matter to look him or her up in a phone book, in a basic reference source like *Who's Who*, or in a publication relating to the person's occupational specialty. Again, it is possible that an archives or manuscript repository can help even if it does not have the papers; the Archives of American Art, for example, may be able to locate artists whose addresses are not easily found. Heirs may, of course, hold the papers of a deceased individual, but if the surnames are not the same the search can be almost hopeless. One of the best ways to proceed in such cases is to try to locate a friend or associate of the person whose papers are sought and see if that friend can, in turn, point the researcher in the right direction. This is research networking at its best.

Research in foreign archives is similar but far from identical to research in archives in the United States. Most archives worldwide use the principle of provenance for modern records, but the arrangement of medieval and earlier records may be idiosyncratic. Many national archives have published guides to their holdings, and most have finding aids similar to typical U.S. inventories and registers.[13] In addition, the United Nations Educational, Scientific, and Cultural Organization (UNESCO) has published a few guides to records of member states and to particular topics in one or more repositories.[14]

A number of U.S. scholars have published books and essays on holdings of foreign archives; Patricia Kennedy Grimsted authored a magisterial guide to archives in the Soviet Union, for instance.[15] Other scholars have produced vol-

umes that survey one topic in several countries, for example a volume on diplomatic archives in various nations.[16]

Some researchers want to use the records of international organizations, such
as the United Nations or the International Labor Organization. To assist scholars
in locating such materials, UNESCO published a directory to the archives of
international organizations, which lists the information obtained by UNESCO
when it surveyed archives around the world.[17]

Finally, some scholars have difficulty obtaining the addresses of archives
outside the United States. Two publications largely solve this problem. First,
the International Council on Archives publishes a directory of national archives
of member nations, which lists virtually every national archives in the world.
Second, the council also publishes a directory of archival associations around
the world, and these organizations can provide addresses of archives within a
nation.[18] Additionally, the National Archives is usually able to provide addresses
of foreign archives.

Research in archives is fun—in fact, many people find researching far more
pleasurable than writing up the results. Samuel Eliot Morison said it well:

Finally, after smoking sundry cigarettes and pacing about the house two or three times,
you commit a lame paragraph or two to paper. By the time you get to the third, one bit
of information you want is lacking. What a relief! Now you must go back to the library
or archives to do some more digging. That's where you are happy! And what you turn
up there leads to more questions and prolongs the delicious process of research.[19]

Like Braudel and Morison, the primary sources for research excite the imagination and stimulate the exploration of the heritage of humanity. With sound
preparation, appreciation of the organization of archives and manuscript repositories, and a thorough understanding of the system of finding aids, every researcher can experience the "delicious process of research."

NOTES

1. Fernand Braudel, *The Mediterranean and the Mediterranean World in the Age of
Philip II*, vol. I, trans. Sian Reynolds (New York: Harper and Row, 1972), 18.

2. See, for example, Thomas J. Schlereth, *Artifacts and the American Past* (Nashville,
Tenn.: AASLH Press, 1982).

3. The National Archives publishes in the *Federal Register* a notice of all new
proposed dispositions of federal records and gives the public the opportunity to comment
on them.

4. All fifty states, the District of Columbia, and the federal government have access
laws called Freedom of Information Acts. The coverage of these laws varies greatly, as
does their effectiveness.

5. A. Hinding, A. S. Bower, and C. A. Chambers, *Women's History Sources: A
Guide to Archives and Manuscript Collections in the United States* (New York: R.R.

Bowker, 1979); Aloha South, *Guide to Materials in U.S. Archives Relating to Africa* (Munich: K.G. Saur, 1989); Richard Dean Burns, ed., *Guide to American Foreign Relations Since 1700* (Santa Barbara, Calif.: ABC-Clio, 1983).

6. Dedra L. Newman, *Black History: A Guide to Civilian Records in the National Archives* (Washington, D.C.: National Archives Trust Fund Board, 1984); Edward E. Hill, *Guide to Records in the National Archives Relating to American Indians* (Washington, D.C.: National Archives Trust Fund Board, 1981); George S. Ulibarri, *Documenting Alaskan History: Guide to Federal Records Relating to Alaska* (Washington, D.C.: National Archives Trust Fund Board, 1982).

7. National Historical Publications and Records Commission, *Directory of Archives and Manuscript Repositories in the United States*, 2d ed. (Phoenix, Ariz.: Oryx Press, 1988). The words "and Records" were added to the Commission's title in 1974.

8. Harriet Ostroff, ed., *Index to Personal Names in the National Union Catalog of Manuscript Collections, 1959–1984* (Alexandria, Va.: Chadwyck-Healey, 1988).

9. Examples of multi-institutional guides are Barbara Teague, ed., *Guide to Kentucky Archival and Manuscript Collections*, vol. 1 (Frankfort, Ky.: Public Records Division, Department for Libraries and Archives, 1988); Raymond Smock, James B. Rhoads, and Dennis Burton, comps., *A Guide to Manuscripts in the Presidential Libraries* (College Park, Md.: Research Materials Corporation, 1985); Francis X. Blouin, Jr., and Robert M. Warner, eds., *Sources for the Study of Migration and Ethnicity* (Ann Arbor, Mich.: Bentley Historical Library, 1979).

10. Purists would argue that in manuscript repositories records are described in inventories and personal papers in registers. In fact, manuscript repositories often use the term *register* to describe the finding aids to both personal papers and records.

11. *National Inventory of Documentary Sources in the United States* (Alexandria, Va.: Chadwyck-Healey, 1985–) is an ongoing effort to capture on film finding aids from the National Archives and Records Service, the Presidential Libraries, the Smithsonian Institution Archives, the Manuscript Division of the Library of Congress, and aids to collections in state archives, state libraries, state historical societies, academic libraries, and other repositories.

12. The Research Libraries Group, Inc., *Government Records in the RLIN Database: An Introduction and Guide* (Mountain View, Calif.: Research Libraries Group, 1990).

13. Margarita Vazquez de Parga, comp., *International Bibliography of Directories and Guides to Archival Repositories* (Munich: K.G. Saur, for the International Council on Archives, 1990).

14. See the list in Frank Evans, "Archives and Research: A Study in International Cooperation Between UNESCO and ICA," in *Archives et bibliothèques de Belgique* 57 (1986).

15. Patricia Kennedy Grimsted, *Archives and Manuscript Repositories in the USSR* (Princeton, N.J.: Princeton University Press, 1972), and *A Handbook for Archival Research in the USSR* (Washington, D.C.: Kennan Institute, 1989).

16. Lewis Hanke, ed., *Guide to the Study of United States History Outside the United States, 1945–1980*, 5 vols. (White Plains, N.Y.: Kraus International Publications, 1985).

17. *Guide to the Archives of International Organizations*, 3 vols. (Paris: UNESCO, 1984–85).

18. *International Council on Archives Directory, 1990* (Paris: International Council on Archives, 1990); *Janus*, vol. 1988.3 (Netherlands: MK's-Hertogenbosch, 1988).

19. Morison's description in his essay, "History as a Literary Art," is quoted in Edward Papenfuse, "Finding Aids and the Historian: The Need for National Priorities and a Standard Approach," *AHA Newsletter* 10, no. 3 (May 1972).

Part IV

Bibliography

Teaching the Bibliography of History: A Selected Annotated Bibliography

Charles A. D'Aniello

What should one read to prepare for teaching students of history the methods of bibliographic and library research? The selective bibliography that follows broadly answers this question. Annotations either present or indicate key points. Entries follow the organization given below, but readers should consider the entire bibliography since cited works often touch on the topics of more than one section. Some entries in this bibliography originally appeared in a bibliography published in *The History Teacher* 17, no. 3 (May 1984): 408–30 and are reprinted by permission.

   I. General Ideas, Issues, and Assumptions

  II. A Selection of Overviews of Historical Research

 III. Historical Research, Library Collections, and the Characteristics of Publication

 IV. Research Methodology: The Humanities

  V. Research Methodology: The Social Sciences

 VI. Relevant Instructional Designs from Other Disciplines

VII. Workbooks, Courses, Exercises, and Instructional Designs

VIII. Early Bibliographic Instruction Programs in History and Related Disciplines

 IX. Electronic Information Sources

  X. Abstracting and Indexing History

 XI. Historians' Use of U.S. Government Documents

XII. Relations Between Historians and Librarians

XIII. Research Guides and Manuals

XIV. Ethical and Intellectual Issues in Documenting Historical Research

I. GENERAL IDEAS, ISSUES, AND ASSUMPTIONS

Brevik, Patricia Senn, and E. Gordon Gee. *Information Literacy: Revolution in the Library*. New York: Macmillan Publishing Company, 1989.

"Information literacy" is a survival skill in the information age. Instead of drowning in the abundance of information that floods their lives, information-literate people know how to find, evaluate, and use information effectively to solve a particular problem or make a decision, whether the information they select comes from a computer, a book, a government agency, a film, or any number of other possible resources. The apparent ease of access through the computer requires an appreciation of the quality of information, and argues for training students to be independent and critical learners. The library is seen as the center of the information universe, and ways for it and librarians to play a role in the changing electronic environment are discussed. See McCrank below for a rejoinder.

Falk, Joyce Duncan. "Librarians and Historians at the American Historical Association"; and Stoan, Stephen K. "Historians and Librarians: A Response." *College & Research Libraries News* 47, no. 8 (September 1986): 501–3.

Historian, librarian, and online search specialist Falk argues that many historians are poorly trained bibliographically, that they are ill-equipped to train their students in bibliography, and that online search specialists are valuable intermediaries for historical researchers. Furthermore, librarians are informed of the uses and value of serendipity and internal logic as well as of librarianship's systematic research models. Historian and librarian Stoan, on the other hand, does not believe in required bibliographic education offered by librarians and believes course-related instruction is the responsibility of faculty, to be offered at their prerogative. He cautions librarians not to assume that failure of a scholar to use a tool is always a result of ignorance.

Feinberg, Richard, and Christine King. "Short-Term Library Skill Competencies: Arguing for the Achievable." *College & Research Libraries* 49 (January 1988): 24–28.

With the limited amount of work undergraduates are asked to do in the library it is impossible to teach them higher-level library research skills. The authors teach only what they consider immediately relevant. They: "(1) teach for short-term research competency; (2) raise students' confidence in using the library so they will develop a positive attitude about libraries in general; and (3) demonstrate that librarians are information specialists."

Frick, Elizabeth. "Information Structure and Bibliographic Instruction." *The Journal of Academic Librarianship* 1, no. 1 (1975): 12–14.

Urges exploration of the "interconnections between information structure, reference source structure and retrieval methods." The achievement of these ends is usually approached in a progression of steps: familiarization with particular sources, an awareness of their distinctive groupings into genres, and a sense of a discipline-specific bibliographic structure. The final step is an understanding of the way in which information is generated and disseminated within a discipline. The development of *Social Sciences Citation Index* is offered as an example of the above and as an indication of the scientific nature of the social sciences—that is, that they are built on previous and ongoing research.

Keresztesi, Michael. "The Science of Bibliography: Theoretical Implications for Bibliographic Instruction." In *Theories of Bibliographic Education: Designs for Teaching*, ed. Cerise Oberman and Katina Strauch, 1–26. New York: R.R. Bowker, 1982.

Describes bibliography as a "comprehensive apparatus" evolving out of the needs of a particular discipline. Ideas are incorporated, reported, and indexed in reference tools; and specific types of tools are either produced or come to serve a discipline in a sequence that parallels the development of the discipline itself. Stages of development are: pioneering, elaboration and proliferation, and establishment. The study of this maturation is topographical.

Kobelski, Pamela, and Mary Reichel. "Conceptual Frameworks for Bibliographic Instruction." *The Journal of Academic Librarianship* 7, no. 2 (May 1981): 73–77. Reprinted in *Conceptual Frameworks for Bibliographic Education: Theory into Practice*, ed. Mary Reichel and Mary Ann Ramey. Littleton, Colo.: Libraries Unlimited, 1987.

An introduction to the various approaches to teaching bibliographic and reference skills. "Type of Reference Tools" permits discussion of the genres of tools such as almanacs, atlases, bibliographies, and handbooks but it does not place them within a research strategy and it is difficult to include "ideas, concepts, and general information about publications that are not reference tools." "Systematic Literature Searching" presents aids within the context of a research strategy and shows when various resources should be used. "Form of Publication" centers on a discussion of the types of information to be found in books, journals, and newspapers, and gives a variety of documents and their access tools. "Primary and Secondary Sources" invites consideration of what constitutes either source in different disciplines and how the number and nature of access tools reflects this. "Citation Patterns" reveals the manner in which research evolves. "Index Structure" can lead to discussion of changing conceptualizations as well as the consideration of different types of indexes and the importance of terminology. "Publication Sequence" traces the "development" of an idea through its expression in a predictable progression of types of reference sources.

McCrank, Lawrence J. "Information Literacy: A Bogus Bandwagon." *Library Journal* 116, no. 8 (May 1, 1991): 38–42.

Medievalist and library administrator McCrank critiques Brevik's concept of "information literacy," arguing that librarians generally do not differentiate between "searching" and "research"; nor do they appreciate the skills necessary for the processes "of evaluating sources, analyzing content, and those methodologies associated with genuine research."

Macdonald, John D. *Reading for Survival*. Washington, D.C.: Library of Congress, 1987.

An eloquent and impassioned argument by a writer and social critic for the broadening of contextual knowledge that results from wide reading. Attributes much of the violence in the world to a lack of knowledge on the part of those who believe that they are right and that everyone who does not believe exactly the same as they do is wrong.

MacGregor, John, and Raymond G. McInnis. "Integrating Classroom Instruction and Library Research: The Cognitive Function of Bibliographic Network Structure." *Journal of Higher Education* 48, no. 1 (1977): 17–38.

Literature networks have a substantive and a bibliographic structure. The former structure is fluid and reflects the perception of a subject; the latter structure is fixed in time, for although an idea may no longer be instrumental it remains recorded. The historian's distinction between secondary and primary sources is analogous to the concepts of substantiative and bibliographic structure respectively. Standing between these sources and structures, and providing access to them, are intermediary sources or reference tools. They provide both locational and topical information; are related to one another by explicit and implicit links; and often perform multiple functions. Most researchers begin with adequate substantive background but possess insufficient bibliographic knowledge. To overcome this deficiency, a specific sequential search strategy is suggested: encyclopedias, reviews of research, citation indexes, abstracts, card catalogs. The manner in which research builds on previous work is illustrated by citation analysis exercises.

McInnis, Raymond G. "Integrating Classroom Instruction and Library Research: An Essay Review." *Studies in History and Society* 4, no. 1 (1974/75): 31–65.

Part 1 discusses the concept of bibliographic and substantive structure in literature networks. Part 2 reviews several major historical bibliographies. The need for reference sources to have explicit and implicit links to other aids is emphasized. Included is an exercise that asks students to trace bibliographically the evolution of a concept to reveal its bibliographic structure.

McInnis, Raymond G. *Perspectives for Reference Service in Academic Libraries*. Westport, Conn.: Greenwood Press, 1978.

A wide range of philosophical and theoretical issues pertinent to bibliographic instruction are discussed. "The Dimensions of the Opportunity: Evidence for Reform in Teaching and Learning in Higher Education," 27–50, covers: anthropology, economics, geography, history (39–43), political science, and sociology.

McNeer, Elizabeth. "Learning Theories and Library Instruction." *Journal of Academic Librarianship* 17, no. 5 (November 1991): 294–97.

Epistemological styles are discussed and appropriate instructional approaches for each group are described. First-year students—literal thinkers or "dualists"—require clarity, structure, and regular feedback. A diversity of "truths" cannot be tolerated. Moderate diversity and experiential learning experiences should be offered as a challenge to development. Upper-division students have moved beyond literalness and require flexible opportunities for analysis and evaluation and for decision making. They are ready to proceed from the known to the only-suspected through the persistent development of analytical skills. Graduate students are relativistic in their thinking and are able to draw inferences and able to transfer knowledge and strategies. They require the opportunity to construct strategies out of which they can construct knowledge. They realize the contextual dimension of knowledge and the validity of both subjective and objective ways of knowing. The librarian should become a resource to them.

Najarian, Suzanne E. "Organizational Factors in Human Memory: Implications for Library Organization and Access Systems." *Library Quarterly* 51, no. 3 (1981): 269–91.

Although she realizes the difficulties with a strictly hierarchical structuring of memory or retrieval system, Najarian notes that there is strong evidence that memory is hierarchically structured. Library tools should be designed to facilitate such an approach. Organizational schemes should be made apparent to users, for instance the structure of the LC classification system should be made clear, enabling a searcher to use the structure as a search plan. The size of categories within organizational schemes should be kept to a minimum because of the limited number of items that can be judged at a single time.

Ortega y Gasset, José. "The Mission of the Librarian." *The Antioch Review* 21, no. 2 (Summer 1981): 133–54.

In 1934, at the meeting of the International Congress of Bibliographers and Librarians in Paris, the Spanish philosopher and political scientist contended that there is an overwhelming flood of publications. People read too fast and they read badly. The reading of books, which is our collective memory, alone satisfies the imperative of historical consciousness. An emerging history of precision will require the accurate and minute analysis of "the structure of human life." He sees this being accomplished by reading "really and effectively all the books of a determined time, to register description of them and most carefully, finally establishing what I would call a 'statistics of ideas'. . . . " Reading too much and reflecting too little fills minds with pseudo-truths, and he proposes the librarian as a "filter interposed between man and the torrent of books." See also Lester Asheim, "Ortega Revisited," *Library Quarterly* 52, no. 3 (July 1982): 215–26; and Jorge F. Sosa and Michael H. Harris, "José Ortega y Gasset and the Role of the Librarian in Post-Industrial America," *Libri* 41, no. 1 (March 1991): 3–21. Asheim cautions against the authoritarianism of Ortega's plea for "a doctor and hygienist of reading." He argues that collections, reflective of the librarian's intellectual openness, be built to be the largest possible store of resources, and that services must be shaped by the users' needs and interests. He argues that librarians can neither define nor eliminate what is useless to users.

Rogers, Sharon J. "Research Strategies: Bibliographic Instruction for Undergraduates." *Library Trends* 29, no. 1 (Summer 1980): 69–81.

Reviews the literature, which considers the epistemological significance of various approaches to bibliographic instruction. Whether to teach process or sources or a blend is explored, and the "logic-in-use" strategies of scholars and the "systematic process" models of librarians are compared and contrasted.

Rogers, Sharon J. "Science of Knowledge." In *Bibliographic Instruction: The Second Generation*, ed. Constance A. Mellon, 125–33. Littleton, Colo.: Libraries Unlimited, 1987.

Argues that the concept of research as a craft places the academic researcher and the librarian in a single dimension. Both activities entail the acquisition of a set of vague but complex skills that are both practical and intuitive. Each discipline has its own peculiar type of primary data and its own techniques for gathering and analysis. Research, though, is not a simple progression. In fact, the decision to find an end point for a piece of research may be defined by a particular research community as a convention that is a social product. Defining a topic for research is a highly creative process, a creative interaction with the material and the problem. Research has creative and craftlike elements. As a tool specialist, the librarian is molded into the research activity in a manner that varies from project to project and within different stages of the process. "As research unfolds, it is informed largely by its own peculiarities. Research, in other words, is an interactive process composed not only of the raw materials (what we sometimes refer to as primary data) that make up the initial problematic situation, but of the character of the research as well."

Rudd, Joel, and Mary Jo Rudd. "Coping with Information Overload: User Strategies and Implications for Libraries." *College & Research Libraries* 47, no. 4 (July 1986): 315–21.

Users organize and sacrifice comprehensiveness to avoid overload. Limiting one's peripheral vision can prevent being swamped by information, but a more sensible approach might be to use the bibliographic and library sources that allow one to scan efficiently a wide universe of potentially useful material. Consultation of informal sources, footnotes, and colleagues dominates the search process and is a mechanism for avoiding overload.

Smalley, Topsy N. "Bibliographic Instruction in Academic Libraries: Questioning Some Assumptions." *The Journal of Academic Librarianship* 3, no. 5 (November 1977): 280–83.

Instruction should be based on conceptual frameworks rather than on the use of specific tools. The user who is unaware of the concepts around which a bibliographic system is built sees only a confusing array of individual parts.

Smalley, Topsy N., and Stephen H. Plum. "Teaching Library Researching in the Humanities and the Sciences: A Contextual Approach." In *Theories of Bibliographic Education: Designs for Teaching*, ed. Cerise Oberman and Katina Strauch, 135–70. New York: R.R. Bowker, 1982.

Relates research differences between the humanities and sciences to differences in their bibliographic apparatus. The humanities and the sciences use different sorts of research methods and study different types of objects. The literature of the humanities is largely monographic and enduring, while the literature of the sciences is largely periodical and characterized by currency. Researchers in the humanities proceed discursively and intuitively. Their task is to study and understand a specific work in context. Their objects of study "have multiple meanings and are incapable of exhaustive explanation." To understand in the sciences "is to understand individual instances as explanatory parts of generalities." In science, work is structured to discount individuality and to be neutral. Experimental validity alone dictates meaningfulness. The scientist's work is discipline-determined and the methods, the theoretical assumptions, and the types of questions pursued are those that science has judged worthy. In the case of the humanities, the structural features of relevant literature exemplify the researcher's concern with the dual aspects of scholarly enterprise: understanding within context and interpretative validity. The researcher is concerned with levels of understanding and is interested in the social and personal experiences characteristic of certain time periods and national traditions. Copies of exercises employed at SUNY-Plattsburgh that reflect the differences between the disciplines are provided. Commenting on the differences between the humanities and the sciences, the authors observe: authors of humanities reference sources reflect interaction of authors with subject matter, whereas authors of scientific reference works attempt to report impartially on observable regularities.

Soper, Mary Ellen. "Characteristics and Use of Personal Collections." *Library Quarterly* 46, no. 4 (October 1976): 397–415.

Reports the responses of 178 questionnaire/interview participants. Respondents felt that their own personal library collections were both more accessible and more available than institutional resources, and that they exist in surroundings in which the respondents preferred to work. Materials in a personal collection were cited more than materials also or only in institutional collections. Researchers in the humanities tended to cite materials in their personal collections to the same extent as materials in the institutional library, and a substantial proportion of their citations were to materials in faraway libraries. A related piece analyzing the contents and "piles" of materials in faculty members' offices is Donald Owen Case, "Collection and Organization of Written Information by Social Scientists and Humanists: A Review and Exploratory Study," *Journal of Information Science* 12 (1986): 97–104.

Stoan, Stephen K. "Research and Library Skills: An Analysis and Interpretation." *College & Research Libraries* 54, no. 2 (March 1984): 99–109.

Bibliographic instruction units often inappropriately become minicourses in the use of reference sources. Librarians assail scholars for not knowing how to do research, which they equate with knowing how to use the library. However, if scholars do not know how to use the library, how do they know how to do research? Studies indicate that footnotes, personal recommendations from other scholars, serendipitous discovery, browsing, personal bibliographic files, and other such techniques that involve no formal use of access tools account for the great majority of citations obtained by scholars. It is not difficult to learn library skills, Stoan declares. However, possessed of neither the extensive background knowledge nor the bibliographic skills of the scholar, undergraduate and graduate students have much to gain from bibliographic instruction, and instruction is also useful for faculty venturing outside of their area(s) of specialization. Bibliographic instruction should be offered in a course context, library skills should not be equated with research skills, and librarians should remember that the faculty alone must decide if, when, and what kind of library instruction should be offered. Many teachers do not give library assignments because they question the wisdom of compelling students to conduct literature searches in disciplines that they barely understand. The importance of footnotes should be emphasized to students. Bibliographic instruction's objective should be to get students into the primary literature as quickly as possible. The importance of browsing receives especially strong endorsement.

Stoan, Stephen K. "Research and Information Retrieval Among Academic Researchers: Implications for Library Instruction." *Library Trends* 39, no. 3 (Winter 1991): 238–57.

Contends that the information-seeking strategies of scholars are both logical and effective. Indexes are seldom used because they cannot capture perspectives and do not offer guidance from peers or intellectual context. An extensive and thoughtful literature review covers information-seeking behavior in the sciences, the social sciences, and the humanities; also considered is the use of personal and library collections. Synthesizing these explorations, the author contends that scholarly research is nonlinear and nonsequential (based on the application of insight to context) and relies heavily on informal channels of communication, and that only the researcher can endow a piece of information with relevance. Two specific references to historical research are made: one to the role of publication as the product rather than transmitter of research, and the other to the inadequacy of indexing systems.

Swanson, Don R. "Undiscovered Public Knowledge." *The Library Quarterly* 56, no. 2 (April 1986): 103–18.

"Independently created pieces of knowledge can harbor an unseen, unknown, and unintended pattern. And so it is that the world of recorded knowledge can yield genuinely new discoveries." One person cannot read every conceivable piece of published information. We read what we identify and perceive as relevant. Indexing is always a compromise, and often while we search for information to solve a problem we do not know what we are searching for: "not only do we seek what we do not understand, we often do not even know at what level an understanding might be achieved." New and different points of view may lead to radically new solutions and perspectives, but indexing and the inability to read every likely item on a problem generally inhibit such discoveries.

Vincent, C. Paul. "Bibliographic Instruction in the Humanities: The Need to Stress Imagination." *Research Strategies* 2, no. 4 (Fall 1984): 179–84.

Technology often makes it seem that technical expertise alone will result in good research. But imagination and toil are essential prerequisites. Indexing tools in the humanities do not cover the entire potentially useful body of material, nor do they make logical and contextual connections. Any index or database is only as reliable as the person who constructs it. Good research is the product of clear and imaginative thought, accompanied by a logical and not overly dependent use of indexing tools and other reference sources. In the end, ''the student must combine the information gained from the reference tool with a knowledge, however limited, of the subject, and then pursue those imaginative connections which are the bedrock of real research.'' Research has not ensued until the results of an index search have been confronted—until a ''meeting-of-the-minds takes place between author and student.''

II. A SELECTION OF OVERVIEWS OF HISTORICAL RESEARCH

Altick, Richard D., ed. *The Scholar Adventurers*. New York: Free Press, 1966.

Fourteen annotated essays explore literary research topics ranging from the dating of manuscripts to using astronomical evidence to the probable solution of a murder mystery by Edgar Allan Poe. The essays demonstrate how problems are identified and sometimes solved, and the degree of chance frequently present in their solution.

Beringer, Richard E. *Historical Analysis: Contemporary Approaches to Clio's Craft*. New York: John Wiley and Sons, 1978.

Methodological introductions, illustrated by a sample of previously published studies, cover the various techniques for approaching and organizing the raw data of history. Under sections devoted to intellectual, psychological, and quantitative history, topics such as the concept of *Zeitgeist*, literary analysis, projection, status and reference groups, Freudian and Eriksonian psychology, quantitative collective biography, and historical demography and cliometrics are considered.

Curtis, L. P., Jr., ed. *The Historians' Workshop: Original Essays by Sixteen Historians*. New York: Alfred A. Knopf, 1970.

How the authors feel as well as think about their work is the subject of this uniquely urbane and introspective exploration. Writing and researching, as well as their own intellectual and professional development are the topics of essays by Carlo M. Cippola, J. G. A. Pocock, John William Ward, and others. Though some of the authors comment on bibliography—and Lyn T. White, Jr., observes that his discovery of the *Princeton Index of Christian Art* was a pivotal point in his career—regrettably, the mundane tools of library research are mentioned only in passing. But the importance of scholarly networks, the influence of mentors, and the power of the reviewing media are clear.

Davidson, James West, and Mark Hamilton Lytle. *After the Fact: The Art of Historical Detection*. New York: Alfred A. Knopf, 1982.

There is no more captivating introduction to historical detective work. In thirteen exciting and zestfully written essays on topics in American history the authors—relying largely on the work of other historians—explore such questions as the decision to drop the atom bomb, the extremely high death rate in seventeenth-century Virginia, possible causes of accusations for witchcraft in seventeenth-century Salem, and the evolution of the Declaration of Independence as a document. There are a number of murder investigations and considerations of the reliability of different forms of evidence in topical contexts. Gathering information is essential, but this book eloquently illustrates that there is more to the ''doing of history.''

Gardner, James B., and George Rolle Adams, eds. *Ordinary People and Everyday Life: Perspectives on the New Social History*. Nashville, Tenn.: Association for State and Local History, 1983.

The outgrowth of a series of five seminars sponsored by the association in 1980 and 1981 entitled "Re-examining America's Past." This is a highly readable synthesis, with further readings suggested, that describes the new social history. Chapters cover: race and ethnicity, women's history, urban history, agriculture and rural life, family history, labor history, the conjunction of political and social history, and the study of social history through artifacts.

Horn, T. C. R., and Harry Ritter. "Interdisciplinary History: A Historiographical Review." *The History Teacher* 19, no. 3 (1986): 427–48.

The evolution of interdisciplinary history is traced through its development in Europe and the United States, with special attention paid to the contributions of Karl Lamprecht and, to lesser extents, James Harvey Robinson, Henri Berr, Marc Bloch, and Lucien Febvre. Contemporary uses of quantification and psychology receive special mention, and the development of the *Journal of the History of Ideas* is discussed. Prize-winning interdisciplinary books are noted, showing that the "interdisciplinary orientation has solidly established itself."

Iggers, Georg G., and Harold T. Parker, eds. *International Handbook of Historical Studies: Contemporary Research and Theory.* Westport, Conn.: Greenwood Press, 1980.

This fine work is composed of separately authored essays on the practice of history in many of the major nations of the world and on such topics as social, economic, and political history. Many are heavily bibliographical and provide a detailed introduction to the breadth and richness of contemporary historical inquiry, that is, to the conceptual constructs that historians utilize and to the types of topics they currently study.

Nevins, Allan. *Gateway to History.* Chicago: Quadrangle Books, 1963.

Developed from a Columbia University methodology seminar. "Modern Materials for History," 97–136, sketches the development of libraries, manuscript repositories, and public archives in the West. Also discussed is the publication of the major documentary sets, which were issued in the nineteenth century.

Ritter, Harry. *Dictionary of Concepts in History.* New York: Greenwood Press, 1986.

A historical approach to the concepts that give method to historical work. Here one will find "Fact," "Evidence," "Explanation," "History," "Past," and "Periodization" traced through their historical evolution. Each essay concludes with extensive references.

Winks, Robin, ed. *The Historian as Detective: Essays on Evidence.* New York: Harper and Row, 1970.

Winks is a historian with a penchant for detective stories. This collection offers twenty-six essays and excerpts from longer works, which "are interesting in themselves and which sometimes rather incidentally, demonstrate different ways in which a historian's mind may work, or should work, or can work." Each piece is preceded by an introduction with suggestions for additional reading and explores such topics as the nature of evidence, problems of testimony and forgery, and eyewitness accounts. Among authors represented are: Allan Nevins, David Donald, Erik H. Erikson, Robin G. Collingwood, and Arthur Schlesinger, Jr.

III. HISTORICAL RESEARCH, LIBRARY COLLECTIONS, AND THE CHARACTERISTICS OF PUBLICATION

Alston, Annie M. "Characteristics of Materials Used by a Selected Group of Historians in Their Research in United States History." M.A. thesis, University of Chicago, 1952.

A local and comparative replication of the content-analysis, type-of-material-used study, which was conducted by Arthur McAnally, is his dissertation, listed below. The work of nine University of Chicago American historians was studied to determine the extent to which the types of sources used differed from the much larger McAnally sample. The diversity of cited titles was greater for the smaller group as was the use of manuscripts as opposed to printed materials.

Bostick, Theodora P. "Microforms: One Historian's Indispensable Assistant." *Microform Review* 20, no. 2 (Spring 1991): 71–73.

A history professor at Christopher Newport College in Newport News, Virginia, observes that primary source material in microform has democratized historical research by making significant material available to scholars at even the smallest institutions. To the benefit of all potential users, micro-publishing has pushed forward cataloging; materials such as newspapers and periodicals work especially well in microform.

Breen, T. H. "Keeping Pace with the Past: Puritans and Planters among the Microforms." *Microform Review* 20, no. 2 (Spring 1991): 57–60.

A history professor at Northwestern University explains how microforms can be used to introduce both graduate and undergraduate students to primary-source research. He advises that expensive collections be bought to match established centers of excellence within a department and warns that narrowly defined, topically oriented, collections run the near-certain risk of not responding fully to new broader contextual emphases.

Brilliant, Richard. "How an Art Historian Connects Art Objects and Information." *Library Trends* 37, no. 2 (Fall 1988): 120–29.

A Columbia University art historian analyzes how he associates art objects with bibliographic and textual information. Intuition comes from immersion in a subject. While online systems are useful, he sees younger colleagues as most dependent upon them and most affected by their lack of retrospective coverage. The development of permeable subject classification schemes will enable one to make connections during a search, and there is a need for flexibility to enable indexes to respond to changing conceptualizations within the discipline. Some indexes, for instance the *Index of Christian Art*, have become important artifacts of scholarship and preserve conceptualizations no longer current.

Broadus, Robert N. "Materials of History: Saving and Discarding." *Collection Building* 10, nos. 1–2 (1990): 3–6.

In an ideal world all records would be saved, since everything tells us something about the human condition. Realizing that this is impossible, representative materials should be preserved through coordinated action across libraries, yet our society has difficulty defining what it considers of probable use to future generations.

Broidy, Ellen. "A Brief Narrative of Primary Research in a Secondary Place." *Microform Review* 20, no. 2 (Spring 1991): 61–66.

A history and film studies librarian and coordinator of library publications at the University of California Library at Irvine, Broidy advises that in newer or smaller institutions microforms alone make primary-source research possible. Major issues in the acquisition of large microform collections are price, quality, and access. While some commentators recommend caution concerning the selectivity exercised by a collection's editor, Broidy notes that topically oriented collections that bring together various materials on the same topic have real value. Examples of directed use of such resources by the author, with a graduate student and a high school student, are given.

Case, Donald Owen. "The Collection and Use of Information by Some American His-
    torians: A Study of Motives and Methods." *Library Quarterly* 61, no. 1 (January
    1991): 61–82.
Twenty historians of the United States, drawn from a large sample, were interviewed
to determine how they choose research topics and how they proceed with research and
writing. Chronology, topic, and geography are reviewed as organizing principles that
define areas of research and determine the behavior of historians. Photocopying is identified as a major innovation, still outdistancing the computer in influence. History emerges
as a back-and-forth kind of scholarship, with different stages of research going on con-
currently. It is guided primarily by a choice of problems or questions. Historians were
found to be methodical in their labors: "Their investigations were guided less by sources
and more by questions or problems that led them to particular sources." Gathered data
is organized in a variety of ways: by author, topic, or chronology. A number of respondents
reported on their attempts to keep up with their files only to give up in the end under the
effort. The "invisible college" (scholars throughout the field sharing ideas and views)
plays a powerful role "in the formulation of research questions," especially early in
one's career, and there is an active exchange of information concerning archival sources.

Chapman, John, with comment by project director R. H. C. Davis. *Information Officer
    in History, University of Birmingham, 1979–1980*. Report to the British Library
    Research and Development Department on Project S1/G/281. June 1981. Bir-
    mingham: School of History, University of Birmingham, 1981.
Chapman was located in the history department of Birmingham from January 1979 to
December 1980; unlike Davis, his counterpart at York University, he did not have an
office in the library or a formal position within it. He performed manual and online
searches, compiled book lists and finding aids, offered user education—later successfully
using the "History Package of the Travelling Workshops Experiment"—and established
a current awareness service. Observations: the information needs of historians are varied
and personal; they are most in need of identifying primary material; they use formal
bibliographies far less than scientists; and they appreciate but are not obsessed with current
awareness services. The slowness of interlibrary loan is troublesome. Online systems are
criticized for imprecise indexing and lack of comprehensiveness and bemoaned for their
failure to provide access to primary material. Reasons for poor relations between the
library and the history department are described, along with the importance to scholars
of the invisible college and the reading of journals and reviews.

Corkill, Cynthia, and Margaret Mann. *Information Needs in the Humanities: Two Postal
    Surveys*. British Library Research and Development Report no. 5455. Sheffield:
    Centre for Research on User Studies, University of Sheffield, 1978.
Based on a postal survey of staff and doctoral students at thirty-five universities in
England and Wales. Cambridge, Oxford, and the Open University were excluded. History
was one of the five disciplines studied. Findings indicate that historians are likely to use
libraries other than the one at their own institutions, and they are heavy users of the
British Library Reference Division. Of all the academics studied, historians are most
likely to use interlibrary loan. Constrained by the requirement of obtaining their degrees,
students are more focused in their research than faculty.

Corkill, Cynthia, Margaret Mann, and Sue Stone. *Doctoral Students in the Humanities:
    A Small-Scale Panel Study of Information Needs and Uses, 1976–1979*. CRUS

Occasional Paper no. 5. Sheffield: Centre for Research on User Studies, University of Sheffield, 1981.

Among the recommendations of the study are possible components of a user education program, which might include: "information on inter-library loan policy, abstracting services, search services, ways to organize material and index it . . . how to enable students to gain quick access to a subject with which they are less familiar, given that overlap with other subjects is not uncommon in humanities research."

Davis, R. H. C. *Information Problems in the Humanities: A Report on the British Library Seminar*. British Library Research and Development Report no. 5259. London: The British Library, 1975.

A brief consideration of the pros and cons of selective and annotated bibliographies and comprehensive lists for students and academics. Historian Davis contends that the most compelling need for bibliographies of current work is not to bring it to the attention of contemporary scholars (in most instances, he believes, this is not a problem), but to make this work available to future generations. He suggests that the books academics use most they buy, and thus, statistical studies of faculty use are flawed when based on circulation statistics.

Handlin, Oscar. "Libraries and Learning." *The American Scholar* 56, no. 2 (Spring 1987): 205–18.

Fiscal challenges are currently faced by libraries, but libraries are too important to be left to librarians, for librarians consider themselves administrators and try to "make do." The struggle for accessibility through retrospective and current cataloging is not a virtue if it locks users into predetermined categories; libraries should provide students with a subversive learning environment. In libraries imaginations roam and syntheses occur in unanticipated ways, constrained only by the imagination of the users and the richness of the collection.

Hazen, Dan C. "Preservation in Poverty and Plenty: Policy Issues for the 1990s." *The Journal of Academic Librarianship* 15, no. 6 (January 1990): 344–51.

Preservation decisions should be based on an understanding of the structure of disciplines and the needs of their practitioners. Historians cast a wide net, and they browse because from this activity "emerge valuable insights, connections, and facts" that allow irrelevant material to be quickly discarded. Strong humanities collections provide a rich infrastructure; strong general collections are reference tools that enable a user to expand references and draw inferences across time, space, and discipline.

Herubel, Jean-Pierre V. M. "The Nature of Three History Journals: A Citation Experiment." *Collection Management* 12, nos. 3/4 (1990): 57–67.

History journals reflect the evolution of historical scholarship. An analysis of the citing patterns of three interdisciplinary history journals (sampling from 1972–73, 1979–80, and 1986–87) was done. The *Journal of Social History*, the *Journal of Interdisciplinary History*, and the *Journal of the History of Ideas* were examined because of their presumed methodological latitude. Among the findings were: a decided emphasis on citing primary sources by all journals, a preponderance of citations to recent pieces, and validation of the multidisciplinary intent of each journal, although authors of history articles tend overwhelmingly to cite other history articles and self-citation is plentiful. Cited articles tend overwhelmingly to be in English.

Herubel, Jean-Pierre V. M. "Materials Used in Historical Scholarship: A Limited Citation
    Analysis of the *Journal of Garden History*." *Collection Management* 14, nos. 1–
    2 (1991): 155–62.
A subfield of art history and landscape architecture, garden history exhibits both humanities and social science citation qualities. The 1989 volume year was examined:
primary materials (city directories, reports, newspapers, and manuscripts) accounted for
40.95 percent of the 962 citations. Monographs accounted for only 37.2 percent of primary
citations. Only 11.64 percent of citations were to journal literature. "One is struck by
the similarity of bibliographic traits here to those in the humanities in general."

Hitchcock, Elaine R. "Materials Used in the Research of State History: A Citation
    Analysis of the 1986 *Tennessee Historical Quarterly*." *Collection Building* 10,
    nos. 1–2 (1990): 52–54.
Archival materials created during the period of time being studied are used most by
the researcher, accounting for 37.4 percent of citations. Overall, primary source materials
account for 61.6 percent of citations. Further broken down, citation counts are: serials,
20.2 percent; newspapers, 15.2 percent; government documents, 12.1 percent; and theses,
3 percent. For slightly different findings see Jeffrey A. Hunt, "Characteristics of Kansas
History Sources: A Citation Analysis of The Kansas Historical Quarterly," Master of
Librarianship thesis, Kansas State College–Emporia, 1975.

Huling, Nancy. "Microforms and the Discipline of History: A Selective Bibliography."
    Microform Review 20, no. 2 (Spring 1991): 67–70.
An annotated bibliography of forty-three periodical articles on specific microform
collections and on issues in micro-publishing and the use of microforms.

Jameson, John Franklin. "An Historian's World: Selections from the Correspondence of
    John Franklin Jameson." *Memoirs of the American Philosophical Society,* vol.
    42 (1956), 95.
In 1906, when he was head of the Bureau of Historical Research of the Carnegie
Institution of Washington, Jameson wrote in support of that organization's continued
publication of *Writings on American History*: "Bibliography holds a more vital relation
to history than to the physical sciences. The latter rest primarily on the observation of
natural processes or tangible objects; the literature, what men have written about these
phenomena, has in research work a secondary position. But in the case of history both
the primary material for observation and the secondary elaboration consist almost wholly
of the written statements of men. Historical bibliographies are guides to both documents
and interpretations, to both the original and secondary material."

Jones, Clyve, Michael Chapman, and Pamela Carr Woods. "The Characteristics of the
    Literature Used by Historians." *Journal of Librarianship* 4, no. 3 (July 1972):
    137–56.
Reports the results of a reference analysis of articles on English history conducted to
identify the nature of materials used by historians. Historians employ a great deal of
recently published material. They make fewer references to monographs and more to
serials than is customary among humanists, but far less reference to them than is customary
among social scientists. Finally, journal use is focused within subdisciplines on core
groups composed of a relatively small number of titles.

Jordan, Philip D., "The Historian and the Contemporary Problem of Bibliographic Tech-
    niques," *American Documentation* 10, no. 4 (October 1959): 267–69.

Presents a historical context for concerns with the volume of historical publication and its bibliographic control; both concerns date to at least the 1880s. To be effective, a historian must know something of the bibliographic past and must be accepting of new techniques offered by emerging technologies.

Kingsley, James. "Bibliographic Organization of American History: Notes on a Continuing Problem," *American Documentation* 10, no. 4 (October 1959): 270–73.

Carries the context for concerns over the volume of publication and its access back to the 1880s. In 1889 historian Paul Leicester Ford wrote: "although knowledge of the literature of the subject is everyday becoming of greater necessity, yet it is, unfortunately, every day becoming more difficult to obtain." Other figures from the period are quoted; the bibliographic apparatus available to a historian working in the 1880s is sketched; and discomfort with the publication schedule of *Writings on American History* is expressed.

McAnally, A. M. "Characteristics of Materials Used in Research in United States History." Ph.D. diss., University of Chicago, 1951.

This study of the sources used by American historians employs citations sampled from works published in the years 1903, 1938, and 1948. Among the findings are: there has been a steady shift away from the use of foreign sources; the use of newspapers has increased steadily; when materials perform a secondary function they are comparatively recently published; the types of resources used differ across specializations; a significant percentage of material cited by historians is not strictly classified as historical; and the library catalog does not adequately capture the bits of pertinent material "hidden" in books, collections, and periodicals.

Morris, Leslie R., Carol M. Kazmierczak, and David Schoen. "A Faculty Bill of Rights for Library Services." *Perspectives* (American Historical Association) 30, no. 3 (March 1992): 1, 6–7.

Describes, perhaps too simplistically, the levels of service faculty can reasonably expect to receive from their institution's library. The tone and intent of the article is captured in its conclusion: "Although the vast majority of librarians are anxious to assist both faculty and students, the library, like any bureaucracy, is prone to make decisions for the benefit of the bureaucracy instead of the patrons." Guidelines are offered for assessing the fairness and appropriateness of budget allocations. Issues in the acquisitions and access of books and periodicals, and standards for evaluating reserve services and interlibrary loan, are considered. Online catalogs are seen as indispensable; the "watchwords for the nineties are 'minimize holdings—maximize access.' "

Pao, Miranda Lee. "Characteristics of American Revolution Literature." *Collection Management* 6, nos. 3/4 (Fall/Winter 1984): 119–28.

It is assumed that with a predictable pattern of literature diversity one can be reasonably assured that one will cover a major portion of the literature by scanning a few known journals. The principal twenty-one journals (9%) contain more than half of the total papers. To retrieve another 25 percent of the literature, one must scan an additional thirty-six journals. Furthermore, the remaining 25 percent or 276 articles were scattered over 167 journals. A similar clustering was found in terms of monographs. "Two hundred and twenty-seven unique publishers were responsible for a total of 1,014 works, published from 1781 through 1971. . . . Ten publishers (each with 23 or more publications) were responsible for 395 (39%) works, 22 (each with 10 or more) for 556 (55%), and 41 (each with 6 or more) for 668 (68%) books." The sample was drawn from John Shy's bibliography *The American Revolution* (Northbrook, Ill.: AHM Publishing, 1973). In addition, the adequacy of coverage in the serial bibliography *Writings in American History* was checked against Shy's work. Twenty-two journals in Shy's bibliography were not covered in WAH. Yet of the top eighteen journals in Shy, which produced 61.6 percent of its articles, only two were missing from WAH.

Perman, Dagmar Horna. "Bibliography and the Historian." In *Bibliography and the Historian: The Conference at Belmont of the Joint Committee on Bibliographical Services in History, May 1967*, ed. Dagmar Horna Perman, 7–19. Santa Barbara, Calif.: Clio, 1968.

Summarizes the results of a survey to determine which bibliographical aids are most used by historians. Three hundred members of the American Historical Association, representing a variety of specializations, were polled. Fifty responded. Questionnaires requested general biographical information, the extent of use of bibliographic tools in one's area of specialization, the techniques used to survey other fields, and respondents were asked to identify perceived deficiencies in bibliographic aids. Generally, the respondents had received their doctoral degrees from good to excellent departments, had used outstanding libraries as students, and were presently employed in less distinguished schools. They were also relatively young, with a median age of thirty-eight. Perhaps this suggests that historians working for promotion and tenure have a utilitarian interest in more efficient research aids. Responses indicated that in their own fields historians desire unannotated and unevaluative comprehensiveness. In fields other than their own, they want highly selective and thoroughly annotated bibliographies. On the whole, they feel bibliographically out of touch with the social sciences and even more so with the humanities. As historical research becomes increasingly interdisciplinary historians will be compelled to rely extensively on indexes and highly annotated bibliographic aids.

Price, Arnold H. "Library Collections and the Historian." *Perspectives* (American Historical Association) 25, no. 5 (May/June 1987): 25–26.

Historians require extensive library collections of great depth and scope. Weak collections in disciplines other than their own hurt historians more than some other scholars. History's sources and findings are cumulative, and the study of history is evolutionary—older interpretations and insights do not become obsolete.

Sheperd, John. *The Information Needs and Information Seeking Behavior of Polytechnic Lecturers in the Subject Area of History*. British Library Research and Development Department Report no. 5743. London: British Library, 1983.

By means of a postal survey the types of materials and methods of obtaining research materials, as well as patterns of library use for Polytechnic history lecturers in thirty-one institutions in England, Wales, and Ulster are considered. Books and journals emerge as overwhelmingly important; for teaching there is a heavy reliance on books and journals owned by the instructor; nearly 25 percent of respondents made heavy use of bibliographic tools for teaching; nearly the same percentage found their institution's library worthless, and for research most found it thoroughly useless. Reviews are heavily used for identifying material for teaching. For research, forms of browsing are employed more, and slightly more use is made of interlibrary loan, bibliographies, abstracts, and indexes. But nearly 80 percent of history lecturers do not use current awareness services, nor are they part of the invisible college of scholars who are sharing ideas. In 1983 computerized searching was ignored by all but 10 percent of the respondents.

Shera, Jesse Hauk. *Historians, Books and Libraries: A Survey of Historical Scholarship in Relation to Library Resources and Services*. 1953. Reprint. New York: Greenwood Press, 1969.

Presents a simple model of the way in which historians work, indicates the kind of sources they need and use, and discusses the relative value of these sources in the solution of various problems. Three exercises are included that are designed to sensitize the library school student to the historian's needs: how to read a history book; how to evaluate such a book for different audiences; and a set of reference questions with a historical orientation are posed. Included are a narrowly defined discussion of the auxiliary sciences, an overview of the evolution of history as a discipline, and consideration of its relationship to the development of bibliographic materials, primary source collections, and libraries.

Stieg, Margaret F. "The Information Needs of Historians." *College & Research Libraries* 42, no. 6 (November 1981): 549–60. Reprinted in Margaret F. Stieg, *The Origin and Development of Scholarly Historical Periodicals*. University, Ala.: University of Alabama Press, 1989.

Reports the result of a survey of historians in a variety of fields. As in the Perman survey, younger historians proved more likely to respond. Among the conclusions are: microform is not a satisfactory substitute for hardcopy; it is discouragingly difficult to obtain dissertations and theses on interlibrary loan, and the service remains a source of considerable frustration. When asked how they identify relevant published materials (given ten choices), historians ranked references in books or journals first and book reviews second; fifth were abstracts or indexes; and tenth was consultation with a librarian. Other findings showed a concentrated use of a relatively small number of journals and a general neglect, in most areas, of research in languages other than English. These findings and the anecdotal comments elicited by the survey reveal a general ignorance of bibliographic aids and their possibilities and suggest that essentially serendipitous research methods are used.

Stoller, Michael E. "Large Manuscript Collections in Microform: Is There a Better Way?" *Microform Review* 20, no. 2 (Spring 1991): 51–55; "Large Manuscript Collections in Microform: A Dubious Library Investment." *Microform Review* 18, no. 1 (Winter 1989): 15–19; and "Large Manuscript Collections in Microform: Yet Again." *Microform Review* 19, no. 1 (Winter 1990): 24–26.

A historian and librarian at Columbia University cautions against purchasing large manuscript collections in microform, as such purchases are seldom justified by use. Even more importantly, the need for publishers to make a profit prohibits the filming of much important material. To make such material available to researchers, Stoller recommends that publishers, scholarly societies, and governments work together. Repositories holding manuscripts must be given financial help to microfilm their material to make it available to others, and the government must assume the burden of making unpublished material available rather than relying on commercial vendors to fulfill this obligation.

Stone, Sue. "Humanities Scholars: Information Needs and Uses." *Journal of Documentation* 38, no. 4 (December 1982): 292–313.

An essay review that covers material published back to 1970. Among the points it makes are: the individual approach characterizes humanistic scholarship; it is serendipitous; historians only reluctantly delegate searching to librarians; and there are strong arguments in favor of browsing. In other disciplines "libraries provide access to reports

of other people's research . . . but in the humanities they may also provide access to the
starting point of research, the raw materials.''

Stone, Sue, ed. *Humanities Information Research, Proceedings of A Seminar; Sheffield
1980*. CRUS Occasional Paper no. 4. Sheffield: Centre for Research on User
Studies, University of Sheffield, Western Bank, 1980.

Stone notes that the history researcher very rarely chooses to delegate searching for
secondary sources, let alone primary sources: ''I believe that the chief reason for this is
that the kinds of questions historians ask about are not answerable from obvious sources.''
In many instances only someone very involved in research would even have the imagination to know where to look. Of course, there is a less profound type of searching for
which librarians would be useful. John Chapman, history information officer at Birmingham University, notes that historians depend to varying degrees on the invisible
college to identify information, distrust the academic credentials of librarians, and are
generally ignorant of library science's vocabulary. But central to why historians do not
delegate searching is the fact that they invest much of themselves in their data. If they
allowed others to search for them beyond a limited extent the interpretation process would
be violated.

Super, R. H. ''A Museum of the Book.'' *Collection Building* 9, nos. 3–4 (1989): 61–
64.

As the museum is to the paleontologist, so the museum of the book may capture the
mind of the researcher in unimaginable ways. A literary historian argues for libraries rich
enough to enable students and scholars to explore, to browse, not merely to search for
answers to specific problems. He complains about the constraining influence of the Library
of Congress classification system and argues that whereas scientists can create their own
laboratories the humanist cannot. Expressing the sentiments he shares with a historian
friend he writes, ''The humanist can only regret the sad lack of humility which reduces
all knowledge to 'information'—information in the sense of our current technology—
and one must hope that in our conceit we do not altogether destroy our past.''

Uva, Peter A. *Information Gathering Habits of Academic Historians: Report of the Pilot
Study*. Syracuse, N.Y.: SUNY Upstate Medical Center Library, 1977. Available
from ERIC's EDRS as ED 142 483.

Reports the results of a survey conducted with forty-two historians from the University
of Rochester and Cornell University. Historians conduct their research in a highly serendipitous manner. Reference aids do not dominate any stage of the research process.
Instead, primary data is the major information source at all stages, and footnotes in
monographs and journal articles are the most frequently used source for ''obtaining''
information. Colleagues are not influential in the selection of a topic for study.

Vondran, Raymond Florian, Jr. ''The Effect of Method of Research on the Information
Seeking Behavior of Academic Historians.'' Ph.D. diss., School of Library Science, University of Wisconsin–Madison, 1976.

Research supports the hypothesis ''that method of research affects some important
aspects of information seeking behavior in the discipline of history. . . . In history, discipline alone is not a sufficient predictor of information seeking behavior; method must
be considered.'' Quantitative historians cite journal articles more frequently than other
historians; they perceive the library as less critical to their work than other historians and
rely more on informal sources of information.

Walters, Edward M. "The Future of the Book: A Historian's Perspective." *Information Technology and Libraries* 1, no. 1 (March 1982): 15–21.

The author is a historian and director of libraries at the University of Texas at Dallas. The cumulative disciplines (the sciences) and the noncumulative disciplines (the humanities and social sciences) will benefit from different types of information delivery systems. The former will be well served by online services while the latter, especially history, will continue to require print sources. This is because historians will require the full informational environment for contextual reasons. The cumulative/noncumulative distinction breaks down in areas of basic as opposed to applied research. The latter requires quick answers and will also be well served by the new technology.

Weil, Eric. "Supporting the Humanities." *Daedalus* 102, no. 2 (Spring 1973): 27–38.

Erudition is necessary in the humanities but "the cultivated man is not he who can quote the contents of an encyclopedia, but he who knows what to look for and where to look for it." Researchers in the humanities demand original sources that they must have available in order to reappraise and rediscover continually. In the humanities, fundamental questions originate from these sources as they apply to us today: "We project our problems on to the men and situations of the past and choose from the past so that the dialogue with its actors may help us in our own predicament through contact with something at the same time different and familiar."

Weintraub, Karl J. "The Humanities Scholar and the Library." *Library Quarterly* 50, no. 1 (January 1980): 22–28.

Written by a cultural historian whose "perspective comes from . . . having to view human existence under the long measure of time and in the large context of cultures." Of special interest are comments on the researchers' dependence upon texts and their characterization of themselves as being more alone with their problems than the scientist: "his objective knowledge is more diffuse; the frontier is less visible, and the dominant current concerns need not be as significant as they are fashionable." "The humanist's work consists less of sequentially interrelated blocks of knowledge than is true of the scientist's work, even if every individual finding may pose a question for the next viewer." Further, "the complex interrelations of insights . . . form at best reasonable patterns of meaning, plausibly arranged views of data in which, one hopes, the major data at least fit one another."

IV. RESEARCH METHODOLOGY: THE HUMANITIES

(See Sections I and III for additional material.)

Brinton, Crane. *Ideas and Men.* 2d ed. Englewood Cliffs, N.J.: Prentice-Hall, 1963.

Distinguishes between two kinds of knowledge: cumulative and noncumulative. Cumulative knowledge is best exemplified by science; noncumulative knowledge, by the humanities. Science is the result of accumulation; at its core are truths accepted by all scientists. Illustrating his point, Brinton writes, "A modern American college student is not wiser than one of the sages of antiquity, has no better taste than an artist of antiquity, but he knows a lot more physics than the greatest Greek scientist ever knew. He knows more *facts* about literature and philosophy than the wisest Greek of 400 B.C. could know; but in physics he not only knows more facts—he understands the relation between facts, that is, the theories and the laws."

Budd, John M. "Research in the Two Cultures: The Nature of Scholarship in Science and the Humanities." *Collection Management* 11, nos. 3/4 (1989): 1–21.

A broad review of pertinent studies and observations with special attention paid to citation indexing. "Empirical evidence shows that humanists rely more on self and less on a systematic search for materials, that they depend on the books to aid analysis and inquiry, and that the nature of humanities scholarship is personal." History is not seen strictly as a discipline in the humanities.

Frye, Northrop. "The Search for Acceptable Words." *Daedalus* 102, no. 2 (Spring 1973): 11–26.

Canadian literary critic points out the inevitable tension between library collections and the needs of the researcher: "The immense resources of modern libraries, which can bring so much to the scholar's doorstep are of course indispensable, but most of them imply that the scholar always knows what he is looking for. If he is doing original research, he may not know."

Gombrich, E. H. "Research in the Humanities: Ideals and Idols." *Daedalus* 102, no. 2 (Spring 1973): 1–10.

By definition the researcher in the humanities possesses and enhances cultural literacy. But humanities scholarship is characterized by a number of obvious pitfalls or traps. *Idola quantitatis* is the cult of "inductivism" or the assumption that "truth emerges in the form of generalizations based on the accumulation of data." Carried to the extreme, this nurtures the scholar who knows more and more about less and less. *Idola novitatis* is the cult of novelty for its own sake. *Idola temporis* is "the lure of newly developed intellectual and mechanical tools which seem to promise prestige to those who 'apply' them to the humanities." Under *idola academica* fall the demands for boundaries between disciplines that prescribe methodologies and techniques. This leads to the overcrowding of some fields and to the elevation of classroom techniques to the status of research methodologies.

Gould, Constance C. *Information Needs in the Humanities: An Assessment.* Stanford, Calif.: Research Libraries Group, 1988.

An assessment of information needs in classical studies, history, art, literature, philosophy, religion, music, and linguistics based on interviews with experts. Discussion of each discipline may be organized, among others, under sections for: general characteristics, access to published material, access to unpublished material, machine-readable data files, and visual materials. Identified for special attention in history are an online bibliography in women's studies, a union list of contemporary accounts of trials, greater online access to monographic literature, the importance of newspapers, and improved access to popular-culture material. Other suggested initiatives include: more cataloging in an automated system of records for archival and manuscript material, completed development of PresNet, nationwide access to local automated catalogs of archival holdings, links to international networks as they are developed, an online catalog of manuscripts on microfilm, the increased cataloging of sources in African-American and women's history, and an automated union catalog and index of oral histories. In addition, online access to the contents of important data files, online access to visual materials of all types, and, specifically, more online cataloging of films.

Guest, Susan S. "The Use of Bibliographic Tools by Humanities Faculty at the State University of New York at Albany." *The Reference Librarian* no. 18 (1987): 157–72.

A survey of humanities faculty; historians were not included. The profile of the humanities researcher does not conform with that presented by much of the literature. Researchers were found to rely heavily on the currency of periodicals and books, journals were of considerable importance as a source of current materials, and library use increased with the age of the researcher. Participants found reviews more important than either abstracts or annotations, that is, more useful than reference sources. They were more current and more contextual. Exhaustive retrospective coverage was not perceived as necessary.

Kanes, Martin. "The Humanities Scholar Views Research and Libraries." *CLi Quarterly* 2, no. 4 (December 1983): 46–49.

An eloquent argument in favor of browsing, citing the role of chance and intuition in knowledge production. Even the twists and turns of manual searching are appreciated for the time they give ideas to germinate and synthesize. The author concludes, concerning computerization, "if everything is the same as everything else on the little green screen, then value systems become impossible, if everything can be known, nothing need be learned."

Meserole, Harrison T. "The Nature(s) of Literary Research." *Collection Management* 13, nos. 1/2 (1990): 65–73.

An English professor briefly describes a literary research methods and bibliography course he teaches, emphasizing the interdisciplinarity of contemporary literary research.

Pastine, Maureen. "Bibliographic Instruction in the Humanities." In *Bibliographic Instruction: The Second Generation*, ed. Constance Mellon, 169–97. Littleton, Colo.: Libraries Unlimited, 1987.

The primary source is the focus of humanities research. Humanities researchers use a wide range of titles, and they are not restricted to a particular time period. They use dictionaries and encyclopedias to assist in the reading and explication of a work, and it is, at some point, useful to know what others have said about it. But as humanities scholarship becomes more interdisciplinary, the substantive and bibliographic challenges to practitioners will increase.

Schweik, Robert C. "Stretching for an Answer: Innovative Research in Literary and Cultural History." *Literary Research Newsletter* 9, nos. 2/3 (Summer 1984): 19–27.

Nothing replaces imagination in research. Of particular interest are comments on ways in which the *Oxford English Dictionary* and *Readers' Guide to Periodical Literature* have been used to explore cultural history. The former has been used to trace the evolution of words, while a study of the latter's subject headings reveals evolving perceptions.

V. RESEARCH METHODOLOGY: THE SOCIAL SCIENCES

Baxter, Pam M. "A View of Academics' Literature Search Methods: The Case of the Social Sciences and Its Implications for Students." *The Reference Librarian* nos. 27/28 (1990): 419–31.

Nonsystematic bibliographic research methods predominate. Personal collections and files are the most likely origin of citations, as revealed by a number of studies. Faculty reluctance to embrace bibliographic instruction is based on its perceived superfluousness for both their own work and that of their students. Several successful exercises and programs are mentioned.

Ben-David, Joseph. "How to Organize Research in the Social Sciences." *Daedalus* 102, no. 2 (Spring 1973): 39–51.

Primary background research is very important to the social scientist. Thus the social scientist requires excellent libraries as well as the retention of social science data and handbooks that will allow ready access to it.

Freides, Thelma. *Literature and Bibliography of the Social Sciences*. Los Angeles: Melville, 1973.

This seminal work presents a philosophical, practical, and historical framework within which to understand the design and function of bibliographic tools, modes of reporting research, and some reference aids. Part 1 broadly discusses the nature and historical evolution of scientific and social scientific methodology. Part 2 considers bibliographic structures or systems—that is, vehicles for reporting and for accessing published research—and presents them as a derivative of a discipline's communications system. In this regard, the roles of various research reporting formats are discussed. Part 3 focuses on comprehensive, selective, and retrospective bibliographies and guides to the literature. Numerous appendixes, in the form of annotated bibliographies representing all the social sciences, illustrate appropriate chapters in parts 2 and 3. Part 4 briefly suggests how a knowledge of bibliographic structures should inform a literature search.

Gould, Constance G., and Mark Handler. *Information Needs in the Social Sciences: An Assessment*. Mountain View, Calif.: Research Libraries Group, 1989.

An assessment of information needs in: economics, political science, psychology, sociology, and anthropology based on interviews with experts. Each discussion is introduced by a brief outline of the general characteristics of the discipline, followed by a consideration of access to published and unpublished material, machine-readable data, and so forth. Strengths and weaknesses of each discipline's bibliographic apparatus are noted. Like the humanities survey (cited in the previous section) the opportunities for improved access via online databases are noted. Examples of recommendations are: "timely access on a national network to comprehensive information on economic working papers" (economics); "more attention to collecting published materials from developing countries, and to disseminating information about them" (political science); "question-level indexing of social science data files" (sociology); "identification of sources of cross-cultural data and information about them through a national network" (psychology); and "a machine-readable index covering the holdings of the Tozzer and Museum of Mankind libraries" (anthropology).

Line, Maurice B. "The Information Uses and Needs of Social Scientists: An Overview of INFROSS." *ASLIB Proceedings* 23, no. 8 (August 1971): 412–34.

Disciplines included in the study were: anthropology, economics, education, political science, psychology, and sociology. History was excluded. Investigation into Information Requirements of the Social Sciences (INFROSS) was designed to acquire information to guide the improvement or design of information systems for the social sciences. An extensive questionnaire was circulated to over two thousand social scientists in Great Britain. (For historians, the Stieg study parallels this effort in the United States.) INFROSS found that to discover current information a quarter of respondents never used abstracts or indexes, library catalogs, the searching of library shelves, or book review indexes. Many clearly did not even know what an abstracting or indexing journal was. Those who did used only one service. Among the conclusions ultimately drawn: the boundaries of the services need to be redefined to capture pertinent literature from other disciplines;

even when a foreign language was read by a practitioner its literature was seldom used; and, generally, the delegation of searching to an information officer was acceptable. Line assumes that this latter point will allow for the development of more sophisticated online systems. See also Perry D. Morrison, "Since Bath: A Review of Published Information Transfer Studies in the Social and Behavioral Sciences, 1974 Through 1978," *Behavioral and Social Sciences Librarian* 1, no. 1 (Fall 1979): 5–22.

Line, Maurice B. "Secondary Services in the Social Sciences: The Need for Improvement and the Role of the Librarian." *Behavioral and Social Sciences Librarian* 1, no. 4 (Summer 1980): 263–73.

Social science services fail to cover a broadly defined area: the literature of sociology, for instance, should be more aptly defined as the literature needed by sociologists. Services also fail to treat monographs, and there are problems inherent in the commercial ownership of many services. The role of ideology in the selection of areas for coverage is raised.

Stoan, Stephen K. "Survey of the Field." In *Sources of Information in the Social Sciences: A Guide to the Literature*, 3d ed., ed. William H. Webb, 3–22. Chicago: American Library Association, 1986.

Sketches the development of the social sciences (history is treated as a social science) and their bibliographic and reference apparatus from the nineteenth century to date. Recent studies of the ways in which social scientists (but not historians in this case) conduct bibliographic research and the characteristics of literature are summarized and expertly synthesized, notably extensive studies, conducted at England's Bath University, of "Technology: Investigation into Information Requirements of the Social Sciences" or INFROSS (1971) and "Design of Information Systems in the Social Sciences" or DISISS (1973–1976, final report in 1980). Patterns of use: research methods are serendipitous and the use of formal tools is sporadic; there is an equal reliance on books and journals; two-thirds of citations in any project refer to either published or unpublished data; much primary data cannot be classified as social science; drawing on many disciplines, "discipline-centered" indexes are of limited value; and research is not linear as in the physical sciences. Characteristics of the literature: the literature has grown faster than either that of the sciences or the humanities; the ratio of published journals to books is about 1.1:1; though there are a large number of indexes, they cover the literature inadequately; only economics and psychology are well served, and they are largely self-citing; terminology is often ambiguous; much research is noncumulative; and the social sciences largely lack reviews of research. Stoan's conceptual framework for social science literature has three categories: scholarly literature (original research, derivative research, synthetic literature, bibliographic literature); primary data in published form (published primary data, access tools to primary data); and incidental professional and scholarly literature (style manuals, directories, etc.).

VI. RELEVANT INSTRUCTIONAL DESIGNS FROM OTHER DISCIPLINES

Beaubien, Anne K. "Bibliographic Instruction in the Social Sciences: Three Models." In *Bibliographic Instruction: The Second Generation*, ed. Constance A. Mellon, 156–68. Littleton, Colo.: Libraries Unlimited, 1987.

The current emphasis on bibliographic instruction is on generalized logic and problem solving. In this light the bibliographic structure and appropriate instruction for psychology, anthropology, and geography and political science are discussed. Psychology is characterized by a tremendous emphasis on the currency of information. Books are less important than other formats. The types of materials needed are fewer than in most disciplines. This simplicity, and the need for currency, have led the discipline to take control of its own indexing and abstracting service. Anthropology, on the other hand, like humanities disciplines, requires retrospective materials. Consequently, it is served well by bibliographies. Of course, there is also an emphasis on cross-cultural research, and it is served by the Human Relations Area Files (HRAF). A comprehensive English-language encyclopedia is lacking, but the way scholars conduct research does not require one. Geography has engendered an array of special tools and a great variety of fact books. Bibliographic control is excellent. Reflecting its wide diversity of concerns, political science is not comprehensively served by a single source.

Blystone, Robert V. "Enhancing Science Courses with BI: Three Approaches." *Research Strategies* 7, no. 2 (Spring 1989): 55–60.

An account by a biology professor of the library exercises he assigns students. One exercise requires students to answer three basic questions concerning the substance, impact, and historical context of a scientific article. In completing this exercise students use: *Science Citation Index*, *Chemical Abstracts*, *Biological Abstracts*, and *Index Medicus*. Another exercise, a scavenger hunt, requires the answering of a series of questions to which the reference source in which the answer may be found is given. The third approach assumes the library is a laboratory and requires students to answer a series of questions about a drug. In addition to finding factual information, students are guided through an exploration of the drug's real-life implications. Reference sources are suggested, and they cut across a wide breadth of disciplines. The course is open to all students and takes them into areas they might not otherwise investigate.

Carpenter, Eric J. "The Literary Scholar, The Librarian, and the Future of Literary Research." *Literary Research Newsletter* 2, no. 4 (October 1977): 143–55.

Discusses the public image of the librarian and the perceptions of students about library-use instruction. Sketches a range of areas in which librarians and literary scholars should cooperate: reference book revision, database design, collection development policies, and library-use instruction. "Librarians and scholars must work together to establish comprehensive programs of instruction in library use which encompass the needs of the freshman composition student, the doctoral candidate preparing a dissertation, and the faculty member beginning research in a discipline outside his own."

Fenstermaker, John J. "The Introductory Course in Research Methods: A Fuller Context for the Eighties." *Literary Research Newsletter* 7, no. 1 (Winter 1982): 3–11.

Comments on his revision of Richard Altick's *Art of Literary Research*. Advises against tampering with Altick's heavy emphasis on bibliographic exercises.

George, Mary W., and Mary Ann O'Donnell. "The Bibliography and Research Methods Course in American Departments of English." *Literary Research Newsletter* 4, no. 1 (Winter 1979): 9–23.

Reports the results of a survey conducted to gather "information about the teaching of basic research tools and techniques in American graduate schools that offer a doctorate in English and American Literature." Data indicated that as many as 25 percent of graduate departments may be offering no such instruction at all and that it is rare for a librarian to be the instructor or coinstructor in such a course. Of 111 responses, 32 departments indicated that they offered such instruction as part of another course. The ultimate conclusion is that the average complete methods course attends to library research half of the time, descriptive bibliography and editing a quarter of the time, and a variety of critical considerations another quarter of the time. The average partial course addresses bibliographic research less than half of the time.

Mellon, Constance A. "Process Not Product in Course-Integrated Instruction: A Generic Model of Library Research." *College & Research Libraries* 45, no. 6 (November 1984): 471–78.

Researching, writing, and editing are recurrent stages in the writing process. Recounts the library component of a process-oriented writing component in freshman composition courses at the University of Tennessee at Chattanooga (UTC). Within the process context a generic approach to library research was taught. There are three stages: prelibrary, library awareness, and library competence. In the first stage writing occurs without recourse to the library. The second stage is reached only after the student recognizes a need to know. As students enter this stage simple instruction is given on how to use the library. This initial library experience should be monitored by instructor and librarian to ensure that it will be successful. In the third stage students return to the library as necessary. As applied at UTC, to ensure success research topics were limited, positive attitudes toward librarians were encouraged, and print materials were prepared to supplement particular tools. Students were walked through the research process in three stages. First, they practiced research by using required readings as research material. They practiced the skills of paraphrasing, summary, and bibliographic form and addressed the issue of plagiarism. The second assignment was a library research project using the familiar Wilson indexes. The approach was generic rather than disciplinary. The third paper differed across the participating composition teachers. Some repeated the second process while others required students to use other library tools. Library anxiety was reduced.

Shapiro, Beth J., and Richard Child Hill. "Teaching Sociology Graduate Students Bibliographic Methods for Document Research." *Journal of Academic Librarianship* 5, no. 2 (September 1979): 75–78.

Describes a course taught by a librarian and a sociology professor at Michigan State University that systematically surveyed source material relevant to historically oriented social science research. Two parallel assignments were given: weekly assignments designed to develop mastery in the use of bibliographic sources and a seminar paper that explored the formulation of a research problem, described the search strategy, and included a list of all bibliographic tools used, a list commenting on sources that proved to be relevant, a comprehensive bibliography of all works consulted, and, finally, an evaluation of the strengths and weaknesses of the assignment itself. Descriptions of the structure of class sessions and of students' reactions are included.

Tuckett, Harold W., and Judith Pryor. "Research Strategy in Political Science." *Research Strategies* 1, no. 3 (Summer 1983): 128–30.

Suggests a search strategy for political science library research that consists not of "neat series of steps, but rather . . . of the interaction between parallel channels of primary and secondary literature." Suggests that the strategy outlined could serve as the framework for a one-hour lecture or for a series of presentations.

VII. WORKBOOKS, COURSES, EXERCISES, AND INSTRUCTIONAL DESIGNS

Workbooks

Furay, Conal, and Michael J. Salevouris. *The Methods and Skills of History: A Practical Guide*. Arlington Heights, Ill.: H. Davidson, 1988.

An outstanding workbook for undergraduates. Readings and exercises explore the meaning and nature of history, history and other disciplines, questions of evidence and context, historical concepts and theories, historical synthesis, writing, the use of secondary sources, historiography, and the use of the library and reference tools.

Lacey, Susan, and Norman McCord. *British History, 1760–1960: A Guide to Sources of Information*. Prepared by the Travelling Workshops Experiment, British Library Research and Development Department/Newcastle-upon-Tyne Polytechnic. Newcastle-upon-Tyne: British Library Board, 1979.

Designed for use with undergraduates by a librarian and a history professor, and originally funded as a British Library research project. In 1979 it became a commercial product of Newcastle-upon-Tyne Polytechnic Products Limited. This extremely well-done guide and self-instructing workbook is part of the larger package, no longer available, titled *British History, 1760–1960: A Learning Package on Sources of Information*, which included "Finding Information in British History," a twenty-minute synchronized program of color slides and audiocassette, and "How to Use the *Arts & Humanities Citation Index*," a twenty-five-minute audiocassette program. Discussion proceeds by type of reference source and corresponding exercises at the end of each chapter. The chapter "Reference Books" discusses: guides, historical atlases, chronologies, dictionaries, encyclopedias, major reference series, special handbooks, biographical reference sources, and yearbooks and directories. Detailed instructions and facsimile pages are included for: the *British Museum Catalog of Printed Books* and *Current Contents: Arts and Humanities*, *Historical Abstracts*, *British Humanities Index*, *Combined Retrospective Index Set to Journals in History*, and *Arts & Humanities Citation Index* and *Social Sciences Citation Index*. Other chapters are: "Theses and Dissertations," "Conferences and Current Research," and "Primary Sources." Instruction in systematic research is given. Originally presented as a workshop conducted on two or three afternoons over successive weeks, or made available in the library over a period of time. See also Sue Lacey-Bryant, "Travelling Workshops Experiment History Package," in *Humanities Information Research, Proceedings of a Seminar; Sheffield 1980*, ed. Sue Stone, CRUS Occasional Paper no. 4 (Sheffield: Centre for Research in User Studies, University of Sheffield, Western Bank, 1980), 69–78. (See entries under John Chapman, D. Clark, and Colin Harris.)

Nugent, Walter T. K. *Creative History: An Introduction to Historical Study*. 2d ed. New York: Harper & Row, 1977.

Designed for use with freshmen and sophomores by a practicing historian, this workbook for skill development is composed of chapters with exercises on such topics as evidence, facts, historical reasoning and methodology, and writing. It recognizes the need for bibliographic knowledge in "The Library: The Historian's Hardware," which contains an exercise of over ten questions, with many components, designed to familiarize students with the layout and use of the reference collection and the organization of the card catalog.

Stoffle, Carla, and Henry F. Dobyns. *Materials and Methods for History Research.* Library edition. Bibliographic Instruction Series. New York: The Libraryworks, a division of Neal-Schuman Publishers, 1979.

Developed at the University of Wisconsin–Parkside as a component of a three-credit undergraduate history methods course. The teacher's edition comes with instructional suggestions and twenty sets of fill-ins, which allow the exercises to be individualized. It follows the categorical mode of discussion employed in Jean Key Gates' *Guide to the Use of Books and Libraries*, 3rd ed. (New York: McGraw-Hill, 1974). Covered are: guides to the literature, handbooks, yearbooks and almanacs, atlases, subject dictionaries, indexes and abstracts, bibliographies, scholarly journals, techniques for evaluating book-length studies, newspapers, government publications, and research paper mechanics and methodology. The latter is complemented by flow charts. There are no tricks in the exercises, and the ease with which they can be done reinforces learning. In fact, instructors may wish to construct more demanding bibliographic exercises to suit their purposes.

Courses, Exercises, and Instructional Designs

Adler, Douglas D. "The Historians' Rites of Passage." *The History Teacher* 6, no. 3 (May 1975): 399–403.

Lists seventy-five reference tools the author believes should be familiar to history students. A partial syllabus and discussion of an undergraduate laboratory course offered at Utah State University, which focuses on library skills and their successful demonstration in the compilation of a resource bibliography, is included. Students proceed each week through a different medium, composing an annotated list of their findings. Considered first are bibliographies, then encyclopedias and encyclopedic sets, professional journals, and so forth. Lecture topics include: definitions of history, what is an archive?, periodical literature, skills (note taking, file systems, writing style, writing a critical bibliography), teachers' aids (criteria for textbook selection, criteria for the use of films, etc.). Slide/tape programs accompany each lecture and enable students to progress at their own pace. A twenty-three-item examination is given in the library and must be completed within a set time. Among the questions asked are: name at least one bibliography on your topic that the library does not hold; find an article relevant to the subject of "revolution" in the *Encyclopedia of the Social Sciences*; find a statistical table on the population of Utah in 1960.

Allen, David Y. "Students Need Help in Learning How to Use the Library." *The Chronicle of Higher Education* 24, no. 15 (9 June 1982): 56.

Historian and librarian Allen contends that undergraduates should be exposed to bibliographic instruction at least twice in their programs, in first-year composition courses and again as upper-division undergraduates; then, as beginning graduate students, they should be exposed to it again. Methodology courses are seen as most appropriate for introducing discipline-specific bibliographic knowledge and skills, and the advisability of making bibliographic learning immediately relevant to course and research needs is emphasized. A close coordination between teaching faculty and librarians is needed to prevent unnecessary duplication of effort, and the active involvement of the former is critical. But the librarian's involvement in teaching students to conceptualize and refine research topics is discouraged. Instead, librarians are urged to devote their energies to explaining the mechanics of reference tools and to explaining bibliographic structures. Limitations of time and pedagogical concerns are seen as mediating against extensive course-integrated instruction, that is, multiple bibliographic sessions within a course culminating in a final project. However, two sessions focusing on an exercise are seen as ideal.

American Historical Association Task Force on the History Major. "Liberal Learning and the History Major." *Perspectives* (American Historical Association) 28, no. 5 (May/June 1990): 14–19.

Report of the American Historical Association Task Force on the History Major in the Association of American College's Project on Liberal Learning, Study in Depth, and the Arts and Sciences Major. History is at the heart of liberal learning, teaching perspective and a sensitivity to the chronology and simultaneity of events. To advance these ends, the report recommends: a foundations course, a course to familiarize students with global diversity, a course in historical methods, a research seminar with a writing requirement, and an integrating or synthesizing course. Every course should require research and writing and use of traditional library resources, and introduction of new technologies will benefit students beyond the requirements of their immediate course work. Faculty are urged to "stress the development of research and writing skills that enable students to move knowledgeably by independent study." Library activities should be coordinated with writing assignments.

Bartul, John C. "Teaching the Value of Inquiry through the Essay Question." *Perspectives* (American Historical Association) 27, no. 8 (November 1989): 18–19.

A question or statement, in this case an essay question, must be understood before it can be answered. Understanding is constructed through questioning and definition; no part of speech should escape examination. Verbs, adjectives, and adverbs, as well as proper nouns require contextual understanding.

Barzun, Jacques. "Teaching and Research in History Today." *The History Teacher* 19, no. 4 (August 1986): 517–25.

The importance of organization, structure, and sequence in historical study is emphasized. A knowledge of history enables one to connect one fact with the next. Contemporary teaching techniques both directly and indirectly foster discontinuity. An elementary episodic library research project for high school students, seemingly without purpose, illustrates the problem.

Beales, Ross W., Jr. and Randall K. Burkett. *Historical Editing for Undergraduates.* Worcester, Mass.: College of the Holy Cross, 1977.

This thirty-eight-page booklet presents an overview of the profession of historical editing and discusses ways in which one can integrate historical editing into undergraduate education. Also included are a bibliography and the policy statement on annotation of the National Historical Publications and Records Commission. For a description of a one-semester undergraduate seminar, see Beales, "Historical Editing and Undergraduate Teaching: A Rationale and a Model," *Teaching History* 3 (Spring 1978): 3–8.

Beaubien, Anne K., Sharon A. Hogan, and Mary W. George. *Learning the Library: Concepts and Methods for Effective Bibliographic Instruction.* New York: R.R. Bowker, 1982.

Practical advice grounded on a theoretical understanding of bibliographic structures. Offers a general model for the analysis of research problems with reference to research aids and a general model of the development of a discipline, its communication network, and its bibliographic control. Chapters relate this structure to search strategies in the humanities and social sciences. The chapter on history, pages 125–34, notes the importance of appreciating the diversity and evolution of historical concerns and advises exploring with students the identification of primary sources and the tools available for accessing them.

Boehm, Eric H. "On the Second Knowledge: A Manifesto for the Humanities." *Libri* 22, no. 4 (1972): 312–23.

Begins with a quotation from Samuel Johnson: "Knowledge is of two kinds. We know a subject ourselves, or we know where we can find information upon it." The humanist is particularly ignorant of the latter; among suggestions to rectify this deficiency in training are a course in reference works and sources of information, a basic social sciences and humanities course, a course on the use of computers, and refresher or updating courses incorporating these teachings after graduation. Workshops, but preferably a year-long methodology course, replete with field trips and laboratory experiences, are recommended as a requirement in history doctoral programs.

Burroughs, Carol. "Civil War Diaries." *Research Strategies* 4, no. 1 (Winter 1986): 32–35.

Describes an exercise focusing on the identification and evaluation of Civil War diaries used with students in Gonzaga University's history department. Its goals are: "to teach students the use of Library of Congress Subject headings in American history; to identify Civil War diaries; to demonstrate the limitations of these headings and the importance of using appropriate bibliographies which include listings of Civil War diaries, and to present some of the kinds of sources available in the library to help students evaluate the diaries and questions about the writers."

Cassara, Ernest. "The Student as Detective: An Undergraduate Exercise in Historical Research." *The History Teacher* 18, no. 4 (August 1985): 581–92.

Discusses a course taught at George Mason University by the author that requires students "to follow in the footsteps of a particular practitioner, to follow him step-by-step in his research, in his use of sources, and to observe his assimilation (synthesis) of material, and the result in his writing." The second volume of Dumas Malone's *Jefferson and the Rights of Man*, paying particular attention to chapter 27, "Hamilton vs. Jefferson," is explored. By tracing the footnotes in this chapter students determined how Malone used his sources. They also, as part of the greater assignment, read pertinent primary and secondary sources. They discovered inaccuracies, examples of bias, and poor writing. It became clear to them that scholars shape their work by the materials they choose to consider and that two scholars examining the same material can come to quite different conclusions.

Chapman, John, with comment by project director R.H.C. Davis. *Information Officer in History, University of Birmingham, 1979–1980*. Report to the British Library Research and Development Department on Project SI/G/281. June 1981. Birmingham: School of History, University of Birmingham, 1981.

Chapman was located in the history department of Birmingham from January 1979 to December 1980; unlike Davis, his counterpart at York University, he did not have an office in the library or a formal position within it. On user education: first-year students did not perceive the "History Package" of the Travelling Workshops Experiment as relevant, but using the package with more advanced students proved useful.

Christensen, Beth and Gerald Hoekstra. "Being Here, Being There: Understanding Early Music Through Historical Research and Analysis." *Research Strategies* 9, no. 2 (Spring 1991): 106–10.

Describes a series of assignments given in the second semester of a three-semester sequence in the music program at St. Olaf College. A faculty–librarian team has students write a fictional account and an entry in a formal journal or a letter that describes the performance of a work composed before 1650. Before the assignment is made the librarian gives a presentation to the class, which concludes with the discussion of a sample research project. Students research historical context across such diverse concerns as: music, architecture, dress, politics, and a full range of motivation. The second assignment, not necessarily supported by library research, is an analysis of the piece from the perspective of a twentieth-century music student.

Clark, D., C.G.S. Harris, P. J. Taylor, A. Douglas, and S.M.J. Lacey. *The Travelling Workshops Experiment in Library User Education.* The British Library Research and Development Report no. 5602. London: British Library Board, 1981.

The Travelling Workshops project was a four-year effort (1975–1978) "to promote and demonstrate library-user education in British institutions of higher learning." During the project's first two years workshops were conducted on biology, mechanical engineering, and social welfare at various schools; during the final two years materials prepared for the workshops were made available for purchase. Packages consist of: a student handbook, which is accompanied by practice questions; an audiotape on citation indexing; and posters. Included are samples of: Biology Information Test, Mechanical Engineering Information Test, Social Welfare Information Test, a generic postworkshop questionnaire, examples of staff and student postworkshop questionnaires. A history package was designed by a librarian and a historian based on this experience on a search strategy for British history, 1760–1960. (See Susan Lacey and Norman McCord at the beginning of this section.)

D'Aniello, Charles A. "A Sociobibliographical and Sociohistorical Approach to the Study of Bibliographic and Reference Sources: A Complement to Traditional Bibliographic Instruction." In *Conceptual Frameworks for Bibliographic Education: Theory and Practice*, ed. Mary Reichel and Mary Ann Ramey, 109–33. Littleton, Colo.: Libraries Unlimited, 1987.

Bibliographic and reference sources can be studied within the context of their creation. Through such study they can be considered as straightforward guides to, or compendiums of, information or knowledge once or still current. Their study reveals the evolution of knowledge and the maturity of the disciplines they serve, and it exercises one's knowledge of cultural and intellectual traditions. The study of reference sources, in this light, shows that knowledge is context-dependent.

Edwards, Susan E. "Faculty Involvement in the University of Colorado Program." In *Faculty Involvement in Library Instruction*, ed. Hannalore B. Rader, 7–22. Ann Arbor, Mich.: Pierian Press, 1976.

Discusses the results of a survey done at Colorado, in conjunction with a five-year grant from the Council on Library Resources and the National Endowment for the Humanities, "to find ways of encouraging high quality library research—within the context of subject matter courses." The departments of economics and history were surveyed as well as a random sample of all departments. Measures were obtained of: students' attitudes toward library instruction, librarian and historian involvement in such instruction, opinions on the settings in which instruction might best be offered, and the willingness of faculty to attend sessions designed to update their knowledge of bibliographic resources and techniques.

Engeldinger, Eugene A. "Bibliographic Instruction and Critical Thinking: The Contribution of the Annotated Bibliography." *RQ* 28, no. 2 (Winter 1988): 195–202.

Recounts the successful approach employed at the University of Wisconsin–Eau Claire. Subject expertise alone will not enable students to evaluate what they read. By writing critical annotations, and ultimately the compilation of an annotated bibliography, students can practice critical thinking skills. Nine basic questions to be addressed in annotations are: Who is the author? What is the purpose for writing the article or doing the research? For what audience is the author writing? Does the author have a bias or make assumptions upon which the rationale of the publication or the research rests? What method of obtaining data or conducting research was employed by the author? What conclusions does the author arrive at? Does the author satisfactorily justify the conclusions from the research or experience? How does the study compare with similar studies? Are there significant attachments or appendixes used such as charts, maps, bibliographies, and so forth?

Fink, Deborah. *Process and Politics in Library Research: A Model for Course Design.* Chicago: American Library Association, 1989.

A superb suggestive outline or guide of "creative learning opportunities" for an undergraduate course that emphasizes the value-laden nature of information and the importance of critically conveying knowledge of library tools and research strategies. Basic practical skills are also well covered. Useful figures or illustrations include instructions for a pathfinder, course project options, mini-project options, in-class essays, various search strategies, and guidelines for evaluating a piece of literature critically. Each chapter consists of a brief but thoughtful contextual introduction, sample learning objectives, discussion questions, in-class activities, take-home exercises, and notes and suggested reading. Among chapter considerations are: critical thinking, reference tools, disciplinary information structures, encyclopedias and dictionaries, creative problem solving and mindmaps, search strategies, note taking and organizational techniques, vocabulary control (issues in index, thesaurus, and LCSH use), finding and evaluating books, the evaluation of information, newspapers, accessing and evaluating periodical literature, and computerized-information access.

Fox, P. K. *User Education in the Humanities in U.S. Academic Libraries.* British Library Research and Development Report no. 5474. London: The British Library, 1979.

Comments on the history workbook used at the University of Wisconsin–Parkside, discusses term paper and doctoral advisement services offered at such institutions as Amherst College, Yale, Stanford, and Columbia. In a section devoted to user education for history students, programs are described: at Dartmouth; at the University of Michigan; the history officer program at the University of Colorado (half-time reference librarian and half-time history department); and the bibliographic assistant program at Mount Holyoke (undergraduate paid by the library and supervised jointly by the library and the history department).

Freeman, Michael Stuart. *Researching Historical Problems: An Introduction to Basic Sources.* Hanover N.H.: Dartmouth College Library, 1979. Slide/tape program. Text available from ERIC's EDRS as ED 165 766 and from LOEX.

A tape and seventy-nine slides logically introduce the tools and strategies for undergraduate historical research. Research steps included require the use of: encyclopedias, bibliographies, the card catalog, specific bibliographies, periodical indexes, and *America: History and Life* and *Historical Abstracts*.

Gerber, David A. "Rethinking the Graduate Research Seminar in American History: The Search for a New Model." *Teaching History* 13, no. 1 (Spring 1988): 8–17.

SUNY–Buffalo history professor Gerber initially included sessions by the library's history bibliographer and government documents specialist in his course. Because these sessions proved of little assistance in helping students frame a topic and conduct research they are no longer held. Instead, students work on a local history topic, and the professor provides them with a syllabus that has an extensive secondary bibliography complete with call numbers. He also makes it clear where resources are available in the area. In place of the session on library instruction he encourages students to take orientation tours of the library and to ask reference librarians focused questions. He suggests that professors make the syllabus available to the library in advance and notes that instruction in bibliography is available to all SUNY–Buffalo graduate history students as part of an introductory course.

Hansen, Forest, and Joann H. Lee. "Ancient Greek History as a Library Instruction Course." *Research Strategies* 3, no. 2 (Spring 1985): 65–74.

Describes an undergraduate course offered at Lake Forest College in Illinois centered on library research and distinguished by team teaching by a librarian and a professor. Copies of the course description, class schedule, research projects, and library exercises are provided.

Harris, Colin, Daphne Clark, and Anne Douglas. "The Travelling Workshops Experiment." In *Progress in Educating the Library User*, ed. John Lubans, Jr., 171–81. New York: R.R. Bowker, 1978.

After the initial workshop offering, lectures were abandoned in favor of a very self-sufficient handbook, which was enhanced to serve "both as a guide to information sources in the subject and as instruction in their use." The introductory lecture was converted to a slide/tape program. Practice exercises became an even more important part of the program. The workshop librarian now served more as a tutor than a teacher. Whereas the first workshops took three days, the final workshops might be completed in five to six hours.

Haywood, C. Robert. *The Doing of History: A Practical Use of the Library-College Concept*. Norman, Okla.: Library-College Associates, 1978.

Despite its title, this work is not methodological and is composed largely of reminiscences of its historian-author. Librarians and teachers are urged to join together to help students "do history." The library-college model involves librarians actively and regularly in instruction as resource people who assist in identifying evidence bibliographically necessary for argumentation and problem solving. The model encourages the development of skills in handling various forms of literature, in recognizing clues that lead from one bibliographic tool to another, and in using the guides that tie bibliography together.

Haywood, C. Robert. "The Teacher-Historian and the Library-Teacher." *Liberal Education* 55, no. 2 (May 1969): 288–95.

History should be taught not as a fund of knowledge, but as an approach or an attitude. To utilize library resources fully teachers should entrust the introduction of materials to librarians and to achieve this, a limited number of topics should be chosen and the librarian should be informed of their selection well in advance in order to allow for adequate preparation time. Librarians' general and interdisciplinary perspective and knowledge of reference sources will increasingly come into play if they realize more than mere assistance in the verification of facts is expected of them. Finally, the librarians' nonevaluative role should make them attractive to students.

"Historians and Using Tomorrow's Research Library: Research, Teaching and Training."
     The History Teacher 17, no. 3 (May 1984): 385–444.

Jane A. Rosenberg, then a librarian at Kent State University, in "New Ways to Find Books: Searching, Locating, and Information Delivery," 387–90, sketches a rapidly evolving electronic environment. Robert P. Swierenga, who had collaborated with Rosenberg, in "Bibliographic Instruction in Historical Methods Courses: Kent State University," 391–96, describes librarian involvement and exercises used to familiarize graduate students with library tools and services. A revision of this essay is the latter part of chapter 3 in this volume. Charles A. D'Aniello, a librarian at the State University of New York at Buffalo, in "An Historical Bibliography and Methods Course: The SUNY at Buffalo Experience," 396–404, describes a four-credit graduate methods course team-taught by a librarian and a historian. Historian Melvin J. Tucker, who has taught with D'Aniello, in "Comments on Cooperative Instruction: The SUNY at Buffalo Experience," 404–8, considers the methodological and historiographic portions of the course. A syllabus and editing exercise are provided and a journal exercise is given from the Kent State course. Charles A. D'Aniello, "A Basic Bibliography of Readings and Course Materials for Bibliographic Instruction in Undergraduate and Graduate History Programs," 408–30, is incorporated into this bibliography.

Isaacson, David. "Library Use as a Learning Skill: Fostering Intellectual Skills Development." *The Journal of Learning Skills* 2, no. 2 (Spring 1983): 51–57.

A former college English teacher and now a librarian, Isaacson sketches a history course in twentieth-century U.S. history that would integrate library skills and a librarian with course objectives. These are to "develop the student's ability to understand the following: what constitutes historical evidence, the difference between statements of fact and interpretations of these statements, the difference between primary and secondary sources, the difference between a scholarly and a popular approach to historical problems, and how to formulate a thesis about an historical subject by doing library research in which that subject is narrowed down to a manageable topic." The author argues that instruction is effective only when it is linked to course objectives and when the librarian is available for informal assistance as students work on the assignments. Suggested assignments, all in some way linked to one another, are: choosing subject headings to search the catalog, using these headings to search the *Readers' Guide to Periodical Literature*, using the *New York Times Index*, using *America: History and Life*, searching for government documents, using biographical dictionaries and encyclopedias. In each instance students would be led to consider the biases and differences between the sources. The concluding exercise would be "the preparation of an annotated bibliography using a variety of different types of sources . . . to support a thesis about a historical subject."

Kirkendall, Carolyn. "Of Princess Di, Richard Dawson, and *The Book Review Digest*."
     Research Strategies 4, no. 1 (Winter 1986): 40–42.

Using book reviews can help students learn to read critically and begin to understand that scholarship requires the questioning of ideas, data, and arguments. For instance, compiling and annotating a bibliography of critical reviews compels students to weigh the pros and cons of particular works and to become sensitive to various points of view.

Kline, Mary-Jo. *A Guide to Documentary Editing*. Baltimore: Johns Hopkins University Press, 1987.

Prepared for the Association for Documentary Editing. For suggestions on the nature and intent of informational annotation (the supplying of facts and contexts to make a document intelligible to the reader), see chapter 9, "Preparing a Documentary Edition for the Printer," 183–203.

Knapp, Patricia. *The Monteith College Library Experiment*. New York: Scarecrow Press, 1966.

A seminal work that recounts and analyzes the 1960–1962 experiment of Wayne State University's Monteith College to involve librarians in curriculum planning and design and to integrate bibliographic instruction into specific courses. The first assignment concerned the chronological development of man. Each student was given a list of books and asked to find the one he or she wished to use. A later freshman assignment asked students to read an autobiography and, using other sources, corroborate its story. In the second semester of the social sciences course students were assigned a series of tasks related to a semester-length research project, were required to use the library to orient themselves to the project, and perhaps also to find primary data. The final assignment required writing a research paper on a social movement.

Landes, David S., and Charles Tilly, eds. *History as Social Science: The Behavioral and Social Sciences Survey*. Prepared for the National Academy of Sciences and the Social Science Research Council. Englewood Cliffs, N.J.: Prentice-Hall, 1971.

Observes that historians are too often compelled to teach courses that cover broad fields or topics and are unable to concentrate their teaching on areas in which they are conducting research and are truly expert. The result is a stream of generalizations based neither on full understanding nor on research. More critical, inquisitive, and specific modes of inquiry are required. Suggestions for the training of undergraduate and graduate students: explicit and systematic instruction in research design and in the selection of appropriate research techniques; systematic exposure to the methodologies of the social sciences; and involvement in the creation, collection, and interpretation of "sources that are expressly valuable in the problems of social-scientific history." They "recommend that departments of history offer formal courses in historical method that include discussion of the appropriate literature of the other social sciences," and they pessimistically conclude that it would barely be an exaggeration to say that most graduate students receive no research instruction.

Lindgren, Jon. "The Idea of Evidence in Bibliographic Inquiry." In *Theories of Bibliographic Education: Designs for Teaching*, ed. Cerise Oberman and Katina Strauch, 27–46. New York: R.R. Bowker, 1982.

Encouraging students to use argument rather than an expository mode in their paper writing will compel them to engage source materials. A page from the *New York Times Index* is used as an example. This approach turns the library into a storehouse of potential evidence. Encyclopedias, dictionaries, abstracts, indexes, and book review sources receive special attention. Concludes with an appendix listing topics and the overview sources that would be useful in exploring them. The manipulation of Library of Congress subject headings and the syndetic nature of the catalog receive special attention.

McDonough, Kristin, and Pauline M. Rothstein. *Fundamentals of Research on the Ethnic Experience in the United States*. New York: Bernard Baruch College, Library Instruction Services, City University of New York, 1981. ERIC ED 229 027.

Designed to assist teaching faculty. A detailed packet of instructional notes, transparencies, bibliography, and exercises that aim at teaching undergraduates how to access and use books, articles, indexes, and abstracts.

Machalow, Robert. *The New York City Subways: The First Ten Years: A Library Research Exercise Using a Computer*. New York: York College, City University of New York, 1984. ERIC ED 255 211.

Documents a library research exercise that uses an Apple IIe and the word-processing software Applewriter to teach library research skills. Students are allowed to approach the problem by different paths, but to satisfy the requirements of the exercise they must consult the library's research collections themselves. Genres and tools introduced are: dictionaries, encyclopedias, indexes, the card catalog, books, periodicals, and newspapers.

McInnis, Raymond G., and Dal S. Symes. "Running Backwards from the Finish Line: A New Concept for Bibliographic Instruction." *Library Trends* 39, no. 3 (Winter 1991): 223–37.

Research, reading, and writing define the process of scholarship, and an appreciation of the function of schemata in the minds of learners is absolutely critical if we are to teach students to teach themselves. Schemata are defined as formal (a text's rhetorical structure) and content (a text's knowledge content). Using a op-ed article by Senator Daniel Patrick Moynihan, the authors lead students in a consideration of the importance of audience to the text; that is, were it written for a scholarly audience, how would it differ? Consideration is then directed to the role that "historical perspective" has on how we interpret information, how we read into a text, and what we see in it and are able to use from it. Believing that students need to practice these skills, sample assignments that have been used are discussed. Graduate students in a creative writing class search for historical and medical information to outline a mystery story set in Houston in the 1950s. History students work with op-ed articles, exploring how a popular piece may be turned into a scholarly article. They analyze its structure and indicate where they believe footnotes are necessary. A detailed consideration of rhetorical structures is done by analyzing actual scholarly articles. Students synthesize and demonstrate their learning through texts they compose around the op-ed article and then share with the class.

Miller, Steven Max, and Marjorie Markoff Warmkessel. "Bibliographic Instruction, History of the Book, and Post-Structuralism: An Unlikely Combination Helps to Expand the Critical Thinking Skills of Undergraduates." *Research Strategies* 8, no. 2 (Spring 1990): 59–65.

Discusses the library component of the undergraduate course titled "Introduction to Techniques of Literary Research and Analysis," offered at Pennsylvania's Millersville University. First, students are introduced to the various versions of the Twenty-third Psalm and to a variety of primary sources from the special collections department to show the mutability and evolution of texts. The second session focuses on the relationship between physical format and content. The result of the sessions is an expanded sense of context.

Milligan, John D. "The Treatment of an Historical Source." *History and Theory* 18, no. 2 (1979): 177–96.

When confronted with a document that does not conform to accepted views and interpretations the historian must determine the validity of the source. Discussion proceeds through the examination of such a document by way of approaches suggested in various methodological texts. Complementing a battery of logical questions the historian should ask is a consideration of the possibility of verifying events and people through other valid primary sources and, although not suggested by the author, the reference sources that make available accepted facts.

Minix, Dean A. "The Briefing Book Concept." *Teaching History: A Journal of Methods* 15, no. 1 (Spring 1990): 3–7.
Students are asked to make believe that they are preparing a briefing book for an ambassador to a country they have chosen to research. They are required to review popular news periodicals and newspapers, scholarly journals, as well as some standard reference serials: *Statesman's Yearbook* and *The Europa Handbook*. Students are to be brought to the library before beginning the assignment. While Minix encourages students to consult with him, there is no mention of systematic library instruction. He does note that most reference librarians will be happy to provide a resource briefing.

Nielsen, Erland Kolding. "On the Teaching of Subject Bibliography in History: Some Experiences and Views on a Methodological Approach to the Discipline with Specific Reference to Danish Conditions." *Libri* 24, no. 3 (1974): 171–208.
A history of instruction in literature searching in history is presented with specific reference to required bibliography courses in Danish university graduate history programs. The need to teach process aligned with content, and not merely reference tools, is discussed. In a discussion of pedagogical concerns, would-be practitioners are urged to design exercises relevant to historical study that demand a synthesis of content and process learnings. Tools should be related to one another logically and ultimately be employed in elucidating a topic, source, or problematic assertion. Such exercises should come from various perspectives of documentation and offer practice in critical skills. Tables are included that illustrate the bibliographical and technical divisions in the bibliography of history, and the search process. (See entry under R. P. Sturges.)

Perkins, Dexter, "We Shall Gladly Teach." *American Historical Review* 62, no. 2 (1957): 291–309.
Of interest to librarians in its plea for a broad historical understanding, its deprecation of an overemphasis on memorization, and its realization of the awesome and ever-growing fund of knowledge. Bibliographic skills positively address each of these concerns. His comment that "a well-trained person is under no great difficulty in getting more and more facts as he goes along" is indicative of the skills expected of an educated person—and of Perkins's ignorance of the extent of bibliographic illiteracy.

Perkins, Dexter, and John L. Snell. *The Education of Historians in the United States.* New York: McGraw-Hill, 1962.
A study, commissioned by the American Historical Association, into the nature of historical instruction in America's colleges and universities. What constitutes a successful seminar? "Introducing students to the bibliographical aids, key sources, and major depositories in his field, the instructor somehow manages to convey to them the intellectual challenge and excitement that he himself finds in his work." For their part, successful seminar students show initiative in finding sources and facts.

Pirsig, Nancy. "What a Historian Should Know." *Change Magazine* 8, no. 2 (1976): 33–36.
Discusses the design and development in Illinois of Sangamon State University's competency-based bachelor's program in history. The program is structured around three

areas of competency: an understanding of the major forces shaping the contemporary world; an understanding of oneself in the contemporary world; and an understanding of the function of culture in one's own and other societies. A prerequisite for the full realization of these goals is a fourth competency: "the ability to identify, locate, and interpret primary and secondary historical materials."

"Public History: State of the Art, 1980." *The Public Historian* 2, no. 1 (Fall 1979): 7–120.

A selection of comments made at the first national conference on public history held in 1979. Includes a survey of college and university programs in public history in existence that year. The survey identifies and describes four programs in institutions where library science plays an integral role: Emporia State University, the University of Maryland, the University of Michigan, and the University of Wisconsin–Madison.

Rayfield, Jo Ann. "Using City Directories to Teach History and Historical Research Methods." *Teaching History: A Journal of Methods* 16, no. 1 (Spring 1991): 14–26.

City directories are standard library reference sources. Consulted across time, they present an immense amount of demographic and economic data for comparative analysis. Five detailed exercises, designed for use with senior high school and beginning college students, guide students through explorations of: population growth, intracity residential mobility, occupational distribution, occupation mobility, and the evaluation of sources (a comparison of directory to census data).

Reddel, Carl W. "Using the Library to Teach History at the United States Air Force Academy." In *A Colorado Response to the Information Society: The Changing Academic Library*. Proceedings of a Conference (Denver, Colorado, October 6–7, 1983), ed. Patricia Senn Bervik. ERIC ED 269 017.

In the historical methods course "students are directly involved in exercises which demonstrate how libraries store and organize historical information and how the library provides the tools to identify and locate this information." In addition, students are provided with the opportunity to use primary source materials, and upper-division offerings familiarize students with information resources for the world's history—encouraging them to approach information problems through the eyes of specialists.

Reitan, E. A. "New Perspectives on Using the Library in History Teaching." *AHA Newsletter* 26, no. 4 (1978): 5–6.

Relates 1976–1977 experiences with a series of workshops designed to encourage cooperation between faculty and librarians in bibliographic instruction held at the Teaching-College Center of Illinois State University. One conclusion was that it is the historian's responsibility to bring students into contact with the special resources and techniques for historical research; another, that the library should play a pivotal role in "inquiry-oriented" instructional designs. Teachers should learn to perceive the library as students do and do library assignments themselves before finalizing them. Courses, and portions of courses, insofar as they relate to the library, should be planned in consultation with a librarian. Finally, faculty leadership in library use has been lost by default.

Rundell, Walter, Jr. "Clio's Ways and Means: A Preliminary Report on the Survey." *The Historian* 30, no. 1 (November 1967): 20–40.

Preliminary report of the Survey on the Use of Original Sources in Graduate History Training begun in 1965 and concluded in early 1967. Comments are based on the author's visits to 112 institutions; 557 interviews with professors, students, librarians, and archivists; and information garnered from nearly 200 questionnaires. Responses on the adequacy of bibliographic and methodological training were mixed and many, including students, felt that students were ill-trained to even handle manuscript materials or use bibliographic aids. Attempting to put some student criticism in perspective the author cautions that appropriate instruction may have been given in many instances but that "Few things are taught or learned once and for all. The ideal situation exists when methodological training coincides with a specific problem, but we cannot always rely on having ideal situations."

Rundell, Walter, Jr. *In Pursuit of American History: Research and Training in the United States*. Norman: University of Oklahoma Press, 1970.

Identifies over seventeen specific graduate programs then offering or having offered a methodology course. Some had a strong bibliographic emphasis. Although some courses had been discontinued, some students interviewed complained about the quality of their methods training. Many complained specifically of inadequate bibliographic skills. At Yale students urged the introduction of a methodology course, while faculty insisted that it was unnecessary. Noted is the failure of historians to take advantage of the technical expertise of archivists and librarians and a need to teach methodological skills broadly and creatively. It is suggested that many historians are so poorly trained bibliographically that they cannot appreciate the importance of such skills and are ill-equipped to pass them on to their students.

Sable, Martin H. "Bibliographic Instruction in Latin American Studies." *Latin American Research Review* 14, no. 1 (1979): 150–53.

Recounts the author's development and offering of an interdisciplinary graduate-level bibliographic research course in Latin American studies, in different iterations, at the University of California, Los Angeles, and later at the University of Wisconsin–Milwaukee. In its latter form the humanities were integrated into the course. Two basic methods of teaching reference sources are noted: the instructor explains each source and then requires students to compose practice questions to be exchanged with classmates for completion; or students are assigned a given number of sources for description on four-by-six-inch cards, some are then reported on orally, and the instructor assigns reference questions to be answered for later classes. Other exercises include the completion of a bibliography on any topic in the social sciences or humanities, and a five-hundred-word evaluative book review on Latin America as a topic in higher education is assigned.

Sanford, Carolyn C. "The Census in One Hour?: The Development of an Effective One-Shot BI Session." *Research Strategies* 9, no. 4 (Fall 1991): 202–5.

Details the seven-year evolution of an assignment designed to teach students to use statistical information to interpret data used by Daniel P. Moynihan in his *Negro Family: The Case for National Action*. In the first two years Sanford lectured students; in the third, students were given a handout and asked to examine the sources listed there; in the fourth year small groups of students were asked to examine the sources placed before them and to then explain them to the class. By the sixth year, students were given sample search topics, with the instructor wandering from group to group. The session's 1991 version had three components: the librarian conducted a sample search; small student groups attempted to carry out the same search; and the librarian reviewed their efforts and showed students where they had gone wrong. Illustrative material from each source was compiled into a handout; these were complemented by overhead transparencies. In

1992 Sanford planned to repeat the previous approach but also planned to distribute an outline of the search process.

Schaus, Margaret. "Hands-on History." *College & Research Libraries News* 51, no. 9 (October 1990): 825–31.

A librarian describes the role of bibliographic instruction in Haverford College's history department's junior year "Seminar on Historical Evidence." The first exercise of the seminar is the "explication" of a physical artifact. In a little less than a month students must: describe the object; explain the process they employed to identify it; and explain its social, cultural, and economic importance. The seminar's second project requires students to select a primary source document and to edit it, providing a full-range of explanatory footnotes as well as noting textual problems. Some completed papers have been published; all are placed in Haverford's archives. The initial bibliographic instruction session lasts ninety minutes. During this meeting librarians encourage students to think about various ways to investigate their historical artifact. Students receive bibliographic guides on historical artifacts as well as on history and related fields. The second library session is devoted to the etiquette of using manuscript material. Beyond these sessions students are encouraged to make private appointments with the library's subject specialists. Bibliographic instruction and consultation with librarians is now an important and integral component of this course, which is highly regarded by Haverford's faculty and students.

Schaus, Margaret, John Spielman, and Susan Stuard. "Introducing Undergraduates to Manuscript Research." *Perspectives* (American Historical Association) 29, no. 5 (May/June 1991): 16–18.

Schaus is a librarian and Spielman and Stuard are history professors. The course described here is much the same as the one described in the previous entry. To those who might wish to develop their own course, the instructors advise: you can use unpublished or poorly edited sources; assess your ability to collect objects and identify a member of the faculty knowledgeable in material culture; have all involved professionals meet before the offering of the course; select documents that are complemented by library holdings; alert librarians and special collections staff at your institution and in the area; accompany the two projects with useful shared readings; encourage individual consultation with experts; remember that two evaluations with written comments take time; and use the exercises to consider the issue of plagiarism.

Schnucker, R. V. "For New Stars Through Learning." *Learning Today* 6, no. 4 (1973): 55–64.

A history professor recounts turning the library into a classroom for a western civilization course. Among the innovations: he moved his office into the library and for a specific period of time required each student to report to him early each morning in the library; and he allocated regular class time for library research and made himself available in the library during that time. The first two class periods were devoted to discussions of the card catalog, various reference sources, and the methodology of building a bibliography. Students worked in teams and each team was required to: define the topic to be presented, give the background of the problem, briefly discuss events associated with the problem, summarize how historians have viewed the problem, and offer an opinion on its importance. There is no mention of formalized bibliographic instruction, and some librarians felt that bibliographic skills were not developed systematically; however, students were very pleased with the experience. The author notes that students turned naturally to him before turning to librarians for assistance.

Stinson, Robert. "Yesterday's News Is Today's History—Or Is It?" *OAH Newsletter* 17, no. 2 (May 1989): 6–7.

Studying history means making an abstraction of the past. That we reorder the past is obviously unavoidable but it can also lead us to mistake our history for history. Examining an old newspaper brings home the simultaneity of history. One experiences a context that is otherwise lost.

Sturges, R. P. "Subject Bibliography in the Service of History." *Library Review* 27 (1978): 90–94.

Elaborates on the Nielson report by explaining in greater detail the logistics and pedagogy of bibliographic instruction in Danish university history programs. The final examinations given at Aarhus, Copenhagen, and Odense are of particular interest. They are given in the library and take between three to four hours to complete. They focus on questions concerning a historical work and require checking facts, verifying bibliographic citations, identifying important secondary work on a given topic, and identifying primary sources. Odense and Copenhagen use a quotation from a historical work about which six questions are asked. The first three involve checking facts concerning matters mentioned in the questions. Questions are chosen so that the answer to each will be found in a different type of reference book. Students are taught to think of categories of reference sources rather than of specific sources. The other three questions are of a bibliographical nature. This exercise leads up to a final examination that is similarly structured and is itself preceded by sessions on various reference tools, first by type and then by period.

Walker, Samuel J. "Teaching the Method of History: A Documentary Exercise." *The History Teacher* 11, no. 4 (August 1978): 471–82.

Describes an exercise requiring students to compare two primary-source documents that give conflicting interpretations of the same event. The use of reference sources is not a part of this exercise, which is designed to take one class period. Included are questions to be asked of the documents that are used as examples (letters describing Tombstone, Arizona, in 1881).

Walter, Robert A. "A Historical Skills Approach to the U.S. History Survey." *AHA Newsletter* 14, no. 1 (1976): 4–7.

Argues that survey courses should concentrate on a conceptual knowledge of topics; far more important than the cramming of facts for such courses are instruction and practice with the tools of rational inquiry. These are identified as reading, writing, analyzing, examining, and synthesizing. Further, students must receive practice in the use of library aids and become familiar with those tools that will allow them independently to extend their knowledge.

Werking, Richard Hume. "Course-Related Instruction for History Majors." In *Putting Library Instruction in Its Place: In the Library and in the School*, ed. Carolyn A. Kirkendall, 44–47. Ann Arbor, Mich.: Pierian Press, 1978.

Librarian and historian Werking writes that faculty identify citations by "cycling" footnotes from "review articles" or from specialized bibliographies. These techniques serve well to keep one informed of what practitioners consider relevant. Students should be taught these methods with such enhancements as citation indexing and "current contents." But the major objective of bibliographic education for advanced history students should be instruction in the identification of primary source materials and in the identification of potentially relevant literature absent from current scholarly conversation be-

cause of its age, form of publication, or ideological slant. Also, instruction in accessing
the literature of other disciplines is necessary.

Werking, Richard Hume. "A Critical Look at Possibilities for and Obstacles to Library
    Use." *RQ* 31, no. 2 (Winter 1991): 162–66.

Librarian and historian Werking originally presented this article as a paper at the 1987
annual meeting of the Organization of American Historians, and it is based, in part, on
his 1978 essay from *Putting Library Instruction in Its Place*. The library, through its
collections, is "a place where conversations among colleagues are going on all the time."
To enable students to tap into these conversations, bibliographic instruction should: teach
them to locate important works, specialized bibliographies, and a review article; put
together a core bibliography through works cited in footnotes; and use citation indexes
to update a bibliography. In addition, instruction should alert students to access tools to
data sources and to material, which, because of its age, format, or disciplinary orientation,
they might not find. Why isn't instruction in library use common? Because faculty assume
such instruction is necessary only in graduate school since undergraduate education often
relies on lectures, textbooks, and reserve rooms; they assume such skills are learned in
high school; separate semester-length courses are offered on some campuses; faculty often
use instruction sessions for baby sitting or do not give assignments dependent on library
use; and often librarians design their instruction on too low a level, turning off both
students and faculty.

Widder, Agnes Haigh, and John Coogan. "Who Was Berut? Using Correspondence
    Between World Statesmen in Bibliographic Instruction." *Research Strategies* 5,
    no. 3 (Summer 1987): 135–38.

Describes a librarian's response to a document-editing exercise assigned by a history
professor. The assignment required that students "use reference materials in the library
to gain a full understanding of each specific reference in the letter." The librarian's
response was a voluntary introductory lecture that focused on reference sources considered
by genre.

VIII. EARLY BIBLIOGRAPHIC INSTRUCTION PROGRAMS IN HISTORY AND RELATED DISCIPLINES

Adams, Herbert B. "Seminary Libraries and University Extension." *Johns Hopkins
    University Studies in Historical and Political Science Series* 5, no. 11 (1887): 7–
    33.

Traces the evolution of the seminary (seminar) method of historical instruction from
its inception under Leopold von Ranke to its adoption in America. In the seminar under
"professional direction students find their own way in the university library to the proper
sources of information . . . fortified by books and documents borrowed from the university
library, and prepared with his brief of points and citations, like a lawyer about to plead
a case in court. Usually members of a seminary take their weekly turn in the presentation
and solution of some historical text, of which all have a copy." Seminary libraries in
Germany were usually owned by the professor, but by the time the method moved to
America expenses argued against this and university libraries placed books on reserve or
maintained separate facilities. The appointment of a librarian of the historical and political
sciences at Columbia University was seen as suggestive of future trends.

Adams, Herbert B. *The Study of History in American Colleges and Universities*. Bureau of Education Circular of Information, no. 2. Washington, D.C.: Government Printing Office, 1987.

Historian Adams explores history instruction in a cross section of the nation's colleges and universities: Harvard, Yale, Columbia, Cornell, Michigan, Johns Hopkins, Vassar, Wellesley, Smith, and Bryn Mawr. Many of the reports devote considerable attention to library matters. Among especially noteworthy information is that Columbia University was proud of a German-educated special librarian attached to the School of Political Science. This librarian offered a course that met once a week:

It gives an introduction, a brief encyclopedic statement of the discipline of political science and the several auxiliary disciplines. It takes up by countries, the material which forms the record of the political, legal, and economic activity of the leading modern states, giving a short sketch of the historiography of each; the special bibliographical works relating to the subject; then a description of all important collections of early chronicles and histories; collections of memoirs; collections and publications of historical and similar societies; general and special collections of treaties and diplomatic papers; statistical collections and other economic publications; government and official publications, including public documents, parliamentary debates, statutes, law reports, and other collective works in the field of public and private law. It is intended to give the title, proper form of citation, history, character of these publications, and the way in which they are indexed and may be used. An account of the archives and public records of each state treated is also given, with a description of their calendars or indexes, printed and unprinted; their general character, arrangement, and regulations for use.

A similar course was offered at Cornell.

Brundin, Robert E. "Justin Winsor of Harvard and the Liberalizing of the College Library." *The Journal of Library History* 10, no. 1 (January 1975): 57–70.

Winsor's career as a historian-librarian-teacher is traced, emphasizing the innovations he brought to the Harvard University Library where he greatly extended the reserve system that had been instituted earlier at the insistence of Professor Henry Adams. Winsor was an early proponent of bibliographic instruction and was convinced that the librarian should possess not only administrative ability but also have sympathy with the scholarly life and a "devotion to intellectual pursuits."

Cunningham, Raymond. "Historian Among the Librarians: Herbert Baxter Adams and Modern Librarianship." *The Journal of Library History* 21, no. 4 (Fall 1986): 704–22.

In late nineteenth-century America historians and librarians worked closely together. The introduction of the seminar demanded the development of seminar or department libraries. Adams was responsible for the development of the history seminar library at Johns Hopkins. He was a friend of many librarians, including Justin Winsor and William Frederick Poole. Profiled are his championship of department or seminar libraries, his influence on the development of the Newberry Library, and his role in the university extension movement as it relates to librarianship. Also discussed are his unrealized nominations to the librarianship of the New York State Library and to the directorship of the Columbia University library school.

Hopkins, Frances L. "A Century of Bibliographic Instruction: The Historical Claims to Professional and Academic Legitimacy." *College & Research Libraries* 43, no. 2 (March 1983): 192–98.

Traces the evolution of bibliographic instruction from the early nineteenth century to date, placing it within the casual context of the development of elective courses, the adoption of the seminary method of graduate instruction, and the emphasis on reference service. Concentration on problem solving and the structure of disciplines was the initial focus of library instruction, and it is appropriate that it be so again.

Hopkins, Frances L. "User Instruction in the College Library: Origins, Prospects, and a Practical Program." In *College Librarianship*, ed. William Miller and D. Stephen Lockwood, 173–204. Metuchen, N.J.: Scarecrow Press, 1981.
Traces the early history of bibliographic instruction arguing for an integration of bibliographic instruction with course content and method. Concludes with a discussion of instructional models: course-related, course-integrated, and curriculum-integrated instruction.

Little, G. T. "Teaching Bibliography to College Students." *Library Journal* 17, no. 8 (August 1892): 87–88.
Describes a bibliography course offered to students of English history in which a series of lectures traced the history of the book and of printing. The hour following each lecture was devoted to practice work in the library that revolved around solving practice reference questions such as, "show that, while Tamerlane was winning his bloody victories, Gutenberg could not have been 'playing ninepins in the streets of Mentz.' " Besides these questions each student spent approximately six hours in the preparation of a bibliographical essay on an assigned subject.

McCaslin, Davida. "The Library and the Department of English." *English Journal* 12, no. 9 (November 1923): 591–98.
Begins with the statement, "Everybody goes to college in these democratic times." Describes instruction in library research offered at Millikin University, which consisted of a detailed library tour, practice library questions, and lectures on the various types of bibliographic and reference sources. Attention is also given to note-taking skills and the issue of plagiarism.

Salmon, Lucy M. "Instruction in the Use of a College Library." *ALA Bulletin* 7 (July 1913): 301–9.
Trained in the seminar method and the use of seminary libraries by Professor Charles Kendall Adams at the University of Michigan, historian Salmon of Vassar explores the question, "Is library use instruction given better as an independent course, or in connection with a regular course?" She contends that bibliographic instruction is most effectively given within the context of a regular course and is best given by the professor. She also maintains, concerning the professor's role, "he cannot separate for the student the bibliography of a subject from the subject itself. Nor can he turn over to the librarian instruction in bibliographical work." A variety of handouts prepared for students are described.

Winsor, Justin. "The Development of the Library." *The Library Journal* 19, no. 11 (November 1894): 370–75.
An address given at the dedication of Northwestern University's library. At the time Winsor was librarian of Harvard University. He discusses the library within the context of the elective system, the seminary method of instruction, and the library's role in supporting independent inquiry, and he urges training for students in the use of books.

IX. ELECTRONIC INFORMATION SOURCES

Alexander, Thomas B. "History's Changing Sources and Techniques." *OAH Newsletter* 17, no. 4 (November 1989): 16.
Considers the way in which the technology of research has changed research topics, noting microfilming and photocopying as examples. Among new sources for historians are: film and television, survey research, and a whole universe of census and economic data. The author describes the pervasive presence of statistics across the profession, noting that future historians will have to be skilled in their interpretation and use.

Allen, David Y. "Computerized Literature Searching, a Do-It-Yourself Activity?" *Perspectives* (American Historical Association) 23, no. 2 (February 1985): 23–24.
After reviewing the advantages and complexities of the databases most suitable for historical researchers, concludes that although "the novice researcher can conduct a search and obtain useful results with practice," it is probable that "only a small minority of historians will want to do much computer literature searching on their own."

Allen, David Y. "A Look At Notebook II." *Perspectives* (American Historical Association) 29, no. 5 (May/June 1991): 10–11.
A detailed review of the database management program for text Notebook II, with a general explanation of how such programs work. Pro-cite is also discussed.

Burton, Vernon Orville. "History's Electric Future." *OAH Newsletter* 17, no. 4 (November 1989): 12–13.
Burton sees computer networks as democratizing historical research, making the same material available at the most prestigious institutions available to those working at smaller institutions. Mentions OCLC, RLIN, DIALOG, and the textual manipulations possible in an electric environment.

Caren, Loretta. "New Bibliographic Instruction for New Technology: 'Library Connections' Seminar at the Rochester Institute of Technology." *Library Trends* 37, no. 3 (Winter 1989): 366–73.
Notes that instruction has always worked best "when faculty corroborated by understanding library resources and incorporating them into coursework and assignments." Recounts a program offering faculty training in: "local connections (online catalog and remote access to it and electronic mail reference services), bibliographic connections (online databases, CD-ROM, access to regional networks), document delivery connections (ILL systems, online ordering through commercial vendors), and future connections—planned or imagined."

Cohen, David A. "Undergraduate On-Line Literature Searching." *Teaching Political Science* 14, no. 2 (Winter 1987): 69–73.
Explores databases useful for political science research and contemporary history, observing that online searches may be made for bibliographic citations, statistical data, or content. The latter receives special attention in the recounting of a particular example. Content analysis occurs when the user requests postings for the number of articles in which a particular word or variation of the word appears—either in the title, in a subject abstract, or in any combination of these three points of access.

Everett, David, and David M. Pilachowski. "What's in a Name? Looking for People Online—Humanities." *Database* 9 (October 1986): 26–34.

America: History and Life, Historical Abstracts, Arts and Humanities Citation Index, and the *MLA International Bibliography* do not have name indexes. Methods to achieve precise name searching are described.

Falk, Joyce Duncan. "Databases for Historical Research: Overview and Implications." *American History: A Bibliographic Review,* 4 (1988): 1–13.
Surveys the variety of bibliographic and nonbibliographic databases of value in historical work; citing specific examples, suggests ways in which computer files will facilitate research. Considered are factors such as the content of databases, the preservation and standardization of electronic data, and the skills historians will need to access computer files.

Falk, Joyce Duncan. "Humanities." In *Women in Online: Research in Women's Studies Using Online Databases,* ed. Steven D. Atkinson and Judith Hudson, 7–72. New York: Haworth Press, 1990.
After conducting searches on a women's studies topic across sixteen databases the author concludes that online databases in the humanities still reveal the limitations of their derivation from print indexes and that there is a decided need for improvements in geographical and historical period indexing. A need for hierarchical geographic indexing is noted. The databases discussed generally, and in light of women's studies, are: *Arts & Humanities Search, Humanities Index, Essay and General Literature Index, Eighteenth Century Short Title Catalogue, Research-In Database, America: History and Life, Historical Abstracts, MLA Bibliography, Philosopher's Index, Religion Index, Art Index, Artbibliographies Modern, Art Literature International, Architecture Database,* AVERY, and *RILM Abstracts.*

Falk, Joyce Duncan. "In Search of History: The Bibliographic Databases." *The History Teacher* 15, no. 4 (1982): 523–44.
Historian, librarian, and former director of the American Bibliographical Center (ABC-CLIO) discusses the strengths and weaknesses of online bibliographic databases by illustrating with sample searches the capabilities of *America: History and Life* and *Historical Abstracts.*

Falk, Joyce Duncan. "The New Technology for Research in European Women's History: 'Online' Bibliographies." *Signs: The Journal of Women in Culture and Society* 9, no. 1 (Autumn 1983): 120–33.
A standard discussion illustrated by sample searches of *Historical Abstracts* for material on "Women's Suffrage" and "Witchcraft in France."

Falk, Joyce Duncan. "OCLC and RLIN: Research Libraries at the Scholar's Fingertips." *Perspectives* (American Historical Association) 27, no. 8 (May/June 1989): 1, 11–13, 17.
Briefly describes the organization, administrative and bibliographic structure of the Research Libraries Information Network (RLIN) and the Online Computer Library Center Online Union Catalog (OCLC). The contents and special projects of each system are briefly described.

Falk, Joyce Duncan. *Survey of Online Searching in the Humanities in Four-Year College and University Libraries.* Irvine: University of California–Irvine University Library, 1985. ERIC ED 261 687.
Results of a survey of 1,160 institutions indicated that at best 10 percent of online searches were in the humanities and that most of these were from the *MLA, America:*

History and Life, and *Historical Abstracts*. Respondents complained of a lack of databases in some areas and limitation of coverage in others. About half of the respondents reported including some online searching in bibliographic instruction.

Grinell, Stuart F. "Reference Service, Online Bibliographic Databases, and Historians: A Review of the Literature." *RQ* 21, no. 1 (Fall 1987): 106–11.

Neither the critical literature on the topic nor on the databases themselves has reached a significant level of maturity. The incompleteness of the literature review prompted a rejoiner from Joyce Duncan Falk in *RQ* 27, no. 4 (Summer 1988): 594–95, which identified categories of material missed by Grinell.

Hannon, Hilary. *Discovering RLIN: An Introduction to the Research Libraries Information Network Database*. Mountain View, Calif.: Research Libraries Group, Inc., 1992.

An engaging and profusely illustrated forty-nine-page introduction to the wealth and diversity of materials and topical collections accessible through RLIN's databases and the CitaDel citation and document-delivery service.

Harter, Stephen P. "Scientific Inquiry: A Model for Online Searching." *Journal of the American Society for Information Science* 35, no. 2 (March 1984): 110–17.

Introduces the scientific inquiry model to describe the successful online search. "The conduct of scientific research . . . is a reiterative, cyclic, trial-and-error process, a process of successive approximation, in which the scientist and science collectively move ever closer to 'truth' but can never really know it, in which today's belief can be rejected at a later time." Beginning with the identification of a problem, scientific inquiry is a complex affair and it proceeds through "conjectures, hunches, intuitive leaps of imagination, evaluation of experiences, and dreams."

Harter, Stephen P., and Susan M. Jackson. "Optical Disc Systems in Libraries: Problems and Issues." *RQ* 27, no. 4 (Summer 1988): 516–27.

Takes a careful look at end-user searching, noting the seductiveness of electronic resources and presenting the sometime contradiction between convenience and efficiency on the one hand and quality and justified end-user satisfaction on the other.

Hurych, Jitka. "After Bath: Scientists, Social Scientists, and Humanists in the Context of Online Searching." *The Journal of Academic Librarianship* 12, no. 3 (July 1986): 158–65.

Reports the results of a survey of 462 university faculty members at Northern Illinois University, who were divided into five groupings: social sciences, medical professions, sciences, humanities, and administration. The most frequent users were social scientists and medical or health professionals. Scientists seem to have the best understanding of Boolean logic. Social scientists tend to define their area of interest in broadest terms. The overwhelming majority of social scientists requested information in English, while both the humanities and the sciences asked for material in other languages. Scientists and humanists expressed their needs most clearly, while social scientists used more databases than researchers in other disciplines.

Johnson, Margaret, Anita Lowry, Lynn Marko, and Katherine Chiang. In *Computer Files and the Research Library*, ed. Constance Gould. Mountain View, Calif.: Research Libraries Group, 1990.

How should libraries position themselves to deal with the burgeoning number of computer files? What are the skills librarians must have and the services libraries should offer? Papers associated with a 1989 RLG workshop of particular interest are Anita

Lowry's "Machine-Readable Texts in the Academic Library: The Electronic Text Service at Columbia University," 15–29, and Katherine Chiang's "Computer Files in the Library: Training Issues," 31–35.

Kenner, Richard M. "Historians in the Information Age: Putting the New Technology to Work." *The Public Historian* 4, no. 3 (Summer 1982): 31–48.
A general overview that focuses somewhat on archival publications, urges the establishment of an ERIC-like clearinghouse for papers, lectures, reports, and monograph-length studies that might not otherwise reach the public or professional communities.

Kiresen, Evelyn-Margaret, and Simone Klugman. "The Use of Online Databases for Historical Research." *RQ* 21, no. 4 (Summer 1982): 342–51.
Discusses some of the mechanical and attitudinal problems that account for low utilization of *America: History and Life* and *Historical Abstracts*. Reviews results of the Computer-Assisted Literature Searching Project at the University of California, Berkeley.

Kollmeier, Harold H., and Kathleen Henderson Staudt. "Composition Students Online: Database Searching in the Undergraduate Research Paper Course." *Computers and the Humanities* 21, no. 3 (July-September 1987): 147–55.
Freshmen see the composition course's research exercise primarily in terms of information gathering, while instructors would prefer them to see this component as part of the writing process. At Drexel University freshmen are taught the basics of online searching in the belief that the research process—definition, narrowing, and question formulation—is taught and practiced in searching. The use of BRS's TERM and CROS databases is discussed. Instruction is one-on-one, with the English instructor trained in online searching meeting the student at the terminal in a session that replaces the standard "so what is your topic?" conference. The logistics of the project are discussed in detail.

Lowry, Anita. "Beyond BI: Information Literacy in the Electronic Age." *Research Strategies* 8, no. 1 (Winter 1990): 22–27.
A graduate-level credit course offered by librarians at Columbia University to humanities students covers "personal information management, the systems of scholarly communication, and computer assisted textual research." One assignment requires students to compile a selected bibliography of at least twenty references on a topic and history students use *America: History and Life* and *Historical Abstracts* both online and in print.

Miller, Connie, and Patricia Tegler. "Online Searching and the Research Process." *College & Research Libraries* 47, no. 4 (July 1986): 370–73.
Contends that the best way scholars work can be described as "cyclical, organic, and intuitive." In trial-and-error searching the process of the search and its products can lead the researcher to alter the original understanding of the problem and may lead to additional sources of information.

Muratori, Fred. "RLIN Special Databases: Serving the Humanist." *Database* 13, no. 5 (October 1990): 48–57.
Databases offered through RLIN are described, and their special features are highlighted: AVERY (*Avery Index*), ESTC (*Eighteenth-Century Short Title Catalogue*), RIPD (*Research in Progress Database*), and SCIPIO (*Sales Catalog Input Project On-Line*).

Nash, Stan and Myoung Chung Wilson. "Value-Added Bibliographic Instruction: Teaching Students to Find the Right Citations." *Reference Services Review* 19, no. 1 (Spring 1991): 87–92.

The flood of inappropriate bibliographic citations that frequently occurs from a CD-ROM search led the authors to ''initiate a preliminary investigation to determine the range of problems that undergraduates face'' in critically evaluating search results. Of the students surveyed, 40 percent did not understand all the elements of the citations (they either misread or did not take advantage of provided information), 20 percent used the wrong databases, and 30 percent would have benefitted from consulting paper indexes. Based upon these findings, a two-tier instructional model is recommended: The first is a consideration of criteria such as an article's language, length, and audience that are useful in evaluating a citation, and the second is an appreciation of the nature of various sources and the relationship between sources, both in paper and on CD-ROM. The authors include a table of criteria to be used in evaluating search citations.

Neavill, Gordon B. ''Electronic Publishing, Libraries, and the Survival Of Information.'' *Library Resources & Technical Services* 28, no. 1 (January/March 1984): 76–89.
Contrasts the permanence of printed matter with the transience of electronic information. Urges that a system be set up to preserve electronic data since one never knows when it will be valuable, and the survival of work at various stages of development makes scholarship possible. Unlike the artifactual book, the computer file may not continue to exist simply because it is an object; nor may it exist as editions frozen in time.

Nicholls, Paul. ''United States History on CD-ROM: A Buyer's Guide.'' *CD-ROM Professional* 5, no. 3 (May 1992): 72–80.
Products discussed include: *America: History and Life*; *Congressional Masterfile*; *The Constitution Papers*; *DiscLit: American Authors*; *National Register of Historic Places Index*; *National Portrait Gallery: Permanent Collection of Notable Americans*; *North American Indians on CD-ROM*; *The Presidents: It All Started with George*; *U.S. Civics/ Citizenship*; *U.S. History on CD-ROM*; *U.S. Presidents*; *U.S.A. Wars: The Civil War*; and *U.S.A. Wars: Vietnam*.

Pastine, Maureen, and Laura Osegueda. ''Computer Databases in Academic Libraries: Implications for Language and Literature Research.'' *Literary Research Newsletter* 8, nos. 2/4 (Summer/Fall 1983): 107–17.
A very general introduction to online bibliographic databases available through Dialog and BRS, the RLIN and OCLC cataloging databases, and online circulation systems, and an assessment of the advantages and disadvantages of online searching.

Reiff, Janice L. *Structuring the Past: The Use of Computers in History*. Washington, D.C.: American Historical Association, 1991.
Online catalogs, bibliographic databases, electronic mail, and spreadsheets and fixed-field databases are discussed in chapters that succinctly convey a good sense of how computers may be used in historical research. In addition, the author provides some examples of various statistical techniques, samples of online catalog records and Boolean searching, and a helpful bibliography with some brief annotations.

Rowe, Judith S. ''Primary Data for Historical Research: New Machine-Readable Resources.'' *RQ* 21, no. 4 (Summer 1982): 351–56.
Discusses various statistical data files useful to historians for the study of such topics as demography, political conflict, public policy, and elections.

Rowney, Don Karl. ''The Microcomputer in Historical Research: Accessing Commercial Databases.'' *The History Teacher* 18, no. 2 (February 1985): 227–42.

In an easily understood manner explains how a computer searches bibliographic files and, perhaps too selectively, outlines commercially available bibliographic databases that should be of special interest to historians.

Shera, Jesse H. "New Tools for Easing the Burden of Historical Research," *American Documentation* 10, no. 4 (October 1959): 274–77.

A variety of new technologies for controlling information are briefly discussed. Particular attention is given to the "microform workstation," but the contemporary computer is not seen as capable of responding effectively to bibliographic problems. Librarian and historian Shera writes: "Doubtless every historian has sighed for the day when he could procure the data he needs with a metaphorical clap of the hands. That day is not yet here, but its advent is, perhaps, no more incredible than would have been the typewriter to those who wrote in cuneiform on tablets of clay."

Shill, Harold. "Bibliographic Instruction: Planning for the Electronic Information Environment." *College & Research Libraries* 48, no. 5 (September 1987): 433–53.

Higher education is being transformed by major changes in society: an increase in nontraditional and foreign students, growing use of computer technology, an expansive vocational curriculum, and the development of partnerships between industry and higher education. The electronic environment presents certain challenges: an erosion of the formal system of communication, gaps in the information structure of some disciplines, and user ignorance of relevant databases. Librarians have a responsibility to instruct patrons in the strengths and weaknesses of online systems, to teach the use of alternative print tools and cost minimization in the use of electronic ones, and to teach electronic browsing or serendipity. "The library's mission can be defined quite simply as the provision of intellectual and physical access to information and knowledge." The primary goal is to instruct users in accessing information, not primarily in microcomputer use. The adoption of "information literacy" as a goal—providing students with skills and conceptual frameworks for lifelong learning—redefines the library's role on campus.

Stern, Peter. "Online in the Humanities: Problems and Possibilities." *The Journal of Academic Librarianship* 14, no. 3 (July 1988): 161–64.

There has not been a revolution in the use of online databases on the part of historians because of "a paucity of suitable subject files; the total lack of a large cumulative databank of historical sources; satisfaction with comfortable and familiar, if haphazard and inadequate, research methods; the lack of a disposition to use new techniques of data retrieval; and, most critically, the lack of money to establish and use such facilities."

Stielow, Frederick, and Helen Tibbo. "The Negative Search, Online Reference, and the Humanities: A Critical Essay in Library Literature." *RQ* 27, no. 3 (Spring 1988): 358–63.

Researchers in the humanities do not ask the factual questions that librarians have traditionally been trained to answer because they consider themselves bibliographic experts. The librarian's opportunity to indicate that online databases have nothing on a topic may encourage the researcher to consult the librarian; determining that nothing has been done on a topic can be extremely valuable.

Still, Julie. "ABC-CLIO's History Databases on CD-ROM." *CD-ROM Professional* 5, no. 3 (May 1992): 83–86.

Describes the content, access points or fields, display options, print/download options, and Boolean search capabilities of the CD-ROM versions of *America: History and Life* and *Historical Abstracts*.

Swanson, Don R. "Information Retrieval as a Trial-and-Error Process." *Library Quarterly* 47, no. 2 (1977): 128–48.

Browsing is a trial-and-error search technique. Classification brings books with at least some shared commonality together where they can be "rapidly examined and rejected until something relevant . . . to the problem at hand is found." In online searching as in browsing, whether it is relevant or irrelevant what one finds has a role in shaping further requests, that is, the nature of further inquiry. This is because the request is nothing more than a guess as to what information may be useful. The relevance of a retrieved citation can only be created by the researcher.

Sweetland, James H. "*America: History and Life—A Wide-Ranging Database.*" *Database* 6 (December 1983): 15–29.

Historian and librarian Sweetland reviews, using tables and sample searches, the basic procedures for searching *America: History and Life* online. Sample searches are illustrated for dissertations, book reviews, concepts, and date of subject.

X. ABSTRACTING AND INDEXING HISTORY

American Historical Association. *AHA Bibliography Report: Toward A Central Bibliographical Service.* 1976. Available upon request from the American Historical Association. Abstracted in the *AHA Newsletter* 14, no. 5 (1976): 2–3.

Summarizes the developments that followed the 1967 Belmont Conference. A record of logistical and financial problems and disappointments. The creation of a central and machine-readable bibliographic service under the control of the AHA is urged. This recommendation was made after a study group concluded that there was then a needless duplication of bibliographic effort at an unwarranted expense. It was further concluded that the recommended central agency should perform a clearinghouse function, evaluating, coordinating, and assisting "many isolated projects" with grant proposals.

Boehm, Eric H. "Dissemination of Knowledge in the Humanities and Social Sciences." *ACLS Newsletter* 15, no. 5 (May 1963): 3–12.

Growth in the number of periodicals has created a dissemination crisis: "The number of scholarly periodicals mankind has given birth to, only 10,000 at the beginning of this century, was nearly 100,000 around the middle of the century and is anticipated to be 1,000,000 at the end of this century." An inventory of available aids should be made and standards for bibliographies established, especially in the humanities (scope and criteria for selection should be clearly stated). Journals in the liberal arts would do well to include abstracts, and a scanning recognition of many languages might better serve many scholars than a thorough knowledge of one language.

Boehm, Eric H. "Twenty-five Years of History Indexing: A Practitioners Report." *The Indexer* 11, no. 1 (April 1978): 33–39.

The founder of *America: History and Life* and *Historical Abstracts* describes the early history of these ventures. The four generations of indexing systems that have been employed are reviewed: a conventional hierarchical system, a decimal system, the cue system, and SPIndex (Subject Profile Index).

Boehm, Ronald J. *ABC-CLIO: A 25 Year History.* Santa Barbara, Calif. and Oxford: ABC-Clio, 1981.

Ronald Boehm, Eric Bochm's son, wrote this general history of the founding of the company and thus of the early years of *America: History and Life* and *Historical Abstracts*. A useful contribution to understanding the politics and commercial factors that have affected the bibliographic control of historical literature. Indexing systems are not covered. Illustrated with photographs.

Falk, Joyce Duncan. "Computer-Assisted Production of Bibliographic Databases in History." *The Indexer* 12, no. 3 (April 1981): 131–39.

An explanation, with facsimiles of editorial paperwork, of how *America: History and Life* and *Historical Abstracts* are produced. The SPindex System is discussed in detail.

Falk, Joyce Duncan. "Why Abstracts?" *Editing History* 5, no. 1 (Spring 1988): 6–8.

Notes that abstracts save the researcher significant amounts of time and may well provide access to information and approaches and methodologies that are not directly and obviously related yet are, nonetheless, pertinent to one's research. In the online environment abstracts provide many access points to the literature. The submission by authors of abstracts along with a manuscript will speed up the entry of contributions into the bibliographic universe. While Falk believes abstracts are best written by professional abstracters, she concludes that author abstracts are most practicable. The most appropriate place for an abstract is at the head of an article, the next most desirable place in the table of contents. Falk advises of abstracts: "The keynotes are accuracy, objectivity, (no comments or added information), and economy of language. The language and syntax should be direct, in the active voice, and easy to read."

Garfield, Eugene. "Is Information Retrieval in the Arts and Humanities Inherently Different from That in Science? The Effect That ISI's Citation Index for the Arts and Humanities Is Expected to Have on Future Scholarship." *Library Quarterly* 50, no. 1 (January 1980): 40–57.

For the humanities researcher, the past is never outdated. In fact, as we try to understand ourselves we project contemporary perceptions onto the past. The range of cited material will thus be far more diverse in this index than in its science counterpart. *Arts and Humanities Citation Index* is seen as a source that will break the insularity of humanities scholarship by encouraging and facilitating its users to cross disciplinary boundaries.

Gilmore, Matthew Benjamin. "Observations on the Indexing of History: The Example of the *Journal of American History.*" *The Indexer* 16, no. 3 (April 1989): 159–62.

Analyzes the evolution of headings through the combination of the current awareness services "Recent Articles" and "Recent Dissertations" into "Recent Scholarship" in the *Journal of American History*. Initially headings for these bibliographies were geographic but, reflecting changes in the discipline, headings are now largely for subjects. The gradual change in emphasis has been from geography to time and topic.

Perman, Dagmar Horna, ed. *Bibliography and the Historian: The Conference at Belmont of the Joint Committee on Bibliographical Services to History, May 1967.* Santa Barbara, Calif.: Clio, 1968.

Records the profession's first introduction to the possibilities of computer technology. In 1965 the Organization of American Historians joined with the American Historical Association in the formation of the Joint Committee on Bibliographical Services to History. Historians, librarians, and bibliographers were represented at the 1967 meeting. The volume comprises twenty-three papers on such topics as computer-produced finding aids and various Library of Congress automation projects. The committee recommended to the American Historical Association that *Writings on American History* be reorganized and that computers be employed in bibliographic projects.

Rosenberg, Jane A. "The Importance of Printing Abstracts: A User's View." *Editing History* 5, no. 2 (Fall 1988): 6.
Emphasizes the time savings to the researcher who uses abstracts. It is difficult without abstracts to review the current journal literature for material that is substantially unrelated but may have some methodological importance. The journal literature is growing so rapidly that there need to be ways to sort out the relevant from the less relevant. The author is suspicious of the quality of work of the volunteer abstracters for *America: History and Life* and *Historical Abstracts*.

Rubanowice, Robert J. "Of Librarians and Historians: Intellectual History and the Organization of Knowledge." *The Journal of Library History* 10, no. 3 (July 1975): 264–71.
Historians classify as they conduct research and immediately understand that history is not isolated in the 900 classification of the Dewey Decimal system but spans the various classifications. Intellectual history is transdisciplinary, and the intellectual historian is served best by a classification system that is exhaustive, analytical, pre-coordinate, and based on facet subject cataloging. In fact, the most thorough form of exhaustive, pre-coordinate indexing possible would include the indexes to all books in a library.

Schnucker, R. V. "The Abstract and the History Journal." *Editing History* 2, no. 2 (December 1985): 2–3.
Not many historical or humanities journals provide abstracts of their articles. The author reports on abstracting by a number of abstracting sources, observes that abstracts could easily be composed by the staff of journals, and explains why abstracts are valuable.

Tibbo, Helen R. "Abstracts, Online Searching, and the Humanities: An Analysis of the Structure and Content of Abstracts of Historical Discourse." Ph.D. diss., University of Maryland, College Park, 1989.
Considers the philosophic and linguistic aspects of historical discourse in relation to a "well-formed" abstract. Comparison is made to the abstracts of other disciplines, and historians were interviewed concerning their information-seeking behaviors and their conception of an ideal abstract. Based on this data a new set of ideal abstracting guidelines is outlined, and the operational specifications for an optimal information storage system are presented. Abstracts should include: specific date and time-span indicators; names of geopolitical units; names of individuals, groups, institutions, and organizations; identification of events; key topical terms; historical and historiographic context; purpose and scope of the text; the author's main theses; description of methodologies; and identification of primary sources.

Wibberly, Stephen E., Jr. "Subject Access in the Humanities and the Precision of the Humanist's Vocabulary." *Library Quarterly* 53, no. 4 (1983): 420–33; and Wibberly. "Names in Space and Time: The Indexing Vocabulary of the Humanities." *Library Quarterly* 58, no. 1 (January 1988): 1–28.
Names of people can be straightforward access points. But conceptual terms can have varying meanings across the disciplines; thus they merit the same careful authority work that is devoted to names and, perhaps, linkage to a controlled vocabulary. The lowest level of precision for names is for general proper nouns that "express a range of meanings, encompass many people, or include a multiplicity of creative works." The degree to which names can be differentiated in place and time distinguishes the precision with which they can be used in indexing.

XI. HISTORIANS' USE OF U.S. GOVERNMENT DOCUMENTS

Hernon, Peter. *Uses of Government Publications by Social Scientists.* Norwood, N.J.:
    Ablex Publishing, 1979.

Interviews suggest that historians, along with other social scientists, utilize comparatively few types of government publications. Those that are used are: statistical publications and census reports, congressional hearings and committee prints, annual reports, court cases, certain foreign policy material, serial set items, and reports of investigations conducted by federal agencies and special commissions.

Morton, Bruce. "U.S. Government Documents as History: The Intersection of Pedagogy
    and Librarianship." *RQ* 24, no. 4 (Summer 1985): 474–81.

The critical element in research is knowing what one needs to know to answer a particular query. Morton suggests that more important than discussing access tools and how to use them is instruction in the "application to history of the information to which those tools might lead." Emphasis should be placed on "the discipline and its information requirements rather than on the reference titles that are the product of those requirements." In framing library instruction, this kind of information is far more important than discussing the kinds of reference tools.

Sears, Jean L. and Marilyn Moody. *Using Government Publications.* Phoenix, Ariz.:
    Oryx Press, 1985–1986. 2 vols.

Profusely and skillfully illustrated and clearly written, chapters of particular interest to history students cover the use of current and retrospective materials and the research process under the chapters: "Historical Searches," "National Archives," "Legislative History," "Treaties," "Foreign Policy Historical Sources," "Genealogy," and "The President: Archives and Manuscript Sources."

Zink, Steven D. "Clio's Blindspot: Historians' Underutilization of United States Gov-
    ernment Publications in Historical Research." *Government Publications Review*
    13, no. 1 (February/March 1986): 67–78.

The failure of historians to utilize the genre fully is attributed to the unsystematic training they receive as graduate students and to the unwillingness of historical journals, until recently, to review U.S. government documents and pertinent bibliographies and indexes.

XII. RELATIONS BETWEEN HISTORIANS AND LIBRARIANS

Allen, David Y. "Historians as Academic Librarians: Proposals and Problems." *AHA
    Newsletter* 28, no. 3 (1980): 10–11.

Historian and librarian Allen argues that the negative perceptions the professions have of one another inhibit their effective cooperation in academic libraries and in the larger academic community. Librarians often carry a self-defeating inferiority complex into their dealings with other academics. Bibliographic instruction is seen as most effective when it is course-integrated, but in such instances historians and librarians are compelled to work as colleagues—a partnership that they too often find uncomfortable and that historians often feel is unwarranted. Nonetheless, suggests one- and two-session library components in history courses and sees the doctoral degree as unnecessary for effective bibliographic work in history, urging the development of special programs by history departments to train librarians for such work.

Gottschalk, Louis. "Possible Readjustments by the Scholar." *Library Quarterly* 23, no. 3 (July 1953): 203–15.

A historian offers a "modest proposal" to facilitate historians' use of primary sources. Argues against the maintenance of special collections and urges libraries to sell their esoteric items, those that are not of exceptional value, to individual scholars and even suggests that libraries subsidize the effort. In the case of an especially esoteric item, argues that librarians are preserving the item for no one in particular, while they may well be inconveniencing the one person who wants to use it. Libraries are advised to rely on microform for archival copies.

Logsdon, Richard H. "The Librarian and the Scholar: Eternal Enemies." *Library Journal* 95, no. 16 (September 15, 1970): 2871—74.

A former dean of libraries of the City University of New York reflects on a conversation he had with Columbia University historian Austin Evans: "the librarian and the scholar are eternal enemies." To the library a group of scholars looks like an anarchy and not a community. Yet libraries cannot function like anarchies, they cannot do everything, they cannot supply anything the moment it is needed, and so forth.

McCrank, Lawrence J. "Public Historians in the Information Professions: Problems in Education and Credentials." *The Public Historian* 7, no. 3 (Summer 1985): 7–22.

A medievalist, library school professor, and library administrator contends that "instead of promoting the cause of history as a strong ally of librarianship, thereby keeping the avenue open to historians seeking alternatives to teaching careers, history departments are failing to teach their students basic skills such as the use of libraries and information sources." Summarizes studies of the bibliographic skills of historians. Career opportunities in archives, information science, and libraries are surveyed.

Rundell, Walter, Jr. "Relations Between Historical Researchers and Custodians of Sources Materials." *College & Research Libraries* 29, no. 2 (November 1968): 466–76.

Reports the results of a survey of various problems encountered by graduate students while doing dissertation research with original sources. Historical researchers are found to have generally good relations with librarians and curators although some points of friction exist. The latter are seen as a consequence either of library shortcomings or of imperfect communications between faculty and the library administration; for instance, materials decisions affecting research are sometimes made by librarians without consulting faculty. For their part, historians are faulted for sometimes giving library assignments to classes without first consulting or even informing the library staff.

XIII. RESEARCH GUIDES AND MANUALS

Altick, Richard D. *The Art of Literary Research.* 3d ed. Rev. by John J. Fenstermaker. New York: W.W. Norton, 1981.

Although this outstanding manual is devoted to literary research, it is applicable to historical work. Techniques for evaluating evidence, determining dates, writing and note-taking skills, and the basic tools for literary research are discussed and illustrated. Forty pages of exercises are included, some demanding extensive work. "Finding Material," 147–73, discusses the uses of the computer in humanities research as well as standard tools. "Libraries," 174–93, surveys libraries of major interest to literary researchers.

American Historical Association. *Guide to Historical Literature*, ed. George Frederick
    Howe. New York: Macmillan, 1961.
Replaces the 1931 edition and will be superseded in 1995 by a two-volume third edition
to be published by Oxford University Press. The new edition will present brief descriptive
and evaluative annotations for citations to sources across a wide array of concerns, and
reference tools will be integrated into each of its sections. It will be exhaustively indexed.
For many years the present guide of over 20,000 briefly annotated entries to important
secondary works, reference aids, and primary source collections—spanning all periods,
places, and topics—has been an invaluable resource. It remains useful as long as one
appreciates its age.

Barzun, Jacques, and Henry F. Graff. *The Modern Researcher*. 5th ed. Fort Worth, Tex.:
    Harcourt Brace Jovanovich, 1992.
This excellent work evolved from a Columbia University history department methodology seminar. "The Searcher's Mind and Virtues," 36–47 stresses imagination: "The
researcher must again and again 'imagine' the kind of source he would like to have before
he can find it." Other virtues are: accuracy, love of order, logic, honesty, and self-
awareness. "Finding the Facts," 48–95, conveys a sense of the capabilities of a research
library and reference collection in a number of brief but well-presented "logic-in-use"
scenarios. Additional topics discussed include the general organization of a library, the
catalog and its uses, and an overview of genres of reference materials. Among the author's
valuable insights: one learns one's ways in libraries by learning the ways of librarians;
the more one knows, the easier it is to imagine how and where to learn still more. The
sections on the limitations of computer use, included in "Finding the Facts" in the
previous edition, has been removed.

Benjamin, Jules R. *A Student's Guide to History*. 4th ed. New York: St. Martin's Press,
    1987.
"How to Research a History Topic" advises that a search begin with a set of well-
defined keywords, and it divides discussion of the card catalog into searches for information on people, places, and general subjects. Also discussed is the nature of usual
schemes for the organization of serials; techniques for bibliographically determining the
value of a monograph, note-taking skills; and how to study for an examination, write
book reviews, and complete reading assignments. "How to Write a Research Paper"
treats writing, organization, and documentation and includes a sample research paper.
These discussions are complemented by Appendix A, "Basic Reference Sources for
Historical Study and Research," which presents the various genres of reference tools,
and lists and selectively annotates major works under the following headings: Dictionaries,
Encyclopedias, Atlases, Yearbooks; Biography Collections; Newspaper Directories and
Indexes; Historical Periodicals; Government Publications and Public Documents; and
Subject Bibliographies that cover the history of Africa, the Near and Middle East, General
Asia, Latin America and the Caribbean, Canada, and the United States—with subdivisions
for Puerto Rican, Black, and Women's history. Appendix B outlines the Dewey and
Library of Congress classification systems.

Collins, Donald E., Dianne B. Catlett, and Bobbie L. Collins. *Libraries and Research:
    A Practical Approach*. 2d ed. Dubuque, Iowa: Kendall/Hall, 1990.
A wide-ranging and very clearly written introduction for undergraduates that focuses
on selecting a research topic, classification systems, periodicals, newspapers, government

publications, manuscripts, developing search strategies, and the preparation of bibliographies. Among topics covered are: online services, manuscripts, and interlibrary loan. Social science and historical examples predominate. Sections are illustrated with flow charts and facsimiles of pages from pertinent sources. A series of library exercises is included.

A Consumer's Guide to the Current Bibliography of Historical Literature: Antiquity, the Middle Ages, Modern Western Europe, North America, and Latin America. Prepared by the Bibliography and Indexes Committee, History Section, Reference and Adult Services Division, American Library Association. RASD Occasional Papers no. 2; Consumer's Guide to Reference Works in History no. 1. Chicago: Reference and Adult Services Division, American Library Association, 1988.

A Consumer's Guide to Ready Reference Sources in History: General Antiquity, the Middle Ages, Modern Western Europe, the United States, and Latin America. Prepared by the Bibliography and Indexes Committee, History Section, Reference and Adult Services Division, American Library Association. RASD Occasional Papers no. 6; Consumer's Guide to Reference Works in History no. 2. Chicago: Reference and Adult Services Division, American Library Association, 1990.

A Consumer's Guide to Research Guides for Historical Literature: Antiquity, the Middle Ages, Modern Europe, the United States, and Latin America. Prepared by the Bibliography and Indexes Committee, History Section, Reference and Adult Services Division, American Library Association. RASD Occasional Papers no. 7; Consumer's Guide to Reference Works in History no. 3. Chicago: Reference and Adult Services Division, American Library Association, 1990.

All are straightforward and critically and comparatively annotated. Entries for each source are at least half a double-spaced page in length, and works in western European languages are included.

Cridland, Nancy C. "History." In *Selection of Library Materials in the Humanities, Social Sciences, and Sciences*, ed. Patricia A. McClung, 78–97. Chicago: American Library Association, 1985.

Advice to neophyte history bibliographers on how to do the job, and in this sense a peek behind office doors for professors and students. Includes a list of important periodicals and historical institutes.

de Graaf, Lawrence B. "Clio's Neglected Tools: A Taxonomy of Reference Works for American History." *The History Teacher* 25, no. 2 (February 1992): 191–231.

Reference tools, electronic and paper, are listed and briefly discussed under twenty-three categories comprising five broad conceptual groupings. Tools are discussed as representatives of these groupings and categories, and they are arranged by the type of material they contain, their scope, and their retrieval techniques. Broad groupings are: Guides to General History Reference Tools; Bibliographical Tools 1: Secondary Works (Primarily Books); Bibliographical Tools 2: Secondary Works (Other Than Books); Informational Reference Works; and Bibliographical Tools 3: Primary Documents, Non-Print Resources (includes newspapers, microforms, and databases). The author concludes with a warning of the potential dangers and inadequacies of online sources.

Freidel, Frank, ed. *Harvard Guide to American History*. Rev. ed., with the assistance of Richard K. Showman. 2 vols. Cambridge: Belknap Press of Harvard University Press, 1974.

"Research Methods and Materials," 3–134, is an extensive discussion of research aids in the field. It is now thoroughly outdated, however, and should be used with Prucha's guide cited later in this section.

Frick, Elizabeth. *Library Research Guide to History: Illustrated Search Strategy and Sources*. Library Research Guide Series, no. 14. Ann Arbor, Mich.: Pierian Press, 1980.

Designed for use with undergraduates. Like McCoy, cited later in this section, Frick takes the reader through the various steps of bibliographic searching by exploring a specific topic. It is generously illustrated with facsimiles of pages from the reference sources it considers. All sources included are well explained in sections that cover topic selection and note taking, topic definition, the use of periodical abstracts and indexes, government documents, biographical sources, guides to historical literature, and interlibrary loan. Concludes with an unannotated bibliography of basic reference sources and a library skills test.

Fritze, Ronald H., Brian E. Coutts, and Louis A. Vyhnanek. *Reference Sources in History: An Introductory Guide*. Santa Barbara, Calif.: ABC-Clio, 1990.

An up-to-date replacement for Helen Poulton's *Historian's Handbook: A Descriptive Guide to Reference Works* (1972) that reflects the dramatic increase in the publication of indexes, microforms, and electronic sources. Well-indexed and containing a detailed table of contents; detailed annotations evaluate, compare, and refer to over 685 reference works and complementing titles. English-language sources are overwhelmingly preferred. While *Walford's Guide to Reference Material* and the *Guide to Reference Books* cover many more titles, their size alone is daunting to undergraduates and beginning graduate students. Advanced researchers, however, must consult them as well as this source. Chapters are introduced by several contextual paragraphs on the type of source under discussion, and sources are discussed in annotated bibliographies. Main chapter headings are: "Guides, Handbooks, and Manuals for History"; "Bibliographies"; "Book Review Indexes"; "Periodical Guides and Core Journals"; "Periodical Indexes and Abstracts"; "Guides to Newspapers, Newspaper Collections, and Newspaper Indexes"; "Dissertations and Theses"; "Government Publications and Legal Sources"; "Dictionaries and Encyclopedias"; "Biographical Sources"; "Geographical Sources and Atlases"; "Historical Statistical Sources"; "Guides to Archives, Manuscripts, and Special Collections"; and "Guides to Microforms and Selected Microform Collections." Each of these main headings is further subdivided; for instance, under "Bibliographies" one finds these subheadings: Bibliographies of Reference Works and National Bibliographies and Library Catalogs. These headings are sometimes further broken down by geography, chronology, and/or type of source.

Gates, Jean Key. *Guide to the Use of Libraries and Information Sources*. 6th ed. New York: McGraw-Hill, 1989.

An excellent general undergraduate handbook, introduced by a brief history of the book and of libraries. Chapters are devoted to each type of reference source. Each genre is clearly defined, and points to consider when evaluating works within the genre are listed along with annotations for representative works. "Information Sources in Subject Fields" includes a chapter on history and geography, and the undergraduate term paper is discussed.

Gore, Daniel. *Bibliography for Beginners*. 2d ed. Englewood Cliffs, N.J.: Prentice-Hall, 1973.

A readable handbook that developed out of the author's teaching of basic bibliography courses at the University of North Carolina–Asheville. Topics covered are: the history of the book, descriptive bibliography, non-book-length sources, reference works, government documents, and search strategies. Sections on the mechanics of cataloging, classification, and the use of the catalog are especially useful. All sections are outdated.

Gottschalk, Louis Reichenthal. *Understanding History: A Primer of Historical Method.* 2d ed. New York: Alfred A. Knopf, 1969.

"How to Find Sources," 70–72, intelligently directs the researcher to standard guides to reference materials. "A Working Bibliography," 72–73, presents an outline of a working bibliography that a researcher would do well to fill in with appropriate encyclopedias, biographical dictionaries, the leading collections of unpublished documents, and so forth. "Where Does Historical Information Come from?" 86–117, is useful in its highlighting of general types of documentary sources. Bibliographic systems and search strategies are not considered.

Hockett, Homer Carey. *The Critical Method in Historical Research and Writing.* 1955. Reprint. Westport, Conn.: Greenwood Press, 1977.

American historian Hockett authored this guide, which deals exclusively with American history. The section on bibliographic tools, 85–129, is badly outdated but it remains useful for its discussion of the history of basic American history research tools. A later section, 254–60, discusses the development of the Library of Congress and the National Archives. A bibliography of general United States reference tools and of bibliographic tools for regional and state history is included.

McCoy, F. N. *Researching and Writing in History: A Practical Handbook for Students.* Berkeley: University of California Press, 1974.

Suitable for use with undergraduates. Like Frick, previously cited in this section, McCoy walks the reader through a term paper on a specific topic. Not only does it clearly outline library search strategies and bibliographic tools most appropriate for each stage of research, as well as note taking and outlining, but it also indicates the internal sequence and amount of time that should be assigned to each stage and its components. While easier to read than Frick, it does not explain the mechanics of use. A bibliography of a suggested "Student's Home Reference Shelf" is included.

McDonough, Kristin, and Eleanor Langstaff. *Access Information: Research in Social Sciences and Humanities.* Dubuque, Iowa: Kendall/Hunt, 1987.

A basic undergraduate guide with numerous facsimiles used to illustrate discussions of how to use a wide range of indexes and abstracts as well as government documents and statistical sources. Guidance is also given on writing, note taking, and online searching. A brief chapter presents a basic strategy for historical research.

McInnis, Raymond G., and James W. Scott. *Social Science Research Handbook.* New York: Barnes and Noble, 1975. Reprint. New York: Garland, 1985.

Bibliographic and reference tools across the social sciences, including area studies, are treated in well-organized bibliographic essays. The discussion for "History" is organized under groupings for atlases and gazetteers, bibliographies, biographical dictionaries and directories, encyclopedias and dictionaries, handbooks and yearbooks, historiographical and methodological works, and statistical sources. There is also a chapter for the "History of Science and Technology." See pages 89–92 for commentary on the way encyclopedias reflect the age and context in which they were written. The handbook is nearly twenty years old, but it is still useful.

Mann, Thomas. *A Guide to Library Research Methods*. New York: Oxford University
	Press, 1987.
	An outstanding, straightforward guide that offers plenty of good advice without getting
bogged down in excessive description and bibliographic detail. The author was an academic researcher at the doctoral level, a graduate student in library science, a private
investigator with a detective agency, a free-lance researcher, a reference librarian at two
university libraries, a specialist in government documents and microforms, a database
searcher, and a reference librarian at the Library of Congress. The utility of various
sources and search techniques is compared and contrasted throughout. Chapter headings
make clear the practical and often innovative character of the work: "Initial Overview:
Encyclopedias"; "Subject Headings and the Card Catalog"; "Systematic Browsing and
the Use of the Classification Scheme"; "Subject Headings and Indexes to Journal Articles"; "Published Bibliographies"; "Computer Searches"; "Locating Material in Other
Libraries"; "Talking to People"; and "Hidden Treasures" (microforms, government
documents). Mann concludes that most people do research by looking at footnotes, general
browsing, and ineffectively using card catalogs. Of librarians he writes, "Even though
they may not know particular titles names within a subject area, they do know beforehand
that they can reasonably expect to find certain types of sources within which they can
reasonably expect to find certain methods of access available, each with its own advantages
and disadvantages. They therefore usually understand the full range of options for finding
information even on unfamiliar subjects; for this reason they can usually provide material
on a subject more efficiently than even full professors within the discipline."

Poulton, Helen J. With the assistance of Marguerite S. Howland. *The Historian's Hand-
	book: A Descriptive Guide to Reference Works*. Foreword by Wilbur S. Shep-
	person. Norman: University of Oklahoma Press, 1972.
	The importance of this work is attested to by the six printings it has gone through since
its first appearance, but Fritze, Coutts, and Vyhnanek's *Reference Sources in History:
An Introductory Guide* is far more up-to-date. Nonetheless, Poulton remains useful for
the contextual and historical discussions that are interwoven throughout the bibliographic
essays that compose its sections. For instance, in its consideration of U.S. government
documents the legislative process is sketched and appropriate reference sources and
government documents are noted. Chapters, subdivided into sections, cover the usual
groupings of catalogs, guides, encyclopedias and dictionaries, geographical aids, and so
forth. Foreign-language sources are only very selectively included, and title and general
indexes are provided.

Prucha, Francis Paul. *Handbook for Research in American History: A Guide to Bibli-
	ographies and Other Reference Works*. Lincoln: University of Nebraska Press,
	1987.
	This guide, written by a historian who has been teaching students American history
for over twenty-four years, should be owned by all students of American history. This
work is characterized by a combination of annotated and unannotated entries for major
bibliographic and reference sources. Items of broad utility are discussed in the text and
more specialized items are listed. Although bibliographic and reference sources are compared and contrasted, the work is short on bibliographic advice. Part 1 is organized under
the following chapters: "Libraries: Catalogs and Guides"; "General Bibliographies";
"Catalogs of Books and Imprints"; "Book Review Indexes"; "Guides to Periodical
Literature"; "Manuscript Guides"; "Guides to Newspapers"; "Lists of Dissertations

and Theses''; ''Biographical Guides''; ''Oral History Materials''; ''Printed Documents of the Federal Government''; ''The National Archives''; ''State and Local Materials''; ''Guides to Legal Sources''; ''Atlases, Maps, and Geographical Guides''; ''Encyclopedias, Dictionaries, and Handbooks''; and ''Databases.'' Part 2 is organized topically: ''Political History''; ''Foreign Affairs''; ''Military History''; ''Social History''; ''Ethnic Groups''; ''Women''; ''Blacks''; ''American Indians''; ''Education''; ''Religion''; ''Economic History''; ''Science, Technology, and Medicine''; ''Regional Material''; ''Travel Accounts''; and ''Chronological Periods.'' An author, title, and subject index provides access to the volume.

Shafer, Robert Jones, ed. *A Guide to Historical Method*. 3d ed. Homewood, Ill.: Dorsey Press, 1980.

Designed for use with undergraduates at Syracuse University. ''Collecting Historical Evidence'' discusses techniques for recording bibliographic information, guides and indexes to government documents, journal and newspaper indexes, manuscript and archival guides, indexes to doctoral dissertations, union lists, and so forth. This treatment is complemented by an appendix that lists bibliographic and reference aids useful when studying specific countries: the United States, Great Britain, France, Germany, Mexico, and Kenya (those actively studied at Syracuse when the guide was published).

Sheehy, Eugene P., ed. *Guide to Reference Books*. 10th ed. Chicago: American Library Association, 1986. Supplemented by Balay, Robert, ed. *Guide to Reference Books, Covering Materials from 1985–1990. Supplement to the Tenth Edition*. Chicago: American Library Association, 1992.

America's ''official'' guide to reference materials across the disciplines. The number of works covered is less than in *Walford's Guide to Reference Material*, and foreign language material is not so well represented. Indexing, however, is superior, and many electronic resources are included in the *Supplement*.

Walford, Albert John, ed. *Walford's Guide to Reference Material*. 5th ed. London: Library Association, 1989–1991. 3 vols. See vol. 2: *Social and Historical Sciences, Philosophy, and Religion*, ed. by Alan Day and Joan M. Harvey.

Britain's ''official'' multivolume guide to reference material across the disciplines, the equivalent of the United States's *Guide to Reference Books*, which it surpasses in size. History is covered in volume 2, *Social and Historical Sciences, Philosophy, and Religion*, 604–766. All nations of the world are covered in English and European languages. While annotations are sometimes brief, references to reviews are often given, and parts of series or the components of multivolume works are consistently noted. Many encyclopedic sets are included, and it is especially useful for its unsurpassed foreign coverage. Examples of foreign guides include: Louise-Noëlle Malclès, *Manual de bibliographie*, 4e éd., rev. et augm. par Andrée Lhéritier (Paris: Presses universitaires de France, 1985) and Wilhelm Totok, *Handbuch de bibliographischen Nachschlagewerke*, Totok, Rolf Weitzel; hrsg. von Hans-Jürgen und Dagmar Kernchen, 6 erw., völlig neu bearb, Aufl. (Frankfurt am Main: V. Klostermann, 1985).

Webb, Walter H., ed. *Sources of Information in the Social Sciences: A Guide to the Literature*. Chicago: American Library Association, 1986.

A superb guide to the bibliographic structure of the social sciences and to its disciplines' major reference works. Each discipline is treated in a separate chapter. Chapters begin with a bibliographic overview of the discipline that cites major monographs, and are followed by a survey of reference works. History's ''Survey of Reference Works,'' 122–

48, contains well-annotated entries that reference additional sources under the general headings: Basic and General Guides; Reviews of the Literature; Online Databases for Historical Research; Bibliographies of Bibliographies; Current Bibliographies; Retrospective Bibliographies; Directories and Biographical Information; Encyclopedias and Encyclopedic Sets; Dictionaries, Handbooks, Manuals, and Compendia; Original Sources; Atlases, Maps, and Pictorial Works; Sources of Scholarly Contributions; and Sources of Current Information. These headings are further subdivided. (For the work's overview of social science research methods and literature, see Stephen Stoan, page 316.)

XIV. ETHICAL AND INTELLECTUAL ISSUES IN DOCUMENTING HISTORICAL RESEARCH

Plagiarism

Shaw, Peter. "Plagiary." *The American Scholar* 51, no. 3 (Summer 1982): 325–37.

Historian Shaw, author of *American Patriots and the Rituals of Revolution* and *The Character of John Adams*, recounts the history of plagiarism, long ago and recent. Citing specific individuals and works, he explores its psychology. Distressed by the literary world's apparent inability to punish reasonably or even take seriously this breach of morality, Shaw counsels: "Where there is an injured party, or where professional advancement over others has been gained through the employment of plagiarism, the issue must be brought out into the open. But when no one has been hurt, those privy to the circumstances, usually the plagiarist's colleagues and peers, ought to be counted on to inflict punishment enough with their personal disapproval." For a thorough overview read Thomas Mallon's *Stolen Words: Forays into the Origins and Ravages of Plagiarism* (New York: Ticknor and Fields, 1989).

The Role of Footnotes

Henige, David. "What Price Economy? The Decline of the Footnote in Historical Scholarship." *Editing History* 4, no. 1 (Spring 1987): 13–16.

The aggregation of footnotes, the reduction of multiple notes into one, endangers the reader's ability to test authors' arguments by following their reasoning through a step-by-step consideration of the data from which they argue. In short, this practice often makes it difficult to match source with argument or assertion. The author/date or "social science system," in addition, makes explanatory footnotes impossible. The author cautions that the increasing extent of interdisciplinary research will require more citations.

McInnis, Raymond G., and Dal Symes. "David Riesman and the Concept of Bibliographic Citation." *College & Research Libraries* 49, no. 5 (September 1988): 387–99.

Summarizes work on the topic, noting that a concept's meaning is valid only if scholars in the same field agree to its meaning. Observes that references have a persuasive function. A cited document is analogous to a subject heading; in fact, citations are enduring footprints on the landscape of scholarly achievement. Argues that the evolution of citation form corresponds with David Riesman's conceptualization of three types of personal character as developed in *The Lonely Crowd*. In the tradition-directed period titles come before authors, since the author is seen as the voice of God. In the transitional inner-directed period, the author's name precedes the title. Today, the other-directed period, the footnote is highly standardized and has become a symbol for substantive content as well as for intellectual ownership or primacy.

Rudolph, Janell, and Deborah Brackstone. "Too Many Scholars Ignore the Basic Rules of Documentation." *The Chronicle of Higher Education* 36, no. 30 (11 April 1990): A56.

Offering their own advice and comments, and citing studies of bibliographic inaccuracy among scholars, two librarians caution that tomorrow's scholars will depend on today's footnotes: "if . . . citations are inaccurate or incomplete, important ideas may be lost simply because they cannot be retrieved."

The Case of David Abraham's *The Collapse of the Weimar Republic: Political Economy and Crisis* (Princeton, N.J.: Princeton University Press, 1981)

Mason, T. W. [Review]. *American Historical Review* 87, no. 4 (October 1982): 1122–23.

A favorable review with praise that in retrospect was an ironic omen: "the argument is sustained throughout by effectively chosen quotations from a wide variety of primary sources."

Turner, Henry A., T. W. Mason, and David Abraham. [Exchange]. *American Historical Review* 88, no. 4 (October 1983): 1143–49.

Turner responds to Mason's review citing four examples of what he terms "slovenliness." He questions the very existence of some sources cited by Abraham and asserts that others "do not say what Abraham claims they do." Mason, who originally reviewed the work favorably, is shocked and affirms Turner's accusations. Abraham defends his conclusions, arguing that they are unaffected by bibliographic errors and that all of his sources do indeed exist.

Feldman, Gerald D., David Abraham, Douglas A. Unfug. "Debate: David Abraham's *The Collapse of the Weimar Republic.*" *Central European History* 17, nos. 2/3 (June/September 1984): 159–293.

An intensely heated and detailed exchange of accusation and defense. Feldman begins by accusing Abraham of "egregious errors, tendentious misconstruals, and outright inventions." He goes on, "It is certainly no less serious than plagiarism. . . . The delinquencies contained . . . are so extensive in number and so extreme in character to make the book a veritable menace to other scholars." Particular attention is directed to the problem of paraphrase and quotation, and he accuses Abraham of "consistently tendentious presentation." He accuses Abraham of frequently misquoting and interpreting secondary sources and, finally, of the "bizarre treatment of statistics." In his reply Abraham refers to the period when "I was a graduate student. While doing that research, I committed the embarrassing and elementary error of hasty and niggardly note-taking. The consequence was that my transcriptions sometimes yielded quotations that were flawed or not precise. My then practice of sometimes translating and transcribing on the spot served me ill, particularly given my technical competence in German at the time. Worst, over the next several years, looking back on my notes, I sometimes mistook summaries of documents for quotations."

The Case of Jayme Sokolow's *Eros and Modernization: Sylvester Graham, Health Reform, and the Origins of Victorian Sexuality in America* (Rutherford, N.J.: Fairleigh Dickinson Press, 1983)

Gray, Ralph D. "A Pinocchio in Academe: A Review, with Elaborations, of Thomas Mallon's *Stolen Words.*" *Editing History* 6, no. 2 (Fall 1990): 7–8.

Adds a few details to the Jayme Sokolow saga recounted below. The author is editor of the *Journal of the Early Republic* and recounts the context in which he received a plagiarized manuscript for consideration from Sokolow and his conversation with an old friend at Sokolow's institution that set in motion an investigation of Sokolow's deceptions.

Mallon, Thomas. *Stolen Words: Forays into the Origins and Ravages of Plagiarism.* New York: Ticknor and Fields, 1989.

See chapter 4, "Quiet Goes the Don: An Academic Affair," 144–93. Recounts the plagiaristic career of former history professor Jayme Sokolow, author of the plagiarized *Eros and Modernization*, and its consequences for Sokolow, as well as the manner in which colleagues and fellow scholars reacted to its discovery.

Index

ABC-Clio (company), 343–44
ABC-Clio Online, 264
ABC POL SCI: Advance Bibliography of Contents, 202
ABI/INFORM (database), 237
Abraham, David, 90, 355
Abstracting, 53, 85–86, 309, 343–45
Abstracts and summaries, 136
Abstracts in Anthropology, 185, 186
Aby, Stephen H., 205
Academic Index (database), 262
Academy and Community: The Foundations of the French Historical Profession (Keylor), 24
Access Information: Research in Social Sciences and Humanities (McDonough and Langstaff), 351
Adams, George Rolle, 302
Adams, Herbert Baxter, 334, 335
Adler, Douglas D., 320
Adler, Mortimer J., 129
Afro-American Encyclopedia (Rywell), 134, 152, 153
After the Fact: The Art of Historical Detection (Davidson and Lytle), 302
Age of Louis XIV, The (Voltaire), 9
Agricola (database), 237
Album of American History, 143
Alderson, Michael, 191
Aldous, Joan, 209,210

Alexander, Thomas B., 337
Allen, David Y., 320, 337, 346
Allgemeine Geschichtswissenschaft (Chliadenius), 20
Alston, Annie M., 303
Altick, Richard D., 218, 219, 302, 347
America: History and Life, 144, 309; abstracting for, 85; annotation of, 79; as a CD-ROM, 341, 342; finding book reviews with, 142; finding review articles with, 141; as an online database, 116–17,232–35, 248–49, 258–59, 340, 343, 358; sample search (Dialog) using, 338
American and French Research on the Treasury of the French Language (ARTFL), 232, 233
American Bibliography (Evans), 83
American Biographical Archive, 135
American Diaries: An Annotated Bibliography of American Diaries Written Prior to the Year 1861 (Mathews), 84
American Diaries: An Annotated Bibliography of Published American Diaries and Journals (Arksey, Pries, and Reed), 86
American Diaries in Manuscript (Mathews), 84
American Economic and Business History Information Sources (Lovett), 193

American Educational History: A Guide
(Sedlak and Walch), 198
American Historical Association, 343,
348
American Historical Association Task
Force on the History Major, 321
American Historical Review, 130, 141
*American History: A Bibliographic
Review*, 130
American Library Association, 349
*American Library Directory: A Classified
List of Libraries in the United States
and Canada*, 132, 151–52
*American Library Resources: A
Bibliographic Guide*, 126
*American Newspapers, 1821–1936: A
Union List of Files Available in the
United States and Canada*, 83, 141,
159
American Quarterly, 179, 182
*American Reference Books Annual
(ARBA)*, 172–73
American Statistics Index (ASI), 122
*American Studies: An Annotated
Bibliography* (Salzman),179, 182
American Working Class History
(Neufeld), 187, 188
*America Votes: A Handbook of
Contemporary American Election
Statistics*, 136, 139
*Ancient Constitution and the Feudal Law:
A Study of English Historical Thought
in the 17th Century, The* (Pocock), 20
Ancient Historians, The (Grant), 23
Ancient Writers: Greece and Rome, 135
Ankersmit, F. R., 21
Annales (school of historiography), 13–
14, 26–27, 40
Annales d'histoire économique et sociale,
26
*Annales: Economies, Sociétés,
Civilisations*, 28
Annotated bibliography (exercise), 324
*Annotated Critical Bibliography of
Feminist Criticism* (Humm), 214
Annual Register of World Events, 139
Anthony, Susan B., 148–49, 161–62
*Anthropological Bibliographies: A

Selected Guide (Smith and Damien),
185, 186
*Anthropological Index to Current
Periodicals in the Museum of Mankind
Library*, 186
Anthropological Literature, 185, 186
Anthropology, reference sources, 183–86
*Applied and Decorative Arts: A Guide to
Basic Reference Works, Histories, and
Handbooks* (Ehresmann), 215, 216
ARBA Guide to Education (Brewer), 195
Archival and manuscript material,
indexes to, 152
Archive and manuscript collections:
automated finding aids, 282–85;
automated records, 285–87; finding
aids, 272–85; published sources, 266–
67; repository organization and
function, 290–91; sources beyond
America or repositories, 290–91;
unpublished sources, 267–68; working
with an archivist, 287–89
Archives, definition of, 267
*Archives and Manuscript Repositories in
the U.S.S.R.*, 290–91
Archivists, working with, 287–89
Aristotle, 20
Arksey, Laura, 86
Arntzen, Etta, 214, 215
Aron, Raymond, 9
Art and history, 14–15, 39–42
Art Index, 217, 260
Art Literature International, 260
Art of Literary Research, The (Altick),
347
*Art Research Methods and Resources: A
Guide to Finding Art Information*
(Jones), 215, 216
Artbibliographies Modern, 260
Articles in American Studies, 1954–1968,
179, 182
Artifactual sources, 54
Artificial collections (archives/
manuscripts), definition of, 268
Arts (fine and applied): and history, 28–
32; reference sources, 214–17
Arts and Humanities Citation Index, 81,
87, 119, 120, 141, 142, 180–82, 344

Arts and Humanities Search (database), 232, 235, 236, 259
Ash, Lee, 126
Asheim, Lester, 299
Atlas of American History, 136
Atlas of Early American History, 136
Atlases and gazetteers, 149–50
Aversa, Elizabeth, 214, 215
Avery Index to Architectural Periodicals (database), 260
Aydelotte, William O., 22, 170

Bachelard, Gaston, 8
Ballou, Patricia K., 213–14
Barnes, Harry Elmer, 23, 28
Barnouw, Erik, 188–89, 220
Barraclough, Geoffrey, 12, 24, 170
Barthes, Roland, 7, 8
Bartul, John C., 321
Barzun, Jacques, 22, 32, 131, 321, 348
Battlefield Atlas of the Civil War, 136
Baxter, Pam M., 203, 314
Beales, Ross W., Jr., 321
Beard, Charles, 28
Beaseley, W. G., 23
Beaubien, Anne K., 316, 321
Behavioral Approach to Historical Analysis, A (Berkhoffer), 22
Ben-David, Joseph, 315
Benjamin, Jules R., 348
Benson, Lee, 170
Berding, Helmut, 19
Berkhoffer, Robert F., 22
Bernheim, Ernst, 21
Berr, Henri, 26
Berringer, Richard H., 302
Berry, John W., 184, 185, 204
Bestermann, Theodore, 81, 178, 182
Bibliographic Index, 81, 114–16, 140, 141, 178, 182, 187
Bibliographic information sources, 168; for anthropology, 185–86; for business and labor, 187–88; for communication, 190; for demography, 191–92; for economics and economic thought, 194–95; for education, 197–98; for fine and applied arts, 217; for general and area studies, 178–82; for history of science

and technology, 226–27; for journalism, 190; for language and literature, 221; for mass media, 190; for philosophy, 223–24; for political science, 201–2, for psychology, 204–5; for quantitative methods, 171–72; for religion, 223–24; for sociology, 207–10; for women's studies, 213–14
Bibliographic instruction (programs or exercises, past and contemporary) at: Amherst College, 324; Bernard Baruch College, 327–28; British universities, 319, 322, 323, 325; Bryn Mawr College, 335; Carleton University (Sanford), 331–32; Columbia University, 324, 334, 335, 340; Cornell University, 335; Danish universities, 329, 333; Dartmouth College, 324–25; Drexel University, 340; Emporia State University, 330; George Mason University, 322; Gonzaga State University, 322; Harvard University, 335; Haverford College, 332; Illinois State University, 330; Johns Hopkins University, 334, 335; Kent State University, 62–66, 326; Lake Forest College, 325; Michigan State University (Widder), 334; Millersville University, 328; Millikin University, 336; Monteith College, Wayne State University, 327; New York College, City University of New York, 328; Northeast Missouri State University, 332; Northwestern University, 336–37; Rochester Institute of Technology, 337; St. Olaf College, 323; Sangamon State University, 329–30; Smith College, 335; Stanford University, 324; State University of New York at Buffalo, 325–26; State University of New York at Stony Brook (Feinberg), 296; United States Air Force Academy, 330; University of Birmingham (Great Britain), 322; University of California, Berkeley, 340; University of California, Los Angeles, 337; University of Colorado, 323–24; University of Houston–

Downtown (Minix), 329; University of
  Maryland, 330; University of
  Michigan, 330, 335; University of
  Wisconsin–Eau Claire, 324; University
  of Wisconsin–Madison, 330;
  University of Wisconsin–Milwaukee,
  331; University of Wisconsin–Parkside,
  320, 324; Utah State University, 320;
  Vassar College, 335, 336; Wellesley
  College, 335; Western Washington
  University (McInnis), 297–98, 328;
  Yale University, 324, 335; York
  University (Great Britain), 322
*Bibliographic Instruction: The Second
  Generation* (Mellon), 314, 316
Bibliographic networks, 297–98
Bibliographic software, 337
Bibliographic structure, 296–97
Bibliographies: retrospective and
  recurrent, 139–40, 163–64
*Bibliographies in American History: A
  Guide to Materials for Research*, 141
*Bibliographies in History: An Index to
  Bibliographies in History Journals and
  Dissertations Covering the United
  States and Canada*, 141
Bibliographies of bibliographies, 140–41
Bibliographie zur Geschichtstheorie
  (Berding), 19
*Bibliography and the Historian: The
  Conference at Belmont of the Joint
  Committee on Bibliographical Services
  to History, May 1967* (Perman), 309,
  344
Bibliography for Beginners (Gore), 350–
  51
Bibliography of Psychohistory
  (DeMause), 203
Biographical dictionaries, 134–35, 148,
  150–51, 153, 160, 163
Biography and Genealogy Master Index,
  135
Biography Index, 114–16
Birkos, Alexander S., 179, 182
*Black Biographical Dictionaries, 1790–
  1950*, 135
Blackwell Dictionary of Historians, The
  (Cannon), 135

*Blackwell Encyclopedia of Political
  Institutions* (Bogdanor), 201
*Blackwell Encyclopedia of Political
  Thought* (Miller),200–201
Blanke, Horst Walter, 20
Blassingame, John, 37
Blazek, Ron, 214, 215
Bloch, Marc, 7, 13, 26, 40
Blystone, Robert V., 317
Bodin, Jean, 20
Boehm, Eric H., 71, 322, 343
Boehm, Ronald J., 343
Bogdanor, Vernon, 201
Bogue, Allan G., 170
Bonnell, Victoria E., 170
Book catalogs, published, 111–14, 140
*Book of Latin Quotations with English
  Translations, A*, 138
Book Review Digest, 81, 142, 326–27
Book review indexes, 142–43
Book reviewing, 130
Books in Print, 87, 237
Boolean logic, 70, 109–10, 240–44
Borgatta, Edgar F., 206, 207
Bostick, Theodora P., 304
Bourdieu, Pierre, 14
Bracken, James F., 219
Brackstone, Deborah, 355
Braudel, Fernand, 265
Breen, T. H., 304
Breisach, Ernst, 19, 22, 23
Brevik, Patricia Senn, 295
Brewer, Deborah, 195
Breysig, Kurt, 6
Bridenbaugh, Carl, 32
Brigham, Clarence S., 83, 141
Brilliant, Richard, 304
Brinton, Crane, 28, 312
Brislin, Richard W., 184, 185, 204
British Biographical Archive, 135
*British Catalogue of Government
  Publications*, 123
British Historical Statistics, 139, 159–60
*British History, 1760–1960: A Guide to
  Sources of Information* (Lacey and
  McCord), 319
British Humanities Index, 182, 190

British Union Catalogue of Periodicals, 121

Broadus, Robert N., 304

Brode, John, 180, 182

Broidy, Ellen, 304

Brown, Norman O., 30

Browsing, in library collections, 58, 310, 311, 312

BRS/Search Service (information retrieval system), 263

BRS/Search Service Database Catalog, 263

Brundin, Robert E., 335

Brush, Stephen G., 225, 226

Buckle, Thomas, 13

Budd, John M., 313

Buenker, John D., 130

Bullock, Alan, 174, 178

Burckhardt, Jacob, 10, 25

Burke, Kenneth, 37

Burke, Peter, 23, 205–6, 207

Burke's Genealogical and Heraldic History of the Peerage, Baronetage, and Knightage, 135, 160

Burkett, Randall K., 321

Burroughs, Carol, 322

Business, reference sources, 186–88

Business Information: How to Find It, How to Use It (Lavin), 186, 187

Business Information Sources (Daniells), 186, 187

Business Periodicals Index, 187–88

Butterfield, Herbert, 23, 24

Buttlar, Lois, 195

Bynagle, Hans E., 221–22

Bynum, W. F., 225, 226

Calendar (archives/manuscripts), definition of, 281

Cambridge Encyclopedia of Africa, 80

Cambridge Encyclopedia of Language (Crystal), 219–20

Cambridge History of Africa, The, 80

Cambridge History of Japan, The, 134

Cambridge History of the British Empire, The, 134

Cannon, John, 135

Carbonell, Charles-Olivier, 23

Caren, Loretta, 337

Carpenter, Eric J., 317

Carter, Sarah, 132, 210–11

Cartographic materials, 124–25

Case, Donald Owen, 72, 300, 305

Cassara, Ernest, 88, 322

Cassell's Encyclopedia of Literature (Steinberg), 220, 221

Catalog (print/online), 99–100; author searching, 103–4; online catalogs, 109–11; principles of description, 100–102; principles of indexing, 102–9, 345; scope, 100; searching by cycling references, 110–11; subject searching, 104–6; title searching, 103

Cates, Jo A., 188

Catholic Periodical and Literature Index, 223

Catholic Periodical Index: A Cumulative Author and Subject Index to a Selected List of Catholic Periodicals, 1930–1960, 223–24

Catlett, Dianne B., 348–49

CD-ROM (technology), 116–17, 339, 341, 342

CD-ROMs In Print, 263

Center for Research Libraries (CRL), 56

Chapman, John, 305, 307, 322

Cheshire, David F., 215

Chiang, Katherine, 339

Chicago Manual of Style, The, 100

Chinese Tradition Historiography (Sidney), 23

Chladenius, Johann Martin, 20

Choice, 130

Christensen, Beth, 323

Chronologies, 137, 149, 150, 158

Chronology of World History: A Calendar of Principal Events from 3000 BC to AD 1976 (Freeman-Grenville), 137

CIS Index, 122

Citation analysis and historians, 52–55, 303–12

Citation indexes, 119, 180–82, 236, 344

Citation patterns (conceptual framework), 76, 87–89, 297

Civilization of the Renaissance in Italy, The (Burckhardt), 25
Clapham, J. H., 32
Clark, Daphne, 323, 325
Clio: A Journal of Literature, History, Philosophy of History, 22
Cliometrics, 13, 33
Clive, John, 38
Clubb, Jerome M., 33, 37, 170–71
Cochrane, Eric, 23
Cohen, David A., 337
Cohen, Ronald, 184, 185
Collapse of the Weimar Republic: Political Economy and Crisis, The (Abraham), 90, 355
Collection development (library), 349
Collingwood, Robin George, 5
Collins, Bobbie L., 348–49
Collins, Donald E., 348–49
Columbia Lippincott Gazetteer of the World, The, 136, 149–50
Combined Retrospective Index Set to Journals in History, 82, 118
Combined Retrospective Index to Book Reviews in Humanities Journals, 1802–1974, 81, 142
Combined Retrospective Index to Book Reviews in Scholarly Journals, 1886–1974, 81, 142
Comini, Alessandra, 31
Commentaries, 136–37, 156, 157, 158, 159
Communication, reference sources, 188–90
Communication: A Guide to Information Sources (Gitter), 188
Companion to the History of Modern Science (Olby), 225, 226
Comprehensive Dissertation Index (CDI), 83, 142
Computer Files and the Research Library (Johnson, Lowry, Marko, and Chiang), 339–40
Computer-Readable Databases, 263
Comte, Auguste, 12
Conceptual Frameworks for Bibliographic Education: Theory into Practice (Reichel and Ramey), 297

Constitution of the United States of America: Analysis and Interpretation: Annotations of Cases Decided by the Supreme Court of the United States to July 2, 1982, 158
Consumer's Guide to Ready Reference Sources in History: General Antiquity, the Middle Ages, Modern Europe, Modern Western Europe, the United States, and Latin America, A, 349
Consumer's Guide to Research Guides for Historical Literature: Antiquity, the Middle Ages, Modern Western Europe, North America, and Latin America, A, 132, 349
Consumer's Guide to the Current Bibliography of Historical Literature: Antiquity, the Middle Ages, Modern Western Europe, North America, and Latin America, A, 349
Coogan, John, 334
Cordasco, Francesco, 198
Corkill, Cynthia, 305
Course-related instruction, 320, 321, 322, 323, 324, 325, 326, 327, 328, 329, 330, 331, 332, 333, 334
Courses (full-length), 322, 324, 326, 329, 331, 332, 333, 334, 335, 336, 340
Coutts, Brian E., 81, 132, 350
Creative History: An Introduction to Historical Study (Nugent), 319–20
Cridland, Nancy C., 349
Critical Method in Historical Research and Writing, The (Hockett), 22, 351
Croce, Benedetto, 5
CROSS (database) (BRS), 238
Crystal, David, 219–20
Cultural Anthropology: A Guide to Reference Sources (Kibbee), 183
Cumulative Subject Index to the Monthly Catalog of U.S. Government Publications, 122
Cumulative Title Index to United States Public Documents, 122
Cunningham, Raymond, 335
Current awareness sources, 141
Current Contents, 141

Current Contents: Arts and Humanities, 141
Current Index to Journals in Education (CIJE), 197
Curriculum-integrated instruction, 75–76
Curtis, Lewis Perry, Jr., 302

Damien, Yvonne, 185, 186
D'Aniello, Charles A., 323, 326
Daniells, Lorna, 186, 187
Darnton, Robert, 14, 15
Database management programs, 337
Davey, Peter, 31
Davidson, James West, 302
Davis, R.H.C., 305, 306, 322
deconstructionism, 8
de Coulanges, Fustel, 10
DeGeorge, Richard T., 221, 222
de Graaf, Lawrence B., 349
Deighton, Lee C., 196, 197
DeLloyd, Guth, 63
DeLoach, Charles, 138, 153–54
Delzell, Charles F., 24
DeMause, Lloyd, 203
DeMiller, Anna L., 218, 219
demography, reference sources, 190–92
Dent, Harold Collett, 23
Derrida, Jacques, 8
de Tocqueville, Alexis, 10
Deutsche Geschichte (Lamprecht), 27
Development of Historiography, The (Fitzsimons), 23
DeVinney, Gemma, 77
Dialindex (Dialog database), 238
Dialog (information retrieval system), 263, 337
Dialog Database Catalog, 263
Dictionaries and encyclopedias, 132–34, 151–52, 153, 155, 156, 157, 161–62, 173, 199–200, 219; difference between, 168
Dictionary of Afro-American Slavery (Miller and Smith),134, 152, 156
Dictionary of American Biography, 81, 134, 148, 150–51, 153, 162, 163
Dictionary of American History, 134
Dictionary of American Literary Biography, 135

Dictionary of American Negro Biography, The, 135
Dictionary of American Portraits, 143
Dictionary of Bible and Religion, The (Gentz), 133, 157
Dictionary of Concepts in Cultural Anthropology (Winthrop), 183, 185
Dictionary of Concepts in History (Ritter), 303
Dictionary of Concepts in Physical Anthropology (Stevenson), 183, 185
Dictionary of Concepts in the Philosophy of Science (Durbin), 174, 178
Dictionary of Demography: Terms, Concepts, and Institutions (Petersen and Petersen), 190–91
Dictionary of Feminist Theory, The (Humm), 212, 213
Dictionary of Historical Concepts (Ritter), 133, 174, 178
Dictionary of Historical Organizations in the United States and Canada, 137
Dictionary of Modern Thought (Bullock and Stallybrass), 174, 178
Dictionary of National Biography, 81, 134–35, 160
Dictionary of Political Analysis (Plano), 173
Dictionary of Political Thought, A (Scruton), 133, 156
Dictionary of Scientific Biography (Gillispie), 225, 226
Dictionary of the History of Ideas (Wiener), 23, 81, 177, 178
Dictionary of the History of Science (Bymum), 225, 226
Dictionary of the Middle Ages (Strayer), 133
Dictionary of the Social Sciences (Gould and Kolb), 174–75, 178
Dilthey, Wilhelm, 5, 6
Dimensions of Quantitative Research in History: Selected Readings (Aydelotte), 22, 170
Dimensions of the Past: Materials, Problems, and Opportunities for Quantitative Work in History (Lorwin and Price), 171

Directories, 137–38, 151–52
Directory of American Scholars: A Biographical Dictionary, 138
Directory of Archives and Manuscript Repositories in the United States, 83, 273–74
Directory of Directories: An Annotated Guide to Business and Industrial Directories, Professional and Scientific Rosters, and Other Lists and Guides, 138
Directory of Historical Organizations in the United States and Canada, 151–52
Directory of History Departments and Organizations in the United States, 137
Directory of Online Databases, 263
Directory of Portable Databases, 263
Discovering RLIN: An Introduction to the Research Libraries Information Network Database (Hannon), 339
Dissertation Abstracts International, 82, 142
Dissertation Abstracts Online, 261
Dissertations and theses, use of, 52
Dobyns, Henry F., 320
Document (archives/manuscripts), definition, 267
Documents in American History, 143, 152
Dodson, Suzanne Cates, 83, 124
Dod's Parliamentary Companion, 135, 160
Doing of History: A Practical Use of the Library-College Concept, The (Haywood), 325
Dollar, Charles N., 169
Douglas, Anne, 232, 325
Down, Robert Bingham, 126
Dray, William, 20
Droysen, J. G., 6, 21
Dubin, Paul T., 174, 178, 224
Duckles, Vincent, 215, 216
Durkheim, Emile, 6

Eatwell, John, 193, 194
Economic Literature Index, 260
Economics: and history, 10 (*see*

Quantitative history); reference sources, 192–95
Editing, 143–65, 321, 324, 327, 332, 333
Education, reference sources, 195–98
Education: A Guide to Reference and Information Sources (Buttlar), 195
Education Index, 197
Education of Historians in the United States, The (Parker and Snell), 329
Edwards, Paul, 222, 223
Edwards, Susan E., 323
Ehresmann, Donald L., 214–15, 216
Eighteenth-Century Short Title Catalogue (ESTC) (database), 83, 233, 261
Electronic information sources: arranging for a mediated search, 250–53; bibliographic instruction and research, 240, 242, 253–56, 337, 338–39; cost of mediated searches, 252–53; databases evaluated for history, 232–34; databases for history, 125, 232–34; database types, 231–32; definitions of computer terms, 230–31; downloading, 117; historians' use of, 54; preservation issues, 341; search techniques and tips, 109–10, 238–44, 246–50; when appropriate, 244; when not appropriate, 244–46
Eliade, Mircea, 222–23
Elkins, Stanley, 32
Elton, G. R., 4, 22
Eminent Contributors to Psychology (Watson), 205
Encyclopaedia Britannica, 134, 158
Encyclopaedia Judaica, 89, 133
Encyclopedia of American Economic History: Studies of the Principal Movements and Ideas (Porter), 187
Encyclopedia of American Facts and Dates, The (Carruth), 137
Encyclopedia of American Political History: Studies of the Principal Movements and Ideas (Greene), 134, 144, 155, 161
Encyclopedia of Associations, 132
Encyclopedia of Education (Deighton), 196, 197

Encyclopedia of Philosophy, The (Edwards), 222, 223
Encyclopedia of Religion (Eliade), 23, 222–23
Encyclopedia of Social Work, 206–7
Encyclopedia of Sociology (Borgatta), 206, 207
Encyclopedia of Southern History: The (Roller and Twyman), 134, 153
Encyclopedia of the American Constitution, 134, 155, 156, 161
Encyclopedia of the Social Sciences (ESS), 79, 175, 178
Encyclopedia of World Art, 216
Encyclopedia of World Cultures (Levinson), 184, 185
Encyclopedia of World Literature (Fleischmann), 220
Encyclopedia Universalis, 134
Encyclopedic Dictionary of Semiotics (Sebeok), 189
Engeldinger, Eugene A., 324
Engerman, Stanley, 13, 32–37
ERIC (database), 237
Ermarth, Michael, 38
Eros and Modernization: Sylvester Graham, Health Reform, and the Origins of Victorian Sexuality in America (Sokolow), 90, 356
Essay and General Literature Index, 81, 114–16
Essay questions, 321
Essays in Modern European Historiography (Halperin), 24
Everett, David, 337
Exhaustive Concordance of the Bible (Strong), 138, 156, 157–58

Facts on File, 139
Faire l'histoire (LeGoff and Nora), 22
Falk, Joyce Duncan, 296, 338, 344
Familiar Quotations (Bartlett's), 138, 154, 158–59, 164
Family in Past Time: A Guide to the Literature, The (Milden), 209–10
Famous Phrases from History (Hemphill), 138
Febvre, Lucien, 13, 26

Feinberg, Richard, 296
Feldman, Gerald D., 355
Feminist Dictionary (Kramarae and Treichler), 212, 213
Feminist Research Method: Exemplary Readings in the Social Sciences (Nielsen), 212–13
Fenstermaker, John J., 317
Ferris, Sharon Paugh, 215–16
Filing unit (archives/manuscripts), definition of, 279–80
Fin-de-Siècle Vienna: Politics and Culture (Schorske), 28–32
Fine Arts: A Bibliographic Guide to Basic Reference Works, Histories, and Handbooks (Ehresmann), 214–15
Fink, Deborah, 89, 324
Finley, Moses, 23
First Stop: The Master Index to Subject Encyclopedias (Ryan), 133, 173–74
Fitch, Nancy H., 171
Fitzsimons, Mathew A., 23
Fleischer, Dirk, 20
Fleischmann, Wolfgang Bernard, 220
Fletcher, John, 192–93
Floud, Roderick, 169
Fogel, Robert, 13, 22, 32–37
Footnotes, use of, 354–55
Foreign Language Index (PAIS), 236–37
Foreign language material, historians' use of, 52
Form of publication (conceptual framework), 76, 84, 297
Foucault, Michel, 7
Foundations of Modern Historical Scholarship: Language, Law, and History in the French Renaissance (Kelley), 20
Fox, Peter K., 324
Franklin, John Hope, 36
Freedom of Information Acts, 271
Freeman, Michael Stuart, 324
Freidel, Frank, 349
Freides, Thelma, 315
French Historical Method: The Annales Paradigm (Stoianovich), 24
French Retrieval Automated Network for

Current Information in Social and Human Sciences (FRANCIS), 232, 259
Freud, Sigmund, 30
Frick, Elizabeth, 296, 350
Frisch, Michael, 22
Fritze, Ronald H., 81, 132, 350
Frye, Northrop, 37, 82, 84, 313
Fueter, Edward, 23
Fulltext Sources Online, 263
Furay, Conal, 319
Furet, François, 24
Future of History, The (Delzell), 24
Fyfe, Janet, 138

Gadamer, Hans-Georg, 20
Gage, Joslyn Matilda, 148–49, 161–62
Gardiner, Patrick, 21
Gardner, Charles Sidney, 23
Gardner, James B., 302
Garfield, Eugene, 344
Gates, Jean Key, 320, 350
Gateway to History (Nevins), 303
Gee, E. Gordon, 295
Geertz, Clifford, 14
General and area studies: sources, 172–83
General Ethnological Concepts (Hultkrantz), 183–84
General History of Africa, 80
Gentz, William H., 133, 157
George, Mary W., 317, 321
Gerber, David A., 325
German Conception of History: The National Tradition of Historical Thought from Herder to the Present, The (Iggers), 24
German Enlightenment and the Rise of Historicism, The (Reill), 20
Geschichte der neueren Historiographie (Fueter), 23
Gilbert, Felix, 23, 24
Gillispie, Charles C., 225, 226
Gilmore, Mathew Benjamin, 344
Gitter, A. George, 188
Glenn, Norval D., 208–9
Goldmann, Lucien, 37
Gombrich, E. H., 313
Gooch, George P., 24
Gore, Daniel, 350

Gottschalk, Louis, 22, 347, 351
Gould, Constance G., 313, 315
Gould, Julius, 174–75, 178
Government documents, 122–23, 346
Government Publications: A Guide to Bibliographic Tools (Palic), 123
Graff, Henry F., 22, 131, 348
Gramsci, Antonio, 12
Grant, Michael, 23
Graubard, Stephen R., 24
Gray, Ralph D., 356
Great American History Machine, The (database), 125
Great Historians from Antiquity to 1800: An International Dictionary (Boia, Nore, Hitchins, Iggers), 135
Great Historians of the Modern Age: An International Dictionary (Boia, Nore, Hitchins, Iggers), 135
Great Soviet Encyclopedia, The, 133, 134
Greek Historians, The (Finley), 23
Greene, Jack P., 134, 144, 155, 161
Greenstein, Fred I., 200, 201
Gregory, Winfred, 83, 141, 159
Grinell, Stuart F., 339
Grossbart, Stephen R., 171, 172
Grun, Bernard, 137, 158
Grunin, Robert, 188
Guest, Susan S., 313
Guides, 131–32, 163–64, 172–73, 347–54; for anthropology, 183; for business and labor, 186–87; for communication, 188; for demography, 190; for economics, 192–93; for education, 195; for fine and applied arts, 214–15; for history of science and technology, 224–25; for journalism, 188; for language, 218–19; for literature, 218–19; for mass media, 188; for philosophy, 221–22; for political science, 198–99; for psychology, 202–3; for quantitative research, 169; for religion, 221–22; for sociology, 205; for women's studies, 210–11
Guide to American Directories, 138
Guide to Basic Information Sources in the Visual Arts (Muesham), 215, 216

Guide to Catholic Literature, 1888–1940,
    223, 224
Guide to Documentary Editing (Kline),
    327
Guide to Historical Literature, 83, 132
Guide to Library Research Methods
    (Mann), 132, 352
Guide to Microforms in Print, 124
Guide to Published Library Catalogs
    (Nelson), 140
Guide to Reference Books (Sheehy), 81,
    129, 132, 353
*Guide to Sources of Educational
    Information* (Woodbury), 195
*Guide to the Archives of International
    Organizations,* 291
*Guide to the Culture of Science,
    Technology, and Medicine* (Durbin),
    224
Guide to the Literature of Art History
    (Arntzen and Rainwater), 214, 215
*Guide to the National Archives of the
    United States,* 273–74
*Guide to the Study of the United States of
    America* (Basler), 140
*Guide to the Study of United States
    History Outside the United States,
    1945–1980* (Hanke), 291
*Guide to the Use of Libraries and
    Information Sources* (Gates), 350

Habermas, Jürgen, 9
Halperin, Samuel William, 24
*Handbook for Archival Research in the
    U.S.S.R., A* (Grimsted), 290–91
*Handbook for Research in American
    History: A Guide to Bibliographies and
    Other Reference Works* (Prucha), 63,
    132, 352–53
Handbook of American Women's History
    (Zophy), 134, 144, 150
Handbook of Business Information
    (Strauss), 186, 187
Handbook of Communication (Pool and
    Schramm), 189
Handbook of Cross-Cultural Psychology
    (Triandis, Lambert, Berry, Lonner,
    Heron, and Brislin), 184, 185, 204

*Handbook of Method in Cultural
    Anthropology* (Naroll and Cohen), 184,
    185
*Handbook of Political Communication,
    The* (Nimmo and Sanders), 201
Handbook of Political Science
    (Greenstein and Polsby), 200, 201
*Handbook of Social and Cultural
    Anthropology* (Honigmann), 184
Handbook of Sociology, The (Smelser),
    206, 207
Handbook to Literature, A (Holman), 219
Handler, Mark, 315
Handlin, Oscar, 306
Hanke, Lewis, 291
Hannon, Hilary, 339
Hanson, Forest, 325
Hardy, Kenneth A., 169
Hareven, Tamara K., 207
Harner, James L., 218–19
Harris, C.G.S., 323
Harris, Colin, 325
Harris, Michael H., 299
Harter, Stephen P., 339
*Harvard Concordance to Shakespeare,
    The,* 138, 153–54
*Harvard Guide to American History,
    The,* 83, 132, 148, 163–64, 349–50
Haselbauer, Kathleen J., 224, 225
Haskins, Loren, 169
Hausen, Donald A., 190
Haywood, Robert C., 325
Hazen, Dan C., 306
Henige, David, 140, 354
Hernon, Peter, 172–73, 346
Herodotus, 9
Herron, Nancy, 190
Herubel, Jean-Pierre V. M., 306, 307
Heyne, Christian, 9
Higham, John, 24
Hill, Richard Child, 318
Hilton, Rodney, 41
Histline (database), 237, 248, 260
L'Histoire et ses méthodes (Samaran), 22
Historian and librarian interactions, 53,
    331–32, 346–47
*Historian as Detective: Essays on
    Evidence, The* (Winks), 303

Historians and Historiography in the Italian Renaissance (Cochrane), 23
Historians and library collections, 306, 308, 309, 311, 312
Historians and library services, 51–57, 308, 309
Historians, Books and Libraries: A Survey of Historical Scholarship in Relation to Library Resources and Services (Shera), 310
Historian's Guide to Statistics (Dollar and Jensen), 169
Historian's Handbook: A Descriptive Guide to Reference Works, The (Poulton), 63, 352
Historians of China and Japan (Beaseley and Pullyblank), 23
Historians of India, Pakistan, and Ceylon (Philips), 23
Historians of Modern Europe (Schmitt), 24
Historians' Workshop: Original Essays by Sixteen Historians (Curtis), 302
Historical Abstracts, 144, 309; abstracting for, 85; as a CD-ROM, 341, 342; finding review articles with, 141; as an online database, 116–17, 232–35, 248–49, 258–59; sample search (Dialog) using, 241–44, 338
Historical Analysis: Contemporary Approaches to Clio's Craft (Beringer), 302
Historical Atlas of South Asia (Schwartzberg), 136
Historical Bibliographies: A Systematic and Annotated Guide, 140
Historical literature, indexing of, 343–45
Historical Periodicals Directory, 84, 138
Historical Social Research: The Use of Historical and Process-Produced Data (Clubb and Scheuch), 170
Historical source, definition of, 9–11
Historical Statistics of the United States, Colonial Times to 1970, 136, 139, 149, 150, 155, 159, 162
Historical Studies Today (Gilbert and Graubard), 24
Historiography: An Annotated

Bibliography of Journal Articles, Books, and Dissertations (Kinnell), 172, 179
Historiography: Ancient, Medieval, Modern (Breisach), 19, 22, 23
Historiography, Methods, History Teaching: A Bibliography of Books and Articles, 1965–1972 (Birkos and Tabb), 179, 182
Historism: The Rise of a New Historical Outlook (Meinecke), 20
History: character of, 38; and culture, 10; definition of, 3, 15n.1; of historical writing, 22–24; and linguistic structuralism, 8; and Marxism, 11–12; and method, 21–22; narrative, 14–15; overviews of historical research, 302–3; philosophy and theory of, 20–21; as poetry, 8, 38; as a science, 3–6; as a social science, 11–14. *See also* Interdisciplinary history
History and Bibliography of American Newspapers (Brigham), 83, 141
History and Criticism (LaCapra), 21
History and Historians in the Nineteenth Century (Gooch), 24
History and Memory, 22
History and Theory (People's Republic of China), 22
History and Theory: Studies in the Philosophy of History, 19, 22
History as Social Science: The Behavioral and Social Sciences Survey (Landes and Tilly), 327
History in a Changing World (Barraclough), 24
History journals, citation studies of, 306, 307
History Journals and Serials: An Analytical Guide (Fyfe),138
History, Man, and Reason: An Answer to Relativism (Mandelbaum), 20
History of American Higher Education (Cordasco), 198
History of Economic Analysis: A Guide to Information Sources (Hutchinson), 193
History of Historical Writing, A (Barnes), 23

History of Historical Writing, A
(Thompson), 23
*History of Ideas: A Bibliographical
Introduction, The* (Tobey), 177–78
History of Manners (Voltaire), 9
*History of Modern Science: A Guide to
the Second Scientific Revolution, 1800–
1950* (Brush), 225–26
History of Muslim Historiography, A
(Rosenthal), 23
*History of Psychology: A Guide to
Information Sources* (Viney), 205
*History of Psychology and the Behavioral
Sciences, The* (Watson), 180, 182
History of Technology (Stinger), 226
*History of the Family and Kinship: A
Select International Bibliography*
(Soliday), 210
History of Woman Suffrage (Stanton,
Anthony and Gage), 148–49, 161–62
*History: Politics or Culture? Reflections
on Ranke and Burckhardt* (Gilbert), 24
*History: The Development of Historical
Studies in the United States* (Higham,
Gilbert, and Krieger), 24
Hitchcock, Elaine R., 307
Hockett, Homer Carey, 22, 351
Hoekstra, Gerald, 323
Hoftsadter, Richard, 24
Hogan, Sharon A., 321
Holler, Frederick L., 198, 199
Holman, Hugh, 219
Honigmann, John Joseph, 184
Hopkins, Frances L., 75, 335, 336
Horn, Thomas Charles Robert, 303
How to Read a Book (Adler and Van
Doren), 129
Huling, Nancy, 307
Hultkrantz, Ake, 183–84
*Humanities: A Selective Guide to
Information Sources* (Blazek and
Aversa), 214, 215
Humanities Index, 77, 82, 114–16, 179–
80, 182, 236, 237, 259
*Human Migration Literature in English,
1955–62* (Mangalamand Morgan), 192
Humm, Maggie, 212, 213, 214
Hunt, Lynn, 22

Huppert, George, 20
Hurych, Jitka, 339
Husen, Torsten, 196, 197
Hutchinson, William K., 193

*Idea of History in the Ancient Near East,
The* (Dent), 23
*Idea of Perfect History: Historical
Erudition and Historical Philosophy in
Renaissance France, The* (Huppert), 20
Ideas and Men (Brinton), 312
Ideas of History (Nash), 21
Iggers, Georg G., 24, 303
Imagination in research, 301–2
Indexes and abstracts (periodicals), 114–
19, 139
Indexing and abstracting: difficulties
with, 53, 345; and *Journal of
American History*, 344; and
undiscovered knowledge, 301
Index Islamicus (Pearson), 223, 224
*Index of Economic Articles in Journals
and Collective Volumes*, 194, 195
Index structure (conceptual framework),
76, 84–86, 297
*Index to Personal Names in the National
Union Catalog of Manuscript
Collections, 1959–1984*, 163
Industry and Labor, 192
*In Pursuit of American History: Research
and Training in the United States*
(Rundell), 331
In the Workshop of the Historian (Furet),
24
Information literacy, 71, 295–96, 297,
340
*Information Literacy: Revolution in the
Library* (Brevik), 295–96
*Information Needs in the Humanities: An
Assessment* (Gould), 313
*Information Needs in the Social Sciences:
An Assessment* (Gould), 315
*Information on Music: A Handbook of
Reference Sources in European
Languages* (Marco and Ferris), 215–16
Information overload, 299
Information Please Almanac, 139

Information retrieval systems (online),
  263–64
Information Sources in Economics
  (Fletcher), 192–93
Information Sources of Political Science
  (Holler), 198, 199
Instructional contexts, 75–76
Instructional exercises and approaches,
  62–66, 316–44; citation patterns
  (conceptual framework), 87–89;
  conceptual frameworks, 76–78; courses
  and exercises, 320–34; in disciplines
  other than history, 316–19; editing,
  143–65, 321, 324, 327, 332, 333;
  form of publication (conceptual
  framework), 84–86; goals, 73–74; in
  literature, 317–18; in political science,
  318–19; primary/secondary sources
  (conceptual framework), 86–87;
  publication sequence (conceptual
  framework), 76–77, 86–87, 89; in
  science, 317; in social science, 316–
  17; sociohistorical analysis (conceptual
  framework), 89; in sociology, 318;
  systematic literature searching
  (conceptual framework), 80–84; type
  of reference tools (conceptual
  frameworks), 78–80; workbooks, 319–
  20. *See also* Bibliographic instruction
Interdisciplinary history: anthropology
  and history, 39–42; arts and history,
  28–39; economics and history, 10; *Fin-
  de-Siècle Vienna: Politics and Culture*
  (Schorske), 28–32; in France, 26–27;
  in Germany, 27; linguistics and
  history, 7–9, 37–39; literature and
  history, 7–9, 28–32; *Metahistory: The
  Historical Imagination in Nineteenth-
  Century Europe* (White), 21, 37–39;
  *Montaillou: The Promised Land of
  Error* (Le Roy Ladurie), 39–42;
  philosophy and history, 37–39;
  political science and history, 10;
  psychology and history, 28–32; *Time
  on the Cross: The Economics of
  American Negro Slavery* (Fogel and
  Engerman), 13, 32–37; in the United
  States, 27–28; women's studies, 210–
  14. *See also* History
Interlibrary loan, 57, 121
*International Bibliography of Directories
  and Guides to Archival Repositories*,
  290
International Bibliography of Economics,
  194, 195
*International Bibliography of Political
  Science*, 201–2
*International Bibliography of Research in
  Marriage and the Family* (Aldous),
  209, 210
*International Bibliography of Social and
  Cultural Anthropology*, 185, 186
International Bibliography of Sociology,
  207–8
*International Communication and
  Political Opinion: A Guide to the
  Literature* (Smith and Smith), 190
*International Council on Archives
  Directory*, 290
*International Encyclopedia of
  Communications* (Barnouw), 188–89,
  220
*International Encyclopedia of Education:
  Research and Studies* (Husen and
  Postlethwaite), 196–97
*International Encyclopedia of Higher
  Education* (Knowles), 196, 197
International Encyclopedia of Population
  (Ross), 191
*International Encyclopedia of Psychiatry,
  Psychology, Psychoanalysis and
  Neurology* (Wolman), 203, 204
International Encyclopedia of Statistics
  (Kruskal and Tanur), 169
*International Encyclopedia of the Social
  Sciences, The* (IESS), 81, 133, 135,
  156, 169, 175, 178
*International Handbook of Historical
  Studies: Contemporary Research and
  Theory* (Iggers and Parker), 24, 303
International Labor Review, 192
International Migration Review, 192
International Mortality Statistics
  (Alderson), 191
International Political Science Abstracts,
  202

International Population Census Bibliography, 192
International Thesaurus of Quotations, The, 138
Internet, 126
Interpreter's Bible: The Holy Scriptures in the King James and Revised Standard Versions with General Articles and Introduction, 137
Interpreter's One-Volume Commentary on the Bible: Introduction and Commentary for Each Book of the Bible Including the Aprocrypha, with General Articles, 137, 156, 157–58
Interuniversity Consortium for Political Science Research (ICPSR), 232
Introduction to Library Research in Anthropology (Weeks), 183
Introduction to Quantitative Methods for Historians, An (Floud), 169
Introduction to the History of Science (Sarton), 225, 226
Introduction to the Study of History (Langlois and Seignobos), 21–22
Inventory of Marriage and Family Literature (Olsen), 209, 210
Isaacson, David, 326
ISIS, 226, 227
ISIS: Cumulative Bibliography, 226, 227
Item (archives/manuscripts), definition of, 280–82

Jakobson, Roman, 37
Jameson, John Franklin, 307
Jarausch, Konrad Hugo, 169
Jeffrey, Kirk, 169
Jensen, Richard J., 169
Johnson, Margaret, 339
Johnson, Samuel, 38, 69
Johnston, William, 31
Jones, Clyve, 307
Jones, Lois, 215, 216
Jordan, Philip D., 307
Journalism, reference sources, 188–90
Journalism: A Guide to the Reference Literature (Cates), 188
Journalism Quarterly, 190

Journal of American History, 130, 141, 344
Journal of Economic Literature, 194, 195
Journal of Interdisciplinary History, 28, 306
Journal of Social History, 306
Journal of the History of Ideas, 306
Journals: cancellation of by libraries, 56; characteristics of, 306–7, 308, 344; historians' choice of, 53

Kammen, Michael, 24
Kanes, Martin, 314
Kann, Robert A., 31
Kazmierczak, Carol M., 308
Kelley, Donald R., 20
Kellner, Hans, 21
Kenner, Richard M., 340
Kernig, Claus Dieter, 177, 178
Keresztesi, Michael, 87, 89, 296
Keylor, William, 24
Keyword: indexing, 118; searching, 108–11
Kibbee, Josephine, 183
King, Christine, 296
Kingsley, James, 308
Kinnell, Susan K., 19, 171–72, 179
Kiresen, Evelyn-Margaret, 340
Kirkendall, Carolyn, 326
Kline, Mary-Jo, 327
Klemanski, John S., 168
Klugman, Simone, 340
Knapp, Patricia, 327
Knowles, Asa S., 196, 197
Kobelski, Pamela, 76–77, 297
Kodansha Encyclopedia of Japan, 79
Kolb, William L., 174–75, 178
Kollmeier, Harold H., 340
Kon, Igor, 20
Kramarae, Cheris, 212, 213
Kraus, Michael, 24
Krieger, Leonard, 24
Kruskel, William H., 169
Kuper, Adam, 175–76, 178
Kuper, Jessica, 175–76, 178

Labor, reference sources, 186–88
Labor History, 188

Lacan, Jacques, 37
LaCapra, Dominick, 21
Lacey, S.M.J., 323
Lacey-Bryant, Sue, 319
Lambert, W. W., 184, 185, 204
Lamprecht, Karl, 6, 12, 27
Landes, David S., 70, 71, 327
Langer, William L., 30
Langlois, Charles V., 21–22
Langstaff, Eleanor, 351
Language, reference sources, 217–21
*Language and Historical Representation:
  Getting the Story Crooked* (Kellner),
  21
Lavin, Michael R., 186, 187
Lawton, Henry, 203
*Learning the Library: Concepts and
  Methods for Effective Bibliographic
  Instruction* (Beaubien, Hogan, and
  George), 321–22
Learning theory, 71–72, 296, 298
Lebergott, Stanley, 33
Lee, Joann H., 325
LeGoff, Jacques, 22
*Lehrbuch der historischen Methode und
  der Geschichtsphilosophie* (Bernheim),
  21
Le Roy Ladurie, Emmanuel, 13, 22, 39–
  42
Levinson, David, 184, 185
Lévi-Strauss, Claude, 7, 40–41
Lexis/Nexis (information retrieval
  system), 263
Libby, Orin G., 32
Librarian and historian interactions, 53,
  331–32, 346–47
*Libraries and Research: A Practical
  Approach* (Collins, Catlett, Collins),
  348–49
Library anxiety, 71
Library collections and historians, 306,
  308, 309, 311, 312; and collection
  development, 349; and services, 51–
  57, 308, 309
Library-college (concept), 325–26
Library Journal, 172–73
Library materials, preservation of, 304,
  306; of computer files, 341

Library of Congress Subject Headings,
  77, 81, 85, 103, 104–6, 115
*Library Research Guide to History:
  Illustrated Search Strategy and Sources*
  (Frick), 350
Library Research in Women's Studies
  (Searing), 210, 211
Library Use: A Handbook for Psychology
  (Reed and Baxter), 203
Library use and historians, 51–55, 303–
  12
Lindgren, Jon, 327
Line, Maurice B., 315, 316
*Linguistics: A Guide to the Reference
  Literature* (DeMiller), 218, 219
Linguistics and history, 7–9, 37–39
*Linguistics and Language Behavior
  Abstracts*, 221
Lipps, Theodor, 27
Literary Research Guide (Patterson), 218,
  219
*Literary Research Guide: A Guide to
  Reference Sources for the Study of
  Literature* (Harner), 218–19
Literature: and history, 7–9, 28–32;
  history as, 7; reference sources, 217–
  21
*Literature and Bibliography of the Social
  Sciences* (Freides), 315
Little, G. T., 336
Logsdon, Richard H., 347
Lonner, Walter, 184, 185, 204
Lopez, Manuel D., 203
Lorwin, Val R., 171
Lovett, Robert W., 193
Lowry, Anita, 339, 340
Lucian, 20
Lukács, Georg, 12
Lytle, Mark Hamilton, 302

McAnally, A. M., 308
McCaslin, Davida, 336
McCord, Norman, 319
McCoy, Florence N., 351
McCrank, Lawrence J., 297, 347
Macdonald, John D., 297
McDonough, Kristin, 327, 351
McGraw-Hill Dictionary of Modern

Economics: A Handbook of Terms and Organizations, 193, 194
MacGregor, James, 297
Machalow, Robert, 328
Machiavelli and Guicciardini: Politics and History in 16th Century Florence (Gilbert), 23
McInnis, Raymond G., 78, 202–3, 297, 298, 328, 351, 354
McNeer, Elizabeth, 298
Magazine ASAP (database), 262
Magazine Index (database), 238, 262
Main Trends of Research in the Social and Human Sciences (Havet), 170, 176, 178
Mallon, Thomas, 356
Mandelbaum, Maurice, 20
Mangalam, J. J., 192
Mann, Margaret, 305
Mann, Thomas, 352
Mannheim, Karl, 9, 30, 37
Man on His Past: The Study of the History of Historical Scholarship (Butterfield), 24
Manuals, 21–22, 131, 347–54
Manuscript (archives/manuscripts), definition of, 268
MARC, 233, 237, 261
MARC/AMC, 283, 284–85
Marco, Guy A., 215–16
Marcuse, Herbert, 30
MARC/VM, 283
Marko, Lynn, 339
Marxism, 11–12, 30
Marxism, Communism, and Western Society (Kernig), 177, 178
Mason, Thomas W., 355
Mass Communication: A Research Bibliography (Hansen), 190
Mass media, reference sources, 188–90
Masters, Roger, 40
Materials and Methods for History Research (Stoffle and Dobyns), 320
Mathews, William, 84, 86
Medline (database), 237
Megill, Allan, 21
Meinecke, Friedrich, 5, 7, 20
Mellon, Constance A., 318

Meserole, Harrison T., 314
Metahistory: The Historical Imagination in Nineteenth-Century Europe (White), 21, 37–39
Methods and Materials of Demography (Shyrock), 190
Methods and Skills of History: A Practical Guide, The (Furay and Salevouris), 319
Meyerhof, Hans, 21
Microform Research Collection: A Guide (Dodson), 83, 124
Microforms, use of, 55–56, 123–24, 304–7
Middle Ages: A Concise Encyclopedia, The (Loyn), 133
Mideast File (database), 238, 260
Milden, James Wallace, 209–10
Miller, Connie, 340
Miller, David, 200–201
Miller, Randall M., 134, 152, 156
Miller, Steven Max, 328
Miller, William G., 126
Milligan, John D., 328
Minix, Dean A., 329
Mitchell, Geoffrey Duncan, 207
MLA International Bibliography, 221, 248, 260
Modern Researcher, The (Barzun and Graff), 22, 131
Momigliano, Arnaldo, 23
Mommsen, Theodor, 7
Montaillou: The Promised Land of Error (Le Roy Ladurie), 39–42
Monteith College Library Experiment, The (Knapp), 327
Monthly Catalog of United States Government Publications, 118, 122
Moody, Marilyn, 346
Morgan, Cornelia, 192
Morison, Samuel Eliot, 291
Morris, Leslie R., 308
Morton, Bruce, 346
Mudge, Isadore Gilbert, 129–30
Muesham, Gerd, 215, 216
Multiple Database Access System (MDAS), 249
Muratori, Fred, 340

Music: and history, 30; reference sources, 7
Music Index, 217
Music Reference and Research Materials (Duckles), 215, 216
"Mythistory," 7

Najarian, Suzanne E., 298
Naroll, Raoul, 184, 185
Nash, Ronald, 21
Nash, Stan, 340
National bibliographies, 112
National Inventory of Documentary Sources in the United States, 163, 279
National Newspaper Index (database), 262
National Union Catalog of Manuscript Collections (NUCMC), 83, 163, 272–75
National Union Catalog Pre–56 Imprints, 112–13
Neavill, Gordon B., 341
Nelson, Bonnie, 81, 140
Neufeld, Maurice F., 187, 188
Nevins, Allan, 303
New American World: A Documentary History of North America to 1612 (Quinn), 143
New Catholic Encyclopedia, 89
New Cultural History, The (Hunt), 22
New Dictionary of the Social Sciences, A (Mitchell), 207
New Directions in European Historiography (Iggers), 24
New Encyclopedia Britannica, The, 133, 134
New Grove Dictionary of Music and Musicians (Sadie), 216
"New History," 6
New History, The (Robinson), 28
New History: The 1980's and Beyond: Studies in Interdisciplinary History (Rabb and Rotberg), 24
New Palgrave: A Dictionary of Economics, The (Eatwell), 193, 194
Newsearch (database), 262
New Serial Titles, 121
Newspaper Abstracts (database), 262

Newspapers, 159, 333
Newspapers in Microfilm: United States, 1948–1983, 141, 159
Newton, Isaac, 4
New Webster's Third International Dictionary of the English Language, 133
New York Public Library Book of Chronologies, The, 137
New York Review of Books, The, 142
New York Times Book Review, The, 142
New York Times Index, The, 139
Nexis (information retrieval system), 263
Nicholls, Paul, 341
Nielsen, Erland Kolding, 329
Nielsen, Joyce McCarly, 212–13
Nietzsche, Friedrich, 7
Nimmo, Dan, 201
Nineteenth Century Readers' Guide to Periodical Literature, 83
Nineteenth Century Society: Essays in the Use of Quantitative Methods for the Study of Social Data (Wrigley), 171
Nonprint media, 53
Nora, Pierre, 22
Notable Americans: What They Did, From 1620 to the Present, 137, 161
Notable American Women, 135, 150–51
Nouvelle Histoire, La, 22
Nugent, Walter T. K., 319

O'Brien, Conor Cruise, 130
O'Donnell, Mary Ann, 317
Olby, R. C., 225, 226
Olsen, David H. L., 209, 210
Online Computer Library Center (OCLC) (information retrieval system), 56, 82, 83, 87, 113, 117, 121, 126, 231, 233, 261, 263, 337, 338
Oral history sources, 22, 54
Ordinary People and Everyday Life: Perspectives on the New Social History (Gardner and Adams), 302–3
Original order, use of (archives/manuscripts), 270
Origin and Development of Scholarly Historical Periodicals, The (Stieg), 310

Ortega y Gasset, José, 298
Osegueda, Laura, 341
Outline of the Principles of History
  (Droysen), 21
*Oxford Companion to American
  Literature, The*, 136
*Oxford Companion to English Literature,
  The*, 136
Oxford Dictionary of Quotations, The,
  138
Oxford English Dictionary, 133, 156,
  314

*Pageant of American History: A Pictorial
  History*, 143
PAIS International, 236, 259
Palic, Vladimir, 123
Pao, Miranda Lee, 308
Parker, Harold T., 24, 303
Parsons, J. Herschel, 190
*Past Before Us: Contemporary Historical
  Writing in the United States, The*
  (Kammen), 24
Pastine, Maureen, 314, 341
Pathfinder exercise, 77, 80–84
Patterson, Margaret C., 218, 219
Pearson, Hilda, 223, 224
Pearson, James Douglas, 223, 224
Penguin Companion to World Literature,
  220
Pepper, Stephen, 37
Periodical issues, locating, 119, 121
Periodical literature: indexes and
  bibliographies, 114–21; index use
  challenges, 61–62
Perkins, Dexter, 329
Perman, Dagmar Horna, 309, 344
Perpetual calendars, 149
Personal papers (archives/manuscripts),
  300; definition, 267–68
Petersen, Renee, 190–91
Petersen, William, 190–91
Philips, Cyril Henry, 23
*Philosopher's Guide to Sources,
  Research Tools, Professional Life, and
  Related Tools, The* (DeGeorge), 221,
  222
Philosopher's Index, 232, 248, 260

*Philosopher's Index: Retrospective Index
  to U.S. Publications from 1940*, 223,
  224
Philosophy: and history, 37–39; reference
  sources, 221–24
*Philosophy: A Guide to the Reference
  Literature* (Bynagle), 221–22
Philosophy of History (Dray), 20
Philosophy of History in Our Time
  (Meyerhof), 21
Photocopier, effect on research, 54
Pictorial reference works, 143
Pilachowski, David M., 337
Pirsig, Nancy, 329
Plagiarism, 90–91, 354, 356
Plano, Jack C., 173
Plum, Stephen H., 300
Pocock, J.G.A., 20
Poetry and history, 8, 38
Pók, Attila, 19
Political science: and history, 10;
  reference sources, 198–202
*Political Science: A Guide to Reference
  and Information Sources* (York), 198,
  199
Polsby, Nelson W., 200, 201
Pool, Ithiel, 189
Poole's Index to Periodical Literature, 83
Popescu, Oreste, 193, 194
Population Index, 191–92
Porter, Glenn, 187
Postlethwaite, T. Neville, 196, 197
Poulton, Helen J., 352
Preservation: of computer files, 341; of
  library materials, 304, 306
PRESNET (database), 283
Price, Arnold H., 309
Price, Jacob M., 171
Pries, Nancy, 86
Primary/secondary sources (conceptual
  framework), 76, 86, 297
Primary sources: automated indexes to,
  286–87; definition of, 4–5, 265–66;
  exercises using, 86, 328; historians'
  choice of, 52; increase of, 56; in
  machine-readable form, 286–87; in
  microform, 286; in scholarly editions,
  143, 285

Problem of Historical Knowledge: An Answer to Relativism, The (Mandelbaum), 20

Process and Politics in Library Research: A Model for Course Design (Fink), 324

Process of Modernization: An Annotated Bibliography on the Sociocultural Aspects of Development (Brode), 180, 182

Progressive Historians, The (Hoftsadter), 24

Provenance (archives/manuscripts), 270–71, 275; definition, 270

Prucha, Francis Paul, 81, 132, 352

Pryor, Judith, 318

Psychohistorian's Handbook (Lawton), 203

Psychological Abstracts, 204–5

Psychology: and history, 28–32; reference sources, 202–5

PsycInfo (database), 233

Public Affairs Information Service Bulletin (PAIS), 82, 236–37, 238

Publication sequence (conceptual framework), 76, 86–87, 296–97, 324

Pulleyblank, E. G., 23

Pulzer, Peter, 31

Quantification in History (Aydelotte), 170

Quantitative historical methods, sources, 169–72

Quantitative history, 13, 32–37

Quantitative Methods for Historians: A Guide to Research, Data, and Statistics (Jarausch and Hardy), 169

Que Sais-Je? (Carbonell), 23

Quotable Shakespeare, The (DeLoach), 138, 153–54

Quotable Woman, 1800–1981, The (Partnow), 138

Quotation dictionaries and concordances, 138, 153–54, 155–56, 157, 158, 159, 164

Rabb, Theodore K., 24, 171

Rainwater, Robert, 214, 215

Ranke, Leopold von, 4, 7, 8, 10, 15 n.1, 21

Rayfield, Jo Ann, 330

Read, Conyers, 28

Readers' Guide to Periodical Literature, 53, 77, 87, 114–16, 262, 314

Reading: consequences of, 297; regulation of, 298–99

Reading for Survival (Macdonald), 297

Recently Published Articles, 141

Record (archives/manuscripts); definition of, 267

Record group (archives/manuscripts); definition of, 275

Reddel, Carl W., 330

Reed, Jeffrey G., 203

Reed, Marcia, 86

Reference books, how to read, 129–31

Reference Services Review, 130

Reference sets, 134, 162

Reference Sources in History: An Introductory Guide (Fritze, Coutts, Vyhnanek), 63, 132, 350

Reference Works in British and American Literature (Bracken), 219

Riechel, Mary, 76–77, 97

Reiff, Janice L., 341

Reill, Peter, 20

Reitan, E. A., 330

Religion, reference sources, 221–24

Religion Index, 232, 248, 261

Religious Index One, 223, 224

Religious Index Two, 223, 224

Renaissance Sense of the Past, The (Burke), 23

Research guides and manuals, 347–54

Research Guide for Psychology (McInnis), 202–3

Research Guide to Philosophy (Tice and Slavens), 221, 222

Research Guide to Religious Studies (Wilson and Slavens), 222

Research Guide to the Health Sciences: Medical, Nutritional, and Environmental (Haselbauer), 224, 225

Research in Education (RIE) (database), 197

Researching and Writing History: A

Practical Handbook for Students
(McCoy), 351
Research in Progress (RIP) (database),
262
Research Libraries Information Network
(RLIN) (information retrieval system),
56, 82, 83, 87, 113–14, 117, 121,
125, 126, 231, 233, 237, 264, 282–85,
337, 338, 339, 340
Research methods and techniques:
characteristics of, 58–59, 72, 97–99,
301; difference between faculty and
students, 60, 72; foreign language use
by historians, 52; and historians, 52,
57–59, 130–31, 296, 303–12; in the
humanities, 312–14; and imagination,
301–2; and librarians, 58,296; in the
social sciences, 314–16; and students,
59–62, 72
Research reviews and book reviews, 141–
42
Review of Religious Research, 223, 224
Reviews in American History, 142
Revue de synthèse historique, 26
Rickert, Heinrich, 6
*RILA, International Repertory of the
Literature of Art*, 217
RILM Abstracts of Music Literature, 217,
261
Ritchie, Maureen, 132, 210–11
Ritter, Harry, 174, 178, 303
Robinson, James Harvey, 28
Rogers, Sharon J., 299
Roller, David C., 134, 153
Roscher, Karl, 6
Rosenberg, Jane A., 64, 71, 72, 326,
345
Rosenthal, Franz, 23
Ross, John A., 191
Rotberg, Robert I., 24
Rothstein, Pauline M., 327
Rowe, Judith, 341
Rowney, Don Karl, 341
Rubanowice, Robert J., 345
Rubino, Carl A., 39
Rudd, Joel, 299
Rudd, Mary Jo, 299
Rudolph, Janell, 355

Rundell, Walter, Jr., 330, 331, 347
Ryan, Joe, 173–74
Rywell, Martin, 134, 152, 153

Sable, Martin H., 331
Sadie, Stanley, 216
Salevouris, Michael J., 319
Salmon, Lucy M., 336
Salzman, Jack, 179, 182
Samaran, Charles, 22
Sanders, Keith R., 201
Sanford, Carolyn C., 331
Sarton, George, 225, 226
Schaus, Margaret, 332
Scheuch, Erwin K., 170–71
Schlesinger, Arthur, Jr., 32
Schmitt, Bernadotte E., 24
Schmitt, Hans A., 24
Schnucker, R. V., 332, 345
Schoen, David, 308
Scholar Adventurers, The (Altick), 302
Schorske, Carl E., 28–32
Schramm, Wilbur, 189
Schweik, Robert C., 314
Science (history of), reference sources,
224–27
Scott, James W., 351
Scruton, Roger, 133, 156
Searing, Susan E., 210, 211
Sears, Jean L., 346
Sebeok, Thomas A., 189
Secondary source: definition of, 265;
increase of, 56
Sedlak, Michael W., 198
Seignobos, Charles, 21–22
*Selected Bibliography of Modern
Historiography, A* (Pók), 19
*Selection of Library Materials in the
Humanities, Social Sciences, and
Sciences, The* (McClung), 349
*Selective Bibliography for the Study of
English and American Literature*
(Altick and Wright), 218, 219
*Serial Bibliographies and Abstracts in
History* (Henige), 140
Series (archives/manuscripts), definition
of, 279
Shafer, Robert Jones, 353

Shapiro, Beth J., 318
Shared Authority: Essays on the Craft and Meaning of Oral and Public History, A (Frisch), 22
Shaw, Peter, 354
Sheehy, Eugene P., 172–73, 353
Sheperd, John, 309
Sheperd's Historical Atlas, 136
Shera, Jesse Hank, 310, 342
Shill, Harold, 342
Shotwell, James T., 28
Shryrock, Henry S., 190
Simiand, François, 6
Skolnick, Arlene, 207
Slavens, Thomas P., 221, 222, 223
Smalley, Topsy N., 299, 300
Smelser, Neil J., 206, 207
Smith, Bruce L., 190
Smith, Chitra H., 190
Smith, John David, 134, 152, 156
Smith, John W., 168
Smith, Margo L., 185, 186
Social Science Encyclopedia, The (Kuper and Kuper), 175–76, 178
Social Science Research Handbook (McInnis and Scott), 132, 351
Social Sciences: A Cross-Disciplinary Guide to Selected Sources (Hernon), 172–73, 190
Social Sciences Citation Index, 81, 119, 141, 142, 180–82, 233
Social Sciences Index, 77, 82, 114–16, 179–80, 182, 236, 237, 259
Social Scisearch (database), 235, 259
Social Stratification: A Research Bibliography (Glenn), 208–9
Sociohistorical Analysis (conceptual framework), 76–77, 89, 297, 323
Sociological Abstracts, 208, 261
Sociology, reference sources, 205–10
Sociology: A Guide to Reference and Information Sources (Aby), 205
Sociology and History (Burke), 205–6, 207
Sokolow, Jayme, 90, 356
Soliday, Gerald L., 210
Some Historians of Modern Europe (Schmitt), 24

Some 20th Century Historians (Halperin), 24
Soper, Mary Ellen, 300
Sosa, Jorge F., 299
Source collections and collected works, 143, 163
Sources of Information in the Social Sciences: A Guide to the Literature (Webb), 132, 172–73, 187, 316, 353
Spencer, Herbert, 12
Spengler, Oswald, 7–8, 15 n.1
Spevack, Melvin, 138
Spielman, John, 332
Stallybrass, Oliver, 174, 178
Stanton, Elizabeth Cady, 148–49, 161–62
Statistical Abstract of the United States, 139
Statistical sources, 139, 149, 150, 155, 159–60, 162–63
Staudt, Kathleen Henderson, 340
Steinberg, S. H., 220, 221
Stern, Fritz, 24
Stern, Peter, 342
Stevenson, Joan, 183, 185
Stieg, Margaret F., 310
Stielow, Frederick, 342
Still, Julie, 342
Stinger, Charles, 226
Stinson, Robert, 333
Stoan, Stephen K., 296, 300, 301, 316
Stockwell, Edward G., 190
Stoffle, Carla, 320
Stoianovich, Troian, 24
Stolen Words: Forays into the Origins and Ravages of Plagiarism (Mallon), 356
Stoller, Michael E., 310
Stone, Lawrence, 14
Stone, Sue, 305, 310, 311
Storia della Storiografia, 24
Strauss, Diane Wheeler, 186, 187
Strong, James, 138, 156, 157–58
Structuralism, 8
Structuring the Past: The Uses of Computers in History (Reiff), 341
Stuard, Susan, 40–41, 332
Student's Guide to History, A (Benjamin), 348

Study of History in American Colleges and Universities, The (Adams), 335
Sturges, R. P., 333
Subject Collections (Ash and Miller), 126
Substantive-bibliographic information sources, 168; for anthropology, 183–85; for business and labor, 187; for communication, 188–89; for demography, 190–91; for economics and economic thought, 193–94; for education, 195–97; for fine and applied arts, 216; for general and area studies, 173–78; for history of science and technology, 225–26; for journalism, 188–89; for language and literature, 219–21; for mass media, 188–89; for religion, 222–23; for philosophy, 222–23; for political science, 200–201; for psychology, 203–4; for quantitative methods, 169–71; for sociology, 205–7; for women's studies, 211–13
Substantive information sources, 168; for general and area studies, 173; for language and literature, 219; for political science, 199–200
Super, R. H., 311
Supermap (computerized mapping program), 125
Survey of Contemporary Literature, 136
Swanson, Don R., 301, 343
Sweetland, James H., 343
Swierenga, Robert P., 171, 326
Symes, Dal S., 328, 354
Systematic Literature Searching (conceptual framework), 76, 80–84, 297

Tamb, Lewis A., 179, 182
Tanur, Judith M., 169
Task Force on the History Major, 71
Taylor, P. J., 323
Technology (history of), reference sources, 224–27
Technology and Culture, 226–27
Teggart, Frederick J., 28
Tegler, Patricia, 340
Télésystèmes-Questel (information retrieval system), 264

Theatre: History, Criticism and Reference (Cheshire), 215
Theoretiker de Aufklädrung (Blanke and Fleischer), 20
Theories of Bibliographic Education: Designs for Teaching (Oberman and Strauch), 296, 300, 327
Theories of History (Gardiner), 21
Thesaurus Linguae Graecae (TLG database), 232, 233
Thomas, Keith, 40
Thomas Jefferson: A Reference Biography (Peterson), 135
Thompson, James Westfall, 23
Thucydides, 9
Tibbo, Helen R., 345
Tice, Terrence N., 221, 222
Tierney, Helen, 211–12, 213
Tilly, Charles, 70, 71, 327
Time on the Cross: The Economics of American Negro Slavery (Fogel and Engerman), 13, 32–37
Times Literary Supplement, The (TLS), 142
Timetables of History: A Horizontal Linkage of People and Events, The (Grun), 137, 158
Tobey, Jeremy L., 177–78
Toews, John, 21
Toomey, Alice F., 82
Toulmin, Stephen, 31
Toward the Scientific Study of History (Benson), 170
Toynbee, Arnold, 15 n.1
Tozzer Library *Catalogue*, 185, 186
Trade catalogs, 112
Travelling Workshop Experiment, 319, 322, 323, 325
Treichler, Paula A., 212, 213
Trends in History: A Review of Current Periodical Literature, 142
Trevelyan, George, 11
Trevor-Roper, Hugh, 31
Triandis, William Wilson Lambert, 184, 185, 204
Trilling, Lionel, 30
Truth and Method (Gadamer), 20
Tucker, Melvin J., 326

Tuckett, Harold W., 318
Turner, Henry A., 355
Twyman, Robert W., 134, 153
Type of reference tool (conceptual
    framework), 76, 78–80, 297

*Ulrich's International Periodicals
    Directory*, 87
*Understanding History: A Primer of
    Historical Method* (Gottschalk), 22,
    351
Understanding Quantitative History
    (Haskins and Jeffrey), 169
Unfug, Douglas A., 355
Union List of Serials, 121
Union lists of catalogs, 141, 159
Urban Politics Dictionary (Smith and
    Klemanski), 168
*U.S. Congressional Committee Hearings
    Index, The*, 122
User Guide Arts and Humanities Search,
    264
*Uses of Government Publications by
    Social Scientists* (Hernon), 346
U.S. History on CD-ROM, 232
Using Government Publications (Sears
    and Moody), 346
U.S. Political Science Documents, 202,
    261
U.S. Serial Set Index, 122
Uva, Peter A., 311

Valla, Lorenzo, 20
Van Doren, Charles, 129
*Varieties of History: From Voltaire to the
    Present* (Stern), 24
Verstehen, Das (Wach), 20
Vico, Giambattista, 20, 37
Vincent, C. Paul, 301–2
Viney, Wayne, 205
Visiting other libraries, 125–26
Voltaire, 9, 20
Vondran, Raymond Florian, Jr., 311
VU/TEXT (information retrieval system),
    264
Vyhnanek, Louis A., 81, 132, 350

Wach, Joachim, 20

Walch, Timothy, 198
Walford, Albert John, 172–73, 353
Walford's Guide to Reference Material,
    81, 132, 172, 173, 353
Walker, Samuel J., 333
Walter, Robert A., 333
Walters, Edward M., 312
Warmkessel, Marjorie Markoff, 328
Watson, Robert Irving, 169, 180, 182,
    205
Webb, William H., 132, 172–73, 187,
    316, 353
Weber, Max, 6, 9, 27
Webster's New Geographical Dictionary,
    136
Weeks, John M., 183
Weil, Eric, 69, 312
Weintraub, Karl J., 312
Werking, Richard Hume, 333, 334
*Which Road to the Past? Two Views of
    History* (Elton and Fogel), 22
White, Hayden, 8, 20–21, 37–39
Whitney, William G., 33
Who's Who, 290
*Who Was When? A Dictionary of
    Contemporaries*, 137
Wibberly, Stephen E., Jr., 345
Widder, Agnes Haigh, 334
Wiener, Philip, 177, 178
Wilson, John F., 222
Wilson, Myoung Chung, 340
Wilsonline (information retrieval system),
    264
Wilson Quarterly, 142
Windelband, Wilhelm, 5, 6
Winks, Robin, 303
Winsor, Justin, 335, 336
Winthrop, Robert, 183, 185
Wolf, Friedrich, 9–10
Wolman, Benjamin B., 203, 204
Woman's Journal, 151
Women: A Bibliography of Bibliographies
    (Ballou), 213–14
Women's studies, reference sources,
    210–14
*Women's Studies: A Guide to Information
    Sources* (Carter and Ritchie), 132,
    210–11

Women's Studies Encyclopedia (Tierney), 134, 144, 211–12, 213
Women Studies Abstracts, 214
Wood, Charles T., 40
Woodbury, Marda, 195
Woods, Pamela Carr, 307
Woodward, C. Vann, 33
Workbooks, 319–20
World Almanac and Book of Facts, 139, 149
World Bibliography of Bibliographies, A (Besterman), 140, 178, 182
Wright, Andrew, 218, 219

Wrigley, E. A., 171
Writing of American History, The (Kraus), 24
Writings on American History, 82, 83, 307, 308–9
Wundt, Wilhelm, 27

Yearbooks and almanacs, 139
York, Henry E., 198–99

Zagorin, Perez, 21
Zink, Steven D., 346
Zophy, Angela Howard, 134, 144, 150

About the Editor and Contributors

DAVID Y. ALLEN, associate librarian, State University of New York at Stony Brook. Dr. Allen is a reference librarian, map librarian, and history bibliographer who has taught history at the college level and has written numerous articles on history, librarianship, and environmental issues. His work has appeared in *Perspectives*, *The Review of Politics*, *Government Publications Review*, and the *Sierra Club Bulletin*. Among his current interests are online searching and bibliographic software.

JOHN ATTIG, authority control librarian, Pennsylvania State University. Mr. Attig is active in the American Library Association, having served on committees responsible for standards for bibliographic description and for coding bibliographic information for computer manipulation. He has published articles in *Information Technology and Libraries*, and a chapter in *The Conceptual Foundations of Descriptive Cataloging* (1989). He compiles an ongoing bibliography on the British philosopher John Locke and has published *The Works of John Locke: A Comprehensive Bibliography, from the Seventeenth Century to the Present* (1985).

CHARLES A. D'ANIELLO, history bibliographer and coordinator for collection development, Lockwood Memorial Library, State University of New York at Buffalo. Mr. D'Aniello for many years team-taught a graduate library research methods course in Buffalo's history department, and he has taught a wide variety of bibliographic research classes. His work has appeared in *RQ*, *Italian Americana*, *The History Teacher*, *Collection Building*, the *Journal of American Ethnic History*, and *American History: A Bibliographic Review*.

JOYCE DUNCAN FALK, independent scholar and consultant based in Santa Barbara, California. Dr. Falk was formerly bibliographic instruction and reference librarian for history, and coordinator of computer-assisted reference, at the University of California, Irvine. Earlier she taught history at the college level and was editor of the bibliographies *America: History and Life* and *Historical Abstracts*, and of the annual *Proceedings of the Western Society for French History*. The author of a user manual and numerous articles about online searching, her most recent publications are "Information Retrieval in Women's History" (ERIC, 1991), and "Humanities," in *Women Online: Research in Women's Studies Using Online Databases* (1990).

GEORG G. IGGERS, Distinguished Professor of History, State University of New York at Buffalo. Major publications include *The Cult of Authority: The Political Philosophy of the Saint-Simonians* (1959); *The German Conception of History* (1968); *New Directions in European Historiography* (1975); ed., with Harold T. Parker, *International Handbook of Historical Studies* (1979); ed., with James M. Powell, *Leopold von Ranke and The Shaping of the Historical Discipline* (1990); ed., *Marxist Historiography in Transformation, East German Social History in the 1980s* (1991); and the foreword to *Historiography: An Annotated Bibliography* (1987).

RAYMOND G. McINNIS, social sciences librarian in the Wilson Library and adjunct professor of history at Western Washington University, Bellingham, Washington. Among the many books and articles he has written on a variety of areas in librarianship are *New Perspectives for Reference Service in Academic Libraries* (1978) and *Research Guide for Psychology* (1982). He edits the Greenwood series "Reference Sources for the Social Sciences and Humanities."

TRUDY HUSKAMP PETERSON, assistant archivist for the National Archives. Dr. Peterson is author of *Basic Archival Workshop Exercises* (1982), *Agricultural Exports, Farm Income, and the Eisenhower Administration* (1979), and editor of *Farmers, Bureaucrats, and Middlemen: Historical Perspectives on American Agriculture* (1980). She served as president of the Society of American Archivists, 1990–1991, and served on the editorial board of *The American Archivist*, 1978–1981.

HARRY RITTER, professor of history at Western Washington University, Bellingham, Washington. Dr. Ritter specializes in modern German and Austrian history, historical methodology, and historiography. He is the author of *Dictionary of Concepts in History* (1986), and his article "Progressive Historians and the Historical Imagination in Austria" won the 1989 Austrian Cultural Institute Prize.

JANE A. ROSENBERG, assistant director for the Reference Materials Program, Division of Research Programs, National Endowment for the Humanities, Washington, D.C. Dr. Rosenberg has had extensive involvement in bibliographic instruction in earlier positions at Indiana University libraries and Kent State University libraries. Her book on the relations between the Library of Congress and the American library community during the first four decades of the twentieth century, *The Library of Congress and American Librarianship*, will be published by the University of Illinois Press in 1993; her work has appeared in the *Journal of Library History* and *Libraries & Culture*, and an article on "Library Management" is in press for the *Encyclopedia of Library History*.

ROBERT P. SWIERENGA, professor of history at Kent State University. Among his major publications are: ed. (with J. W. Schulte Nordholt) *A Bilateral Bicentennial: A History of Dutch-American Relations, 1782–1982* (1982); ed. *History and Ecology: James C. Malin's Studies of the Grassland* (1984); gen. ed., *Netherlanders in America: A Study of Emigration and Settlement in the Nineteenth and Twentieth Centuries in the United States*, by J. Van Hinte (1985); ed. *The Dutch in America: Immigration, Settlement, and Cultural Change* (1985); and *Belief and Behavior: Essays in the New Religious History* (1991). He served as co-editor of *Social Science History*, the journal of the Social Science History Association, from 1976 to 1990.